Advances, Tools and Techniques of Digital Image Processing

Advances, Tools and Techniques of Digital Image Processing

Edited by **Niceto Salazar**

WILLFORD PRESS

New York

Published by Willford Press,
118-35 Queens Blvd., Suite 400,
Forest Hills, NY 11375, USA
www.willfordpress.com

Advances, Tools and Techniques of Digital Image Processing
Edited by Niceto Salazar

International Standard Book Number: 978-1-68285-296-5 (Hardback)

Contents

Preface

Digital image processing is the application of computer programs and algorithms to process digital images. This book includes topics such as image recognition and identification, restoration and segmentation techniques, different types of images, enhancing digital images, etc. The objective of this book is to give a comprehensive overview of the different aspects of digital image processing and the various tools and technologies used in this field. It will serve as a reference to a broad spectrum of readers.

The researches compiled throughout the book are authentic and of high quality, combining several disciplines and from very diverse regions from around the world. Drawing on the contributions of many researchers from diverse countries, the book's objective is to provide the readers with the latest achievements in the area of research. This book will surely be a source of knowledge to all interested and researching the field.

In the end, I would like to express my deep sense of gratitude to all the authors for meeting the set deadlines in completing and submitting their research chapters. I would also like to thank the publisher for the support offered to us throughout the course of the book. Finally, I extend my sincere thanks to my family for being a constant source of inspiration and encouragement.

Editor

Face liveness detection using dynamic texture

Tiago de Freitas Pereira[1*], Jukka Komulainen[2], André Anjos[4], José Mario De Martino[3], Abdenour Hadid[2], Matti Pietikäinen[2] and Sébastien Marcel[4]

Abstract

User authentication is an important step to protect information, and in this context, face biometrics is potentially advantageous. Face biometrics is natural, intuitive, easy to use, and less human-invasive. Unfortunately, recent work has revealed that face biometrics is vulnerable to spoofing attacks using cheap low-tech equipment. This paper introduces a novel and appealing approach to detect face spoofing using the spatiotemporal (dynamic texture) extensions of the highly popular local binary pattern operator. The key idea of the approach is to learn and detect the structure and the dynamics of the facial micro-textures that characterise real faces but not fake ones. We evaluated the approach with two publicly available databases (Replay-Attack Database and CASIA Face Anti-Spoofing Database). The results show that our approach performs better than state-of-the-art techniques following the provided evaluation protocols of each database.

Keywords: Anti-spoofing; Liveness detection; Countermeasure; Face recognition; Biometrics

1 Introduction

Because of its natural and non-intrusive interaction, identity verification and recognition using facial information are among the most active and challenging areas in computer vision research. Despite the significant progress of face recognition technology in the recent decades, a wide range of viewpoints, ageing of subjects and complex outdoor lighting are still research challenges. Advances in the area were extensively reported in [1] and [2].

Unfortunately, the issue of verifying if the face presented to a camera is indeed a face from a real person and not an attempt to deceive (spoof) the system has mostly been overlooked. It was not until very recently that the problem of spoofing attacks against face biometric system gained attention of the research community. This can be attested by the gradually increasing number of publicly available databases [3-6] and the recently organized IJCB 2011 competition on countermeasures to 2-D facial spoofing attacks [7] which was the first competition conducted for studying best practices for non-intrusive spoofing detection.

A spoofing attack consists in the use of forged biometric traits to gain illegitimate access to secured resources protected by a biometric authentication system. The lack of resistance to direct attacks is not exclusive to face biometrics. The findings in [8], [9] and [10] indicate that fingerprint authentication systems suffer from a similar weakness. The same shortcoming on iris recognition systems has been diagnosed [11-13]. Finally, in [14] and [15], the spoofing attacks to speaker biometrics are addressed. The literature review for spoofing in face recognition systems will be presented in Section 2.

In authentication systems based on face biometrics, spoofing attacks are usually perpetrated using photographs, videos or forged masks. While one can also use make-up or plastic surgery as means of spoofing, photographs and videos are probably the most common sources of spoofing attacks. Moreover, due to the increasing popularity of social network websites (Facebook, Flickr, YouTube, Instagram and others), a great deal of multimedia content - especially videos and photographs - is available on the web that can be used to spoof a face authentication system. In order to mitigate the vulnerability of face authentication systems, effective countermeasures against face spoofing have to be deployed.

Micro-texture analysis has been effectively used in detecting photo attacks from single face images [3,16,17]. Recently, the micro-texture-based analysis for spoofing detection was extended in the spatiotemporal domain in

*Correspondence: tiagofrepereira@gmail.com
[1]CPqD Telecom & IT Solutions, School of Electrical and Computer Engineering, University of Campinas (UNICAMP), Campinas, São Paulo 13083-970, Brazil
Full list of author information is available at the end of the article

[18] and [19]. In both papers, the authors introduced a compact face liveness description that combines facial appearance and dynamics using spatiotemporal (dynamic texture) extensions of the highly popular local binary pattern (LBP) approach [20]. More specifically, local binary patterns from three orthogonal planes (LBP-TOP) were considered. This variant has shown to be very effective in describing the horizontal and vertical motion patterns in addition to appearance [21].

Even though authors of [18] and [19] considered LBP-TOP-based dynamic texture analysis for face spoofing detection, very dissimilar strategies were introduced for exploring the temporal dimension. In [18], the LBP-TOP-based face liveness description was extracted from relatively short time windows using the dense sampling of multiresolution approach, whereas an average of LBP-TOP features over longer temporal windows was used in [19]. Moreover, the experimental setups had significant differences because different face normalization techniques were applied in each work. Furthermore, the evaluations were performed on different databases (Replay-Attack Database [3] and CASIA Face Anti-Spoofing Database [6], respectively). In this article, we consolidate the methods proposed in [18] and [19], isolating the different variables and studying the potential of the different LBP-TOP countermeasures in different settings on both datasets. Furthermore, we demonstrate that our principled approach is able to consistently outperform prior work on the same databases and following the same evaluation protocols. We also provide an open-source framework that makes our research fully reproducible with minimal effort.

This work provides an in-depth analysis on the use of dynamic texture for face liveness description. We apply a unified experimental setup and evaluation methodology for assessing the effectiveness of the different temporal processing strategies introduced in [18] and [19]. The remainder of the paper is organized as follows: in Section 2, a brief review of the relevant literature is provided. The basic theory of local binary patterns in spatiotemporal domain is introduced in Section 3. Our dynamic texture-based face liveness description is described in Section 4. Section 5 presents the two publicly available databases which are used for evaluating the proposed countermeasure. In Section 6, we report on the experimental setup and results. Finally, in Section 7, we summarize this work highlighting its main contributions.

2 Literature review

Considering the type of countermeasures for face anti-spoofing that does not require user collaboration, Chakka et al. in [7] propose a classification scheme based on the following cues:

- Presence of vitality (liveness)
- Differences in motion patterns
- Differences in image quality assessment

Presence of vitality or liveness detection consists of search for features that only live faces can possess. For instance, Pan et al. in [4] exploited the observation that humans blink once every 2 to 4 s and proposed an eye blink-based countermeasure. Experiments carried out with the ZJU Eye Blink Database (http://www.cs.zju.edu.cn/~gpan/database/db_blink.html) showed an accuracy of 95.7%.

The countermeasures based on differences in motion patterns rely on the fact that real faces display a different motion behaviour compared to a spoof attempt. Kollreider et al. [22] present a motion-based countermeasure that estimates the correlation between different regions of the face using optical flow field. In this approach, the input is considered a spoof if the optical flow field on the center of the face and on the center of the ears present the same direction. The performance was evaluated using the subset 'Head Rotation Shot' of the XM2VTS database whose real access was the videos of this subset, and the attacks were generated with hard copies of those data. Using this database, which was not made publicly available, an equal error rate (EER) of 0.5% was achieved. Anjos and Marcel [23] present a motion-based countermeasure measuring the correlation between the face and the background through simple frame differences. Using the PRINT ATTACK database, that approach presented a good discrimination power (half total error rate (HTER) equals to 9%).

Countermeasures based on differences in image quality assessment rely on the presence of artefacts intrinsically present at the attack media. Such remarkable properties can be originated from media quality issues or differences in reflectance properties of the object exposed to the camera. Li et al. [24] hypothesize that fraudulent photographs have less high-frequency components than real ones. To test the hypothesis, a small database was built with four identities containing both real access and printed photo attacks. With this private database, an accuracy of 100% was achieved. Assuming that real access images concentrate more information in a specific frequency band, Tan et al. [5] and Zhang et al. [6] used, as countermeasure, a set of difference of Gaussian filters (DoG) to select a specific frequency band to discriminate attacks and non-attacks. Evaluations carried out with the CASIA Face Anti-Spoofing Database and NUAA Photograph Imposter Database (http://parnec.nuaa.edu.cn/xtan/data/NUAAImposterDB.html) showed an equal error rate of 17% and an accuracy of 86%, respectively.

Because of differences in reflectance properties, real faces very likely present different texture patterns compared with fake faces. Following that hypothesis, Määttä et al. [17] and Chingovska et al. [3] explored the power of local binary patterns (LBP) as a countermeasure. Määttä et al. combined three different LBP configurations ($LBP_{8,2}^{u2}$, $LBP_{16,2}^{u2}$ and $LBP_{8,1}^{u2}$) in a normalized face image and trained a support vector machine (SVM) classifier to discriminate real and fake faces. Evaluations carried out with NUAA Photograph Impostor Database [5] showed a good discrimination power (2.9% in EER). Chingovska et al. analysed the effectiveness of $LBP_{8,1}^{u2}$ and set of extended LBPs [25] in still images to discriminate real and fake faces. Evaluations carried out with three different databases, the NUAA Photograph Impostor Database, Replay-Attack database and CASIA Face Anti-Spoofing Database [6], showed a good discrimination power with a HTER equal to 15.16%, 19.03% and 18.17%, respectively.

3 LBP-based dynamic texture description

Määttä et al. [17] and Chingovska et al. [3] propose a LBP-based countermeasures to spoofing attacks based on the hypothesis that real faces present different texture patterns in comparison with fake ones. However, the proposed techniques analyse each frame in isolation, not considering the behaviour over time. As pointed out in Section 2, motion is a cue explored in some works and in combination with texture can generate a powerful countermeasure. For describing the face liveness for spoofing detection, we considered a spatiotemporal representation which combines facial appearance and dynamics. We adopted the LBP-based spatiotemporal representation because of its recent convincing performance in modelling moving faces and facial expression recognition and also for dynamic texture recognition [20].

The LBP texture analysis operator, introduced by Ojala et al. [26,27], is defined as a gray-scale invariant texture measure, derived from a general definition of texture in a local neighbourhood. It is a powerful texture descriptor, and among its properties in real-world applications are its discriminative power, computational simplicity and tolerance against monotonic gray-scale changes. The original LBP operator forms labels for the image pixels by thresholding the 3×3 neighbourhood with the center value and considering the result as a binary number. The histogram of these $2^8 = 256$ different labels is then used as an image descriptor.

The original LBP operator was defined to only deal with the spatial information. However, more recently, it has been extended to a spatiotemporal representation for dynamic texture (DT) analysis. This has yielded to the so-called volume local binary pattern operator (VLBP) [21]. The idea behind VLBP consists of looking at dynamic texture (video sequence) as a set of volumes in the (X, Y, T)

space where X and Y denote the spatial coordinates and T denotes the frame index (time). The neighborhood of each pixel is thus defined in a three-dimensional space. Then, similar to basic LBP in spatial domain, volume textons can be defined and extracted into histograms. Therefore, VLBP combines motion and appearance into a dynamic texture description.

To make VLBP computationally treatable and easy to extend, the co-occurrences of the LBP on the three orthogonal planes (LBP-TOP) was also introduced [21]. LBP-TOP consists of the three orthogonal planes - XY, XT and YT - and the concatenation of local binary pattern co-occurrence statistics in these three directions. The circular neighbourhoods are generalized to elliptical sampling to fit to the space-time statistics. The LBP codes are extracted from the XY, XT and YT planes, which are denoted as XY-LBP, XT-LBP and YT-LBP, for all pixels, and statistics of the three different planes are obtained and concatenated into a single histogram. The procedure is shown in Figure 1. In this representation, DT is encoded by the XY-LBP, XT-LBP and YT-LBP.

Using equal radii for the time and spatial axes is not a good choice for dynamic textures [21], and therefore, in the XT and YT planes, different radii can be assigned to sample neighbouring points in space and time. More generally, the radii R_x, R_x and R_t, respectively, in axes X, Y and T and the number of neighbouring points P_{XY}, P_{XT} and P_{YT}, respectively, in the XY, XT and YT planes can also be different. Furthermore, the type of LBP operator on each plane can vary; for example, the uniform pattern ($u2$) or rotation invariant uniform pattern ($riu2$) variants [20] can be deployed. The corresponding feature is denoted as LBP-$TOP_{P_{XY},P_{XT},P_{YT},R_x,R_y,R_t}^{operator}$.

Assuming we are given a $X \times Y \times T$ dynamic texture ($x_c \in \{0, \cdots, X-1\}$, $y_c \in \{0, \cdots, Y-1\}$, $t_c \in \{0, \cdots, T-1\}$), i.e. a video sequence. A histogram of the DT can be defined as

$$H_{i,j} = \sum_{x,y,t} I\left\{f_j(x,y,t) = i\right\}, i = 0, \cdots, n_j - 1; j = 0, 1, 2$$

(1)

where n_j is the number of different labels produced by the LBP operator in the jth plane ($j = 0 : XY$, $1 : XT$ and $2 : YT$), and $f_i(x,y,t)$ expresses the LBP code of the central pixel (x,y,t) in the jth plane.

Similar to the original LBP, the histograms must be normalized to get a coherent description for comparing the DTs:

$$N_{i,j} = \frac{H_{i,j}}{\sum_{k=0}^{n_j-1} H_{k,j}}.$$

(2)

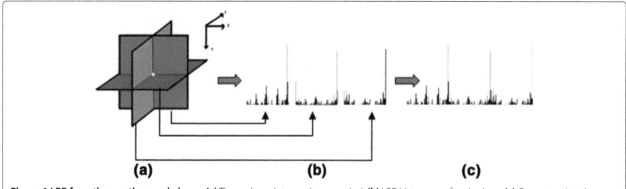

Figure 1 LBP from three orthogonal planes. (a) Three planes intersecting one pixel. **(b)** LBP histogram of each plane. **(c)** Concatenating the histograms (courtesy of [21]).

In addition to the computational simplification, compared with VLBP, LBP-TOP has the advantage to generate independent histograms for each of the intersecting planes, in space and time, which can be treated in combination or individually. Because of the aforementioned complexity issues on the implementation of a VLBP-based processor, the developed spatiotemporal face liveness description uses LBP-TOP to encode both facial appearance and dynamics.

Our key idea is to learn and detect the structure and the dynamics of the facial micro-textures that characterise real faces but not fake ones. Due to its tolerance against monotonic gray-scale changes, LBP-based representation is adequate for measuring the facial texture quality and determining whether degradations due to recapturing process, e.g. the used spoofing medium, are observed. Instead of just applying static texture analysis, we exploit also several dynamic visual cues that are based on either the motion patterns of a genuine human face or the used display medium.

Unlike photographs and display devices, real faces are indeed non-rigid objects with contractions of facial muscles which result in temporally deformed facial features such as eye lids and lips. Therefore, it can be assumed that the specific facial motion patterns (including eye blinking, mouth movements and facial expression changes) should be detected when a live human being is observed in front of the camera. The movement of the display medium may cause several distinctive motion patterns that do not describe genuine faces. As shown in Figure 2, the use of (planar) spoofing medium might cause sudden characteristic reflections when a photograph is warped or because of a glossy surface of the display medium. As it can be seen, warped photo attacks may cause also distorted facial motion patterns. It is likely that hand-held attacks introduce synchronized shaking of the face and spoofing medium which can be observed as excessive relative motion in the view and facial region if the

distance between the display medium and the camera is relatively short. In this work, we try to exploit the aforementioned visual cues for face spoofing detection by exploring the dynamic texture content of the facial region. We adopted the LBP-based spoofing detection in spatiotemporal domain because LBP-TOP features have been successfully applied in describing dynamic events, e.g. facial expressions [21].

4   The proposed countermeasure

Figure 3 shows a block diagram of the proposed countermeasure. First, each frame of the original frame sequence was gray-scaled and passed through a face detector using modified census transform (MCT) features [28]. Only detected faces with more than 50 pixels of width and height were considered. The detected faces were geometric normalized to 64×64 pixels. In order to reduce the face detector noise, the same face bounding box was used for each set of frames used in the LBP-TOP calculation. As can be seen in the Figure 4, the middle frame was chosen. Unfortunately, the face detector is not error free, and in case of error in the middle frame face detection, the nearest detection was chosen; otherwise, the observation was discarded. After the face detection step, the LBP operators were applied for each plane (XY, XT and YT) and the histograms were computed and then concatenated. After the feature extraction step, binary classification can be used to discriminate spoofing attacks from real access attempts.

Face liveness is rather difficult to be determined based on the motion between a couple of successive frames. The used volume can be expanded along the temporal dimension by increasing R_t, as aforementioned in Section 3. This way to deal with dynamic texture is called single resolution approach, since only one histogram per LBP-TOP plane is accumulated. However, this leads to rather sparse sampling on the temporal planes XT and YT; thus, we might loose valuable details. In order to explore the

Figure 2 Example sequence of a warped photo attack from the CASIA Face Anti-Spoofing Database [6]. This describes the characteristic reflections (flickering) of a planar spoofing medium and the distorted motion patterns.

dynamic texture information more carefully, we proposed the multiresolution approach.

The multiresolution approach can be performed by concatenating the histograms in the time domain (XT and YT) for different values of R_t. The notation chosen to represent these settings is using brackets for the multiresolution data. For example, $R_t = [1 - 3]$ means that the LBP-TOP operator will be calculated for $R_t = 1$, $R_t = 2$ and $R_t = 3$ and all resultant histograms will be concatenated. With the multiresolution approach, dense sampling on the temporal planes XT and YT is achieved.

The proposed countermeasure was implemented using the free signal processing and machine learning toolbox Bob [29], and the source code of the algorithm is available as an add-on package to this framework (http://pypi.python.org/pypi/antispoofing.lbptop). After installation, it is possible to reproduce all results reported in this article.

5 Spoofing databases

In this section, we give an overview of the two largest and most challenging face spoofing databases, Replay-Attack Database [3] and the CASIA Face Anti-Spoofing Database [6], consisting of real access attempts and several fake face attacks of different natures under varying conditions. Instead of still images, both datasets contain short video recordings which makes them suitable for evaluating countermeasures that exploit also temporal information.

5.1 Replay-Attack Database

The Replay-Attack Database (http://www.idiap.ch/dataset/replayattack) [3] consists of short video (~10s) recordings of both real-access and attack attempts to 50 different identities using a laptop. It contains 1,200 videos (200 real-access and 1,000 attacks), and the attacks were taken in three different scenarios with two different illumination and support conditions. The scenarios of attack include the following:

1. *Print*: the attacker displays hard copies of high-resolution photographs printed on A4 paper
2. *Mobile*: the attacker displays photos and videos taken with an iPhone 3GS using the phone screen
3. *Highdef*: the attacker displays high-resolution photos and videos using an iPad screen with a resolution of $1,024 \times 768$.

The illumination conditions include the following:

1. *Controlled*: the background of the scene is uniform and the light of a fluorescent lamp illuminates the scene
2. *Adverse*: the background of the scene is non-uniform and daylight illuminates the scene

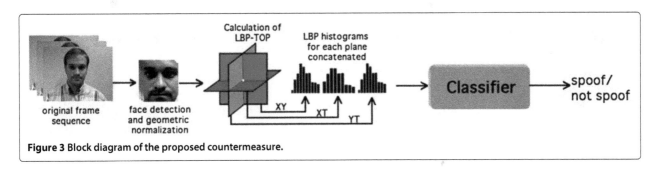

Figure 3 Block diagram of the proposed countermeasure.

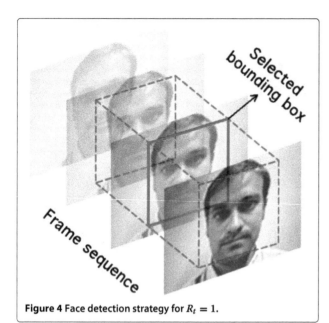

Figure 4 Face detection strategy for $R_t = 1$.

The support conditions include the following:

1. *Hand-based*: the attacker holds the attack media using his own hands
2. *Fixed*: the attacker sets the attack device in a fixed support so it does not move during the spoofing attempt

Figure 5 shows some examples of real accesses and attacks in different scenarios. The top row shows samples from the controlled scenario. The bottom row shows samples from the adverse scenario. Columns from left to right show examples of real access, printed photograph, mobile phone and tablet attacks.

The Replay-Attack Database provides a protocol for objectively evaluating a given countermeasure. Such protocol defines three non-overlapping partitions for training, development and testing countermeasures (see Table 1). The training set should be used to train the countermeasure, and the development set is used to tune the countermeasure and to estimate a threshold value to be used in the test set. The test set must be used only to report results. As a performance measurement, the protocol advises the use of HTER (Equation 3).

$$ \text{HTER} = \frac{\text{FAR}(\tau, D) + \text{FRR}(\tau, D)}{2}, \qquad (3) $$

where τ is a threshold, D is the dataset, FAR is the false acceptance rate and FRR is the false rejection rate. In this protocol, the value of τ is estimated on the EER using the development set.

5.2 CASIA Face Anti-Spoofing Database

The CASIA Face Anti-Spoofing Database (http://www.cbsr.ia.ac.cn/english/FaceAntiSpoofDatabases.asp [6] contains 50 real clients, and the corresponding fake faces are captured with high quality from the original ones. The variety is achieved by introducing three imaging qualities (low, normal and high) and three fake face attacks which include warped photo, cut photo (eyeblink) and video attacks. Examples from the database can be seen in Figure 6. Altogether, the database consists of 600 video clips, and the subjects are divided into subsets for training and testing (240 and 360, respectively). Results of a baseline system are also provided along the database for fair comparison. The baseline system considers the high-frequency information in the facial region using multiple DoG features and SVM classifier and is inspired by the work of Tan et al. [5].

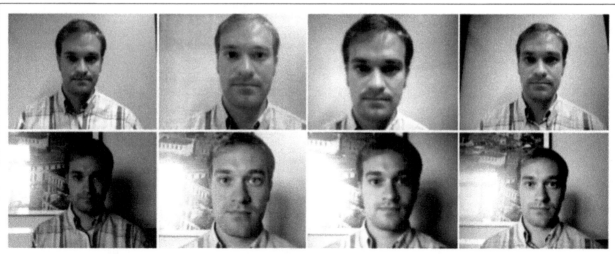

Figure 5 Some frames of real access and spoofing attempts (courtesy of [3]).

Table 1 Number of videos in each subset

Type	Train	Devel.	Test	Total
Real access	60	60	80	200
Print attack	30 + 30	30 + 30	40 + 40	100 + 100
Mobile attack	60 + 60	60 + 60	80 + 80	200 + 200
Highdef attack	60 + 60	60 + 60	80 + 80	200 + 200
Total	360	360	480	1200

Numbers displayed as sums indicate the amount of hand-based and fixed support attack available in each subset [3].

Since the main purpose of the database is to investigate the possible effects of different fake face types and imaging qualities, the test protocol consists of seven scenarios in which particular train and test samples are to be used. The quality test considers the three imaging qualities separately, low (1), normal (2) and high quality (3), and evaluates the overall spoofing detection performance under a variety of attacks at the given imaging quality. Similarly, the fake face test assesses how robust the anti-spoofing measure is to specific fake face attacks, warped photo (4), cut photo (5) and video attacks (6), regardless of the imaging quality. In the overall test (7), all data are used to give a more general evaluation. The results of each scenario are reported as detection error trade-off (DET) curves and EERs, which is the point where FAR equals FRR on the DET curve.

6 Experiments

This section provides an in-depth analysis on the proposed LBP-TOP-based face liveness description using the Replay-Attack Database [3] and the CASIA Face Anti-Spoofing Database [6]. First, we study the effect of different classifiers and LBP-TOP parameters by following the evaluation method proposed in [18]. The LBP-TOP representation is computed over relatively short temporal windows, and the results are reported using the overall classification accuracy for the individual volumes. Altogether, four experiments were carried out evaluating the effectiveness of

1. Each LBP-TOP plane individually and in combination
2. Different classifiers
3. Different LBP operators
4. The multiresolution approach

In order to study the effect of the different variables, each parameter was tuned solely (fixing other elements) using the development set of each face spoofing database. It should be noted that unlike the Replay-Attack Database, the CASIA Face Anti-Spoofing Database is lacking a specific development set. Therefore, the first 4 experiments were performed in this database using cross-validation by randomly dividing the training data into fivefold. Hence, the results presented for CASIA Face Anti-Spoofing Database are actually the average HTER on the test set over five iterations of the algorithm with different folds playing the role of a development set.

Finally, we also studied the accumulation of facial appearance and dynamics information over longer time windows and perform an evaluation at system level. The access attempt-based results presented in Section 6.5 were obtained using the official protocol of each database.

Inspired by [3], the LBP-TOP operator chosen to start the evaluation was LBP-TOP$^{u2}_{8,8,8,1,1,R_t}$.

6.1 Effectiveness of each LBP-TOP plane individually and in combination

In this experiment, we analysed the effectiveness of each individual plane and their combinations when the multiresolution area is increased. Figure 7 shows the HTER evolution, on the test set, considering individual and combined histograms of LBP-TOP planes for each database. We used, as binary classifier, a linear projection derived from linear discriminant analysis (LDA) as in [3].

The results indicate differences in the performance between the two databases. The temporal components (XT and YT) are a decisive cue for the Replay-Attack Database, and the combination of all three planes (XY, XT and YT) gives the best performance. Conversely, for the CASIA Face Anti-Spoofing Database, the addition of

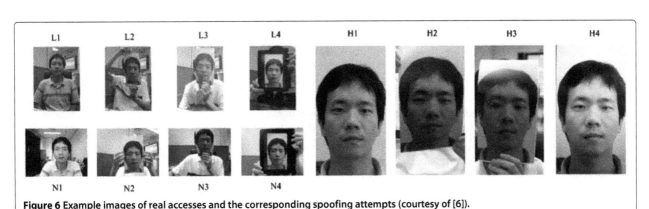

Figure 6 Example images of real accesses and the corresponding spoofing attempts (courtesy of [6]).

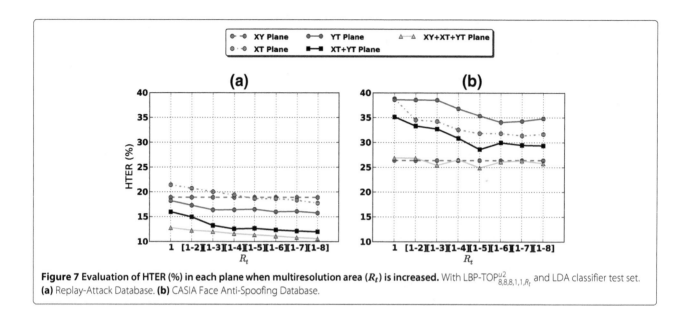

Figure 7 Evaluation of HTER (%) in each plane when multiresolution area (R_t) is increased. With LBP-TOP$^{u2}_{8,8,8,1,1,R_t}$ and LDA classifier test set. **(a)** Replay-Attack Database. **(b)** CASIA Face Anti-Spoofing Database.

temporal planes improves the performance only slightly compared to the spatial LBP representation (considering only the XY plane). These observations can be explained by taking a closer look at the differences in the databases and their spoofing attack scenarios. 2-D fake face attacks can be categorized into two groups, close-up and scenic attacks, based on how the fake face is represented with the spoofing medium.

A close-up spoof describes only the facial area which is presented to the sensor. The main weakness with the tightly cropped fake faces is that the boundaries of the spoofing medium, e.g. a video screen frame, photograph edges or the attacker's hands, are usually visible during the attack and thus can be detected in the scene [19]. However, these visual cues can be hidden by incorporating the background scene in the face spoof and placing the resulting scenic fake face very near to the sensor as performed on the Replay-Attack Database. In such cases, the description of facial appearance leads to rather good performance because the proximity between the spoofing medium and the camera causes the recaptured face image to be out-of-focus also revealing other facial texture quality issues, like degradation due to the used spoofing medium. Furthermore, the attacks in Replay-Attack Database are performed using two types of support conditions, fixed and hand-held. Naturally, the LBP-TOP-based face representation can easily detect fixed photo and print attacks since there is no variation in the facial texture over time. On the other hand, the hand-held attacks introduce synchronized shaking of the face and spoofing medium. This can be observed as excessive relative motion in the view, again, due to the proximity between the display medium and the sensor. Since the distinctive global motion patterns are

clearly visible also on the facial region, they can be captured even by computing the LBP-TOP description over relatively short temporal windows, i.e. low values of R_t.

In contrast, the CASIA Face Anti-Spoofing Database consists of close-up face spoofs. The distance between the camera and the display medium is much farther compared to the attacks on Replay-Attack Database. The display medium does not usually move much in the attack scenarios. Therefore, the overall translational movement of a fake face is much closer to the motion of a genuine head. Due to the lack of distinctive shaking of the display medium, the CASIA Face Anti-Spoofing Database can be considered to be more challenging from the dynamic texture point of view. Because the motion cues are harder to explore in some attack scenarios using small values of R_t, we investigated in Section 6.5 whether the use of longer time windows helps to reveal the disparities between a genuine face and a fake one.

6.2 Effectiveness of different classifiers

In this experiment, we analysed the effectiveness of different classifiers when the multiresolution area is increased. Figure 8 shows the HTER evolution, on the test set, under three different classification schemes. The first one uses χ^2 distance, since the feature vectors are histograms. The same strategy reported in [3] was carried out. A reference histogram only with real accesses was created averaging the histograms in the training set. The last two selected classification schemes analysed were LDA and SVM with a radial basis function kernel (RBF).

The SVM classifier with an RBF kernel provided the best performance on the Replay-Attack Database and the CASIA Face Anti-Spoofing Database (7.97% and 20.72%

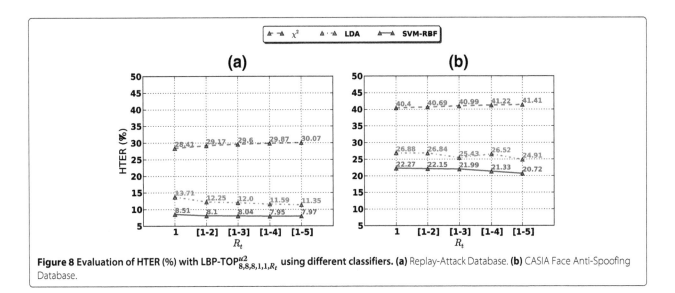

Figure 8 Evaluation of HTER (%) with LBP-TOP$^{u2}_{8,8,8,1,1,R_t}$ using different classifiers. **(a)** Replay-Attack Database. **(b)** CASIA Face Anti-Spoofing Database.

in terms of HTER, respectively). However, it is important to remark that the same LBP-TOP configuration with an LDA classifier resulted in comparable performance (11.35% and 24.91% in terms of HTER). This is not a huge gap, and the classification scheme is far simpler. As similar findings have been reported [3,30], the use of simple and computationally efficient classifiers should be indeed considered when constructing real-world anti-spoofing solutions.

6.3 Effectiveness of different LBP operators

The size of the histogram in a multiresolution analysis, in time domain, increases linearly with R_t. The choice of an appropriate LBP representation in the planes is an important issue since it impacts the size of the histograms. Using uniform patterns or rotation invariant extensions, in one or multiple planes, may bring a significant reduction in computational complexity. In this experiment, the effectiveness of different LBP operators in the three LBP-TOP planes (XY, XT and YT) was analysed. Figure 9 shows the performance, in HTER terms, configuring each plane as basic LBP (with 256 bins for $P = 8$), LBP^{u2} (uniform patterns) and LBP^{riu2} (rotation invariant uniform patterns) when the multiresolution area (R_t) is increased in both databases. Results must be interpreted with the support of Figure 10, which shows the number of bins on the histograms used for classifications in each configuration.

When the multiresolution area is increased, the HTER saturates for LBP^{riu2} and LBP^{u2} on both datasets. For the basic LBP operator, a minimum can be observed in

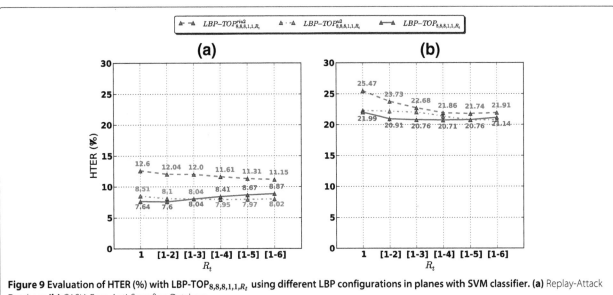

Figure 9 Evaluation of HTER (%) with LBP-TOP$_{8,8,8,1,1,R_t}$ using different LBP configurations in planes with SVM classifier. **(a)** Replay-Attack Database **(b)** CASIA Face Anti-Spoofing Database.

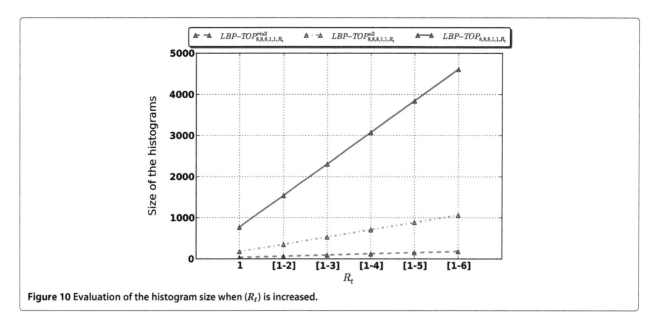

Figure 10 Evaluation of the histogram size when (R_t) is increased.

7.60% and 20.71% on the Replay-Attack Database and CASIA Face Anti-Spoofing Database, respectively. On both databases, basic LBP and LBP^{u2} presented similar performance. Even though the use of regular LBP leads to the best results, the LBP^{u2} operator seems to provide a reasonable trade-off between computational complexity (see Figure 10) and performance. Hence, we will still proceed with LBP^{u2}.

6.4 Effectiveness of the multiresolution approach
In this experiment, we analysed the effectiveness of the multiresolution approach in comparison with the single resolution approach. The single resolution approach consists of using only fixed values for R_t, without

concatenating histograms for each R_t. With this approach, the size of the histograms will be constant for different values of R_t, which decreases the computational complexity compared to the multiresolution approach. Figure 11 shows the HTER evolution for different values of R_t in both databases comparing both approaches.

On both datasets, the HTER of the single resolution approach increases with R_t, whereas the multiresolution approach helps to keep the HTER low when the multiresolution area is increased. This suggests that the increase of R_t causes more sparse sampling in the single resolution approach when valuable motion information is lost. In contrary, the more dense sampling of the multiresolution approach is able to provide a more detailed description

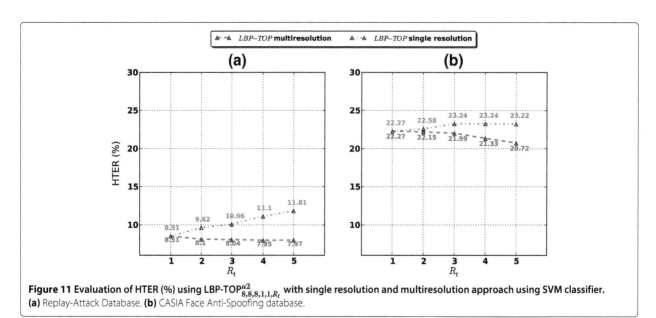

Figure 11 Evaluation of HTER (%) using LBP-TOP$^{u2}_{8,8,8,1,1,R_t}$ with single resolution and multiresolution approach using SVM classifier.
(a) Replay-Attack Database. **(b)** CASIA Face Anti-Spoofing database.

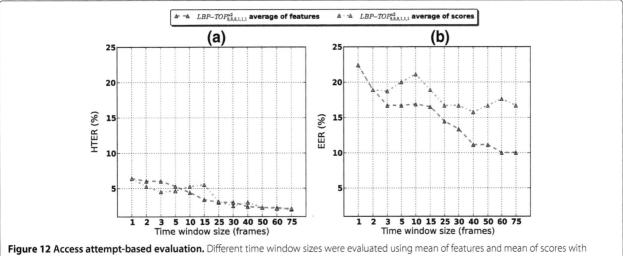

Figure 12 Access attempt-based evaluation. Different time window sizes were evaluated using mean of features and mean of scores with LBP-TOP$_{8,8,8,1,1,1}^{u2}$. **(a)** Replay-Attack Database (HTER %). **(b)** CASIA Face Anti-Spoofing Database (EER %).

of the motion patterns, thus improving the discriminative power.

6.5 Access attempt-based analysis

In the previous experiments, the importance of the temporal dimension was studied using the single resolution and the multiresolution approaches. As seen in Section 6.1, the multiresolution approach is able to capture well the nature of fixed photo attacks and the excessive motion of display medium, especially on the

Replay-Attack Database. However, in some attack scenarios, the motion patterns were harder to explore using small values of R_t. Therefore, we now study how the used temporal window size affects the performance when the facial appearance and dynamics information are accumulated over time. The face description of the single resolution and multiresolution methods can be accumulated over longer time periods either by averaging the features within a time window or by classifying each subvolume and then averaging the scores within the current

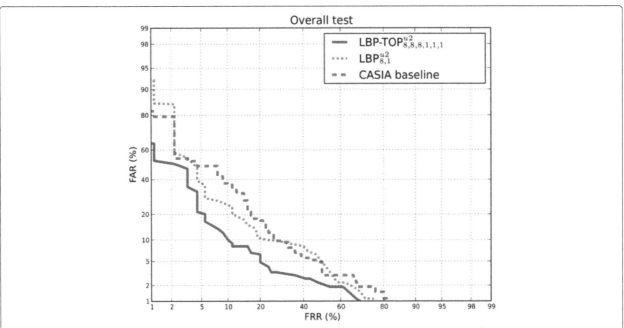

Figure 13 Overall test protocol on the CASIA Face Anti-Spoofing Database. Overall performance of LBP-TOP$_{8,8,8,1,1,1}^{u2}$ using the average of features compared to the DoG baseline method and LBP$_{8,1}^{u2}$.

Table 2 Comparison of EER (%)

Scenario	Low	Normal	High	Warped	Cut	Video	Overall
DoG baseline [6]	13	13	26	16	6	24	17
LBP$^{u2}_{8,1}$	11	17	13	13	16	16	16
LBP-TOP$^{u2}_{8,8,8,1,1,1}$	10	12	13	6	12	10	10

This table shows comparison between the DoG baseline method, LBP$^{u2}_{8,1}$ and LBP-TOP$^{u2}_{8,8,8,1,1,1}$ using the average of features on the CASIA Face Anti-Spoofing Database.

window. In this manner, we are able to provide dense temporal sampling over longer temporal windows without excessively increasing the size of the feature histogram.

To follow the method used in previous experiments, we begin evaluating the two averaging strategies with the LBP-TOP$^{u2}_{8,8,8,1,1,1}$ operator and a SVM classifier with RBF kernel. In order to determine the video-based system performance, we applied both the average of features and scores on the first valid time window of N frames from the beginning of each video sequence. It should be noted that the following access attempt-based analysis is based on the official protocol of each database. Thus, the results on Replay-Attack Database are reported in terms of HTER, whereas the performance on CASIA Face Anti-Spoofing Database is described using EER.

The access attempt-based performance of both averaging strategies on the two databases is presented in Figure 12. The results indicate that when the amount of temporal information increases, the better we are able to discriminate real faces from fake ones. This is the case especially on the CASIA Face Anti-Spoofing Database in which the distinctive motion clues, such as the excessive shaking of the display medium, cannot be exploited. However, when longer video sequences are explored, we are more likely to observe other specific dynamic events, such as different facial motion patterns (including eye blinking, lip movements and facial expression changes) or sudden characteristic reflections of planar spoofing media which can be used for differentiating real faces from fake ones. It is also interesting to notice that by averaging features,

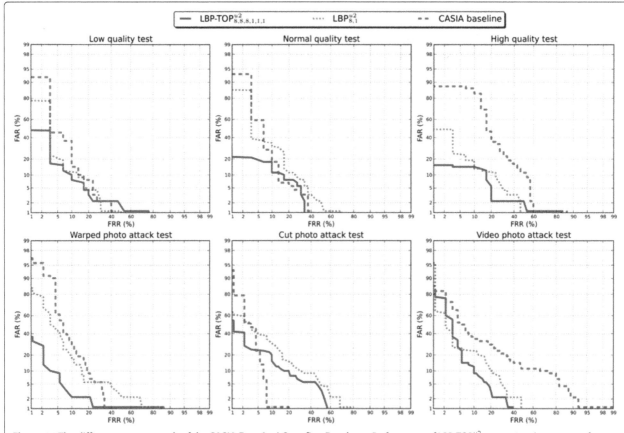

Figure 14 The different test protocols of the CASIA Face Anti-Spoofing Database. Performance of LBP-TOP$^{u2}_{8,8,8,1,1,1}$ using the average of features compared to the DoG baseline method and LBP$^{u2}_{8,1}$.

more stable and robust spoofing detection performance is achieved on both databases. The averaging scores of individual subvolumes seem to suffer from outliers; thus, more sophisticated temporal processing of scores might lead to more stable behaviour.

According to the official test protocol of CASIA Face Anti-Spoofing, also the DET curves and the EERs for the seven scenarios should be reported. Based on the previous analysis, we chose to use the average of features within a time window of 75 frames which corresponds to 3 s of video time. As it can be seen in Figure 13 and Table 2, the use of only facial appearance (LBP) leads to better results compared to the baseline method (CASIA baseline). More importantly, when the temporal planes XT and YT are also considered for spatiotemporal face description (LBP-TOP), a significant performance enhancement is obtained (from 16% to 10% in terms of EER), thus confirming the benefits of encoding and exploiting not only the facial appearance but also the facial dynamics information.

More detailed results for each scenario are presented in Figure 14 and in Table 2. The results indicate that the proposed LBP-TOP-based face description yields best results in all configurations except under cut-photo attacks. As described in [6], the DoG filtering baseline method is able to capture the less variational nature of the cut eye regions well. However, the difference in the motion patterns seems to be too small for our LBP-TOP-based approach as mainly eye blinking occurs during the cut-photo attacks and no other motion is present. The EER development presented in Table 3 supports this conclusion since the performance under cut-photo attacks does not improve that much if longer temporal window is applied compared to the other scenarios.

On the other hand, the spatiotemporal face description is able to improve the major drawbacks of DoG-based countermeasure. Unlike the baseline method, our approach performs almost equally well at all three imaging qualities. Furthermore, the performance under warped photo and video attacks is significantly better. Especially the characteristic specular reflections (flickering) and

Table 3 Effect of different time window sizes on CASIA Face Anti-Spoofing Database

Frames	Low	Normal	High	Warped	Cut	Video
1	17	27	23	29	16	20
5	13	20	20	19	14	14
10	14	20	19	18	16	14
25	13	13	10	10	14	12
50	13	11	10	7	13	10
75	10	12	13	6	12	10

This table shows EER development of LBP-TOP$^{u2}_{8,8,8,1,1,1}$ using the average of features.

Table 4 HTER (%) of the best results on the Replay-Attack Database

	Dev	Test
Motion Correlation [23]	11.78	11.79
LBP$^{u2}_{8,1}$ + SVM	14.84	15.16
LBP$_{3×3}$ + SVM [3]	13.90	13.87
LBP-TOP$^{u2}_{8,8,8,1,1,1}$ + SVM	8.17	8.51
LBP-TOP$_{8,8,8,1,1,[1-2]}$ + SVM	7.88	7.60

This table shows the HTER of the best results achieved on the Replay-Attack Database (following the database protocol) compared with the provided baseline.

excessive and distorted motion of warped photo attacks can be described very well.

6.6 Summary

Tables 4 and 5 summarize all the results obtained for each database following their provided protocols. In order to be comparable with still frame analysis presented for example in [3], the results for the Replay-Attack Database represent the overall classification accuracy considering each frame individually. The access attempt-based results are reported only for the CASIA Face Anti-Spoofing Database as requested in its test protocol.

Table 4 shows also the results for the LBP (http://pypi.python.org/pypi/antispoofing.lbp) [3] and the Motion Correlation (http://pypi.python.org/pypi/antispoofing.motion) [23] based countermeasures whose source code is freely available. Table 5 contains the provided DoG-based baseline and the holistic LBP-based face description. It can be seen that the proposed countermeasure presented the best results, overtaking the baseline results in both databases, thus confirming the benefits of encoding and exploiting not only the facial appearance but also the facial dynamics information. Unfortunately, our comparison is limited to these countermeasures due to the lack of publicly available implementations of other state-of-the-art techniques presented in the literature.

During these experiments, we observed that the general performance of the proposed countermeasure was consistently better on the Replay-Attack Database compared to the CASIA Face Anti-Spoofing Database. As mentioned

Table 5 EER (%) of the best results on the CASIA Face Anti-Spoofing Database

	Test
DoG baseline [6]	17
LBP$^{u2}_{8,1}$ + SVM	16
LBP-TOP$^{u2}_{8,8,8,1,1,1}$ with average of features + SVM	10

This table shows the EER of the best results achieved on the CASIA Face Anti-Spoofing Database (following the database protocol) compared with the provided baseline.

in Section 6.1, the nature of the attack scenarios is different between the two datasets. In the Replay-Attack Database, our LBP-TOP-based face description was able to capture motion patterns of fixed photo attacks and scenic fake face attacks already when only relatively short time windows were explored. Performances below 10% (HTER) were achieved. On the other hand, the CASIA Face Anti-Spoofing Database turned out to be more challenging from the dynamic texture point of view. Due to the lack of motion, analysis of longer temporal windows was required in order to find out distinctive motion patterns between genuine faces and fake ones. As it can be seen in Table 5, by extending the micro-texture-based spoofing detection into the spatiotemporal domain, an improvement from 16% to 10% in terms of EER was obtained. The results also indicate that the proposed dynamic texture-based face liveness description was able to improve the state of the art on both datasets.

7　Conclusion

Inspired by the recent progress in dynamic texture, the problem of face spoofing detection was recently investigated in two independent articles using spatiotemporal local binary patterns. The key idea of the proposed countermeasures consists of analysing the structure and the dynamics of the micro-textures in the facial regions using LBP-TOP features that provide an efficient and compact representation for face liveness description. However, very dissimilar strategies were introduced for exploring the temporal dimension even though the same features were utilized. Furthermore, the experiments were carried out using different face normalization techniques and different databases. In this article, we consolidated the methods proposed in the previous studies, isolating the different variables and studying the potential of the different LBP-TOP countermeasures in different settings on the two publicly available datasets. Furthermore, we also provided an open-source framework that makes our research fully reproducible with minimal effort.

Experiments carried out with a unified experimental setup and evaluation methodology showed that the dynamic texture-based countermeasure was able to consistently outperform prior work on both datasets. Best results were achieved using a nonlinear SVM classifier, but it is important to note that experiments with a simpler LDA-based classification scheme resulted in comparable performance under various spoofing attack scenarios. Thus, the use of simple and computationally efficient classifiers should be indeed considered when constructing real-world anti-spoofing solutions. In a future work, we will study the generalization capabilities of the proposed countermeasure using multiple face anti-spoofing databases. In other words, we plan to perform cross-database experiments by training and tuning the

LBP-TOP-based face description solely on one dataset and test on another one.

Competing interests
The authors declare that they have no competing interests.

Acknowledgements
This work has been performed within the context of the TABULA RASA project, part of the 7th Framework Research Programme of the European Union (EU), under the grant agreement number 257289. The financial support of FUNTTEL (Brazilian Telecommunication Technological Development Fund), Academy of Finland and Infotech Oulu Doctoral Program is also gratefully acknowledge.

Author details
[1]CPqD Telecom & IT Solutions, School of Electrical and Computer Engineering, University of Campinas (UNICAMP), Campinas, São Paulo 13083-970, Brazil. [2]Center for Machine Vision Research, Department of Computer Science and Engineering, University of Oulu, Oulu FI-90014, Finland. [3]School of Electrical and Computer Engineering, University of Campinas (UNICAMP), Campinas, São Paulo 13083-970, Brazil. [4]IDIAP Research Institute, Martigny CH-1920, Switzerland.

References
1. P Flynn, A Jain, A Ross, *Handbook of Biometrics* (Springer Science+Business Media, LLC, New York, USA, 2008)
2. S Li, A Jain, *Handbook of Face Recognition* (Springer London Dordrecht Heidelberg, New York, 2011)
3. I Chingovska, A Anjos, S Marcel, On the effectiveness of local binary patterns in face anti-spoofing, in *IEEE International Conference of the Biometrics Special Interest Group* (Darmstadt, 6–7 September 2012)
4. G Pan, L Sun, Z Wu, S Lao, Eyeblink-based anti-spoofing in face recognition from a generic webcamera, in *IEEE 11th International Conference on Computer Vision* (Rio de Janeiro, 14–21 October 2007), pp. 1–8
5. X Tan, Y Li, J Liu, L Jiang, Face liveness detection from a single image with sparse low rank bilinear discriminative model, in *11th European Conference on Computer Vision: Part VI. ECCV'10* (Heraklion, Crete, Greece, 5–11 September 2010), pp. 504–517
6. Z Zhang, J Yan, S Liu, Z Lei, D Yi, SZ Li, A face antispoofing database with diverse attacks, in *Proceedings of 5th IAPR International Conference on Biometrics (ICB'12)* (New Delhi, India, 29 March – 1 April 2012)
7. M Chakka, A Anjos, S Marcel, R Tronci, D Muntoni, G Fadda, M Pili, N Sirena, G Murgia, M Ristori, F Roli, J Yan, D Yi, Z Lei, Z Zhang, ZS Li, WR Schwartz, A Rocha, H Pedrini, LJ Navarro, C-M Santana, J Määttä, A Hadid, M Pietikäinen, Competition on counter measures to 2-D facial spoofing attacks, in *IAPR IEEE International Joint Conference on Biometrics* (Washington DC, USA, 11–13 October 2011)
8. U Uludag, A Jain, Attacks on biometric systems: a case study in fingerprints, in *Proc. SPIE-EI* (San Rose CA, USA, 18–22 January 2004), pp. 622–633
9. J Leyden, Gummi bears defeat fingerprint sensors. The Register **16** (2002). http://www.theregister.co.uk/2002/05/16/gummi_bears_defeat_fingerprint_sensors/
10. T Matsumoto, H Matsumoto, K Yamada, S Hoshino, Impact of artificial gummy fingers on fingerprint systems, in *Proceedings of SPIE, Volume 4677* (San Jose, CA, USA, 24–25 January 2002), pp. 275–289
11. P Johnson, B Tan, S Schuckers, Multimodal fusion vulnerability to non-zero effort (spoof) imposters, in *IEEE Informational Workshop on Information Forensics and Security* (Seattle, USA, 12–15 December 2010), pp. 1–5
12. M Kanematsu, H Takano, K Nakamura, Highly reliable liveness detection method for iris recognition, in *International Conference on Instrumentation, Control and Information Technology* (Takamatsu, 17–20 September 2007), pp. 361–364
13. A Pacut, A Czajka, A liveness detection for iris biometrics, in *40th Annual IEEE International Carnahan Conferences Security Technology* (Lexington, KY, October 2006), pp. 122–129
14. G Chetty, M Wagner, Liveness verification in audio-video speaker authentication, in *Proceeding of International Conference on Spoken*

Language Processing ICSLP , Volume 4 (Jeju Island, Korea, 4–8 October 2004), pp. 2509–2512

15. N Eveno, L Besacier, A speaker independent "liveness" test for audio-visual biometrics, in *9th European Conference on Speech Communication and Technology* (Lisbon, 4–8 September 2005)

16. J Bai, TT Ng, X Gao, YQ Shi, Is physics-based liveness detection truly possible with a single image?, in *IEEE International Symposium on Circuits and Systems (ISCAS)* (Paris, 30 May - 2 June 2010), pp. 3425–3428

17. J Määttä, A Hadid, M Pietikäinen, Face spoofing detection from single images using micro-texture analysis, in *IAPR IEEE International Joint Conference on Biometrics* (Washington DC, USA, 11–13 October 2011)

18. TF Pereira, A Anjos, JM De Martino, S Marcel, LBP-TOP based countermeasure against facial spoofing attacks, in *International Workshop on Computer Vision With Local Binary Pattern Variants - ACCV* (Daejeon, Korea, 5–6 November 2012)

19. J Komulainen, A Hadid, M Pietikäinen, Face spoofing detection using dynamic texture, in *International Workshop on Computer Vision With Local Binary Pattern Variants - ACCV* (Daejeon, Korea, 5–6 November 2012)

20. M Pietikäinen, A Hadid, G Zhao, T Ahonen, *Computer Vision Using Local Binary Patterns, Volume 40* (Springer, 2011)

21. G Zhao, M Pietikäinen, Dynamic texture recognition using local binary patterns with an application to facial expressions. IEEE Trans. Pattern Anal. Mach. Intell. **29**, 915–928 (2007)

22. K Kollreider, H Fronthaler, J Bigun, Non-intrusive liveness detection by face images. Elsevier Image and Vision Computing **27**, 233–244 (2009)

23. A Anjos, S Marcel, Counter-measures to photo attacks in face recognition: a public database and a baseline, in *IAPR IEEE International Joint Conference on Biometrics* (Washington DC, USA, 11–13 October 2011)

24. J Li, Y Wang, T Tan, A Jain, Live face detection based on the analysis of fourier spectra. Biometric Technology for Human Identification **5404**, 296–303 (2004)

25. J Trefný, J Matas, Extended set of local binary patterns for rapid object detection, in *15th Computer Vision Winter Workshop, Volume 2010* (Czech Republic, 3–5 February 2010)

26. T Ojala, M Pietikäinen, D Harwood, A comparative study of texture measures with classification based on feature distributions. Pattern Recognit. **29**, 51–59 (1996)

27. T Ojala, M Pietikäinen, T Mäenpää, Multiresolution gray-scale and rotation invariant texture classification with local binary patterns. Pattern Analysis and Machine Intelligence, IEEE Transactions on. **24**(7), 971–987 (2002). IEEE

28. B Froba, A Ernst, Face detection with the modified census transform, in *Automatic Face and Gesture Recognition, 2004. Proceedings. Sixth IEEE International Conference on* (Seoul, South Korea, 17–19 May 2004), pp. 91–96

29. A Anjos, L El Shafey, R Wallace, M Günther, C McCool, S Marcel, Bob: a free signal processing and machine learning toolbox for researchers, in *20th ACM Conference on Multimedia Systems* (Nara, Japan, 22–24 February 2012)

30. J Komulainen, A Anjos, A Hadid, S Marcel, M Pietikäinen, Complementary countermeasures for detecting scenic face spoofing attacks, in *6th IAPR International Conference on Biometrics* (Madrid, 4–7 June 2013)

2

Some fast projection methods based on Chan-Vese model for image segmentation

Jinming Duan[*], Zhenkuan Pan, Xiangfeng Yin, Weibo Wei and Guodong Wang

Abstract

The Chan-Vese model is very popular for image segmentation. Technically, it combines the reduced Mumford-Shah model and level set method (LSM). This segmentation problem is solved interchangeably by computing a gradient descent flow and expensively and tediously re-initializing a level set function (LSF). Though many approaches have been proposed to overcome the re-initialization problem, the low efficiency for this segmentation problem is still not solved effectively. In this paper, we first investigate the relationship between the L^1-based total variation (TV) regularizer term of Chan-Vese model and the constraint on LSF and then propose a new technique to solve the re-initialization problem. In detail, four fast projection methods are proposed, i.e., split Bregman projection method (SBPM), augmented Lagrangian projection method (ALPM), dual split Bregman projection method (DSBPM), and dual augmented Lagrangian projection method (DALPM). These four methods without re-initialization are faster than the existing approaches. Finally, extensive numerical experiments on synthetic and real images are presented to validate the effectiveness and efficiency of these four proposed methods.

Keywords: Variational level set method; Chan-Vese model; Re-initialization; Projection method

1. Introduction

Image segmentation is a popular research topic in image processing, as it has a number of significant applications in object detection and moving object tracking, resources classification in SAR images, organs segmentation and 3D reconstruction in medical images, etc. Among the segmentation approaches, the variational models [1-4] are one of the influential and effective methods. In detail, the Snake model [5] and Mumford-Shah model [6] are two fundamental models for image segmentation using variational method. The first one is a typical parametric active contour model based on image edges and fast for segmentation. However, this parametric model is not very effective for images with weak edge and meanwhile fails to deal with adaptive topologies. The second one is a typical region-based model, which aims to replace the original image with a piecewise smooth image and a minimum contour for image segmentation by minimizing an energy functional. Theoretically, it is very difficult to optimize this Mumford-Shah functional as it includes two energy terms defined

in two-dimensional image space and one-dimensional contour space respectively. In order to implement this model numerically, Aubert et al. [7-9] introduced the concept of shape derivative and transformed the two-dimensional energy term into one-dimensional one. Consequently, the original model becomes a parametric active contour model. Different from [5], authors in [7-9] developed a level set scheme [10] to achieve curve evolution for adaptive topologies. Another routine to optimize the Mumford-Shah model is to transform the term in contour space into the one in image space, which can be achieved via introducing a proper characteristic function for each different phase that represents different feature in an image. An equivalent energy functional of the original Mumford-Shah model was proposed in [11] via elliptic function approximation based on Gamma-convergence theory. Then, this new Gamma-convergence approximated Mumford-Shah model was extended to segment multiphase images [12-14], which forms the first Gamma-convergence family for variational image segmentation. The second family is variational level set method (VLSM) [15] that combines classical LSM and variational method. The most famous model of this family is Chan-Vese model [16], the first one making use of

---
* Correspondence: duanmujinming@126.com
College of Information Engineering, Qingdao University, Qingdao 266071, China

Heaviside function of LSF to design characteristic function and then realize two-phase piecewise constant image segmentation. Also, this model has been successfully extended for a great number of multiphase image segmentation [17-19]. The third family is variational label function method (VLFM) sometimes also called piecewise constant level set method [20-22] or fuzzy membership function method [23]. However, if the Heaviside function of LSF is considered as a label function, the third family is actually an extended version of the second one.

Technically, the energy functional minimization for image segmentation results in a set of partial differential equations (PDEs), which must be solved numerically. Compared with other traditional methods, the computational efficiency of variational image segmentation model is much slower, so developing its fast numerical algorithms is always a challenging task in this area. Traditionally, the models in the first two families are usually solved by gradient descent flow. Therefore, the resulting Euler equations always include complicated curvature term, which usually leads to slow computational efficiency. Previously, some fast algorithms for optimizing L^1-based total variation (TV) term have already been efficiently applied to the models of third family (VLFM). For example, novel split Bregman algorithm [24,25], dual method [26,27], and augmented Lagrangian method [21,22,28], and these fast algorithms all avoid computing complex curvature associated with TV regularizer term. Therefore, these proposed algorithms can improve the convergent rate to a great extent.

For the second family, the VLSM for image segmentation usually uses zero level set of a continuous sign distance function (SDF) to represent a contour and the geometric features (i.e., normal and curvature) can be calculated naturally via SDF. Along this way, the post-processing of curves and surfaces will be very convenient. However, the LSF is not preserved as a SDF anymore in the contour evolution and thus the geometric virtue on zero level set will be lost. There are two methods [29,30] to overcome this problem: the traditional one is periodically re-initializing the LSF as a SDF by solving a static eikonal equation or a dynamical Hamilton-Jacobi equation using upwind scheme [29,31-33]. However, this is very expensive and tedious and may make the zero level set moving to undesired positions. The novel one is by constraining LSF to remain a SDF during the contour evolution through adding penalty terms into the original energy functional [30,34]. However, the penalty parameter limits the time step for the LSF evolution due to Courant-Friedrichs-Lewy (CFL) condition [35] and thus the SDF cannot be preserved unless penalty parameter is very large, which cannot guarantee the stability of numerical computation. In order to avoid CFL condition, researchers in [36] proposed completely augmented Lagrangian method

by introducing eight auxiliary variables and four penalty parameters, leading to numerous sub-minimization and sub-maximization problems for every introduced variable. Therefore, the resulting models are very complicated.

In this paper, we investigate the relationship between the TV regularizer term of Chan-Vese model and the constraint of LSF as a SDF and then propose a new model with fewer auxiliary variables in comparison with [36]. In this case, we can transform the constraint into a very simple algebra equation that can be explicitly implemented via direct projection approach without re-initialization. Based on this explicit model and novel technique, three algorithms in the third family (i.e., split Bregman algorithm, dual method, and augmented Lagrangian method) for optimizing the variational models can be conveniently extended to Chan-Vese model in second family, and thus four fast algorithms are developed (i.e., split Bregman projection method, augmented Lagrangian projection method, dual split Bregman projection method, and dual augmented Lagrangian projection method). Technically, the resulting equations in the proposed four algorithms include four components: (1): a simple Euler-Lagrange equation for LSF and this Euler-Lagrange equation can be solved via fast Gauss-Seidel iteration, (2): a generalized soft thresholding formula in analytical form, (3): a fast iterative formula for dual variable, and (4): a very simple projection formula. These four components can be used elegantly to avoid computing the complex curvature in [16,30,34]. In addition, all the four proposed fast projection methods can preserve full LSF as a SDF precisely without a very large penalty parameter due to the introduced Lagrangian multiplier and Bregman iterative parameter. So a relatively large time step is allowed to be employed to speed up LSF evaluation in comparison with [30,34]. Most importantly, even if the LSF is initialized as a piecewise constant function, it can be corrected automatically due to the iterative projection computation. Therefore, our proposed methods have both higher computational efficiency and better SDF fidelity than those reported in [30,34,36]. What is worth mentioning here is that our proposed algorithms are quite generic and can be easily extended to all models using VLSM for multiphase image segmentation, motion segmentation, 3D reconstruction etc. For example, the case [37] for multiphase image segmentation has been investigated by using augmented Lagrangian projection method in our recent work.

This paper is organized as follows: in Section 2, we first present the Chan-Vese model under VLSM framework and then review some previous approaches with constraint of LSF as a SDF. In Section 3, the fast split Bregman projection method (SBPM), augmented Lagrangian projection method (ALPM), dual split Bregman projection method (DSBPM), dual augmented Lagrangian projection method (DALPM) are presented. In Section 4, extensive numerical experiments have been conducted to compare our proposed fast methods with some existing approaches. Finally, concluding remarks and outlooks are given.

2. The Chan-Vese model and its traditional solution scheme

2.1 Mumford-Shah model

We first introduce the Mumford-Shah model that is the basic of this paper, and it can be discussed below. For a scalar image $f(x)$: $\Omega \to R$, the Mumford-Shah model can be stated as the following energy functional minimization problem

$$\underset{u,\Gamma}{\text{Min}}\left\{ E(u,\Gamma) = \alpha\int_{\Omega}(u-f)^2 dx + \beta\int_{\Omega/\Gamma}|\nabla u|^2 dx + \gamma\int_{\Gamma} ds \right\} \tag{1}$$

where f is the original input image. The objective of this model is to find a piecewise smooth image u and a minimum contour Γ to minimize (1). α, β, and γ are three positive penalty parameters. This problem is hard to solve due to inconsistent dimension μ and Γ. In order to solve Equation 1 approximately, Chan and Vese [16] first combined the reduced Mumford-Shah model [6] and VLSM [10] and proposed the following Chan-Vese model with an idea of dividing an image into two regions

$$\underset{u,\Gamma}{\text{Min}}\left\{ E(u,\Gamma) = \alpha_1\int_{\Omega_1}(u_1-f)^2 dx + \alpha_2\int_{\Omega_2}(u_2-f)^2 dx + \gamma\int_{\Gamma} ds \right\} \tag{2}$$

where $u = (u_1, u_2)$ stands for piecewise constant image mean value in regions Ω_1 and Ω_2, respectively, and $\Omega = \Omega_1 \cup \Omega_2$, $\Omega_1 \cap \Omega_2 = \varnothing$.

2.2 Traditional LSM

In order to understand the Chan-Vese model clearly, let us first recall some concepts of traditional LSM. $\Gamma(t)$ is defined as a closed contour that separates two regions $\Omega_1(t)$ and $\Omega_2(t)$, and a Lipschitz continuous LSF $\phi(x,t)$ is defined as

$$\begin{cases} \phi(x,t) > 0 & x \in \Omega_1(t) \\ \phi(x,t) = 0 & x \in \Gamma(t) \\ \phi(x,t) < 0 & x \in \Omega_2(t) \end{cases} \tag{3}$$

where $\Gamma(t)$ corresponds to zero level set $\{x{:}\phi(x, t) = 0\}$ and its evolution equation can be transformed into zero level set of $\phi(x,t)$. Then, we differentiate $\phi(x,t) = 0$ with respect to t and obtain the following LSF evolution equation

$$\phi_t + \frac{dx}{dt} \cdot \nabla\phi = 0 \tag{4}$$

As the normal on $\{x : \phi(x,t) = 0\}$ is $\vec{N} = \nabla\phi/|\nabla\phi|$, Equation 4 can be rewritten as the following standard level set evolution equation:

$$\phi_t + v_N|\nabla\phi| = 0 \tag{5}$$

where normal velocity v_N of $\Gamma(t)$ is $\frac{dx}{dt} \cdot \frac{\nabla\phi}{|\nabla\phi|}$.

Usually, $\phi(x,t)$ is defined as a SDF

$$\begin{cases} \phi(x,t) = d(x,\Gamma(t)) & x \in \Omega_1(t) \\ \phi(x,t) = 0 & x \in \Gamma(t) \\ \phi(x,t) = -d(x,(t)) & x \in \Omega_2(t) \end{cases} \tag{6}$$

Where $d(x, \Gamma(t))$ denotes the Euclidean distance from x to $\Gamma(t)$. An equivalent constraint to Equation 6 is the eikonal equation

$$|\nabla\phi(x,t)| = 1 \tag{7}$$

In order to satisfy Equation 7, an iterative re-initialization scheme [16] is used to solve the steady state of following equation:

$$\begin{cases} \phi_t + \text{sign}(\phi_0)(|\nabla\phi|-1) = 0 & \text{in } \Omega \times R \\ \phi(x,0) = \phi_0 & \text{in } \Omega \end{cases} \tag{8}$$

where ϕ_0 is the function to be reinitialized and $\text{sign}(\phi_0)$ denotes the sign function of ϕ_0.

2.3 The Chan-Vese model under VLSM framework and its solution

By using Heaviside function of LSF and its total variation form, Chan and Vese [16] transformed the model (2) into VLSM. In fact, a Heaviside function is defined as

$$H(x) = \begin{cases} 1 & x \geq 0 \\ 0 & \text{otherwise} \end{cases} \tag{9}$$

Its derivative in the distributional sense is the Dirac function

$$\delta(x) = \frac{\partial H(x)}{\partial x} \tag{10a}$$

According to Equation 9, the characteristic function of Ω_1 and Ω_2 can be defined as

$$\chi_1(x) = H(\phi(x)) = \begin{cases} 1 & x \in \Omega_1 \\ 0 & \text{otherwise} \end{cases} \tag{10b}$$

$$\chi_2(x) = 1 - H(\phi(x)) = \begin{cases} 1 & x \in \Omega_2 \\ 0 & \text{otherwise} \end{cases} \tag{10c}$$

Based on the co-area formula [38] of characteristic functions, the length term in Equation 2 can be approximately defined in image space Ω as

$$\gamma \int_\Gamma ds = \gamma \int_\Omega |\nabla H(\phi)| dx = \gamma \int_\Omega |\nabla \phi| \delta(\phi) dx \qquad (11)$$

Therefore, Equation 2 can be rewritten as the following VLSM:

$$\underset{\phi,u}{\text{Min}} \left\{ E(\phi, u_1, u_2) = \alpha_1 \int_\Omega (u_1 - f)^2 H(\phi) dx \right.$$
$$+ \alpha_2 \int_\Omega (u_2 - f)^2 (1 - H(\phi)) dx$$
$$\left. + \gamma \int_\Omega |\nabla \phi| \delta(\phi) dx \right\} \qquad (12)$$

Equation 12 is a multivariate minimization problem and usually solved via alternative optimization procedure. First fix ϕ to optimize u and then fix u for optimizing ϕ. In detail, when ϕ is fixed, we obtain

$$u_1 = \frac{\int_\Omega f H(\phi) dx}{\int_\Omega H(\phi) dx}, \qquad u_2 = \frac{\int_\Omega f(1 - H(\phi)) dx}{\int_\Omega (1 - H(\phi)) dx} \qquad (13)$$

On the other hand, when u is fixed, the sub-problem of optimization with respect to ϕ is as follows:

$$\underset{\phi}{\text{Min}} \left\{ E(\phi) = \int_\Omega Q_{12}(u_1, u_2) H(\phi) dx + \gamma \int_\Omega |\nabla H(\phi)| dx \right\} \qquad (14)$$

where $Q_{12}(u_1, u_2) = \alpha_1(u_1 - f)^2 - \alpha_2(u_2 - f)^2$. In order to solve Equation 14, we need to compute the evolution equation of ϕ via gradient descent flow as

$$\begin{cases} \dfrac{\partial \phi}{\partial t} = \left(\gamma \nabla \cdot \left(\dfrac{\nabla \phi}{|\nabla \phi|} \right) - Q_{12}(u_1, u_2) \right) \delta(\phi) & \text{in } \Omega \\ \dfrac{\partial \phi}{\partial \vec{n}} = 0 & \text{on } \partial\Omega \end{cases} \qquad (15)$$

In order to avoid singularity in numerical implementation for Equation 15, the Heaviside function and Dirac function are usually approximated by their regularized version with a small positive regularized parameter ε as

$$H_\varepsilon(\phi) = \frac{1}{2} + \frac{1}{\pi} \arctan\left(\frac{\phi}{\varepsilon}\right) \qquad (16a)$$

$$\delta_\varepsilon(\phi) = \frac{1}{\pi} \frac{\varepsilon}{\phi^2 + \varepsilon^2} \qquad (16b)$$

As both the energy functional (12) and the evolution Equation 15 do not include any exact definition of LSF ϕ as a SDF, the ϕ will not be preserved as a SDF during the contour evolution, which leads to accuracy loss in curve or surface expression.

The first correction approach to preserve the LSF as a SDF is solving Equation 8 using upwind scheme after

some iterations of ϕ using Equation 15. However, this method is expensive and may cause the interface to shrink and move to undesirable positions. In order to make comparisons with other methods, we name this re-initialization approach as gradient descent equation with re-initialization method (GDEWRM).

The second correction approach, which was proposed by [30] as following, is to add the constraint Equation 7 as a penalty term into Equation 14 in order to avoid the tedious re-initialization process

$$\underset{\phi}{\text{Min}} \left\{ E(\phi) = \int_\Omega Q_{12} H_\varepsilon(\phi) dx + \gamma \int_\Omega |\nabla H_\varepsilon(\phi)| dx \right.$$
$$\left. + \frac{\mu}{2} \int_\Omega (|\nabla \phi| - 1)^2 dx \right\} \qquad (17)$$

Theoretically, μ should be a large penalty parameter in order to sufficiently penalize the constraint $|\nabla \phi| = 1$ as a SDF. However, under such circumstance, we cannot choose a relatively large time step to improve the computational efficiency due to the CFL stability condition [35]. Here, we name this method as gradient descent equation without re-initialization method (GDEWORM).

As an extension of (17), an augmented Lagrangian method (ALM) and a projection Lagrangian method (PLM) are proposed by [34] to remain the LSF as a SDF during the LSF evolution. These two extensions can be expressed as follows, respectively:

$$\underset{\phi}{\text{Min}} \left\{ E(\phi, \lambda) = \int_\Omega Q_{12} H_\varepsilon(\phi) dx + \gamma \int_\Omega |\nabla H_\varepsilon(\phi)| dx \right.$$
$$\left. + \int_\Omega \lambda (|\nabla \phi| - 1) dx + \frac{\mu}{2} \int_\Omega (|\nabla \phi| - 1)^2 dx \right\} \qquad (18)$$

$$\underset{\phi,\vec{w}}{\text{Min}} \left\{ E\left(\phi, \vec{w}\right) = \int_\Omega Q_{12} H_\varepsilon(\phi) dx + \gamma \int_\Omega |\nabla H_\varepsilon(\phi)| dx \right.$$
$$\left. + \int_\Omega \lambda \left(|\vec{w}| - 1\right) dx + \frac{\mu}{2} \int_\Omega \left(\vec{w} - \nabla \phi\right)^2 dx \right\} \qquad (19)$$

Different from GDEWORM, ALM (18) enforces the constraint $|\nabla \phi| = 1$ via Lagrangian parameter λ. Therefore, a relatively small penalty parameter μ can be chosen to improve the stability of numerical calculation of Equation 18. The PLM (19) is actually proposed by combining variable splitting and penalty approach, so it is more efficient than GDEWORM due to the split technique. However, one drawback still exists: as μ becomes very large, the intermediate minimization process of PLM becomes increasingly ill-conditioned as happened for GDEWORM.

Using the similar idea, [36] introduced four auxiliary variables and four Lagrangian multipliers to deal with the same constrained optimization problem. The minimization problem is reformulated as following, and here, we name it as completely augmented Lagrangian method (CALM).

$$
\begin{aligned}
E\left(\phi, \varphi, s, \vec{v}, \vec{w}\right) = & \int_{\Omega} Q_{12} s dx + \gamma \int_{\Omega} |\vec{v}| dx \\
& + \int_{\Omega} \lambda_2 (s - H_\varepsilon(\varphi)) dx + \frac{\mu_2}{2} \int_{\Omega} (s - H_\varepsilon(\varphi))^2 dx \\
& + \int_{\Omega} \vec{\lambda}_3 \cdot \left(\vec{v} - \nabla s\right) dx + \frac{\mu_3}{2} \int_{\Omega} \left(\vec{v} - \nabla s\right)^2 dx \\
& + \int_{\Omega} \lambda_1 (\varphi - \phi) dx + \frac{\mu_1}{2} \int_{\Omega} (\varphi - \phi)^2 dx \\
& + \int_{\Omega} \vec{\lambda}_4 \cdot \left(\vec{w} - \nabla\phi\right) dx + \frac{\mu_4}{2} \int_{\Omega} \left(\vec{w} - \nabla\phi\right)^2 dx
\end{aligned}
\tag{20}
$$

$$
s.t \left|\vec{w}\right| = 1. \tag{21}
$$

Note that all of the above methods, GDEWRM (8, 14), GDEWORM (17), ALM (18), and PLM (19), only take efforts in how to add the constraint $|\nabla\phi| = 1$ into the original functional and ignore the TV regularizer term $\int_{\Omega} |\nabla H(\phi)| dx$. Therefore, their resulting evolution equations bring about complex curvature terms, and the computational efficiency will be very slow due to such complicated finite difference scheme for the curvature. Through introducing eight variables in CALM (20), each sub-minimization or sub-maximization problem of this model becomes very simple because there is no curvature term in these sub-problems. However, as we know, every variable including Lagrangian multiplier is defined in the domain of image space, which implies the more variables the model has, the less efficient it will become. Moreover, there are five penalty parameters setting up in the CALM, so the choices of these parameters are more difficult. In order to avoid computing curvature and meanwhile decrease the number of the introduced variables and parameters, we will design fast algorithms in the next section, by taking into full consideration the relationship between regularization term $\int_{\Omega} |\nabla H(\phi)| dx$ and constraint term $|\nabla\phi| = 1$.

3. Four fast projection methods

The fast split Bregman method [24,25], dual method [26], and augmented Lagrangian method [28] proposed for TV model for image restoration have been successfully extended to the Chan-Vese model under VLFM framework [20,38], but they cannot be directly applied to Chan-Vese model under VLSM framework due to the complex constraint $|\nabla\phi| = 1$. In this section, inspired by these fast algorithms, we aim to design some new fast algorithms for Chan-Vese model [16] without re-initialization under VLSM framework. Through

introducing two or three auxiliary variables, the constraint is transformed into a very simple projection formula so that our proposed fast methods are able to avoid both expensive re-initialization process and complex curvature appearance in the evolution equations. Therefore, the proposed methods are faster than their counterparts with higher performance.

In order to state the problem clearly, we rewrite the traditional Chan-Vese model (14) and the constraint (7) as the following:

$$
\underset{\phi}{\text{Min}}\left\{E(\phi) = \int_{\Omega} Q_{12}(u_1, u_2) H_\varepsilon(\phi) dx + \gamma \int_{\Omega} |\nabla\phi| \delta_\varepsilon(\phi) dx\right\} \tag{22a}
$$

$$
s.t. |\nabla\phi| = 1. \tag{22b}
$$

Next, we will introduce each fast algorithm separately.

3.1 Split Bregman projection method

Unlike Equations 18 and 19, we do not put the constraint Equation 22b directly into functional Equation 22a. Instead, we introduce an auxiliary splitting variable $\vec{w}$ to replace the $\nabla\phi$ in the TV regularizer term $\int_{\Omega} |\nabla\phi| \delta_\varepsilon(\phi) dx$. Therefore, the constraint Equation 22b becomes constraint $\left|\vec{w}\right| = 1$ and another constraint $\vec{w} = \nabla\phi$ is produced. Then, we use the Bregman distance technique [25] by introducing Bregman iterative parameter $\vec{b}$ to satisfy the constraint $\vec{w} = \nabla\phi$, so we can transform Equation 22a, b into the following optimization problem:

$$
\begin{aligned}
\underset{\phi, \vec{w}}{\text{Min}}\Big\{E\left(\phi, \vec{w}\right) = & \int_{\Omega} Q_{12}(u_1, u_2) H_\varepsilon(\phi) dx + \gamma \int_{\Omega} |\vec{w}| \delta_\varepsilon(\phi) dx \\
& + \frac{\theta}{2} \int_{\Omega} \left(w - \nabla\phi - \vec{b}\right) dx\Big\},
\end{aligned}
$$

$$
s.t. \left|\vec{w}\right| = 1,
$$

In order optimize the above problem, we use the iterative technique as

$$
\begin{aligned}
\left(\phi^{k+1}, \vec{w}^{k+1}\right) = & \arg \underset{\phi, \vec{w}}{\text{min}} \left\{E\left(\phi, \vec{w}\right)\right. \\
= & \int_{\Omega} Q_{12}(u_1, u_2) H_\varepsilon(\phi) dx \\
& + \gamma \int_{\Omega} |\vec{w}| \delta_\varepsilon(\phi) dx + \frac{\theta}{2} \int_{\Omega} \\
& \times \left. \left(w - \nabla\phi - \vec{b}^{k+1}\right) dx\right\},
\end{aligned}
\tag{23a}
$$

$$
s.t. \left|\vec{w}\right| = 1, \tag{23b}
$$

where $\theta > 0$ is a penalty parameter, $\vec{w}$ and $\vec{b}$ are vectors, $\vec{b}^{k+1} = \vec{b}^k + \nabla\phi^k - \vec{w}^k$, $\vec{b}^0 = \vec{w}^0 = \vec{0}$. The alternating minimization of $E(\phi, \vec{w})$ with respect to ϕ and $\vec{w}$ leads to the Euler-Lagrange equations, respectively

$$\begin{cases} Q_{12}(u_1, u_2)\delta_\varepsilon(\phi) + \gamma|\vec{w}^k|\dfrac{\partial\delta_\varepsilon(\phi)}{\partial\phi} + \theta\nabla\cdot\left(\vec{w}^k - \nabla\phi - \vec{b}^{k+1}\right) = 0 & \text{in } \Omega \\ \left(\vec{w}^k - \nabla\phi - \vec{b}^{k+1}\right)\cdot\vec{n} = 0 & \text{on } \partial\Omega \end{cases}$$

(24)

$$\begin{cases} \gamma\dfrac{\vec{w}}{|\vec{w}|}\delta_\varepsilon(\phi) + \theta\left(\vec{w} - \nabla\phi^{k+1} - \vec{b}^{k+1}\right) = 0 \\ \text{s. t. } |\vec{w}| = 1 \end{cases}$$

(25)

Equation 24 can be solved using semi-implicit difference scheme and Gauss-Seidel iterative method, and the first equation of Equation 25 can be expressed as a following generalized soft thresholding formula in analytical form

$$\vec{w}^{k+1} = \text{Max}\left(\left|\nabla\phi^{k+1} + \vec{b}^{k+1}\right| - \dfrac{\gamma}{\theta}\delta_\varepsilon(\phi^{k+1}), 0\right)\dfrac{\nabla\phi^{k+1} + \vec{b}^{k+1}}{\left|\nabla\phi^{k+1} + \vec{b}^{k+1}\right|}.$$

(26)

Then, $|\vec{w}| = 1$ can be guaranteed via a simple projection technique as the following:

$$\vec{w}^{k+1} = \dfrac{\vec{w}^{k+1}}{\left|\vec{w}^{k+1}\right|}.$$

(27)

Note that after computing the projection (27), the constraint $|\vec{w}| = 1$ is precisely guaranteed so that the constraint $|\nabla\phi| = 1$ is indirectly adjusted by this projection technique when evolution Equation 24 for LSF reaches its steady state.

3.2 Augmented Lagrange projection method

The ALPM proposed in this part is different from previous ALM (18) and CALM (20). Here, we add the constraint $\vec{w} = \nabla\phi$ in energy functional through augmented Lagrangian method and let the constraint $|\nabla\phi| = 1$ as a simple projection of auxiliary variable $\vec{w}$. Compared with CALM (20) including eight variables and four parameters, our augmented Lagrangian projection method is introduced only by two auxiliary

variables and one parameter θ. Similar to the Subsection 3.1, we introduce an auxiliary splitting variable $\vec{w}$ such that $\vec{w} \approx \nabla\phi$ when the following energy functional approaches reach minimum.

$$\left(\phi^{k+1}, \vec{w}^{k+1}, \vec{\lambda}^{k+1}\right) = \underset{\vec{\lambda}}{\text{Arg Max}} \underset{\phi, \vec{w}}{\text{Min}}$$

$$\begin{cases} E\left(\phi, \vec{w}, \vec{\lambda}\right) = \displaystyle\int_\Omega Q_{12}(u_1, u_2)H_\varepsilon(\phi)dx + \gamma\displaystyle\int_\Omega|\vec{w}|\delta_\varepsilon(\phi)dx \\ \quad + \displaystyle\int_\Omega \vec{\lambda}\cdot\left(\vec{w} - \nabla\phi\right)dx + \dfrac{\theta}{2}\displaystyle\int_\Omega\left(\vec{w} - \nabla\phi\right)^2 dx \end{cases}$$

(28a)

$$s.t. \left|\vec{w}\right| = 1,$$

(28b)

where $\vec{\lambda}$ is the Lagrangian multiplier and θ is a positive penalty parameter. The augmented Lagrangian method reduces the possibility of ill-conditioning and makes the numerical computation stable through iterative Lagrangian multiplier during the process of the minimization. Therefore, different from the previous penalty methods (17, 19) which need a very large penalty parameter to penalize the constraint effectively, the constraint $\vec{w} = \nabla\phi$ of this method can be guaranteed without increasing θ to a very large value. Here, we minimize $E\left(\phi, \vec{w}, \vec{\lambda}\right)$ with respect to ϕ and $\vec{w}$ and maximize $E\left(\phi, \vec{w}, \vec{\lambda}\right)$ with respect to $\vec{\lambda}$. A saddle point of the min-max problems satisfies the following:

$$\begin{cases} Q_{12}(u_1, u_2)\delta_\varepsilon(\phi) + \gamma|\vec{w}^k|\dfrac{\partial\delta_\varepsilon(\phi)}{\partial\phi} + \nabla\cdot\vec{\lambda}^k + \theta\nabla\cdot\left(\vec{w}^k - \nabla\phi\right) = 0 & \text{in } \Omega \\ \left(\vec{\lambda}^k + \theta\left(\vec{w}^k - \nabla\phi\right)\right)\cdot\vec{n} = 0 & \text{on } \partial\Omega \end{cases}$$

(29)

$$\begin{cases} \gamma\dfrac{\vec{w}}{|\vec{w}|}\delta_\varepsilon(\phi^{k+1}) + \vec{\lambda}^k + \theta\left(\vec{w} - \nabla\phi^{k+1}\right) = 0 \\ \text{s. t. } |\vec{w}| = 1 \end{cases}$$

(30)

$$\vec{\lambda}^{k+1} = \vec{\lambda}^k + \theta\left(\vec{w}^{k+1} - \nabla\phi^{k+1}\right), \vec{\lambda}^0 = 0$$

(31)

Equation 29 can be solved using the same method as Equation 24, and the first equation of Equation 30 can be solved using the following generalized soft thresholding formula in analytical form

$$\vec{w}^{k+1} = \text{Max}\left(\left|\nabla\phi^{k+1} - \vec{\lambda}^k/\theta\right| - \dfrac{\gamma}{\theta}\delta_\varepsilon(\phi^{k+1}), 0\right)\dfrac{\nabla\phi^{k+1} - \vec{\lambda}^k/\theta}{\left|\nabla\phi^{k+1} - \vec{\lambda}^k/\theta\right|}$$

(32)

Then, the second equation of Equation 30 can be implemented as same as Equation 27.

3.3 Dual split Bregman projection method

The dual method [26] is another fast algorithm proposed in recent years for TV model for image restoration, and it has been extensively applied to variational image segmentation models [20] under VLFM framework. In Equation 22a, $\int_\Omega |\nabla\phi|\delta_\varepsilon(\phi)dx$ is not the total variation of ϕ, but its equivalent formula $\int_\Omega |\nabla H_\varepsilon(\phi)|dx$ is the total variation of $H_\varepsilon(\phi)$. Based on this observation, we can introduce a dual variable to replace $\int_\Omega |\nabla H_\varepsilon(\phi)|dx$ with its dual formula $\mathrm{Sup}_{\vec{p}:|\vec{p}|\leq 1}\int_\Omega H_\varepsilon(\phi)\nabla\cdot\vec{p}\,dx$.

Thus, Equation 22a can be rewritten as following min-max functional:

$$\left(\phi^{k+1},\vec{p}^{k+1}\right) = \underset{\phi}{\mathrm{Arg\,Min}}\,\underset{\vec{p}:|\vec{p}|\leq 1}{\mathrm{Sup}}$$

$$\left\{E\left(\phi,\vec{p}\right) = \int_\Omega Q_{12}(u_1,u_2)H_\varepsilon(\phi)dx + \gamma\int_\Omega H_\varepsilon(\phi)\nabla\cdot\vec{p}\,dx\right\} \tag{33}$$

For the constraint $|\nabla\phi| = 1$ (22b), we first introduce an auxiliary variable $\vec{w}$ and add the new constraint $\vec{w} = \nabla\phi$ into (33) through Split Bregman iterative method, which is expressed as following

$$\left(\phi^{k+1},\vec{p}^{k+1},\vec{w}^{k+1}\right) = \underset{\phi,\vec{w}}{\mathrm{Arg\,Min}}\,\underset{\vec{p}:|\vec{p}|\leq 1}{\mathrm{Sup}}$$

$$\left\{\begin{array}{l}E\left(\phi,\vec{p},\vec{w}\right) = \int_\Omega Q_{12}(u_1,u_2)H_\varepsilon(\phi)dx + \gamma\int_\Omega H_\varepsilon(\phi)\nabla\cdot\vec{p}\,dx \\ \qquad + \dfrac{\theta}{2}\int_\Omega \left(\vec{w}-\nabla\phi-\vec{b}^{k+1}\right)^2 dx\end{array}\right\} \tag{34}$$

Then the constraint $|\nabla\phi| = 1$ can be replaced by the constraint $\left|\vec{w}\right| = 1$ so that we can conveniently use the projection formula in Equation 27. Actually, the effect of vector Bregman iterative parameter $\vec{b}$ is used to reduce the dependence on the penalty parameter θ, as the same role of Lagrangian multiplier λ in augmented Lagrangian projection method (28a). The Bregman iterative parameter $\vec{b}$ can be updated by $\vec{b}^{k+1} = \vec{b}^k + \nabla\phi^k - \vec{w}^k$, where $\vec{b}^0 = \vec{w}^0 = \vec{0}$. The Euler-Lagrange equation of ϕ in Equation 34 is derived as

$$\left\{\begin{array}{ll}\left(Q_{12}(u_1,u_2)+\gamma\nabla\cdot\vec{p}^k\right)\delta_\varepsilon(\phi)+\theta\nabla\cdot\left(\vec{w}^k-\nabla\phi-\vec{b}^{k+1}\right)=0 & \text{in }\Omega \\ \left(\vec{w}^k-\nabla\phi-\vec{b}^{k+1}\right)\cdot\vec{n}=0 & \text{on }\partial\Omega\end{array}\right. \tag{35}$$

After ϕ^{k+1} is obtained, we can solve $\vec{p}\,k+1$ via the gradient descent method

$$\frac{\partial\vec{p}}{\partial t} = -\gamma\nabla H\left(\phi^{k+1}\right), \left|\vec{p}\right|\leq 1 \tag{36}$$

By using semi-implicit difference scheme and the Karush-Kuhn-Tucker (KKT) conditions in [26], we can update $\vec{p}$, and get following fast iterative formula for this dual variable $\vec{p}\,k+1$

$$\vec{p}^{k+1} = \frac{\vec{p}^k - \tau\nabla H\left(\phi^{k+1}\right)}{1+\tau\left|\nabla H\left(\phi^{k+1}\right)\right|} \tag{37}$$

where $\tau \leq 1/8$ is a time step as in [26].

Then, we can get a simple analytical form for auxiliary variable as the following:

$$\vec{w}^{k+1} = \nabla\phi^{k+1} + \vec{b}^{k+1} \tag{38}$$

Finally, we use projection formula of $\vec{w}^{k+1}$ as same as Equation 27 in order to satisfy the constraint $\left|\vec{w}\right| = 1$.

3.4 Dual augmented Lagrangian projection method

The same idea in Subsection 3.3 can be extended to combine dual method and augmented Lagrangian projection method in Subsection 3.2, and this will lead to the dual augmented Lagrangian projection method. In detail, by introducing auxiliary variable $\vec{w}$ and putting the constraint $\vec{w} = \nabla\phi$, we can transform Equation 33 into following iterative minimization formulation:

$$\left(\phi^{k+1},\vec{p}^{k+1},\vec{w}^{k+1}\right) = \underset{\phi,\vec{w}}{\mathrm{Arg\,Min}}\,\underset{\vec{p}:|\vec{p}|\leq 1}{\mathrm{Sup}}$$

$$\left\{\begin{array}{l}E\left(\phi,\vec{p},\vec{w}\right) = \int_\Omega Q_{12}(u_1,u_2)H_\varepsilon(\phi)dx + \gamma\int_\Omega H_\varepsilon(\phi)\nabla\cdot\vec{p}\,dx \\ \qquad + \int_\Omega \vec{\lambda}\cdot\left(\vec{w}-\nabla\phi\right)dx + \dfrac{\theta}{2}\int_\Omega\left(\vec{w}-\nabla\phi\right)^2 dx\end{array}\right\} \tag{39}$$

The constraint $|\nabla\phi| = 1$ can be also expressed as the constraint $\left|\vec{w}\right| = 1$. By using the similar procedure, we can obtain the Euler-Lagrange equation of ϕ as the following;

$$\left\{\begin{array}{ll}\left(Q_{12}(u_1,u_2)+\gamma\nabla\cdot\vec{p}^k\right)\delta_\varepsilon(\phi)+\nabla\cdot\vec{\lambda}^k+\theta\nabla\cdot\left(\vec{w}^k-\nabla\phi\right)=0 & \text{in }\Omega \\ \left(\vec{\lambda}^k+\theta\left(\vec{w}^k-\nabla\phi\right)\right)\cdot\vec{n}=0 & \text{on }\partial\Omega\end{array}\right. \tag{40}$$

The $\vec{p}^{k+1}$ is updated as same as Equation 38, and $\vec{w}^{k+1}$ is the following analytical form

$$\vec{w}^{k+1} = \nabla\phi^{k+1} - \frac{\vec{\lambda}^k}{\theta} \tag{41}$$

Table 1 Abbreviations, full names, and their corresponding energy functionals of all methods for comparison

No.	Abbreviations	Full name	Energy functional
1	GDEWRM	Gradient descent equation with re-initialization [16]	$E(\phi) = \int_\Omega Q_{12} H(\phi) dx + \gamma \int_\Omega |\nabla H(\phi)| dx$ and $\begin{cases} \phi_t + \text{Sign}(\phi_0)(|\nabla\phi|-1) = 0 \\ \phi(x,0) = \phi_0 \end{cases}$
2	GDEWORM	Gradient descent equation without re-initialization [30]	$E(\phi) = \int_\Omega Q_{12} H_\varepsilon(\phi) dx + \gamma \int_\Omega |\nabla H_\varepsilon(\phi)| dx + \frac{\mu}{2} \int_\Omega (|\nabla\phi|-1)^2 dx$
3	ALM	Augmented Lagrangian method [34]	$E(\phi,\lambda) = \int_\Omega Q_{12} H(\phi) dx + \gamma \int_\Omega |\nabla H(\phi)| dx + \int_\Omega \lambda(|\nabla\phi|-1) dx + \frac{\mu}{2}\int_\Omega (|\nabla\phi|-1)^2 dx$
4	PLM	Projection Lagrangian method [34]	$E(\phi,\vec{w}) = \int_\Omega Q_{12} H(\phi) dx + \gamma \int_\Omega |\nabla H(\phi)| dx + \int_\Omega \lambda(|\vec{w}|-1) dx + \frac{\mu}{2}\int_\Omega (\vec{w}-\nabla\phi)^2 dx$
5	CALM	Completely augmented Lagrangian method [36]	$E(\phi,\varphi,s,\vec{v},\vec{w}) = \int_\Omega Q_{12} s\, dx + \gamma\int_\Omega |\vec{v}| dx + \int_\Omega \lambda_2(s-H_\varepsilon(\varphi)) dx$ $+\frac{\mu_2}{2}\int_\Omega (s-H_\varepsilon(\varphi))^2 dx$ $+\int_\Omega \vec{\lambda_3}\cdot(\vec{v}-\nabla s) dx + \frac{\mu_3}{2}\int_\Omega (\vec{v}-\nabla s)^2 dx$ s. t. $|\vec{w}|=1$ $+\int_\Omega \lambda_1(\varphi-\phi) dx + \frac{\mu_1}{2}\int_\Omega (\varphi-\phi)^2 dx$ $+\int_\Omega \vec{\lambda_4}\cdot(\vec{w}-\nabla\phi) dx + \frac{\mu_4}{2}\int_\Omega (\vec{w}-\nabla\phi)^2 dx$
6	SBPM	Split Bregman projection method	$E(\phi,\vec{w}) = \int_\Omega Q_{12} H_\varepsilon(\phi) dx + \gamma\int_\Omega |\vec{w}| \delta_\varepsilon(\phi) dx + \frac{\theta}{2}\int_\Omega (\vec{w}-\nabla\phi-\vec{b}^{k+1})^2 dx$ s. t. $|\vec{w}|=1$
7	ALPM	Augmented Lagrangian projection method	$E(\phi,\vec{w},\vec{\lambda}) = \int_\Omega Q_{12} H_\varepsilon(\phi) dx + \gamma\int_\Omega |\vec{w}| \delta_\varepsilon(\phi) dx + \int_\Omega \vec{\lambda}\cdot(\vec{w}-\nabla\phi) dx + \frac{\theta}{2}\int_\Omega (\vec{w}-\nabla\phi)^2 dx$ s. t. $|\vec{w}|=1$
8	DSBPM	Dual Split Bregman projection method	$E(\phi,\vec{p},\vec{w}) = \int_\Omega Q_{12} H_\varepsilon(\phi) dx + \gamma\int_\Omega H_\varepsilon(\phi)\nabla\cdot\vec{p}\, dx + \frac{\theta}{2}\int_\Omega (\vec{w}-\nabla\phi-\vec{b}^{k+1})^2 dx$ s. t. $|\vec{w}|=1$
9	DALPM	Dual augmented Lagrangian method	$E(\phi,\vec{p},\vec{w},\vec{\lambda}) = \int_\Omega Q_{12} H_\varepsilon(\phi) dx + \gamma\int_\Omega H_\varepsilon(\phi)\nabla\cdot\vec{p}\, dx + \int_\Omega \vec{\lambda}\cdot(\vec{w}-\nabla\phi) dx + \frac{\theta}{2}\int_\Omega (\vec{w}-\nabla\phi)^2 dx$ s. t. $|\vec{w}|=1$
10	FMM	Fuzzy membership method [38]	$E(\phi,\vec{w}) = \int_\Omega Q_{12}\phi\, dx + \gamma\int_\Omega |\vec{w}| dx + \frac{\theta}{2}\int_\Omega (w-\nabla\phi-\vec{b}^{k+1}) dx$ s. t. $\phi\in[0,1]$

Then, we project $\vec{w}^{k+1}$ as in Equation 27. Finally, the Lagrangian multiplier $\vec{\lambda}$ can be updated as the following:

$$\vec{\lambda}^{k+1} = \vec{\lambda}^k + \theta\left(\vec{w}^{k+1} - \nabla\phi^{k+1}\right) \qquad (42)$$

The advantages of the proposed four projection methods can be summarized as follows. (1): By introducing fewer auxiliary variables (i.e., two for SBPM, ALPM and three for DSBPM, DALPM) and considering the relationship between TV regularization term $\int_\Omega |\nabla H_\varepsilon(\phi)|dx$ or its equivalent form $\int_\Omega |\nabla\phi|\delta_\varepsilon(\phi)dx$ in Equation 22a and constraint term $|\nabla\phi| = 1$ in Equation 22b, we developed a very simple projection formula (27) in order to skillfully avoid expensive re-initialization process. (2): The proposed methods do not have many sub-minimization and sub-maximization problems and penalty parameters due to the fewer auxiliary variables, so it is very easy and efficient to implement. (3): The final Euler-equations of proposed fast projection algorithms only include a simple Euler-Lagrange equation (24, 29, 35, 40) that can be solved via fast Gauss-Seidel iteration, a generalized soft thresholding formula in analytical form (26, 32), a fast iterative formula for dual variable (37), and a very simple projection formula (27). This technique can elegantly avoid computing the complex curvature and thus improve the efficiency. (4): All the proposed methods can preserve full LSF as a SDF precisely without a very large penalty parameter. This is due to the introduced Bregman iterative parameters (23a, 34) and Lagrangian multipliers (28a, 39) and the

projection computation, so a relatively large time step is allowed to be employed to speed up LSF evaluation as we will use semi-implicit gradient descent flow for (24, 29, 35, 40). (5): Even if the LSF is initialized as a piecewise constant function, it can be corrected automatically and precisely due to the projection computation. In conclusion, our proposed four projection methods will have both higher computational efficiency and better SDF fidelity, which can be validated in the next experimental Section.

4. Numerical experiments

In this section, we present some numerical experiments to compare the effectiveness and efficiency of our methods (i.e., SBPM, ALPM, DSBPM, and DALPM) with five previous ones (i.e., GDEWRM, GDEWORM, ALM, PLM, and CALM). In addition, we also compare the proposed four methods with the fast algorithm proposed in [38] for Chan-vese model under VLFM framework [20], which is named in this paper as fuzzy membership method (FMM). Therefore, there are totally ten algorithms involved in this paper. In order to make it easier to assess the exact differences between these models, we list the abbreviations of all methods, their full name, and corresponding energy functionals in Table 1.

In order to make the comparisons fair among different methods, we solve the PDEs in Equations 15, 17, 18, 19, 24, 29, 35, and 40 by semi-implicit difference scheme based on their gradient descent equations. As for FMM, we here adopt the method proposed in [38]. For CALM, we use the Gauss-Seidel fixed point iteration for solving

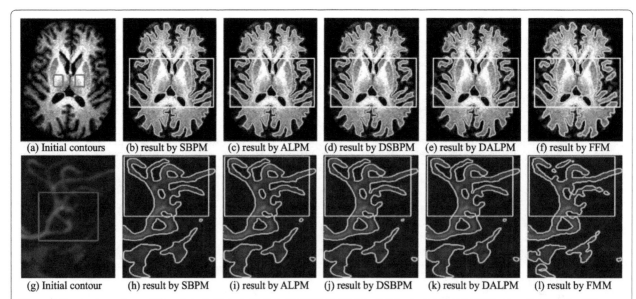

| (a) Initial contours | (b) result by SBPM | (c) result by ALPM | (d) result by DSBPM | (e) result by DALPM | (f) result by FFM |
| (g) Initial contour | (h) result by SBPM | (i) result by ALPM | (j) result by DSBPM | (k) result by DALPM | (l) result by FMM |

Figure 1 Comparison of our different projection methods with FMM. By their application to segment an MR image of brain and a CT image of vessel. **(a and g)** Original image with red initial contour. **(b-f and h-l)** The final segmentation results (i.e., green contours) by SBPM, ALPM, DSBPM, DALPM, and FMM, respectively.

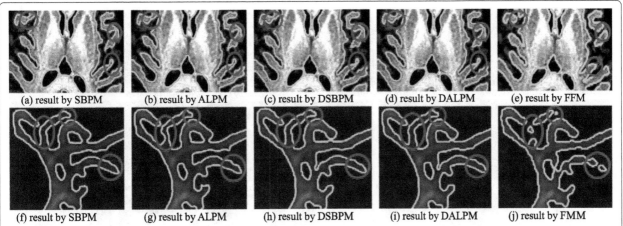

(a) result by SBPM   (b) result by ALPM   (c) result by DSBPM   (d) result by DALPM   (e) result by FFM

(f) result by SBPM   (g) result by ALPM   (h) result by DSBPM   (i) result by DALPM   (j) result by FMM

Figure 2 Zoom in small sub-regions of images in Figure 1 for detail comparisons. (a-j) The enlarged region of panels b to l of Figure 1, respectively.

the LSF ϕ instead of fast Fourier transformation (FFT) for fair comparison with others. The initial LSF ϕ^0 is initialized as a same piecewise constant function for all the methods except initializing a SDF for GDEWRM. Equation 8 is solved by using the first order upwind scheme in every five iterations. In experiments 1 and 2, we set a one-step iteration for inside loop computation of ϕ for all the methods. However, ten-step iterations for ϕ in experiment 3 are required to achieve the final 3D SDFs fast. The parameter γ is usually formatted by $\gamma = \eta \times 255^2$, $\eta \in (0,1)$. We set the spatial step $h = 1$ and $\alpha_1 = \alpha_2 = 1$, $\tau = 0.125$, $\varepsilon = 3$. The stopping criterion is based on the relative energy error formula $|E^{k+1} - E^k|/E^k \leq \xi$, where ξ is a small prescribed tolerance and here we set 10^{-3} in all numerical experiments. All experiments are performed using Matlab 2010b on a Windows 7 platform with an Intel Core 2 Duo CPU at 2.33GHz and 2GB memory.

4.1 Experiment 1

In this experiment, we aim to compare the proposed four methods with the fast algorithm FMM. As FMM uses binary or label functions and continuous convex relaxation technique, it is very robust for initialization and fast and guaranteed to find a global minimizer. Our methods and FMM are applied to segment two medical images. One is MRI image of brain in the first row of Figure 1, and the other is CT image of vessel in the second row. The five methods are initialized with the same piecewise constant function (0 and 1). Here, we draw the red contours to represent their initial contours in the first column of Figure 1. Columns 2, 3, 4, 5, and 6 are the final segmentation results (i.e., green contours) by SBPM, ALPM, DSBPM, DALPM, and FMM, respectively. In order to make detailed comparisons, we crop a part of region indicated by the yellow rectangle in Figure 1 and enlarge them in Figure 2 where the first four columns are the results by the proposed four methods, respectively, and the last column is by FMM. One can observe from Figures 1 and 2 that the white matter in the brain and the vessel are extracted correctly and perfectly by the four methods. However, the results by FMM are less desirable. This can be clearly observed in column 5 of Figure 2, where some undesirable results of structure segmentation are marked with blue circles. However, we cannot tell easily some major differences among those segmentation results by all the four proposed methods. Further, fewer iterations and fast computational time shown in Table 2 demonstrate that the four methods are comparatively efficient as the fast FMM. In fact, the SBPM, ALPM, DSBPM, and DALPM are just different iterative schemes to solve the same system. The authors in [28] have proven their equivalence for the TV model. The segmentation results in Figure 1 and iterations and CPU times in Table 2 demonstrate consistency with their conclusion.

Table 2 Comparisons of iterations and computation time among our proposed fast methods

Image (size)	SBPM		ALPM		DSBPM		DALPM		FMM	
	Iterations	CPU time (s)	Iterations	CPU time (s)	Iterations	CPU time (s)	Iterations	CPU time (s)	Iterations	CPU time (s)
Brain (123 × 155)	19	0.327	19	0.331	20	0.308	20	0.325	22	0.326
Vessel (95 × 152)	23	0.313	22	0.306	22	0.309	22	0.303	24	0.329

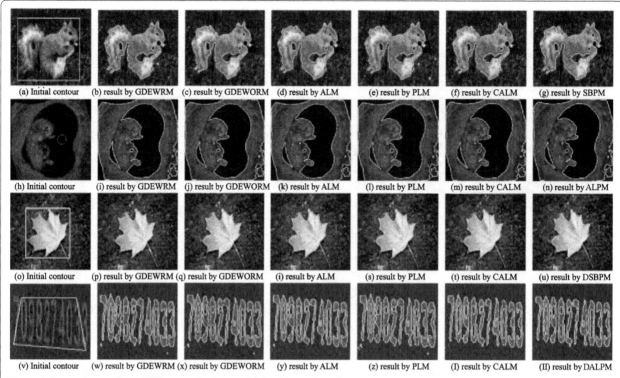

Figure 3 Comparisons of our different projection methods with previous five ones. To segment a squirrel image, an ultrasound baby image, a leaf image, and a synthetic noise number image. **(a, h, o, v)** Original image with initial green contour. **(b, i, p, w)** Results by GDEWRM. **(c, j, q, w)** Results by GDEWORM. **(d, k, i, y)** Results by ALM. **(e, l, s, z)** Results by PLM. **(f, m, t, I)** Results by CALM. **(g, n, u, II)** Results by our projection methods (from top to bottom is SBPM, ALPM, DSBPM, and DALPM, respectively).

4.2 Experiment 2

In this experiment, we will compare the efficiency of our methods with that of GDEWRM, GDEWORM, ALM, PLM, and CALM. All nine methods are run on four real and synthetic images including squirrel, ultrasound baby, leaf, and synthetic noise number images, respectively. In the first column of Figure 3, we initialize piecewise constant function (0 and 1) for all methods except GDEWRM, which is initialized with a SDF. Columns 2, 3, 4, 5, and 6 of Figure 3 are the results by GDEWRM, GDEWORM, ALM, PLM, and CALM respectively. In the last column of Figure 3, we only present the final segmentation result of squirrel, ultrasound baby, leaf, and number image by SBPM, ALPM, DSBPM, and DALPM respectively, because the visual effect and computational efficiency for all the four proposed methods

Table 3 Comparison of iterations and computation time using different segmentation methods

Methods	Iterations				CPU time (s)			
	Squirrel (155 × 122)	Ultrasound baby (180 × 175)	Leaf (128 × 87)	Numbers (128 × 127)	Squirrel (155 × 112)	Ultrasound baby (180 × 175)	Leaf (128 × 87)	Number (128 × 127)
GDEWRM	165	372	98	100	4.296	12.769	3.070	4.230
GDEWORM	166	108	85	38	2.543	4.905	1.978	1.666
ALM	46	100	64	31	1.243	3.803	1.163	0.945
PLM	109	92	69	34	1.211	2.813	0.738	0.596
CALM	32	39	62	26	0.696	1.365	0.685	0.498
SBPM	24	28	28	14	0.389	0.723	0.256	0.202
ALPM	23	26	27	15	0.372	0.707	0.237	0.212
DSBPM	24	25	29	13	0.381	0.692	0.258	0.192
DALPM	22	26	28	14	0.351	0.701	0.262	0.208

are very similar on these images. From Figure 3, we can see that all the methods do a relatively good performance for segmenting both real and noise synthetic images. However, compared with other methods, all the four proposed methods perform better, which can be observed in the last column of Figure 3. In addition, we record total iterations and computation time of all nine methods for segmenting these images in Table 3. In order to make the experimental data in Table 3 meaningful, we draw Figure 4 to illustrate the differences regarding iterations and computation time. Figure 4a,b,c,d shows the total iterations with bar chart of all nine methods for segmenting squirrel, ultrasound baby, leaf, and number images, respectively, and Figure 4e,f,g,h draws the total CPU time for segmenting these images. According to Figure 4e,f,g,h, the computational time of the nine methods can be clearly ranked in the following order: SBPM ≈ ALPM ≈ DSBPM ≈ DALPM < CALM < PLM < ALM < GDEWORM < GDEWRM. The reason leading to this rank can be justified as follows. (1) All the methods compute faster than the GDEWRM due to its expensive re-initialization process. (2) Among these methods without re-initialization, ALM, PLM, and CALM are running faster than GDEWORM. For GDEWORM, the CFL condition limits its time step so that it cannot be fast, while ALM improves convergence rate by introducing Lagrange multiplier λ. PLM uses Lagrangian method and variable splitting technique to enhance the evolution

Table 4 Comparison of iterations, computation time, and SDF fidelity using different segmentation methods

Methods	Iterations	CUP time (s)	SDF fidelity value
GDEWRM	200	77.236	0.0385
GDEWORM	2000	224.094	0.4407
ALM	600	69.624	1.9005
PLM	500	46.644	0.0441
CALM	200	18.545	0.0259
SBPM	50	5.296	0.0149
ALPM	50	5.197	0.0149
DSBPM	50	4.924	0.0153
DALPM	50	5.213	0.0153

speed, so PLM is faster than ALM. However, both ALM and PLM are limited by CFL condition and their speed is slowed. CALM introduces many scalar or vector auxiliary variables and Lagrangian multipliers to make each subproblem very simple as well as can avoid CFL condition, so it computes faster than ALM and PLM. (3) All the proposed methods can achieve the best efficiency and satisfactory segmentation results because the nonlinear curvature is replaced by the linear Laplace operator in Equations 24 and 29 or the dual divergence operator in Equations 35 and 40 as simple projection technique (27)

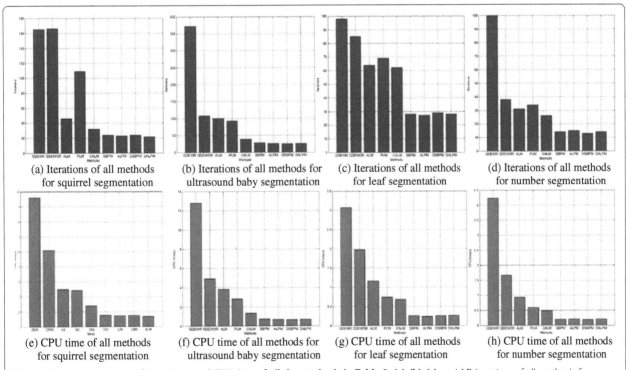

(a) Iterations of all methods for squirrel segmentation

(b) Iterations of all methods for ultrasound baby segmentation

(c) Iterations of all methods for leaf segmentation

(d) Iterations of all methods for number segmentation

(e) CPU time of all methods for squirrel segmentation

(f) CPU time of all methods for ultrasound baby segmentation

(g) CPU time of all methods for leaf segmentation

(h) CPU time of all methods for number segmentation

Figure 4 Graph Expression of iterations and CPU time of all the methods in Table 3. (a), **(b)**, **(c)**, and **(d)** Iterations of all methods for segmenting squirrel, ultrasound baby, leaf and synthetic noise number images respectively. **(e)**, **(f)**, **(g)**, and **(h)** Record of their CPU time.

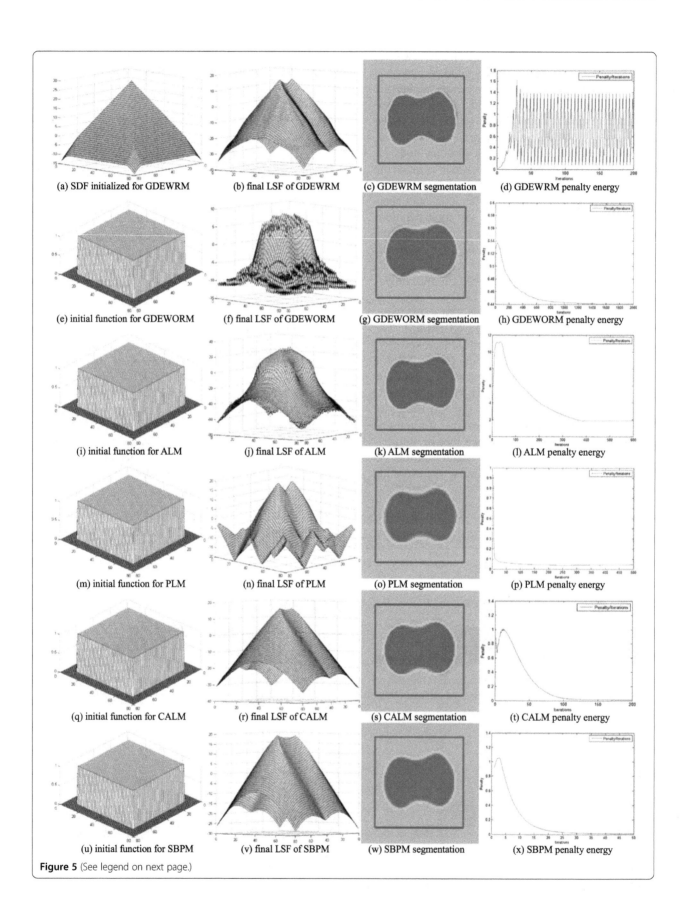

(a) SDF initialized for GDEWRM (b) final LSF of GDEWRM (c) GDEWRM segmentation (d) GDEWRM penalty energy

(e) initial function for GDEWORM (f) final LSF of GDEWORM (g) GDEWORM segmentation (h) GDEWORM penalty energy

(i) initial function for ALM (j) final LSF of ALM (k) ALM segmentation (l) ALM penalty energy

(m) initial function for PLM (n) final LSF of PLM (o) PLM segmentation (p) PLM penalty energy

(q) initial function for CALM (r) final LSF of CALM (s) CALM segmentation (t) CALM penalty energy

(u) initial function for SBPM (v) final LSF of SBPM (w) SBPM segmentation (x) SBPM penalty energy

Figure 5 (See legend on next page.)

(See figure on previous page.)
Figure 5 SDF fidelity comparisons of our projection methods with previous methods. (a, e, i, m, q, u) Initial LSFs. **(b, f, j, n, r, v)** Final LSFs. **(c, g, k, o, s, w)** Initial contours marked by red rectangle and final segmentation results indicated by green contours. **(d, h, l, p, t, x)** Mean value of penalty energy plots $\int_{\Omega}(|\nabla\phi| - 1)^2 dx$ (closeness measure between LSF and SDF).

is used. In comparison with CALM, our projection methods have fewer sub-problems, so it is very efficient. In addition, by introducing the Bregman iterative parameters (23a, 34) and Lagrangian multipliers (28a, 39), a relatively large time step can be used to speed up LSF evaluation. Therefore, our methods compute faster than CALM and their efficiency ranks first. (4) The proposed four fast methods (i.e., SBPM, ALPM, DSBPM, and DALPM) are actually equivalent, which is validated in [25]. Therefore, these projection methods have very similar computation speed.

4.3 Experiment 3
In this experiment, we aim to compare SDF fidelity produced by our four methods and the other five. We segment a synthetic image (100×100) to obtain the SDF fidelity value in Table 4 as explained below. The first column of Figure 5 is the initial LSFs for all the methods. As there is no constraint of LSF as a SDF in GDEWRM, panel a is initialized as a SDF for this method. However, if it is initialized as a piecewise constant function, the LSF will be far away from SDF during the contour evaluation, even though the re-initialization process may be not able to pull LSF back to SDF. In this case, the comparisons of SDF preservation with other methods without re-initialization are not very fair. Based on the above observation, Figure 5e,i,m,q,u is initialized as the same piecewise constant function for GDEWORM, ALM, PLM, CALM, and SBPM, respectively. As all of our four projection methods achieve almost the same results, here, we only give the experimental data for SBPM in the last row of Figure 5. In the second column of

Figure 5b,f,j,n,r,v are the final 3D LSFs of GDEWRM, GDEWORM, ALM, PLM, CALM, and SBPM, respectively. In the third column of Figure 5c,g,k,o,s,w are the same initial contours marked by red rectangle and the final segmentation results marked by green contours of above methods. In the last column, we draw the plots of mean value of penalty energy $\int_{\Omega}(|\nabla\phi| - 1)^2 dx$ by the above corresponding methods, which is used to measure the closeness between LSF and SDF. We denote SDF fidelity value as mean value in the last iteration for every method. The smaller this value is, the closer the LSF and SDF will be. We also put all these results in Table 4 for easy comparison.

Note that the final LSF of GDEWRM in Figure 5b is very close to SDF, which is validated by its very small SDF fidelity value (0.0385) in Table 4. However, the final green segmentation contour in Figure 5c shows that the zero level set of Figure 5b by this GDEWRM shrinks and cannot reach the exact location of the object. In fact, in order to obtain Figure 5b, this GDEWRM needs 300 re-initialization iterations after every five-step iteration of LSF evolution. So it is very expensive (total 77.236 s reported in Table 4), and this re-initialization leads to large jumps in its penalty energy plots in Figure 5d. For GDEWORM and PLM, their experimental results are displayed in the second and fourth row, respectively. Although their final SDF fidelity values are close to zero (i.e., 0.4407 for GDEWORM and 0.0441 for PLM), their final SDFs as shown in Figure 5f,n are not preserved nicely. Moreover, due to CFL condition, we need to choose a very small time step 10^{-4} and a very large penalty parameter 2×10^4 for GDEWORM and

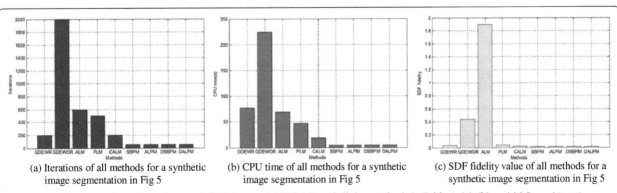

(a) Iterations of all methods for a synthetic image segmentation in Fig 5

(b) CPU time of all methods for a synthetic image segmentation in Fig 5

(c) SDF fidelity value of all methods for a synthetic image segmentation in Fig 5

Figure 6 Graph expression of iterations and CPU time and SDF fidelity of all the methods in Table 4. (a), (b), and **(c)** Record iterations, CPU time, and SDF fidelity value of all methods, respectively.

PLM, respectively. This selection is aimed to guarantee the closeness between the LSF and SDF and stability of LSF evolution, but this leads to a large number of total iterations (i.e., respective 2,000 and 500). As we analyzed in experiment 2, PLM adopts variable splitting technique and therefore its total computation time and iterations are much less than GDEWORM. As large penalty parameters are employed in PLM and GDEWORM, we find that the final green contours by these two methods cannot segment the object precisely. For ALM, it improves convergence rate by introducing Lagrange multiplier λ so that we can choose a slightly larger time step 10^{-2} and a relatively smaller penalty parameter 10^{-1} to evolve the LSF. However, we conducted a great number of experiments for this method and note that it is very sensitive to parameters selection. Also, its final SDF fidelity value is always the largest among all the methods. This may be due to the fact that the introduced Lagrangian multiplier in ALM breaks the CFL condition. The fourth row of Figure 5 that demonstrates CALM is able to achieve a better 3D SDF (shown in Figure 5f) and a smaller SDF fidelity value (0.0259 shown in Table 4) than those by other methods except our methods. The computation speed of this method has been improved to a great extent as observed in Table 4 and Figure 5t. The last row of Figure 5 presents the experimental data by our proposed SBPM. Here, we emphasize that the other three proposed methods can achieve almost that same SDF and efficiency as SBPM. From Figure 5v, the final 3D LSF is perfectly preserved as SDF fidelity value is only 0.0149, the smallest one among all the methods in Table 4. Most impressively, we find that penalty parameter 10 can be large enough to penalize accurately the full LSF as SDF due to the introduced Lagrangian multiplier, Bregman iterative parameter, and the precise projection computation. In this case, a relatively large time 10^{-2} can be employed to speed up LSF evolution as shown in Figure 5x. In addition, even if the LSF is initialized as a piecewise constant function for SBPM, it can be corrected automatically and precisely due to the projection formula (27).

Lastly, we present Figure 6 that includes three bar graphs which correspond to iterations, CUP time, and SDF fidelity value in Table 4, respectively. However, Figure 6b shows that the slowest method is GDEWORM rather than GDEWRM, which is inconsistent with the conclusion in experiment 2. In fact, the time step in GDEWRM is set 10^{-2}, 100 times larger than that set for GDEWORM. We find that this time step together with 300 re-initialization iterations would not broke the stability of LSF evolution and simultaneously is able to achieve a very desirable SDF. In contrast, for the purpose of preserving distance feature, we should choose a very large penalty parameter for GDEWORM, which limits the speed of LSF evolution. Therefore, in this experiment, on the premise of preserving distance feature, the GDEWRM is faster than GDEWORM. From Figure 6c, the ability of SDF fidelity can be ranked as SBPM ≈ ALPM ≈ DSBPM ≈ DALPM > CALM > GDEWORM > PLM > GDEWRM > ALM. In conclusion, this experiment validates that the four projection methods perform excellently in both accuracy and speed of preserving SDF.

5. Conclusions

In this paper, by investigating the relationship between the L^1-based TV regularizer term of Chan-Vese model and the constraint on LSF and introducing some auxiliary variables, we design fast split Bregman projection method (SBPM), augmented Lagrangian projection method (ALPM), dual split Bregman projection method (DSBPM), and dual augmented Lagrangian projection method (DALPM). All these methods can skillfully avoid the expensive re-initialization process and simplify computation of curvatures. In our methods, there are fewer subproblems and penalty parameters, so they can be solved efficiently. Moreover, the full LSF can be preserved as a SDF precisely without a very large penalty parameter so that a relatively large time step can be used to speed up LSF evaluation. In addition, even if the LSF is initialized as a piecewise constant function, it can be corrected automatically and accurately due to analytical projection computation. Simulation experiments have validated the efficiency and performance of proposed methods in terms of computational cost and SDF fidelity.

Abbreviations

ALM: augmented Lagrangian method; ALPM: augmented Lagrangian projection method; CALM: completely augmented Lagrangian method; CFL: Courant-Friedrichs-Lewy; DALPM: dual augmented Lagrangian method; DSBPM: dual split Bregman projection method; FFT: fast Fourier transformation; FMM: fuzzy membership method; GDEWORM: gradient descent equation without re-initialization; GDEWRM: gradient descent equation with re-initialization; KKT: Karush-Kuhn-Tucker; LSF: level set function; LSM: level set method; PDEs: partial differential equations; PLM: projection Lagrangian method; SBPM: split Bregman projection method; SDF: sign distance function; TV: total variation; VLFM: variational label function method; VLSM: variational level set method.

Competing interests

The authors declare that they have no competing interests.

Acknowledgments

This work was supported by the National Natural Science Foundation of China (nos.61305045, 61170106, and 61303079), National 'Twelfth Five-Year' Development Plan of Science and Technology (no.2013BAI01B03), and Qingdao Science and Technology Development Project (no. 13-1-4-190-jch).

References

1.   JM Morel, S Solimini, *Variational Methods in Image Segmentation* (Birkhauser, Boston, 1994)

2.   TF Chan, M Moelich, B Sandberg, Some recent developments in variational image segmentation, in *Image Processing Based on Partial Differential Equations*, ed. by XC Tai, KA Lie, TF Chan, S Osher (Springer, Heidelberg, 2006), pp. 175–210

3. S Osher, N Paragios, *Geometric Level Set Methods in Imaging, Vision, and Graphics* (Springer, Heidelberg, 2003)

4. A Mitiche, IB Ayed, *Variational and Level Set Methods in Image Segmentation* (Springer, Heidelberg, 2010)

5. M Kass, A Witkin, D Terzopoulos, Snakes: active contour models. Int. J. Comput. Vis. **4**(1), 321–331 (1987)

6. D Mumford, J Shah, Optimal approximations by piecewise smooth functions and associated variational problems. Commun. Pure Appl. Math. **42**(5), 577–685 (1989)

7. G Aubert, M Barlaud, O Faugeras, S Jehan-Besson, Image segmentation using active contours: calculus of variations or shape gradient. SIAM J. Appl. Math. **63**(6), 2128–2154 (2003)

8. G Aubert, M Barlaud, S Duffner, A Herbulot, S Jehan-Besson, Segmentation of vectorial image features using shape gradients and information measures. J. Math. Imaging Vis. **25**(3), 365–386 (2006)

9. G Aubert, M Barlaud, E Debreuve, M Gastaud, Using the shape gradient for active contour segmentation: from the continuous to the discrete formulation. J. Math. Imaging Vis. **28**(1), 47–66 (2007)

10. S Osher, JA Sethian, Fronts propagating with curvature-dependent speed: algorithms based on Hamilton-Jacobi formulations. J. Comput. Phys. **79**(1), 12–49 (1988)

11. L Ambrosio, VM Tortorelli, Approximation of functionals depending on jumps by elliptic functionals via gamma-convergence. Commun. Pur. Appl. Math. **43**(8), 999–1036 (1990)

12. S Esedoglu, YH Tsai, Threshold dynamics for the piecewise constant Mumford-Shah functional. J. Comput. Phys. **211**(1), 367–384 (2006)

13. YM Jung, SH Kang, JH Shen, Multiphase image segmentation by Modica-Mortola phase transition. SIAM J. Appl. Math. **67**(5), 1213–1232 (2007)

14. I Posirca, YM Chen, CZ Barcelos, A new stochastic variational PDE model for soft Mumford-Shah segmentation. J. Math. Anal. Appl. **384**(1), 104–114 (2011)

15. HK Zhao, TF Chan, B Merriman, S Osher, A variational level set approach to multiphase motion. J. Comput. Phys. **127**(1), 179–195 (1996)

16. TF Chan, LA Vese, Active contours without edges. IEEE Trans. image process. **10**(2), 266–277 (2001)

17. LA Vese, TF Chan, A multiphase level set framework for image segmentation using the Mumford and Shah model. Int. J. Comput. Vis. **50**(3), 271–293 (2002)

18. C Samson, L Blanc-Feraud, G Aubert, A level set model for image classification. Int. J. Comput. Vis. **40**(3), 187–197 (2000)

19. G Chung, LA Vese, Energy minimization based segmentation and denoising using a multilayer level set approach. LNCS, Springer-Verlang **3757**, 439–455 (2005)

20. X Bresson, S Esedoglu, P Vandergheynst, JP Thiran, S Osher, Fast global minimization of the active contour/snake model. J. Math. Imaging Vis. **28**(2), 151–167 (2007)

21. J Lie, M Lysaker, XC Tai, A binary level set model and some applications to Mumford-Shah image segmentation. IEEE Trans. Image process. **15**(5), 1171–1181 (2006)

22. J Lie, M Lysaker, XC Tai, A variant of the level set method and applications to image segmentation. Math. Comput. **75**(255), 1155–1174 (2006)

23. F Li, K Michael, T Zeng, C Shen, A multiphase image segmentation method based on fuzzy region competition. SIAM J. Imaging Sci. **3**(3), 277–299 (2010)

24. T Goldstein, S Osher, The split Bregman method for L1 regularized problems. SIAM J. Imaging Sci. **2**(2), 323–343 (2009)

25. T Goldstein, X Bresson, S Osher, Geometric applications of the split Bregman method: segmentation and surface reconstruction. J. Sci. Comput. **45**(1–3), 272–293 (2009)

26. A Chambolle, An algorithm for total variation minimization and applications. J. Math. Imaging Vis. **20**(1), 89–97 (2004)

27. ES Brown, TF Chan, X Bresson, Completely convex formulation of the Chan-Vese image segmentation model. Int. J. Comput. Vis. **98**(1), 103–121 (2012)

28. C Wu, XC Tai, Augmented Lagrangian method, dual methods, and split Bregman iteration for ROF, vectorial TV, and high order models. SIAM J. Imaging Sci. **3**(3), 300–339 (2010)

29. YHR Tsai, LT Cheng, S Osher, HK Zhao, Fast sweeping algorithms for a class of Hamilton-Jacobi equations. SIAM J. Numer. Anal. **41**(2), 673–694 (2003)

30. C Li, C Xu, C Gui, MD Fox, Level set evolution without re-initialization: a new variational formulation, in *Proceedings of IEEE conference on Computer Vision and Pattern Recognition (CVPR)*, 1st edn. San Diego **20–25**, 430–436 (2005)

31. D Adalsteinsson, JA Sethian, The fast construction of extension velocities in level set methods. J. Comput. Phys. **148**(1), 2–22 (1999)

32. D Peng, B Merriman, S Osher, HK Zhao, M Kang, A PDE-based fast local level set method. J. Comput. Phys. **155**(2), 410–438 (1999)

33. M Sussman, E Fatemi, An efficient, interface preserving level set re-distancing algorithm and its application to interfacial incompressible fluid flow. SIAM J. Sci. Comput. **20**(4), 1165–1191 (1999)

34. C Liu, F Dong, S Zhu, D Kong, K Liu, New variational formulations for level set evolution without reinitialization with applications to image segmentation. J. Math. Imaging Vis **41**(3), 194–209 (2011)

35. R Courant, K Friedrichs, H Lewy, On the partial difference equations of mathematical physics. IBM J **11**(2), 215–234 (1967)

36. V Estellers, D Zosso, R Lai, S Osher, JP Thiran, X Bresson, An efficient algorithm for level set method preserving distance function. IEEE Trans. Image Process. **21**(12), 4722–4734 (2012)

37. C Liu, Z Pan, J Duan, New algorithm for level set evolution without re-initialization and its application to variational image segmentation. J Software **8**(9), 2305–2312 (2013)

38. X Bresson, A Short Guide on a Fast Global Minimization Algorithm for Active Contour Models (Online). https://googledrive.com/host/0B3BTLeCYLunCc1o4YzV1Ui1SeVE/codes_files/xbresson_2009_short_guide_global_active_contours.pdf. Accessed 22 Apr 2009

3

Shadow extraction and application in pedestrian detection

Junqiu Wang[1]* and Yasushi Yagi[2]

Abstract

We find shadows in many images and videos. Traditionally, shadows are considered as noises because they make hurdles for visual tasks such as detection and tracking. In this work, we show that shadows are helpful in pedestrian detection instead. Occlusions make pedestrian detection difficult. Existing shape-based detection methods can have false-positives on shadows since they have similar shapes with foreground objects. Appearance-based detection methods cannot detect heavily occluded pedestrians. To deal with these problems, we use appearance, shadow, and motion information simultaneously in our method. We detect pedestrians using appearance information of pedestrians and shape information of shadow regions. Then, we filter the detection results based on motion information if available. The proposed method gives low false-positives due to the integration of different features. Moreover, it alleviates the problem brought by occlusions since shadows can still be observable when foreground objects are occluded. Our experimental results show that the proposed algorithm provides good performance in many difficult scenarios.

1 Introduction

Shadows can be found in many images and videos. Shadows are formulated when direct light from a light source cannot reach due to obstruction by an opaque object. Traditionally, shadows are regarded as noises for vision tasks such as detection and tracking. In this work, we propose a detection algorithm considering shadows as helpful information in pedestrian detection.

Pedestrian detection in images and videos is a key issue for many applications such as autonomous vehicles and visual surveillance. A large number of pedestrian detection algorithms have been proposed in recent years. Among them, various features, descriptors, and classification methods have been investigated. Despite of the good performance achieved by many detection methods, pedestrian detection is still an open problem. For example, pedestrian detection methods usually have a low detection rate when many pedestrians are occluded. Appearance variations due to viewpoint or illumination also bring problems to pedestrian detection.

We classify image features into four categories: shape, appearance, motion, and depth features. Shape features are employed in many detection algorithms due to their invariance to viewpoint changes [1]. Shape features are very sparse in detection and modeling processes. Therefore, shape-based detection methods can be efficient. However, it is rather difficult to extract accurate shape features because of background clutters. Appearance features are successfully applied in sliding window-based detection systems [2,3]. They compute contrast information and describe such information using various descriptors. Histograms of gradient orientations (HOGs) have achieved good performance in pedestrian detection [3]. Unfortunately, it is rather difficult to detect heavily occluded objects using appearance-based methods.

In visual surveillance scenarios, stationary cameras are widely used. Background subtraction is the first step to understand the scene. Object detection and tracking can be performed based on background subtraction results. In a crowded environment, motion blobs found by comparison with the learned background is informative [4]. In this work, we also perform background subtraction in video sequences.

Although background modeling and subtraction is helpful, pedestrian detection is still difficult since subtraction result can contain many errors. Background subtraction is far from perfect: one blob in the subtraction

*Correspondence: jerywangjq@gmail.com
[1] Aviation Industry Cooperation China, Beijing, China
Full list of author information is available at the end of the article

results may merge several objects; one object may be split into a few blobs. Incorrect background model updating tends to introduce incorrect models because of motion ambiguities. The problem becomes more difficult when foreground objects have similar appearance with its background.

In surveillance and many other scenarios, we can find cast shadows easily [5]. Shadows are regions where direct light cannot reach due to obstruction by an object. The space behind an opaque object is occupied by the shadow. The shape and position of the shadow are determined by the shape of the object and the position of the light sources. We can calculate the position and the shape of shadows approximately if we know the light source and the rough shape of the object. Therefore, shadows are informative in telling the existence of an object. We will detect shadows in background subtraction results based on the properties of shadows. To be specific, we compute the position of the Sun using the location and timing information. Then, we predict the orientation, position, and shape of an object in images.

Detection-based appearance information has achieved great success in the last decades. However, detection of an occluded object is still very difficult. For example, in Figure 1, there are five people in two groups in the image. The two girls in the left group have certain occlusion. Detection is still possible in this case. In the right group, the last two people are heavily occluded. It is rather difficult to reason the number and the position of the persons based on appearance information. Fortunately, the problem becomes easy if we consider the shadow information in Figure 1c. Shadow information is not noise. It is helpful in visual tasks such as tracking and detection.

The rest of this paper is organized as follows. After a brief review of important related works in Section 2, we discuss feature extraction in our algorithm in Section 3. Then, we will give the geometric transforms for feature extraction in Section 4. Detection method using foreground and shadow information is given in Section 5. Motion filtering is described in Section 6. Experimental results on real image sequences are demonstrated in Section 7. Section 8 explains the difficulty in applying shadow information in indoor environments. Section 9 concludes this work.

2   Related work

Pedestrian detection has been intensively investigated in the last decades. Gavrila [1] proposed a shape-based pedestrian detection method. Dalal and Triggs [3] proposed an appearance-based object detection method using histogram of gradient orientations. Their approach is very effective for detecting articulated objects such as pedestrians. Tuzel et al. [6] found that covariance description has nice properties for object detection. All of the above detection methods are carried out based on appearance information only. Bertozzi et al. [7] detect pedestrians in infrared images using active contours and neural networks.

Motion information has been noticed to be helpful in detecting objects. Dalal et al. [8] normalized optical flow in video frames and applied motion information into pedestrian detection. Other works also looked at pedestrian detection from video sequences. Actually, motion information has been used in a few previous works before Dalal et al. [8]. Viola and Jones [9] detect pedestrians using patterns of motion and appearance. They model both of the motion and appearance using Haar-like features. Cutler et al. [10] proposed a detection method using long-term periodic motion information. In order to find periodicity, they analyzed long video sequences. Their system can be applied in image sequences with very low resolutions. Jones and Snow [11] extended the original pedestrian detection algorithm. They analyzed a moderate number of frames in a batch processing.

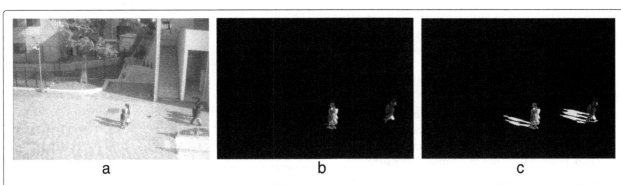

Figure 1 Shadow information is important. (a) Input image. **(b)** Foreground of our background subtraction result. **(c)** Foreground and shadows of our background subtraction result. It is difficult to discriminate how many persons in the right group in **(a)** with appearance information only. The shadows of the persons provide helpful information to remove the ambiguities.

Depth information has also been adopted for pedestrian detection. Gavrila and Munder [12] designed a detection algorithm for driving aid. This algorithm integrates various techniques for finding pedestrians including the use of stereo cameras. Ess et al. [13] explicitly use depth information and projected two-dimensional (2D) detection results onto the three-dimensional (3D) space.

Part-based detection can be successfully applied in pedestrian detection under the condition that the resolution of images is sufficiently high. Felzenszwalb et al. [14] presented a general object detection algorithm that is able to detect objects in partial occlusions. Lempitsky [15] applied a similar idea in object detection using HOGs.

There are some works combining detection and tracking in an integrated framework, e.g., Leibe et al. [16] presented a detection and tracking algorithm in which object detection and trajectory estimation are coupled.

We detect pedestrians using appearance information of pedestrians and shape information of shadow regions. Motion information is used if available. The focus of our work is to show the power of shadow information. Therefore, we do not combine all the features in our work.

3 Feature extraction

We model the background using Gaussian mixture models for each pixel. In addition, we also model possible shadows using available time and region information. We segment input images into three kinds of regions: foreground, shadows, and background.

3.1 Background modeling

We represent each pixel using one Gaussian mixture model. Other representations such as texture or nonparametric representations [17,18] can also be used.

We update the background using a recursive filter [19,20]. We assume that $\eta(t)$ is a learning rate set for our recursive filter. We calculate the parameter of each pixel using this learning rate:

$$\mu(t) = (1-\eta(t)) \times \mu(t-1) + (I(t)-\mu(t-1)) \times \eta(t) \quad (1)$$

where $I(t)$ is the pixel value in the input image, and $\mu(t-1)$ and $\mu(t)$ are the mean values calculated at $t-1$ and t. Here, we set $\eta(t)$ to 0.03. The learning of other parameters follows the similar approach in [19].

3.2 Shadow detection

One of the difficulties in using shadow information is detecting shadows in input images. Invariant color properties have been used in shadow detection, e.g., normalized RGB color space and a lightness measure are employed in shadow detection [17]. Pixels with similar hue and saturation values and lower luminosity in hue-saturation-value (HSV) color space are classified as cast shadows [21].

In surveillance scenarios, an object casts shadows on surfaces. Shadow regions tend to have lower intensities due to the obstruction of the direct light source. Given a color vector without cast shadows, many shadow detection algorithms assume that the vector under cast shadows keeps the original vector direction. This assumption is not correct in outdoor environments because the ambient light source is blue. The values in different color channels are attenuated differently.

Background subtraction results include foreground objects and shadows. To separate shadows from foreground blobs, we apply a morphological close filter on background subtraction results to fill the gaps. Then, we convert the input images into HSV space which explicitly separates chromaticity and luminosity channels. A pixel in background subtraction results is considered as a possible shadow pixel when it has lower luminosity and similar hue values compared with the mode in the background model. After the classification, we calculate pixels that can be confidently classified into shadows. We use the Canny edge detection algorithm to find edges. The edges on shadow boundaries are found by comparing the hue and luminosity values. When shadows are projected on textured background, many edges are found including texture edges. The gradient orientations of such pixels are similar to those in the background model.

4 Geometry properties of shadows

Shadows are helpful for pedestrian detection. However, shadows tend to vary according to the relative position between a pedestrian and the Sun. The Sun angle varies according to timing, latitude, and aptitude of the camera [22].

4.1 Shadows in the 3D world coordinate

It is possible to infer time based on shadow direction and length. The reverse inference is much easier since we can get precise timing and location information.

The setting of the coordinates related to shadows is shown in Figure 2a. The Sun zenith angle θ_S is calculated by [22-24]

$$\theta_S = 90 - e_0 - \frac{P}{1010} \times \frac{283}{273+T} \times \frac{1.02}{60\tan(e_0 + \frac{10.3}{e_0+5.11})},$$
$$(2)$$

where P is the local pressure, T the time, and e_0 the Sun's topocentric elevation angle without atmospheric refraction correction. e_0 is calculated by

$$e_0 = \arcsin(\sin\phi_o \sin\delta' + \cos\phi_o \cos\delta' \cos H'), \quad (3)$$

where ϕ_o is the observer geometric latitude calculated using the local latitude; δ', the topocentric sun declination calculated using the geocentric sun declination from the

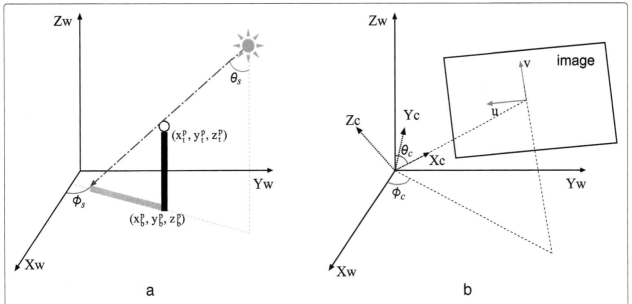

Figure 2 Coordinate transformation. The coordinates' setting and geometry relationship between the Sun angles and objects. **(a)** The 3D camera coordinate system is set to have the same origin with the 3D world coordinate system. **(b)** The shadow length and angles are determined by the Sun angles and the object height.

local longitude and current time; H', the topocentric local hour angle from the current time.

The Sun topocentric azimuth angle is calculated using

$$\phi_S = \arctan\left(\frac{\sin H'}{\cos H' \sin \phi_o - \tan \delta' \cos \phi_o}\right) + 180. \quad (4)$$

4.2 Camera projection matrix

The setting of the coordinates of the camera is shown in Figure 2b. The projected coordinates of 3D points in the image can be obtained by multiplying its 3D coordinates with the camera projection matrix $\mathbf{u} = \mathbf{Mx}$. We calibrate the cameras that are used for video capture. Both camera intrinsic and extrinsic parameters are known. For single images, we obtain camera lens length from the EXIF of these images. Then, we calibrate the image using the method introduced in [25].

The camera projection matrix $\mathbf{M}$ is calculated by multiplying the camera intrinsic matrix $\mathbf{A}$ and the extrinsic matrix

$$\mathbf{M} = \mathbf{A}\begin{bmatrix} \mathbf{R} & \mathbf{t} \\ \mathbf{0}^T & 1 \end{bmatrix}, \quad (5)$$

where $\mathbf{R}$ is the rotation matrix; $\mathbf{t}$, the translation vector. According to the setting in Figure 2, the translation vector $\mathbf{t} = [0 \quad 0 \quad 0]^T$.

Similarly, according to the setting of the coordinates, we calculate the rotation matrix by

$$\mathbf{R} = \begin{bmatrix} \cos\phi_C \cos\theta'_C & \sin\phi_C \cos\theta'_C & -\sin\theta'_C \\ -\sin\phi_C & \cos\phi_C & 0 \\ \cos\phi_C \sin\theta'_C & \sin\phi_C \sin\theta'_C & \cos\theta'_C \end{bmatrix}, \quad (6)$$

where $\theta'_C = \theta_C - \frac{\pi}{2}$.

We use a simple camera model which has no skewness. The pixels obtained are assumed as squares. The camera intrinsic matrix is described by

$$\mathbf{A} = \begin{bmatrix} f_c & 0 & 0 \\ 0 & f_c & 0 \\ 0 & 0 & 1 \end{bmatrix}. \quad (7)$$

4.3 Shadows in images

To estimate the shape of a shadow, we need the height of the obstruction object and the Sun angle. We calculate the Sun angle based on the all sky model [22-24]. We define a world coordinate $(\mathbf{x}_w, \mathbf{y}_w, \mathbf{z}_w)$. We assume the 3D coordinates of the Sun, $\mathbf{s}$. The Sun position is determined by its zenith angle θ_S and azimuth angle ϕ_S. The two angles decide the shadow projection in the image. We denote the camera local frame by $(\mathbf{x}_c, \mathbf{y}_c, \mathbf{z}_c)$, which is rotated by angles (θ_C, ϕ_C).

We calculate the length of the shadow of an object by

$$L_p^s = z_t^p \tan\theta_S. \quad (8)$$

The 3D coordinates of the shadow of the head is $\mathbf{x}_t = [x_t\, y_t\, z_t]^{\mathrm{T}}$. It is calculated by

$$x_t^s = x_b^p - L_p^s \cos \phi_S$$
$$y_t^s = y_b^p - L_p^s \sin \phi_S,$$

and $z_t^s = -Z_C$ since shadows are on the ground.

5 Detection

Appearance, shadow, and motion information are used simultaneously in our method. We detect pedestrians using appearance information of pedestrians and shape information of shadow regions. We also filter the detection results based on motion information if available. The flow charts of our method and typical traditional detection methods are illustrated in Figure 3.

5.1 Detection in foreground regions

We compute detection probabilities in foreground regions using appearance information. First, we train a Hough forest to model pedestrians. The Hough forest consists of many Hough trees that are efficient in matching descriptors. In testing stages, we calculate histograms of orientations for images in different scales. After that, we accumulate voting probabilities in a Hough space similar to the approach in [15]. The probabilistic formulation in [15] fits into our framework quite well.

There are many pedestrian detection approaches in the literature. We select the Hough forest due to a few merits of this approach. First, the Hough forest can detect multiple pedestrians under heavy occlusions. According to the survey by Dollar et al. [26], occlusion is one of the major difficulties for pedestrian detection. Second, the Hough forest detection model has a probabilistic nature. It can be easily integrated with other knowledge. Pedestrian detection has been considered in a Hough-based framework using object segmentation and an MDL prior [27]. The implicit shape model (ISM) interleaves pedestrian detection and segmentation. Therefore, the probabilistic aspect of this work is not very clear because of the interleaving. DPM [14] is a multi-scale sliding window object detector. It is good at dealing with pose variations and small occlusions. It usually gets multiple overlapping detections for a pedestrian. Non-maximum suppression has to be carried out on the initial detection results. A greedy procedure is adopted in DPM for discarding repeated pedestrian detections. Some of the true detection can be eliminated in this procedure. In contrast, the non-maximum suppression in the Hough forest detector is more reasonable since it accumulates detection probabilities according to the comparison of the voting in the iterations. This strategy can lead to a good performance for occluded pedestrians. There are other approaches for pedestrian detection. However, most of them perform non-maximum suppression as the DPM method. Therefore, they are not very good at dealing with heavy occlusions. The Hough forest is better in this aspect. Our approach improves such ability by incorporating shadow information.

Let $\mathbf{g} = \{g_i\}$ be random variables describing correspondences between voting elements in the Hough spaces and hypothesis and $\mathbf{f} = \{f_h\}$ be binary variables representing

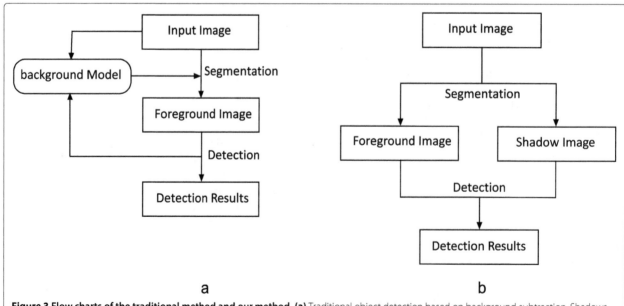

Figure 3 Flow charts of the traditional method and our method. (a) Traditional object detection based on background subtraction. Shadows are considered as noises. **(b)** Our pedestrian detection approach takes shadows as informative cues.

whether the hypotheses h actually correspond to a real pedestrian. We calculate

$$p(\mathbf{g}, \mathbf{f}|\mathbf{L}_A) \propto p(\mathbf{L}_A|\mathbf{g}, \mathbf{f})p(\mathbf{g}, \mathbf{f}), \qquad (9)$$

where $\mathbf{L}_A$ denotes HOG descriptors obtained from the appearance information. The details of the calculation can be found in [15].

5.2 Shape representation and matching in shadows

We construct a simple 3D model [4,28] for pedestrian detection. Since we can calculate geometry properties of shadows, we can generate specific shape templates according to different timing and locations. To be specific, we project the 3D model onto 2D space based on shadow geometries. The shape templates generated are matched with shadow silhouettes.

We perform matching based on the chamfer distance function. We match contours of the shadow mask for two reasons. First, we can use distance transform to accelerate the matching process. Shape matching is very efficient using distance transform results [29]. Second, the contours detected around shadows contain similar information with the region. We have a set of templates described by points $\Upsilon_M = \{\alpha_M^i\}_{i=1}^{N_{\Upsilon_M}}$. We detect shadow boundaries consisting sets of points $\Lambda_S = \{\beta_S^i\}_{i=1}^{N_{\Lambda_S}}$. We calculate the average of the minimum distances between each points of the templates and the edge detection results:

$$d(\Upsilon, \Lambda) = \frac{1}{N_\Upsilon} \sum_{\alpha \in \Upsilon} \min \|\alpha - \beta\|^2. \qquad (10)$$

We can accelerate the matching process using a distance transform for the chamfer function. This transformation takes the set of points on the detected edges as input. The nearest boundary point to each location is calculated, and the minimum distance is assigned to the locations. The chamfer function (Equation 10) for a single template can be obtained by assigning the distance directly on the transformed results. To increase the robustness against partial occlusion, the distance is limited to a predefined threshold $d_{\min}$.

$$d_{\Upsilon,\Lambda} = \frac{1}{N_\Upsilon} \sum_{i=1}^{N_\Lambda} \sum_{\alpha \in \Upsilon} \min(\min \|\alpha - \beta\|^2, d_{\min}). \qquad (11)$$

We define the probability of an object by

$$p(\mathbf{g}, \mathbf{f}|\mathbf{L}_S) = \exp(-\lambda \|d_{\Upsilon,\Lambda}\|) \qquad (12)$$

where $\exp(-\lambda \|d_{\Upsilon,\Lambda}\|)$ considers the overlapping between the modeling and shadow regions.

5.3 Fusing detection probabilities

We fuse the detection probabilities calculated based on appearance and shadow information. We check the probabilities in Equations 9 and 12. We favor large probabilities

based on both shadow and appearance information. However, since pedestrians can be occluded in many cases, we calculate the fused probability using a maximization procedure,

$$p(\mathbf{g}, \mathbf{f}|\mathbf{L}_S, \mathbf{L}_A) = \max(p(\mathbf{g}, \mathbf{f}|\mathbf{L}_S), p(\mathbf{g}, \mathbf{f}|\mathbf{L}_A)). \qquad (13)$$

When the appearance cue of a pedestrian is available and the shadow cue is unavailable (e.g., a pedestrian's shadow is in another large shadow region), the probability calculated based on the shadow cue is zero (or a very small value). We get an extremely low probability (or zero) if we use a simple product probability fusion method. In fact, we can infer the existence of this pedestrian based on the appearance cue only. The probability using a product of probabilities from the shadow and the appearance can be misleading. We meet a similar problem when the shadow cue is available and the appearance cue is unavailable (e.g., a pedestrian walks outside of the image, but his/her shadow is still in the image). The probability using a max of probabilities can detect pedestrians successfully when either an appearance cue or a shadow cues are available. We select the cue which is more informative when both of the cues are available.

In case of multiple pedestrians having overlaps in the image, the probabilities of the appearance given the state cannot be simply considered as a probability of a single pedestrian. Instead, a joint likelihood of the whole image, given all pedestrians, needs to be considered. The exact normalization of the probabilities' distributions based on appearance and shadow is not easy. We carry out the normalization using a heuristic way. First, We discard those probabilities in both distributions less than p_{TA} or p_{TS}. Then, we normalize the remaining probabilities in $[0, 1]$.

6 Filtering based on motion information

We improve detection performance by filtering detection results using motion information. In images with low resolutions, a pedestrian is roughly a blob moving following a curve. It is difficult to discriminate motion of arms in this resolution. Motion information is more complicated in high resolutions. Despite of the complexity, we found that false-positive detection results usually have different motion patterns with true-positives. Many false-positive detection results are due to the appearance similarity with the object models. However, they do not have any motion in long time durations. We apply the motion filters described in [9] in the blobs that possible hypothesis exits. We learn a pattern library off-line using real pedestrian motion. Then, we compare the motion patterns of possible detections with the modeling motion patterns. We discard those detections when they are very different from the pattern models.

a   b   c

Figure 4 Detection results in outdoor environments. The detection results using the part-based method [11] **(a)**, the voting method [1] **(b)**, and the proposed method **(c)**.

7 Experimental results

We implemented the proposed method and tested it on a data set collected from several video sequences and single images. We have 4,230 images in the data set. Among them, we randomly select 126 images. We label the subset of the images to make the ground truth for quantitative analysis. We detect shadows in the images captured by stationary cameras using the method described in Section 3.2. We estimate shadow regions in single images using the method described in [30].

We compare our algorithm with two detection methods. The first one is a part-based detection algorithm [14] that integrates appearance and spatial information using part representation and assembly. One of the nice properties of their method is that it can detect objects in partial occlusions. The second one is the Hough transform-based method that is also very good at detecting objects in partial occlusions [15].

The qualitative analysis of our experimental results are shown in Figure 4. The detection results of the part-based [14], Hough transform-based [15], and our detectors are show in the first, second, and third columns, respectively. The detection task in the first row is not very difficult since there is almost no occlusion. However, the part-based method gives a few false-positives. The Hough transform-based method provides better results. Our detector gives better performance in this simple detection task. In the second row, one person is partially occluded. The part-based detector [14] gives correct detection results. However, it also has many false-positives. The Hough transform-based detector [15] merges the two persons into one object and provides a wrong detection result. The input image in the third row is relatively more difficult since several persons walk in a crowd. The part-based detector gives four correct detections and a few false-positives. The Hough transform-based detector

gives three correct detections and one false-positive. Our detector misses one object because the information is incomplete. The input in the fourth and fifth rows are single images. We detect shadows using the method in [30]. The motion filtering is not applicable in these images since motion information is not available. The proposed method gives fewer false-positives than the part-based and the Hough transform-based methods in the third and fourth rows. The Hough transform-based method provides a bad performance in the fourth row due to invalid scale estimation. The problem can be partially solved in our formulation because the shadows give hints for scale estimation.

We show the recall-precision curves of the three methods in Figure 5. To demonstrate the power of the shadow and motion cues, We calculate multiple ROC curves for (a) detection results with only shadow cues, (b) with motion cue, and (c) with both shadow and motion cues. We found that shadow cue plays an important role in pedestrian detection. The detection results using shadow cues are better than the results without shadow and motion cues. The part-based and Hough transform-based methods fail to achieve high recall curve values in the data set. Our detector outperforms the other two detectors because the other two detectors omit shadow and motion information. This confirms our expectation that fusing different kinds of information is important for pedestrian detection.

8 Detection using shadow information in indoor environments

We have demonstrated the power of shadow information for pedestrian detection in outdoor environments. It seems that detecting people in indoor environments is simpler. However, it is much more difficult to apply shadow information in indoor environments. The major

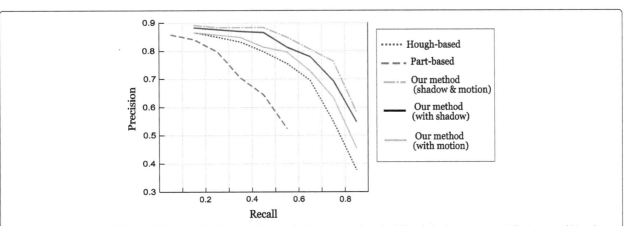

Figure 5 Detection precision-recall curves. Precision-recall curves for the proposed method (the dash-dot green curve), the improved Hough transform method (the dashed blue curve), and the part-based method (the red solid curve). Our method achieves better performance on the data set.

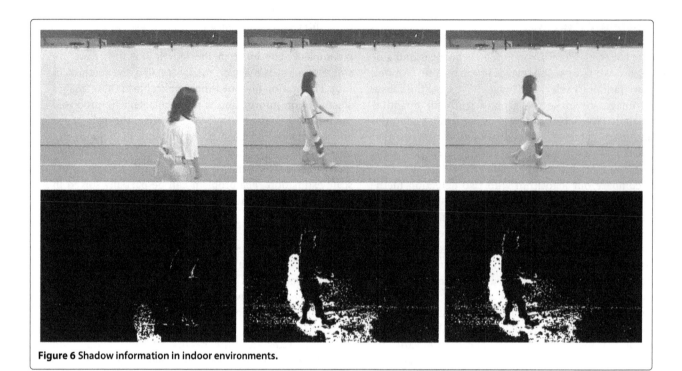

Figure 6 Shadow information in indoor environments.

difficulty for using shadow information is due to the complicated lighting conditions in indoor environments. There can be many different kinds of light sources in an indoor environment. Moreover, inter-reflections are common in indoor environments. The inter-reflections can be very strong in many cases. Due to these reasons, shadows formulated in an indoor environment can be very complicated. We add a few examples in Figure 6. In these examples, shadows are detected. However, it is not easy to apply the shadow information in the detection. The examples are captured in the environments with relatively 'simple' lighting conditions. Although we believe shadow information cannot be easily applied in object detection in indoor environments, we did not say that such application is not possible. There are two ways to solve this problem. First, we can apply shadow information in an indoor environment if the lighting conditions and the geometry are known. We use the similar strategy in the detection. Second, in most cases, there are fewer objects in indoor environments. We can claim a detection if we can relax the detection condition to 'moving object with shadows might be walking people.' Basically, detecting pedestrians in outdoor environments is more difficult in general. We introduce shadow information in the detection, which is helpful in improving the detection performance.

9   Conclusions

We show that integration of multiple cues is helpful in designing an effective object detection system. To be specific, we found that shadow information should be considered as informative instead of noise. In addition, motion information-based filtering process finds false-positives and improves the performance of our detection system. The experimental results confirm our expectation that fusing multiple information is important for object detection.

Our method has a few limitations. First, it is rather difficult to improve its performance in overcast or raining days. Second, a pedestrian's shadow cannot be extracted reliably when his/her shadow is merged into a large shadow formulated by a large object. Third, shadow cues are not very informative when the zenith angle is very small. We consider shadow as informative features in good weather.

Competing interests
The authors declare that they have no competing interests.

Author details
[1] Aviation Industry Cooperation China, Beijing, China. [2] The Institute of Scientific and Industrial Research, Osaka University, 8-1 Mihogaoka, Ibaraki, Osaka 567-0047, Japan.

References
1. D Gavrila, V Philomin, Real-time object detection for smart vehicles, in *Proc. Int. Conf. Computer Vision* (IEEE, Corfu, 1999), pp. 87–93
2. P Viola, M Jones, Rapid object detection using a boosted cascade of simple features, in *Proc. of Conf. on Computer Vision and Pattern Recognition* (IEEE, Kauai, 2001), pp. 511–518
3. N Dalal, B Triggs, Histograms of oriented gradients for human detection, in *Proc. of Conf. on Computer Vision and Pattern Recognition* (IEEE, San Diego, 2005), pp. 886–893

4. T Zhao, R Nevatia, Tracking multiple humans in complex situations. IEEE Trans. Pattern Anal. Mach. Intell. **26**(9), 1208–1221 (2004)

5. J Wang, Y Yagi, Pedestrian detection based on appearance, motion, and shadow information, in *Proc. of Int. Conf. on Systems, Man, Cybernetics* (IEEE, Seoul, 2012)

6. O Tuzel, F Porikli, P Meer, Human detection via classification on Riemannian manifolds, in *Proc. of Conf. on Computer Vision and Pattern Recognition* (IEEE, Minneapolis, 2007), pp. 1–8

7. M Bertozzi, P Cerri, M Felisa, S Ghidoni, MD Rose, Pedestrian validation in infrared images by means of active contours and neural networks. EURASIP J. Adv. Signal Process. **2010**(5), (2010)

8. N Dalal, B Triggs, C Schmid, Human detection using oriented histograms of flow and appearance, in *Proc. of European Conf. on Computer Vision* (Springer, Graz, 2006), pp. 428–441

9. PA Viola, MJ Jones, D Snow, Detecting pedestrians using patterns of motion and appearance. Int. J. Comput. Vis. **63**(2), 153–161 (2005)

10. R Cutler, L Davis, Robust real-time periodic motion detection: analysis and applications. IEEE Trans. Patt. Anal. Mach. Intell. **22**(7), 781–796 (2000)

11. M Jones, D Snow, Pedestrian detection using boosted features over many frames, in *Proc. of Int. Conf. on Pattern Recognition* (IEEE, Tampa, 2008), pp. 1–4

12. DM Gavrila, S Munder, Multi-cue pedestrian detection and tracking from a moving vehicle. Int. J. Comput. Vis. **73**, 41–59 (2007)

13. A Ess, B Leibe, LJV Gool, Depth and appearance for mobile scene analysis, in *Proc. of Int. Conf. on Computer Vision* (IEEE, Rio de Janeiro, 2007), pp. 1–8

14. PF Felzenszwalb, RB Girshick, McDA Allester, D Ramanan, Object detection with discriminatively trained part-based models. IEEE Trans. Pattern Anal. Mach. Intell. **32**(9), 1627–1645 (2010)

15. O Barinova, V Lempitsky, P Kohli, On detection of multiple object instances using hough transforms, in *Proc. of Conf. on Computer Vision and Pattern Recognition* (IEEE, San Francisco, 2010), pp. 2233–2240

16. B Leibe, K Schindler, L Gool, Coupled detection and trajectory estimation for multi-object tracking, in *Proc. of Int. Conf. on Computer Vision* (IEEE, Rio de Janeiro, 2007), pp. 1–8

17. AM Elgammal, R Duraiswami, D Harwood, LS Davis, Background and foreground modeling using non-parametric Kernel density estimation for visual surveillance. Proc. IEEE. **10**(7), 1151–1163 (2002)

18. AM Elgammal, D Harwood, LS Davis, Non-parametric model for background subtraction, in *Proc. of European Conf. on Computer Vision* (Springer, Marseille, 2000), pp. 751–767

19. N Friedman, S Russell, Image segmentation in video sequences: a probabilistic approach, in *Proc. 13th Conf. on Uncertainty in Artificial Intelligence* (AUAI, Providence, 1997), pp. 175–181

20. B Stenger, V Ramesh, N Paragios, F Coetzee, JM Buhmann, Topology free hidden Markov models: application to background modeling, in *Proc. of Int. Conf. on Computer Vision* (IEEE, Vancouver, 2001), pp. 294–301

21. R Cucchiara, C Grana, M Piccardi, A Prati, Detecting moving objects, ghosts, and shadows in video streams. IEEE Trans. Pattern Anal. Mach. Intell. **25**(10), 1337–1342 (2003)

22. M Blanco-Muriel, DC Alarcon-Padilla, T Lopez-Moratalla, M Lara-Coira, Computing the solar vector. Solar Energy. **70**(5), 431–441 (2001)

23. AJ Preetham, P Shirley, B Smits, A practical analytic model for daylight, in *Proceedings of ACM SIGGRAPH* (ACM, Los Angeles, 1999), pp. 91–100

24. I Reda, A Andreas, *Solar position algorithm for solar radiation applications.* Technical report NREL/TP-560-34302, National Renewable Energy Laboratory, USA, (2005)

25. D Hoiem, A Efros, M Hebert, Putting objects in perspective. Int. J. Comput. Vis. **80**, 3–15 (2008)

26. P Dollar, C Wojek, B Schiele, P Perona, Pedestrian detection: an evaluation of the state of the art. IEEE Trans. Pattern Anal. Mach. Intell. **34**(4), 743–761 (2012)

27. B Leibe, A Leonardis, B Schiele, Robust object detection with interleaved categorization and segmentation. Int. J. Comput. Vis. **77**(3), 259–289 (2008)

28. T Zhao, R Nevatia, B Wu, Segmentation and tracking of multiple humans in crowded environments. IEEE Trans. Pattern Anal. Mach. Intell. **30**(7), 1198–1211 (2008)

29. K Toyama, A Blake, Probabilistic tracking in a metric space, in *Proc. of Int. Conf. on Computer Vision, Corfe* (IEEE, Corfu, 2001), pp. 50–59

30. R Guo, Q Dai, D Hoiem, Single-image shadow detection and removal using paired regions, in *Proc. of Conf. on Computer Vision and Pattern Recognition* (IEEE, Colorado Springs, 2011), pp. 2033–2040

4

A no-reference objective image quality metric based on perceptually weighted local noise

Tong Zhu and Lina Karam[*]

Abstract

This work proposes a perceptual based no-reference objective image quality metric by integrating perceptually weighted local noise into a probability summation model. Unlike existing objective metrics, the proposed no-reference metric is able to predict the relative amount of noise perceived in images with different content, without a reference. Results are reported on both the LIVE and TID2008 databases. The proposed no-reference metric achieves consistently a good performance across noise types and across databases as compared to many of the best very recent no-reference quality metrics. The proposed metric is able to predict with high accuracy the relative amount of perceived noise in images of different content.

Introduction

Reliable assessment of image quality plays an important role in meeting the promised quality of service (QoS) and in improving the end user's quality of experience (QoE). There is a growing interest to develop objective quality assessment algorithms that can predict perceived image quality automatically. These methods are highly useful in various image processing applications, such as image compression, transmission, restoration, enhancement, and display. For example, the quality metric can be used to evaluate and control the performance of individual system components in image/video processing and transmission systems.

One direct way to evaluate video quality is through subjective tests. In these tests, a group of human subjects are asked to judge the quality under a predefined viewing condition. The scores given by observers are averaged to produce the mean opinion score (MOS). However, subjective tests are time-consuming, laborious, and expensive. Objective image quality (IQA) assessment methods can be categorized as full reference (FR), reduced reference (RR), and no reference (NR) depending on whether a reference, partial information about a reference, or no reference is used for calculation. Quality assessment without a reference is challenging. A no-reference metric is not relative to a reference image, but rather an absolute value is computed based on some characteristics of the test image.

Of particular interest to this work is the no-reference noisiness objective metric. Noisiness and blurriness are two key distortions in multiple applications, and typically there is a tradeoff to balance between noisiness and blurriness. For example, in soft-thresholding for image denoising [1], the image could be blurry when the threshold is high, while the image could remain noisy when the threshold is low. Also, in Wiener-based super-resolution [2], too much regularization will result in less noise at the expense of more blur. The reconstructed image could be blurry when the auto-correlation function is modeled to be too flat, while the reconstructed image could be noisy when the auto-correlation function is modeled to be too sharp. No-reference image sharpness/blur metrics have been widely discussed [3,4]. However, these image sharpness/blur metrics typically fail in the presence of noise. The sharpness metric may increase when noise increases. A no-reference noise-immune image sharpness metric was also proposed [5]. Furthermore, all the edge-based sharpness metrics can be easily applied in the wavelet domain as described in [5] to provide resilience to noise. Still, it lacks the ability to assess the impairment due to noise. For visual quality assessment of noisiness, many full-reference metrics are presented in [6], such as peak signal-to-noise ratio (PSNR), multi-scale structural similarity (MS-SSIM) [7], noise quality measure (NQM) [8], and information fidelity criterion (IFC) [9].

*Correspondence: karam@asu.edu
School of Electrical, Computer & Energy Engineering, Arizona State University, Tempe, AZ 85287, USA

However, these full-reference metrics require the reference image for calculation. There is a need to develop a no-reference noisiness quality metric. Furthermore, such noisiness metric could be further combined with the no-reference blur metrics [3,4] to provide a better prediction of image quality for several applications including super-resolution, image restoration, and other multiply distorted images. A global estimate of image noise variance was used as a no-reference noisiness metric in [10]. The histogram of the local noise variances is used to derive the global estimate. However, the locally perceived visibility of noise is not considered. Similarly in [11], noisiness is expressed by the sum of estimated noise amplitudes and the ratio of noise pixels. Both the metrics of [10,11] do not account for the effects of locally varying noise on the perceived noise impairment and they do not exploit the characteristics of the human visual system (HVS).

To tackle this issue, this paper firstly presents a full-reference image noisiness metric which integrates perceptually weighted local noise into a probability summation model. This proposed metric can predict the perceptual noisiness in images with high accuracy. In addition, a no-reference objective noisiness metric is derived based on local noise standard deviation, local perceptual weighting, and probability summation. The experimental results show that the proposed FR and NR metrics show better and more consistent performance across databases and distortion types, when compared with several very recent FR and NR metrics.

The remainder of this paper is organized as follows. A perceived noisiness model based on probability summation is presented first followed by details on the contrast sensitivity thresholds computation. A full-reference perceptually weighted noise (FR-PWN) metric is proposed next based on perceptual weighting using the computed contrast sensitivity thresholds and probability summation. After that, a no-reference perceptually weighted noise (NR-PWN) metric is further derived. Performance results and comparison with existing metrics are presented followed by a conclusion.

Perceptual noisiness model based on probability summation

The PSNR simply calculates the difference point by point. However, the human visual system should be taken into consideration since the visual impairment due to the same noise could be perceived differently based on the local characteristics of the visual content. Contrast is a key concept in vision science because the information in the visual system is represented in terms of contrast and not in terms of the absolute level of light. So, the relative changes in luminance are important rather than the absolute ones [3]. The contrast sensitivity threshold measures the smallest contrast or the just-noticeable difference (JND) that yields

a visible signal over a uniform background. The proposed metric makes use of JND for calculating the probability of noise detection. Even when the noise is uniform, the impact of the noise will be more visible in image regions with a relatively lower JND. Consider the noisy signal y as

$$y(i,j) = y'(i,j) + \text{error}(i,j) \tag{1}$$

where $y'(i,j)$ is the original undistorted image. The probability of detecting a noise distortion at location (i,j) can be modeled as an exponential having the following form

$$P(i,j) = 1 - \exp\left(-\left|\frac{\text{error}(i,j)}{\text{JND}(i,j)}\right|^{\beta}\right) \tag{2}$$

where $\text{JND}(i,j)$ is the JND value at (i,j) and it depends on the mean intensity in a local neighborhood region surrounding pixel (i,j). β is a parameter whose value is chosen to maximize the correspondence of (2) with the experimentally determined psychometric function for noise detection. In psychophysical experiments that examine summation over space, a value of about 4 has been observed to correspond well to probability summation [12].

A less-localized probability of noise detection can be computed by adopting the 'probability summation' hypothesis which pools the localized detection probabilities over a region of interest, R [13]. The probability summation hypothesis is based on the following two assumptions: (1) A noise distortion is detected if and only if at least one detector senses the presence of a noise distortion; (2) The probabilities of detection are independent; i.e., the probability that a particular detector will signal the presence of a distortion is independent of the probability that any other detector will. The measurement of noise detection in a region R is then given by

$$P_{\text{noise}}(R) = 1 - \prod_{i,j \in R}(1 - P(i,j)). \tag{3}$$

Substituting (2) into (3) yields

$$P_{\text{noise}}(R) = 1 - \exp(-D_R^{\beta}) \tag{4}$$

where

$$D_R = \left(\sum_{i,j \in R}\left|\frac{\text{error}(i,j)}{\text{JND}(i,j)}\right|^{\beta}\right)^{1/\beta} \tag{5}$$

From (4), it can be seen that $P_{\text{noise}}(R)$ increases if D_R increases and vice versa. So D_R can be used as a noisiness metric over region R. However, the probability of noise detection does not directly translate to noise annoyance level. In this work, the β parameter in (4) and (5) is replaced with $\alpha = \beta \times s$, which has the effect of steering the slope of the psychometric function in order to translate noise detection levels into noise annoyance levels. The factor s was found experimentally to be $1/16$ resulting in a value of 0.25 for α. More details about how $\text{JND}(i,j)$ is computed is given in the Section 'Perceptual contrast sensitivity threshold model and JND computation'.

Perceptual contrast sensitivity threshold model and JND computation

Multiple parameters including screen resolution, the viewing distance, the minimum display luminance, and the maximum display luminance are considered in the contrast sensitivity model [14]. The thresholds are computed locally for each block. Firstly, the contrast sensitivity threshold t_{128} is generated for a region with a mean grayscale value of 128 as follows:

$$t_{128} = \frac{T M_g}{L_{\max} - L_{\min}} \tag{6}$$

where $L_{\min}$ and $L_{\max}$ are the minimum and maximum display luminances, M_g is the total number of gray scale levels, and T is given by the following parabolic approximation [15]:

$$T = \min(10^{g_{0,1}}, 10^{g_{1,0}}), \tag{7}$$

$$g_{0,1} = \log_{10} T_{\min} + K \left(\log_{10} \frac{1}{2 N \omega_y} - \log_{10} f_{\min} \right)^2, \tag{8}$$

$$g_{1,0} = \log_{10} T_{\min} + K \left(\log_{10} \frac{1}{2 N \omega_x} - \log_{10} f_{\min} \right)^2. \tag{9}$$

In (8) and (9), $T_{\min}$ is the luminance threshold at frequency, $f_{\min}$, where the threshold is minimum. ω_x and ω_y represent, respectively, the horizontal width and the vertical height of a pixel in degrees of visual angle, K is the steepness of the parabola. N is the local neighborhood size and is set to 8. $T_{\min}, f_{\min}$, and K can be computed as [15]:

$$T_{\min} = \begin{cases} \dfrac{L_T}{S_0} \left(\dfrac{L}{L_T} \right)^{\alpha_T}, L \le L_T \\[3mm] \dfrac{L}{S_0}, L > L_T \end{cases} \tag{10}$$

$$f_{\min} = \begin{cases} f_0 \left(\dfrac{L}{L_f} \right)^{\alpha_f}, L \le L_f \\[3mm] f_0, L > L_f \end{cases} \tag{11}$$

$$K = \begin{cases} K_0 \left(\dfrac{L}{L_K} \right)^{\alpha_K}, L \le L_K \\[3mm] K_0, L > L_K \end{cases} \tag{12}$$

The values of the constants in (10) - (12) are [15] $L_T = 13.45 \text{ cd/m}^2$, $S_0 = 94.7$, $\alpha_T = 0.649$, $\alpha_f = 0.182$, $f_0 = 6.78 \text{ cycle/deg}$, $L_f = 300 \text{ cd/m}^2$, $K_0 = 3.125$, $\alpha_K = 0.0706$ and $L_K = 300 \text{ cd/m}^2$. Equations 10 to 12 give $T_{\min}$, $f_{\min}$, and K as functions of local background luminance L. For a background intensity value of 128, given a gamma-corrected display, the corresponding local background luminance is computed as follows:

$$L = L_{\min} + 128 \frac{L_{\max} - L_{\min}}{M_g} \tag{13}$$

where $L_{\min}$ and $L_{\max}$ denote the minimum and maximum luminances of the display. Once the JND for a region with mean grayscale value of 128, t_{128}, is calculated using (6), the JND for regions with other mean grayscale values are approximated as follows [16]:

$$\begin{aligned} \text{JND}(i,j) &= t_{128} \left(\frac{\sum_{n_1=0}^{N-1} \sum_{n_2=0}^{N-1} I_{n_1,n_2}}{N^2 (128)} \right)^{\alpha_T} \\[3mm] &= t_{128} \left(\frac{\text{Mean}(I_{n_1,n_2})}{128} \right)^{\alpha_T} \end{aligned} \tag{14}$$

where I_{n_1,n_2} is the intensity level at pixel location (n_1, n_2) in a $N \times N$ region surrounding pixel (i,j). It should be noted that the indices (n_1, n_2) are used to denote the location with respect to the top left corner of the $N \times N$ region, while the indices (i,j) are used to denote the location with respect to the top left corner of the whole image. $\text{Mean}(I_{n_1,n_2})$ is the mean value over the considered $N \times N$ region surrounding pixel (i,j). α_T is a correction exponent that controls the degree to which luminance masking occurs and is set to $\alpha_T = 0.649$, as given in [16]. $\text{JND}(i,j)$ in (5) is computed using (14). In our implementation, $N = 8$ was used for the $N \times N$ region.

Full-reference noisiness metric

This work firstly presents a full-reference noisiness metric based on the probability summation model presented in the previous sections. Figure 1 shows the block diagram of the proposed full-reference FR-PWN metric. The input image is first divided into blocks of $M \times M$. The block will be the region of interest R_b. The block size is chosen to correspond with the foveal region. Let r be the visual resolution of the display in pixels per degree, v the viewing distance in centimeters, and d the display resolution in pixels per centimeter. Then the visual resolution can be calculated as follows [17]:

$$r = d \cdot v \cdot \tan(\pi/180) \approx d \frac{v \pi}{180} \approx d \frac{v}{57.3}. \tag{15}$$

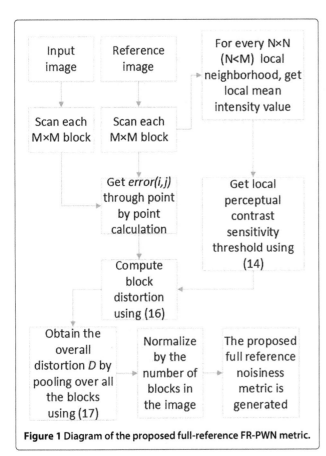

Figure 1 Diagram of the proposed full-reference FR-PWN metric.

In the HVS, the foveal region has the highest visual acuity and corresponds to about 2° of visual angle. The number of pixels contained in the foveal region can be computed as $(2\lfloor r\rfloor)^2$ [17]. For example, for a viewing distance of 60 cm and 31.5 pixels/cm display, the number of pixels contained in the foveal region is $(64)^2$, corresponding to a block size of 64×64. Using (5), the perceived noise distortion within a block R_b is given by

$$D_{R_b} = \left(\sum_{i,j\in R_b}\left|\frac{error(i,j)}{JND(i,j)}\right|^{\alpha}\right)^{1/\alpha} \quad (16)$$

where $JND(i,j)$ is the JND at location (i,j) and is computed using (14). Using the probability summation model as discussed previously, the noisiness measure D for the whole image I is obtained by using a Minkowski metric for inter-block pooling as follows:

$$D = \left(\sum_{R_b}\left|D_{R_b}\right|^{\alpha}\right)^{1/\alpha} \quad (17)$$

The resulting distortion measure, D, normalized by the number of blocks, is adopted as the proposed full-reference metric FR-PWN. This full-reference metric not only works for noisiness, but could also work for other additive distortions.

No-reference noisiness metric

In the previous section, a full-reference quality metric is presented based on the probability summation model and JND. However, in many cases, the reference image is not available, so error(i,j) in (16) can not be computed. Therefore, there is a need to develop a no-reference noisiness quality metric. Figure 2 shows the block diagram which summarizes the proposed no-reference NR-PWN metric. From (14), it can be seen that $JND(i,j)$ depends on the local mean of the neighborhood surrounding (i,j). For the proposed NR metric, the local mean for a pixel (i,j) belonging to a region R_N is taken to be the mean of region R_N and is denoted by mean(R_N). Consequently, Equation 14 can be written as follows:

$$JND(i,j) = JND(R_N)$$
$$= t_{128}\left(\frac{\text{Mean}(R_N)}{128}\right)^{\alpha_T}, \text{for all } (i,j) \text{ belongs to } R_N. \quad (18)$$

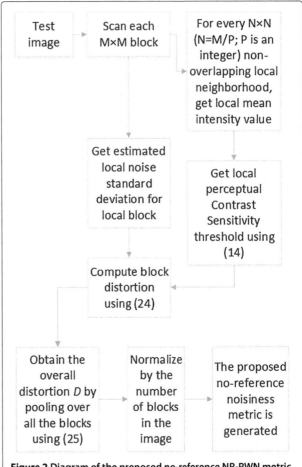

Figure 2 Diagram of the proposed no-reference NR-PWN metric.

Now only one $JND(R_N)$ will be calculated for all pixel (i, j) belonging to the same R_N, and different $JND(R_N)$ will be calculated separately for each R_N within the considered region of interest block R_b. The size of the block R_b is chosen to approximate a foveal region (e.g., 64×64 as discussed previously). Using p, q as the indices within a local neighborhood R_N, the proposed NR metric is derived from the presented FR metric (16) as follows:

$$D_{R_b} = \left(\sum_{R_N \in R_b} \sum_{p,q \in R_N} \left| \frac{error(p, q)}{JND(p, q)} \right|^\alpha \right)^{1/\alpha}$$

$$= \left(\sum_{R_N \in R_b} \frac{\sum_{p,q \in R_N} |error(p, q)|^\alpha}{(JND(R_N))^\alpha} \right)^{1/\alpha} \quad (19)$$

In (19), $\sum_{p,q \in R_N} |error(p, q)|^\alpha$ can be approximated by $N^2 E[|(error(p, q)|^\alpha]$ under the ergodicity assumption, where $N \times N$ is the size of each local neighborhood R_N. Also, if $error(p, q)$ is a Gaussian distribution process with a mean of 0 and a standard deviation of σ_{R_N}, using the central absolute moments of a Gaussian distribution process [18], it can be shown that

$$E\left[|error(p, q))|^\alpha \right] = \sigma_{R_N}^\alpha \frac{2^{\alpha/2} \Gamma(\frac{\alpha+1}{2})}{\pi^{1/2}}, \text{for } \alpha > -1 \quad (20)$$

where $\Gamma(t)$ is the gamma function

$$\Gamma(t) = \int_0^\infty x^{t-1} e^{-x} dx. \quad (21)$$

Using (20), D_{R_b} in (19) can be written as follows:

$$D_{R_b} = \left(\sum_{R_N \in R_b} \frac{N^2 \sigma_{R_N}^\alpha \frac{2^{\alpha/2} \Gamma(\frac{\alpha+1}{2})}{\pi^{1/2}}}{(JND(R_N))^\alpha} \right)^{1/\alpha} \quad (22)$$

For a given α, define a constant C as

$$C = \frac{2^{\alpha/2} \Gamma(\frac{\alpha+1}{2})}{\pi^{1/2}}. \quad (23)$$

Then, the proposed NR noisiness metric over the region R_b is given by

$$D_{R_b} = \left(\sum_{R_N \in R_b} \frac{C \cdot N^2 \cdot \sigma_{R_N}^\alpha}{(JND(R_N))^\alpha} \right)^{1/\alpha}. \quad (24)$$

As in (17), the noisiness metric over the image I can be computed as follows:

$$D = \left(\sum_{R_b} |D_{R_b}|^\alpha \right)^{1/\alpha}. \quad (25)$$

The resulting noise measure D, normalized by the number of blocks, is adopted as the proposed no-reference NR-PWN metric.

In (24), the noise variance σ_{R_N} is estimated directly from the test image, without the reference image. Multiple methods are available to estimate the noise variance, such as fast noise variance estimation (FNV) [19] and generalized cross validation (GCV)-based method [20,21]. In our implementation, the GCV method was used for computing the local noise variance. Similar results were also obtained using the FNV [19] noise estimation method.

Performance results

The performance of the proposed FR-PWN and NR-PWN metrics is assessed using the LIVE [6] and TID2008 [22] databases. The LIVE database [6] consists of 29 RGB color image. The images are distorted using different distortion types: JPEG2000, JPEG, Gaussian blur, white noise, and bit errors. The difference mean opinion score (DMOS) for each image is provided. The white noise part of the LIVE database includes 174 images with a noise standard deviation ranging from 0 to 2. White noise was added to the RGB components of images after scaling between 0 and 1. All of the white noise images (174 images) from the LIVE database are used in our experiments. The TID2008 database [22] consists of 25 reference images (512×384) and 1,700 distorted images. The images are distorted using 17 types of distortions, including additive Gaussian noise, high-frequency noise, JPEG2000, and Gaussian blur. The MOS was obtained using a total of 838 observers with 256,428 comparisons of the visual quality of distorted images. All of the additive Gaussian noise image (100 images) and high-frequency noise images (100 images) from the TID2008 database are used in our experiments. As mentioned in [22], additive zero-mean noise is often present in images and it is commonly modeled as a white Gaussian noise. This type of distortion is included in most studies of quality metric effectiveness. High-frequency noise is an additive non-white noise which can be used for analyzing spatial frequency sensitivity of the HVS [23]. High-frequency noise is typical in lossy image compression and watermarking.

To measure how well the proposed metrics correlate with the provided subjective scores, the correlation coefficients adopted by VQEG [24] are used, including the Pearson's linear correlation coefficient (PLCC) and the Spearman rank-order correlation coefficient (SROCC). A four-parameter logistic function as suggested in [24] is used prior to computing the Pearson's linear correlation coefficient:

$$MOS_{P_i} = \frac{\beta_1 - \beta_2}{1 + \exp\left(\frac{M_i - \beta_3}{|\beta_4|}\right)} + \beta_2 \quad (26)$$

where M_i is the quality metric for image i, MOS_{P_i} is the predicted MOS or DMOS. Figure 3 shows the DMOS

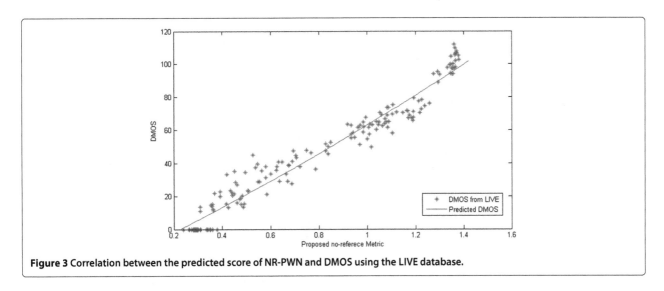

Figure 3 Correlation between the predicted score of NR-PWN and DMOS using the LIVE database.

score and predicted DMOS obtained using NR-PWN for the LIVE database.

Table 1 shows the evaluation results for the LIVE database. In addition to the proposed FR-PWN and NR-PWN metrics, the performance results of various existing metrics are presented for comparison, including seven full-reference metrics, DCTune [25], picture quality scale (PQS) [26], NQM [8], Fuzzy S7 [27], blockwise spectral distance measure (BSDM) [28], MS-SSIM [7], IFC [9], one reduced reference metric quality-aware images (QAI) [29], and seven no-reference metrics, blind image integrity notator using DCT statistics (BLINDS-II) (SVM) [30], BLINDS-II (Prob.) [30], hybrid no-reference (HNR) [31], blind/referenceless image spatial quality evaluator (BRISQUE) [32], naturalness image quality evaluator (NIQE) [33], blind image quality index (BIQI) [34], and learning a blind measure of perceptual image quality (LBIQ) [35]. The benchmarks of full-reference metrics are obtained from [6], and the others are obtained from their respective authors or available implementations. The shown 'N/A' in Table 1 means the value is not provided in the literature.

Table 2 shows the performance of the proposed FR-PWN and NR-PWN metrics using images with different types of distortion as provided by the TID2008

Table 1 Performance evaluation for the LIVE database

	Metrics	PLCC	SROCC
FR	DCTune [25]	0.9288	0.9324
	PQS [26]	0.9603	0.9535
	NQM [8]	0.9885	0.9854
	Fuzzy S7 [27]	0.9038	0.9199
	BSDM (S4) [28]	0.9559	0.9327
	MS-SSIM [7]	0.9737	0.9805
	IFC [9]	0.9766	0.9625
	FR-PWN (proposed)	0.9846	0.9835
RR	QAI [29]	0.8889	0.8639
NR	BLINDS-II(SVM) [30]	0.9799	0.9691
	BLINDS-II(Prob.) [30]	0.9854	0.9783
	HNR [31]	0.962	N/A
	BRISQUE [32]	0.9851	0.9786
	NIQE [33]	0.9773	0.9662
	BIQI [34]	0.9538	0.9510
	LBIQ [35]	0.9761	0.9702
	Estimated noise standard deviation	0.9497	0.9713
	NR-PWN (proposed)	0.9770	0.9816

Table 2 Performance evaluation using SROCC for the TID2008 database

	Metrics	Additive Gaussian noise	High-frequency noise
FR	MS-SSIM [7]	0.8094	0.8685
	DCTune [25]	0.8415	0.8721
	NQM [8]	0.7679	0.9015
	FR-PWN (proposed)	0.8818	0.9194
NR	BLINDS-II (SVM) [30]	0.6600	N/A
	BLINDS-II (Prob.) [30]	0.6956	0.7454
	BRISQUE [32]	0.829	0.6234
	NIQE [33]	0.7775	0.8539
	GRNN [36]	0.7532	N/A
	Li et al. [37]	0.7043	N/A
	NR-PWN (proposed)	0.8020	0.9136

database [22]. The proposed metric is compared with three full-reference metrics DCTune [25], NQM [8], MS-SSIM [7], and six very recent no-reference metrics that reported results for TID2008: BLINDS-II (SVM) [30], BLINDS-II (Prob.) [30], BRISQUE [32], NIQE [33], general regression neural network (GRNN) [36], and Li et al. [37]. The benchmarks of full-reference metrics are obtained from [22], and the others are obtained from their respective authors or available implementations. The shown N/A in Table 2 means the value is not provided in the literature. The proposed metric uses the same parameters as used with the LIVE database without any training.

From Table 1, it can be observed that the proposed FR-PWN metric outperforms the existing FR metrics for the LIVE database while achieving a similar performance as the NQM [8] metric. Table 2 shows that the proposed FR-PWN metric outperforms the existing FR metrics for the TID2008 database, on both Gaussian noise and high-frequency noise. The proposed NR-PWN metric comes close in performance to the proposed FR-PWN metric for both the LIVE and the TID2008 databases. In particular, Table 1 shows that the proposed NR-PWN metric performs better than existing NR metrics except for the Blinds-II and BRISQUE metrics in terms of PLCC. The proposed NR-PWN metric outperforms all the considered NR metrics in terms of SROCC and even existing FR metrics except the full-reference NQM [8] for the LIVE database. Table 2 shows that the proposed NR-PWN metric surpasses existing NR metrics except BRISQUE [32] for additive Gaussian noise, and that it significantly outperforms existing FR and NR metrics for high-frequency noise. Particularly, it should be noted that the performance of BRISQUE [32] drops dramatically on high-frequency noise and is significantly lower than the proposed metric. In addition, many of the shown state-of-the-art metrics including BLINDS-II [30], NIQE [33], and BRISQUE [32] use 80% of the data for training [30,32,33]. Consequently, these may not perform well on new distortions outside the training set, such as high-frequency noise (Table 2). In contrast, the proposed NR-PWN does not require training and still performs well on this new distortion.

Furthermore, it is worth indicating that as shown in Tables 1 and 2, the existing metrics exhibit differences in performance across different databases and types of distortions. It is noted in [38] that the performance of many image quality metrics could be quite different across databases. The difference in performance can be attributed to the differences in quality range, distortions, and contents across databases. Despite this, the results obtained show that the proposed FR-PWN and NR-PWN metrics achieve consistently a good performance across noise types (white noise and high-frequency noise) and

across databases as compared to the existing quality metrics. For example, the proposed FR-PWN metric exhibits a performance similar to NQM [8] for the LIVE database, while it significantly outperforms NQM [8] for white noise images from TID2008. Also, the existing BLINDS-II [30] performs fairly well for the LIVE database, but its performance significantly decreases when applied to TID2008. It is also interesting to note that although the mathematical derivations for the proposed NR-PWN is based on white noise, the proposed NR-PWN metric performs consistently well for high-frequency noise, a non-white noise.

The performance results presented in Tables 1 and 2 for the proposed NR-PWN metric are obtained using the GCV method [20,21] for local variance estimation. If the local variance is estimated using the FNV method [19], the resulting SROCC values are 0.9627 for the LIVE database additive Gaussian noise, 0.7850 for the TID2008 database additive Gaussian noise, and 0.9210 for the TID2008 database high-frequency noise, respectively.

Finally, the calculation of the proposed FR-PWN and NR-PWN metrics involves parameters of viewing conditions such as maximum luminance L_{max} of the monitor. However, the performance of the proposed metrics are resilient to different L_{max} values. In Tables 1 and 2, the proposed metrics are calculated using $L_{max} = 175$ cd/m^2. The L_{max} in real viewing conditions may vary from 100 cd/m^2 for CRT monitors to 300 cd/m^2 for LCD monitors. Table 3 shows the performance of the proposed metric in terms of SROCC using different values of L_{max}, for both the LIVE and the TID2008 databases. It can be observed that the proposed metrics are not sensitive to the selection of L_{max}.

Conclusions

This paper proposed both a full-reference and a no-reference noisiness metrics. The no-reference noisiness metric is derived from the proposed full-reference metric

Table 3 SROCC of the proposed metrics using different L_{max}

	L_{max} (cd/m^2)	100	175	300
LIVE additive	FR-PWN	0.9835	0.9835	0.9835
Gaussian noise	NR-PWN	0.9816	0.9816	0.9816
TID2008 additive	FR-PWN	0.8816	0.8818	0.8818
Gaussian noise	NR-PWN	0.8020	0.8020	0.8020
TID2008 high-	FR-PWN	0.9194	0.9194	0.9197
frequency noise	NR-PWN	0.9136	0.9136	0.9136

and integrates noise variance estimation and perceptual contrast sensitivity thresholds into a probability summation model. The proposed metrics can predict the relative noisiness in images based on the probability of noise detection. Results show that the proposed metrics achieve a consistently good performance across noise types and across databases as compared to the existing quality metrics. Further work can be performed to develop a no-reference quality metric for multiply distorted images.

Competing interests

The authors declare that they have no competing interests.

References

1. D Donoho, De-noising by soft-thresholding. IEEE Trans. Inf. Theory. **41**(3), 613–627 (1995)
2. R Hardie, A fast image super-resolution algorithm using an adaptive Wiener Filter. IEEE Trans. Image Process. **16**(12), 2953–2964 (2007)
3. R Ferzli, L Karam, A no-reference objective image sharpness metric based on the notion of just noticeable blur (JNB). IEEE Trans. Image Process. **18**(4), 717–728 (2009)
4. N Narvekar, L Karam, A no-reference image blur metric based on the cumulative probability of blur detection (CPBD). IEEE Trans. Image Process. **20**(9), 2678–2683 (2011)
5. R Ferzli, L Karam, No-reference objective wavelet based noise immune image sharpness metric, in *IEEE International Conference on Image Processing, ICIP 2005*, vol. 1 (IEEE, Piscataway, 2005), pp. I–405–8
6. H Sheikh, M Sabir, A Bovik, A statistical evaluation of recent full reference image quality assessment algorithms. IEEE Trans. Image Process. **15**(11), 3440–3451 (2006)
7. Z Wang, E Simoncelli, A Bovik, Multiscale structural similarity for image quality assessment, in *Proceedings of the Thirty-Seventh Asilomar Conference on Signals, Systems and Computers, 2004*, vol. 2 (Pacific Grove, 9–12 November 2003), pp. 1398–1402
8. N Damera-Venkata, T Kite, W Geisler, B Evans, A Bovik, Image quality assessment based on a degradation model. IEEE Trans. Image Process. **9**(4), 636–650 (2000)
9. H Sheikh, A Bovik, G De Veciana, An information fidelity criterion for image quality assessment using natural scene statistics. IEEE Trans. Image Process. **14**(12), 2117–2128 (2005)
10. MCQ Farias, S Mitra, No-reference video quality metric based on artifact measurements, in *IEEE International Conference on Image Processing, ICIP 2005*, vol. 3 (IEEE, Piscataway, 2005), pp. III–141–144
11. MG Choi, JH Jung, JW Jeon, No-reference image quality assessment using blur and noise. Int. J. Electrical Electron. Eng. **3**, 318–322 (2009)
12. I Hontsch, L Karam, Locally adaptive perceptual image coding. IEEE Trans. Image Process. **9**(9), 1472–1483 (2000)
13. JG Robson, N Graham, Probability summation and regional variation in contrast sensitivity across the visual field. Vis. Res. **21**, 409–418 (1981)
14. L Karam, N Sadaka, R Ferzli, Z Ivanovski, An efficient selective perceptual-based super-resolution estimator. IEEE Trans. Image Process. **20**(12), 3470–3482 (2011)
15. A Ahumada, H Peterson, Luminance-model-based DCT quantization for color image compression. Human Vision, Visual Processing, and Digital Display III, SPIE Proc. **1666**, 365–374 (1992)
16. AB Watson, DCT quantization matrices visually optimized for individual images. Human Vision, Visual Processing, and Digital Display IV, SPIE Proc. **1913**, 202–216. (SPIE, San Jose, 1993)
17. Z Liu, L Karam, A Watson, JPEG2000 encoding with perceptual distortion control. IEEE Trans. Image Process. **15**(7), 1763–1778 (2006)
18. A Wilkelbauer, Moments and absolute moments of the normal distribution. (2012), http://arxiv.org/abs/1209.4340. (Accessed 15 April 2013)
19. J Immerkær, Fast noise variance estimation. Comput. Vis. Image Underst. **64**(2), 300–302 (1996). http://www.sciencedirect.com/science/article/pii/S1077314296900600.

20. G Wahba, Estimating the smoothing parameter, in *Spline Models for Observational Data* (Society for Industrial Mathematics, Philadelphia, 1990), pp. 45–65
21. D Garcia, Robust smoothing of gridded data in one and higher dimensions with missing values. Comput. Stat. Data Anal. **54**(4), 1167–1178 (2010)
22. N Ponomarenko, V Lukin, A Zelensky, K Egiazarian, M Carli, F Battisti, TID2008-A database for evaluation of full-reference visual quality assessment metrics. Adv. Mod. Radioelectronics. **10**, 30–45 (2009)
23. N Ponomarenko, F Silvestri, K Egiazarian, M Carli, J Astola, V Lukin, On between-coefficient contrast masking of DCT basis functions, in *Proceedings of the Third International Workshop on Video Processing and Quality Metrics*, vol. 2007 (Scottsdale, January 2007)
24. VQEG, Final report from the Video Quality Experts Group on the validation of objective models of video quality assessment (2000). http://www.vqeg.org/. (Accessed 15 April 2013)
25. AB Watson, DCTune: A technique for visual optimization of DCT quantization matrices for individual images. Soc. Inf. Display Dig. Tech. Papers. **24**, 946–949 (1993)
26. M Miyahara, K Kotani, V Algazi, Objective picture quality scale (PQS) for image coding. IEEE Trans. Commun. **46**(9), 1215–1226 (1998)
27. DV Weken, M Nachtegael, EE Kerre, Using similarity measures and homogeneity for the comparison of images. Image Vis. Comput. **22**(9), 695–702 (2004)
28. I Avcibas, I Avcıbaş, B Sankur, K Sayood, Statistical evaluation of image quality measures. J. Electron. Imaging. **11**, 206–223 (2002)
29. Z Wang, G Wu, H Sheikh, E Simoncelli, EH Yang, A Bovik, Quality-aware images. IEEE Trans. Image Process. **15**(6), 1680–1689 (2006)
30. M Saad, A Bovik, C Charrier, Blind image quality assessment: a natural scene statistics approach in the DCT domain. IEEE Trans. Image Process. **21**(8), 3339–3352 (2012)
31. J Shen, Q Li, G Erlebacher, Hybrid no-reference natural image quality assessment of noisy, blurry, JPEG2000, and JPEG images. IEEE Trans. Image Process. **20**(8), 2089–2098 (2011)
32. A Mittal, A Moorthy, A Bovik, No-reference image quality assessment in the spatial domain. IEEE Trans. Image Process. **21**(12), 4695–4708 (2012)
33. A Mittal, R Soundararajan, A Bovik, Making a completely blind image quality analyzer. IEEE Signal Process. Lett. **20**(3), 209–212 (2013)
34. A Moorthy, A Bovik, A two-step framework for constructing blind image quality indices. IEEE Signal Process. Lett. **17**(5), 513–516 (2010)
35. H Tang, N Joshi, A Kapoor, Learning a blind measure of perceptual image quality, in *2011 IEEE Conference on Computer Vision and Pattern Recognition (CVPR)* (IEEE, Piscataway, 2011), pp. 305–312
36. C Li, A Bovik, X Wu, Blind image quality assessment using a general regression neural network. IEEE Trans. Neural Netw. **22**(5), 793–799 (2011)
37. C Li, G Tang, X Wu, Y Ju, No-reference image quality assessment with learning phase congruency feature. J. Electrical Inf. Technol. **35**(2), 484–488 (2012)
38. S Tourancheau, F Autrusseau, Z Sazzad, Y Horita, Impact of subjective dataset on the performance of image quality metrics, in *15th IEEE International Conference on Image Processing* (IEEE Piscataway, 2008), pp. 365–368

5

Efficient robust image interpolation and surface properties using polynomial texture mapping

Mingjing Zhang and Mark S Drew[*]

Abstract

Polynomial texture mapping (PTM) uses simple polynomial regression to interpolate and re-light image sets taken from a fixed camera but under different illumination directions. PTM is an extension of the classical photometric stereo (PST), replacing the simple Lambertian model employed by the latter with a polynomial one. The advantage and hence wide use of PTM is that it provides some effectiveness in interpolating appearance including more complex phenomena such as interreflections, specularities and shadowing. In addition, PTM provides estimates of surface properties, i.e., chromaticity, albedo and surface normals. The most accurate model to date utilizes multivariate Least Median of Squares (LMS) robust regression to generate a basic matte model, followed by radial basis function (RBF) interpolation to give accurate interpolants of appearance. However, robust multivariate modelling is slow. Here we show that the robust regression can find acceptably accurate inlier sets using a much less burdensome 1D LMS robust regression (or 'mode-finder'). We also show that one can produce good quality appearance interpolants, plus accurate surface properties using PTM before the additional RBF stage, provided one increases the dimensionality beyond 6D and still uses robust regression. Moreover, we model luminance and chromaticity separately, with dimensions 16 and 9 respectively. It is this separation of colour channels that allows us to maintain a relatively low dimensionality for the modelling. Another observation we show here is that in contrast to current thinking, using the original idea of polynomial terms in the lighting direction outperforms the use of hemispherical harmonics (HSH) for matte appearance modelling. For the RBF stage, we use Tikhonov regularization, which makes a substantial difference in performance. The radial functions used here are Gaussians; however, to date the Gaussian dispersion width and the value of the Tikhonov parameter have been fixed. Here we show that one can extend a theorem from graphics that generates a very fast error measure for an otherwise difficult leave-one-out error analysis. Using our extension of the theorem, we can optimize on both the Gaussian width and the Tikhonov parameter.

Keywords: Polynomial texture mapping; Photometric stereo; Radial basis functions; Hemispherical harmonics; Robust regression

1 Introduction

Polynomial texture mapping (PTM) [1] uses a single fixed digital camera at constant exposure, with a set of n images captured using lighting from different directions. A typical rig would consist of a hemisphere of xenon flash lamps imaging an object, where directions to each light is known (Figure 1a). The basic idea in PTM is to improve on a simple Lambertian model for matte

content, whereby the three components of the light direction are mapped to luminance, by extending the model to include a low-order polynomial of lighting-direction components. The strength of PTM, in comparison to a simple Lambertian photometric stereo (PST) [2] is that PTM can better model real radiance and to some extent grasp intricate dependencies due to self-shadowing and interreflections. Usually, some 40 to 80 images are captured. The better capture of details is the driving force behind the interest in this technique evinced by many museum professionals, with the original least squares

*Correspondence: mark@cs.sfu.ca
School of Computing Science, Simon Fraser University, Vancouver, British Columbia V5A 1S6, Canada

(LS)-based PTM method already in use at major museums in the USA, including the Smithsonian, the Museum of Modern Art and the Fine Arts Museums of San Francisco, and is planned for the Metropolitan and the Louvre (M. Mudge, personal communication, Cultural Heritage Imaging). As well, some work has involved applying PTM *in situ* for such applications as imaging palaeolithic rock art [3]. In such situations, one has to *recover* lighting directions from the specular patch on a reflective sphere [4]; such a 'highlight' method [5] can also be applied to museum capture of small objects or to microscopic image capture.

PTM generates a matte model for the surface, where luminance (or RGB) is modelled at each pixel via a polynomial regression from light-direction components to luminance. Say, e.g. there are $n = 50$ images, with n known normalized light-direction three-vectors $\boldsymbol{a}$. Then in the original embodiment, a six-term polynomial model is fitted at each pixel separately, regressing onto that pixel's n luminance values using LS regression. The main objectives of PTM are the ability to *re-light* pixels using the regression parameters obtained, as well as the recovery of surface properties: surface normal, colour and albedo. For re-lighting, the idea is simply that if the regression from the n in-sample light-directions $\boldsymbol{a}$ to n luminance values, L is known then substituting a new $\boldsymbol{a}$ will generate a new L, thus yielding a simple interpolation scheme for new, out-of-sample, light directions $\boldsymbol{a}$.

In [6], we extend PTM in three ways: First, the six-term polynomial is changed so as to allow purely linear terms to model purely linear luminance exactly. Secondly, the LS regression for the underlying matte model is replaced by a robust regression, the least median of squares (LMS) method [7]. This means that only a majority of the n pixel values obtained at each pixel need be actually matte, with specularities and shadows automatically identified as outliers. With correctly identified matte pixels in hand, surface normals, albedos and pixel chromaticity are more accurately recovered. Thirdly, authors in [6] further add an additional interpolation level by modelling the part of in-sample pixel values that is not completely explained by the matte PTM model via a radial basis function (RBF) interpolation. The RBF model does a much better job of modelling features such as specularities that depend strongly on the lighting direction. As well, the RBF approach can make use of any shadow information to help model interpolated shadows, which change abruptly with lighting direction. The interpolation is still local to each pixel and, thus, does not attempt to bridge non-specular locales as in reflectance sharing, for example [8,9]. In reflectance sharing, a *known* surface geometry is assumed, as opposed to the present paper. Here, we rely on the idea that there is at least a small contribution to specularity at any pixel, e.g. the sheen on skin or paintwork, so that we need not share across neighbouring pixels and can employ the RBF approach from [6]. For cast shadows, a more difficult feature to model, at each pixel the RBF model will utilize whatever shadow content is actually present across the whole set of n images from n lights.

The current study is aimed at further refining and improving the PTM + RBF pipeline as was employed in [6], as well as exploring different combinations of basis functions. The main contributions of this work are three-fold:

1. We introduce a more efficient, 'mode-finder' regression method to replace the computationally intensive multivariate LMS regression in the matte modelling stage. Compared to the 6D LMS regression, the mode-finder effectively reduces the number of unknowns from 6 to 1 and thus greatly reduces the processing time from $O(n^6 \log n)$ to $O(n \log n)$ ([7], p. 206). We found that this simplification introduces little reduction of accuracy. Although technically the mode-finder regression approach can be applied to the mode of either luminance or any colour components, we show that the mode of luminance provides the highest accuracy. How a robust mode-finder works is simple: from the n luminance values at the current pixel, select one randomly; continue and adopt as the best estimate of the 'mode' that luminance which delivers the least median of squared residuals. What makes the LMS method powerful is that it provides strong mathematical guarantees on the performance given by choosing a much smaller subset than a simple exhaustive search and it also delivers an inlier band, automatically, thus classifying luminance values as usable or not. The multivariate version of LMS is similar: for 6D LMS, e.g., we randomly select six luminances and find residuals for a polynomial regression. Again, the number of selections is tremendously smaller than an exhaustive search, but nonetheless is very slow compared to a 1D search.

2. We explore different combinations of basis functions for PTM. Firstly, we extend the classical polynomial models from 6D to 16D. Moreover, due to another observation we made that luminance reconstruction has a far greater impact on the re-lighted image quality than the reconstruction of chromaticity, we can reduce the dimension for chromaticity modelling with little loss of accuracy. Reducing the number of float regression coefficients makes a difference, when we multiply by millions of pixels. We found that 16D for luminance + 9D for chromaticity is a good balance between dimensionality and accuracy.

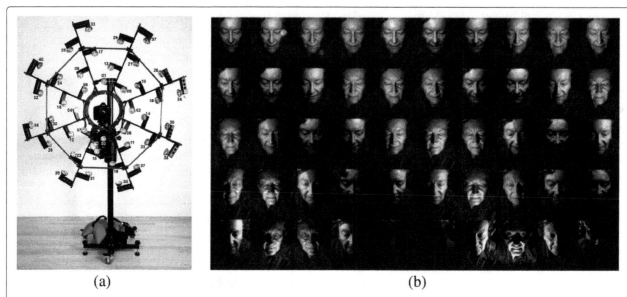

Figure 1 A typical PTM rig and an example dataset. (a) A 40-light rig for capturing PTM datasets (courteously supplied by Cultural Heritage Imaging). **(b)** A PTM dataset of 50 images (courteously supplied by Tom Malzbender, Hewlett-Packard).

Secondly, we compared the performance of the hemiSpherical harmonics (HSH) basis against the polynomial basis of the same order and found that, surprisingly, the polynomial model outperforms HSH in terms of the quality of appearance reconstruction, especially at large incident angles.

3. We adopt a method to mathematically determine the optimal parameters used for the RBF interpolation stage. Previously in [6], we made use of an RBF network consisting of Gaussian radial functions to model the non-Lambertian contribution. The parameters in this model, including the Gaussian dispersion σ and Tikhonov regularization coefficient τ, were taken heuristically and remained constant across all pixels. In this work, we start off from a theorem that minimizes error in a leave-one-out analysis by optimizing the Gaussian dispersion parameter. Such a theorem is not new, but here we extend its use to whole images and three-channel colour. More importantly, however, we also extend the theorem to optimize over the Tikhonov regularization. For the fairly large size matrices being inverted, these optimizations matter and make a substantial difference to results obtained.

Note that contributions 1 and 3 are direct improvements over the methodology of the PTM + RBF pipeline: Contribution 1 is aimed at increasing the efficiency of the first stage - matte modelling; contribution 3 is devoted to the optimization of the second stage - RBF interpolation. On the other hand, the goal of contribution 2 is to find an optimal set of basis functions. The discoveries made in contribution 2 can be applied to the matte modelling stage of PTM + RBF, as well as regular PTM with no RBF interpolation.

This paper is organized as follows: In Section 2 we review previous work in this area, and in Section 3 we provide a brief recapitulation of the PTM method. In Section 4 we introduce the notion of our contribution 1 - using a robust mode-finder instead of a full multivariate robust regression and explicate how we use the mode-finder and trimmed LS to realize outlier detection and recover surface properties. In Section 5, focusing on contribution 2, we test the appearance reconstruction with PTM separately applied to luminance and chromaticity and compare the reconstructed matte appearance for PTM and for HSH. In Section 6 we describe our contribution 3, i.e. how to use an optimized version of the RBF framework to interpolate specularity and shadows on reconstructed images. Finally, Section 7 presents concluding remarks.

2 Related work

Many methods for detecting outlier pixels in photometric methods have been proposed. Early examples include a four-light PST approach in which the values yielding significantly differing albedos are excluded [10-12]. In a similar five-light PST method [13], the highest and the lowest values, presumably corresponding to highlights and shadows, are simply discarded. Another four-light method [14] explicitly includes ambient illumination and surface integrability and adopts an iterative strategy using current surface estimates to accept or reject each additional light based on a threshold indicating a shadowed value. The problem with these methods is that they rely on throwing away only a small number of outlier pixel values, whereas our robust methods in the current and previous studies allow up to 50% of the pixel values discarded as outliers.

More recently, Willems et al. [15] used an iterative method to estimate normals. Initially, the pixel values within a certain range (10 to 240 out of 255) were used to estimate an initial normal map. In each of the following iterations, error residuals in normals for all lighting directions are computed and the normals are updated based only on those directions with small residuals. Sun et al. [16] showed that at least six light sources are needed to guarantee that every location on the surface is illuminated by at least three lights. They proposed a decision algorithm to discard only doubtful pixels, rather than throwing away all pixel values that lie outside a certain range. However, the validity of their method is based on the assumption that out of the six values for each pixel, there is at most one highlight pixels and two shadowed pixels. Julia et al. [17] utilized a factorization technique to decompose the luminance matrix into surface and light source matrices. The shadow and highlight pixels are considered as missing data, with the objective of reducing their influence on the result. Wu et al. [18] formulated the problem of surface normal recovery as a rank minimization problem, which can be solved via convex optimization. Their method is able to handle specularities and shadows as well as other non-Lambertian deviations. Compared to these methods, the algorithm proposed here is a good deal simpler, while producing excellent results.

A small number of recent studies utilize probability models as a mechanism to try to incorporate handling shadows and highlights into the PST formulation. Tang et al. [19] model normal orientations and discontinuities with two coupled Markov random fields (MRFs). They proposed a tensorial belief propagation method to solve the *maximum a posteriori* problem in the Markov network. Chandraker et al. [20] formulate PST as a shadow labelling problem where the labels of each pixel's neighbours are taken into consideration, enforcing the smoothness of the shadowed region, and approximate the solution via a fast iterative graph-cut method. Another study [21] employs a maximum-likelihood (ML) imaging model for PST. In their method, an inlier map modelled via MRF is included in the ML model. However, the initial values of the inlier map would directly influence the final result, whereas our methods do not depend on the choice of any prior.

Yang et al. [22] include a dichromatic reflection model into PST and associated method for both estimating surface normals as well as separating the diffuse and specular components, based on a surface chromaticity invariant. Their method is able to reduce the specular effect even when the specular-free observability assumption (that is, each pixel is diffuse in at least one input image) is violated. However, this method does not address shadows and fails on surfaces that mix their own colours into the reflected highlights, such as metallic materials. Moreover, their method also requires knowledge of the lighting chromaticity - they suggest a simple white-patch estimator - whereas in our method, we have no such requirement. Kherada et al. [23] proposed a component-based mapping method. They decompose the captured images into direct and global components - single bounce of light from a surface, as opposed to illumination onto a point that is interreflected from all other points of the scene. They then model matte, shadow and specularity separately within each component. Their method is stated to provide a better appearance reconstruction than the original PTM [1], although at the cost of a much heavier computational load, but depends on a training phase and requires accurate disambiguation of direct and global contributions.

Aside from the polynomial basis, it is possible to use other types of basis function in PTM, as long as they provide a good approximation of the light-reflectance interaction. Spherical harmonics (SH), the angular portion of a set of solutions to the Laplace's equations defined on a sphere, appear to be a good candidate for this purpose. Due to their appealing mathematical properties, they have been extensively applied in a great variety of topics in computer graphics, such as the modelling of BRDFs [24], early work on image-based rendering and re-lighting [25,26], BRDF shading [27], irradiance environment maps [28], precomputed radiance transfer [29,30], distant lighting [31,32] and lighting-invariant object recognition [33]. However, in the context of PTM, we note that the incoming and outgoing lights are defined only on the upper hemisphere. Therefore, representation of such a hemispherical function using basis functions defined over the full spherical domain introduces discontinuities at the boundary of the hemisphere and requires a large number of coefficients [34]. Thus, it is more natural to map these functions to a basis set defined only over the upper hemisphere. In [34], a HSH basis derived from SH using shifted associated Legendre polynomials was proposed. This basis has been applied in surface modelling under distant illumination [35] and in shape description and reconstruction of surfaces [36]. Recent progress on HSH includes a HSH-based Helmholtz bidirectional reflectance basis [37] and noise-resistant Eigen hemispherical harmonics. In this study, we incorporate the HSH basis as proposed in [34] into the framework of PTM and compare its performance with the polynomial basis.

PTM and other similar reflectance transformation imaging (RTI) methods have found extensive applications in cultural heritage imaging and art conservation. Earl et al. use PTM to capture and visually examine a great variety of ancient artefacts, including bronze busts, coins, paintings, ceramics and cuneiform inscriptions [38-41]. Duffy [42] employed a highlighted RTI method to record the prehistoric rock inscriptions and carvings at the Roughting Linn rock site, UK. Padfield et al. [43] adopted PTM to digitally capture paintings in order to monitor their physical changes during conservation. These applications demonstrate the ability of PTM to visually enhance the captured images via different display modes, most notably specular enhancement and diffuse gain, allowing for inspection of features such as fingerprints and erasure marks that are otherwise much less visually prominent in regular images.

3 Matte modelling using PTM

3.1 Luminance

PTM models smooth dependence of images on lighting direction via polynomial regression. Here we briefly recapitulate PTM as amended by [6]: Suppose n images of a scene are taken with a fixed-position camera and lighting from $i = 1..n$ different lighting directions $a^i = (u^i, v^i, w^i)^T$. Let each RGB image acquired be denoted ρ^i, and we also make use of luminance images, $L^i = \sum_{k=1}^{3} \rho_k^i$. Colour is re-inserted later, as is described in Section 3.4. It is also possible to 'multiplex' illumination by combining several lights at once in order to decrease noise [44], but here we simply use one light at a time.

In [6] we use a 6D vector polynomial p for each normalized light direction three-vector a as follows:

$$p(a) = (u, v, w, u^2, uv, 1), \quad \text{where } w = \sqrt{1 - u^2 - v^2} \tag{1}$$

This differs from the original PTM formulation [1] in that originally the polynomial used had been $(u, v, u^2, v^2, uv, 1)$, which unfortunately does not model a true Lambertian (linear) surface well since it must warp a non-linear model to suit linear data.

Then at each pixel (x, y) separately, we can seek a polynomial regression six-vector of coefficients $c(x, y)$ in a simple model, regressing lighting directions onto luminance:

$$\begin{bmatrix} p(a^1) \\ p(a^2) \\ \cdots \\ p(a^n) \end{bmatrix} c(x, y) = \begin{bmatrix} L^1(x, y) \\ L^2(x, y) \\ \cdots \\ L^n(x, y) \end{bmatrix} \tag{2}$$

E.g. if $n = 50$, then we could write this as

$$\underset{50 \times 6}{P} \; \underset{6 \times 1}{c(x, y)} = \underset{50 \times 1}{L(x, y)} \tag{3}$$

An example dataset (code named *Barb*) for PTM is displayed in Figure 1b, which was captured with a 50-light dome (i.e. $n = 50$) similar to the one shown in Figure 1a. The dataset *Barb* has large specular and shadowed regions, which cannot be well addressed by the classical PTM model, and such datasets have typically been avoided. Thus, we find *Barb* an ideal representative dataset to test the accuracy and/or robustness of a re-lighting method. On other such difficult datasets we have tried, very similar results were found (see [6] for depictions of shiny and shadowed datasets).

3.2 Robust 6D regression

In our recent version of PTM [6], we solve Equation 3 using a robust LMS regression [7]. The purpose of robust regression is to (1) isolate the matte and specular/shadow components and allow the latter to be more cleanly modelled with an additional RBF interpolation stage and (2) identify the non-matte outliers so that more accurate surface normals as well as other reflectance properties can be obtained with LS. The LMS algorithm as applied in [6] is summarized as follows [7]:

While the 6D LMS regression is slow, it is guaranteed to omit distracting features such as specularities and shadows. Due to the 50% breakdown point of LMS, it requires that at least half plus 1 of the luminance observations belong to a base matte reflectance that can be sufficiently addressed by a polynomial model. Fortunately, this requirement is satisfied for most pixels in real-world datasets. This regression method will be referred to Method:LMS in the following text.

3.3 Re-lighting

The re-lighting of images for PTM is fairly straightforward. Given a new light direction a' and estimated polynomial coefficients $c(x, y)$, the approximated luminance can be expressed as:

$$L'(x, y) = \max[p(a') c(x, y), 0] \tag{10}$$

Note that with Method:LMS, $c(x, y)$ was obtained from a trimmed LS where only the matte observations are used. Therefore, the resulting $L'(x, y)$ is expected to show matte-only contents as well, and non-matte components can be later addressed by other methods (such as the RBF interpolation we will describe in Section 6). This contrasts the robust methods with Method:LS, which uses only PTM to capture both the matte and non-matte components (to some degree) at the same time. Also note that in Equation 10 only luminance is recovered. Colour would

Algorithm: LMS

1. Initialize the iteration counter $q = 1$.
2. Sample a random subset of d indices: $J_q \subset \{1, 2, \ldots, n\}$ ($|J_q| = d$). In our 6D PTM model, $d = 6$. Get the subset of the polynomial of lighting directions and their corresponding luminance observations indexed by J_q, denoted by P_{J_q} and L_{J_q} respectively.
3. Use LS on this subset of observations/lighting directions to estimate the polynomial coefficients c_{J_q}:

$$c_{J_q} = P_{J_q}^\dagger L_{J_q} \qquad (4)$$

4. Use the current estimation c_{J_q} to approximate the real observation L and calculate the squared residuals $r_1^2, r_2^2, \ldots, r_n^2$ for the n observations in L, collectively stored as $R^2 = (r_1^2, r_2^2, \ldots, r_n^2)$:

$$R = L - P c_{J_q} \qquad (5)$$

$$R^2 = R^T R \qquad (6)$$

5. Get the median M_{J_q} of the n residuals $r_1^2, \ldots, r_n^2$ in R^2:

$$M_{J_q} = \text{median}_{i=1,\ldots,n}\, r_i^2 \qquad (7)$$

6. Let $q \leftarrow q + 1$ and go back to Step 2 until $q > m$. Here we choose $m = 1,500$ for our typical datasets where $n = 50$ and $d = 6$.
7. Find the smallest median of squared residuals $M_{\min}$ such that:

$$M_{\min} = \min_{q=1,\ldots,m} M_{J_q} \qquad (8)$$

and keep the estimation of coefficient set $c_{\min}$ that yields $M_{\min}$.

8. Calculate the robust standard deviation σ:

$$\sigma = 1.4826 \left(1 + \frac{5}{n-d}\right) \sqrt{M_{\min}} \qquad (9)$$

9. Obtain the squared residuals r_i^2 ($i = 1, \ldots, n$) with respect to $c_{\min}$ for each of the n observations. Maintain a binary weight vector ω of n elements, where $\omega_i = 1$ if $r_i^2 \leq (2.5\sigma)$ and $\omega_i = 0$ otherwise.
10. Perform trimmed LS using only the observations L_i and polynomial of lighting vector $p(a^i)$ with $\omega_i = 1$.

be re-introduced by multiplying the chromaticity and the albedo as in Equation 11 as discussed next.

3.4 Colour, normals and albedo

The luminance L consists of the sum of colour components: $L = R + G + B$. Luminance is given by the shading s (e.g. this could in the simplest case be Lambertian shading, meaning surface normal dotted into light direction) times

albedo α: i.e. $L = s\alpha$. The chromaticity χ is defined as RGB colour ρ, made independent of intensity by dividing by the L_1 norm:

$$\rho = L\chi, \quad L = s\alpha, \quad \chi \equiv \{R, G, B\}/(R + G + B) \qquad (11)$$

Suppose our robust regression below delivers binary weights ω, with $\omega = 0$ for outliers. As in [6], once inliers are identified we recover a robust estimate of chromaticity χ as the median of inlier values, for $k = 1..3$:

$$\chi_k = \underset{i \in (\omega \equiv 1)}{\text{median}} \left(\rho_k^i / L^i\right) \qquad (12)$$

In addition, an estimate of surface normal n is given by a trimmed PST: with the collection of directions a stored in the $n \times 3$ matrix A, suppose ω^0 is an index variable giving the inlier subset of light directions: $\omega^0 = (\omega \equiv 1)$. Using just the inlier subset, a trimmed version of PST gives an estimate of normalized surface normal $\hat{n}$ and albedo α via

$$\tilde{n} = \left(A(\omega^0)\right)^\dagger L(\omega^0); \quad \alpha = \|\tilde{n}\|, \quad \hat{n} = \tilde{n}/\alpha \qquad (13)$$

where $A^\dagger$ is the Moore-Penrose pseudoinverse. Other weighting functions are also possible, such as the triangular function used by Method:QUANTILE which we will briefly describe in Section 4.1.

With chromaticity χ in hand, Equation 11 gives RGB pixel values ρ for the interpolated luminance L, and (13) above also gives us the properties albedo α and surface normal $\hat{n}$ intrinsic to the surface.

Institutional users of the PTM approach are indeed interested in appearance modelling for re-lighting, but they are also separately interested in surface properties, especially accurate surface normals, which carry much of the shape information.

4 Robust chromaticity/luminance modes

In this section, we present our first main contribution. As we mentioned in Section 3.2, despite its high robustness LMS can be very slow. Therefore, it is necessary to find a less computationally expensive robust method. Here, we suggest a simplified form of LMS - the mode-finder approach.

4.1 Robust mode-finder algorithm

The basic idea of a mode-finder is first to identify a central value of either luminance or chromaticity, termed 'mode' across all the observations at every pixel then perform trimmed LS only using the observations that are with a certain range around the mode. This is a far simpler problem than LMS. For reference, we call this new method Method:MODE, which can be achieved with the following algorithm [7]:

Algorithm: MODE

1. Initialize the iteration counter $q = 1$.
2. Compute the n squared residuals r_i^2 ($i = 1, \ldots, n$) with respect to the scalar observation indexed by q:

$$r_i^2 = (L_i - L_q)^2 \qquad (14)$$

3. Find the median M_q of r_i^2:

$$M_q = \text{median}_{i=1,\ldots,n} \, r_i^2 \qquad (15)$$

4. Let $q \leftarrow q + 1$ and go back to step 2 until $q > n$ ($n = 50$ for our typical datasets).
5. Find the smallest median of squared residuals $M_{\min}$ such that

$$M_{\min} = \min_{q=1,\ldots,n} M_q \qquad (16)$$

and keep the observation of $L_{\min}$ that yields $M_{\min}$.
6. Same as steps 8 to 10 in Algorithm: LMS, except that in mode-finder, the dimensionality $d = 1$ and the residuals are calculated with respect to $L_{\min}$.

The rationale of Method:MODE is that non-matte outlier observations usually take extreme values in luminance (for instance, shadowed and specular pixels may have an intensity close to 0 and 1, respectively), or their chromaticity may deviate from other matte observations (for instance, specular observations are usually more desaturated whereas shadowed regions appear darker).

Method:MODE may seem to be merely another example of previous thresholding methods. In a typical method of this type [45], the top 10% and the bottom 50% of luminance observations are simply discarded. Then, coefficient values sought are found using a triangular function to weight lighting directions in the resulting range. As in [6], we refer to this simple method as Method:QUANTILE and denote the original PTM method as Method:LS. However, Method:MODE is different from Method:QUANTILE in that the inlier range is calculated based on the distribution of the observation values rather than the empirical values and heuristic triangle functions previously employed. Simply put, Method:MODE lets the data itself dictate what values are in- and outliers.

4.2 Mode-finder versus LMS

In essence, both Method:LMS and Method:MODE attempt to fit a mathematical model to as many data points as possible by minimizing the median of residuals and then identify an inlier range around the fitted model. All observations that fall outside of this range are deemed outliers. The only difference between the two methods is the mathematical model used: Method:LMS fits the data with a 6D polynomial model, whereas Method:MODE approximates the observations with one single scalar constant, i.e. a 1D mathematical model.

To see how the outlier identification works in the two methods, we study a particular pixel in the *Barb* dataset (marked by a yellow cross in Figure 2a). In Figure 2b,c, the actual luminance observations at this pixel location from 50 lighting conditions are represented as either black solid dots (if they are identified as inliers) or red crosses (for outliers) and are sorted in ascending order. For comparison, the approximated luminance values are shown as blue circles. An observation is classified as outlier if (1) its value is outside the inlier band, marked with green shade enclosed by blue dashed lines or (2) its *approximated* value (blue circle) is negative. Note that the major difference between Method:LMS (Figure 2b) and Method:Mode (Figure 2c) is that the 6D polynomial model in LMS generates an inlier band that closely approximates the actual data curve, whereas the 1D constant model in Method:MODE creates a wider, horizontal band. Despite this seemingly crucial difference, Method:MODE as a matter of fact correctly captures most of the outliers identified by Method:LMS. Although Method:MODE may throw away more data points than necessary, it would not negatively affect the accuracy of estimated polynomial coefficients since these unnecessarily excluded data points are matte anyway and a robust method is not affected by the sum of squared residuals as in LS.

Figure 3 shows a more detailed comparison on outlier estimation and surface property recovery using LMS and mode-finder. Since there is no ground truth data for these properties available, we simply adopt the results obtained with the full 6D LMS method as our 'gold standard' [6] and compare the relative performance of mode-finder against it. Figure 3a displays accuracy of outlier detection in terms of precision, recall and f-statistic, and shows that as long as we use modes for luminance we can achieve a very accurate set of outliers. Results using luminance are shown using white bars. The black bars represent the results obtained by the chromaticity mode, which will be covered in Section 4.3. Figure 3b shows the results for recovered surface normal vectors using outlier detection based on the simpler mode-finder, compared to Method:LMS: the median angular error is 3.03°, which is quite small. Figure 3c shows error in three-vector chromaticity, again measured in terms of angle: the median error is 5.93°, which is quite acceptable. Figure 3d shows errors in albedo - the median is only 0.0037 (where the maximum correct albedo is 1.5855). Such small differences are quite reasonable as a tradeoff with having a much less complex algorithm.

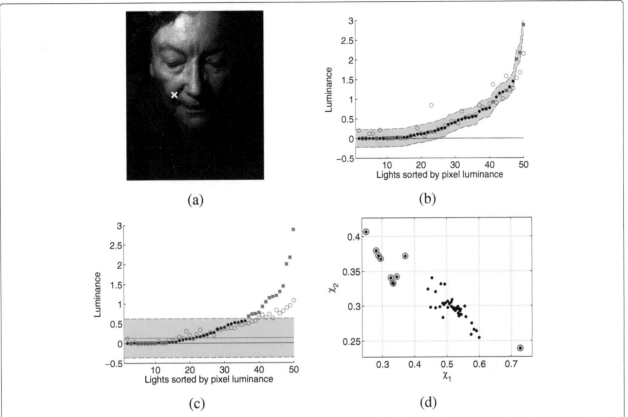

(a)   (b)

(c)   (d)

Figure 2 Comparison of outlier detection with LMS and with mode-finding approach. (a) One original image; consider pixel at yellow 'x'. **(b)** Outlier detection with 6D to 1D LMS regression. Here, the pixels are displayed in ascending order sorted by luminance. The approximated values are shown as blue circles. Inlier pixel values (at this 1 pixel, over the set of 50 lights) with estimated $\hat{L}$ values that fall within the green inlier band are displayed as black dots and outlier measured luminances, including values with negative luminance estimates that fall below the horizontal line at $L = 0$, as black dots with red crosses. The blue dashed lines indicate the boundaries of the inlier band automatically identified by LMS. **(c)** Outlier detection with luminance-mode finder. Here the blue solid line shows the location of the (scalar) mode, bracketed by a horizontal inlier band; inliers also exclude negative-$\hat{L}$ lights. **(d)** Red vs. green chromaticity, with outliers for green mode showing red circles (see Section 4.3).

4.3 Luminance versus chromaticity modes

As mentioned earlier in Subsection 4.1, the mode-finder can be applied on luminance but as well could be applied to colour components, since non-matte observations tend to have an altered chromaticity. For example, in Figure 2c, we have shown the outliers identified by Method:MODE on luminance. In Figure 2d, we apply mode-finder on green chromaticity only and find that the observations with outlying green components (red circles) tend to have outlying red chromaticities as well. In addition, the chromaticity outliers are also expected to largely overlap with the luminance outliers.

It is also possible to combine outliers obtained from different chromaticities or even mix luminance/chromaticity outliers in the hope of getting a more accurate outlier estimation. For example, we can estimate outliers using green chromaticity (this subset of outlier indices are denoted c_{green}) and red chromaticity (c_{red}) at the same time, and then take the outliers c that appear in both c_{green} and c_{red},

i.e. $c = c_{\mathrm{green}} \cap c_{\mathrm{red}}$. We refer to such a combined method as 'green & red'.

Now the question is: which combination of modalities gives the best approximated appearance? We found [46] that in terms of peak signal-to-noise ratio (PSNR) accuracy of the reconstructed appearance for Method:MODE, we have an ordering:

$$\text{Lum} > (\text{green \& red \& lum}) > \text{green} > (\text{green \& red})$$
$$> \text{lum (Method:QUANTILE)}$$

where '>' means better accuracy; using luminance alone is always best, (green & red) seems to be slightly worse than green only, and (green & red & lum) is between green and luminance. In comparison, using luminance with Method:QUANTILE has the worst performance.

5 Higher-dimensional LS-based PTM and hemispherical harmonics

In this section, we present our second contribution. First, we investigate what can be gained by increasing the

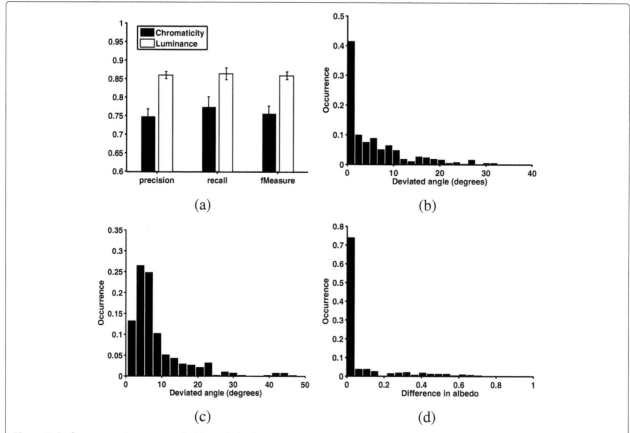

Figure 3 Surface properties recovered with mode-finder compared with 6D LMS. **(a)** Accuracy of outlier detection of mode-finder compared to 6D LMS. **(b,c,d)** The deviation in surface normal, chromaticity and albedo, respectively.

dimensionality of the classical PTM model above 6D without including robust regression. In addition, we apply PTM with different dimensions to model luminance and chromaticity separately. The objective of this part of the investigation is to show that one can, in fact, go quite a long way towards accuracy of appearance modelling using only high-dimensional smooth regression, without the final step of RBF modelling, provided we separate modelling of luminance and chrominance.

Secondly, aside from polynomials, other sets of basis functions can be used to model lighting-surface interaction. One notable example is HSH [34] - it has also been suggested that one could replace a PTM polynomial basis by HSH instead [47]. HSH is mathematically very similar to SH which have already been extensively employed in computer graphics. The key difference between HSH and SH is that HSH is only defined for light directions that live on an upper hemisphere, making it more appropriate for our experimental setup.

The conclusions we reach are that (1) a higher dimension does indeed substantially improve the quality of the reconstructed appearance; (2) if we *split* the problem into modelling luminance and chrominance separately,

rather than applying PTM to each component of colour, then we can reduce the dimensionality for chrominance, compared to that for luminance - we find that 16D for luminance and 9D for chrominance work well; and (3) surprisingly, PTM works better than HSH. Note that every dataset we tried behaved this same way.

5.1 Separation of luminance and chromaticity using LS-based PTM

Our first observation is that the quality of the reconstructed images has a positive correlation with the dimensionality of PTM. Suppose we model luminance only, using an LS-based simple PTM. Figure 4a shows accuracy of the approximated input image set, in terms of PSNR, for different dimensionalities d. In order to calculate the overall PSNR between the original and the approximated set of images, we make the individual images into collages, as the one shown in Figure 1b, and compute the similarity between the original and approximated collages. Here we traverse d values 1, 4, 6, 9 and 16. We see that the reconstructed image quality improves steadily as dimensionality increases for both PTM and HSH (which will be covered in Section 5.2), and in fact PTM produces an

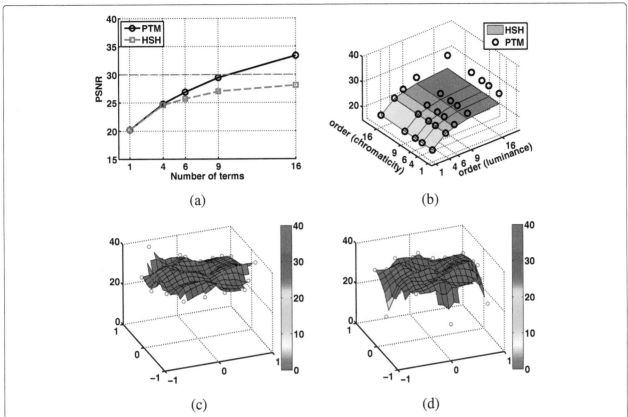

Figure 4 Quality of entire image set reconstructed with non-robust, LS-based PTM and HSH over range of dimensionalities. (a) PSNRs for PTM (black curve) and HSH (red, dashed curve), for luminance images, over values of the basis set dimension; the horizontal blue dashed line indicates PSNR = 30. Here the PSNR value displayed is for the entire set of input images compared to the approximated set. **(b)** PSNRs for PTM (scattered circles) and HSH (surface) in RGB images versus the dimensions for luminance and chromaticity. **(c,d)** PSNRs for approximated images for each of the lighting direction images, for PTM and HSH, respectively. PSNR is plotted as against the x and y components of the lighting direction. Blue circles indicate PSNRs for individual reconstructed image in the dataset, and the coloured surface shows an interpolation surface. Here, 16D for luminance and 9D for chromaticity are used.

acceptable (chosen to be PSNR $\geq$ 30 dB) reconstruction at $d = 16$.

Second, we also investigate modelling the luminance and chromaticity separately, using different dimensionalities for each. (Note that only two of the components of χ need be modelled, since $\sum_{k=1}^{3} \chi_k \equiv 1$). Figure 4b shows results for dimension of luminance versus chrominance, for HSH (coloured surface) and PTM (black circles). We see that while a higher dimension for luminance is important (as in Figure 4a), the accuracy of approximation of chrominance is only mildly dependent upon dimension. The actual PSNR values plotted in Figure 4b are shown in Table 1.

Due to the two observations made above, we conclude that the quality of the reconstructed images is mainly determined by the luminance, rather than the chromaticities. Hence, in order to achieve a high PSNR with a given dimensionality, it is reasonable to assign a higher dimensionality for luminance and a relatively lower dimensionality for chromaticities. Here we adopt $d = 16$ for

luminance and $d = 9$ for chromaticities, making the total number of dimensions $16 + 9 \times 2 = 34$.

5.2 Comparison of higher-dimension PTM and HSH

Using the LS-based approach, we use either a polynomial matrix P or an HSH equivalent, which we denote as S. When we solve Equation 3, we also prudently include some Tikhonov regularization [48] in solving for c. The solution of Equation 3 is thus

$$c = P^{\dagger}L \quad \text{or} \quad c = S^{\dagger}L \tag{17}$$

where † indicates forming a pseudoinverse using a small amount of regularization, with Tikhonov parameter (denoted τ) of, say, $\tau = 10^{-3}$.

We relegate the definition of HSH to Appendix 1. There we list explicitly the definition of the first 16 HSH basis functions, along with the first 16 PTM polynomials.

Recall that in Figure 4a, HSH is consistently outperformed by PTM of the same dimension. Even at a high

Table 1 Comparison of PTM and HSH over various dimensionalities

| | Chrom terms | Lum terms | | | | |
		1	4	6	9	16
PTM basis	1	19.66	24.19	26.15	28.40	31.15
	4	19.84	24.50	26.53	28.74	31.55
	6	19.82	24.48	26.55	28.79	31.73
	9	19.77	24.45	26.50	28.99	*32.27*
	16	19.75	24.37	26.45	28.96	32.59
HSH basis	1	19.66	24.02	25.03	26.27	27.16
	4	19.81	24.20	25.19	26.39	27.28
	6	19.79	24.19	25.24	26.45	27.38
	9	19.76	24.17	25.22	26.54	27.50
	16	19.75	24.14	25.21	26.54	27.57

PSNR values for least-squares matte regression over ranges of dimensionalities for luminance and chromaticity. The italicized value is obtained with the combination of dimensionalities 16D for luminance and 9D for chromaticity.

dimension $d = 16$, HSH still cannot produce an acceptable result. Similar results are shown in Figure 4b and Table 1.

We further compare the PSNR for each individual image in the dataset. Figure 4c,d shows PSNR for approximation of each image in the colour image set, using PTM and HSH, respectively. Here, as described in Section 5.1, $d = 16$ for luminance and $d = 9$ for chrominance are used. We see that as well as producing higher PSNR values, PTM also does not lose too much accuracy for lighting directions with large incident angles (lights low to the object), whereas HSH does very poorly at these boundary points.

In Table 2 we summarize statistics for PSNRs in Figure 4c,d and as well include results for applying PTM or HSH to each component of RGB separately: to be comparable with dimensionality of 16 for luminance and 9 for chromaticity (for each of two components), making a total of 34 dimensions, here we model R,G,B with 11D each.

For comparison, we also include results for the RBF modelling in Section 6 below: the PSNR values are not (machine-) infinite because Tikhonov regularization moves the approximation slightly away from exactly reproducing input images.

6 Specularities and shadows: RBF modelling

Following [6] we adopt an RBF network approach for the remaining luminance not explained by the matte model Equation 3. For N-pixel images, the 'excursion' H is defined as the set of $(N \times 3 \times n)$ non-matte colour values not explained by the R_{matte} given by the basic PTM matte Equation 3, now extended to functions of the colour channel as well: the approximated colour matte image is given by

$$R_{\mathrm{matte}} = P C \chi, \tag{18}$$

where C is the collection of all luminance-regression slopes. Since we include colour, all RBF quantities become functions of the colour channel as well. Throughout, we use the mode-finder efficient robust outlier finder to determine coefficients C.

Then a set of non-matte excursion colour values H is defined for our input set of colour images, via $H = R - R_{\mathrm{matte}}$ where R is the $(N \times 3 \times n)$ set of input images. We follow [6] in carrying out RBF interpolation for interpolant light directions. But here we use the much

Table 2 Comparison of modelling luminance + chromaticity and RGB

		Mean	Median	Mean bottom quartile	Mean top quartile
Lum + Chrom (16D + 9D×2)	PTM	32.60	32.80	28.58	36.37
	HSH	31.80	32.86	24.67	36.51
RGB (11D×3)	PTM	30.35	30.49	25.71	34.20
	HSH	30.33	31.28	23.68	34.95
RBF	47.94	46.47	36.60	61.63	

PSNR statistics for PTM and HSH, using LS + regularization, for dimensionalities 16 and 9 for luminance and chromaticity and similarly for modelling R,G,B separately with 11D each. For completeness, we also show values for RBF modelling.

faster luminance-mode approach Method:MODE for generating matte images and also for recovering the surface chromaticity, surface normal and albedo.

For a particular input dataset, the RBF network models the interpolated excursion solely based on the direction to a new light a': an estimate is given by $\hat{\eta} = \text{RBF}(a')$. Thus, one arrives at an overall interpolant

$$\hat{R} = \hat{R}_{\text{matte}}(a') + \hat{\eta}(a') \tag{19}$$

Since in general we do not possess ground-truth data for acquired image sets, we can characterize the accuracy of appearance-interpolation methods by a leave-one-out analysis. In this approach, we carry out the entire image modelling task but omit, in turn, each of the input set images, thus yielding a modelling dimensionality decreased by 1. Since we know the left-out image's appearance, we can generate an error characteristic by comparing the interpolated image with the actual one.

We will summarize how to use RBF interpolation and appearance reconstruction in Sections 6.1 and 6.2, respectively. Then in Section 6.3, we present a method to optimize the parameters of the radial Gaussian function, which serves as the third contribution in this work.

6.1 RBF

A brief recapitulation of the RBF calculation is in order, so as to explain the mechanism of developing a leave-one-out error measurement below.

As in [6], we first generate a matte interpolation structure from in-sample input images and then use RBF to model the excursion H, for the part of the input image which cannot be explained by a matte model. So first we model the luminance L, using either PTM or HSH. E.g. if we decide to use a 16D polynomial $p(A)$, then luminance for in-sample images is modelled by $L_{\text{matte}} = C\,(p(A))^\dagger$, where C is the set of polynomial coefficients. If there are N pixels and n lights, then L_{matte} is $N \times n$ and C is $N \times 16$, and the polynomial term above is $16 \times n$.

We obtain an $N \times 3$ set of chromaticities as in Equation 12 from which we can generate a matte colour image model for in-sample images R_{matte}, for each if the $i = 1..n$ lighting directions, via

$$R^i_{\text{matte}} = \text{diag}\left(L^i_{\text{matte}}\right) \chi \,, \; i = 1..n \tag{20}$$

The dimensionality of R_{matte} is $N \times 3 \times n$. The set of excursions for all the input images H has this same dimensionality, and $H = R - R_{\text{matte}}$. Because the RBF modelling adopted in [6] includes a so-called polynomial term (actually, linear here), we have to extend H with a set of $N \times 3 \times 4$ zeros. Call this extended excursion H'.

For interpolation, we need a set of RBF coefficients Ψ', with dimensionality $N \times 3 \times (n + 4)$. We adopt Gaussian RBF basis functions $\phi(\|a - a^i\|), i = 1..n$ (although of course other functions might be tried, such as multiquadric or inverse-multiquadric). We call the set $\phi(\|a^i - a^j\|)$ matrix Φ. Then Φ is extended into an $(n+4) \times (n+4)$ matrix Φ' as in [6].

Then we calculate and store the RBF coefficients Ψ' over all the input lights as follows:

$$\Psi' = H'\,(\Phi')^\dagger \tag{21}$$

where the † means the Moore-Penrose pseudoinverse, guarding against reduced rank.

However, here we also extend the pseudoinverse to include some Tikhonov regularization:

$$(\Phi')^\dagger = \left(\Phi'^T \Phi' + \tau I_{(n+4)}\right) \Phi'^T \tag{22}$$

with Tikhonov parameter τ. Below, we mean to optimize this parameter using a clever mathematical theorem borrowed for this work.

6.2 Appearance reconstruction

Given a novel lighting direction a, appearance reconstruction from PTM coefficients C and RBF coefficients Ψ' is quite straightforward: we generate a matte image by multiplying PTM coefficient matrix C by its corresponding combination of polynomial $p(a)$ and then use recovered chromaticity χ to form a colour matte image. Then we form a new Gaussian function ϕ from new lighting direction a and simply multiply ϕ times the prestored RBF excursion coefficient set Ψ' to generate a single-image excursion value η. The Gaussian radial basis function has the explicit form $\phi(a_i, a_j, \sigma) = \exp(-r^2/\sigma^2)$, with radius r for light-direction vectors a_i and a_j given by $r = \|a_i - a_j\|$.

6.3 Optimization of dispersion σ and of Tikhonov parameter τ

In this subsection, we describe our third contribution, i.e. finding the best values for the Gaussian dispersion σ and the Tikhonov coefficient τ so as to optimize the reconstructed appearance. Since we have no ground truth for real input image sets, we test the accuracy of appearance modelling by simply leaving out one of the n input images at a time and attempting to reconstruct the left-out image.

To this end, here we borrow the work in [49] in determining a best value of the Gaussian dispersion parameter σ to minimize the leave-one-out error. However, here we mean to apply the method given in [49] to a whole image at once and include colour, extend RBF modelling to include the additional polynomial term and, finally and importantly, extend [49] to include Tihkonov regularization and its optimization.

The work [49] defines the optimum σ as that yielding the smallest error in reconstructing a leave-one-out image, using only the information from the other images.

E.g. if the input set consists of 50 images, then we follow through matte and then RBF modelling using only 49 images and attempt to reconstruct the 50th image, and then repeat for each of the 50 light directions.

Modelling on the theorem given in [49] in Appendix 2, we generalize the theorem, which is aimed at optimizing RBF over the dispersion parameter σ, to also optimize over Tikhonov parameter τ. The resulting calculation from this theorem is so fast that it is simple to run any unconstrained non-linear optimizer such as the subspace trust-region method [50].

We find that an approximate colour image reconstruction, for the kth leave-one-out image, is simply as follows:

$$E = \Psi'/\nu$$

$$\hat{R} = R - E \tag{23}$$

where the *error image* E is simply formed from the RBF coefficients Ψ', and a vector ν generated as the solution to the following simple equation in terms of the $(n + 4) \times (n + 4)$ identity matrix I:

$$\Phi'\nu = I \tag{24}$$

This theorem means that one can very rapidly assess the error generated in a leave-one-out analysis of RBF modelling. Figure 5a shows the PSNR between the actual input image set and the result of matte plus RBF modelling, for an optimal choice of σ and τ. Unsurprisingly, we see that RBF interpolation does best in the center of the cluster of lighting directions and worse when there is less supporting information, near the boundary of the cluster of light directions. We take as the optimum dispersion σ and Tihkonov parameter value τ as those which deliver the highest leave-one-out median PSNR over the set overall.

Table 3 shows PSNR statistics for this leave-out-out RBF test. In comparison, we show in Figure 5b and also in the second line of Table 3 the results of a leave-one-out test using PTM matte modelling alone for dimensions 16 and 9 for luminance and chrominance, with no RBF stage. We notice that in a challenging leave-one-out test for interpolation, PTM does reasonably well. To put these plots in perspective, in Figure 5c, we also show the results for PTM + RBF in a leave-all-in setting: of course, the PSNR for PTM + RBF for leave-all-in is by far the best accuracy. In Figure 5d we show the in-sample correct image closest to the mean value of PSNR values for all leave-one-out RBF

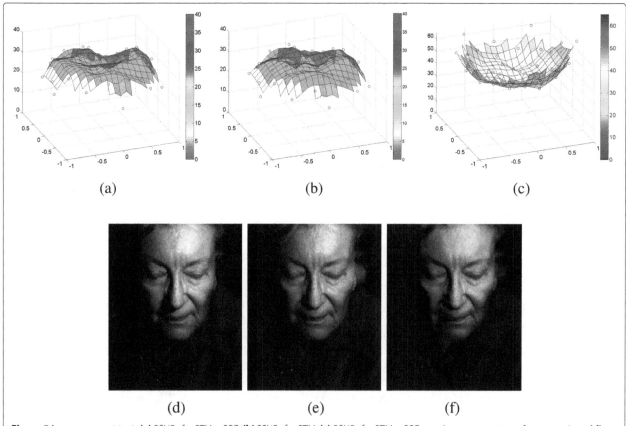

(a)   (b)   (c)

(d)   (e)   (f)

Figure 5 Leave-one-out test. (a) PSNRs for PTM + RBF. **(b)** PSNRs for PTM. **(c)** PSNRs for PTM + RBF, non-leave-one-out test, for comparison. **(d)** Correct interpolant for lighting direction **(e)** PTM + RBF interpolant, PSNR = 30.803 (note camera flare from other images in the set). **(f)** PTM interpolant: the PSNR = 30.763, which is acceptable, but not using RBF results in poor modelling of specular content and wrong shadows.

Table 3 PSNR statistics for leave-one-out test, using PTM + RBF, and using only PTM

	Mean	Median	Mean bottom quartile	Mean top quartile
PTM + RBF	30.18	31.24	22.77	35.68
PTM	29.15	29.54	22.23	34.16

modelling, and in Figure 5e,f, we show the interpolants from using PTM + RBF and from using just PTM, respectively. Clearly, RBF provides a substantial boost in visual appearance, although PTM itself (with no RBF stage), with the higher dimensions we have specified, does produce a reasonable image. Nevertheless, qualitatively, using RBF does much better in that, without RBF, specularities are not well modelled and the shadows are wrong.

7 Conclusions

In this paper, we have set out tests and conclusions that improve PTM modelling for appearance interpolation and surface property recovery. We found that increasing PTM dimensionality has a substantial effect on accuracy, more for the luminance channel than for colour. We found that a dimension of 16 for luminance and 9 for chromaticity, modelling luminance and chromaticity separately, delivered good performance. We found that for determining outliers, we could have almost as good accuracy using a much less burdensome robust 1D 'location finder' as in a more accurate but slower robust multivariate processing.

A second stage of modelling using RBF interpolation provides a large boost in accuracy of appearance modelling. Here we showed that Tikhonov regularization in calculating RBF coefficients was important, since we are inverting large matrices; and moreover we incorporated optimizing the Tikhonov parameter into an optimization theorem that had been initially aimed at only generating a best choice of Gaussian dispersion parameter for radial basis function networks.

Future work will include developing a real-time viewer including the new insights gained here.

Appendix 1: hemispherical harmonics

HSH are derived from spherical harmonics (SH) as an alternative set of basis functions on the unit sphere that are particularly aimed at non-negative function values. The familiar SH are defined as [51]

$$Y_l^m(\theta, \phi) = K_l^m e^{im\phi} P_l^{|m|} \cos(\theta), l \in N, -l \le m \le l \tag{25}$$

where $\theta \in [0, \pi]$ is the altitude angle, and $\phi \in [0, 2\pi]$ the azimuth angle. P_l^m are the associated Legendre

polynomials, orthogonal polynomial basis functions over $[-1, +1]$, and K_l^m are the normalization factors for these.

$$P_l^m(x) = \frac{(-1)^m}{2^l l!} \sqrt{(1-x^2)^m} \frac{d^{(l+m)}}{dx^{(l+m)}} (x^2 - 1)^l$$
$$K_l^m = \sqrt{\frac{(2l+1)(l-|m|)!}{4\pi(l+|m|)!}} \tag{26}$$

In the context of computer graphics, real-valued functions as follows are often preferred:

$$Y_l^m = \begin{cases} \sqrt{2}K_l^m \cos(m\phi)P_l^m(\cos\theta), & m > 0 \\ \sqrt{2}K_l^m \sin(-m\phi)P_l^{-m}(\cos\theta), & m < 0 \\ K_l^0 P_l^0(\cos\theta), & m = 0 \end{cases} \tag{27}$$

However, since in graphics the incident and reflected lights are all distributed on an upper hemisphere, it requires a large number of coefficients to handle the discontinuities at the boundary of the hemisphere when the mapping is represented with basis defined on a full sphere [34]. Thus, it is more natural to use an HSH basis instead. In this study, we used the HSH model proposed in [34]n:

$$H_l^m = \begin{cases} \sqrt{2}\tilde{K}_l^m \cos(m\phi)\tilde{P}_l^m(\cos\theta) & m > 0 \\ \sqrt{2}\tilde{K}_l^m \sin(-m\phi)\tilde{P}_l^{-m}(\cos\theta) & m < 0 \\ \tilde{K}_l^0 \tilde{P}_l^0(\cos\theta) & m = 0 \end{cases} \tag{28}$$

where $\tilde{P}_l^m$ and $\tilde{K}_l^m$ are the 'shifted' associated Legendre polynomials and the hemispherical normalization factors, respectively, defined as follows:

$$\tilde{P}_l^m(x) = P_l^m(2x - 1)$$
$$K_l^m = \sqrt{\frac{(2l+1)(l-|m|)!}{2\pi(l+|m|)!}} \tag{29}$$

Now the hemispherical functions are defined only over the upper hemisphere, $\theta \in [0, \pi/2], \phi \in [0, 2\pi]$.

Figure 6 shows the first three 'bands' of the HSH, i.e. $l = 0..2$, and the first 16 functions are stated explicitly in Equation 31.

Similarly, we can also consider the polynomial basis in Equation 1 as a set of functions defined on the hemisphere by representing the lighting direction (u, v, w) with spherical polar coordinates: $u = \sin\theta\cos\phi$, $v = \sin\theta\sin\phi$, $w = \cos\theta$, so e.g. the PTM basis functions in Equation 1 are given by

$$(\sin\theta\cos\phi, \sin\theta\sin\phi, \cos\theta, \sin^2\theta\cos^2\phi, \sin^2\theta\cos\phi\sin\phi, 1) \tag{30}$$

For comparison, a selection of nine polynomial terms are visualized as surface plots in Figure 7, and the first 16 polynomial terms are listed in Equation 32

$H_i = H_l^m; i = ((l+1)l - m) + 1;$ Order $= (l+1)$:

Order 1:

$H_1(\theta, \phi) = 1/\sqrt{(2\pi)}$

Order 2:

$H_2(\theta, \phi) = \sqrt{(6/\pi)}(\cos(\phi)\sqrt{(\cos(\theta) - \cos(\theta)^2)})$

$H_3(\theta, \phi) = \sqrt{(3/(2\pi))}(-1 + 2\cos(\theta))$

$H_4(\theta, \phi) = \sqrt{(6/\pi)}(\sin(\phi)\sqrt{(\cos(\theta) - \cos(\theta)^2)})$

Order 3:

$H_5(\theta, \phi) = \sqrt{(30/\pi)}(\cos(2\phi)(-\cos(\theta) + \cos(\theta)^2))$

$H_6(\theta, \phi) = \sqrt{(30/\pi)}(\cos(\phi)(-1 + 2\cos(\theta))$
$\qquad \sqrt{(\cos(\theta) - \cos(\theta)^2)})$

$H_7(\theta, \phi) = \sqrt{(5/(2\pi))}(1 - 6\cos(\theta) + 6\cos(\theta)^2)$

$H_8(\theta, \phi) = \sqrt{(30/\pi)}(\sin(\phi)(-1 + 2\cos(\theta))$
$\qquad \sqrt{(\cos(\theta) - \cos(\theta)^2)})$

$H_9(\theta, \phi) = \sqrt{(30/\pi)}((-\cos(\theta) + \cos(\theta)^2)\sin(2\phi))$

$$(31)$$

Order 4:

$H_{10}(\theta, \phi) = 2\sqrt{(35/\pi)}\cos(3\phi)(\cos(\theta) - \cos(\theta)^2)^{3/2}$

$H_{11}(\theta, \phi) = \sqrt{(210/\pi)}\cos(2\phi)$
$\qquad (-1 + 2\cos(\theta))(-\cos(\theta) + \cos(\theta)^2)$

$H_{12}(\theta, \phi) = 2\sqrt{(21/\pi)}\cos(\phi)\sqrt{(\cos(\theta) - \cos(\theta)^2)}$
$\qquad (1 - 5\cos(\theta) + 5\cos(\theta)^2)$

$H_{13}(\theta, \phi) = \sqrt{(7/(2\pi))}(-1 + 12\cos(\theta) - 30$
$\qquad \cos(\theta)^2 + 20\cos(\theta)^3)$

$H_{14}(\theta, \phi) = 2\sqrt{(21/\pi)}\sin(\phi)\sqrt{(\cos(\theta) - \cos(\theta)^2)}$
$\qquad (1 - 5\cos(\theta) + 5\cos(\theta)^2)$

$H_{15}(\theta, \phi) = \sqrt{(210/\pi)}(-1 + 2\cos(\theta))(-\cos(\theta) +$
$\qquad \cos(\theta)^2)\sin(2\phi)$

$H_{16}(\theta, \phi) = 2\sqrt{(35/\pi)}\sin(3\phi)(\cos(\theta) - \cos(\theta)^2)^{3/2}$

Constant term:

$P_1 = 1$

Linear terms:

$P_2 = u = \sin(\theta)\cos(\phi)$

$P_3 = v = \sin(\theta)\sin(\phi)$

$P_4 = w = \cos(\phi)$
$\qquad\qquad\qquad\qquad\qquad\qquad\qquad (32)$

Quadratic terms:

$P_5 = u^2 = \sin^2(\theta)\cos^2(\phi)$

$P_6 = uw = \sin(\theta)\cos^2(\phi)$

$P_7 = uv = \sin^2(\theta)\cos(\phi)\sin(\phi)$

$P_8 = vw = \sin(\theta)\cos(\phi)\sin(\phi)$

$P_9 = v^2 = \cos^2(\phi)$

Cubic terms:

$P_{10} = u^3 = \sin^3(\theta)\cos^3(\phi)$

$P_{11} = u^2v = \sin^3(\theta)\cos^2(\phi)\sin(\phi)$

$P_{12} = u^2w = \sin^2(\theta)\cos^3(\phi)$

$P_{13} = uvw = \sin^2(\theta)\cos^2(\phi)\sin(\phi)$

$P_{14} = v^2u = \sin^3(\theta)\sin^2(\phi)\cos(\phi)$

$P_{15} = v^2w = \sin^2(\theta)\sin^2(\phi)\cos(\phi)$

$P_{16} = v^3 = \sin^3(\theta)\sin^3(\phi)$

Appendix 2: leave-one-out optimization in RBF

It is useful to state explicitly how the optimization theorem in [49] goes over to the situation when Tikhonov regularization comes into play.

Firstly, we utilize three-band colour image data, rather than scalar data, and process whole images at once using vectorized programming in Matlab. However for clarity, below we state matters as they pertain to a single pixel and in one colour band.

Suppose there are n lights and n input values at a pixel, e.g. for our exemplar dataset $n = 50$. Then we make $(n + 4) \times (n + 4)$ matrix $\mathbf{\Phi}(\sigma)$, where here we are explicitly including dependence on a variable dispersion value σ. For the $(n + 4)$ vector of excursion values $\mathbf{H}$ (extended by four zeros to include the 'polynomial' RBF part), we begin by solving for the $(n + 4)$ vector set of RBF coefficients $\boldsymbol{\psi}$, which is the vector solution for the modelling equation

$$\mathbf{H} = \mathbf{\Phi}\,\boldsymbol{\psi}$$

However, instead of simply using a matrix inverse in order to guard against numerical instability, we make use of the Tikhonov regularized inverse from Equation 22:

$$\boldsymbol{\psi} = \mathbf{\Phi}(\sigma, \tau)^\dagger \mathbf{H}$$

so that in fact we generate only approximate, not exact, approximations $\hat{\mathbf{H}}$ for in-sample lighting directions:

$$\hat{\mathbf{H}} = \mathbf{\Phi}\,\boldsymbol{\psi} = \mathbf{\Phi}\mathbf{\Phi}^\dagger \mathbf{H}$$

Then the main task is interpolation to any new light $\boldsymbol{a}'$ via

$$\eta' = \sum_{j=1}^{(n+4)} \psi_j^T \,\phi(\boldsymbol{a}_j - \boldsymbol{a}')$$

where η' is the scalar value of interpolated excursion (for this pixel and colour channel).

Now we mean to consider the leave-one-out problem, meaning that all the matrices and vectors have extent $(n + 3)$ because the kth input-image case has been omitted. Suppose we denote this case using superscript (k). That is, we aim for a solution $\boldsymbol{\psi}^{(k)}$ of

$$\mathbf{H}^{(k)} = \mathbf{\Phi}^{(k)}\,\boldsymbol{\psi}^{(k)} \qquad (33)$$

Firstly, consider the following *Lemma*: if vector $\boldsymbol{v}$ has $v_k = 0$, then

$$\text{if } \boldsymbol{A}\boldsymbol{v} = \boldsymbol{b}, \text{ then } \boldsymbol{A}^{(k)}\boldsymbol{v}^{(k)} = \boldsymbol{b}^{(k)}$$

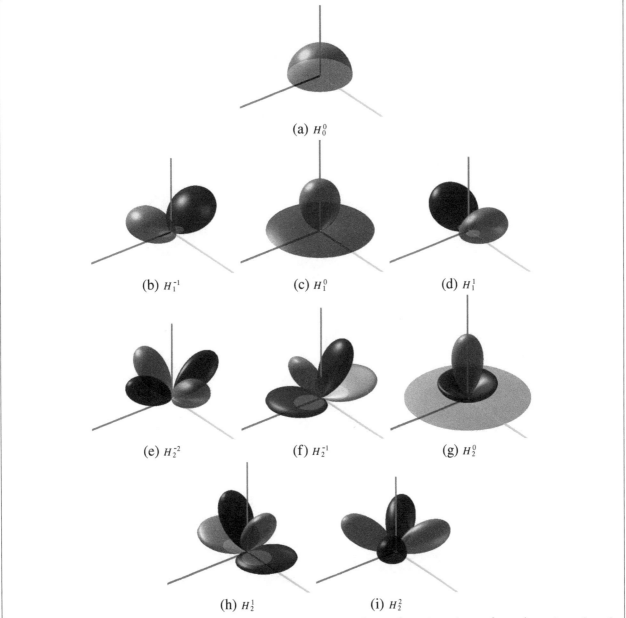

Figure 6 Visualization of the first three bands of hemispherical harmonics. (a) H_0^0. **(b)** H_1^{-1}. **(c)** H_1^0. **(d)** H_1^1. **(e)** H_2^{-2}. **(f)** H_2^{-1}. **(g)** H_2^0. **(h)** H_2^1. **(i)** H_2^2. The distance r from the origin to any point (θ, ϕ, r) on the plot surface is proportional to the value of H_l^m at direction (θ, ϕ), with cyan indicating positive values and purple negative. Red, green and blue indicate x, y and z axes, respectively.

That is, if we know the not-reduced-dimension equation holds, then for the special situation in which $\boldsymbol{v}_k = 0$, we can simply omit whatever value b_k may take on, for the reduced-dimension problem indicated by (k).

Now consider an auxiliary full-dimension vector $\boldsymbol{v}$ defined such that

$$\boldsymbol{v} = \boldsymbol{\Phi}^+ \boldsymbol{e}_k$$

where $\boldsymbol{e}_k$ is the kth column of the unit matrix.

Now define a new vector

$$\boldsymbol{\beta} = \boldsymbol{\psi} - (\psi_k / v_k) \boldsymbol{v}$$

Notice that the kth component of $\boldsymbol{\beta}$ is zero.
Now evaluate $\boldsymbol{\Phi\beta}$:

$$\boldsymbol{\Phi\beta} = \boldsymbol{\Phi\psi} - (\psi_k / v_k)\boldsymbol{\Phi v} = \hat{\boldsymbol{\eta}} - (\psi_k / v_k)\boldsymbol{e}_k$$

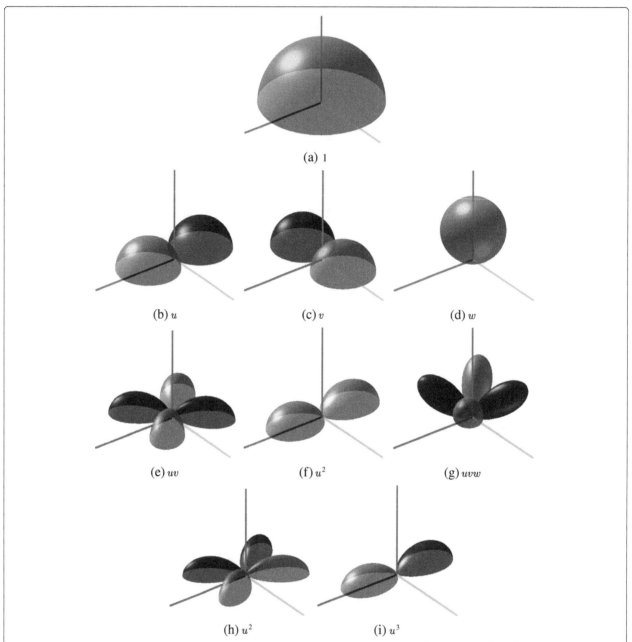

Figure 7 Visualization of selected polynomial basis functions. (a) 1, **(b)** u, **(c)** v, **(d)** w, **(e)** uv, **(f)** u^2, **(g)** uvw, **(h)** u^2, **(i)** u^3. The distance r from the origin to any point (θ, ϕ, r) on the plot surface is proportional to the value of the polynomial term P at direction (θ, ϕ), with cyan indicating positive values and purple negative. Red, green, blue indicate x, y, z axes, respectively.

Hence, by our lemma, $\boldsymbol{\beta}$ is the sought solution for the leave-one-out set of coefficients $\boldsymbol{\psi}^{(k)}$; however, this statement is approximate and not exact because $\hat{\eta}$ is only approximately (but very close to being equal to) η.

So in order to optimize on σ and τ, we need only to generate the error estimate E_k for the kth case,

$$E_k = -(\psi_k / \nu_k)$$

for each of the $k = 1..n$ left-out lights, and apply some appropriate error measure such as median (E_k) for choosing the least-error solution:

$$\min_{\{\sigma, \tau\}} \operatorname*{median}_{k=1}^{n} E_k(\sigma, \tau) \tag{34}$$

In practise, we found that utilizing this leave-one-out calculation is very fast and generates smaller interpolation errors when the resulting solution pair $\{\sigma, \tau\}$ is used for general interpolation for the dataset being optimized for by this leave-one-out procedure.

Competing interests

The authors declare that they have no competing interests.

References

1. T Malzbender, D Gelb, H Wolters, Polynomial texture maps, in *Proceedings of Computer Graphics, SIGGRAPH*, vol. 2001 (ACM Los Angeles, California, 2001), pp. 519–528

2. RJ Woodham, Photometric method for determining surface orientation from multiple images. Opt. Eng. **19**, 139–144 (1980)

3. M Mudge, T Malzbender, C Schroer, M Lum, New reflection transformation imaging methods for rock art and multiple-viewpoint display, in *7th International Symposium on Virtual Reality, Archaelogy and Cultural Heritage* (Eurographics, Nicosia, Cyprus, 2006)

4. K Sunkavalli, T Zickler, H Pfister, Visibility subspaces: uncalibrated photometric stereo with shadows, in *11th European Conference on Computer Vision–ECCV 2010* (Springer Heraklion, 2010), pp. 251–264

5. G Earl, K Martinez, T Malzbender, Archaeological applications of polynomial texture mapping: analysis, conservation and representation. J. Archaeological Sci. **37**, 1–11 (2010)

6. M Drew, Y Hel-Or, T Malzbender, N Hajari, Robust estimation of surface properties and interpolation of shadow/specularity components. Image Vis. Comput. **30**(4-5), 317–331 (2012)

7. PJ Rousseeuw, AM Leroy, *Robust Regression and Outlier Detection*. (Wiley, New York, 1987)

8. T Zickler, S Enrique, R Ramamoorthi, P Belhumeur, Reflectance sharing: image-based rendering from a sparse set of images, in *Eurographics Symposium on Rendering Techniques* (Konstanz, Germany, 2005), pp. 253–265

9. T Zickler, R Ramamoorthi, S Enrique, P Belhumeur, Reflectance sharing: predicting appearance from a sparse set of images of a known shape. IEEE Trans. Patt. Anal. Mach. Intell. **28**, 1287–1302 (2006)

10. EN Coleman Jr, R Jain, Obtaining 3-dimensional shape of textured and specular surfaces using four-source photometry. Comput. Graph. Image Process. **18**, 309–328 (1982)

11. F Solomon, K Ikeuchi, Extracting the shape and roughness of specular lobe objects using four light photometric stereo. IEEE Trans. Patt. Anal. Mach. Intell. **18**, 449–454 (1996)

12. S Barsky, M Petrou, The 4-source photometric stereo technique for three-dimensional surfaces in the presence of highlights and shadows. IEEE Trans. Patt. Anal. Mach. Intell. **25**(10), 1239–1252 (2003)

13. H Rushmeier, G Taubin, A Guéziec, Applying shape from lighting variation to bump map capture, in *Eurographics Rendering Techniques 97* (Springer Vienna, 1997), pp. 35–44

14. A Yuille, D Snow, Shape and albedo from multiple images using integrability, in *Proceedings of the IEEE Computer Society Conference on Computer Vision and Pattern Recognition 1997* (San Juan, Puerto Rico, 1997), pp. 158–164

15. G Willems, F Verbiest, W Moreau, H Hameeuw, K Van Lerberghe, L Van Gool, Easy and cost-effective cuneiform digitizing, in *Proceedings of 6th International Symposium on Virtual Reality, Archaeology and Cultural Heritage (Short and Project Papers)* (Pisa, Italy, 2005), pp. 73–80

16. J Sun, M Smith, L Smith, S Midha, J Bamber, Object surface recovery using a multi-light photometric stereo technique for non-Lambertian surfaces subject to shadows and specularities. Image Vis. Comput. **25**, 1050–1057 (2007)

17. Julià C, F Lumbreras, AD Sappa, A factorization-based approach to photometric stereo. Int. J. Imag. Syst. Tech. **21**, 115–119 (2011)

18. L Wu, A Ganesh, B Shi, Y Matsushita, Y Wang, Y Ma, Robust photometric stereo via low-rank matrix completion and recovery, in *Computer Vision – ACCV 2010*, ed. by Kimmel R, Klette R, Sugimoto A, and Lecture notes in computer science, no. 6494. (Springer Berlin Heidelberg, 2011), pp. 703–717

19. KL Tang, CK Tang, TT Wong, Dense photometric stereo using tensorial belief propagation, in *IEEE Computer Society Conference on Computer Vision and Pattern Recognition 2005*, vol. 1 (San Diego, California, 2005), pp. 132–139

20. M Chandraker, S Agarwal, D Kriegman, ShadowCuts: photometric stereo with shadows, in *IEEE Computer Society Conference on Computer Vision and Pattern Recognition 2007* (Minneapolis, Minnesota, 2007), pp. 1–8

21. F Verbiest, L Van Gool, Photometric stereo with coherent outlier handling and confidence estimation, in *IEEE Computer Society Conference on Computer Vision and Pattern Recognition 2008* (Anchorage, Alaska, 2008), pp. 1–8

22. Q Yang, N Ahuja, Surface reflectance and normal estimation from photometric stereo. Comput. Vis. Image Underst. **116**(7), 793–802 (2012)

23. S Kherada, P Pandey, A Namboodiri, Improving realism of 3D texture using component based modeling, in *2012 IEEE Workshop on Applications of Computer Vision (WACV)* (Breckenridge, Colorado, 2012), pp. 41–47

24. SH Westin, JR Arvo, KE Torrance, Predicting reflectance functions from complex surfaces, in *Proceedings of the 19th Annual Conference on Computer Graphics and Interactive Techniques*, SIGGRAPH '92 (New York, 1992), pp. 255–264

25. TT Wong, PA Heng, SH Or, WY Ng, Image-based rendering with controllable illumination, in *Proceedings of the Eurographics Workshop on Rendering Techniques 1997* (Springer Vienna, 1997), pp. 13–22

26. JS Nimeroff, E Simoncelli, J Dorsey, Efficient re-rendering of naturally illuminated environments, in *Photorealistic Rendering Techniques, Focus on Computer Graphics* (Springer Berlin Heidelberg, 1995), pp. 373–388

27. J Kautz, PP Sloan, J Snyder, Fast, arbitrary BRDF shading for low-frequency lighting using spherical harmonics, in *Proceedings of the 13th Eurographics Workshop on Rendering Techniques* (Pisa, Italy, 2002), pp. 291–296

28. R Ramamoorthi, P Hanrahan, An efficient representation for irradiance environment maps, in *Proceedings of the 28th Annual Conference on Computer Graphics and Interactive Techniques* (Los Angeles, California, 2001), pp. 497–500

29. PP Sloan, J Kautz, J Snyder, Precomputed radiance transfer for real-time rendering in dynamic, low-frequency lighting environments, in *ACM Transactions on Graphics (TOG)*, vol. 21 (ACM, New York, 2002), pp. 527–536

30. PP Sloan, J Sloan, J Hart, J Snyder, Clustered principal components for precomputed radiance transfer. ACM Trans. Graph. **22**(3), 382–391 (2003)

31. R Basri, DW Jacobs, Lambertian reflectance and linear subspaces. IEEE Trans. Patt. Anal. Mach. Intell. **25**, 218–233 (2003)

32. R Basri, D Jacobs, I Kemelmacher, Photometric stereo with general, unknown lighting. Int. J. Comput. Vis. **72**, 239–257 (2007)

33. L Zhang, D Samaras, Pose invariant face recognition under arbitrary unknown lighting using spherical harmonics, in *Biometric Authentication. Lecture notes in computer science, vol 3087* (Springer Heidelberg, 2004), pp. 10–23

34. P Gautron, J Křivánek, SN Pattanaik, K Bouatouch, A novel hemispherical basis for accurate and efficient rendering, in *Eurographics Symposium on Rendering Techniques 2004* (Eurographics Association, Norköping, Sweden, 2004), pp. 321–330

35. S Elhabian, H Rara, A Farag, 2011 Canadian Conference on Computer and Robot Vision (CRV) (St. Johns, Newfoundland, 2011), pp. 293–300

36. H Huang, L Zhang, D Samaras, L Shen, R Zhang, F Makedon, J Pearlman, Hemispherical harmonic surface description and applications to medical image analysis, in *Third International Symposium on 3D Data Processing, Visualization, and Transmission* (Chapel Hill, North Carolina, 2006), pp. 381–388

37. S Elhabian, H Rara, A Farag, Towards accurate and efficient representation of image irradiance of convex-Lambertian objects under unknown near lighting, in *2011 IEEE International Conference on Computer Vision (ICCV)* (Barcelona, Spain, 2011), pp. 1732–1737

38. G Earl, K Martinez, T Malzbender, Archaeological applications of polynomial texture mapping: analysis, conservation and representation. J. Archaeol. Sci. **37**(8), 2040–2050 (2010)

39. G Earl, G Beale, K Martinez, H Pagi, Polynomial texture mapping and related imaging technologies for the recording, analysis and presentation of archaeological materials, in *ISPRS Commission V Midterm Symposium* (Newcastle, 21–24 June 2010), pp. 218–223

40. G Earl, PJ Basford, AS Bischoff, A Bowman, C Crowther, J Dahl, M Hodgson, K Martinez, L Isaksen, H Pagi, KE Piquette, E Kotoula, Reflectance transformation imaging systems for ancient documentary artefacts, in *EVA London 2011: Electronic Visualisation and the Arts* (London, 2011)

41. R Bridgman, G Earl, Experiencing lustre: polynomial texture mapping of medieval pottery at the Fitzwilliam Museum, in *Proceedings of the 7th International Congress of the Archaeology of the Ancient Near East (7th ICAANE)*, ed. by R Matthews, J Curtis, M Symour, A Fletcher, A Gascoigne, C Glatz, SJ Simpson, H Taylor, J Tubb, R Chapman, and Ancient & Modern Issues in Cultural Heritage. Colour & Light in Architecture, Art & Material Culture. Islamic Archeology. (Harrasowitz, London, 2012), pp. 497–512

42. S Duffy, Polynomial texture mapping at Roughting Linn rock art site, in *Proceedings of the ISPRS Commission V Mid-Term Symposium: Close Range Image Measurement Techniques* (Newcastle, 21–24 June 2010), pp. 213–217

43. J Padfield, D Saunders, T Malzbender, Polynomial texture mapping: a new tool for examining the surface of paintings. ICOM Comm. Conserv. **1**, 504–510 (2005)

44. Y Schechner, S Nayar, P Belhumeur, Multiplexing for optimal lighting. IEEE Trans. Patt. Anal. Mach. Intell. **29**(8), 1339–1354 (2007)

45. A Wenger, A Gardner, C Tchou, J Unger, T Hawkins, P Debevec, Performance relighting and reflectance transformation with time-multiplexed illumination. ACM Trans. Graph. **24**(3), 756–764 (2005)

46. M Zhang, MS Drew, Robust luminance and chromaticity for matte regression in polynomial texture mapping, in *Workshops and Demonstrations in Computer Vision–ECCV 2012* Springer Firenze, Italy, 2012), pp. 360–369

47. M Mudge, J Davis, R Scopigno, M Doerr, A Chalmers, O Wang, P Gunawardane, T Malzbender, Image-based empirical information acquisition, scientific reliability, and long-term digital preservation for the natural sciences and cultural heritage, in *Eurographics Tutorials* (Crete, 14–18 April 2008

48. A Tikhonov, V Arsenin, *Solutions of Ill-Posed Problems*. Wiley, New York, 1977)

49. S Rippa, An algorithm for selecting a good value for the parameter c in radial basis function interpolation. Adv. Comput. Math. **11**(2–3), 193–210 (1999)

50. T Coleman, Y Li, An interior, trust region approach for nonlinear minimization subject to bounds. SIAM J. Optimiz. **6**, 418–445 (1996)

51. M Abramowitz, I Stegun, *Handbook of Mathematical Functions: with Formulas, Graphs, and Mathematical Tables* (Dover, New York, 1965)

6

Multiscale texture retrieval based on low-dimensional and rotation-invariant features of curvelet transform

Bulent Cavusoglu

Abstract

Multiscale-based texture retrieval algorithms use low-dimensional feature sets in general. However, they do not have as good retrieval performances as those of the state-of-the-art techniques in the literature. The main motivation of this study is to use low-dimensional multiscale features to provide comparable retrieval performances with the state-of-the-art techniques. The proposed features of this study are low-dimensional, robust against rotation, and have better performance than the earlier multiresolution-based algorithms and the state-of-the-art techniques with low-dimensional feature sets. They are obtained through curvelet transformation and have considerably small dimensions. The rotation invariance is provided by applying a novel principal orientation alignment based on cross energies of adjacent curvelet blocks. The curvelet block pair with the highest cross energy is marked as the principle orientation, and the rest of the blocks are cycle-shifted around the principle orientation. Two separate rotation-invariant feature vectors are proposed and evaluated in this study. The first feature vector has 84 elements and contains the mean and standard deviation of curvelet blocks at each angle together with a weighting factor based on the spatial support of the curvelet coefficients. The second feature vector has 840 elements and contains the kernel density estimation (KDE) of curvelet blocks at each angle. The first and the second feature vectors are used in the classification of textures based on nearest neighbor algorithm with Euclidian and Kullback-Leibler distance measures, respectively. The proposed method is evaluated on well-known databases such as, Brodatz, TC10, TC12-t184, and TC12-horizon of Outex, UIUCTex, and KTH-TIPS. The best performance is obtained for kernel density feature vector. Mean and standard deviation feature vector also provides similar performance and has less complexity due to its smaller feature dimension. The results are reported as both precision-recall curves and classification rates and compared with the existing state-of-the-art texture retrieval techniques. It is shown through several experiments that the proposed rotation-invariant feature vectors outperform earlier multiresolution-based ones and provide comparable performances with the rest of the literature even though they have considerably small dimensions.

Keywords: Texture retrieval; Low dimension; Multiresolution; Curvelet transform; Rotation invariance; Principle orientation

1. Introduction

Texture classification and retrieval has been investigated by many researchers. Recognizing textures is essential in content-based image retrieval (CBIR) applications since images are actually constructed of many texture combinations. Unfortunately, textures rarely exist in a fixed orientation and scale. Hence, defining rotation-invariant features is important and rotation invariance is a hot research topic since 1980s. In one of the early works [1], rotation-invariant matched filters are used for rotation-invariant pattern recognition. The authors of [2] applied a model-based approach, in which they used statistical features of textures for classification. Using the statistics of spatial features as in [1,2] may provide good results, however, it may include great interclass variations depending on the recording conditions of textures such as contrast, illumination, etc. Hence, multiscale techniques which have the capability of representing the feature in one or more resolution with lesser effect of these recording conditions

Correspondence: bulent.cavusoglu@gmail.com
Electrical-Electronics Engineering Department, Ataturk University, Erzurum 25240, Turkey

have been used since 1990s. The main idea behind multiscale analysis in image processing is to provide the views of the same image in different resolutions to enhance the feature that can be more apparent in a specific resolution. In this way, it is easier to analyze or classify the image based on certain properties and certain scales. Nonstationary structures such as images require their multiscale transforms to be well localized both in time and frequency. However, according to Heisenberg's uncertainty principle, it is impossible to have localization both in time and frequency simultaneously. In other words, one cannot find a particular frequency to represent a certain point in time. Hence, frequency localizations require the time to be defined over a particular time window. It is also important that these localizations can be performed over orthogonal basis of tight frames. Wavelets [3] can address all these requirements. They are generated from one mother wavelet through translations and scalings. In one of the earliest works [4], the authors used statistics of Gabor wavelet as the features over Brodatz database while performing multiscale analysis for texture retrieval. However, the effects of rotations are not considered in this work. Another drawback of this work is such that wavelet transform is able to capture singularities around a point. The textures which have curvature-like structures may not provide good results by using the wavelet transform. Other transforms such as ridgelet [5] which extends wavelets to capture singularities along a line and curvelets [6,7] which can capture singularities around a curve are proposed to overcome such issues. One promising result of curvelet is that it can capture the edge around a curve in terms of very few coefficients. This creates new opportunities in the area of image processing. Curvelets with their nice features are also used in texture retrieval [8]. However, rotation invariance is not considered in [8]. Rotation invariance in the multiscale framework was first investigated in [9] for Gabor wavelet features. In a similar work, the authors used Gaussianized steerable pyramids for providing rotation-invariant features in [10]. Wavelet-based rotation invariance is introduced in [11] using rotated complex wavelet filters and in [12] using wavelet-based hidden Markov trees. These works show the effectiveness of their methods on the average performance. The details of their work also reveal that the textures with curvature-like structures perform worse than other textures. Hence, curvelet is a good alternative to overcome such issues. However, the authors of [8] realized that curvelet is actually very orientation-dependent and sensitive to rotation. Then, they provided rotation-invariant curvelet features in [13,14] based on comparison of energies of curvelet coefficients and realigning the curvelet blocks by cycle-shifting them with reference to the highest energy curvelet block. They showed that this scheme creates great advantage when compared to rotation-variant curvelet features. They

also showed that their features provide better results when compared to wavelets and rotation-invariant Gabor filters. However, the authors of [15] indicated that the provided method of [13,14] does not work for all the images, and they proposed another method based on modeling the curvelet coefficients as generalized Gaussian distributions (GGD) and then providing a distance measure by using Kullback-Leibler divergence between the statistical parameters of curvelets. It should be noted that they also use the highest energy curvelet block for circular shifting with the exception that they use only one reference point instead of using different reference points for each scale. This approach may provide good fits for higher scales of curvelet coefficients; however, lower levels of curvelet coefficients tend to not behave as Gaussian. In this study, we investigate the distributions of curvelet coefficients and use kernel density estimation (KDE) which provides better fits for lower scales as well. Although the complexity increases with density estimations, better results are obtained. There are also some latest and comprehensive works in texture retrieval trying to address both the scale invariance and rotation invariance issues. For instance in [16], Harris-Laplace detector [17] is used for salient region detection and then scale-invariant feature transformation (SIFT) [18] is used in order to provide scale invariance and rotation-invariant feature transformation (RIFT) [19] is used for rotation invariance. The results are pretty good; however, feature vector sizes are considerably large, 5,120 (40×128) for SIFT descriptor with earth mover distance (EMD). In [20], local binary pattern (LBP) variance is used for rotation invariance, in which two principle orientations are found and local binary pattern variances are used for texture retrieval. The feature dimensions of [20] with feature reduction are in the range of 1,000 s. In [21], both the scale and rotation variance are considered together using LBP, and it provides promising results again with feature sizes around LBP variants.

The main motivation of this study is to provide good retrieval performance with low-dimensional feature sets. The multiresolution structure in the literature has low-dimensional feature sets but not in the desired range of performances. In this study, we provide solutions for low-dimensional rotation-invariant multiresolution features with good retrieval performances by using curvelet transformation. First, a novel method is introduced for obtaining rotation-invariant curvelet features. The proposed method is based on cross energy principle. Second, the low-dimensional feature set based on mean and standard deviation of curvelet coefficients, used in the literature [13,14], is modified to reflect its support region. The size of this feature vector is 84, and the increase in the performance by this modification is also shown. Third, we use kernel density estimate, a nonparametric density estimation, of curvelet coefficients to estimate the densities and use symmetric Kullback-Leibler distance as the distance measure. Although this feature set has higher dimension, 840, it provides better results and still remains in the low complexity region when compared with the other methods in the literature. It is shown through experiments that the results of the proposed feature sets are better than those of the state-of-the-art techniques in low dimension and comparable in medium dimension feature sets. The organization of the paper is as follows. First, multiresolution transforms are introduced in Section 2. Second, Section 3 explains the proposed texture retrieval scheme. Third, the proposed rotation invariance method is provided in Section 4, and classification is explained in Section 5. Fourth, the experimental results are presented in Section 6. Then, Section 7 includes discussions and comparisons with state-of-the-art texture retrieval techniques. Finally, Section 8 includes conclusions.

2. Background

Multiscale transforms are widely used in CBIR and texture retrieval. Hence, in order to better appreciate and understand the multiscale transforms, especially the curvelet transform, we briefly define wavelets, ridgelets, and curvelet transforms in this section.

2.1. Wavelets

Given that $\Psi_{s,\tau}(x, y)$ is a wavelet function for scale s and translation τ, wavelet transform of a function $f(x, y)$ and the inverse transform can be obtained by using Equations 1 and 2, respectively.

$$W_f(s, \tau) = \iint f(x,y)\Psi^*_{s,\tau}(x,y)dxdy \qquad (1)$$

$$f(x,y) = \iint W_f(s, \tau)\Psi_{s,\tau}(x,y)d\tau ds \qquad (2)$$

where Ψ is a two-dimensional mother wavelet. Other wavelets can be generated by scaling the mother wavelet function by s and shifting in the x or y direction by τ_x or τ_y, respectively, as given in Equation 3. In wavelet transform, only the transformation framework is outlined and the wavelet functions are left to the choice of the designer. Commonly used Mexican hat wavelet is depicted

in Figure 1. The isometric shape of the wavelet can be seen from the figure. The projection of the function of interest (i.e., an image) to this isometric wavelet results in capturing point singularities very well. However, the singularities in images are generally continuous around a line or a curve. In order to provide a better solution for the detection of line-shaped geometries, the ridgelets are proposed.

$$\Psi_{s,\tau_x,\tau_y}(x,y) = \frac{1}{\sqrt{s}}\Psi\left(\frac{x-\tau_x}{s}, \frac{y-\tau_y}{s}\right) \qquad (3)$$

2.2. Ridgelets

Ridgelets are proposed for effectively describing anisotropic elements such as lines or curves with small number of coefficients. In order to have the ability of detecting lines or curves, it is necessary to define functions with directional geometry. Such a function is constant along lines of $x\cos(\theta) + y\sin(\theta)$. A sample ridgelet is given in Figure 2. The ridgelet is obtained by scaling and translating the mother wavelet function $\Psi(x, y)$. The ridgelet in Equation 4 is defined for angle θ, scale s, and translation τ. Ridgelets can be used to identify the singularities along lines.

$$\Psi_{s,\tau,\theta}(x,y) = \frac{1}{\sqrt{s}}\Psi\left(\frac{x\cos(\theta) + y\sin(\theta) - \tau}{s}\right) \qquad (4)$$

Using the ridgelet functions defined in Equations 4, the ridgelet transform and inverse ridgelet transform can be performed using Equations 5 and 6, respectively.

$$\mathcal{R}f(s, \tau, \theta) = \int\int f(x,y)\Psi^*_{s,\tau,\theta}(x,y)dxdy \qquad (5)$$

$$f(x,y) = \int_0^{2\pi}\int_{-\infty}^{\infty}\int_0^{\infty}\mathcal{R}f(s, \tau, \theta)\Psi_{s,\tau,\theta}(x,y)\frac{ds}{s^3}d\tau\frac{d\theta}{4\pi} \qquad (6)$$

2.3. Curvelets

Curvelet transformation enables the detection of singularities along a curvature, while the ridgelets are not sufficient enough for the identification of curves due to

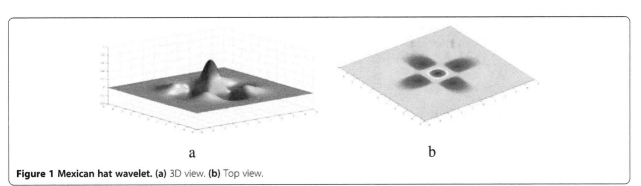

Figure 1 Mexican hat wavelet. (a) 3D view. **(b)** Top view.

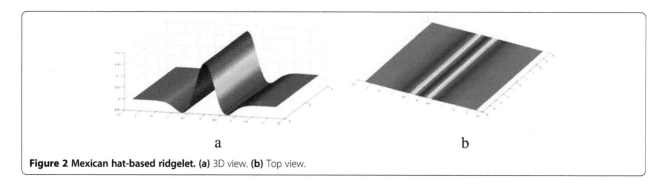

a

b

Figure 2 Mexican hat-based ridgelet. (a) 3D view. **(b)** Top view.

their line-directional geometry. Basically, a curvelet function is also a wavelet function which is rotated, scaled, and translated for different angles, scales, and shifts, respectively. A curvelet function can also be defined as a ridgelet function with various rotation angles. Figure 3 shows a curvelet function for specific scale, rotation, and translation. If the translations on $\mathbf{Z}^2$ are defined by $\mathbf{k} = (k_1, k_2)$, rotations are given by $\theta_\ell = 2\pi.2^{-s} \cdot \ell$ where $\ell = 0, 1,....., 2^s$ such that $0 \le \theta_\ell < 2\pi$, parabolic scaling matrix D_s is given by Equation 7 and rotation operator is given by Equation 8, then the curvelet function is defined by Equation 9.

$$D_s = \begin{bmatrix} 2^{2s} & 0 \\ 0 & 2^s \end{bmatrix} \tag{7}$$

$$R_{\theta_\ell} = \begin{bmatrix} \cos\theta_\ell & \sin\theta_\ell \\ -\sin\theta_\ell & \cos\theta_\ell \end{bmatrix} \tag{8}$$

$$\Psi_{s,l,\mathbf{k}}(x,y) = 2^{3s/2}\Psi_s\left(D_s R_{\theta_l}\begin{bmatrix} x \\ y \end{bmatrix} - \begin{bmatrix} k_1 \\ k_2 \end{bmatrix}\right) \tag{9}$$

where Ψ_s is a mother wavelet function. Based on the above definitions, the curvelet coefficient is given by Equation 10.

$$C(s, l, \mathbf{k}) = \int \int f(x, y)\Psi_{s,l,k}^*(x, y)dxdy \tag{10}$$

A graphical explanation of the curvelet can be depicted as in Figure 4. Here, the image is represented by a red curve over which the curvelet transform is calculated, and the blue line in black ovals represents the cross-sectional magnitude of curvelet operator. The dot product of the line, originally the image, and the curvelet function becomes maximum when the image and the signal are aligned, in other words, have the maximum number of common points (pixels). On the other end, the curvelet coefficients become zero if the two do not cross each other for any rotational and/or translational change. Hence, it is possible to follow the orientation and location of the image, red line, by just determining the maximum of curvelet coefficients. Due to this efficient property, it is possible to use curvelets for edge detection, object detection,

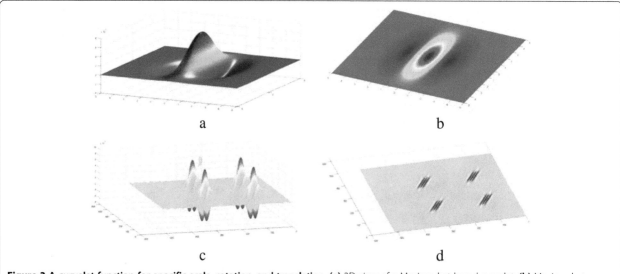

a

b

c

d

Figure 3 A curvelet function for specific scale, rotation, and translation. (a) 3D view of a Mexican hat based curvelet. **(b)** Mexican hat curvelet, top view. **(c)** 3D view of a Meyer-based curvelet. **(d)** Meyer curvelet, top view.

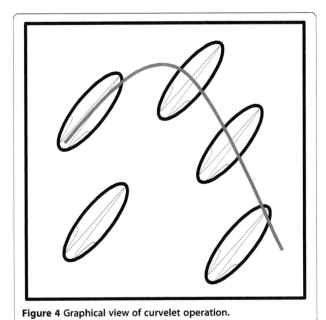

Figure 4 Graphical view of curvelet operation.

noise removal, texture identification, etc. Since orientation is an important feature of curvelet transformation, curvelet coefficients may significantly vary with rotation. Hence, the direct use of curvelet coefficients as the image features introduce rotation dependency and overall texture classification performance may deteriorate if rotated replica of a texture exists in the database. So, it is necessary to utilize curvelet coefficients in a rotation-invariant manner to overcome this downside.

3. Proposed texture retrieval scheme

The proposed texture retrieval scheme is depicted in Figure 5. In the proposed scheme, first, the query and training images are selected from the image database. Second, curvelet transform is applied to both sets of images. Third, principle orientation (PO) of each image is detected by analyzing the cross energies of the curvelet coefficients. Then, the extracted features are realigned by cycle-shifting all the features around the PO. Finally, PO-aligned features are compared for classification. Each step of the algorithm is explained in the following subsections.

3.1. Feature extraction

Broad range of feature sets are used in the literature such as entropy, energy, first- and second-order statistics, and many more. In this study, we propose and evaluate two different feature vectors. The first one is called as mean and standard deviation feature vector, $\mathbf{F}_{\mu\sigma}$, and the second one is called as kernel density feature vector, $\mathbf{F}_{\mathrm{KDE}}$. $\mathbf{F}_{\mu\sigma}$ includes the mean and standard deviation of curvelet coefficients, which belong to different levels and angles, scaled with a support coefficient. Similar features previously used in [13,14] without a scaling factor. Using only the first- and second-order statistics may describe the distribution fully only if the distribution is Gaussian. However, as indicated in earlier works [15], the Gaussian probability density function (PDF) may not be a perfect fit for curvelet data. Moreover, the curvelet coefficients at lower levels deviate from the Gaussian distribution as it can be seen from Figure 6, which presents second level curvelet coefficients

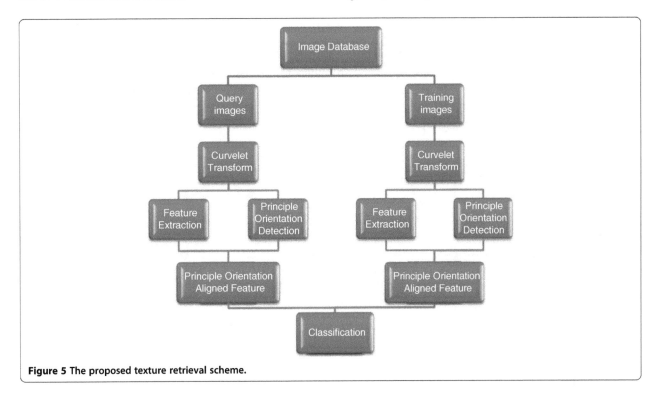

Figure 5 The proposed texture retrieval scheme.

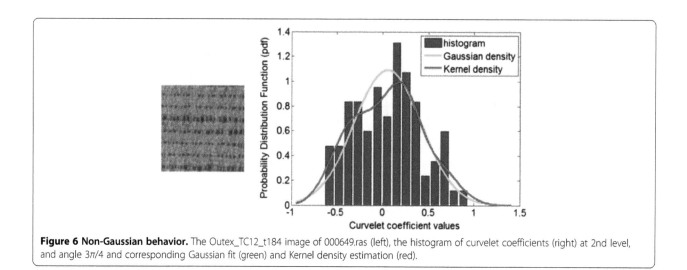

Figure 6 Non-Gaussian behavior. The Outex_TC12_t184 image of 000649.ras (left), the histogram of curvelet coefficients (right) at 2nd level, and angle $3\pi/4$ and corresponding Gaussian fit (green) and Kernel density estimation (red).

of an image. Hence, kernel density feature, $\mathbf{F}_{KDE}$, which estimates the PDF of curvelet coefficients using KDE, is also proposed. It is expected to obtain better classification results when the PDF of curvelet coefficients is used since it represents full statistics. An alignment step is needed in both approaches to provide rotation invariance. Before going into the details of the alignment step, the feature vectors of this study are defined first.

3.2. Mean standard deviation feature vector $\mathbf{F}_{\mu\sigma}$
A feature vector which includes the first- and second-order statistics of curvelet coefficients for five levels is given by Equation 11.

$$\mathbf{F}'_{\mu\sigma} = [\mu_{1,1}, \sigma_{1,1}, \mu_{2,1}, \sigma_{2,1}, \mu_{2,2}, \sigma_{2,2}, \ldots, \mu_{2,8}, \sigma_{2,8}, \mu_{3,1},$$
$$\sigma_{3,1}, \mu_{3,2}, \sigma_{3,2}, \ldots \mu_{3,16}, \sigma_{3,16}, \mu_{4,1}, \sigma_{4,1}, \mu_{4,2},$$
$$\sigma_{4,2}, \ldots, \mu_{4,16}, \sigma_{4,16}, \mu_{5,1}, \sigma_{5,1}]$$

$$(11)$$

where $\mu_{s,\ell}$ and $\sigma_{s,\ell}$ are the mean and standard deviation of curvelet coefficients at scale s and angle ℓ, respectively. It should be noted that it is enough to consider only the first half plane of the curvelet coefficients since curvelet transform is even symmetric around π. This feature vector is depicted for 5 scales and includes 84 elements. The feature vector of Equation 11 is used in [13] as well. Since the feature vector includes robust features such as the first- and second-order statistics, it can be used for comparison purposes. As it can be seen from Figure 7, the number of wedges doubles every other scale going from the lower to the higher frequencies. This means that the spatial support is halved every other scale as well. In other words, curvelet transformation is applied over a narrower region going from the lower to the higher scales. A larger special support region means that it is more likely to have dissimilarities. Thus, the statistics carried out from dissimilarities should be penalized. A similar approach is also used in [22], where the authors use spatially obtained

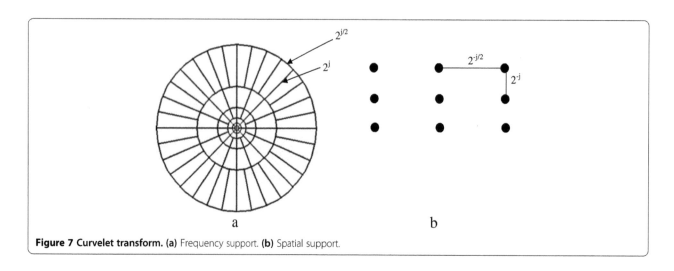

Figure 7 Curvelet transform. (a) Frequency support. **(b)** Spatial support.

features for classification of various scene categories. In order to reflect the size of the spatial support, we apply a weighting factor, α_s, given by Equation 12 and obtain the scaled mean-standard deviation feature vector, $\mathbf{F}_{\mu\sigma}$, given by Equation 13.

$$\alpha_s = \left\{ \begin{array}{ll} 1 & , s = 1 \\ 2^{\mathrm{ceil}(s/2)} & , s > 1 \end{array} \right\} \tag{12}$$

$$\mathbf{F}_{\mu\sigma} = [\alpha_1(\mu_{1,1}, \sigma_{1,1}), \alpha_2(\mu_{2,1}, \sigma_{2,1}, \mu_{2,2}, \sigma_{2,2}, \dots,$$
$$\mu_{2,8}, \sigma_{2,8}), \dots, \alpha_N(\mu_{N,1}, \sigma_{N,1})] \tag{13}$$

where N is the total number of scales and s is the scale. The 'ceil' function rounds up the number to the nearest integer. If there are five scales, then the corresponding feature vector is given by the following:

$$\mathbf{F}_{\mu\sigma} = [2^0(\mu_{1,1}, \sigma_{1,1}), 2^1(\mu_{2,1}, \sigma_{2,1}, \mu_{2,2}, \sigma_{2,2}, \dots, \mu_{2,8}, \sigma_{2,8}),$$
$$2^2(\mu_{3,1}, \sigma_{3,1}, \mu_{3,2}, \sigma_{3,2}, \dots \mu_{3,16}, \sigma_{3,16}), 2^2(\mu_{4,1},$$
$$\sigma_{4,1}, \mu_{4,2}, \sigma_{4,2}, \dots, \mu_{4,16}, \sigma_{4,16}), 2^3(\mu_{5,1}, \sigma_{5,1})] \tag{14}$$

The images we use are either 128×128 or converted to 128×128 in the preprocessing stage during our work, and the feature vector used in this study has five scales. Considering 8 angles at 2nd, 16 angles at 3rd and 4th, and 1 for 1st and 5th scales, the size of the feature vector is $(1 + 8 + 16 + 16 + 1) \times 2 = 84$.

3.3. Kernel density feature vector F$_{KDE}$

Probability density of curvelet coefficients is very close to normal distribution. However, earlier works have showed that the coefficients may not exactly be modeled by using a normal PDF. It is shown in [15] that modeling curvelet coefficients by GGD provides a better fit than that of the normal PDF. In this study, we use a nonparametric approach for estimating the density of curvelet coefficients due to the fact the Gaussianity assumption gets even weaker for lower levels. One may notice non-Gaussian behavior by observing Figure 6. Nonparametric estimation is widely used when parametric modeling of the distribution becomes infeasible. We obtain the proposed kernel density feature vector, $\mathbf{F}_{KDE}$, through KDE. It is given by Equation 15.

$$\mathbf{F}_{KDE} = [f_{1,1}, f_{2,1}, f_{2,2}, \dots, f_{2,8}, f_{3,1}, f_{3,2}, \dots, \tag{15}$$
$$f_{3,16}, f_{4,1}, f_{4,2}, \dots, f_{4,16}, f_{5,1}]$$

where each element of $\mathbf{F}_{KDE}$, which represents the density of curvelet coefficients at a particular scale and angle, is estimated through KDE. The feature vector of Equation 15 is given for five scales and can be extended to include higher number of scales. In KDE, first, a kernel function is

defined [23]. Then, using n data points ($X_1, X_2, \dots, X_n$) of a random variable x, the kernel estimator for PDF $p(x)$ is given by Equation 16:

$$\hat{p}(x) = \frac{1}{nh} \sum_{i=1}^{n} K\left(\frac{x - X_i}{h}\right) \tag{16}$$

where K is the kernel function and h is the smoothing parameter called bandwidth. The kernel function used in this study is normal kernel with zero mean and unity variance. Each kernel is placed on the data points and normalized over the data to obtain the kernel estimation. A more depth analysis on KDE is given in [23]. The histogram of the curvelet coefficients, corresponding Gaussian fit, and KDE is shown in Figure 6. As it can be seen from the figure, KDE provides much better fit than Gaussian. The non-Gaussian structure of curvelet coefficients can be observed for second-level coefficients of a sample image given in Figure 6. We have evaluated the kernel density at 20 bins, resulting in a feature vector dimension of 840 (42×20).

4. Rotation invariance

4.1. Effect of rotation on curvelet transform

Following the curvelet transformation, curvelet coefficients for different orientations and specific scales are obtained. Hence, the curvelet coefficients reflect the effect of the rotation. Let us consider a particular scale s with rotation angles represented by $\{\theta_1, \theta_2, \dots, \theta_n\}$. For each rotation angle, there exists a curvelet coefficient matrix. The elements of this matrix are obtained following a translation in x and y direction. Curvelet transformation of two different images and their rotated versions are given in Figure 8. These images are in the size of 128×128 and have 5 scales in curvelet domain. Four of those scales are shown in Figure 8. The fifth scale is the highest resolution and is not divided into angles. The most inner box and the most outer box represent the lowest and highest resolutions, respectively. We can follow that the rotation is captured in all scales. It is difficult to notice the rotation by just looking at the curvelet domain image. However, high energy areas are really noticeable. The authors of [13,14] realized this feature and proposed to synchronize them by aligning the highest energy curvelet coefficients while cycle-shifting the others not to change the relative order among all. Since the curvelet coefficients are arranged in a cyclic fashion, applying this idea gave promising results. However, the obvious energy compaction is not valid for all images as the authors of [15] pointed out. It is also possible that the high energy area may exist at some other location in the rotated image after curvelet transformation is applied, especially in the figures where a nice uniform texture does not exist.

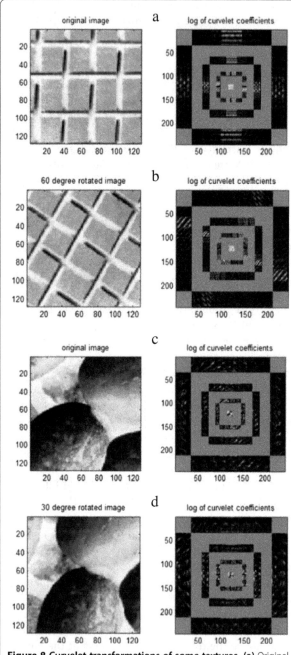

Figure 8 Curvelet transformations of some textures. (a) Original image (left) and its curvelet coefficients (right). **(b)** 60° rotated image (left) and its curvelet coefficients (right). **(c)** Original image (left) and its curvelet coefficients (right). **(d)** 30° rotated image (left) and its curvelet coefficients (right).

This nonuniformity can be observed in Figure 8c,d. In order to overcome this issue, first, we propose to find the most robust area of the image against rotation based on curvelet transform and mark that point as principle orientation; then perform an alignment by cycle-shifting the feature vector with reference to principle orientation. In order to find the least affected rotation angle, we

perform cross-correlation check for two adjacent curvelet coefficients at each scale.

4.2. Principle orientation detection

In order to minimize the effect of rotation in the texture, it is necessary to find a reference point, namely, principle orientation, so that all feature vectors can be synchronized by reordering the features. The rotation dependence is expected to be eliminated after the synchronization. The authors of [13,14] suggest a synchronization routine by means of the curvelet block with the maximum energy. We propose to use cross energy of adjacent curvelet blocks for the principle orientation detection, and the procedure is explained in the following subsection.

4.3. Cross-correlation and cross energy of curvelet coefficients at adjacent angles

The cross-correlation of two adjacent curvelet blocks for angles ℓ and $\ell + 1$ is given as follows:

$$R_{s,\ell}(n_1, n_2) = \sum_{k_1} \sum_{k_2} \left(\left| C(s, \ell, k_1, k_2) \right| . \left| C(s, \ell + 1, k_1 + n_1, k_2 + n_2) \right| \right)$$

$$(17)$$

The cross-correlation function actually reflects the cross energies for different lags. In obtaining the latter curvelet coefficient on the right hand side of Equation 17, only a rotation is applied to curvelet operator while the image stands still. Also, as it can be seen from Equation 9 that this rotation operator is not supposed to cause a lag in the latter coefficient. Hence, it is expected to get the maximum value of cross-correlation function at 0th lag, that is $R_{s,\ell}(0, 0)$. As a result, Equation 17 can be used to detect the highest cross-energy blocks. Another view can be expressed as follows: by analyzing the adjacent blocks of curvelet transform in terms of their cross-correlation quantities, one may find the orientation for each scale which is the least affected by rotation. In other words, getting a high correlation between two adjacent blocks means that the directional change has little effect on curvelet coefficients for the specific two orientations at hand. In short, if curvelet coefficients of two adjacent blocks of an image at specific orientation give the highest values, they will also be the ones with the highest correlation values for the rotated version of original texture. The proposed method is structured based on this approach. Since rotation of curvelet operator and rotation of image has the same effect, the observed angle between the curvelet operator and the image for the highest correlation value remains fixed. Based on this principle, we determine the fixed angle by searching for the highest cross correlation and take the first of the

Figure 9 Image D1 of Brodatz database.

highest cross-energy (correlated) blocks as the principle block (orientation) and then cycle-shift all the coefficients in reference to the principle orientation. Hence, this operation provides an alignment based on the highest cross-energy principle. Once the cross-correlation functions are obtained for all scales except the coarsest and finest due to the fact that there is only one coefficient matrix for them, the curvelet coefficients are aligned with reference to the highest 0th lag value of cross-correlations in each scale. The dimension mismatch is generally the case faced for two coefficient matrices of adjacent orientations. If there are not enough coefficients to match the larger sized coefficient block, then the smaller sized coefficient block is padded with zero coefficients in order to overcome the dimension mismatch problem. This zero-filling solves the dimension mismatch problem and does not affect the cross energy.

4.3. Closer look on principle orientation alignment based on cross energy

In this subsection, we outline some examples to better understand the contribution of this study. In the first example, we consider an image taken from the Brodatz database as shown in Figure 9. The corresponding curvelet coefficients of this image and its 30° and 60° rotated versions are given in Figure 10. The yellow boxes on each scale show the principle orientations obtained by the proposed algorithm. Similarly, Figure 11 shows the same curvelet transforms with yellow boxes representing the reference points based on the algorithm of [13]. A close look immediately reveals that both algorithms have common reference points. But it can also be observed that the proposed algorithm captures the boxes where orientation at each scale is the same, whereas the algorithm of [13] may not detect the correct orientation at the scale 2 for this particular example. This is due to the fact that the texture of this figure does not have a uniform pattern, and rotation may cause the curvelet transform to capture the most dominant edges for that orientation. Since the proposed algorithm focuses on the amount of change in the rotation, it manages to capture the correct orientation at each scale.

In the second example, we consider the image '000480. ras' of Outex TC12_t184 database and its rotated image of '000649.ras'. The images and their corresponding kernel density estimations are given in Figure 12. As can be observed from the figure, coefficients of right column are cycle-shifted around the highest cross-energy coefficient block, second from the top and highlighted by a bold frame. As a result, this coefficient block, level = 2 and angular parameter = 2, is reordered (cycle-shifted) in a way that this set gets angular parameter value of 1 (the one at the top of the middle column) and all the others move into the position of prior angular parameter in a cyclic manner.

It should also be noted that the curvelet coefficients of unrotated and rotated images show some differences

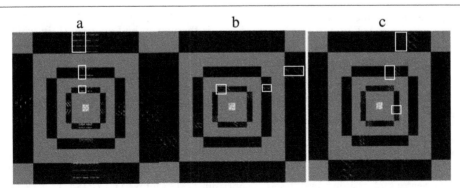

Figure 10 Reference rotation points marked by yellow boxes based on the proposed principle orientation. **(a)** 0° (no rotation). **(b)** 30° rotation. **(c)** 60° rotation.

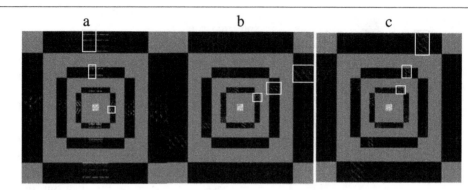

Figure 11 Reference rotation points marked by yellow boxes based on the rotation invariance of [13]. **(a)** 0° (no rotation). **(b)** 30° rotation. **(c)** 60° rotation.

even after principle orientation alignment. This can also be observed by comparing the first and second columns of Figure 12. This is due to the fact that the curvelet coefficients of these images may be similar; however, it is hardly likely that they will be the same. Hence, the purpose of the alignment is to make the curvelet coefficients of two images comparable as much as possible.

4.5. PO-aligned feature vectors

The mean standard deviation, $\mathbf{F}_{\mu\sigma}$, and kernel density, $\mathbf{F}_{\mathrm{KDE}}$, feature vectors are aligned according to principle orientation, following the principle orientation detection. The aligned feature vectors are cycle-shifted versions of the initial ones. The PO-aligned mean-standard deviation feature vector and kernel density feature vector are denoted as $\mathbf{F}_{\mu\sigma}^{\mathrm{PO}}$ and $\mathbf{F}_{\mathrm{KDE}}^{\mathrm{PO}}$, respectively. The rotation-invariant mean-standard deviation feature vector without scaling, $\mathbf{F}_{\mu\sigma}^{',\mathrm{PO}}$, is also used in our simulations for comparison purposes. The proposed PO-aligned feature vectors are used in the classification process in this study.

5. Classification

The classification is performed based on nearest neighbor (NN) classifier. In NN, the query image is compared against the training images of all the classes and the image is assigned to the class which has the minimum distance with. Separate distance measures are used in this study for each proposed feature vector. Euclidian distance is used with the mean and standard deviation feature vector and Kullback-Leibler distance measure with kernel density feature vector.

5.1. Distance measures

Euclidian distance

The PO-aligned feature vectors of training and query images are compared to find the best match based on Euclidian distance measure. The Euclidian distance, d_{ij}^{euc},

between the ith query image and the jth database image is calculated by Equation 18.

$$\left(d_{ij}^{\mathrm{euc}}\right)^2 = \left(\mathbf{F}_{i,\mu\sigma}^{\mathrm{PO}} - \mathbf{F}_{j,\mu\sigma}^{\mathrm{PO}}\right)\left(\mathbf{F}_{i,\mu\sigma}^{\mathrm{PO}} - \mathbf{F}_{j,\mu\sigma}^{\mathrm{PO}}\right)^T, i \neq j \qquad (18)$$

where $\mathbf{F}_{i,\mu\sigma}^{\mathrm{PO}}$ and $\mathbf{F}_{j,\mu\sigma}^{\mathrm{PO}}$ are the feature vector of query image (ith image of the database) and the training image (the feature vector of the jth database image), respectively.

Symmetric Kullback-Leibler distance

Kullback-Leibler divergence is a common method to measure the distance between two PDFs and is given by Equation 19:

$$d_{pp'}^{\mathrm{KL}} = \int p(x)\ln\left(\frac{p(x)}{p'(x)}\right)dx \qquad (19)$$

Since $d_{pp'}^{\mathrm{KL}}$ is not necessarily equal to $d_{p'p}^{\mathrm{KL}}$, it is more appropriate to use symmetric Kullback-Leibler (SKL) distance, given by Equation 20;

$$d_{pp'}^{\mathrm{SKL}} = \left|\frac{1}{2}\int p(x)\ln\left(\frac{p(x)}{p'(x)}\right)dx + \frac{1}{2}\int p'(x)\ln\left(\frac{p'(x)}{p(x)}\right)dx\right| \qquad (20)$$

The SKL distance between the kernel density feature vectors of query image, $\mathbf{F}_{i,\mathrm{KDE}}^{\mathrm{PO}}$, and the training images, $\mathbf{F}_{j,\mathrm{KDE}}^{\mathrm{PO}}$ is then given by Equation 21, in which n is the dimension of the feature vector.

$$d_{\mathbf{F}_{i,\mathrm{KDE}}^{\mathrm{PO}}, \mathbf{F}_{j,\mathrm{KDE}}^{\mathrm{PO}}}^{\mathrm{SKL}} = \sum_{m=1}^{n} d_{F_{i,\mathrm{KDE}}^{\mathrm{PO}}(m), F_{j,\mathrm{KDE}}^{\mathrm{PO}}(m)}^{\mathrm{SKL}}, i \neq j \qquad (21)$$

6. Experimental results

The proposed algorithm is evaluated over various databases, Brodatz [24], Outex TC10 [25], Outex TC12-horizon [25], Outex TC12-t184 [25], KTH-TIPS [26], and UIUCTex [19]. The setup for each database is as follows: 100 simulations are run for each database, and

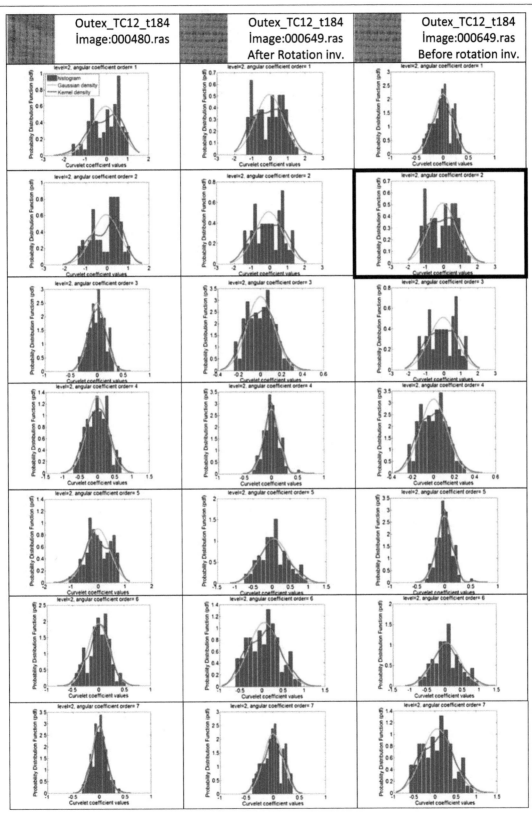

Figure 12 The effect of the proposed rotation invariance. Unrotated figure (left column), rotated figure (middle column) with PO alignment, and rotated figure without PO alignment (right column).

average precision-recall and classification performances are reported for all the simulation setups.

(a) Training images: They are selected randomly from each class of each database. Number of training images is varied from 10 to 70 in increments of 10 s. The results are reported separately for various numbers of training images.

(b) Query images: Training images are excluded from the database, and the remaining images are used as queries. The average classification and precision-recall results are reported.

(c) Brodatz database: The database is proposed in [24] and includes 112 classes, each with 192 images. In order to create large enough database with translations and rotations, first nonrotated test images are created by dividing each original 512 ×

512 image into 16 nonoverlapping 128 × 128 regions; then, 12 rotated test images are obtained for multiple of 30° rotations. The reason for 30° rotations is to obtain results, comparable with [24] which uses the same database with the same setup. A database of 21,504 images (112 × 16 × 12) is constructed in this way. In this setup, each class includes 192 images.

(d) Outex TC10 database: The database is proposed in [25] and includes 24 classes each with 180 images. The images are recorded under incandescent (inca) illumination. Each class consists of 20 non-overlapping portions of the same texture with 9 different orientations (0, 5, 10, 15, 30, 45, 60, 75, 90). The database includes a total of 4,320 images (24 × 20 × 9).

(e) Outex TC12-horizon database: The database is proposed in [25] and includes 24 classes and 180

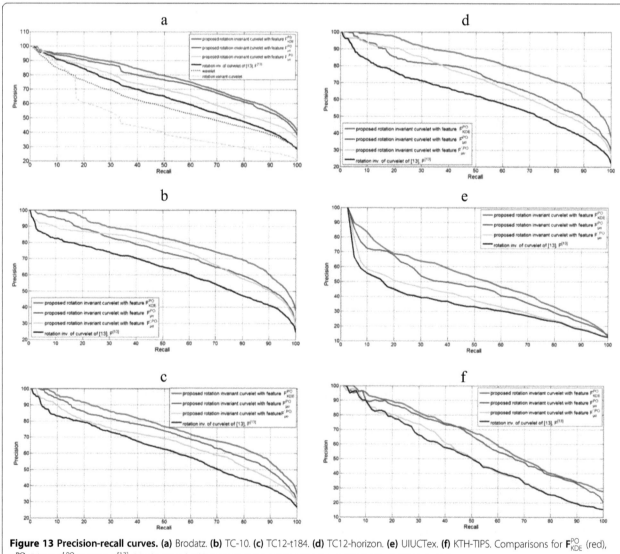

Figure 13 Precision-recall curves. (a) Brodatz. **(b)** TC-10. **(c)** TC12-t184. **(d)** TC12-horizon. **(e)** UIUCTex. **(f)** KTH-TIPS. Comparisons for $\mathbf{F}^{PO}_{KDE}$ (red), $\mathbf{F}^{PO}_{\mu\sigma}$ (blue), $\mathbf{F}'^{PO}_{\mu\sigma}$ (green), $\mathbf{F}^{[13]}$ (black), Wavelet (magenta) and rotation-variant curvelet (yellow) are included.

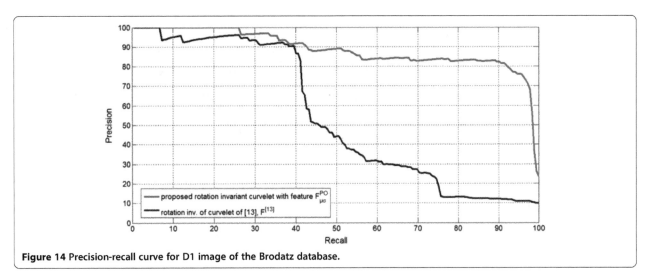

Figure 14 Precision-recall curve for D1 image of the Brodatz database.

images for each class. The same setup of Outex TC10 database is used except that the images are recorded under horizon (horizon sunlight) illumination.

(f) Outex TC12-t184 database: The database is proposed in [25] and includes 24 classes and 180 images for each class. Same setup is used as Outex TC10 database except that the images are recorded under t184 (fluorescent 184) illumination.

(g) KTH-TIPS database: The database is proposed in [26] and includes 10 classes and 81 images for each class. The images are recorded under varying illumination, pose, and scale. The database includes total of 810 images (10×81).

(h) UIUCTex database: The database is proposed in [19] and includes 25 classes and 40 images for each class. The images include significant scale and viewpoint variations as well as rotations. The database includes a total of 1,000 images (25×40).

The experimental results are reported under two main performance measurement categories, precision-recall curves and classification accuracies. The studies in the literature make use of both performance measures. In order to make our work easily comparable with future works as well as the literature, we have provided our results under these two categories. In order to see only the effect of principle orientation alignment and performance of two feature vectors of this study, the results of the proposed methods are compared generally with only one reference from the literature. The results of [13] are used for general comparison purposes with our results since the authors of [13] also use curvelet features. We make a broader comparison with the literature in the discussion section.

6.1. Precision-recall curves

Precision is the ratio of number of relevant retrieved images to number of all retrieved images whereas recall is the ratio of number of relevant retrieved images over total number of relevant images in the database. The precision-recall curves for all the databases are provided in Figure 13. Figure 13a compares the performances of the proposed rotation-invariant $\mathbf{F}_{KDE}^{PO}$ and $\mathbf{F}_{\mu\sigma}^{PO}$ features with the feature $\mathbf{F}_{\mu\sigma}^{',PO}$ where scaling is not used, the

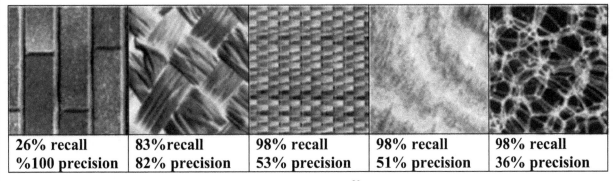

| 26% recall | 83%recall | 98% recall | 98% recall | 98% recall |
| %100 precision | 82% precision | 53% precision | 51% precision | 36% precision |

Figure 15 Mixed classes for the query image of D1 when rotation-invariant $\mathbf{F}_{\mu\sigma}^{PO}$ is used.

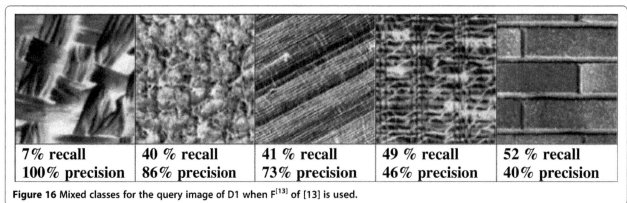

| 7% recall | 40 % recall | 41 % recall | 49 % recall | 52 % recall |
| 100% precision | 86% precision | 73% precision | 46% precision | 40% precision |

Figure 16 Mixed classes for the query image of D1 when $F^{[13]}$ of [13] is used.

Table 1 Classification rates (%)

	Classification	TC10	TC12-horizon	TC12-t184	KTH-TIPS	Brodatz	UIUCTex
Train 10	F^{PO}_{KDE}	91.94	92.06	90.24	80.70	95.39	65.63
	$F^{PO}_{\mu\sigma}$	91.15	91.48	88.37	75.41	92.73	65.21
	$F'^{,PO}_{\mu\sigma}$	89.47	89.39	85.78	69.21	90.86	52.10
	$F^{[13]}$	82.97	82.48	78.23	68.11	82.27	46.82
Train 20	F^{PO}_{KDE}	94.87	95.66	93.59	86.69	97.24	71.41
	$F^{PO}_{\mu\sigma}$	94.80	95.15	93.32	82.56	95.81	70.36
	$F'^{,PO}_{\mu\sigma}$	92.83	92.81	90.22	76.36	94.23	57.95
	$F^{[13]}$	88.72	87.94	84.78	76.20	88.69	51.73
Train 30	F^{PO}_{KDE}	96.60	96.64	95.25	88.31	98.02	74.08
	$F^{PO}_{\mu\sigma}$	96.12	96.50	95.06	87.92	96.88	73.79
	$F'^{,PO}_{\mu\sigma}$	94.62	94.46	91.91	79.57	95.72	61.81
	$F^{[13]}$	90.77	90.99	87.39	77.37	91.08	53.95
Train 40	F^{PO}_{KDE}	97.53	97.53	95.94	90.83	98.47	
	$F^{PO}_{\mu\sigma}$	96.86	97.49	95.86	89.42	97.70	
	$F'^{,PO}_{\mu\sigma}$	95.24	95.41	92.85	83.27	96.71	
	$F^{[13]}$	92.58	92.36	88.89	82.15	93.04	
Train 50	F^{PO}_{KDE}	97.82	98.05	96.62	92.19	98.91	
	$F^{PO}_{\mu\sigma}$	97.60	97.82	96.46	91.10	98.05	
	$F'^{,PO}_{\mu\sigma}$	95.90	95.99	93.74	84.32	97.53	
	$F^{[13]}$	93.30	93.20	90.23	82.77	94.01	
Train 60	F^{PO}_{KDE}	98.00	98.40	97.20	92.84	99.04	
	$F^{PO}_{\mu\sigma}$	97.73	98.22	96.92	91.52	98.37	
	$F'^{,PO}_{\mu\sigma}$	96.16	96.40	94.54	84.00	97.64	
	$F^{[13]}$	94.10	93.74	91.03	83.14	94.76	
Train 70	F^{PO}_{KDE}	98.33	98.46	97.44	93.09	99.18	
	$F^{PO}_{\mu\sigma}$	98.22	98.29	97.28	92.36	98.72	
	$F'^{,PO}_{\mu\sigma}$	96.52	96.44	94.86	86.00	98.10	
	$F^{[13]}$	94.40	94.63	91.79	85.64	95.34	

All the databases are evaluated for various (10,20,…,70) number of training images except the UIUCTex database since it only includes 40 images per class.

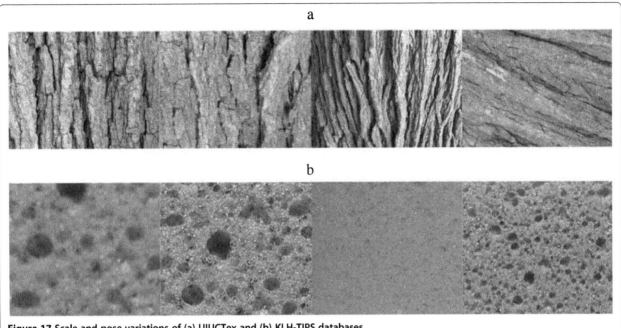

Figure 17 Scale and pose variations of (a) UIUCTex and (b) KLH-TIPS databases.

algorithm of [13] represented by **F** [13], wavelet, and rotation-variant features of curvelet in Brodatz database. Since the algorithm of [13] is already better than Gabor and ridgelet transforms and shown in detail in the literature, they are not included in this figure. As can be seen from this figure, the performance of F_{KDE}^{PO} is better than that of the other methods. It should be kept in mind that using F_{KDE}^{PO} instead of $F_{\mu\sigma}^{PO}$ increases the complexity due to the increased feature size. Hence, the better performance against $F_{\mu\sigma}^{PO}$ comes in the expense of complexity. The results for Outex TC10, TC12-t184, and TC12-horizon are given in Figure 13b,c,d, respectively. It can be observed from these figures that the proposed algorithm with the feature vector F_{KDE}^{PO} provides the best results followed by the feature vector $F_{\mu\sigma}^{PO}$. Although the same performance order is preserved for the results of UIUCTex and KTH-TIPS, given in Figure 13e,f, respectively, a lower precision-recall performance is observed compared to that of Outex database. The reason for that both UIUCTex and KTH-TIPS databases include scale and viewpoint variations and the proposed algorithm does not perform as well

under viewpoint and scale variations as it does for rotation variations.

We now provide a more depth analysis based on the precision-recall curve for a particular image taken from Brodatz database. Figure 14 shows the precision-recall curve of D1 query image of Brodatz database given in Figure 9. As it can be followed from Figure 14, the proposed feature vector $F_{\mu\sigma}^{PO}$ with rotation invariance provides much better precision-recall curve on this particular image. Figure 15 includes intermediate results and gives the mixed classes that are not relevant with the query image and the point where they are included in the precision-recall curve. Figure 15 shows that the first irrelevant image comes at the 26% recall and 100% precision point. It means that 50 relevant images (192 × 0.26) are retrieved before an irrelevant image is retrieved. This break point can also be seen on the blue line in Figure 14. Similarly, Figure 16 provides intermediate results for the algorithm of [13]. The first irrelevant image is retrieved at 7% recall and 100%. It means that 13 relevant images (192 × 0.07) are retrieved before an irrelevant one is retrieved.

Table 2 Comparison of classification rates with KLD of [15] for number of training images of 60 and 70

	Train 60	Train 70
Classification	KTH-TIPS	KTH-TIPS
F_{KDE}^{PO}	92.84	98.40
$F_{\mu\sigma}^{PO}$	91.52	98.22
KLD of [15]	83.60	86.90

6.2. Classification rates

In this section, classification rates are provided. If the query image is classified to its own class, then this classification is marked as true, if not, then it is marked as false. The percentage of correctly marked ones gives the classification rate. The training images are selected randomly from each class, and then, the remaining images are used as queries to get the classification rate. This

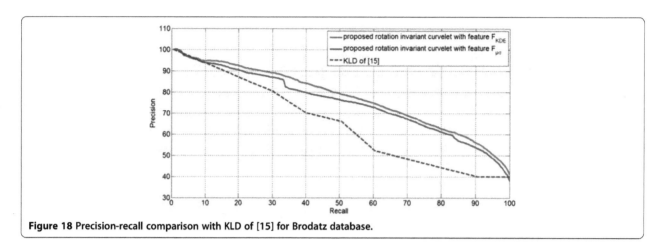

Figure 18 Precision-recall comparison with KLD of [15] for Brodatz database.

process is repeated 100 times, and the average results are reported in Table 1 where classification rates of the proposed feature vectors $\mathbf{F}_{KDE}^{PO}$ and $\mathbf{F}_{\mu\sigma}^{PO}$ and nonscaled feature vectors $\mathbf{F}_{\mu\sigma}^{',PO}$ and $\mathbf{F}^{[13]}$ of [13] are included. As can be seen from the table, $\mathbf{F}_{KDE}^{PO}$ has the superior performance followed by $\mathbf{F}_{\mu\sigma}^{PO}$. Brodatz database provides the highest performance in terms of classification since it only contains the rotated replica of the cropped images. Outex database provides the next best results followed by TC12-horizon, TC10, and TC12-t184 with slight differences. The differences among the subclasses of Outex database are not much, and overall performance for this database is good since it also includes only rotations and does not have scale or viewpoint variations. The UIUCTex and KTH-TIPS databases are the ones with the worst results among all. This is due to the fact that both databases include scale and pose variations as can be seen from Figure 17. The proposed feature vectors perform well for these databases as well, as can be seen from Table 1.

Table 3 Comparison of classification rates with LBP variants of [20] for training number of 20

Classification	Feature dimension	TC10	TC12-horizon	TC12-t184
$\mathbf{F}_{KDE}^{PO}$	840	94.87	95.66	93.59
$\mathbf{F}_{\mu\sigma}^{PO}$	84	94.80	95.15	93.32
$\mathbf{F}_{KDE}^{PO}$ out of class	840	94.87	87.35	86.25
$\mathbf{F}_{\mu\sigma}^{PO}$ out of class	84	94.80	86.73	85.51
$LBP_{24,3}^{riu2}/VAR_{24,3}$ [20]	416	98.15	87.03	87.15
$LBP_{8,1}^{riu2}/VAR_{8,1}$ [20]	160	96.66	77.98	79.25
$LBP_{24,3}^{u2}GM_{ES}$ [20]	13251	97.76	95.57	95.39
$LBP_{8,1}^{u2}GM_{ES}$ [20]	451	73.64	76.57	72.47
$LBPV_{24,3}^{u2}GM_{PD2}$ [20]	2211	97.55	94.18	94.23
$LBPV_{8,1}^{u2}GM_{PD2}$ [20]	227	72.99	76.15	72.19

7. Discussion

In this section, a broader comparison with the most recent and successful works in the literature is provided. The proposed rotation-invariant texture retrieval algorithm is evaluated by using the proposed PO-aligned feature vectors $\mathbf{F}_{KDE}^{PO}$ and $\mathbf{F}_{\mu\sigma}^{PO}$ and observed that they really perform well even though the feature dimensions are considerably low compared to those of the literature. In [15], following an energy-based cycle shift based on only one level, GGD estimations of curvelet coefficients are used with Kullback-Leibler distance (KLD) measure. Although the size of the feature dimensions is not elaborated in [15], we presume that it is close to size of $\mathbf{F}_{KDE}^{PO}$ which is 840 in our case. As can be seen from Table 2, both proposed methods outperform KLD in KTH-TIPS database. The precision recall curve is also provided in Figure 18 for comparison in the Brodatz database. The superior performance of the proposed methods over KLD can be observed from this figure.

In [20], LBP variance features provide really promising results. We compare our results with the results of [20] in Table 3. The classification results for $\mathbf{F}_{KDE}^{PO}$ and $\mathbf{F}_{\mu\sigma}^{PO}$ reflect in-class training. That is, the training images and the query images belong to the same class. However, the authors of [20] used in-class training for TC10 while they use out of class training for TC12-horizon and TC12-t184 for which they choose 20 images from TC10 database and use it for the queries of the other databases. Hence, we have run the simulations for these settings as well. '$\mathbf{F}_{KDE}^{PO}$ out of class' and '$\mathbf{F}_{\mu\sigma}^{PO}$ out of class' reflect the results of these simulations. As can be seen from Table 3, variants of LBP with low feature sizes perform worse than the proposed algorithm, but for high feature sizes, they outperform our algorithm especially in out of class classifications. The main reason for this outcome is that our algorithm is computationally efficient with its small feature size, and good results of LBP come in the expense of increased computational complexity.

Table 4 Comparison of classification rates with [16] for indicated training numbers

Classification	Feature size	UIUCTex	KTH-TIPS	Brodatz
$\mathbf{F}_{KDE}^{PO}$	840	71.41	90.83	92.00
$\mathbf{F}_{\mu\sigma}^{PO}$	84	70.36	89.42	90.78
HSR + LSR SIFT [16]	$40 \times 128 = 5{,}120$	98.00	92.70	94.00
HSR + LSR RIFT [16]	$40 \times 100 = 4{,}000$	96.00	86.70	89.60

Number of training images for UIUCTex, 20; KTH-TIPS, 40; Brodatz, 3.

The authors of [16] use Laplace and Harris detectors for salient region detection. SIFT is also used for scale invariance, and RIFT is used for rotation invariance. Although the results are good, feature vector dimensions are considerably large, 5,120 (40×128) for SIFT descriptor with EMD. It should also be noted that support vector machine (SVM) classification, a strong classifier requiring learning effort, is used in [16]. Since we are not using SVM, we are not exactly able to tell how much of the better performance is obtained due to SVM. It is worth noting that using rotation-invariant technique RIFT and decreasing the feature size in their work also cause decrease in performance, and this effect can be seen from HSR + LSR of RIFT [16] in Table 4 where our proposed algorithm has better performance in KTH-TIPS and Brodatz databases.

Table 5 is included for easy comparison with the literature in terms of computational load and performance. The proposed algorithms, especially mean and standard deviation feature vector, have small feature dimensions. This is important as execution of the distance calculation at each comparison is proportional to the feature size. The computational complexity based on feature sizes are depicted as low, medium, and high in Table 5,

and the table is arranged in an increasing complexity manner. That is, top rows have lower complexity and bottom rows have higher complexity. Since the computational complexity of SVM is much higher than that of NN, SVM-based algorithms are placed at the bottom of Table 5. The proposed $\mathbf{F}_{\mu\sigma}^{PO}$ feature vector has quite low dimension, 84, and it provides really good results. The other proposed vector $\mathbf{F}_{KDE}^{PO}$ also provides good results with 840 feature dimension.

Table 5 gives a comparison of the proposed algorithm with the rest of the literature in terms of performance, dimension, and complexity in related databases. The algorithms in the top three rows are based on curvelet transformation, which are shown to outperform earlier multiscale-based texture classification methods. It is clear from the table that although they have similar feature sizes and complexities with the proposed algorithms, the proposed algorithms outperform all of them. The variants of LBP proposed in [20] are given in the table as well. It is seen that for dimension size of 160, $LBP_{8,1}^{riu2}/VAR_{8,1}$ algorithm provides worse results than the proposed algorithms in TC12-horizon and TC12-t184 databases but better result in TC-10 database. The performance of the proposed algorithms are better than $V_{8,1}^{u2}GM_{PD2}$, whose dimension size is 227, in all of the compared databases. $LBPV_{8,1}^{u2}GM_{PD2}$ and $LBP_{24,3}^{u2}GM_{ES}$ whose dimensions are 2,211 and 13,251, respectively, provide better results than the proposed algorithms at a high cost of increased feature size. The algorithms of [16] are provided in the 10th and 11th rows. It should be noted that their classification algorithm is based on SVM, an algorithm with higher computational complexity. Moreover, their feature vectors have higher dimensions

Table 5 Performance comparison of the proposed algorithms with the literature

	Algorithm	Feature size	Comput. complexity of feature	Class. method	Better than the proposed algorithms	Comparable with the proposed algorithms	Worse than the proposed algorithms
1	$\mathbf{F}_{\mu\sigma}'$	84	Low	NN	-	-	a,b,c,d,e,f
2	$\mathbf{F}^{[13]}$	84	Low	NN	-	-	a,b,c,d,e,f
3	$LBP_{8,1}^{riu2}/VAR_{8,1}$ [20]	160	Medium	NN	b	-	c,d
4	$LBPV_{8,1}^{u2}GM_{PD2}$ [20]	227	Medium	NN	-	-	b,c,d
5	$LBP_{24,3}^{riu2}/VAR_{24,3}$ [20]	416	Medium	NN	b	c,d	-
6	$LBP_{8,1}^{u2}GM_{ES}$ [20]	451	Medium	NN	-	-	b,c,d
7	KLD [15]	840	Medium	NN	-	-	a,e
8	$LBPV_{24,3}^{u2}GM_{PD2}$ [20]	2,211	High	NN	b,c,d	-	-
9	$LBP_{24,3}^{u2}GM_{ES}$ [20]	13,251	High	NN	b,c,d	-	-
10	HSR + LSR [16] RIFT	4,000	High	SVM	f	-	a,e
11	HSR + LSR [16] SIFT	5,120	High	SVM	a,e,f	-	-

The table does not include the proposed algorithms and is ordered in the increasing complexity and feature size order (top to bottom). The databases are represented with as follows: a, Brodatz; b, TC10, c, TC12-horizon; d, TC12-t184; e, KTH-TIPS; f, UIUCTex. The italicized letters indicate the databases where the proposed methods are superior.

than those of the proposed algorithms. Even though their algorithm provides better results for HSR + LSR + SIFT, the proposed algorithms outperform HSR + LSR + RIFT in Brodatz and KTH_TIPS databases. This result is suspected to arise from the deduced feature size and less satisfactory performance of RIFT in scale-variant database (KTH-TIPS). In general, the proposed algorithms of this study outperform all of the multiscale-based texture classification algorithms. They also outperform LBP variants of [20] with small dimensions. The performance of the algorithm of [20] with high dimensions is better as expected. Proposed algorithms also outperform the algorithms of [16] in smaller dimensions especially in rotation-variant databases.

Finally, we mention one of the latest works in the rotation and scale-invariant texture retrieval published by Li et al. [21]. They provide scale invariance by finding optimal scale of each pixel. They modify Outex and Brodatz databases to include enough scale and rotation variations and report their results on these databases. For scale and rotation invariance feature, they report average precision rates around 69% for Brodatz and 60% for Outex database. Since they use a modified database, including this database will extend the scope of this study considerably, and we are leaving the scale invariance and the comparison with their database as our future work.

8. Conclusions

Low-dimensional and rotation-invariant curvelet features for multiscale texture retrieval are proposed through two feature vectors in this study. This study is important since it provides the best results for multiscale texture retrieval in the literature to the best of our knowledge. Moreover, the results are comparable with the state-of-the-art techniques in low and medium feature dimension sizes. Rotation invariance is provided by using the cross energies of curvelet blocks at adjacent orientations. The orientations with maximum cross energy are defined as the principle orientation of an image, which is the least affected location by rotation. The corresponding location is selected as the reference point for the image, and the feature vector is cycle-shifted based on this reference point. The feature vector $\mathbf{F}_{\mu\sigma}^{\mathrm{PO}}$ has 84 elements. The other proposed feature vector $\mathbf{F}_{\mathrm{KDE}}^{\mathrm{PO}}$ uses KDE, and it has 840 elements. It provides better results than $\mathbf{F}_{\mu\sigma}^{\mathrm{PO}}$ in the expense of increased complexity. The texture retrieval results of the proposed method are better than earlier works which make use of other rotation-invariant curvelet features and are comparable with the state-of-the-art works in the literature, especially in the low and medium feature dimension ranges. As a result, we provide a novel rotation invariance method for curvelets and two separate feature vectors for texture retrieval in this study. The proposed methods suggest highly effective discriminative power for texture retrieval. The comparisons with the literature show the effectiveness of the proposed algorithms since they provide good performances with low complexity. Addition of scale invariance for curvelet features may provide better results. Thus, we plan to extend this study for scale-invariant features of curvelet transform as our future work.

Competing interests
The author declares that he has no competing interests.

References
1. HH Arsenault, YN Hsu, K Chalasinskamacukow, Rotation-invariant pattern-recognition. Opt. Eng. **23**, 705–709 (1984)
2. RL Kashyap, A Khotanzad, A model-based method for rotation invariant texture classification. IEEE T. Pattern Anal. **8**, 472–481 (1986)
3. SG Mallat, A theory for multiresolution signal decomposition - the wavelet representation. IEEE T. Pattern Anal **11**, 674–693 (1989)
4. BS Manjunath, WY Ma, Texture features for browsing and retrieval of image data. IEEE T. Pattern Anal. **18**, 837–842 (1996)
5. MN Do, M Vetterli, The finite ridgelet transform for image representation. IEEE T. Image Process. **12**, 16–28 (2003)
6. EJ Candes, DL Donoho, Curvelets, multiresolution representation, and scaling laws. Wavelet Appl Signal Image ProcessViii Pts 1 and 2 **4119**, 1–12 (2000)
7. EJ Candes, DL Donoho, New tight frames of curvelets and optimal representations of objects with piecewise C-2 singularities. Commun. Pur. Appl. Math. **57**, 219–266 (2004)
8. IJ Sumana, M Islam, DS Zhang, GJ Lu, *Content based image retrieval using curvelet transform, vol. 1 and 2 (2008 IEEE 10th Workshop on Multimedia Signal Processing, 2008)* (Queensland, Australia, 2008), pp. 11–16
9. GM Haley, BS Manjunath, Rotation-invariant texture classification using a complete space-frequency model. IEEE T. Image Process. **8**, 255–269 (1999)
10. G Tzagkarakis, B Beferull-Lozano, P Tsakalides, Rotation-invariant texture retrieval with Gaussianized steerable pyramids. IEEE T. Image Process. **15**, 2702–2718 (2006)
11. M Kokare, PK Biswas, BN Chatterji, Rotation-invariant texture image retrieval using rotated complex wavelet filters. IEEE T. Syst. Man. Cy. B **36**, 1273–1282 (2006)
12. VR Rallabandi, VPS Rallabandi, Rotation-invariant texture retrieval using wavelet-based hidden Markov trees. Signal Process **88**, 2593–2598 (2008)
13. DS Zhang, MM Islam, GJ Lu, IJ Sumana, Rotation invariant curvelet features for region based image retrieval. Int. J. Comput. Vision **98**, 187–201 (2012)
14. MM Islam, DS Zhang, GJ Lu, *Rotation invariant curvelet features for texture image retrieval, Presented at the Icme, vol. 1–3 (2009 IEEE International Conference on Multimedia and Expo* (New York, NY, USA, 2009)
15. F Gomez, E Romero, Rotation invariant texture characterization using a curvelet based descriptor. Pattern Recogn Lett **32**, 2178–2186 (2011)
16. J Zhang, M Marszalek, S Lazebnik, C Schmid, Local features and kernels for classification of texture and object categories: a comprehensive study. Int. J. Comput. Vision **73**, 213–238 (2007)
17. K Mikolajczyk, C Schmid, Scale & affine invariant interest point detectors. Int. J. Comput. Vision **60**, 63–86 (2004)
18. D Lowe, Distinctive image features from scale-invariant keypoints. Int. J. Comput. Vision **60**, 91–110 (2004)
19. S Lazebnik, C Schmid, J Ponce, A sparse texture representation using local affine regions. IEEE T. Pattern Anal. Mach. Intel. **27**, 1265–1278 (2005)
20. ZH Guo, L Zhang, D Zhang, Rotation invariant texture classification using LBP variance (LBPV) with global matching. Pattern Recogn **43**, 706–719 (2010)
21. Z Li, GZ Liu, Y Yang, JY You, Scale- and rotation-invariant local binary pattern using scale-adaptive texton and subuniform-based circular shift. IEEE T. Image Process. **21**, 2130–2140 (2012)
22. S Lazebnik, C Schmid, J Ponce, *Beyond bags of features: spatial pyramid matching for recognizing natural scene categories, in Computer Vision and Pattern Recognition (IEEE Computer Society Conference on, 2006* (New York, NY, USA, 2006), pp. 2169–2178

23. B Silverman, *Density Estimation for Statistics and Data Analysis* (Chapman & Hall, London, 1986)
24. P Brodatz, *Textures: A Photographic Album for Artists and Designers* (Dover, NewYork, 1966)
25. T Ojala, T Maenpaa, M Pietikainen, J Viertola, J Kyllonen, S Huovinen, *Outex - new framework for empirical evaluation of texture analysis algorithms, in Pattern Recognition, 2002, vol. 1 (Proceedings. 16th International Conference on, 2002)* (Quebec City, QC, Canada), pp. 701–706
26. E Hayman, B Caputo, M Fritz, J-O Eklundh, On the significance of real-world conditions for material classification, in *Computer Vision*, ed. by T Pajdla, J Matas (Springer, Berlin Heidelberg, 2004), pp. 253–266

7

Parallelization of the optical flow computation in sequences from moving cameras

Antonio Garcia-Dopico[*], José Luis Pedraza, Manuel Nieto, Antonio Pérez, Santiago Rodríguez and Juan Navas

Abstract

This paper presents a flexible and scalable approach to the parallelization of the computation of optical flow. This approach is based on data parallel distribution. Images are divided into several subimages processed by a software pipeline while respecting dependencies between computation stages. The parallelization has been implemented in three different infrastructures: shared, distributed memory, and hybrid to show its conceptual flexibility and scalability. A significant improvement in performance was obtained in all three cases. These versions have been used to compute the optical flow of video sequences taken in adverse conditions, with a moving camera and natural-light conditions, on board a conventional vehicle traveling on public roads. The parallelization adopted has been developed from the analysis of dependencies presented by the well-known Lucas-Kanade algorithm, using a sequential version developed at the University of Porto as the starting point.

Keywords: Optical flow; Parallelization; Cluster; MPI; Threads; Onboard camera

1 Introduction

Optical flow is an image analysis technique used to detect motion in video sequences. The detection can be performed in real time while images are being captured, or afterwards, when they are already stored in video format. Therefore, the optical flow works on an image sequence. For each image of the sequence, it generates a vector at each image pixel representing the apparent motion in the corresponding sampling period.

To determine the apparent motion of objects in an image, the information generated by the optical flow and by a separate process that identifies the different objects can be used. However, the apparent simplicity by which the human eye interprets movement in a three-dimensional space represents a highly complex task when trying to emulate it with computers - even in the case of a single motion.

The movement represented by the optical flow is considered an apparent movement since, in fact, the set of vectors generated is obtained from a two-dimensional image arising from projecting the real image (three-dimensional) on the plane of the camera. Moreover, optical flow computation techniques are based on analyzing the brightness variations of each pixel, making it impossible to distinguish between true and apparent motion. In fact, it is not possible to determine whether a velocity vector is obtained due to an actual motion of an object or a movement of the camera that has captured the image or a variation of luminosity due to some environmental condition such as reflections or shadows.

Technically, optical flow computation is based on assumptions rarely observed in real cases, but they can be partially met and so be considered as valid approximations. These are, as described by Beauchemin and Barron [1], (a) uniform illumination, (b) surfaces with Lambertian reflectance, and (c) movement limited to the plane of the image. Since most applications rarely meet the aforementioned conditions, it is considered that the method is approximate and that it does not allow the reconstruction of the original movement produced in the three-dimensional scene. However, in many occasions, the optical flow allows obtaining valid approximations of the movement being actually recorded.

Determining optical flow is a subject that has been studied by means of computers for several decades, and it has been employed in applications, such as (a) three-

*Correspondence: dopico@fi.upm.es
DATSI, Facultad de Informática, Universidad Politécnica de Madrid
Boadilla del Monte, Madrid 28660, Spain

dimensional image segmentation [2], (b) support for navigation of autonomous robots or, in general, the detection of obstacles to avoid collisions [3-6], (c) synchronization and/or 'matching' of video scenes [7], and (d) fluid dynamics analysis [8]. In any case, the problem is computationally very complex, so most of the proposed solutions are based on strong simplifications adapted to the technology available at the time or to the specific applications they intend to solve. In some cases, the size of the images is so small that can hardly represent a real-life scene [9-12]. In other cases, determining parameters in the generation of optical flow such as the light source (source, intensity, variation, etc.) or the motion of objects within the scene are restricted [13-15]. Except for some recent articles normally associated with the movement of conventional vehicles [16,17], mobile robots [18,19], and handheld cameras [20,21], the majority of papers describe systems in which the variation of the scene is limited. This limitation is determined because they work with images with a static background and taken with a static camera.

This article focuses on the parallelization of an optical flow computing system based on the well-known Lucas-Kanade algorithm [22,23]. The system is applied to an environment which is particularly hostile in terms of optical flow computation and has rarely been described by other authors [19]. It aims to determine the motion visually perceived by the driver of a conventional vehicle through roads or streets under real conditions: with real traffic and moving at speeds ranging from a few kilometers per hour to 120 km/h. Not only do these conditions rule out the parameter restrictions applied to other systems (i.e., regarding image size, controlled light sources), but they in fact all act simultaneously in generating the optical flow. Thus, image resolution must be sufficient (in the order of 500 × 300 pixels) to capture multiple objects of different sizes. Also, the camera moves with the car because it is located inside it. Finally, the light conditions are natural and highly variable. Hence, applying the restriction used in other systems is largely impossible. Moreover, obtaining the optical flow directly during the driving session requires the analysis of medium- or high-resolution video sequences in real time which requires significant computing capacity. This aspect may be exacerbated when working with large volumes of information coming from complete sessions previously stored, for which the corresponding optical flow has to be obtained. In these cases, it may be necessary to work faster than real time to obtain the optical flow of all the stored video in a reasonable amount of time.

The requirements described above prompted the authors to choose a well-tested and verified algorithm, providing the required accuracy. Considering all these factors and in accordance with the analysis of different algorithms and their benefits [24,25], the Lucas-Kanade method, which has good quality results with moderate computational cost, has been chosen. Specifically, the sequential implementation by Correia at the Biomedical Engineering Institute, Engineering School of the University of Porto [26,27] has been used.

Other authors have addressed the parallelization of optical flow computing systems. However, in most of the cases, the chosen solutions require specific hardware, such as those based on FPGA, on which there is abundant literature [5,28]. By contrast, this article presents three implementations of a parallelization approach which relies solely on low-cost general-purpose computers. The implemented versions are all based on the sequential implementation from Correia [26] and are the following: (a) distributed, supported by a cluster of computers; (b) parallel, supported by a shared memory multiprocessor; (c) hybrid, supported by a cluster of multiprocessors. The paper describes the characteristics of the three parallelizations mentioned and analyzes them from the point of view of their performance, because all of them perform the same computations as the sequential algorithm and thus produce the same results. The specific details of the sequential implementation of the Lucas-Kanade algorithm and the results obtained can be found in [26,27].

2 Parallelization of the optical flow

There is a variety of algorithms to perform the computation of the optical flow. Most of them are based on the classical and well-established algorithms analyzed in [24], which usually have an initial premise for their correct operation, the assumption that the illumination intensity is constant along the analyzed sequence.

Each algorithm presents some advantages and disadvantages; the main drawback of most of the algorithms is their high computational and memory costs. Some of them try to reduce these costs by sacrificing accuracy of results, i.e., they balance the cost of the algorithm against the level of accuracy.

Over the years, a lot of research has been carried out in the field of optical flow algorithms and the latter have been continuously improved, sometimes by concentrating on the algorithm itself [19,29-31], sometimes by combining two of them [32,33], and sometimes by combining with other techniques [4,16,34]. Although most optical flow algorithms were designed with the main objective of obtaining accurate results, the trade-offs between efficiency and accuracy in optical flow algorithms are highlighted in [35] as well as the importance of an efficient optical flow computation in many real-world applications. They also analyze several classical algorithms under both criteria. Alternative algorithms, designed for implementation on computers with multiple processors, have been proposed since the first steps of development of this technique.

There have been many alternatives and they have evolved along with the technology. In some cases, SIMD processor arrays with specific chips, either existing [36] or designed *ad hoc* for the computation of optical flow [13,17,37-39], have been used. General-purpose MIMD as the connection machine [40,41], networks of transputers [42], or cellular neural networks [43,44] were also used in the past.

In recent years, there have also been many implementations based on FPGA [5,15,28,45-48] and graphic processor units (GPU) [6,8,49-51]. The results of a comparative study of both technologies for real-time optical flow computation are presented in [52]. They conclude that both have similar performance, although their FPGA implementation took much longer to develop.

Some of the above methods for computing optical flow can be highlighted since they are based on the same Lucas-Kanade method used in this paper or their application appears to be similar to that described in this paper.

A system for driving assistance is presented in [17]. It detects vehicles approaching from behind and alerts the driver when performing lane change maneuvers. The system is based on images taken by a camera located in the rear of a vehicle circulating through cities and highways, i.e., under the same hostile conditions as our system. However, their model is simpler because it is limited to detecting large objects near the camera and moving in the same direction and sense. Their method is based on the determination of the vanishing point of flow from the lane mark lines and calculating the optical flow along straight lines drawn from the vanishing point. The optical flow is computed by a block-matching method using SAD (sum of absolute differences). The entire system is based on a special purpose SIMD processor called IMAPCAR implemented in a single CMOS chip that includes an array of 1×128 8-b VLIW RISC processing elements. It processes 256×240 pixel images at 30 fps. Their experimental results show 98% detection of overtaking vehicles, with no false positives, during a 30-min session circulating on a motorway in wet weather. A real-time implementation of the Lucas-Kanade algorithm on the graphics processor MaxVideo200 is presented in [51]. Due to hardware limitations, some of the calculations are performed on 8- and 16-b integer. Consequently, the results obtained are substantially worse than those obtained by Barron et al. for the same Lucas-Kanade method. In terms of real-time performance, they are able to process 252×316 pixel images in 47.8 ms, equivalent to a throughput of 21 fps.

Another implementation of the Lucas-Kanade algorithm is presented in [28], this time based on FPGA. Their method is based on the use of high-performance cameras that capture high-speed video streams, e.g., 90 fps. Using this technology, they are able to reduce the motion of objects in successive frames. Additionally, variations in light conditions are smaller due to the high frame rate, thus moving closer to meeting the constant illumination condition. In summary, a high frames-per-second rate allows simplifying the optical flow computation model and allows obtaining accurate results in real time. The division of the Lucas-Kanade algorithm into tasks is similar to that used in our method, although in [28], the pipeline is implemented using specific and reconfigurable FPGA hardware (Virtex II XC2V6000-4 Xilinx FPGA; Xilinx Inc., San Jose, CA, USA). Each pipeline stage is subdivided into simpler substages, resulting in over 70 substages using fixed point arithmetic for the most part. The throughput achieved is 1 pixel per clock cycle. Their system is capable of processing up to 170 fps with 800×600 pixel images and, although its real-time performance should be measured relative to the acquisition frame rate, it appears to be significantly high for the current state of technology.

In recent years, cluster computing technology has spread to the extent of becoming the basic platform for parallel computing. In fact, today, most powerful supercomputers are based on cluster computing [53]. However, it is unusual to find references to parallel optical flow algorithms designed to exploit the possibilities offered by clusters of processors to suit the size of the problems. In [54-56] some solutions are presented based on clusters and will be discussed in more detail.

A preliminary version of this paper [54] presents a parallelization of the Lucas-Kanade algorithm applied to the computation of optical flow on video sequences taken from a moving vehicle in real traffic. These types of images present several sources of optical flow: road objects (lines, trees, houses, panels,...), other vehicles, and also heavily changing light conditions. The method described is based on dividing the Lucas-Kanade algorithm into several tasks that must be processed sequentially, each one using a different number of images from the video sequence. These tasks are distributed among cluster nodes, balancing the load of their processors and establishing a data pipeline through which the images flow. The paper presents preliminary experimental results using a cluster of eight dual processor nodes, obtaining throughput values of 30 images per second with 502×288 pixel images and 10 fps with 720×576 pixel images. An interpolation method is also proposed to improve the quality of the optical flow obtained from video sequences taken by interlaced cameras.

The work by [55] presents a variational method based on the domain decomposition paradigm that minimizes the communication between processes and therefore is suitable for implementation in PC clusters. The implementation is based on dividing the problem into $n \times n$ subimages and sending each portion to a processor in the cluster. Two criteria for decomposition into subdomains are analyzed: the Neumann-Neumann (NN) and the balancing-Neumann-Neumann (BNN) preconditioners which are applied to a pair of synthetic 2,000 × 2,000 pixel images. Their experimental results show that the NN approach provides better results than the non-parallel version on the basis of a decomposition into 5 × 5 subdomains, obtaining increasing speed-up factors from 1.23 (5 × 5) to 3.67 (12 × 12) using between 25 and 144 processors. Processing time per frame goes from 10 down to 2 s.

The work in [56] addresses the optical flow calculation with three-dimensional images by an extension of the Horn-Shunck model to three-dimensional. They study three different multigrid discretization schemes and compare them with the Gauss-Seidel method. They conclude that the multigrid method based on Garlekin discretization very significantly improves the results obtained using Gauss-Seidel method. They also perform a parallelization of the algorithm aimed at its execution in clusters and apply it to the calculation of three-dimensional motion of the human heart using sequences of two 256 × 256 × 256 and 512 × 512 × 512 images taken by C-arm computed tomography. Their method is based on subdividing the image into several three-dimensional subsets and processing each one in a different processor. The analyzed method is well suited to the proposed application because the image just include a single object (heart), with highly localized relative movements of expansion and contraction. This fact, along with the uniformity of illumination, requires a very low communication overhead due to parallelization. The speedup using 8, 12, and 16 processors is excellent: 7.8, 11.52, and 15.21, with an efficiency close to 1, but it starts to decrease when reaching 32 processors: 28.46. The experiments were performed on an eight-node quad-processor cluster.

3 The Lucas and Kanade algorithm

The Lucas and Kanade algorithm [22,23] takes a digital video as the only data source and computes the optical flow for the corresponding image sequence. The result is a sequence of two-dimensional arrays of optical flow vectors, with each array associated to an image of the original sequence and each vector associated to an image pixel. The algorithm analyzes the sequence frame by frame and performs several tasks. Some of them require some previous and some following images of the image being processed, so the optical flow is not computed for some of the images at the beginning and at the end of the sequence.

The Lucas and Kanade algorithm computes the optical flow using a gradient based approach, so it calculates the spatiotemporal derivatives of intensity of the images. This method assumes that image intensity remains constant between frames of the sequence, a common assumption in many algorithms:

$$I(x, y, t) = I(x + u\Delta t, y + v\Delta t, t + \Delta t) \quad (1)$$

This expression, using a Taylor series and assuming differentiability, can be expressed by the motion constraint equation:

$$I_x u\delta t + I_y v\delta t + I_t \delta t = \mathcal{O}\left(u^2\delta t^2, v^2\delta t^2\right) \quad (2)$$

In a more compact form, taking δt as the time unit:

$$\nabla I(\mathbf{x}, t) \cdot \mathbf{v} + I_t(\mathbf{x}, t) = \mathcal{O}\left(\mathbf{v}^2\right) \quad (3)$$

where $\nabla I(\mathbf{x}, t)$ and $I_t(\mathbf{x}, t)$ represent the spatial gradient and temporal derivative of image brightness, respectively, and $\mathcal{O}\left(\mathbf{v}^2\right)$ indicates second order and above terms of the Taylor series expansion.

In this method, the image sequence is first convolved with a spatiotemporal Gaussian operator to eliminate noise and to smooth high contrasts that could lead to poor estimates of image derivatives. Then, according to the Barron et al. implementation, the spatiotemporal derivatives I_x, I_y, and I_t are computed with a four-point central difference.

Finally, the two velocity components, $\mathbf{v} = \left(v_x, v_y\right)$, are obtained by a weighted least squares fit with local first-order constraints, assuming a constant model for $\mathbf{v}$ in each spatial neighborhood $\mathcal{N}$ and by minimizing

$$\sum_{x \in \mathcal{N}} \mathbf{W}^2(\mathbf{x}) \left[\nabla I(\mathbf{x}, t) \cdot \mathbf{v} + I_t(\mathbf{x}, t)\right]^2 \quad (4)$$

where $\mathbf{W}(\mathbf{x})$ denotes a window function that assigns more weight to the center. The solution is obtained from

$$\mathbf{v} = \left(\mathbf{A}^T \mathbf{W}^2 \mathbf{A}\right)^{-1} \mathbf{A}^T \mathbf{W}^2 \mathbf{b} \quad (5)$$

where, for n points $\mathbf{x}_i \in \mathcal{N}$ at a single time t

- $\mathbf{A} = [\nabla I(\mathbf{x}_1), ..., \nabla I(\mathbf{x}_n)]^T$
- $\mathbf{W} = \text{diag}[\mathbf{W}(\mathbf{x}_1), ..., \mathbf{W}(\mathbf{x}_n)]$
- $\mathbf{b} = -(I_t(\mathbf{x}_1), ..., I_t(\mathbf{x}_n))^T$

The product $\mathbf{A}^T \mathbf{W}^2 \mathbf{A}$ is a 2 × 2 matrix given by:

$$\mathbf{A}^T \mathbf{W}^2 \mathbf{A} = \begin{bmatrix} \sum \mathbf{W}^2(\mathbf{x}) I_x^2(\mathbf{x}) & \sum \mathbf{W}^2(\mathbf{x}) I_x(\mathbf{x}) I_y(\mathbf{x}) \\ \sum \mathbf{W}^2(\mathbf{x}) I_y(\mathbf{x}) I_x(\mathbf{x}) & \sum \mathbf{W}^2(\mathbf{x}) I_y^2(\mathbf{x}) \end{bmatrix} \quad (6)$$

where all the sums are taken over points in the neighborhood $\mathcal{N}$.

3.1 Implementation

In this section, the sequential implementation of the Lucas-Kanade algorithm proposed by Correia [26,27] is described because this implementation has been used as the starting point for the parallelization.

This implementation starts by smoothing the image sequence with a spatiotemporal Gaussian filter to attenuate temporal and spatial aliasing, as shown in [24]. As it applies a smoothing Gaussian filter with $\sigma = 3.2$, it requires 25 pixels: the central pixel and 4σ (12) pixels on each side of this center pixel:

$$\frac{1}{\sqrt{2\pi}\sigma} e^{-\frac{x^2}{2\sigma^2}} \tag{7}$$

This one-dimensional symmetric Gaussian filter is applied three times, first on the temporal 't' dimension, then on the spatial 'X' dimension, and finally on the spatial 'Y' dimension. Therefore, it needs 12 pixels on each side of the center pixel, and 4σ images (12) previous and next to the image being processed.

The result of applying the smoothing Gaussian filter on an image can be seen in Figure 1, which shows the original image, Figure 1a, and the three steps, the result for the temporal filter, Figure 1b, for the spatial filters, Figure 1c, and the global result, Figure 1d.

After smoothing, the next step of the Lucas and Kanade algorithm is to compute the spatiotemporal derivatives for the three dimensions: t, x and y (I_t, I_x, I_y). Using the previously computed image, smoothed on t, X and Y, and applying a numerical approximation, the derivatives (I_t, I_x, I_y) are computed separately. The method used is the 5-point central differences of Gregory-Newton and the derivative function for the central point is

$$f'(x_3) = \frac{f(x_1) - 8f(x_2) + 8f(x_4) - f(x_5)}{12h} \tag{8}$$

Taking $h = 1$ because the distance between two consecutive pixels is 1, the one-dimensional array to be used as convolution coefficient mask in the computation of the partial derivatives is obtained as follows:

$$\left[\frac{1}{12}, \quad \frac{-8}{12}, \quad 0, \quad \frac{8}{12}, \quad \frac{-1}{12} \right] \tag{9}$$

Then, for each pixel of the image $I_{x,y}^t$, two additional pixels on each side of the central one are needed on each dimension. Two pixels to the right and left $\left(I_{x-2,y}^t, I_{x-1,y}^t, I_{x,y}^t, I_{x+1,y}^t, I_{x+2,y}^t \right)$ are taken, as well as two pixels above and below $\left(I_{x,y-2}^t, I_{x,y-1}^t, I_{x,y}^t, I_{x,y+1}^t, I_{x,y+2}^t \right)$, and one pixel in the two previous and in the two following images $\left(I_{x,y}^{t-2}, I_{x,y}^{t-1}, I_{x,y}^t, I_{x,y}^{t+1}, I_{x,y}^{t+2} \right)$. Thus, the temporal gradient of an image requires at least five consecutive images of the sequence. The results of these convolutions are the estimates of the partial derivatives, which are shown in Figure 2, and represent the temporal, Figure 2a, horizontal, Figure 2b, vertical, Figure 2c, and global intensity changes, Figure 2d.

Finally, the velocity vectors associated to each pixel of the image are computed from the spatiotemporal partial derivatives previously computed. This is done by using a spatial neighborhood matrix of 5×5 pixels, centered

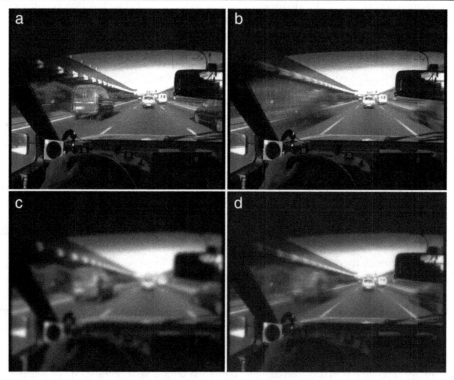

Figure 1 Image smoothing in three dimensions: t, x, and y. **(a)** Original image. **(b)** Smoothing in t. **(c)** Smoothing in x and y. **(d)** Smoothing in t, x, and y.

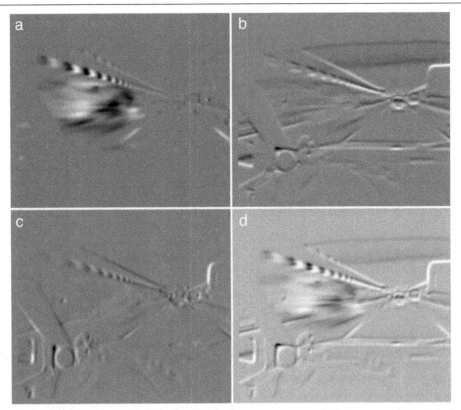

Figure 2 Partial derivatives of an image in three dimensions: *t*, *x* and *y*. (a) Derivative in *t*. **(b)** Derivative in *x*. **(c)** Derivative in *y*. **(d)** Derivatives in *t*, *x*, and *y*.

on each pixel, and a one-dimensional weight matrix, $(0.0625, 0.25, 0.375, 0.25, 0.0625)$, [24]. The noise parameters used are $\sigma_1 = 0.08$, $\sigma_2 = 1.0$, and $\sigma_p = 2.0$ [57]. The estimated velocity vectors whose highest eigenvalue of $A^T W^2 A$ is less than 0.05 are considered unreliable (noise) and are discarded [24].

3.2   Results of the sequential algorithm

Figure 3 shows the optical flow computed for the image of Figure 1a. The processing steps have been analyzed and are shown in Figures 1 and 2. The original image corresponds to a three-lane highway. The vehicle carrying the camera is overtaking the vehicle on the right while it is being overtaken (quite fast) by the vehicle on the left. This introduces some noise in the results, since it would require a higher temporal resolution to correctly handle the movement of objects at such speed.

Figure 4 shows two images of a video sequence that has been processed with this algorithm and also the optical flow obtained after applying this algorithm. In this sequence, a vehicle can be observed on the right going slower than the vehicle where the camera is installed, and a second vehicle on the left is changing lanes. Finally, a traffic light panel can be seen above. The optical flow generated by these three objects and by the road

lines and other elements on the shoulder are shown in Figure 4.

4   Sequential algorithm tasks and dependencies

This section analyzes in some detail the dependencies among the tasks of the sequential algorithm described in Section 3.1. The pseudocode of the algorithm's main loop is shown below, including the task list with the task parameters.

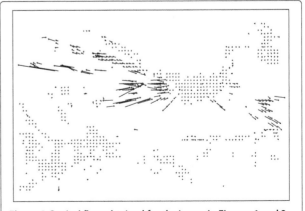

Figure 3 Optical flow obtained for the image in Figures 1 and 2.

```
/* Sequential algorithm main loop */
while (readfile (fname, time, raw_pic, ...)> 0) {
   T_Smooth (raw_pic, s_T_buff, ...);
   X_Smooth (s_T_buff, s_TX_buff, ...);
   Y_Smooth (s_TX_buff, s_TXY_buff, ...);
   t_derivate (s_TXY_buff, diff_buff.It, ...);
   x_derivate (s_TXY_buff, diff_buff.Ix, ...);
   y_derivate (s_TXY_buff, diff_buff.Iy, ...);
   velocities (diff_buff.Ix, diff_buff.Iy, diff_buff.It, vels_pic, ...);
   out_velocities (full_name, "Full", vels_pic, ...);
}
```

The tasks mentioned in the algorithm's main loop are as follows:

- **read_file** reads images from disk and passes them to `T_smooth`.
- **T_smooth** receives images from `read_file` and passes them to `X_smooth`. Performs the temporal smoothing, using the current image as well as the n previous images and n following images, with $n = 4 \cdot \sigma$. This calculation involves *a very strong dependence* between each image and all those around it. In fact, every image depends on another $8 \cdot \sigma$ images. With a value of $\sigma = 3.2$ that means the 12 previous and the 12 following frames.
- **X_smooth** receives images from `T_smooth` and passes them to `Y_smooth`. Performs the spatial smoothing of the images on the x coordinate.
- **Y_smooth** receives images from `X_smooth` and passes them to `t_derivative`, `x_derivative`, and `y_derivative`. Performs the spatial smoothing of the images on the y coordinate.
- **t_derivative** receives images from `Y_smooth`, calculates the partial derivative of the images with respect to t (`It`), and passes it to `velocities`. Five images are required, two previous and two following the current one. This calculation is affected by a *very strong dependency* of each image with the four images surrounding it.
- **x_derivative** receives images from `Y_smooth`, calculates the partial derivative of the images with respect to x (`Ix`), and passes it to `velocities`.
- **y_derivative** receives images from `Y_smooth`, calculates the partial derivative of the images with respect to y (`Iy`), and passes it to `velocities`.
- **velocities** receives the partial derivatives with respect to t, x, and y of the images (`It`, `Ix`, and `Iy`) from `t_derivative`, `x_derivative`, and

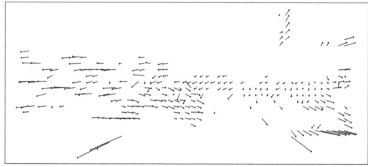

Figure 4 Frames 10 and 20 and optical flow from frame 15.

y_derivative. Using these partial derivatives, it calculates each pixel velocity as a pair (v_x, v_y) and passes it to out_velocities.

- **out_velocities** receives velocity vectors from velocities and processes them to generate the appropriate output. For example, it calculates statistics (splitflow) or converts them to PostScript (psflow) to visualize the results. Finally, it writes the calculated speeds to disk.

Reviewing the major tasks that make up the application reveals a problem: the execution of the tasks must follow a strict order. Therefore, the parallel execution of the tasks inside a single iteration is not possible because their order must be respected. However, it is possible to overlap the execution of tasks over different images. Moreover, there are strong dependencies between the input data, as T_smooth and t_derivatives need to know not only the image being processed but also the neighbouring ones. Therefore, the optical flow from different images cannot be calculated in parallel without processing the other images.

5 Parallel algorithm

In order to parallelize the Lucas-Kanade algorithm, the dependencies described in Section 4 were the starting point to build a hybrid scheme. Data and computation have been parallelized by dividing the input image into subimages and distributing the tasks to be performed on each pixel. This form of combined algorithm is much more flexible than using parallelization on data or on tasks separately.

If only data parallelization were considered by dividing the images and executing the algorithm on every data subset on a medium-sized cluster (64 or more processors), very small images have to be considered. Even if large images are taken into account (2,000 × 1,200 pixels), the size of the subimages (250 × 150) is too small. On the other hand, to obtain correct results, pixel dependencies have to be considered for smoothing on all three coordinates and also when calculating the derivatives. Solving these dependencies requires introducing additional pixels, usually known as border pixels. If many subpictures are used, the number of border pixels (ghost or halo pixels) increases and the overhead costs of this algorithm would become unacceptable.

If only the tasks parallelization analyzed in Section 4 is considered, the task number is too low, even when the larger tasks are distributed between several nodes for load balancing. Initially, there are seven starting tasks, not including I/O. Even if some of those tasks are doubled or tripled, the execution does not benefit from a cluster with more than 14 to 16 processors. Furthermore,

in this scheme, dependencies do not have to be taken into account between pixels but between tasks. T_smooth and t_derivative tasks require knowing all of the images because previous and further images are needed when performing these computations. The best way to solve these dependencies is by using a pipeline. Images have to progress through the pipeline stages. To balance the duration of different stages, the longer stages have to be replicated. This solution solves one of the problems, dependencies between tasks, but not the scalability problem.

If both solutions are combined, establishing a task pipeline and partitioning input images, an easily scalable and flexible scheme is obtained. The idea is to have a full pipeline for each subimage, i.e., several pipelines of N stages, with some of these replicated. The algorithm dependencies are solved and the border overhead is minimized because images are divided into a small number of subimages. Adding the border pixels allows treating each subimage independently. Smoothing on the X and Y coordinates uses 25 pixels, 12 on each side of the central pixel, hence, each subimage needs 12 more pixels. Therefore, to divide 1,280 × 1,024 images into four subimages (2 × 2), four 652 × 524 subimages are necessary, by adding 12 pixels on the X and Y axis. In this way, the border pixels are overlapped, and every subimage is completely independent of others.

If the number of processors available is small, the use of a single pipeline is sufficient. If the number of processors is lower than the number of pipeline stages, several tasks can be grouped to balance the load of the stages. This analysis will be addressed in Subsection 6.1.

If there are many processors available, several pipelines have to be built so that all processors can work in parallel. The number of pipelines is calculated by dividing the number of available processors by the number of pipeline stages.

Section 6 shows how the pipeline could be increased up to 16 stages. If every image is divided into 64 subimages, 1,024 processors can be used due to the scalability of this model. Obviously, using 1,024 processors would make sense for working with a high number of large images (large sequences or very high temporal resolution). In most cases, a 16 to 64 processor cluster will be enough to process the input sequences in a reasonable time.

To show the flexibility of the proposed algorithm, three different implementations using 4, 8, and 16 processors, respectively, are presented in Sections 7, 8, and 9. The first implementation runs on a shared memory computer, the second one on a distributed memory computer, and the last one is a hybrid implementation executed on a distributed system in which each node is a shared memory multiprocessor.

6   Pipeline structure

As shown in Section 5, a pipeline structure is proposed as the main idea to exploit parallelism. The optical flow application is divided into independent modules to be connected in the same sequential order of the tasks to be executed for each single image. When a module finishes its processing task for an image, it starts executing the same task for the next image. This way, each module is working on a different image at a certain time.

The objective of this structure is to create a thread for each of the tasks shown in Section 4. This way, a different thread is assigned to each task and will execute its function on each of the images, in parallel with other threads that will be executing their function on different images.

The derivatives computation is not too demanding. However, the three tasks that solve the derivatives are grouped in order to simplify communication because the three tasks get the same input information from `Y_smooth` and send the results to `velocities`. Consequently, the mapping task-thread is as follows:

- `in_th` executes the task `read_file`.
- `smoothT_th` executes the task `T_smooth`.
- `smoothX_th` executes the task `X_smooth`.

- `smoothY_th` executes the task `Y_smooth`.
- `diff_th` executes the task `derivatives` that includes the derivative computation in `t`, `x`, and `y`.
- `vels_th` executes the task `velocities`.
- `out_th` executes the task `out_velocities` that includes the `psflow`, `splitflow`, and writes results to the disk.

Because the time taken for each stage is different, several synchronizations will be introduced in the pipeline. As usual, buffers with synchronization mechanisms have to be introduced between threads to allow communication between them. Figure 5 shows threads and buffers used for communication in the shared memory pipeline.

In order to measure the time spent on each task, a sequential implementation has been run on a single cluster node. Two image sizes have been used as input data: 720×576 and 502×288 pixels. The most important result is the relationship between the times spent by different tasks, but not the time each task spends individually. Table 1 shows the amount of time spent on each task and its weight on the total time spent by the algorithm.

An important aspect to be pointed out is that the execution time ratio for the tasks is constant even when

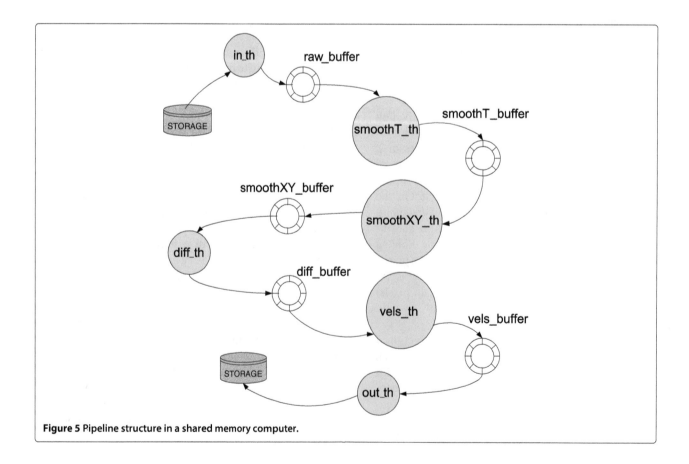

Figure 5 Pipeline structure in a shared memory computer.

Table 1 Execution time per task (ms)

Task	Time 502 × 288		Time 720 × 576	
read_file	0.9 ms	0.1%	0.9 ms	0%
T_smooth	12 ms	6.9%	40 ms	7.6%
X_smooth	8 ms	4.6%	30 ms	5.7%
Y_smooth	7 ms	4.1%	25 ms	4.8%
t_derivative	7 ms	4.1%	25 ms	4.8%
xy_derivatives	3 ms	1.7%	10 ms	1.9%
velocities	130 ms	74.4%	370 ms	70.4%
out_velocities	7 ms	4.1%	25 ms	4.8%

changing the image size. This fact allows using the same approach when parallelization is addressed, without taking into account the image size.

Another aspect to be considered is that the temporal smooth is slower than the spatial smooth tasks. This is because spatial smooth works with just a single image, while temporal smooth requires several images preceding and following the one being processed. The main difference between the smooth on the X axis and the smooth on the Y axis is that the image can be in cache memory when the latter is executed. In the same way that temporal smooth is slower than spatial smooth, the computation of the temporal derivative is slower than the computation of spatial derivatives. The reason is again the need of the temporal derivative to use several images, clearly spoiling the memory hierarchy behavior.

6.1 Pipeline stages

Table 1 shows that the execution times for different tasks are not well balanced, and this situation has to be changed. Taking into account the time spent on each task, a new organization of tasks is proposed. The main reason supporting the redesign of the pipeline stages is the high execution time for the velocities function. The proposed solution is to parallelize the slower task (velocities) since it does not depend on other images, but on the derivatives with respect to t, x, and y, i.e., It, Ix, and Iy.

With the purpose of obtaining a higher speedup, the pipeline has initially been proposed for 16 processors, even if there are fewer processors. The scheme is valid as it is flexible enough to allow grouping tasks to adapt to

Table 2 Pipeline times (ms) and theoretical speedups

Nodes	Distribution	ms per 502 × 288 image	ms per 720 × 576 image
16	4 nodes execute the _smooth and _derivatives tasks	$T = \max(12, 8, 7, 7 + 3) = 12$	$T = \max(40, 30, 25, 25 + 10) = 40$
	12 nodes execute the velocities and out_velocities tasks	$T = 137/12 = 12$ $T_{img} = \max(12, 12) = 12$ ms Max speedup $= 174/12 = 14.5$	$T = 395/12 = 33$ $T_{img} = \max(40, 33) = 40$ ms Max speedup $= 525/40 = 13.1$
8	1 node executes the T_smooth and X_smooth tasks	$T = 12 + 8 = 20$	$T = 40 + 30 = 70$
	1 node executes the Y_smooth and _derivatives tasks	$T = 7 + 7 + 3 = 17$	$T = 25 + 25 + 10 = 60$
	6 nodes execute the velocities and out_velocities tasks	$T = 137/6 = 23$ $T_{img} = \max(20, 17, 23) = 23$ ms Max speedup $= 174/23 = 7.6$	$T = 395/6 = 66$ $T_{img} = \max(70, 60, 66) = 70$ ms Max speedup $= 525/70 = 7.5$
4	1 node executes every task except velocities	$T = 12 + 8 + 7 + 7 + 3 = 37$	$T = 40 + 30 + 25 + 25 + 10 = 130$
	3 nodes execute the velocities and out_velocities tasks	$T = 137/3 = 46$ $T_{img} = \max(37, 46) = 46$ ms Max speedup $= 174/46 = 3.8$	$T = 395/3 = 132$ $T_{img} = \max(130, 132) = 132$ ms Max speedup $= 525/132 = 4$

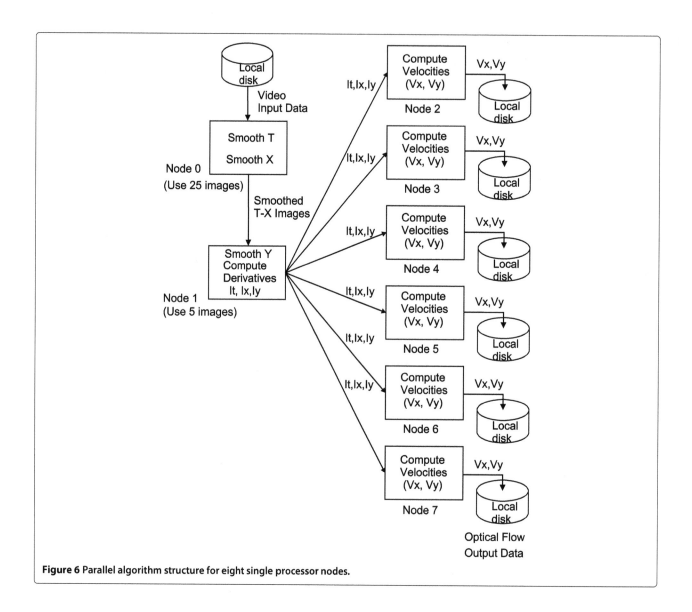

Figure 6 Parallel algorithm structure for eight single processor nodes.

other situations. Table 2 shows how the task distribution is scheduled in the pipeline for 4, 8, and 16 nodes and the pipeline time per image for every case. Figure 6 details the task scheduling for each node when using an 8-node computer.

If a distributed memory computer is used, the communication time has to be taken into account and will depend on the network used (Gigabit, Myrinet,...). However, this time is not negligible and tends to be around several milliseconds. This approach is also valid for a shared memory multiprocessor, minimizing the communication overhead.

7   Shared memory version with hyperthreading

The first implementation described used a shared memory biprocessor with hyperthreading (i.e., four virtual

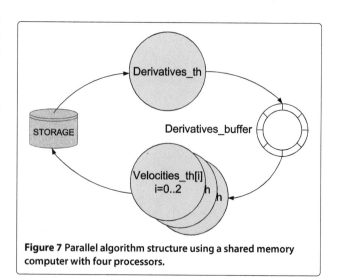

Figure 7 Parallel algorithm structure using a shared memory computer with four processors.

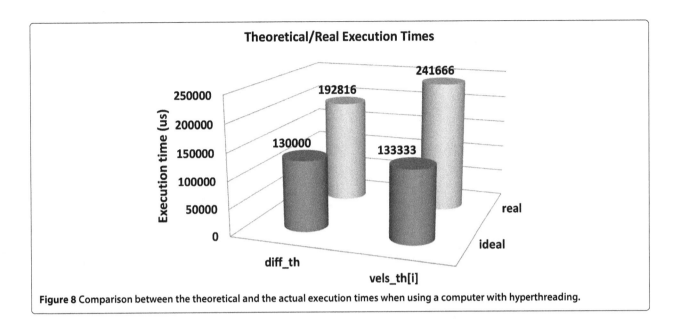

Figure 8 Comparison between the theoretical and the actual execution times when using a computer with hyperthreading.

processors). Taking into consideration the parallel algorithm proposed in Section 6.1 for four processors, the following grouping of tasks has been made:

- **diff_th** performs the tasks `read_file`, `T_smooth`, `X_smooth`, `Y_smooth` and `derivatives`.

- **vels_th** performs tasks `velocities` and `out_velocities`.

As the `vels_th` takes three times as long as `diff_th`, the idea is to execute three `vels_th` threads so that the delay is compensated. Furthermore, this structure can be carried out because tasks `velocities` and `out_velocities` do not depend on other images, instead, they only depend on the partial derivatives of a single image, `It`, `Ix`, and `Iy`. In this way, execution times are better balanced and there is a better fit to the architecture used with four threads running in four virtual processors. The communication scheme between threads is shown in Figure 7.

When measuring the execution times, it can be observed that the behavior of the threads is greatly influenced by the hyperthreading technology of the processors. Figure 8 shows the differences between the execution times theoretically calculated in Section 6 and the actual execution times measured when executing the application.

In Figure 8, it can be seen that actual execution times are much longer than theoretical times. Moreover, it can be seen that threads `vels_th` suffer higher delays (81% slower) than `diff_th` threads (48% slower). This is because these threads, being all clones, compete for

the same functional units of virtual processors, producing conflicts and delays.

8 Message-passing version

The second implementation of the parallelized Lucas-Kanade algorithm is based on distributed memory with message-passing communications. This version has been developed and implemented on an eight-node cluster.

The tasks mentioned in Table 1 have been assigned to the eight nodes of the cluster, and the MPI message-passing standard has been used for communications.

To optimize the communications between nodes, asynchronous non-blocking messages have been used so that communications and computing are overlapped. Consequently, while a node is processing image i, it has already started a non-blocking send with the results of processing the previous image (i-1), and it has also started a non-blocking reception to simultaneously receive the next image to be processed (i+1). In this way, simultaneous submissions, receptions, and computing are allowed in each node.

Moreover, persistent messages have been used to avoid building and destroying the data structures used for each message. This design decision has been possible because the information traveling between two given nodes always has the same structure and the same size so that the skeleton of the message can be reused.

The general communication scheme between different nodes is shown in Figure 6.

The scheme employed for the distribution of tasks over nodes was as follows:

- **Node 0**: Its pseudocode follows

```
/* Node-0 code. Use persistent messages and asynchronous communications */
   ...
  while (n_bytes = readfile (fname, raw_pic, ...)){
  MPI_Wait(&request[comp], &status); /* Wait for the oldest send to finish */

  T_smooth(raw_pic, s_T_buff[comp], ...);
  X_smooth(s_T_buff[comp], s_TX_buff[comp], ...);

  comp = (comp + 1) % N_SMOOTH_T_BUFFERS;
  out = (out + 1) % N_SMOOTH_T_BUFFERS;

  MPI_ISend(&request[out]); /* Start the next asynchronous sending op. */
}
```

Node-0 code performs the following tasks: it reads the images of the video sequence from the disk, then it performs the temporal smoothing (using the current image as well as the previous 12 and the next 12 images) and performs the spatial smoothing on the x coordinate. Finally, it sends the image smoothed on t and on x to node 1.

- **Node 1**: The pseudocode representing the job completed at node 1 follows

Node-1 performs the following tasks: it receives the images already smoothed on t and x, from node 0, then it performs the spatial smoothing on the y coordinate, and computes the partial derivative with respect to t of the image (using five images, the current one, plus the previous two and the next two). Finally, it sends the processed image to the other nodes, from 2 to 7, selecting the target in a cyclical way.

- **Rest of the nodes**: The pseudocode that describes the work done at the rest of the nodes follows

```
/* Node-0 code. Start an asynchronous receiving operation */
MPI_IRecv(&request_in[in]);

/* Start send/recv operations to overlap communication & computation */
...
while (working) {
   in = (in + 1) % N_SMOOTH_Y_BUFFERS;

   MPI_IRecv(&request_in[in]); /* Start the next asynchronous receiving operation */

   MPI_Wait(&request_in[comp_in], &status); /* Wait for the previous
    receive to finish*/

   if ((status.MPI_TAG == END) ||
       (status.MPI_ERROR != 0)) end();

   MPI_Wait(&request_out[dest][comp_out], &status); /* Wait for the oldest send */

   Y_smooth(X_s_buff[comp_in], Y_s_buff[comp_in], ...);
   t_derivatives(s_Y_buff[comp_in], buff[dest][comp_out].It, ...);

   MPI_ISend(&request_out[dest][comp_out]); /* Start the next asynchronous sending
operation*/

   comp_in = (comp_in + 1) % N_SMOOTH_Y_BUFFERS;
   if (++dest == nprocs) {
      dest = FIRST_PROC_VELS;
      comp_out = (comp_out + 1) % N_DIFF_BUFFERS;
      out = (out + 1) % N_DIFF_BUFFERS;
   }
}
```

```
/* Rest of the nodes. Start an asynchronous receiving operation */
MPI_IRecv(&buff[comp], ...);

while (working) {
    in = (in + 1) % N_DIFF_BUFFERS;

    MPI_IRecv(&request_in[in]); /* Start the next asynchronous receiving operation */

    MPI_Wait(&request_in[comp], &status); /* Wait for the previous receive to finish*/

    if ((status.MPI_TAG == END) ||
        (status.MPI_ERROR != 0)) end();

    x_derivative (buff[comp].s_TXY, Ix, ...);
    y_derivative (buff[comp].s_TXY, Iy, ...);
    velocities (Ix, Iy, buff[comp].It, vels_pic, ...);
    out_velocities(full_name, vels_pic, ...);
    comp = (comp + 1) % N_DIFF_BUFFERS;
}
```

Each node from 2 to 7 performs the following tasks: it receives images already smoothed in t, x, and y, as well as the derivative with respect to t (It) of the image from node 1, then it calculates the partial derivatives with respect to x and y of the image, (Ix and Iy). Starting from the derivatives in t, x , and y (It, Ix, and Iy) of the image, it computes the speed of each pixel as a pair (v_x, v_y) and formats the computed velocities (statistics, etc.) before writing them to disk.

Task xy_derivatives has been taken from the intermediate node to the end nodes to reduce the size of the messages. Instead of sending three matrices per image (It, Ix, and Iy), two matrices are sent, (It and the image smoothed on t, x, and y). The task loads are not so well balanced but, by reducing the network traffic, the performance improves due to the communication time being shorter.

Table 3 shows the mean values for the time spent on each task and the global computing time spent by each node with every image.

From the data shown at Table 3, it can be observed that regardless of the waiting time spent on communication calls, the load is fairly well balanced between nodes 0 and 2 to 7. Node 1 is out of balance, as envisaged in the previous

paragraph, and in actual terms the imbalance is even higher as will be shown. The theoretical estimates were made from the times obtained by executing the sequential version, which executes everything within the same node (and the same processor). Processing multiple images in the sequential version implies a heavy use of memory that can sometimes produce a high rate of page replacements, and even thrashing. The use of memory is not so heavy in the message-passing version, since the number of images handled by each node is much smaller.

9 Message-passing and threads

This section looks at a third implementation, implemented with 16 processors. The idea is based on maximizing the use of resources available in the machine. As already mentioned, a cluster of eight dual processors with hyperthreading nodes is used. However, due to the bad results obtained with hyperthreading shown in Section 7, only the real processors have been used instead of the virtual ones.

This implementation is based on threads and MPI. The goal is to run several threads in each node, thereby taking advantage of the existence of two processors on every single node. The threads in the different nodes communicate using MPI.

Due to the single-threaded MPI implementation used, it is only possible to make invocations to the MPI library from a single thread. Thus, a single thread responsible for communications has been assigned to each node to send and receive messages, and it is the only one interacting with the MPI library. This thread is normally suspended and only wakes up when data to send or receive are available.

The communication between nodes is asynchronous to overlap communication and computation. Also, messages

Table 3 Mean time per task (ms)

Node	0		1		2-7	
Time	read_file	1.05	Y_smooth	21.82	xy_derivatives	9.92
per	T_smooth	36.29	t_derivative	21.55	velocities	369.88
task	X_smooth	25.37			out_velocities	24.92
Global		62.71		43.37		404.72

are persistent to reuse their skeleton, as in the implementation described in Section 8.

A sending window has been implemented in order to maximize the overlapping of data communication and computation. A variable pointing to the next element to be sent and a variable pointing to the next message to be confirmed by node are maintained. The communication buffers are circular allowing the same memory locations to be reused for different images along the execution of the program.

The division of tasks is based on the algorithm for 16 processors described in Subsection 6.1. In any case, the distribution of tasks to nodes is the same as in the previous version, shown in Figure 6. The differences are found inside each node as described in the following subsections, since multiple threads run in each node as shown in Figure 9.

9.1 Node 0

Three of the tasks described in Section 6 run on node 0. The first two, `read_file` and `T_smooth`, are grouped in

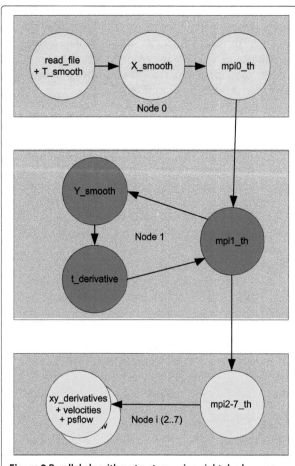

Figure 9 Parallel algorithm structure using eight dual processor nodes, with MPI and threads.

a single thread, since the former takes a very short time, and `X_smooth` runs on another thread. A third thread, `mpi0_th`, is responsible for communication of this node with the next one (node 1).

9.2 Node 1

Two of the tasks described in Section 6 run on node 1. One thread executes the task `Y_smooth` and an other thread executes the task `t_derivative`. A third thread, `mpi1_th`, is responsible for communication of this node with node 0 and with nodes 2 to 7.

9.3 Nodes 2 to 7

Three of the tasks described in Section 6 run on each of the nodes 2 to 7. An important difference from the other nodes is the absence of dependencies between images within these tasks. Consequently, a single thread can handle all three tasks for a given image, reusing the data in memory.

Specifically, there will be one thread per processor (`velocities_th[0-1]`). Each is responsible for the computation of the derivatives in X and Y (`xy_derivatives`), the computation of the velocity vectors (`velocities`), the formatting of the output (using `psflow` and `splitflow`), and dumping the output to disk (`out_velocities`). An additional thread, `mpi2-7_th`, will handle communications with node 1.

10 Results

Figure 10 shows the speedup reached by different versions. This section analyzes the results for each version implemented.

10.1 Cluster architecture

Parallelization has been carried out in a generic way in order to be sufficiently general to serve for different architectures, either based on distributed or on shared memory. Performance measures have been obtained using an architecture based on distributed multiprocessor nodes so that the evaluation of the different implementations has been possible.

Specifically, a cluster of eight identical nodes has been used. Each node contains two Intel Xeon 2.4 GHz processors and 4 GB of main memory. The system runs under a Linux operating system - Ubuntu distribution. The nodes are connected to a Gigabit network, through a conventional switch. This architecture was chosen because distributed memory systems are economical, easy to assemble, and of widespread use. Each node is a dual processor using hyperthreading, so that it apparently has four processors. However, although four virtual processors apparently run as four physical processors, the target performance cannot be as high because only some processor

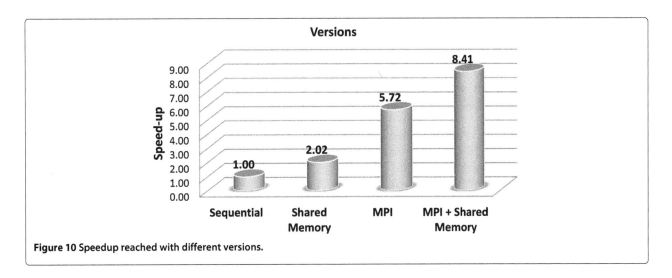

Figure 10 Speedup reached with different versions.

components are replicated while others must be shared between processes or threads.

10.2 Shared memory version

With the shared memory version, a speedup of 2.02 was obtained, i.e., it runs twice as fast as the sequential version. Without taking into account the type of operations performed by the application and the details of the processors, a higher improvement would be expected.

A first reason to explain the relatively low speedup is the amount of memory needed by the application. The sequential version needs a much lower amount of memory than the threads version, and memory accesses are performed in a more sequential way so that processing of an image finishes before moving on to the next one. In the case of shared memory, several images are handled simultaneously, each one corresponding to a different processing time. It also needs to access scattered memory positions, so it requires a larger memory and uses it in a less efficient way because of the irregular memory access pattern.

Another cause for the low speedup is the use of hyperthreading technology. While every node apparently has four processors (dual-hyperthreading processor), there are just two actual processors. Analyzing the application code, it can be noted that the calculations basically consist of floating point operations (floating point square roots, multiplications, etc.). Considering the usual structure of current processors, it is clear that the floating point functional units are not sufficiently replicated.

In an attempt to distinguish inefficiencies due to the parallel implementation - such those due to distribution of tasks - from speed-up limitations due to the supporting architecture, a common, highly parallelizable application example has been used as a reference. The example is the matrix multiplication and the speedup reached in this case is 2.7, far from the theoretical maximum 4. From

this result, the application speedup obtained, 2.02, can be considered as reasonable.

10.3 Message-passing version

Sending a message from one node to another may be very time-consuming, depending on the network characteristics and the amount of information being transferred. However, communication between nodes is asynchronous so, at least in part, it may be possible to overlap communication operations (both sending and receiving) with CPU processing time. Due to the non-blocking characteristics of the application communications, the program does not need to wait for sending or receiving operations to finish, but instead it immediately begins to perform the calculation on the data already available.

With this communication scheme based on non-blocking and persistent messages, a higher speedup than the one shown in Figure 10 could be expected. The analysis of the execution time of all tasks, both in the sequential and in the message-passing versions, shows that the time spent was very similar, which points to communications as the origin of the performance problem. Lower than expected performance of the message-passing implementation is mainly due to the large volume of data exchanged.

There are two types of messages: those exchanged between nodes 0 and 1 and the messages that node 1 sends to the end nodes (2 to 7). Node 0 sends data after applying a smooth function to the image on coordinates T and X. The amount of data sent for each image is then equivalent to a floating point number per image pixel. The image resolution used for experimentation is 720×576 pixels, so the total data sent per image are $720 \cdot 576 = 414,720$ float elements, or $414,720$ float $\cdot 4$(bytes/float) $= 1,658,880$ B.

The network used is a Gigabit-Ethernet. The performance measured for this network was found to be between 770 and 880 Mbps. Taking an average rate of 800

Mbps, the delivery time per message sent from node 0 to node 1 would be

$$1,658,880 \text{ B} \cdot 8(\text{bits/byte})/800 \text{ Mbps} = 16.58 \text{ ms}.$$

As for the size of the message sent by node 1 to provide end nodes with the data they need, it must be noted that it is sent after t derivatives are computed (I_t). In fact, not only such derivatives but also smoothed images have to be sent to allow computing x and y derivatives. Therefore, two matrices as large as the matrix sent from node 0 to node 1 have to be sent, needing twice as much time.

Summarizing, the large amount of data transferred explains why the performance achieved is lower than the theoretical maximum.

Anyway, with this parallelization scheme, the computation of the optical flow achieves a throughput of 30 images per second with 502×288 pixel images. For 720×576 pixel images, the throughput obtained is ten images per second.

10.4 Message-passing and shared memory version

The last version considered tries to take advantage of the previous two. This combined version parallelizes at node-level using threads and at the network level by making use of MPI.

Comparing this version with the message-passing one, it must be noted that the task distribution among nodes is the same in both versions. It was considered important to compare both versions in order to analyze the benefit of introducing shared memory mechanisms. In this case, the number of threads created, as well as their features, makes it easier to appreciate the performance reachable with this technique. In comparison with the message-passing version, the speedup of the final version is 1.47, which is quite significant.

With this version, the computation of the optical flow achieves a throughput of 45 images per second with 502×288 pixel images. For the 720×576 resolution, 15 images per second throughput is obtained. Note that in both cases the optical flow is computed for every image.

11 Conclusion

This paper addresses the parallelization of optical flow calculation. A flexible and scalable parallelization scheme has been described, based on dividing each image into several subimages in order to process each one through a software pipeline. This pipeline allows to respect dependencies between different computation stages. Each pipeline step performs an optical flow computation stage. Stages exhibiting a greater need for computation are replicated to balance the time spent on each pipeline stage. The number of subimages which each image is divided into depends on the number of processors available, thus ensuring high scalability. This parallelization scheme has

been developed starting from a dependency analysis of the Lucas-Kanade algorithm, using a sequential implementation developed at the University of Porto.

Three different versions of the proposed scheme have been implemented and executed on a cluster of dual hyperthreading processor nodes to evaluate its flexibility and scalability. These versions are as follows:

- A shared memory version, using threads. It yields a speedup of 2.02 on a four-processor system.
- A distributed memory version using MPI. In an eight-processor system it yields a speedup of 5.72.
- A hybrid version, using threads and MPI to take advantage of the fact that each node is a multiprocessor - a dual hyperthreading processor. In an eight-node system, with two processors per node, the speedup reached is 8.41.

The speedup obtained in all three cases is very satisfactory, clearly showing the feasibility of the proposed scheme, as well as its flexibility and scalability. If more than 16 processors are going to be used, this task pipeline can be combined with image partitioning, having a full pipeline consisting of 16 stages per subimage.

Once implemented, these versions have been used to calculate optical flow video sequences taken in variable natural-light conditions and with a moving camera. In fact, the camera was installed on board a vehicle traveling on conventional open roads. Despite the challenging conditions of these experiments, the results obtained were satisfactory.

This parallelization scheme can be combined with GPUs. Each task of the pipeline can be implemented as a kernel in a GPU to improve the performance, as current GPUs are very powerful and affordable. As three different versions of the task pipeline have been proposed, with 4, 8, or 16 processors, the solution can be easily adapted to a different number of GPUs to take advantage of a GPU cluster.

Also this parallelization scheme can be easily transported to many processor architectures as the Intel MIC (Many Integrated Core) architecture (Intel Corp, Santa Clara, CA, USA). The Intel MIC has 60 cores, it is based on 4-way SMT (simultaneous multithreading) cores, each one containing a 512-b vector unit (SIMD). In this architecture, both vectorization and a high degree of parallelism (240 threads) are required to achieve good performance. The proposed parallelization that we have described in this paper can be easily adapted to this Intel MIC architecture because image pixels are contiguous in memory allowing to use vectorization, and combining task-pipelining with image partitioning a high degree of parallelism can be achieved (15 subimages, each one having a full pipeline of 16 stages, imply 240 threads).

The use of these kinds of coprocessors, MICs or GPUs, can improve drastically the performance of the parallelization scheme described in this paper.

Competing interests
The authors declare that they have no competing interests.

References

1. SS eauchemin, JL Barron, The computation of optical flow. ACM Comput. Surv. **27**(3), 433–466 (1995)
2. X Feng, P Perona, Scene segmentation from 3D motion, in *IEEE Computer Society Conference on Computer Vision and Pattern Recognition*, Santa Barbara, 23–25 June 1998 (IEEE Computer Society Los Alamitos, 1998), pp. 225–231
3. S Temizer, *Optical flow based local navigation*. (PhD thesis, Massachusetts Institute of Technology, Cambridge, MA, 2001)
4. JS Zelek, Towards Bayesian real-time optical flow.Image Vis. Comput. **22**(12), 1051–1069 (2004)
5. Z Wei, DJ Lee, BE Nelson, KD Lillywhite, Accurate optical flow sensor for obstacle avoidance, in *Proceedings of the 4th International Symposium on Advances in Visual Computing*, Las Vegas, 1–3 December 2008, LNCS, vol. 5358 (Springer Berlin, 2008), pp. 240–247
6. J Marzat, Y Dumortier, A Ducrot, Real-time dense and accurate parallel optical flow using CUDA, in *17th International Conference WSCG*, Plzen, 2–5 February 2009, pp. 105–111
7. P Sand, SJ Teller, Video matching. ACM Trans, Graph. **23**(3), 592–599 (2004)
8. F Champagnat, A Plyer, G Le Besnerais, B Leclaire, B Davoust, Y Le Sant, Fast and accurate PIV computation using highly parallel iterative correlation maximization. Exp. Fluids. **50**(4), 1169–1182 (2011)
9. F Valentinotti, GD Caro, B Crespi, Real-time parallel computation of disparity and optical flow using phase difference. Mach Vis. Appl. **9**(3), 87–96 (1996)
10. F Weber, H Eichner, H Cuntz, A Borst, Eigenanalysis of a neural network for optic flow processing. New J. Phys. **10**(1), 015013 (2008)
11. K Sakurai, S Kyo, Okazaki S, Overtaking vehicle detection method and its implementation using IMAPCAR highly parallel image processor. IEICE Trans. **91-D**(7), 1899–1905 (2008)
12. T Röwekamp, M Platzner, L Peters, Specialized architectures for optical flow computation: a performance comparison of ASIC, DSP, and multi-DSP, in *Proceedings of the 8th ICSPAT*, San Diego, 14–17 September 1997, pp. 829–833
13. J Kramer, Compact integrated motion sensor with three-pixel interaction. IEEE Trans. Pattern Anal. Mach. Intell. **18**(4), 455–460 (1996)
14. M Fleury, AF Clark, AC Downton, Evaluating optical-flow algorithms on a parallel machine. Image Vis. Comput. **19**(3), 131–143 (2001)
15. JH Barrón-Zambrano, FM del Campo-Ramírez, M Arias-Estrada, Parallel processor for 3D recovery from optical flow, in *International Conference on Reconfigurable Computing and FPGAs*, Cancun, 3–5 December 2008 (IEEE Computer Society Los Alamitos, 2008), pp. 49–54
16. S Tan, J Dale, A Anderson, A Johnston, Inverse perspective mapping and optic flow: a calibration method and a quantitative analysis. Image Vis. Comput. **24**(2), 153–165 (2006)
17. K Sakurai, S Kyo, S Okazaki, Overtaking vehicle detection method and its implementation using IMAPCAR highly parallel image processor. IEICE Trans. **91-D**(7), 1899–1905 (2008)
18. C Braillon, C Pradalier, J Crowley, C Laugier, Real-time moving obstacle detection using optical flow models, in *2006 IEEE Intelligent Vehicles Symposium*, Tokyo, 13–15 June 2006, pp. 466–471
19. K Pauwels, MM Van Hulle, Optic flow from unstable sequences through local velocity constancy maximization. Image Vis. Comput. **27**(5), 579–587 (2009)
20. G Zhang, J Jia, HBao WHua, Robust bilayer segmentation and motion/depth estimation with a handheld camera. IEEE Trans. Pattern Anal. Mach. Intell. **33**(3), 603–617 (2011)
21. YS Hsieh, YC Su, LG Chen, Robust moving object tracking and trajectory prediction for visual navigation in dynamic environments, in *IEEE International Conference on Consumer Electronics (ICCE)*, Las Vegas, 13–16 June 2012, pp. 696–697
22. B Lucas, T Kanade, An iterative image registration technique with an application to stereo vision, in *Proceedings of the 7th International Joint Conference on Artificial Intelligence (IJCAI)*, Vancouver, 24–28 August 1981, pp. 674–679
23. B Lucas, *Generalized image matching by method of differences*. (PhD thesis, Department of Computer Science, Carnegie-Mellon University, 1984)
24. J Barron, D Fleet, SS Beauchemin, Performance of optical flow techniques. Int. J. Comput. Vis. **12**(1), 43–47 (1994)
25. A Bainbridge-Smith, R Lane, Determining optical flow using a differential method. Image Vis. Comput. **15**(1), 11–22 (1997)
26. M Correia, A Campilho, J Santos, L Nunes, Optical flow techniques applied to the calibration of visual perception experiments, in *Proceedings of the 13th International Conference on Pattern Recognition, ICPR96*, Vienna, 25–29 August 1996 vol.1, (1996), pp. 498–502
27. M Correia, A Campilho, Implementation of a real-time optical flow algorithm on a pipeline processor, in *Proceedings of the International Conference of Computer Based Experiments, Learning and Teaching*, Szklarska Poreba, 28 September to 1 October, (1999)
28. J Díaz, E Ros, R Agís, JL Bernier, Superpipelined high-performance optical-flow computation architecture. Comput. Vis. Image Underst. **112**(3), 262–273 (2008)
29. T Brox, A Bruhn, N Papenberg, J Weickert, High accuracy optical flow estimation based on a theory for warping, in *European Conference on Computer Vision (ECCV)*, Prague, 11–14 May 2009, *LNCS*,vol. 3024, ed. by T Pajdla, J Matas (Springer Berlin, 2004), pp. 25–36
30. SN Tamgade, VR Bora, Motion vector estimation of video image by pyramidal implementation of Lucas Kanade optical flow, in *2nd International Conference on Emerging Trends in Engineering and Technology (ICETET)*, 16–18 December 2009 (IEEE Computer Society Piscataway, 2009), pp. 914–917
31. A Doshi, AG Bors, Smoothing of optical flow using robustified diffusion kernels. Image Vis. Comput. **28**(12), 1575–1589 (2010)
32. A Bruhn, J Weickert, C Schnörr, Lucas/Kanade meets Horn/Schunck: combining local and global optic flow methods. Int. J. Comput. Vis. **61**(3), 211–231 (2005)
33. M Drulea, IR Peter, S Nedevschi, Optical flow a combined local-global approach using L1 norm, in *Proceedings of the 2010 IEEE 6th International Conference on Intelligent Computer Communication and Processing, ICCP '10*, Cluj-Napoca, 26–28 August 2010 (IEEE Computer Society Piscataway, 2010), pp. 217–222
34. T Brox, J Malik, Large displacement optical flow: descriptor matching in variational motion estimation. IEEE Trans. Pattern Anal. Mach. Intell. **33**(3), 500–513 (2011)
35. H Liu, TH Hong, M Herman, R Chellappa, Accuracy vs. efficiency trade-offs in optical flow algorithms, in *4th European Conference on Computer Vision*, Cambridge, 15–18 April 1996, *LNCS*, vol. 1065, ed. by B Buxton, R Cipolla (Springer Berlin, 1996), pp. 271–286
36. B Buxton, B Stephenson, H Buxton, Parallel computations of optic flow in early image processing. Commun. Radar Signal Process. IEE Proc. F. **131**(6), 593–602 (1984)
37. PE Danielsson, P Emanuelsson, K Chen, P Ingelhag, C Svensson, Single-chip high-speed computation of optical Flow, in *MVA'90 IAPR Workshop on Machine Vision Applications*, Tokyo, 28–30 November 1990, pp. 331–336
38. G Adorni, S Cagnoni, M Mordonini, Cellular automata based optical flow computation for "just-in-time" applications, in *International Conference on Image Analysis and Processing*, Venice, 27–29 September 1999, pp. 612–617
39. A Stocker, R Douglas, *Computation of Smooth Optical Flow in a Feedback Connected Analog Network*. (MIT Press, Cambridge, 1998). http://cogprints.org/82/
40. H Bulthoff, J Little, T Poggio, A parallel algorithm for real-time computation of optical flow. Nature. **337**(6207), 549–553 (1989)
41. Del Bimbo A, P Nesi, Optical flow estimation on Connection-Machine 2, in *Proceedings of Computer Architectures for Machine Perception, New Orleans, 15–17 December 1993*, pp. 267–274
42. H Wang, J Brady, I Page, A fast algorithm for computing optic flow and its implementation on a transputer array, in *Proceedings of the British Machine Vision Conference - BMVC90*, Oxford, 24–27, September 1990, pp. 175–180

43. C Colombo, A Del Bimbo, S Santini, A multilayer massively parallel architecture for optical flow computation, in *Proceedings of the 11th IAPR International Conference on Pattern Recognition, 1992. Vol. IV. Conference D: Architectures for Vision and Pattern Recognition,* The Hague, 30 August to 3 September 1992, pp. 209–213

44. MG Milanova, AC Campilho, MV Correia, Cellular neural networks for motion estimation, in *15th International Conference on Pattern Recognition (ICPR'00),* Barcelona, 3–7 September 2000 (IEEE Computer Society Los Alamitos, 2000), pp. 819–822

45. H Niitsuma, T Maruyama, High speed computation of the optical flow, in *Proceedings of the 13th International Conference Image Analysis and Processing - ICIAP 2005,* Cagliari, 6–8 September 2005, *LNCS,* vol. 3617, ed. by F Roli, S Vitulano (Springer Berlin, 2005), pp. 287–295

46. J Sosa, J Boluda, F Pardo, R Gómez-Fabela, Change-driven data flow image processing architecture for optical flow computation. J. Real-Time Image Process. **2**(4), 259–270 (2007)

47. T Browne, J Condell, G Prasad, T McGinnity, An investigation into optical flow computation on FPGA hardware, in *International Conference on Machine Vision and Image Processing, 2008. IMVIP '08,* Portrush, 3–5, September 2008, pp. 176–181

48. N Devi, V Nagarajan, FPGA based high performance optical flow computation using parallel architecture. Int. J. Soft Comput. Eng. **2**(1), 433–437 (2012)

49. Y Mizukami, K Tadamura, Optical flow computation on compute unified device architecture, in *Proceedings of the 14th International Conference Image Analysis and Processing - ICIAP 2007,* Modena, 10–14 September 2007, pp. 179–184

50. M Gong, Real-time joint disparity and disparity flow estimation on programmable graphics hardware. Comput Vis. Image Underst. **113**(1), 90–100 (2009)

51. MV Correia, AC Campilho, A pipelined real-time optical flow algorithm, in *Proceedings of Image Analysis and Recognition ICIAR (2),* Porto, 29 September to 1 October 2004, *LNCS,* vol. 3212, ed. by AC Campilho, MS Kamel (Springer Berlin, 2004), pp. 372–380

52. J Chase, B Nelson, J Bodily, Z Wei, DJ Lee, Real-time optical flow calculations on FPGA and GPU architectures: a comparison study, in *16th International Symposium on Field Programmable Custom Computing Machines,* Palo Alto, 14–15 April 2008 (IEEE Los Alamitos, 2008), pp. 173–182

53. (2014). http://www.top500.org Accessed 6 Mar 2014

54. A García Dopico, M Correia, J Santos, L Nunes, Distributed computation of optical flow, in *4th International Conference on Computational Science (ICCS 2004): 6-9 Jun 2004; Krakow, LNCS,* vol. 3037, ed. by M Bubak, G van A Ibada, P Sloot, J Dongarra (Springer Berlin, 2004), pp. 380–387

55. T Kohlberger, C Schnorr, A Bruhn, J Weickert, Domain decomposition for variational optical-flow computation. IEEE Trans. Image Process. **14**(8), 1125–1137 (2005)

56. EM Kalmoun, H Köstler, U Rüde, 3D optical flow computation using a parallel variational multigrid scheme with application to cardiac C-arm CT motion. Image Vis. Comput. **25**(9), 1482–1494 (2007)

57. E Simoncelli, E Adelson, D Heeger, Probability distributions of optical flow, in *Proceedings of the IEEE Conference on Computer Vision and Pattern Recognition,* Maui, 3–6 June 1991, pp. 310–315

8

Local spatiotemporal features for dynamic texture synthesis

Rocio A Lizarraga-Morales[1*], Yimo Guo[2], Guoying Zhao[2], Matti Pietikäinen[2] and Raul E Sanchez-Yanez[1]

Abstract

In this paper, we study the use of local spatiotemporal patterns in a non-parametric dynamic texture synthesis method. Given a finite sample video of a texture in motion, dynamic texture synthesis may create a new video sequence, perceptually similar to the input, with an enlarged frame size and longer duration. In general, non-parametric techniques select and copy regions from the input sample to serve as building blocks by pasting them together one at a time onto the outcome. In order to minimize possible discontinuities between adjacent blocks, the proper representation and selection of such pieces become key issues. In previous synthesis methods, the block description has been based only on the intensities of pixels, ignoring the texture structure and dynamics. Furthermore, a seam optimization between neighboring blocks has been a fundamental step in order to avoid discontinuities. In our synthesis approach, we propose to use local spatiotemporal cues extracted with the local binary pattern from three orthogonal plane (LBP-TOP) operator, which allows us to include in the video characterization the appearance and motion of the dynamic texture. This improved representation leads us to a better fitting and matching between adjacent blocks, and therefore, the spatial similarity, temporal behavior, and continuity of the input can be successfully preserved. Moreover, the proposed method simplifies other approximations since no additional seam optimization is needed to get smooth transitions between video blocks. The experiments show that the use of the LBP-TOP representation outperforms other methods, without generating visible discontinuities or annoying artifacts. The results are evaluated using a double-stimulus continuous quality scale methodology, which is reproducible and objective. We also introduce results for the use of our method in video completion tasks. Additionally, we hereby present that the proposed technique is easily extendable to achieve the synthesis in both spatial and temporal domains.

Keywords: Dynamic texture synthesis; Spatiotemporal descriptor; Non-parametric synthesis

Introduction

Texture synthesis is an active research area with wide applications in fields like computer graphics, image processing, and computer vision. The texture synthesis problem can be stated as follows: given a finite sample texture, a system must automatically create an outcome with similar visual attributes of the input and a predefined size. Texture synthesis is a useful alternative way to create arbitrarily large textures [1]. Furthermore, since it is only necessary to store a small sample of the desired texture, the synthesis can bring great benefits in memory storage. Most texture synthesis research has been focused on the enlargement of static textures. However, dynamic texture synthesis is receiving a growing attention during recent years.

Dynamic textures are essentially textures in motion and have been defined as video sequences that show some kind of repetitiveness in time or space [2,3]. Examples of these textures include recordings of smoke, foliage and water in motion. Comparatively to the static texture synthesis, given a finite video sample of a dynamic texture, a synthesis method must create a new video sequence which looks perceptually similar to the input in appearance and motion. The temporal domain synthesis comprises the duration of the video, while the spatial domain synthesis consists of enlarging the frame size. The synthesis in both domains must keep a natural appearance, avoiding discontinuities, jumps and annoying artifacts.

The number of methods for dynamic texture synthesis that have been proposed can be separated into

---
*Correspondence: rocio_lizarraga@laviria.org
[1] Universidad de Guanajuato DICIS, Salamanca, Guanajuato 36885, Mexico
Full list of author information is available at the end of the article

two groups: parametric and non-parametric. Parametric methods address the problem as a modeling of a stationary process, where the resulting representation allows to generate a new video with similar characteristics as the input sample [2-7]. A clear disadvantage of these methods is that the estimation of the parameters may not be straightforward, being time-consuming and computationally demanding. Besides, the synthetic outputs may not be realistic enough, showing some blurred results. In contrast, we have the non-parametric methods, also known as exemplar-based techniques, which actually have been the most popular techniques up to now. The success of these methods comes from their outcomes, which look more natural and realistic than those of the parametric methods. Considerable work in non-parametric methods has been developed for dynamic texture synthesis along the time domain. Nevertheless, the synthesis in the spatial domain has not received the same attention.

Non-parametric techniques for texture synthesis were born only for static textures and are categorized into two types: pixel-based and patch-based. Pixel-based methods are the pioneers in non-parametric sampling for static texture synthesis, starting with the innovating work by Efros and Leung [8]. As their name says, the pixel-based methods grow a new image outward from an initial seed one pixel at a time, where each pixel to be transferred to the output is selected by comparing its spatial neighborhood with all neighborhoods in the input texture. This method is time-consuming, and an extension to dynamic texture synthesis might be impractical. In order to attend this issue, Wei and Levoy [9] proposed an acceleration method, and the synthesis of dynamic texture can be achieved. However, the pixel-based methods are susceptible to deficient results because one pixel might not be sufficient to capture the large-scale structure of a given texture [10]. On the other hand, we have the patch-based methods. These techniques select and copy whole neighborhoods from the input, to be pasted one at a time onto the output, increasing the speed and quality of the synthesis results. In order to avoid discontinuities between patches, their representation, selection, and seaming processes become key issues. The main research trend in these methods is to minimize the mismatches on the boundaries between patches, after their placement in the corresponding output. The new patch can be blended [11] with the already synthesized portion, or an optimal cut can be found for seaming the two patches [12,13]. The patch-based methods have shown the best synthesis results up to now. However, some artifacts are still detected in their outputs. The reason is that in these methods, there has been more attention on the patch seaming than in the patch representation for a better selection and matching. We must select the patch that matches the best with the preceding one, depending on a given visual feature. Usually, only the color features have been considered. This assumption may result in structural mismatches along the synthesized video. Recent approaches for static texture synthesis have proposed the use of structural features [10,14], thereby preserving the texture appearance by improving the representation and selection of patches. Nonetheless, an extension of these methods to dynamic texture synthesis has not been considered. To our knowledge, there are no synthesis methods of dynamic texture that explore the use of features that consider structure, appearance, and motion for the patch representation and selection.

In this paper, we propose the use of local spatiotemporal patterns [15], as features in a non-parametric patch-based method for dynamic texture synthesis. The use of such features allows us to capture the structure of local brightness variations in both spatial and temporal domains and, therefore, describe appearance and motion of dynamic textures. In our method, we take advantage of these patterns in the representation and selection of patches. With this improvement, we capture more structural information for a better patch matching, preserving properly the structure and dynamics of the given input sample. In this way, we can simplify the synthesis method with a very competitive performance in comparison with other patch-based methods. The main contributions of this paper are the following: (1) the extension of a patch-based approach, previously applied only for static texture, for its use in dynamic texture synthesis; (2) the dynamic texture description through local spatiotemporal features, instead of using only the color of the pixels. With this improvement, we capture the local structural information for a better patch matching, preserving properly the appearance and dynamics of a given input texture. (3) A simplified method, where the computation of an optimal seam between patches can be omitted. This can be achieved because of the fitting and matching of patches. (4) A robust and flexible method that can lead to different kinds of dynamic texture videos, ranging from videos that show spatial and temporal regularity, those conformed by constrained objects and videos that contain both static and dynamic elements, showing irregularity in both appearance and motion. (5) A combination with a temporal domain synthesis method in such a way that we can perform the synthesis in both the spatial and temporal domains. (6) The use of such method for video completion tasks.

It must be mentioned that this is a formal review and an extension of our previous work on synthesis only in the spatial domain [16]. In this study, we have carried out new tests that show our contribution more objectively. New results were obtained to test the boundaries of our proposal, using different types of dynamic textures for synthesis. For the evaluation of the results, the previous work only includes personal comments of the quality achieved, while in the current manuscript, the results are evaluated using a double-stimulus continuous quality scale (DSCQS) methodology for the video quality assessment, which is reproducible and objective. A comparison with other state-of-the-art parametric and non-parametric approaches, following the same assessment methodology, is also presented in this manuscript. Furthermore, we hereby present results for the use of our method in constrained synthesis tasks, where missing parts in a given video can be considered as holes that must be filled. Moreover, we also propose results for the combination of our technique with a temporal synthesis method, in order to achieve the synthesis in both spatial and temporal domains. This last change is important since previous methods are mainly focused only on synthesis in temporal domain.

This paper is organized as follows: in the section 'Dynamic texture synthesis using local spatiotemporal features', the local spatiotemporal features used in this work and the proposed approach are defined. In the 'Experiments and results' section, we include a set of tests using a standard database of dynamic textures, a comparison with other parametric and non-parametric approaches in order to validate our method, and the application of our algorithm in constrained synthesis tasks. Finally, 'Conclusions' section presents a summary of this work and our concluding remarks.

Dynamic texture synthesis using local spatiotemporal features

In this section, the spatiotemporal features used for the representation of dynamic texture patches are defined. Also, the proposed method for the texture synthesis in the spatial domain is described. After that, with the combination of a method in spatial domain and a temporal domain approach, we can achieve a full synthesis in both spatial and temporal domains.

The spatiotemporal descriptor

The local binary pattern from three orthogonal planes (LBP-TOP) [15] is a spatiotemporal descriptor for dynamic textures. The LBP-TOP considers the co-occurrences in three planes XY, XT and YT, capturing information about space-time transitions. The LBP-TOP is an extension of the local binary patterns (LBP) presented by Ojala et al. [17]. As it is known, the LBP is a theoretically simple yet an efficient approach to characterize the spatial structure of a local texture. Basically, the operator labels a given pixel of an image by thresholding its neighbors in function of the pixel intensity and summing the thresholded values weighted by powers of two. According to Ojala et al., a monochrome texture image T in a local neighborhood is defined as the joint

distribution of the gray levels of $P(P > 1)$ image pixels $T = t(g_c, g_0, \ldots, g_{P-1})$, where g_c is the gray value of the center pixel and $g_p(p = 0, 1, \ldots, P - 1)$ are the gray values of P equally spaced pixels on a circle radius $R(R > 0)$ that form a circularly symmetric neighbor set. If the coordinates of g_c are (x_c, y_c), then the coordinates of g_p are $(x_c - R\sin(2\pi p/P), y_c + R\cos(2\pi p/P))$. The LBP value for the pixel g_c is defined as in Equation 1:

$$\text{LBP}_{P,R}(g_c) = \sum_{p=0}^{P-1} s(g_p - g_c)2^p, \quad s(t) = \begin{cases} 1, & t \geq 0, \\ 0, & \text{otherwise.} \end{cases}$$

$$(1)$$

More details can be further consulted in [17].

For the spatiotemporal extension of the LBP, named as LBP-TOP, the local patterns are extracted from the XY, XT, and YT planes, with XY the frame plane and XT and YT the temporal variations planes. Each code is denoted as XY-LBP for the space domain, and XT-LBP and YT-LBP for space-time transitions [15]. In the LBP-TOP approach, the three planes intersect in the center pixel, and three different patterns are extracted in function of that central pixel (see Figure 1). The local pattern of a pixel from the XY plane contains information about the appearance. In the local patterns from XT and YT planes, statistics of motion in horizontal and vertical directions are included. In this case, the radii in axes X, Y, and T are R_X, R_Y, and R_T, respectively, and the number of neighboring points in each plane is defined as P_{XY}, P_{XT}, and P_{YT}. Supposing that the coordinates of the center pixel $g_{t_c,c}$ are (x_c, y_c, t_c), the coordinates of the neighbors $g_{XY,p}$ in the plane XY are given by $(x_c - R_X\sin(2\pi p/P_{XY}), y_c + R_Y\cos(2\pi p/P_{XY}), t_c)$. Analogously, the coordinates of $g_{XT,p}$ in the plane XT are $(x_c - R_X\sin(2\pi p/P_{XT}), y_c, t_c - R_T\cos(2\pi p/P_{XT}))$, and the coordinates of $g_{YT,p}$ on the plane YT are $(x_c, y_c - R_Y\cos(2\pi p/P_{YT}), t_c - R_T\sin(2\pi p/P_{YT}))$.

For the implementation proposed in this paper, each pixel in the input sequence V_{in} is analyzed with the

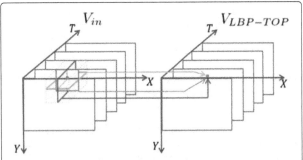

Figure 1 Creation of the LBP-TOP-coded sequence. Each pixel in the corresponding LBP-TOP sequence is obtained by extracting the LBPs from the three orthogonal planes in the input sequence.

LBP-TOP$_{P_{XY},P_{XT},P_{YT},R_{XY},R_{XT},R_{YT}}$ operator, in such a way that we obtain a LBP-TOP-coded sequence $V_{\text{LBP-TOP}}$. Each pixel in the $V_{\text{LBP-TOP}}$ sequence is coded by three values, comprising each of the space-time patterns of the local neighborhood, as can be seen in Figure 1. As we said before, in patch-based methods, each patch must be carefully selected, depending on a given visual feature. To accomplish this task, we use $V_{\text{LBP-TOP}}$ as a temporary sequence for the patch description in the selection process. This means that instead of comparing the similarity of patches using only the intensity, we compare them using their corresponding LBP values in $V_{\text{LBP-TOP}}$.

Dynamic texture synthesis in spatial domain

In this paper, as we said before, we propose the synthesis of dynamic textures using local spatiotemporal features [15] in a patch-based method for dynamic texture synthesis. As mentioned, patch-based algorithms basically select regions from the input as elements to build an output. Since our method synthesize textures in motion, we take video volumes as such building blocks to obtain the desired sequence. The selection of these volumes is crucial, in order to obtain a high quality synthesis and smooth transitions. In our approach, we achieve this by including local structural information for a better video volume matching. The use of this information allows us to consider the local spatial and temporal relations between pixels and, therefore, get more insight about the structure of a given dynamic texture.

In general, our method can be described in an algorithmic manner: the synthesized output video is built by sequentially pasting video volumes or blocks in raster scan order. In each step, we select a video block B_k from the input video V_{in} and copy it to the output V_{out}. To avoid discontinuities between adjacent volumes, we must carefully select B_k based on the similarity of its spatiotemporal cues and the features of the already pasted neighbor B_{k-1}. At the beginning, a volume B_0 of $W_x \times W_y \times W_t$ pixel size is randomly selected from the input V_{in} and copied to the upper left corner of the output V_{out}. The following blocks are positioned in such a way that they are partially overlapped with the previously pasted ones. The overlapped volume between two blocks is of size $O_x \times O_y \times O_t$ pixels. If the input sample V_{in} is of $V_x \times V_y \times V_t$ pixel size, we set the synthesis block size as $W_x \times W_y \times W_t$, and the overlapped volume of two adjacent blocks as $O_x \times O_y \times O_t$. In this process we consider $V_t = W_t = O_t$.

In Figure 2, the following elements are illustrated: a video block, the boundary zone, where two video blocks should match, and an example of the overlapped volume between two blocks. In Figure 2b, the selected block B_k has a boundary zone E_{B_k}, and the previously pasted volume in V_{out} has a boundary zone E_{out}.

According to our method and in order to avoid discontinuities, E_{B_k} and E_{out} should have similar local spatiotemporal structure properties. It could be easy to think that the video block that matches the best is selected to be pasted on the output. However, as it was pointed out by Liang et al. [11], for the case of static texture synthesis, this can lead to a repeatability of patterns, and some randomness in the output is desirable.

In order to accomplish a better video block selection and preserve a certain degree of randomness in the outcome, we build a set of candidate video patches A_B. This set is built by elements which are considered to match with previously pasted volumes with some tolerance. Then, we select one block randomly from this set. Let $B_{(x,y,t)}$ be a volume whose upper left corner is at (x, y, t) in V_{in}. We construct

$$A_B = \{B_{(x,y,t)} \,|\, d(E_{B_{(x,y,t)}}, E_{\text{out}}) < d_{\max}\}, \qquad (2)$$

where $E_{B_{(x,y,t)}}$ is the boundary zone of $B_{(x,y,t)}$, and $d_{\max}$ is the distance tolerance between two boundary zones. Details on how to compute $d(\cdot)$ are given later.

When we have determined all the potential blocks, we pick one randomly from A_B to be the kth video block B_k to be pasted on V_{out}. The cardinality of A_B depends on how many video blocks form the input satisfy the similarity constraints given by $d_{\max}$. With a low value of $d_{\max}$, the output will have a better quality, but few blocks will be considered to be part of A_B. By contrast, with a high tolerance, a big number of blocks will be part of the set and there will be more options to select, but the quality of the output will be compromised. For a given $d_{\max}$, the set A_B could be empty. In such case, we choose B_k to be the block $B_{(x,y,t)}$ from V_{in}, whose boundary zone $E_{B_{(x,y,t)}}$ has the smallest distance to the boundary zone of the output E_{out}. In our implementation, the similarity constrain $d_{\max}$ is set to be $d_{\max} = 0.01\,VL$, where V is the number of pixels in the overlapped volume and L is the maximum LBP value in the sequence.

The final computation of the overlapping distance between a given block $E_{B_{(x,y,t)}}$ and the output E_{out} is estimated by using the L2 norm through the corresponding LBP values for each pixel. As it was mentioned before, we use the $V_{\text{LBP-TOP}}$ representation as a temporary sequence for the patch description. The input sequence V_{in} is analyzed with the LBP-TOP$_{P_{XY},P_{XT},P_{YT},R_{XY},R_{XT},R_{YT}}$ operator, in such a way that we obtain a LBP-TOP-coded sequence $V_{\text{LBP-TOP}}$. Here, we set the operator to be LBP-TOP$_{8,8,8,1,1,1}$, and therefore, each pixel from the V_{in} sequence is coded in $V_{\text{LBP-TOP}}$ by three basic LBP values, one for each orthogonal plane. The overlapping distance is defined as

$$d(E_{B_{(x,y,t)}}, E_{\text{out}}) = \left[\frac{1}{V} \sum_{i=1}^{V} \sum_{j=1}^{3} \left[p_{B_{(x,y,t)}}^{j}(i) - p_{\text{out}}^{j}(i) \right]^2 \right]^{1/2}, \qquad (3)$$

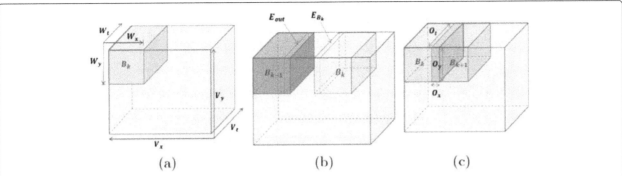

Figure 2 Illustration of the building blocks. Examples of **(a)** a video block, **(b)** the boundary zone of two different video volumes, and **(c)** the overlapped volume between two blocks. The boundary zones must have similar LBP-TOP features.

where V is the number of pixels in the overlapped volume. $p^j_{B_{(x,y,t)}}(i)$ and $p^j_{out}(i)$ represents the LBP values of the ith pixel on the jth orthogonal plane, respectively. For color textures, we compute the LBP-TOP codes for each color channel. In this paper, we use the RGB color space, and the final overlapping distance is the distance average for all the color components.

In summary, the creation of the output is shown in Figure 3, where the three possible configurations of the overlapping zones are also shown. Figure 3a presents the step where the second block is pasted, and the boundary zone is taken only on the left side. Figure 3b shows when B_k is the first block in the second or subsequent rows, and the boundary is taken on the upper side of it. The third case, illustrated in Figure 3c, is when B_k is not the first on the second or subsequent rows. Here, the total distance is the addition of the distances from the above and left boundaries.

It is important to mention that the size of a given block and the overlapped volumes are dependent on the properties of a particular texture. The size of the video block must be appropriate; it must be large enough to represent the structural composition of texture, but at the same time, small enough to avoid redundancies. This

characteristic makes our algorithm flexible and controllable. In our proposal, this parameter is adjusted empirically, but still, it can be automatically approximated with methods to obtain the fundamental pattern or texel size, like the ones proposed in [18,19]. In the same way, the boundary zone should avoid mismatching features across the borders, but at the same time, be tolerant to the border constraints. The overlapping volume is a small fraction of the block size. In our experiments, we take one sixth of the total patch size volume.

On the overlapped volume, in order to obtain smooth transitions and minimize artifacts between two adjacent blocks, we blend the volumes using a feathering algorithm [20]. This algorithm set weights to the pixels for attenuating the intensity around the blocks' boundaries using a ramp style transition. As a result, possible discontinuities are avoided, and soft transitions are achieved.

Experiments and results

In this section, we present series of tests that have been accomplished in order to evaluate the performance of our method. At first, an assessment of performance is made on a variety of dynamic textures. Next, comparisons between the proposed approach with other four state-of-

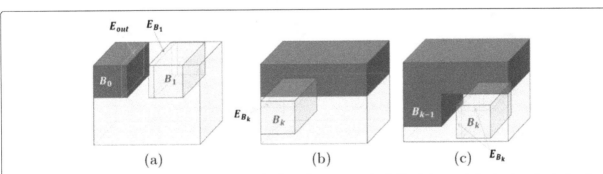

Figure 3 Illustration of our patch-based method process for dynamic texture synthesis. The darker zone is the already synthesized portion of video. Implicitly, three possible overlapping zones between the output E_{out} and the new block E_k are also shown: **(a)** the overlapping zone is on the left side of E_k, **(b)** the overlapping zone is taken from the upper side of E_k, and **(c)** the overlapping zone is taken from the upper and left sides.

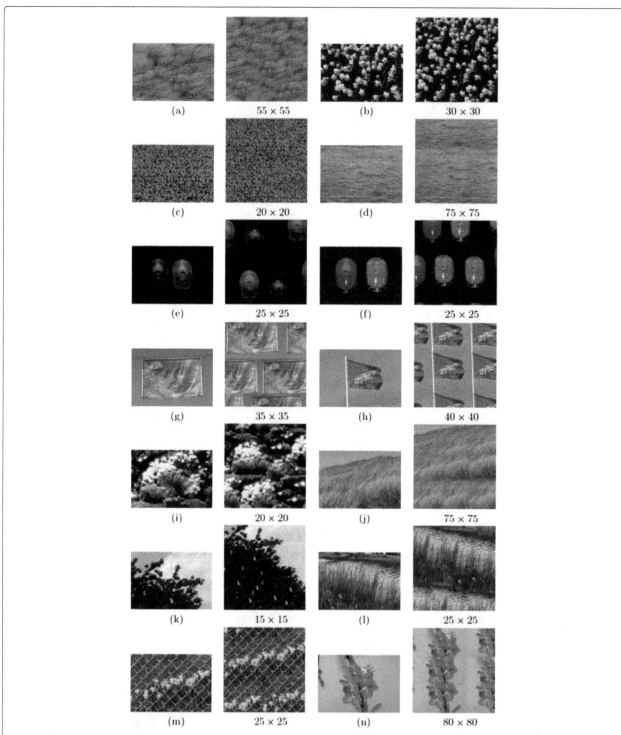

Figure 4 Results of the synthesis in spatial domain. (a to n) Frames taken from the original sequence and the corresponding synthesis results. The block size used for obtaining such results is shown for each sequence.

the-art methods are made to validate its application. The comparison is carried out with both parametric and non-parametric methods. The parametric methods presented are proposed by Bar-Joseph et al. [21] and by Costantini et al. [4]. For comparison with non-parametric methods, we have included the pixel-based technique proposed by Wei and Levoy [9] and the patch-based approach introduced by Kwatra et al. [13]. The selected baseline methods were selected for their impact to the dynamic texture synthesis field. Specifically, the method presented in [13]

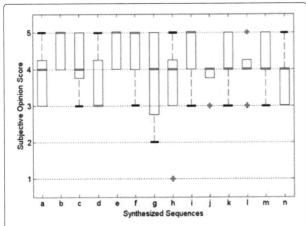

Figure 5 Box plot of the subjective opinion scores of the synthesized sequences in Figure 4. The outliers are presented as red crosses.

is the most popular and recent approach that achieves the synthesis of dynamic textures in both time and space domains using a non-parametric technique. Moreover, it is more similar to our proposal, since it uses a patch-based sampling. Afterwards, we also consider our method for a video completion task. All the resulting videos are available on the website https://dl.dropboxusercontent.com/u/13100121/SynResults.zip.

Performance on a variety of dynamic textures

In the first experiment, a set of 14 videos was selected for evaluating our approach performance on different types of dynamic textures. The videos were selected from the DynTex database [22], which provides a comprehensive range of high-quality dynamic textures and can be used for diverse research purposes. In Figure 4, a frame (176×120 pixel size) taken from each original video is presented. The selected sequences correspond to videos that show spatial and temporal regularities (a to d), constrained objects with temporal regularity (e to h), and videos that show some irregularity in either appearance or motion (i to n). In this context, the term regularity can be interpreted as the repeatability of a given pattern along one dimension, such as of a texture primitive or a movement cycle. Next to each original frame, the resulting synthesized outputs, enlarged to 200×200 pixel size, are presented. The spatial dimensions of the block $W_x \times W_y$ used for synthesis are shown below each image. The temporal dimension W_t of each block corresponds to the time duration of the given

input sample, so that from now the W_t parameter will be obviated.

As we can observe in Figure 4a,b,c,d, our method preserves the spatiotemporal regularity of the input, and the borderlines between blocks are practically invisible. It is worth mentioning that in our method, we do not need to compute an additional optimal seam on the borders between the adjacent video volumes to achieve smooth transitions, such as the optimal cut used in [13]. This soft transition in our outcomes is achieved through the proper selection of blocks that have similar spatiotemporal features using the LBP-TOP representation. The sequences shown in Figure 4e,f,g,h are different in the sense that they are composed by constrained objects. In these examples, it is important that the structure of these objects can be maintained in the output, where we aim to generate an array of these objects. As it is pointed out by the results, our method can keep the shape and structure of a given object without generating any discontinuity.

The last set of examples, shown in Figure 4i,j,k,l,m,n, is of great interest since it shows videos that contain both static and dynamic elements, showing irregularity in both appearance and motion. This is a very common characteristic in real sequences. As far as we know, there are no proposals to handle this kind of videos since in general, previous methods for dynamic texture synthesis assume some spatial homogeneity. Specifically, the example shown in Figure 4m is interesting because it contains a lattice in front of the flowers in motion. In the resulting video, we can see that the structure of the lattice is completely maintained without any discontinuity. Furthermore, the appearance and dynamics of the rest of the elements, both static and in motion, from the original video are preserved.

A quantitative and reliable evaluation of texture synthesis is not an easy task. The final goal of synthesis is to achieve a high-quality result, able to trick the human visual perception. However, the perception of quality differs from person to person, and moreover, there are usually more than one acceptable outcome. Therefore, in this paper, we consider that a subjective evaluation is the most appropriate. We propose to carry a subjective assessment, where a set of test subjects are asked to give their opinion about the perceived quality of a given video. The synthetic sequences are subjectively evaluated using the DSCQS methodology [23], provided by the International Telecommunication Union through the recommendation ITU-R BT.500-11, for a subjective assessment of

Table 1 Average performance of our method

	a	b	c	d	e	f	g	h	i	j	k	l	m	n	Average
μ	3.8	4.6	4.1	3.6	4.5	4.5	3.6	3.6	4.4	3.7	4.3	4.1	4.3	3.7	4.1
σ	0.78	0.5	0.78	0.86	0.52	0.72	1.22	1.22	0.72	0.44	0.70	0.60	0.70	0.66	0.74

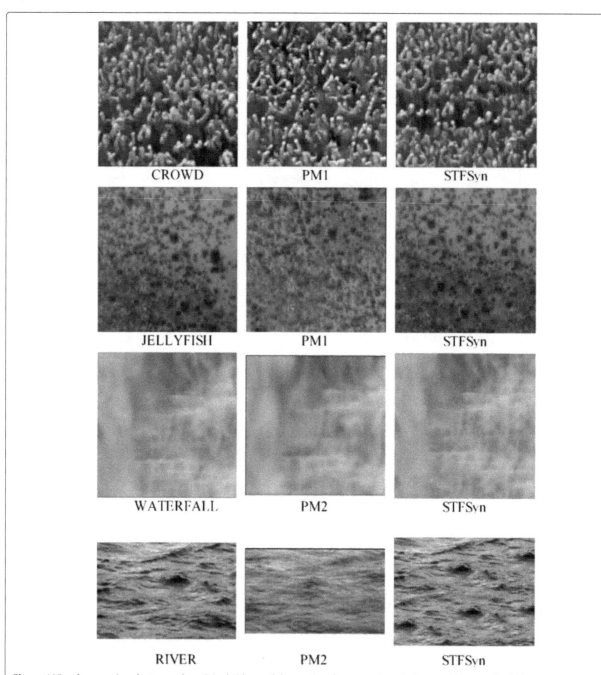

Figure 6 Visual comparison between the original video and the results of parametric techniques and our method. The original video is presented in the first column, while the resulting clips of the parametric techniques PM1 and PM2 are shown in the second column. The resulting sequence of our method STFSyn is presented in the third column.

the quality of videos. This is a measure given by a number of subjects on how well the image characteristics of the original clip are faithfully preserved in the synthesized video. The measure is presented as a five-point quality scale. The scores correspond to the following: 1 BAD, 2 POOR, 3 FAIR, 4 GOOD, and 5 EXCELLENT. The main advantage of this evaluation method is that it turns the subjective tests in reproducible and objective evaluations.

The testing protocol is described as follows. We asked for 15 non-expert volunteers to participate in the experiments. All of these subjects neither were part of our team nor are related to texture synthesis work. This is important to mention since non-expert observers yield more

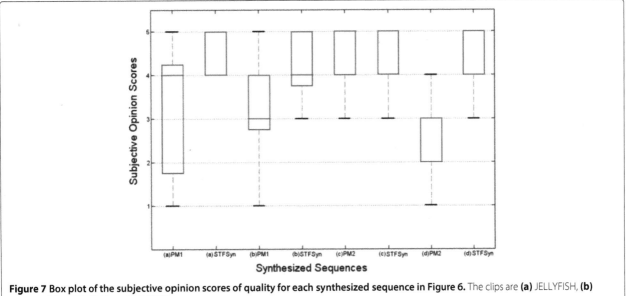

Figure 7 Box plot of the subjective opinion scores of quality for each synthesized sequence in Figure 6. The clips are **(a)** JELLYFISH, **(b)** CROWD, **(c)** WATERFALL, and **(d)** RIVER.

critical evaluations about the synthesis quality. We placed the input texture video and the corresponding output on a screen side by side and asked our subjects to rate the quality of the video.

The results for the opinion scores of the synthesized videos are presented in Figure 5, where each box is the result of subjective opinions for each sequence presented in Figure 4. The box plots help indicate the degree of dispersion of the corresponding data samples, and the median and outliers (red cross) of the samples can be easily identified. In this box plot, we can see that the median of the opinion scores of most of our sequences ranges between 4 (GOOD) and 5 (EXCELLENT). It was observed that only the synthetic video (d) has a median on FAIR. The corresponding output of video (g) not only has received the lowest score of 2 (POOR) but also has received the highest of 5 (EXCELLENT). A very low outlier of 1 (BAD) is detected in the synthetic video (h). This means that only one subject considers this video as bad. The opinion scores were also statistically evaluated; the mean value (μ) and standard deviation (σ) of the opinions are computed to determine the total average results. These data can be consulted on Table 1, where we can see that the total mean quality achieved by our method is of 4.1, interpreted as 4 (GOOD), for all the test sequences. We can also observe that there is a low variation of opinions, with a value of σ of 0.74.

Performance comparison

The second experiment is a comparison with other state-of-the-art methods. We have compared our approach (called STFSyn from now on, for spatiotemporal

feature-based synthesis) with both parametric and non-parametric approaches. We have borrowed the sequences used by other methods for testing their approaches and feed our method with such inputs. This is to compare the resulting quality achieved by the different methods. All the synthetic videos created for comparison purposes were also assessed with the DSCQS methodology. Each synthetic video is placed next to the original one and submitted for evaluation of the same 15 non-expert subjects who would score the perceived quality in comparison with the original one. In this part of the experiment, each stimulus is randomly presented to the subjects, without telling them the method implemented to obtain such outcome. The parameters used by our method STFSyn are reported in each description.

For comparison with parametric methods, we have borrowed the sequences presented by Bar-Joseph et al. [21] and used by Costantini et al. [4] for their experiments, and execute STFSyn algorithm with such inputs. In Figure 6, a

Table 2 Performance comparison of our method with the parametric approaches

	JELLYFISH	CROWD	WATERFALL	RIVER	Average
PM1$_\mu$	3.23	3.23	-	-	3.23
PM2$_\mu$	-	-	4.41	2.64	3.53
STFSyn$_\mu$	4.32	4.0	4.58	4.29	*4.32*
PM1$_\sigma$	1.56	1.25	-	-	1.40
PM2$_\sigma$	-	-	0.71	0.93	0.82
STFSyn$_\sigma$	0.49	0.74	0.61	0.58	*0.60*

The best average results are italicized.

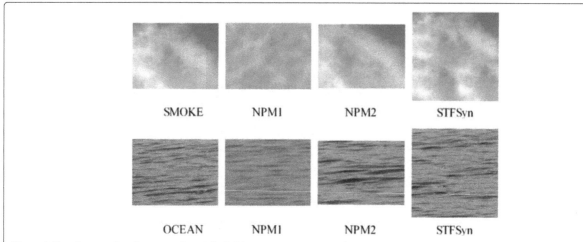

Figure 8 Visual comparison between the original video, non-parametric techniques and our method. The original video is presented in the first column. The resulting clips of the non-parametric techniques NPM1 and NPM2 are shown in the second and third columns, respectively. Finally, the sequence resulting from our method STFSyn is presented in the fourth column.

frame extracted from the original sequences CROWD and JELLYFISH (256 × 256 pixel size) used by Bar-Joseph et al. (called as PM1 for parametric method 1) is presented. Next to the original frame, a frame extracted from the sequence obtained from PM1 is also shown. In the third column, a frame from STFSyn results is displayed. In our method, the video CROWD was synthesized with a block of 70 × 70 pixel size, and the JELLYFISH video synthesis required a 80 × 80 pixel size volume. In Figure 6, we also present a frame of the original sequences, WATERFALL and RIVER, reported by Costantini et al. (PM2) in their experiments. A frame from STFSyn results is also displayed. The video WATERFALL was synthesized with

a block of 85 × 85 pixel size, and the RIVER video synthesis required a 90 × 90 pixel size block. Here, it is observed that both parametric methods present artifacts, discontinuities, and are blurred, while the videos generated by the proposed method STFSyn keep a natural look in comparison with the original.

The resulting subjective opinion scores for each synthetic sequence are shown in Figure 7. In this figure, we can see that STFSyn method achieves better performance than the parametric methods. The median of the perceived quality of STFSyn is ranked as 4 (GOOD) and 5 (EXCELLENT), while the median by the Bar-Joseph method (PM1) [21] is only between 3 (FAIR) and 4

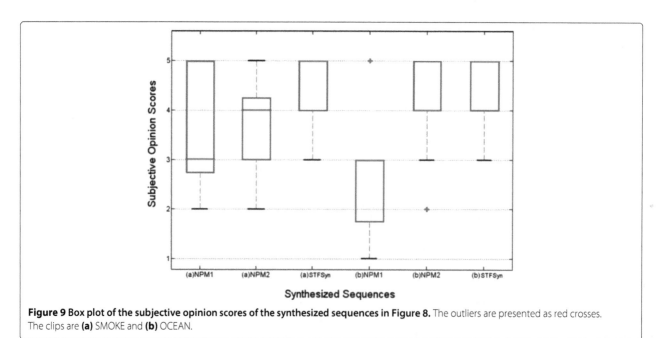

Figure 9 Box plot of the subjective opinion scores of the synthesized sequences in Figure 8. The outliers are presented as red crosses. The clips are **(a)** SMOKE and **(b)** OCEAN.

(GOOD). The sequence WATERFALL synthesized by the PM2 [4] has received the same median punctuation than our method as 5 (EXCELLENT). For the video RIVER, the PM1 received a median ranking of 3 (FAIR), while STF-Syn was punctuated as 4 (GOOD). The mean (μ) and the standard deviation (σ) were also computed from the data obtained by each method (PM1, PM2, and our STFSyn) for each video clip. The results are presented in Table 2, where the best results are highlighted in italics. In this table, we can see that the STFSyn approach gets the best average score of 4.32, in comparison to the 3.23 and 3.53 for the PM1 and PM2, respectively. Besides, our approach presents a lower variation in the perceived quality by the subjects, with a σ value of 0.6, in comparison with the 1.40 and 0.82 presented by the PM1 and PM2, respectively.

We have also compared our approach with non-parametric methods. The selected proposals were the two most representative methods, the pixel-based technique proposed by Wei and Levoy [9] and the well-known patch-based method proposed by Kwatra et al. [13]. We have borrowed the sequences named OCEAN and SMOKE used by both Wei and Levoy (NPM1) and Kwatra (NPM2) in their experiments for spatiotemporal synthesis and made a comparison of their quality with our results. The

video OCEAN was synthesized with the STFSyn using a block of 75 × 75 pixel size, and the SMOKE video synthesis required a 95 × 95 pixel size block. In Figure 8 frames extracted from the original sample, the result from Wei and Levoy (NPM1) [9], the outcomes by Kwatra et al. (NPM2) [13], and our results are presented. Here, it is observed that the videos obtained by NPM1 are considerably blurred, while the videos generated by NPM2 and by our method keep a natural appearance and motion of the two phenomena.

The corresponding assessment of the results by NPM1 [9] and NPM2 [13] with the DSCQS methodology is presented in Figure 9. In this figure, we can see that for the two sequences, the NPM1 receives a median score of 3 (FAIR); the NPM2 resulting sequences have their median ranked as 4 (GOOD), while our method achieves a median score of 5 (EXCELENT) in both cases.

In a third comparison (see Figure 10), we have borrowed more video sequences reported only by Kwatra et al. (NPM2) for spatiotemporal synthesis. Here, the tested sequences are CLOUDS, WATERFALL, and RIVER. The video CLOUDS was synthesized with a video patch of 80×80 pixel size; WATERFALL and RIVER, as it was mentioned before, required a block of 85 × 85 and 90 × 90 pixel

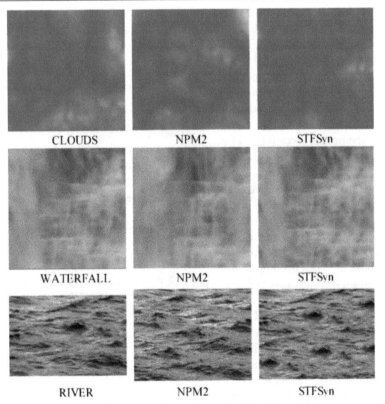

Figure 10 Visual comparison between the original sequence, the non-parametric technique NPM2 and our method. The original sequence is shown in the first column. The resulting outcome of the non-parametric method NPM2 is presented in the second column, and our method resulting video is shown on the third column.

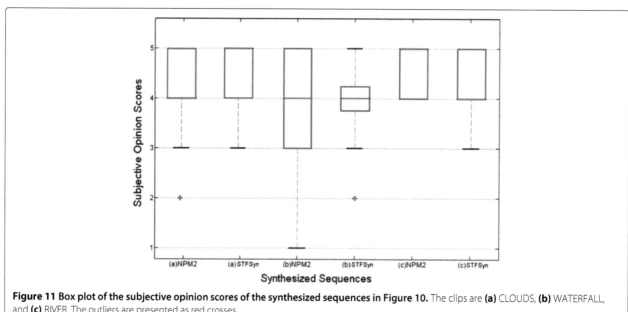

Figure 11 Box plot of the subjective opinion scores of the synthesized sequences in Figure 10. The clips are **(a)** CLOUDS, **(b)** WATERFALL, and **(c)** RIVER. The outliers are presented as red crosses.

size, respectively. As it can be seen from the results shown in Figure 10, both NPM2 and our method have generated very competitive and pleasant results for the dynamic texture synthesis. It is very difficult to see if any of the methods generates artifacts or discontinuities. However, the assessment carried out with the DSCQS methodology (see Figure 9 and Figure 11) highlights the differences in quality achieved by each method. In Figure 11, we can observe that both approaches performed with median rankings of 4 (GOOD) and 5 (EXCELENT). However, the NPM2 in the WATERFALL sequence has received evaluations as low as 1 (POOR). It is important to highlight that the clip RIVER was the only one considered by NPM2 for increasing the spatial resolution, process that we have done to every video presented in these comparisons. From all these comparisons, we can observe that the only method that achieves similar quality results is the one presented by Kwatra et al. (NPM2) [13]. The main difference and advantage of our method in comparison with NPM2 is that because of the proper representation of building blocks, our method does not need to compute an optimal seam. This characteristic allows us to simplify the synthesis method.

The corresponding mean (μ) values and standard deviation (σ) for each video achieved by each non-parametric method (NP1, NP2, and and STFSyn) are detailed in Table 3, where the best average performance is highlighted in italics. In this table, we can see that our method STFSyn in most cases receives higher opinion values than the other non-parametric approaches. Only the NP2 with the clip WATERFALL achieves a slightly superior mean value of 4.58 in comparison with our 4.29 mean opinion score.

The total average for the NP1 is a low 2.99; the average for NP2 is 4.1, while our STFSyn method reaches a total average mean value of 4.32. In the same manner for the standard deviation, the STFSyn approach has the lower value of variation in the scores with a 0.72 total average, in comparison with the 1.23 value by NP1 and 0.91 obtained by NP2.

Dynamic texture synthesis in both space and time domains

An extension of the proposed method to achieve a final synthesis in both spatial and temporal domains was also considered in this study. Our method provides the flexibility to be integrated with other existing approaches for synthesis in the temporal domain, like those previously mentioned in the introduction section [13,24,25].

The idea behind these techniques for extending the duration of a video is straightforward yet very effective. The general proposal is to find sets of similar frames that

Table 3 Performance comparison of our method with non-parametric proposals

	SMOKE	OCEAN	CLOUDS	WATERFALL	RIVER	Average
$NPM1_\mu$	3.47	2.52	-	-	-	2.99
$NPM2_\mu$	3.82	4.05	4.58	3.82	4.23	4.1
$STFSyn_\mu$	4.23	4.58	4.29	3.82	4.58	*4.32*
$NPM1_\sigma$	1.23	1.23	-	-	-	1.23
$NPM2_\sigma$	0.88	0.96	0.50	1.38	0.83	0.91
$STFSyn_\sigma$	0.66	0.71	0.58	1.07	0.61	*0.72*

The best average results are italicized.

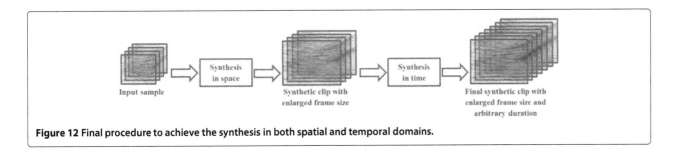

Figure 12 Final procedure to achieve the synthesis in both spatial and temporal domains.

could work as transitions and then loops in the original video to generate a new video stream, making jumps between such matching frames. In the first step of these type of algorithms, the video structure is analyzed for the existence of matching frames within the sequence. The frame similarity is measured in a given image representation, e.g., the intensities of all pixels [13,25] or the intrinsic spatial and temporal features [24]. Depending on the nature of the input video texture, the chosen frame representation method, and the similarity restrictions, the number of matching frames can be either large or small. The implication of this number of frames is that if it is large, a varied number of combinations/transitions can be reached; otherwise, the variability of the transferred clips to the output is compromised. Moreover, under certain motion circumstances, as it is pointed out in [26], some dynamic textures can be pleasantly synthesized in the temporal domain, while others may be not. The reasons include the motion speed and motion periodicity of the input sample. In general, texture synthesis methods in temporal domain are more capable to synthesize dynamic texture that shows repetitive motions, motions with regularity or random motions with fast speed.

The extension presented here is executed by using the algorithm proposed by Guo et al. [24], which has shown to provide high-quality synthesis besides applying LBP-TOP

features in the frame representation. The use of LBP-TOP features in the method by Guo et al. proves to capture the characteristics of each frame more effectively, and thus, the most appropriate pairs of frames are found to be stitched together. Additionally, this method is able to preserve temporal continuity and motion without adding annoying jumps and discontinuities.

As is illustrated in Figure 12, for the complete spatiotemporal synthesis, we apply our method and the method of Guo et al. [24] in cascade. We first execute our method for spatial synthesis and the enlargement of the frame size; after that, we perform the extension in the temporal domain.

In the experiments, we take sample videos from the DynTex database that have a duration of 10 s (150 frames), with a frame size of 176 × 120 pixel size. The final result after the spatiotemporal synthesis is a video with 20 s (300 frames) of duration and a frame of 200 × 200 pixel size, noticing that any duration and size can be achieved. In Figure 13, we show an example of the result. More results can be consulted in the results repository at the web page previously cited.

Video completion with dynamic texture synthesis

Video completion is the task of filling in the missing or damaged regions (in either spatial or temporal domain),

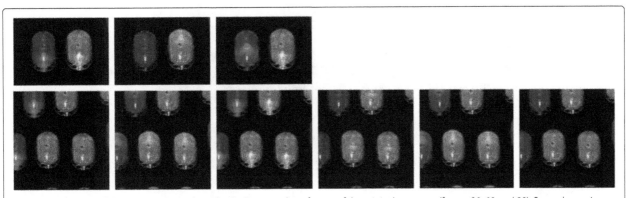

Figure 13 Example of the spatiotemporal synthesis. First row: three frames of the original sequence (frames 30, 60, and 90). Second row: six frames of the synthesized sequence (frames 30, 60, 120, 180, 240, and 300).

with the available information from the same video. This, with the goal of generating a perceptually smooth and satisfactory result. There is a number of applications for this task. Such applications may include the following: video post-production and to fill large holes in damaged videos for restoration. Also, it can be applied to the problem of dealing with boundaries after a convolution process. The most common approach to deal with these problems is the tiling and reflection of the information in the border; however, this may introduce discontinuities not present in the original image. In many cases, texture synthesis can be used to extrapolate the image by sampling from itself, in order to fill these missing areas.

For testing purposes, we execute our method with simple examples for video completion. The goal of these examples consists on fulfill the boundaries (missing parts) on videos. The boundary constraint is related to the texture that is surrounding the area to be synthesized. This constraint is taken into account in order to avoid subjectively annoying artifacts at the transition between synthetic and natural textures. Two different examples for this task are shown in Figure 14. In these cases, the process is conducted to start the synthesis only for the black holes. In this way, the original video is preserved, while the missing parts are completed with information available in the same sequence. The results show that our method can be also considered for video completion tasks.

Conclusions

In this paper, the use of local spatiotemporal features for dynamic texture synthesis has been studied. This method explores a patch-based synthesis approach, where the video patch selection is accomplished by taking the corresponding LBP-TOP features, instead of just making use of the intensity of pixels. The LBP-TOP features have the capability of describing the appearance and dynamics of local texture, and thus, a better video block representation can be achieved. The use of this representation leads us to a better matching of adjacent building blocks; as a result, the visual characteristics of the input can be successfully preserved. Moreover, the proposed method is neither difficult to implement nor intricate, since no additional seam optimization is needed to get smooth transitions between video blocks. A final extension to the synthesis in both spatial and temporal domains has been also considered. This extension can be achieved, applying first the synthesis in space and after that, the elongation in the temporal domain. As the experimental results show, this method produces good synthetic clips on a wide range of types of natural videos. We tested video sequences that show spatiotemporal regularity, videos conformed by constrained objects and those constituted by both static and dynamic elements. According to the results of the evaluation, the performance of the proposed method has shown to be better than other parametric and non-parametric methods. We have also shown that this proposal can be considered for applications requiring video completion.

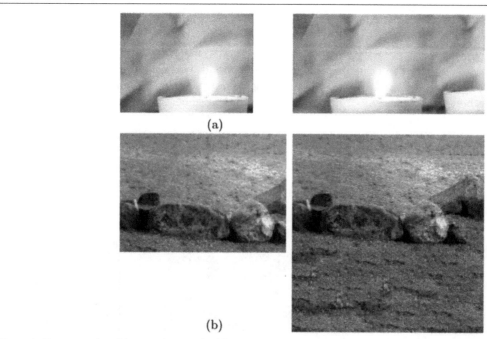

Figure 14 Two examples of the use of our method for video completion tasks. (a) The frame of the original video of 140 × 100 pixels size is completed, in order to be of 200 × 100 pixels size. (b) The frame of 176 × 120 pixels size is completed to 200 × 200 pixels size.

Abbreviations

DSCQS: double-stimulus continuous quality scale methodology; LBP: local binary patterns; LBP-TOP: local binary patterns from three orthogonal planes; NPM1: non-parametric method 1; NPM2: non-parametric method 2; PM1: parametric method 1; PM2: parametric method 2; STFSyn: spatiotemporal features-based synthesis.

Competing interests

The authors declare that they have no competing interests.

Authors' contributions

RAL-M carried out the experiments and drafted the manuscript. YG, GZ and MP conceived of the study and participated in the design of the proposal and the experiments. In addition, they developed the temporal synthesis approach. RES-Y contributed in the design of the experiments and in the revision of the manuscript. All authors read and approved the final manuscript.

Acknowledgements

The authors would like to thank the Academy of Finland, Infotech Oulu, and the Finnish CIMO for the financial support. In addition, Lizarraga-Morales would like to thank the Mexican CONCyTEG and CONACyT for the grants provided and to the Universidad de Guanajuato through the PIFI 2013 for the financial support.

Author details

[1] Universidad de Guanajuato DICIS, Salamanca, Guanajuato 36885, Mexico.
[2] Center for Machine Vision Research, Department of Computer Science and Engineering, University of Oulu, P.O. Box 4500, Oulu FI-90014, Finland.

References

1. LY Wei, S Lefebvre, V Kwatra, G Turk, State of the art in example-based texture synthesis, Eurographics 2009 State of the Art Report (EG-STAR), European Association for Computer Graphics, 2009, pp. 93–117

2. B Ghanem, N Ahuja, Phase PCA for dynamic texture video compression. Paper presented at the IEEE international conference on image processing, San Antonio, TX, USA, 16 Sept–19 Oct 2007, vol. 3, pp. 425–428. doi: 10.1109/ICIP.2007.4379337

3. G Doretto, E Jones, S Soatto, Spatially homogeneous dynamic textures, in Computer Vision- ECCV'04. ed. by T. Pajdla and J. Matas. 8th European Conference on Computer Vision, Prague, Czech Republic, May 2004. Lecture Notes in Computer Science. vol. 3022 (Springer, Heidelberg, 2004), pp. 591–602. doi: 10.1007/978-3-540-24671-8_47

4. R Costantini, L Sbaiz, S Susstrunk, Higher order SVD analysis for dynamic texture synthesis. IEEE Trans. Image Process. **17**(1), 42–52 (2008). doi: 10.1109/TIP.2007.910956

5. CB Liu, RS Lin, N Ahuja, MH Yang, Dynamic textures synthesis as nonlinear manifold learning and traversing. Paper presented in the British machine vision conference, Edinburgh, 4–7 Sept 2006, pp. 88.1–88.10. doi: 10.5244/C.20.88

6. L Yuan, F Wen, C Liu, HY Shum, Synthesizing dynamic texture with closed-loop linear dynamic system, in Computer Vision-ECCV'04, ed. by T Pajdla, J Matas, vol. 3022 (Springer, Heidelberg, 2004), pp. 603-616. doi: 10.1007/978-3-540-24671-8_48

7. B Ghanem, N Ahuja, Phase based modelling of dynamic textures. Paper presented at the 11th IEEE international conference on computer vision, Rio de Janeiro, Brazil, 14–21 Oct 2007, pp. 1–8. doi: 10.1109/ICCV.2007.4409094

8. A Efros, T Leung, Texture synthesis by non-parametric sampling. Paper presented at the 7th IEEE international conference on computer vision, Kerkyra, Greece, 20–27 Sept 1999, vol. 2, pp. 1033–1038. doi: 10.1109/ICCV.1999.790383

9. LY Wei, M Levoy, Fast texture synthesis using tree-structured vector quantization. Paper presented at the 27th annual conference on computer graphics and interactive techniques, New Orleans, LA USA, 23–28 July 2000 pp. 479–488. doi: 10.1145/344779.345009

10. Y Gui, M Chen, Z Xie, L Ma, Z Chen, Texture synthesis based on feature description. J. Adv. Mech. Des. Syst. Manuf. **6**(3), 376–388 (2012). doi: 10.1299/jamdsm.6.376

11. L Liang, YQ Xu, B Guo, HY Shum, Real-time texture synthesis by patch-based sampling. ACM Trans. Graph. **20**(3), 127–150 (2001). doi: 10.1145/501786.501787

12. AA Efros, WT Freeman, Image quilting for texture synthesis and transfer. Paper presented at the 28th annual conference on computer graphics and interactive techniques, Los Angeles, CA USA, 12–17 Aug 2001, pp. 341–346. doi: 10.1145/383259.383296

13. V Kwatra, A Schödl, I Essa, G Turk, A Bobick, Graphcut textures: image and video synthesis using graph cuts. ACM Trans. Graph. (TOG) **22**(3), 277–286 (2003). doi: 10.1145/882262.882264

14. Q Wu, Y Yu, Feature matching and deformation for texture synthesis. ACM Trans. Graph. (TOG) **23**(3), 364–367 (2004). doi: 10.1145/882262.882264

15. G Zhao, M Pietikäinen, Dynamic texture recognition using local binary patterns with an application to facial expressions. IEEE Trans. Pattern Anal. Mach. Intell. **29**(6), 915–928 (2007). doi: 10.1109/TPAMI.2007.1110

16. RA Lizarraga-Morales, Y Guo, G Zhao, M Pietikäinen, Dynamic texture synthesis in space with a spatio-temporal descriptor, in Computer Vision-ACCV'12 Workshops, ed. Jong-Il Park and Junmo Kim. ACCV 2012 International Workshops, Daejeon, Korea, Nov 2012. Part I, LNCS 7728, 2013, pp. 38–49. doi: 10.1007/978-3-642-37410-4_4

17. T Ojala, M Pietikäinen, T Mäenpää, Multiresolution gray-scale and rotation invariant texture classification with local binary patterns. IEEE Trans. Pattern Anal. Mach. Intell. **24**(7), 971–987 (2002). doi: 10.1109/TPAMI.2002.1017623

18. V Asha, P Nagabhushan, N Bhajantri, Automatic extraction of texture-periodicity using superposition of distance matching functions and their forward differences. Pattern Recognit. Lett. **33**(5), 629–640 (2012). doi: 10.1016/j.patrec.2011.11.027

19. RA Lizarraga-Morales, RE Sanchez-Yanez, V Ayala-Ramirez, Fast texel size estimation in visual texture using homogeneity cues. Pattern Recognit. Lett. **34**(4), 414–422 (2013). doi: 10.1016/j.patrec.2012.09.022

20. R Szeliski, HY Shum, Creating full view panoramic image mosaics and environment maps. Paper presented at the 24th annual conference on computer graphics and interactive technique, Los Angeles, CA USA, 3–8 Aug 1997, pp. 251-258. doi: 10.1145/258734.258861

21. Z Bar-Joseph, R El-Yaniv, D Lischinski, M Werman, Texture mixing and texture movie synthesis using statistical learning. IEEE Trans. Vis. Comput. Graph. **7**(2), 120–135 (2001). doi: 10.1109/2945.928165

22. R Péteri, S Fazekas, MJ Huiskes, DynTex : a comprehensive database of dynamic textures. Pattern Recognit. Lett. **31**, 1627–1632 (2010). doi: 10.1016/j.patrec.2010.05.009

23. JR Ohm, Multimedia Communication Technology (Springer, Berlin, 2004)

24. Y Guo, G Zhao, J Chen, M Pietikainen, Z Xu, Dynamic texture synthesis using a spatial temporal descriptor. Paper presented at the 16th IEEE international conference on image processing, Cairo, Egypt, 7–10 Nov 2009, pp. 2277–2280. doi: 10.1109/ICIP.2009.5414395

25. A Schödl, R Szeliski, DH Salesin, I Essa, Video textures. Paper presented at the 27th annual conference on computer graphics and interactive techniques, New Orleans, LA, USA, 23–28 July 2000, pp. 489–498. doi: 10.1145/344779.345012

26. Y Guo, G Zhao, Z Zhou, M Pietikäinen, Video texture synthesis with multi-frame LBP-TOP and diffeomorphic growth model. IEEE Trans. Image Process. **22**(10), 3879–389 (2013). doi: 10.1109/TIP.2013.226314

9

Explore semantic pixel sets based local patterns with information entropy for face recognition

Zhenhua Chai[1*], Heydi Mendez-Vazquez[2], Ran He[1], Zhenan Sun[1] and Tieniu Tan[1]

Abstract

Several methods have been proposed to describe face images in order to recognize them automatically. Local methods based on spatial histograms of local patterns (or operators) are among the best-performing ones. In this paper, a new method that allows to obtain more robust histograms of local patterns by using a more discriminative spatial division strategy is proposed. Spatial histograms are obtained from regions clustered according to the semantic pixel relations, making better use of the spatial information. Here, a simple rule is used, in which pixels in an image patch are clustered by sorting their intensity values. By exploring the information entropy on image patches, the number of sets on each of them is learned. Besides, Principal Component Analysis with a Whitening process is applied for the final feature vector dimension reduction, making the representation more compact and discriminative. The proposed division strategy is invariant to monotonic grayscale changes, and shows to be particularly useful when there are large expression variations on the faces. The method is evaluated on three widely used face recognition databases: AR, FERET and LFW, with the very popular LBP operator and some of its extensions. Experimental results show that the proposal not only outperforms those methods that use the same local patterns with the traditional division, but also some of the best-performing state-of-the-art methods.

1 Introduction

Face recognition is a popular biometric technique, mainly because it is considered as non-intrusive and it can be applied in a wide range of applications such as access control, video surveillance and human computer interaction [1]. Feature extraction is one of the most important steps in the face recognition process, but to obtain discriminative and robust features for describing face images is still an open problem [2]. Several methods have been proposed toward this aim, that can mainly be divided into two groups: local feature-based methods and global appearance-based methods [1]. In general, local feature-based methods exhibit a better behavior and have some advantages over the global ones [3-5]. Among existing local descriptors, Gabor wavelet-based methods are one of the best performing, mainly due to their spatial locality

and orientation selectivity [6]. However, although different strategies have been proposed, they are still computationally intensive and consume too much time in feature extraction [7], being not suitable for real-time and mobile applications. On the other hand, histograms of local patterns, such as Local Binary Patterns and its different extensions, which are also very popular local descriptors [8], are very simple and fast to compute.

The Local Binary Patterns (LBP) operator was first proposed for texture classification and was then applied to face recognition using a regular regions division [9]. Many extensions of the original operator have appeared afterwards [10-16]; however most of them have focused on obtaining more discriminative descriptors, while few methods have been proposed to get a more robust division strategy.

Recently, the semantic pixel set-based LBP (spsLBP) [17] was proposed for this aim. By clustering the pixels in an image region into a number of sets according to their semantic meanings instead of using a regular division, it

---

*Correspondence: zhchai@nlpr.ia.ac.cn
[1] National Laboratory of Pattern Recognition, Institute of Automation, Chinese Academy of Science, P.O. Box 2728, Beijing 100190, People's Republic of China
Full list of author information is available at the end of the article

makes better use of the spatial information when constructing the local histograms. It was shown in [17] that this strategy can alleviate to some extent the pixel-shifting problem caused by some face deformations like variations in expression. However, only the original LBP operator was tested with the proposed strategy in [17], while more robust LBP variants can be used for improving the overall performance.

In this paper, we aim at extending the proposal in [17] to a more general framework, in which more robust local operators can be applied, such as Local Ternary Patterns (LTP) and Three-Patch LBP (TP-LBP). Moreover, we believe that the amount of information in different face regions is different, then using a fixed number of sets for all regions, like in [17], could not be appropriate. Hence, a different number of sets should be used in different regions according to their specific information quantity. Taking this into account, we propose in this paper a method for automatically learning the number of sets in which each region should be divided, by using information entropy. When including more sets, the feature vector dimensionality increases, so a dimensionality reduction method is needed. We have considered to apply the Principal Component Analysis with a Whitening process (WPCA) [18] in our framework. This method not only reduces the dimension of the feature vector, making it more compact, but also can be used even on small-sample-size cases [18].

The rest of this paper is organized as follows: in section 2, related work is analyzed; in section 3, the proposed framework is introduced, and the strategy to learn the number of clusters in a region is presented; section 4 shows experimental results of the proposed method in comparison with some related state-of-the-art descriptors; finally, conclusions are given in section 5.

2 Related work

LBP is one of the most popular face image descriptors [19,20]. It was introduced in this area in 2004, motivated by the fact that faces can be seen as a composition of micro-patterns which can be well described by this operator [9]. The original LBP [21] describes these local texture patterns by thresholding the comparison results between the intensity value of the center pixel and its 3×3 neighborhood. The resulted binary values are then concatenated together and encoded as an integer. This encoding process is illustrated on Figure 1. The operator is invariant to grayscale monotonic variations since it only takes into account if the surrounding pixels values are brighter or darker than the center pixel value. The original method was later extended for using a circular neighborhood of different radius sizes and considering different numbers of equally spaced pixels on the defined circle [22]. In the same work [22], it was shown that more than 90% of the texture information (lines, edges, corners) is contained on 58 patterns which have at most two bitwise 0 to 1 or 1 to 0 transitions; so these patterns were called uniform LBP and, in this case, a single label is assigned to all remaining patterns.

In the past few years, a number of variants of the original operator have been proposed for improving different aspects of the method [20]. Some of the extensions aim at enhancing the discriminative capability of the operator, such as the improved LBP (ILBP) [10], in which both the pixels in the circular neighborhood and the center pixel are compared against the mean intensity value of them. Another is the extended LBP (ELBP) [23], which encodes the gradient magnitude image in addition to the original image in order to represent the velocity of local variations. There are some extensions that have been proposed for improving the robustness, such as the local ternary patterns (LTP) [16] which includes a 3-level generalization coding scheme and is more resistance to noise. However, this operator is no longer invariant to monotonic grayscale transformations. There are also some extensions which have concentrated on choosing an appropriate neighborhood for the encoding process (e.g. the number and distribution of the sampling points as well as the shape and size of the neighborhood). One of the examples is the Multi-scale Block LBP (MB-LBP) [24], in which the average intensity values of neighboring rectangular blocks are compared rather than single pixels. This allows to capture macro-structures of face images. Three-Patch LBP and Four-Patch LBP [25] are also patch-based operators, and their experimental results are very promising.

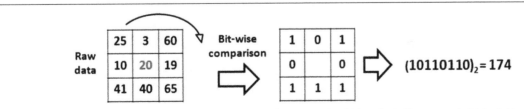

Figure 1 LBP encoding process. This figure describes the LBP encoding process in which each pixel is compared with its eight neighbor pixels and the comparisons are encoded in a binary number representing the LBP code.

Most of the descriptors mentioned above use the original strategy of Ahonen et al. [9] for facial representation. The scheme consists of dividing the face image into rectangular regions, from which local histograms of the extracted local patterns are obtained. Afterwards, the histograms of all regions are concatenated into a single spatially enhanced feature histogram that encodes both the local texture and the global shape of face images. Under this strategy, deciding the number and size of blocks is usually a problem, especially when there are different appearance variations on the face. A finer division usually makes the descriptor more discriminative but sometimes, for example when there are expression variations, will bring some problems. This is illustrated on Figure 2, where it can be appreciated that in the case of expression variations, a finer division can affect the recognition process because small blocks around some face areas, such as mouth and eyes, are shifted to neighbor blocks. Just a few methods on the literature aim at modifying the spatial division strategy. In [26] and [27], many subregions are obtained by shifting and scaling a rectangular region over the face image and boosting is used for selecting the most discriminative regions of different sizes at different positions. Overlapped subregions have also been used [28]; as well as circular [29] and triangular [30] regions.

The spsLBP method [17] is another approach proposed to solve the blocks division problem. It uses a simple clustering method to segment the pixels in a region by considering their intensity values. In spsLBP, the face image is first divided into a few coarse rectangular regions and then the pixels in each region are regrouped by their semantic meanings. Histograms of LBP codes are computed from the obtained sets and concatenated as in the traditional scheme. It is a very simple idea in which the local patterns are associated with their semantic meaning instead of their spatial position only. This strategy allows to group most of the relevant pixels into corresponding sets even in the presence of some shifting. It should be noticed that, for simplicity, intensity values were used for associating the pixels, but some other attributes such as contrast, luminance, texton, etc., could also be used. It was shown in [17] that this strategy outperforms the traditional regular division. However, more robust LBP variants were not considered in that work. On the other hand, the number of pixel sets for each region was set equal which can be inappropriate in some cases. In Figure 3, it is shown that different face regions can contain a different amount of variable information. By intuition, some regions rich in texture, like areas around eyes, should contain more information; thus, a large number for pixel groups with different semantic meanings should be set while others, like cheek, can be almost homogenous. Hence, we believe both, more robust descriptors and proper number of sets for each region, can boost the performance of this framework.

3 Face feature extraction using semantic pixel set-based local patterns

The most often used strategy for obtaining face descriptors is based on spatial histograms of local patterns. However, the grouping statistical process only considers the spatial information of the pixels, and this may be the reason for non-corresponding sub-blocks matching when there are large expression variations. Hence, we present

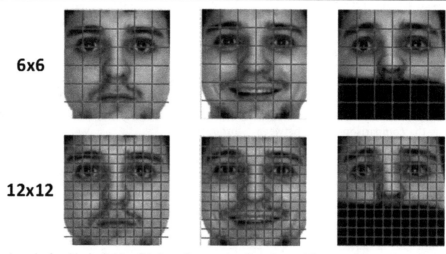

Figure 2 Traditional regular face blocks division. This figure illustrates the effect of using different sizes for regular blocks division. It is shown that when there are occlusions on faces, a finer division allows to have more blocks for comparisons (valid areas); meanwhile, in the case of expression variations, a finer division produces a decrease on the recognition rates because small blocks around some face areas, such as mouth and eyes, are shifted to neighbor blocks.

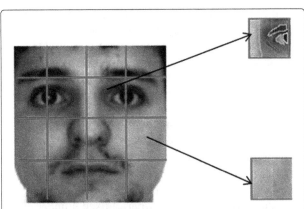

Figure 3 Illustration of the different amount of information contained in different face regions. The figure shows an example of the amount of information contained in different face regions. It can be seen that in regions around eyes, there are more variations according to pixel intensities than in cheek regions.

a strategy for associating local patterns in a face region by their semantic meaning in an adaptive way, in order to exploit better the information within each rectangular face region.

The process of face feature extraction using the general framework of semantic pixel set-based local patterns is illustrated on Figure 4. First, a face image is divided into a few regular blocks of a given size, and the number of pixel sets (N_i) for block i, is learned according to the information entropy of the block. Then, pixels in this block are re-grouped into N_i sets according to their semantic meaning. Once we have different sets of pixels for each block,

histograms of local patterns are extracted from each of them. Finally, all features are concatenated together and enhanced by the WPCA method.

3.1 Learning the number of sets based on the information entropy

The entropy is a term defined in information theory as a measurement of the uncertainty associated with a random variable [31]. It is relevant to the quantity and variability of the information. Here, we assume that the pixel intensity value is a random variable; thus, we can use the histogram of the intensities in each face block to approximate the probability density function (PDF) for computing the information entropy. Applied to our case, the larger the entropy value is, the more information a face block should contain, and thus more clusters should be set.

The entropy value of the face block i can be then defined as

$$S(i) = \sum_{k=1}^{n} p(x_k) \log_2 \left(\frac{1}{p(x_k)} \right) = - \sum_{k=1}^{n} p(x_k) \log_2 p(x_k) \quad (1)$$

where $p(x_k)$ is the probability of the pixel x with intensity value k in the histogram of the block.

In our proposal, the entropy following Equation 1, is computed from the intensity histograms of the coarse-divided regions for all face images in the training set. Then, the average entropy value of a block in all images is used as the corresponding regional entropy. Although some images in the training set might be affected by noise, the average entropy values can still reflect the information quantity differences among different facial regions.

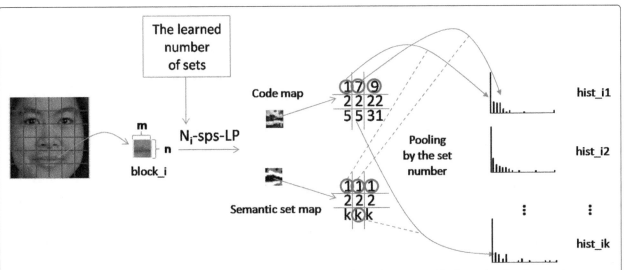

Figure 4 The flowchart of the semantic pixel set-based local patterns using information entropy. This figure describes the complete flowchart of the proposed method. First, a face image is coarsely divided into a few blocks of a given size. With the learned number of pixel sets for each face block according to the information entropy, pixels are re-grouped to different sets according to their semantic meaning. Histograms of local patterns are then extracted from each set. Finally, all features are concatenated together and enhanced by the WPCA method.

Finally, a monotonic transform function is used for mapping the entropy value to the number of sets. The whole process is described in Figure 5.

The monotonic transform function $F(x_i)$ in this paper, is implemented by using a linear function as follows:

$$F(x_i) = (x_i - x_{min})/(x_{max} - x_{min})$$
$$\times (new_{max} - new_{min}) + new_{min}, \quad (2)$$

where x_i is the average entropy for block i, x_{min} and x_{max} are the minimum and the maximum entropy values from all regions, new_{min} is the least sets the region should be divided while new_{max} is the maximum number of sets that can be obtained in a region. If the output of $F(x_i)$ is not an integer number, it can be rounded to be an integer value.

In this work, we have decided to use $new_{min} = 2$ and $new_{max} = 8$ and a coarse blocks division of 6×6, aiming at having a good trade-off between the computational cost and the proper use of the local spatial information.

Illustrated in Figure 6 is the number of sets learned with the proposed algorithm, using the mentioned configuration, for a given training set. In the image, the brightest parts represent those regions with number of sets equal to 8 and the darkest parts correspond to the number of sets 2, while the gray parts represent integers between 2 and 8. It can be seen that those blocks corresponding to the eyes and nose contain more information than the rest of the parts. This corresponds to our intuition and also obeys the traditional weighted maps used for face recognition. Hence, we believe that using different number of sets for each block will enhance the discriminant ability of the method proposed in [17], where a fixed number of sets was used. Besides, it can also help to make better use of the spatial information.

3.2 Semantic pixel sets based local patterns

Once the number of pixel sets (N_i) in each face block is learned on the training phase, the proposed semantic

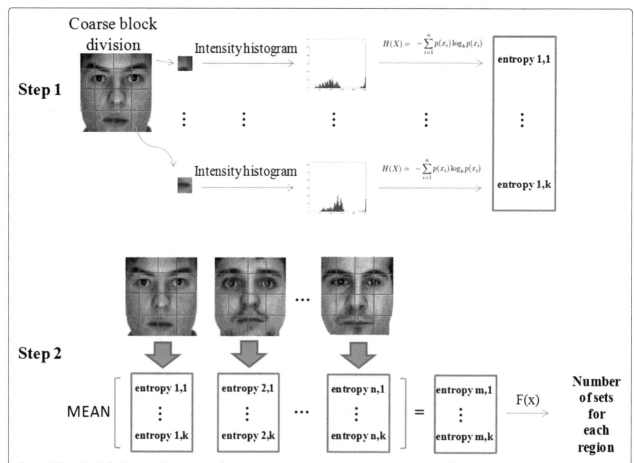

Figure 5 The details for learning the number of sets in each face block using information entropy. This figure describes the process of learning the number of sets for each face block using the information entropy. First, the pixel intensity value in each face block is treated as a random variable; thus, we can use the histogram of the intensities in each face block to approximate the probability density function (PDF) for computing the information entropy. Then, the average entropy value of all face images is used as the regional corresponding entropy. Finally, a linear function is used as a mapping from the entropy value to the number of sets.

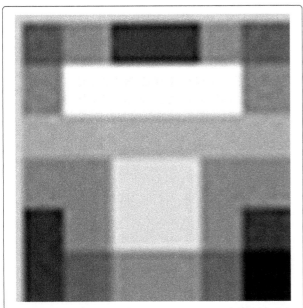

Figure 6 The learning results of set number in each face block. In the figure, the number of sets learned with the proposed algorithm based on entropy, for a given face division, is shown. It can be seen that those blocks corresponding to the eyes and nose contain more information than the rest of the parts.

pixel set-based strategy for obtaining the histogram features can be used in the recognition process. First, the pixel intensity values on block i are sorted and clustered uniformly in N_i sets, as it is illustrated in Figure 7. Under this strategy, for a fixed number of sets, the division of a block will always be the same although some have monotonic variations; so if the used local pattern operator, such as LBP, is invariant to monotonic grayscale variations, the final descriptor will also inherit this property (Additional file 1).

As was mentioned before, not only the LBP operator but also any other local pattern-based encoding method can be used with our strategy since the final representation will be given by the histograms of codes computed from each pixel set. So, we will have for each coarse block the corresponding semantic set map and the codes map computed by the encoding method (e.g. LBP, LTP, TPLBP, etc.).

Using both, the semantic set map and the computed codes map, the histogram for the set $S(i, n)$, with $n \in [1, .., N_i]$, can be obtained by

$$H_{i,n}(l) = \sum_{x,y \in S(i,n)} I\{\text{codes\_map}(x,y) = l\}, l = 0, 1, \ldots, m-1 \tag{3}$$

where codes_map(x, y) is the local pattern obtained at position (x, y) and m is the number of code labels.

Finally, all feature vectors from all sets of all blocks $(1 : t)$ will be concatenated together to represent a face image:

$$X = [H_{1,1}\, H_{1,2}\, \ldots\, H_{1,N_1}\, \ldots\, H_{t,N_t}]. \tag{4}$$

In the following, we will call this face image descriptor, semantic pixel set-based local patterns using information entropy (en-spsLP). As have been explained, the local patterns (LP) can be any histogram descriptor based on a local operator such as LBP and its different extensions.

3.3 Dimensionality reduction using WPCA

In order to take more advantage of the spatial information, overlapping regions can be used to extract the en-spsLP features. However, this increases the total dimension of the feature vector and can bring the curse of dimensionality. Hence, a feature reduction method should be applied in this case, in order to get a more compact representation.

There are different methods in the literature for dimensionality reduction. Most of the supervised methods usually applied in face recognition like LDA, although have shown good results, require more than two images per person for training, which cannot be always satisfied in real applications. It was proposed in [18] to apply Principal Component Analysis with a Whitening process (WPCA) to solve the so-called 'Single Sample per Person' problem. This method has been recently used with different face descriptors such as Local Gabor Binary Patterns [32] and POEM [33], showing a very good performance even when only one or a few images are available per person. For those reasons, we decided to apply WPCA for the dimensionality reduction in our framework.

Under this method, after a feature vector, X, is projected into the lower dimensional feature space found by PCA, $u = W_{\text{PCA}}X$, it is normalized with a whitening transformation:

$$w = \Lambda_M^{-1/2} u, \tag{5}$$

where $\Lambda_M^{-1/2} = \text{diag}\left\{\lambda_1^{-1/2}, \lambda_2^{-1/2}, \ldots, \lambda_M^{-1/2}\right\}$ and λ_i are the eigenvectors of the covariance matrix. This process aims at reducing the negative influences of the leading eigenvectors, as well as magnifies the discriminating details encoded in the trailing ones.

4 Experimental evaluation

Verification and identification experiments were conducted in order to evaluate the performance of the proposed method. Two popular databases: FERET [34] and AR [35], were used for identification experiments, while the LFW [36] database was used for verification. In those experiments where WPCA was not applied, the χ^2 distance was used to compare the obtained descriptors from face images, otherwise cosine distance will be used. In the case of identification, the nearest neighbor classifier

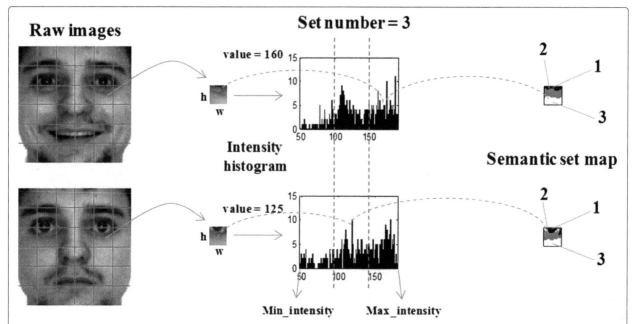

Figure 7 The details of computing the semantic set map. This figure shows the detailed process for clustering the semantic pixel sets in one face block. First, the pixel intensity value distribution is computed. It can be viewed as a simplified sorting process. Then, it is quantified into k sets according to the learned number. Finally, according the raw pixel intensity values and the sets they belong to, a semantic set map for one face block can be obtained.

was applied, and the top-rank recognition rate was used to measure the performance of the methods. In the case of verification on LFW, we have followed the evaluation protocol, and the estimated mean classification accuracy with the standard error ($\hat{u}\pm$SE) was used for the evaluation. All images were photometric normalized with the preprocessed sequence proposed by Tan and Triggs [16].

The two databases used for identification are composed by images captured under controlled environments. The FERET database [34] contains images with a lot of variations in expression, lighting and aging, divided into five subsets: Fa (gallery set), composed by frontal images of 1,196 subjects; Fb containing 1,195 face images with variations in expression; Fc subset, which contains 194 images with variations in lighting; Dup-I with 722 face images taken with an elapsed time with respect to the images in the gallery set; and Dup-II, a subset of Dup I, which contains 234 images in which the elapsed time is at least 1 year. On the other hand, the AR database [35] was created to test face recognition methods in front of various expressions, different illuminations and occlusions. It contains more than 3,200 face images of 126 people captured on two different sessions. Each person has up to 13 images per session. We randomly selected 100 different subjects (50 males and 50 females) and the neutral expression image of every person in each session was used as gallery and the rest of them with different expressions, lighting and occlusions were used for testing. Images from both

databases were cropped to 114×114. Thus, using a coarse block division of 6×6, the blocks size will be 19×19.

Different from the former two databases, the LFW [36] database contains 13,233 images that were obtained under different unconstrained environments. The images are from 5,749 different individuals, and 1,680 of them have two or more images. In our experiment, we follow the standard training and testing protocol. We have used here the 'View 1' for learning the number of sets for each face block, and the 'View 2' for the final testing. Under this protocol, 6,000 pairs of images are compared in the evaluation; the half of them correspond to images from the same person and the other half not. The testing data are divided into 10 evenly distributed sets and the test is repeated 10 times, using one set for testing and the others for training. It should be noted that our proposal was tested with the original data, without correcting the few labeling errors in the database. Besides, the aligned version (provided by [37]) of face images was used, and all of them were cropped to 126×110. In this case, overlapped coarse blocks of 18×22 were used.

4.1 The contribution of semantic pixel sets to different LBP based descriptors

The aim of the first experiment is to show that the semantic pixel set (sps)-based strategy, makes not only the original LBP but also other LBP-based descriptors, more robust and stable under different variations of facial appearance. It is expected that by using more robust descriptors, better results can be achieved. In order to make a fair comparison with [17], we use in this experiment the same fixed number of sets for each region, i.e. 6 or 8 sets. Besides, the original uniform LBP, the Local Ternary Patterns (LTP) [16] and the Three-Patch LBP (TP-LBP) [25] with the coarse initial division are tested. The obtained results on the FERET database are listed on Table 1. It can be seen that almost on all cases, the sps outperforms the traditional regular division. Moreover, the more robust the descriptor, the better the results achieved with our proposal. In general, the best performing descriptor is LTP.

In order to have an in-depth comparison between the sps strategy and the traditional block division, we test the LTP descriptor, with each strategy during histogram estimation. In order to make the comparison fair, we do not use the illumination preprocessing in this experiment. Given a coarse blocks division of 6 × 6, we compare the results of using LTP directly over this division (LTP), dividing those coarse blocks into more n sub-blocks (n-blockLTP) and dividing them into n sets according to our proposal (n-spsLTP). The results obtained in each subset of AR database with different kinds of variations are listed on Table 2.

As was explained in the Introduction, a finer regular block division is good for some cases (e.g. occlusions) but degrades for some others, especially for expression variations. It can be seen from Table 2, that although the blockLTP presents slightly better results than our proposal for occlusion variations, in the case of expressions, the performance drops off by a significant margin, even worse than the original LTP. In general, our sps strategy has a more stable behavior. In any case, we have to admit the disadvantages of our method in the case of unpredicted occlusions. For instance, the pixel intensities of the original cheek region occluded by sunglasses will not be as dark as the black sunglasses. This will definitely change

Table 2 Top rank recognition rates on the AR database

Method	Expression	Lighting	Scarf	Sunglasses	Average
LTP	88.66	94.66	74.00	64.83	79.70
6-blockLTP	83.50	99.66	93.83	91.16	92.04
8-blockLTP	82.83	99.33	92.66	89.33	91.04
6-spsLTP	90.00	98.66	91.33	88.83	91.83
8-spsLTP	90.66	99.33	92.33	86.66	92.63

The advantage and disadvantage between sps and regular blocks division.

the sorting results of the pixel intensity values. The pooling process will thus go wrong. So, in the future, we will try some appearance-based methods for clustering in order to get a more stable block division result.

4.2 The contribution of entropy-based learning algorithm for estimation the number of sets in each block

The aim of the this experiment is to demonstrate the contribution of using the information entropy for learning the number of sets for each face block. In this case, we compare the results of the same three descriptors with a fixed number of sets for each block (best results from Table 1) and using information entropy for learning the number of sets (en-sps). The obtained results are shown on Table 3. It can be appreciated that by using different number of sets for each region, better results are achieved in almost all cases. Besides, it can be said that the proposed learning method is useful for deciding the number of sets in each face block.

4.3 Face recognition using information entropy based spsLTP

In order to further exploit the capabilities of the proposed descriptor and to make better use of the spatial information, in this experiment we use the overlapping regions to derive the face features. Since in both experiments above, the LTP-based descriptor performs the best, we are going to use it in this experiment. In this case, keep the same blocks size but with five pixels of overlapping between neighbor blocks. When more blocks are involved, the final

Table 1 Top rank recognition rates on the FERET database

Method	Fb	Fc	DupI	DupII	Average
uLBP	91.96	93.29	58.86	49.14	77.61
6-spsLBP	95.73	95.36	69.52	62.39	84.30
8-spsLBP	95.56	95.36	68.28	60.68	83.66
LTP	95.73	96.90	69.39	61.96	84.34
6-spsLTP	97.07	96.90	72.71	67.94	86.65
8-spsLTP	97.15	96.90	71.88	65.38	86.18
TPLBP	91.54	88.14	65.51	55.55	79.65
6-spsTPLBP	95.73	92.26	71.32	64.10	84.77
8-spsTPLBP	95.56	91.23	70.08	62.39	84.05

The contribution of semantic pixel sets to different LBP-based descriptors.

Table 3 Top rank recognition rates on the FERET database

Method	Fb	Fc	DupI	DupII	Average
6-spsLBP	95.73	95.36	69.52	62.39	84.30
en-spsLBP	96.31	96.39	71.60	67.52	85.84
6-spsLTP	97.07	96.90	72.71	67.94	86.65
en-spsLTP	97.23	96.39	74.93	70.94	87.67
6-spsTPLBP	95.73	92.26	71.32	64.10	84.77
en-spsTPLBP	97.74	96.90	72.02	65.38	86.52

The contribution of entropy based learning algorithm for the estimation of the number of sets in each face block.

feature vector size becomes many times the original one. Hence, the use of a feature reduction method is needed. As it was explained above, the WPCA method is applied in this case. The obtained results, compared with some other face descriptors on FERET database are shown on Table 4. It can be seen that for spsLTP, better results can be achieved with the overlapping version (spsLTP-ov). Besides, when the learned number of sets for each block is used, the results can get further improvement, compared with the results obtained by using a fixed number of sets for all blocks. Moreover, the benefits of using WPCA are demonstrated. In this database, when using overlapping blocks, we have found a total of 1,298 sets. This means that the descriptor (en-set-spsLTP-ov) has a dimension of 153,164 (1,298 × 59 × 2). We have selected only 850 features by using WPCA (en-set-spsLTP-ov-WPCA) and a better result is obtained. So, by applying WPCA, we get a more compact and discriminative descriptor.

It can also be seen on the table that our results are comparable with some of the state-of-the-art methods such as the Local Gabor Binary Patterns Histograms Sequence (LGBPHS) [32], the Learned Local Gabor Patterns (LLGP) [39], the Histograms of Gabor Ordinal Measures (HOGOM) [40], the Patterns of Oriented Edge Magnitudes (POEM) [42] and Discriminative Local Binary Patterns (DLBP) [41].

4.4 Descriptors comparison in unconstrained environment

The aim of this last experiment is to show the effectiveness of our proposal in a more challenging face database, the LFW, for the uncontrolled face verification task. Since our method is unsupervised, only related works are compared. All images of the aligned version [36] are cropped to be 126 × 110 around the center. Blocks of 18 × 22 pixels are used to extract the en-spsLTP features, overlapped by six pixels in the rows and eight pixels in the columns. During model selection, the training set in 'View 1' was used to learn the number of sets for each block by using the information entropy. For testing in 'View 2', the training set is used to train the WPCA axes and find the best threshold for determining if a comparison corresponds to the same person or not. In Table 5, we compare our method with other descriptors evaluated in [37] and [43] under the same protocol. We can find that in the list of unsupervised methods, our proposed method is comparable with the other descriptors. Since this dataset is very challenging, we believe our method can achieve a better result by using a more complex nonlinear classifier learned from a supervised way.

5   Conclusions

This paper proposes a face representation framework called histogram of semantic pixel set-based local patterns using information entropy (en-spsLP). First, the number of pixel sets is learned according to the information entropy in each face block. Then, during the histogram estimation, the code of the local pattern is pooled according to the original pixel intensity distribution. Finally, all the histograms are concatenated together and enhanced by the WPCA. The proposed method is easy to implement and the speed of the feature extraction is very fast. At the same time, the results are comparable with some of the state-of-the-art methods. Future work is to try other clustering criterion (e.g. by texton) in order to achieve more robustness to unpredicted occlusions. Besides, the optimal values for initial block size and position based on face landmarks can be further analyzed.

Table 4 Top rank recognition rates on the FERET database

Method	Fb	Fc	DupI	DupII
LGBPHS [32]	94.00	97.00	68.00	53.00
LGBPWP [18]	98.10	98.90	83.80	81.60
POEM [33]	97.60	96.00	77.80	76.50
POEM + WPCA [38]	99.60	99.48	88.78	85.00
LLGP [39]	99.00	99.00	80.00	78.00
HOGOM [40]	98.10	99.50	83.60	82.00
DLBP [41]	99.00	99.00	86.00	85.00
6-spsLTP-ov	97.65	99.48	76.73	72.22
en-spsLTP-ov	98.41	99.48	79.36	76.92
6-spsLTP-ov + WPCA	99.41	99.48	84.90	81.62
en-spsLTP-ov + WPCA	99.74	99.48	88.78	85.89

Face recognition using entropy based spsLTP-ov + WPCA in controlled environment.

Table 5 Mean scores on the LFW database on 'image-restricted configuration' and aligned images

Method	Performance
uLBP [37]	0.6824
Gabor (C1) [37]	0.6849
TPLBP [37]	0.6926
FPLBP [37]	0.6818
SIFT [37]	0.6986
V1-like [43]	0.6421 ± 0.0069
V1-like+ [43]	0.6808 ± 0.0044
LARK [44]	0.7223 ± 0.0049
POEM [33]	0.7520 ± 0.0073
POEM + WPCA [45]	0.8113 ± 0.0053
en-spsLTP-ov + WPCA	0.8050 ± 0.0033

Face recognition using entropy based spsLTP-ov + WPCA in uncontrolled environment.

Additional file

Additional file 1: Proof of the monotonic grayscale invariant property of the semantic pixel set strategy.

Competing interests
The authors declare that they have no competing interests.

Acknowledgement
This work is funded by the Strategic Priority Research Program of the Chinese Academy of Sciences (Grant No. XDA06030300), National Basic Research Program of China (Grant No. 2012CB316300), National Natural Science Foundation of China (Grant No. 61075024, 61273272, 61103155) and International S&T Cooperation Program of China (Grant No.2010DFB14110).

Author details
[1]National Laboratory of Pattern Recognition, Institute of Automation, Chinese Academy of Science, P.O. Box 2728, Beijing 100190, People's Republic of China. [2]Advanced Technologies Application Center, 7th Avenue #21812 b/ 218 and 222, Havana, Cuba.

References

1. AK Jain, SZ Li, *Handbook of Face Recognition*. (Springer-Verlag New York, Inc., Secaucus, NJ, USA,2005)
2. W Zhao, R Chellappa, PJ Phillips, A Rosenfeld, Face recognition: a literature survey. ACM Comput. Surv. **35**(4), 399–458 (2003)
3. B Heisele, P Ho, J Wu, T Poggio, Face recognition: component-based versus global approaches. Comput. Vis. Image Underst. **91**(1–2), 6–21 (2003)
4. X Tan, S Chen, Z Zhou, F Zhang, Face recognition from a single image per person: a survey. Pattern Recognit. **39**(9), 1725–1745 (2006)
5. R He, BG Hu, WS Zheng, XW Kong, Robust principal component analysis based on maximum correntropy criterion. IEEE Trans. Image Process. **20**(6), 1485–1494 (2011)
6. Á Serrano, IM de Diego, C Conde, E Cabello, Recent advances in face biometrics with Gabor wavelets: a review. Pattern Recognit. Lett. **31**(5), 372–381 (2010)
7. Z Lei, S Liao, M Pietikäinen, SZ Li, Face recognition by exploring information jointly in space, scale and orientation. IEEE Trans. Image Process. **20**, 247–256 (2011)
8. M Pietikäinen, A Hadid, A Zhao, T Ahonen, *Computer Vision Using Local Binary Patterns*. (Springer-Verlag, London Ltd, 2011)
9. T Ahonen, A Hadid, M Pietikäinen, Face recognition with local binary patterns, in *European Conference on Computer Vision (ECCV)*. Prague, Czech Republic, 11–14 May 2004, pp. 469–481
10. H Jin, Q Liu, H Lu, X Tong, Face detection using improved LBP under Bayesian framework, in *International Conference on Image and Graphics (ICIG)*. Hong Kong, 18–20 Dec 2004, pp. 306–309
11. S Liao, ACS Chung, Face recognition by using elongated local binary patterns with average maximum distance gradient magnitude, in *Asian Conference on Computer Vision (ACCV)*. Tokyo, 18–22 Nov 2007, pp. 672–679
12. S Liao, X Zhu, Z Lei, L Zhang, SZ Li, Learning multi-scale block local binary patterns for face recognition, in *International Conference on Biometrics (ICB)*. Seoul, 27–29 Aug 2007, pp. 828–837
13. Z Guo, L Zhang, D Zhang, X Mou, Hierarchical multiscale LBP for face and palmprint recognition, in *International Conference on Image Processing (ICIP)*. Hong Kong, 26–29 Sept 2010, pp. 4521–4524
14. S Liao, M Law, A Chung, Dominant local binary patterns for texture classification. IEEE Trans. Image Process. **18**(5), 1107–1118 (2009)
15. Z Guo, L Zhang, D Zhang, A completed modeling of local binary pattern operator for texture classification. IEEE Trans. Image Process. **19**(6), 1657–1663 (2010)
16. X Tan, B Triggs, Enhanced local texture feature sets for face recognition under difficult lighting conditions. IEEE Trans. Image Process. **19**(6), 1635–1650 (2010)
17. Z Chai, H Mendez, R He, Z Sun, T Tan, Semantic pixel sets based local binary patterns for face recognition, in *acepted in Asian Conference on Computer Vision (ACCV)*. Daejeon, 5–9 Nov 2012
18. W Deng, J Hu, J Guo, Gabor-eigen-whiten-cosine: a robust scheme for face recognition, in *AMFG*. Beijing, 16 Oct 2005, pp. 336–349
19. S Marcel, Y Rodriguez, G Heusch, On the recent use of local binary patterns for face authentication. Tech. Rep, 06–34, Idiap, 2006
20. D Huang, C Shan, M Ardabilian, Y Wang, L Chen, Local binary patterns and its application to facial image analysis: a survey. IEEE Trans. Syst. Man Cybernetics-Part C: Appl. Rev. **41**(6), 765–781 (2011)
21. T Ojala, M Pietikäinen, D Harwood, A comparative study of texture measures with classification based on featured distributions. Pattern Recognit. **29**, 51–59 (1996)
22. T Ojala, M Pietikäinen, Mäenpää T, Multiresolution gray-scale and rotation invariant texture classification with local binary patterns. IEEE Trans. Pattern Anal. Mach. Intell. **24**(7), 971–987 (2002)
23. X Huang, SZ Li, Y Wang, Shape localization based on statistical method using extended local binary pattern, in *International Conference on Image and Graphics (ICIG)*, (2004), pp. 184–187
24. S Liao, X Zhu, Z Lei, L Zhang, SZ Li, Learning multi-scale block local binary patterns for face recognition, in *International Conference on Biometrics (ICB)*. Seoul, 27–29 Aug 2007, pp. 828–837
25. L Wolf, T Hassner, Y Taigman, Descriptor based methods in the wild, in *Faces in Real-Life Images workshop at the European Conference on Computer Vision (ECCV)*. Marseille, 12–18 Oct 2008
26. G Zhang, X Huang, S Li, Y Wang, X Wu, Boosting local binary pattern (LBP)-based face recognition, in *Advances in Biometric Person Authentication, Volume 3338 of Lecture Notes in Computer Science*, ed. by S Li, J Lai, T Tan, G Feng, and Wang Y (Springer Berlin Heidelberg, 2005), pp. 179–186
27. C Shan, S Gong, Owan McP, Conditional mutual information based boosting for facial expression recognition, in *Proceedings of British Machine Vision Conference*. Oxford, UK, Sept 2005
28. T Gritti, C Shan, V Jeanne, R Braspenning, Local features based facial expression recognition with face registration errors, in *Proceedings of IEEE International Conference on Automatic Face and Gesture Recognition*. Amsterdam, The Netherlands, 17–19 Sept 2008
29. T Ahonen, A Hadid, M Pietikäinen, Face description with local binary patterns: Application to face recognition. IEEE Trans. Pattern Anal. Mach. Intell. **28**(12), 2037–2041 (2006)
30. H Mendez-Vazquez, E Garcia-Reyes, Y Condes-Molleda, A new image division for LBP method to improve face recognition under varying lighting conditions, in *Proceedings of International Conference on Pattern Recognition*. Tampa, Florida, 8–11 Dec 2008, pp. 1–4
31. TM Cover, JA Thomas, *Elements of Information Theory (Wiley Series in Telecommunications and Signal Processing)*. (Wiley, New York, 2006)
32. W Zhang, S Shan, W Gao, X Chen, H Zhang, Local Gabor binary pattern histogram sequence (LGBPHS): a novel non-statistical model for face representation and recognition, in *International Conference on Computer Vision (ICCV)*. Beijing, 17–20 Oct 2005, pp. 786–791
33. NS Vu, A Caplier, Face recognition with patterns of oriented edge magnitudes, in *European Conference on Computer Vision (ECCV)*. Heraklion, Crete, 5–11 Sept 2010, pp. 313–326
34. JP Phillips, H Moon, SA Rizvi, PJ Rauss, The FERET evaluation methodology for face-recognition algorithms. IEEE Trans. Pattern Anal. Mach. Intell. **22**(10), 1090–1104 (2000)
35. A Martínez, R Benavente, The AR face database. Tech. Rep. #24, CVC 1998
36. GB Huang, M Ramesh, T Berg, E Learned-Miller, Labeled faces in the wild: a database for studying face recognition in unconstrained environments. Tech. Rep, 07–49, (University of Massachusetts, Amherst, 2007)
37. L Wolf, T Hassner, Y Taigman, Similarity scores based on background samples, in *Asian Conference on Computer Vision (ACCV)*. Xi'an, China, 23–27 Sept 2009, pp. 88–97
38. NS Vu, A Caplier, Enhanced patterns of oriented edge magnitudes for face recognition and image matching. IEEE Trans. IP. **21**(3), 1352–1365 (2012)
39. S Xie, S Shan, X Chen, X Meng, W Gao, Learned local Gabor patterns for face representation and recognition. Signal Process. **89**(12), 2333–2344 (2009)
40. Z Chai, R He, Z Sun, T Tan, H Mendez-Vazquez, Histograms of Gabor ordinal measures for face representation and recognition, in *IAPR International Conference on Biometrics (ICB),*. New Delhi, India, 29 March–1 April 2012, pp. 52–58

41. D Maturana, D Mery, A Soto, Learning discriminative local binary patterns for face recognition, in *International Conference on Automatic Face and Gesture Recognition (FG)*. Santa Barbara, CA, 21–25 March 2011, pp. 470–475

42. NS Vu, HM Dee, A Caplier, Face recognition using the POEM descriptor. Pattern Recogn. **45**(7), 2478–2488 (2012)

43. N Pinto, JJ DiCarlo, DD Cox, Establishing good benchmarks and baselines for face recognition, in *Faces in Real-Life Images workshop at the European Conference on Computer Vision (ECCV)*. Marseille, 12–18 Oct 2008

44. HJ Seo, P Milanfar, Face verification using the LARK representation. IEEE Trans. Inform. Forensics Secur. (TIFS). **6**(4), 1275–1286 (2011)

45. NS Vu, A Caplier, Enhanced patterns of oriented edge magnitudes for face recognition and image matching. IEEE Trans. Image Process. **21**(3), 1352–1365 (2012)

10

Locating moving objects in car-driving sequences

Antonio Garcia-Dopico[*], José Luis Pedraza, Manuel Nieto, Antonio Pérez, Santiago Rodríguez and Luis Osendi

Abstract

This paper presents a system for the search and detection of moving objects in a sequence of images previously captured by a camera installed in a conventional vehicle. The objective is the design and implementation of a software system based on optical flow analysis to detect and identify moving objects as perceived by a driver, taking into account that these objects could interfere with the driver's behavior, either through distraction or by posing an actual danger that may require an active response. The problem presents significant difficulties because the vehicle travels on conventional roads, open to normal traffic. Consequently, the scenes are recorded with natural lighting, i.e., under highly variable conditions (intensity, shadows, etc.). Furthermore, the use of a moving camera makes it difficult to properly identify static objects such as the road itself, signals, buildings, landscapes, and moving objects of the same speed, such as pedestrians or other vehicles. The proposed method consists of three stages. First, the optical flow is calculated for each image of the sequence, as a first estimate of the apparent motion. In a second step, two segmentation processes are addressed: the optical flow itself and the images of the sequence. Finally, in the last stage, the results of these two segmentation processes are combined to obtain the movement of the objects present in the sequence, identifying both their direction and magnitude. The quality of the results obtained with different sequences of real images makes this software suitable for systems to study driver behavior and to help detect danger situations, as various international traffic agencies consider in their research projects.

Keywords: Optical flow; Optical flow segmentation; Image segmentation; Real traffic; Driver behavior; Natural lighting

1 Introduction

This paper addresses the detection of moving objects that could interfere with driver behavior, either through distraction or by posing an actual danger. The scene is recorded as seen by the driver, i.e., with a moving camera. The optical flow obtained from these video sequences is computed to obtain an estimate of the apparent motion present in the scene. The camera is installed inside a conventional vehicle driving on public roads. The moving camera and the variable natural lighting pose a serious challenge for calculating optical flow. Taking the sequences while driving on actual roads also implies a large number of objects captured by the images (vehicles, vegetation, signs, buildings, etc.). This makes it difficult to correctly determine optical flow.

The main novelty present in our solution is the combined use of two independent and complementary segmentation processes, optical flow segmentation and raw image segmentation. Once both processes are finished, an additional computation stage is dedicated to find matches between both segmented image results. This stage also identifies objects with relatively high apparent motion to detect and point out any danger situation. All these processes require highly computing-intensive operations. Due to this fact, a parallel real-time version of this system has been developed and implemented as described in [1]. In this parallel version, all processing stages are carried out at a 45-frames per second (fps) rate when applied to 502×288 small images or at a 15-fps rate when high-resolution 720×576 images are used. These data come from a rather basic prototype, but we envisage running these processes on a powerful up-to-date multi-core quad processor PC to achieve 30 fps for full HD $1,920 \times 1,080$ images.

*Correspondence: dopico@fi.upm.es
DATSI, Facultad de Informática, Universidad Politécnica de Madrid, Boadilla del Monte 28660, Spain

Apparent motion identified in this way is similar to apparent motion as estimated by a human driver. Therefore, potential dangers that could be identified by a driver who is aware of his activity can be identified by a system based on the techniques described in this paper.

Once OF has been computed, all similar optical flow vectors are grouped together, because they probably belong to be the same object. The complexity of the process is increased by the fact that the camera is also moving, because all objects in the image sequence seem to move away from a given point, the focus of expansion (FOE), and there is no static object that can be used as a reference. In fact, depending on the movement of the camera relative to the rest of the objects, three situations can be distinguished:

1. Static camera with moving objects: this is the simplest case since the images have a fixed background, which helps differentiate the moving objects more clearly. An example of this case could be the sequences captured by roadside traffic cameras.
2. Moving camera with static objects: this scenario presents more difficulties, since there is no static background to easily determine the moving objects. However, the knowledge that the objects in the scene are static makes it easier to establish reference points for movement. Examples of this case could be the landscape sequences in commercial movies.
3. Moving camera with moving objects: this is the special case addressed in this paper, in which both the camera and the objects are moving in the scene. It is the most complex case since there is no available reference. The camera is installed on board a vehicle traveling at a regular speed, ranging from a few kilometers per hour to 120 km/h.

In the sequences taken with the moving camera, all of the pixels seem to recede from a given point which is known as the FOE. The FOE is the point on the horizon at which the camera is aimed. It seems to be static and, therefore, does not generate optical flow. As the distance of the pixels from the FOE increases, they create a higher optical flow vector, i.e., if an object is near the edge of the image, it appears to move faster than if it is close to the FOE. Even the direction of the vector is affected, since all objects appear to radially move away from the FOE. This means that vectors from the same object could present different magnitudes or directions, making the task of grouping them highly complex.

Moreover, due to the camera movement, optical flow can be rather high even when all the objects in the scene are static. This optical flow can be determined and the pattern of movement established, but it is not uniform or constant because the vehicle speed and direction change considerably. Depending on the speed of the camera and on the direction of its motion, the apparent pixel movement or movement pattern is obtained, determining the velocity of a static object relative to the camera. Furthermore, the images are taken outdoors with variable light conditions, so shadows and reflections constantly appear and disappear as the car moves, interfering with the optical flow calculation.

In addition to calculating and segmenting the optical flow, the image is also segmented in search of the objects composing it. Although a specific kind of image sequences is used, restrictions have not been applied, as the aim is to obtain general solutions applicable to any kind of sequences. The system tries to locate moving objects and to assign them vectors with its velocity with respect to the camera, based solely on the video sequences taken from the inside of a moving car traveling along a road.

Two approaches were used in analyzing the images: (1) static, i.e., the size and shape of the objects are identified; and (2) dynamic, i.e., analyzing the motion in the sequence to obtain velocity vectors. In a subsequent phase, these partial results are combined so that the objects are mapped to velocity vectors as shown in Figure 1.

By combining the best of each approach, satisfactory results can be obtained, since only the edges of uniform objects generate optical flow. Consequently, correct shapes of uniform objects can not be obtained using only

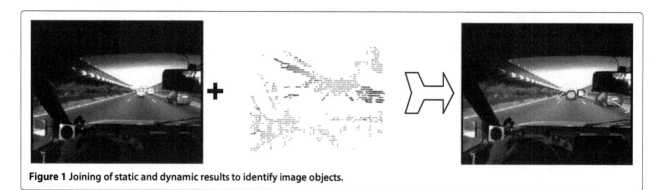

Figure 1 Joining of static and dynamic results to identify image objects.

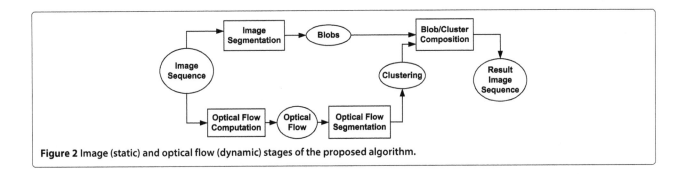

Figure 2 Image (static) and optical flow (dynamic) stages of the proposed algorithm.

velocity vectors. On the other hand, static images alone do not allow obtaining velocity vectors of moving objects.

The general approach followed is shown in Figure 2, in which the stages of the process are represented by rectangular shapes, and the results obtained by elliptical shapes. The images used for this work have been taken with a camera located inside the vehicle simulating the driver's point of view as shown in Figure 3.

2 Related work

This section briefly describes the basis on which the system analyzed in this paper is supported. As indicated earlier, the main novelty of our solution is the combined use of optical flow segmentation and raw image segmentation. Moreover, these processes should ideally be carried out in real time. Consequently, several of the application areas involved deserve to be placed in context, specifically, algorithms for optical flow computation and their parallelization, and segmentation of the optical flow results.

2.1 Algorithms for optical flow computation

There is a variety of algorithms to perform the computation of the optical flow. Most of them are based on the

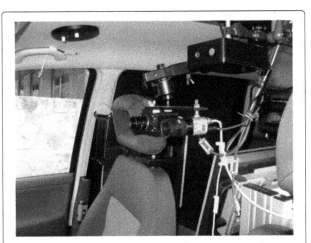

Figure 3 Scene camera inside the vehicle. The picture is taken from the driving seat, and the camera is located between the driver and passenger seats.

classical and well-established algorithms analyzed in [2], which usually have an initial premise for their correct operation, the assumption that the illumination intensity is constant along the analyzed sequence.

Each algorithm shows some advantages and disadvantages; the main drawback of most of the algorithms is their high computational and memory costs. Some of them try to reduce these costs by sacrificing accuracy of results, i.e., they balance the cost of the algorithm against the level of accuracy.

Over the years, a lot of research has been carried out in the field of optical flow algorithms. It has been continuously improved, sometimes by concentrating on the algorithm itself [3-6], sometimes by combining two of them [7,8], and sometimes by combining with other techniques [9-11].

Although most optical flow algorithms were designed with the main objective of obtaining accurate results, the trade-offs between efficiency and accuracy in optical flow algorithms are highlighted in [12] as well as the importance of an efficient optical flow computation in many real world applications. They also analyze several classical algorithms under both criteria. However, a search of the literature did not identify any previous studies or comparisons of the efficiency of recent algorithms or of their potential for parallelization or real-time capabilities.

2.2 Parallelization of optical flow

Over the last decades, the computation of optical flow has always posed a challenge in terms of processor computing power. Alternative algorithms, designed for implementation on computers with multiple processors, have been proposed since the first steps of development of this technique.

There have been many alternatives, and they have evolved along with the technology. In some cases, single-instruction multiple data (SIMD) processor arrays with specific chips, either existing [13] or designed *ad hoc* for the computation of optical flow [14], have been used. General-purpose MIMD as the connection machine [15,16], networks of transputers [17], or cellular neural networks [18,19] were also used in the past.

In recent years, there have also been many implementations based on field-programmable gate array (FPGA) [20-22] and graphic processor units (GPU) [23-25]. The results of a comparative study of both technologies for real-time optical flow computation are presented in [26]. They conclude that both have similar performance, although their FPGA implementation took much longer to develop. A very thorough comparison of both technologies applied to real-time vision computing is done by Pauwels et al. [27]. They examine several algorithms common in vision computing under many aspects, such as speed, cost, accuracy, power consumption, design time, and their general behavior on specific computations such as Gabor filtering, optical flow, and warping. Although the more adequate technology for each studied aspect is suggested, they conclude that the GPU surpasses the FPGA in most of their comparisons and agree with [26] about the FPGA requiring much developing time than the GPU. Some of the methods mentioned previously for computing optical flow are based on the Lucas-Kanade [28,29] method used in this paper or their application appears to be similar to that described in this paper.

A system for driving assistance is presented in [14]. It detects vehicles approaching from behind and alerts the driver when performing lane change maneuvers. The system is based on images taken by a camera located in the rear of a vehicle circulating through cities and highways, i.e., under the same hostile conditions as those in our system. However, their model is simpler because it is limited to detecting large objects near the camera and moving in the same direction and sense. Their method is based on the determination of the vanishing point of flow from the lane mark lines and calculating the optical flow along straight lines drawn from the vanishing point. The optical flow is computed by a block matching method using sum of absolute differences (SAD). The entire system is based on a special-purpose SIMD processor called IMAP-CAR implemented in a single CMOS chip that includes an array of 1×128 8-bit VLIW RISC processing elements. It processes 256×240 pixel images at 30 fps. Their experimental results show 98% detection of overtaking vehicles, with no false positives, during a 30-min session circulating on a motorway in wet weather.

Another implementation of the Lucas-Kanade algorithm is presented in [21]; this time, based on FPGA. Their method is based on the use of high-performance cameras that capture high-speed video streams, e.g., 90 fps. Using this technology, they are able to reduce the motion of objects in successive frames. Additionally, variations in light conditions are smaller due to the high frame rate, thus moving closer to meeting the constant illumination condition. In summary, a high fps rate allows simplifying the optical flow computation model and allows obtaining accurate results in real time. The division of the Lucas-Kanade algorithm into tasks is similar to that used in our method, although in [21], the pipeline is implemented by using specific and reconfigurable FPGA hardware (Virtex II XC2V6000-4 Xilinx FPGA; Xilinx, Inc., San Jose, CA, USA). Each pipeline stage is subdivided into simpler substages, resulting in over 70 substages using fixed-point arithmetic for the most part. The throughput achieved is one pixel per clock cycle. Their system is capable of processing up to 170 fps with 800×600 pixel images and, although its real time performance should be measured relative to the acquisition frame rate, it appears to be significantly high for the current state of technology.

In recent years, cluster computing technology has spread to the extent of becoming the basic platform for parallel computing. In fact, today, most powerful supercomputers are based on cluster computing [30]. However, it is unusual to find references to parallel optical flow algorithms designed to exploit the possibilities offered by clusters of processors to suit the size of the problems. In [31-34], some solutions are presented based on clusters.

In [32] and [1], we present a parallelization of the Lucas-Kanade algorithm applied to the computation of optical flow on video sequences taken from a moving vehicle in real traffic. These types of images present several sources of optical flow: road objects (lines, trees, houses, panels, etc.), other vehicles, and also highly variable light conditions. The method described is based on splitting the Lucas-Kanade algorithm into several tasks that must be processed sequentially, each one using a different number of subimages from the video sequence. These tasks are distributed among cluster nodes, balancing the load of their processors, and establishing a data pipeline through which the images flow. The method is implemented in three different infrastructures, (shared, distributed memory, and hybrid) to show its conceptual flexibility and scalability. A significant improvement in performance is obtained in all three cases. The paper presents experimental results using a cluster of 8 dual-processor nodes, obtaining throughput values of 45 fps with 502×288 pixel images and 15 fps with 720×576 pixel images, reaching speedups of 8.41. This is the parallel implementation of the Lucas-Kanade algorithm that we use in the segmentation system described later in this paper.

In [34], the optical flow calculation with three-dimensional images by an extension of the Horn-Schunck model to 3D is used. They study three different multigrid discretization schemes and compare them with the Gauss-Seidel method. Their experimental results show that under the conditions of their application, the multigrid method based on Galerkin discretization very significantly improves the results obtained using Gauss-Seidel. They also perform a parallelization of the algorithm aimed at its execution in clusters and apply it to the calculation of 3D motion of the human heart using sequences of two $256 \times 256 \times 256$ and $512 \times 512 \times 512$ images taken by C-arm computed tomography. Their method is based on subdividing the image into several 3D subsets and processing each one in a different processor. The analyzed method is well suited to the proposed application, because the image just includes a single object (heart), with highly localized relative movements of expansion and contraction. This fact, along with the uniformity of illumination, requires a very low communication overhead due to parallelization. The speedup[a] using 8, 12, and 16 processors is excellent: 7.8, 11.52, and 15.21, with an efficiency close to one, but it starts to decrease when reaching 32 processors: 28.46. The experiments were performed on an eight-node quad-processor cluster.

2.3 Segmentation of optical flow

Many authors have used the optical flow as a starting point for the segmentation of moving objects in many applications under different scenarios such as robotics, collision avoidance, navigation, video coding, and driving assistance. Our system is devoted to helping with driver behavior analysis [35]. Optical flow provides apparent motion information, so it is usually combined with other techniques to obtain accurate and useful results.

An early approach for detecting moving object segmenting the optical flow generated by moving cameras is presented by Adiv in [36]. The first processing step partitions the flow field into connected segments of flow vectors that are consistent with a rigid motion of a roughly planar surface. Each segment is assumed to correspond to a portion of only one rigid object. In the second processing step, segments which are consistent with the same 3D motion parameters are combined as induced by one rigid object, either because of its real movement or because of the moving camera. The results of its method are analyzed using synthetic and real 128×128 video images, according to the technology of the time.

Thompsom and Pong [37] analyzed four techniques for detecting moving objects based on optical flow with the help of additional knowledge about camera motion or scene structure. Each one being suitable for a specific situation, they suggested that a reliable detecting method will require combining several techniques that were appropriately selected.

In [38], Choia and Kim addressed optical flow segmentation using a region growing technique, in which the motion constraints are relaxed, applying a hierarchy of motion models. They perform multi-stage processing to detect uniform subregions, according to simple motion models, which are grouped in uniform regions with respect to a complex model. In a first stage, the optical flow is segmented in subregions with similar motion vectors, called 2D translational patch. Next, 2D translational

patches consistent with planar rigid motion are grouped in a 3D planar patch. In the last stage, the 3D planar patches are grouped into homogeneous regions generated by roughly parabolic rigid objects with 3D motion (parabolic patches). A pre-processing stage is performed to detect the static background combining null and near-null optical flow fields with a change detection technique.

In [39], Chung et al. combined region-based and boundary-based techniques on optical flow to perform spatially coherent object tracking. Their approach uses feed-forward inside frame-processing steps (region-based information to boundary-based computations) and feedback between subsequent frames. The region-based technique is based on gradient-based motion constraints and intensity-consistency constraints. The boundary-based technique is based on the distance-transform active contour improved by feed-forwarded intensity consistency data. The motion constraints within the contour are fed backed to be used as initial motion estimates in the region-based module for the next frame. They report its method as suitable for accurate segmentation in sequences with a moving background or camera and multiple moving objects, taking 1 to 2 s of processing time per frame using MATLAB (The MathWorks, Inc., Natick, MA, USA) on a 2.6-GHz dual Xeon computer.

In [40], Klappstein et al. studied the detection of moving objects as a part of a driver assistant system using either a monocular or a stereoscopic system that captured real-world vehicle image sequences. Their approach tries to detect and distinguish between the 'static motion' generated by the motion of the camera, usually known as ego-motion, and the 'dynamic objects motion'. It is based on tracking feature points in sequential images and estimating depth information from 3D reconstructed images. Their method consists of five processing stages, in which different techniques are performed according to the vision system in use. The optical flow computation is the starting point of both processing sequences, although an initial 3D reconstruction is also performed in the stereoscopic system. In the second step, the ego-motion is estimated based on optical flow and 3D information, which is necessary to estimate or enhance the 3D reconstruction prior to motion detection and final object segmentation. The 3D stereo reconstruction is enhanced by fusing the optical flow and stereo information using a Kalman filter. The detection of moving objects is based on individual tracked feature points. In the monocular system, this is done by looking for inconsistencies of feature points in the 3D reconstructed image, according to several constraints that must be satisfied by a static 3D point. In the stereoscopic system, this is done by analyzing the velocity of feature points. The segmentation stage is based on a globally optimal graph-cut algorithm. The stereoscopic system is reported to offer similar but more accurate results than the monocular system; however, it suffers from a problem of decalibration of the stereo cameras and has higher computational costs.

In [41], Pauwels et al. tried to reproduce the processes carried out by the human brain while segmenting moving objects. They identify six interdependent feature extraction stages and propose a GPU-based architecture that emulate the processing tasks and the information flow in the dorsal visual stream. The extracted features are Gabor pyramid, binocular disparity, optical flow, edge structure, egomotion and ego-flow, and independent flow segments. They perform reliable motion analysis of real-world driving video sequences in real time achieving 30 fps with 320×256 pixels and 21 fps with 640×512 pixels.

In [42], Samija et al. addressed the segmentation of dynamic objects in 360° panoramic image sequences from an omnidirectional camera. They improve the segmentation results projecting the optical flow vectors geometrically on a sphere centered in the camera projection center. The camera is on a mobile robot where the movement on the horizontal plane is known; hence, the ego-motion is also known. Their approach is based on the differences between the estimated optical flow generated by two subsequent images and the expected optical flow computed by applying the ego-motion to the first image.

In [43], Namdev et al. combined motion potentials from optical flow and from geometry in an incremental motion segmentation system for a vision-based simultaneous localization of moving objects and mapping of the environment (SLAM). A dense tracking of features from optical flow results in dense tracks for which multiview geometric constraints are calculated with the help of the ego-motion supplied by the VSLAM module. Then, motion potentials due to geometry are calculated using the geometric constraints. The motion segmentation is performed by a graph-based clustering algorithm that processes a graph structure created using the geometric motion potentials along with the optical flow motion potentials. They show the results obtained from several private and public datasets. A standard laptop running MATLAB was used, taking up to 7 min of processing time for each frame, which was mainly due to the time required by the optical flow computation.

3 The Lucas-Kanade algorithm

The Lucas-Kanade algorithm [28,29] takes a digital video as the only data source and computes the optical flow for the corresponding image sequence. The result is a sequence of 2D arrays of optical flow vectors, each array associated to an image of the original sequence and each vector associated to an image pixel. The algorithm analyzes the sequence frame by frame and performs several tasks. In some cases, a task may require a certain number of images preceding and following the image being

processed; therefore, the optical flow is not computed for some of the images at the beginning and at the end of the sequence.

The Lucas-Kanade algorithm computes the optical flow using a gradient-based approach, i.e., it calculates the spatio-temporal derivatives of intensity of the images. This method assumes that image intensity remains constant between the frames of the sequence, a common assumption in many algorithms:

$$I(x, y, t) = I(x + u\Delta t, y + v\Delta t, t + \Delta t) \tag{1}$$

This expression, using Taylor series and assuming differentiability, can be expressed by the motion constraint equation:

$$I_x u\delta t + I_y v\delta t + I_t \delta t = \mathcal{O}\left(u^2 \delta t^2, v^2 \delta t^2\right) \tag{2}$$

In a more compact form, taking δt as the time unit,

$$\nabla I(\mathbf{x}, t) \cdot \mathbf{v} + I_t(\mathbf{x}, t) = \mathcal{O}\left(\mathbf{v}^2\right) \tag{3}$$

where $\nabla I(\mathbf{x}, t)$ and $I_t(\mathbf{x}, t)$ represent the spatial gradient and temporal derivative of image brightness, respectively, and $\mathcal{O}\left(\mathbf{v}^2\right)$ indicates second order and above terms of the Taylor series expansion.

In this method, the image sequence is first convolved with a spatio-temporal Gaussian operator to eliminate noise and to smooth high contrasts that could lead to poor estimates of image derivatives. Then, following from the implementation in [2], the spatio-temporal derivatives I_x, I_y, and I_t are computed with a four-point central difference.

Finally, the two velocity components, $\mathbf{v} = \left(v_x, v_y\right)$, are obtained by a weighted least squares fit with local first-order constraints, assuming a constant model for $\mathbf{v}$ in each spatial neighborhood $\mathcal{N}$ and by minimizing

$$\sum_{x \in \mathcal{N}} \mathbf{W}^2(\mathbf{x}) \left[\nabla I(\mathbf{x}, t) \cdot \mathbf{v} + I_t(\mathbf{x}, t)\right]^2 \tag{4}$$

where $\mathbf{W}(\mathbf{x})$ denotes a window function that assigns more weight to the center. The resulting solution is

$$\mathbf{v} = (\mathbf{A}^T \mathbf{W}^2 \mathbf{A})^{-1} \mathbf{A}^T \mathbf{W}^2 \mathbf{b} \tag{5}$$

where for n points, $\mathbf{x}_i \in \mathcal{N}$ at a single time t

- $\mathbf{A} = \left[\nabla I(\mathbf{x}_1), \ldots, \nabla I(\mathbf{x}_n)\right]^T$
- $\mathbf{W} = \text{diag}\left[\mathbf{W}(\mathbf{x}_1), \ldots, \mathbf{W}(\mathbf{x}_n)\right]$
- $\mathbf{b} = -\left(I_t(\mathbf{x}_1), \ldots, I_t(\mathbf{x}_n)\right)^T$

The product $\mathbf{A}^T \mathbf{W}^2 \mathbf{A}$ is a 2×2 matrix given by

$$\mathbf{A}^T \mathbf{W}^2 \mathbf{A} = \begin{bmatrix} \sum \mathbf{W}^2(\mathbf{x}) I_x^2(\mathbf{x}) & \sum \mathbf{W}^2(\mathbf{x}) I_x(\mathbf{x}) I_y(\mathbf{x}) \\ \sum \mathbf{W}^2(\mathbf{x}) I_y(\mathbf{x}) I_x(\mathbf{x}) & \sum \mathbf{W}^2(\mathbf{x}) I_y^2(\mathbf{x}) \end{bmatrix} \tag{6}$$

where all the sums used are points in the neighborhood $\mathcal{N}$.

3.1 Implementation

In this section, the implementation of the Lucas-Kanade algorithm proposed by Correia [44,45] is described because this implementation has been used to compute the optical flow prior to being segmented. All the parameters used in this section are obtained from the original sequential implementation by Correia presented in [44,45].

This implementation starts by smoothing the image sequence with a spatio-temporal Gaussian filter to attenuate temporal and spatial aliasing, as shown in [2]. It applies a smoothing Gaussian filter:

$$\frac{1}{\sqrt{2\pi}\sigma}e^{-\frac{x^2}{2\sigma^2}} \tag{7}$$

In this implementation σ is 3.2, and therefore, 25 pixels are required: the central one and 4σ [45] pixels at each side. This one-dimensional (1D) symmetrical Gaussian filter is applied three times, first on the temporal 't' dimension, then on the spatial 'X' dimension, and finally on the spatial 'Y' dimension.

The result of applying the Gaussian smoothing filter to an image can be seen in Figure 4, which shows the original image (Figure 4a) and three steps: the result for the temporal filter (Figure 4b), for the spatial filters (Figure 4c), and the final result (Figure 4d).

After smoothing, the next step of the Lucas-Kanade algorithm is to compute the spatio-temporal derivatives for the three dimensions: t, x, and y (I_t, I_x, I_y). Using the previously computed image, smoothed on t, X and Y, and applying a numerical approximation, the derivatives (I_t, I_x, I_y) are separately computed making use of the five-point central finite differences method, used to compute the first order of derivative with fourth order of accuracy on one-dimensional grid, based on central finite differences [46]:

$$f'(x_3) = \frac{f(x_1) - 8f(x_2) + 8f(x_4) - f(x_5)}{12h} \tag{8}$$

Taking $h = 1$ because the distance between two consecutive pixels is one, the one-dimensional array to be used as the convolution coefficient mask in the computation of the partial derivatives is obtained as follows:

$$\left[\frac{1}{12}, \frac{-8}{12}, 0, \frac{8}{12}, \frac{-1}{12}\right] \tag{9}$$

The results of the convolutions are the estimates of the partial derivatives, which are shown in Figure 5, and represent the temporal (Figure 5a), horizontal (Figure 5b), vertical (Figure 5c), and combined intensity changes (Figure 5d).

Finally, the velocity vectors associated to each pixel of the image are computed from the spatio-temporal partial derivatives previously computed. This is done by using a spatial neighborhood matrix of 5×5 pixels, centered on each pixel and a one-dimensional weight kernel with the following coefficients: $(0.0625, 0.25, 0.375, 0.25, 0.0625)$

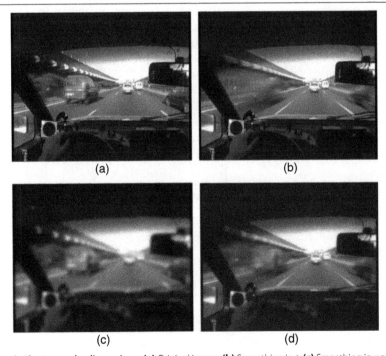

(a)

(b)

(c)

(d)

Figure 4 Image smoothing in the t, x, and y dimensions. (a) Original image. **(b)** Smoothing in t. **(c)** Smoothing in x and y. **(d)** Smoothing in t, x, and y.

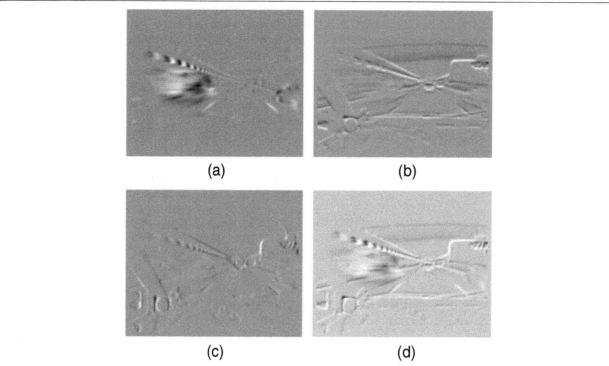

Figure 5 Partial derivatives of an image in the *t*, *x*, and *y* dimensions. **(a)** Derivative in *t*. **(b)** Derivative in *x*. **(c)** Derivative in *y*. **(d)** Derivatives in *t*, *x*, and *y*.

[2]. Noise parameters are $\sigma_1 = 0.08$, $\sigma_2 = 1.0$, and $\sigma_p = 2.0$ [47]. The estimated velocity vectors whose highest eigenvalue of $A^T W^2 A$ is less than 0.05 are considered unreliable (noise) and are discarded [2].

3.2   Results of the optical flow algorithm

Figure 6 shows the optical flow computed for the image of Figure 4a. The processing steps have been analyzed

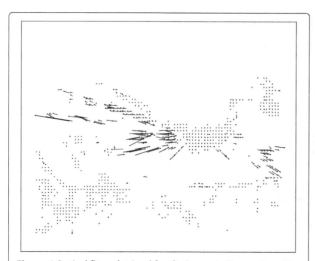

Figure 6 Optical flow obtained for the image in Figures 4 and 5.

and are shown in Figures 4 and 5. The original image corresponds to a three-lane highway. The vehicle carrying the camera is overtaking the vehicle on the right while it is being overtaken (quite fast) by the vehicle on the left. This introduces some noise in the results, since it would require a higher temporal resolution to correctly handle the movement of objects at such speed.

Figure 7 shows two images of a video sequence that has been processed with this algorithm and also the corresponding optical flow. In this sequence, a vehicle can be observed on the right going slower than the vehicle carrying the camera, and a second vehicle on the left is changing lanes. Also visible is a traffic information panel on the upper-right corner of the image. The optical flow generated by these three objects, road markings, and other elements in the image is also shown in Figure 7.

4   Optical flow segmentation

Segmentation is performed once the optical flow has been calculated and assuming that a speed vector has been associated with each pixel of the image. During segmentation of the optical flow, nearby vectors with similar speeds are combined in clusters. A cluster is a group of vectors with similar properties which collects information on its position within the image, its area, the average vector,

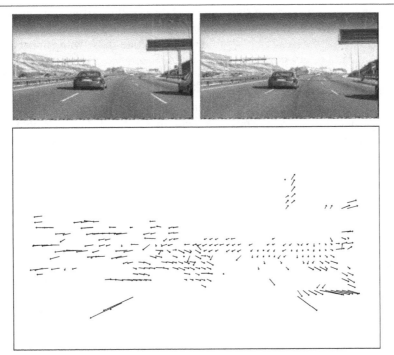

Figure 7 Frames for example session and optical flow. Frames 10 (upper left) and 20 (upper right) of an example session and the optical flow for frame 15 (bottom center).

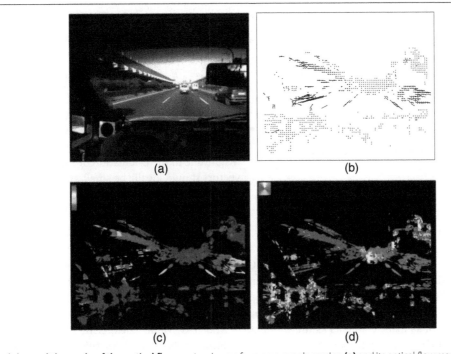

Figure 8 Modulus and the angle of the optical flow vector. Image from an example session **(a)** and its optical flow result **(b)**. Optical flow components **(c and d)**. **(a)** Image, **(b)** optical flow, **(c)** modulus, and **(d)** angle.

etc. The underlying assumption is that when a set of similar and closely grouped vectors is found, they should correspond to the same object.

The purpose of grouping similar vectors is the ability to assign a cluster to every object with independent movement and associate the cluster's average velocity vector to that object. This makes it easier to study the optical flow, since no multiple one-to-one vector comparisons are needed. Instead, representative vectors from different clusters are compared.

Similar, in this context, means similar in both magnitude and angle. Figure 8 shows the modulus and the angle of the optical flow vector, thereby illustrating the complexity of the problem. In Figure 8c, colors are applied according to the color bar in the upper-left corner, with modulus ranging from zero in black to its maximum value in red. In Figure 8d, the vector angle is colored according to the color circle in the upper-left corner, with blue, yellow, red, and green corresponding to the directions left, top, right, and bottom, respectively.

- Even within the same object, the vector modulus varies according to the distance from the camera, i.e., the closer a pixel, the greater the modulus. This is as expected, because considering similar velocity objects, motion perception increases as the object approaches the camera (i.e., as the depth Z coordinate decreases).
- Large differences can be found between different optical flow vector moduli. This is due to large actual differences in velocity between static objects and vehicles traveling in the same or in opposite directions.
- In general, the vector diverges by forming a conical shape, in such a way that its focus is the FOE, i.e., the imaginary point where the vectors originate and which the camera is focusing on. Consequently, static objects in the scene emerge from the FOE, and they move away towards the image edges.
- The closer a vector is to the image edges, the higher its modulus.
- Some very close vectors have rather different moduli and angles, as is the case with most of the vectors located inside the vehicle, i.e., close to the camera. These vectors represent noise and should be discarded.

4.1 Segmentation method implemented

The segmentation method implemented is based on an iterative algorithm operating on the optical flow vector matrix. This matrix consists of as many elements as there are pixels in the image matrix. Each of these elements is a vector which originates from a single pixel. Many matrix elements will be null due to the absence of an optical flow vector starting from the corresponding pixel. The algorithm tries to identify optical flow vector clusters by selecting those with similar properties and lying close to each other. To this end, the array of optical flow vectors is traversed from left to right and from top to bottom, i.e., in the storage order, so that for each non-zero vector, the distance - or similarity - to each of the previously identified clusters is obtained and the current vector is associated to the closest cluster. If none is found with similar characteristics, the current vector is used as the first element of a new cluster. To perform this task, the similarity function described below has been defined:

$$similVect\left(\vec{u}, \vec{v}\right).$$

4.1.1 Similarity of vectors

To calculate the distance or similarity between a vector and an optical flow vector cluster, every cluster is represented by its average vector. The similarity is then obtained by taking vector pairs, each pair being constituted by the vector candidate to be assigned to a cluster and the vector representing the average of each cluster previously created. Calculating the similarity between vector pairs is based on the three magnitudes described below. The general principle may be summarized as follows: the smaller the differences between these values, the shorter the distance between vectors (and the higher the similarity). They are as follows:

- Modulus difference.
  $$m = \left|\left|\vec{u}\right| - \left|\vec{v}\right|\right| = \left|\sqrt{u_x^2 + u_y^2} - \sqrt{v_x^2 + v_y^2}\right|$$
- Minimum angle between the two vectors, given by its scalar product.
  $\vec{u} \cdot \vec{v} = \left|\vec{u}\right| \cdot \left|\vec{v}\right| \cdot cos\alpha$ and hence
  $$\alpha = \arccos\left(\frac{\vec{u} \cdot \vec{v}}{\left|\vec{u}\right| \cdot \left|\vec{v}\right|}\right) = \arccos\left(\frac{u_x \cdot v_x + u_y \cdot v_y}{\sqrt{u_x^2 + u_y^2} \cdot \sqrt{v_x^2 + v_y^2}}\right)$$
- Euclidean distance between the positions of the two vector origins in the image. The weight of this magnitude in the calculation of similarity between vectors should ideally be small. In fact, this magnitude is considered as a rule to facilitate discarding vectors located far from the cluster.

$$d = \sqrt{(x_2 - x_1)^2 + (y_2 - y_1)^2}$$

Given two vectors $\vec{u}$ and $\vec{v}$, the $similVect\left(\vec{u}, \vec{v}\right)$ function returns a scalar value that is used as a similarity measure. Like any other distance, it is zero when both vectors are identical and grows as they become less similar. A MaxGAP value is experimentally determined as the maximum return value for this function. Vectors are not considered as belonging to the same cluster if the similVect function returns the MaxGAP value.

$$\text{similVect}\left(\overrightarrow{u}, \overrightarrow{v}\right) = \begin{cases} \text{if} & (d > \text{thresholdDist} \lor \alpha > \text{thresholdAng} \lor m > \text{thresholdMag}) \\ \text{then} & = (\text{MaxGAP}) \\ \text{else} & = (\alpha \cdot k\text{Ang} + m \cdot k\text{Mag} + d \cdot k\text{Dist}) \end{cases}$$

4.1.2 Algorithm

The algorithm used for building the vector clusters is as follows:

1. The starting point is an optical flow vector matrix $m\text{OpticalFlow}(i, j)$ and an empty cluster list $l\text{Cluster} = \Phi$.

2. For each non-empty optical flow vector $\overrightarrow{v}$ belonging to the $m\text{OpticalFlow}(i, j)$ matrix, reading it from left to right (j) and from top to bottom (i), the following steps are performed:

   (a) The function $\text{similVect}\left(\overrightarrow{u}, \overrightarrow{v}\right)$ is called for each of the clusters of the list, so as to obtain the cluster which is most similar to the current vector. similVect is called with the following parameters:

   $\overrightarrow{v}$: current optical flow vector
   $l\text{Cluster}(k).\overrightarrow{\text{avgVector}}$: average vector of the cluster

   (b) If the previous step does not return any value smaller than MaxGAP, there are no matching clusters for the current vector. This may be because the vector is far from all clusters or due to the lack of correspondence between the two vectors in terms of their modulus or angle. In this event, a new cluster $\overrightarrow{v}$ is created containing only one vector. The new cluster is registered on the cluster list.

   (c) If similar clusters are found, the current vector is associated to the maximum similarity cluster, i.e., the cluster with the smallest return value in similVect. Once associated, the average vector and other characteristic properties of this cluster are recalculated.

To minimize the time spent on calculating the similarity function, the algorithm avoids calculating the distance of each vector $\overrightarrow{v}$ from all the other vectors within each cluster. Instead, a cluster bounding box containing all the vectors in the same cluster is defined and an initial filtering step performed. If the vector distance from any of the bounding box polygons is greater than a predefined value peakDist, then MaxGAP is returned.

Not only peakDist but also the maximum thresholds peakAng and peakMag must be defined. If the comparison returns values above these thresholds, the vectors are not considered similar. It is also necessary to determine the values of certain constant parameters to weight the angle ($k\text{Ang}$), magnitude difference ($k\text{Mag}$), and distance ($k\text{Dist}$) between vectors.

Determining all these values formed part of an experimental process considering different kinds of video sequences. From these experiments, the values obtained were as follows: the maximum distance or peakDist was fixed as 10 pixels. This means that optical flow vectors belonging to the same cluster are separated less than 10 pixels. A higher value for this parameter would lead to interpret several clusters as being the same. A lower value for the parameter would artificially lead to a cluster being interpreted as several independent clusters.

The maximum value for the angle differences peakAng was set to $\frac{\Pi}{3} = 60°$. Consequently, no optical flow vector can be associated to a cluster if its angle difference from the average cluster vector is greater than 60°. This peak value may seem to be excessive, but it is derived from the actual use of a moving camera. The camera movement can generate optical flow vectors with fast changing directions, especially if the observed objects are close to the optical axis of the camera.

The peak difference in terms of magnitude, peakMag, is also experimentally set at a value of 2. This is justified by the small differences observed when comparing the optical flow vectors generated from different pixels of the same object.

Finally, the weights used for the expression in Section 4.1.1 have been assigned the following values: $k\text{Ang} = 0.8$, $k\text{Mag} = 0.15$, and $k\text{Dist} = 0.05$. This means that a much greater importance is assigned to the difference between angles, while the magnitudes are considered significantly less important and the distances within the image almost negligible. The overall similarity measure is thus established in the system as $\alpha \cdot 0.8 + m \cdot 0.15 + d \cdot 0.05$.

4.1.3 Filtering

Once all of the optical flow vectors present in the original matrix are grouped into clusters, the classification using the algorithm can be considered completed. However, using this approach, without a post-filtering stage can generate many clusters that are irrelevant to the study of stationary or moving objects in the field of view of the moving camera. These clusters are usually derived from image noise, caused by shadows or differences in lighting. This noise can also be due to the detection of almost completely static clusters, i.e., clusters moving with the same speed and direction as the camera used, so presumably are part of the vehicle itself, such as the dashboard and mirror.

Based on these considerations, the segmentation method includes a final step for cluster filtering. In this step, clusters consisting of a small number of vectors are interpreted as noise and consequently removed. Those clusters whose average vector modulus is less than a pre-set value are also removed, as they are interpreted as being part of the vehicle in which the camera is installed.

Figure 9 shows the result of applying cluster filtering with the following parameters:

- minimum number of vectors in a cluster $= 180$
- minimum value for the modulus of the average vector $= 0.2$

Figure 9a shows the result prior to filtering, in which 2,149 clusters are identified. However, a significant proportion of irrelevant clusters can be observed. By contrast, Figure 9b shows the 31 clusters obtained after filtering.

4.2 Optical flow segmentation results

This section presents the results of applying the optical flow segmentation method to multiple images from different video sequences, all of them taken with the camera installed on board a moving car. Ideally, the best result would be a single cluster for each object in the scene, regardless of its shape or whether the cluster completely covers the object. This is because the geometrical shape of the object is derived from the segmentation of the image itself, not from the segmentation of its optical flow. But, this is not always possible, and several clusters for each object with slight variations in direction or in the modulus are usually found. Furthermore, since the camera is in motion, the same single object can provide optical flow vectors with different directions, depending on their relative positions with respect to the FOE. For example, on a

straight road segment, a traffic sign in front of the camera can take up the whole width of the scene, generating optical flow in all directions, though always moving away from the FOE.

4.2.1 Highway with traffic in both directions

In this sequence, the vehicle is driving along a four-lane highway in which other vehicles driving in both directions can be seen. For vehicles moving in the same direction, the closest vehicle to the camera is slower than the rest, so it is overtaken in the initial images of the sequence. The remaining vehicles move at a very similar pace as the vehicle with the camera. For vehicles moving in the opposite direction, a large truck and several small vehicles are approaching the camera. The result of the segmentation of the optical flow for this sequence is shown in Figure 10.

In this experiment, clusters are detected for the oncoming truck and for the vehicle moving in the same direction. Clusters can not be obtained for the remaining vehicles, or only intermittently. However, some clusters appear in some frames, such as for the vehicles in the background which are driving in the same direction as the camera. For these vehicles, a cluster has been found as shown in Figure 10a. This is mainly because the vehicle group moves at a similar speed to the vehicle with the camera, so perceived motion is negligible. In the last frame, the vehicles behind the truck and driving in the opposite direction are detected. This is because their distance from the camera is shorter than those in the previous frames. However, the vehicle group is treated as a single cluster. Furthermore, certain clusters can be discontinuously observed near the edges of the windshield throughout the sequence. These clusters are clearly related to noise and are removed during the cluster-object aggregation stage as they are usually clearly separate from any objects.

4.2.2 Highway with traffic in both directions (2)

Once again, the vehicle is driving along a four-lane highway. However, this case is characterized by the presence

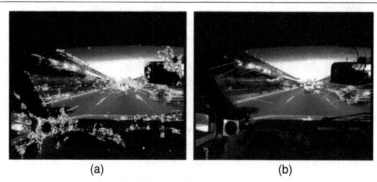

(a)   (b)

Figure 9 Filtering stage to eliminate clusters consisting of a small number of vectors. **(a)** Clusters found without filtering. **(b)** Clusters after filtering.

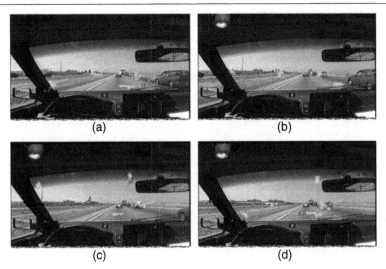

Figure 10 Optical flow segmentation of the first highway sequence example. **(a)** Image 1. **(b)** Image 2. **(c)** Image 3. **(d)** Image 4.

of a truck at close distance filling a great proportion of the image. Both sides of the road are lined with trees, and a bridge can be seen at a distance.

The bridge over the road can help us examine the impact of a large object on the optical flow sequence. The result of the optical flow segmentation for this sequence is shown in Figure 11.

The first thing to note is that, as expected, the truck is not interpreted as a single cluster, instead there are several, up to eight in the first image. This is mainly because the truck consists of several parts, and each one generates a slightly different optical flow vector, especially in terms of its modulus. Moreover, given that optical flow vectors are obtained only for the contours (or, more

specifically, for changes in the image intensity) of the parts that comprise the truck and the differences in the direction of the optical flow vectors due to camera movement, it is reasonable to obtain several clusters for a single large vehicle.

Distant vehicles moving in the same direction as the camera do not generate any cluster, precisely due to their distance, their low relative speeds, and their small apparent size. For vehicles approaching in the opposite direction, clusters are continuously obtained throughout the sequence, sometimes resulting in misinterpretations of the bridge over the road. However, this should not cause any problem once the clusters are combined with the objects.

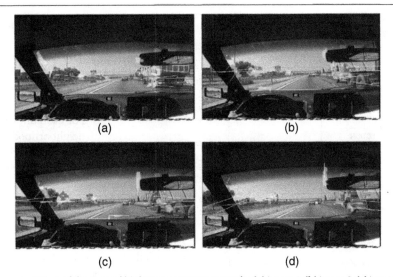

Figure 11 Optical flow segmentation of the second highway sequence example. **(a)** Image 1. **(b)** Image 2. **(c)** Image 3. **(d)** Image 4.

Finally, it can be noted that some clusters are obtained near the windshield edges of the vehicle in which the camera is installed. These clusters clearly represent noise due to the high contrast between the vehicle and the road. There are also clusters obtained for the trees located on one side of the road. However, this is a correct detection because even though they are static, they present an apparent motion with respect to the camera and, hence, generate optical flow.

5   Image segmentation

In addition to segmenting the optical flow, the images are also segmented since the optical flow does not preserve the shape and size of objects, so this information has to be retrieved from the original images. An edge-based segmentation scheme using a modified Canny algorithm [48] has been chosen with the following characteristics:

- It minimizes edge detection errors: this is important to avoid false detections.
- Good edge location: minimizes distance between the detected edge and the actual edge.
- A single answer for each edge: the transition that conforms the edge may be large, but this scheme seeks the maximum gradient to render a clearly defined edge.

The segmentation scheme consists of six steps, as shown in Figure 12. It takes the source image as input and generates a list of blobs as output. A blob represents a uniform region of the image, containing information such as its size in pixels, the smallest rectangle containing it, and its average intensity. Segmentation is divided into the following steps:

- Smoothing: the image is smoothed using a Gaussian filter to remove noise.
- Edge extraction: a Sobel operator was chosen because it has low computational cost and low noise sensitivity (very important for the type of images used).

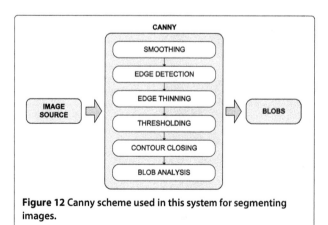

Figure 12 Canny scheme used in this system for segmenting images.

- Thinning edges: the edges obtained have to be homogenized by thinning them to a pixel's width, choosing only those with maximum intensity gradient.
- Thresholding: in this step, the image is binarized, and most of the edges generated by noise are eliminated (although a few real edges are also eliminated). A segmentation algorithm based on the k-means with $k = 2$ is used. This algorithm, unlike the Bayesian ones, does not need a *priori* information of the classes, it only needs the number of classes (k) into which to divide the histogram (bottom and edges).
- Closing contours: this avoids discontinuities in the edges and facilitates subsequent detection of objects. The Deriche and Cocquerez algorithm [49] is used, which is based on the assumption that an open-edge section can be closed following the direction of maximum gradient. However, the search for the next edge pixel is limited so that the maximum angle between two consecutive edge pixels is 45°.
- Blob analysis: this last step identifies the objects. The following recursive algorithm is used:

1. It starts from the binarized image and a mask for each pixel indicating whether it has been processed (initially, the mask values for the pixels are all false).
2. The image is explored from left to right and top to bottom.

   (a) If the pixel has not been processed and does not correspond to an edge, a blob is created, initialized, and appended to the list of blobs.
   (b) A recursive search is started from the pixel indicated.

      (i) The pixel is marked as processed and added to the blob.
      (ii) The blob parameters are updated, i.e., number of pixels, maximum and minimum coordinates, center of gravity, etc.
      (iii) For each unprocessed pixel in the neighborhood that is not an edge, the search is repeated recursively, i.e., it returns to step (b).

3. The result is a list of blobs.

Filtering the blobs based on their size is the next step. Any blobs above or below certain size limits are discarded, since small blobs are associated with noise, and very large blobs are associated with background details. As a consequence, some quite far away vehicles can be discarded, but due to their distance, they are not relevant for the driver.

5.1 Results of image segmentation

This section presents the results of applying the algorithm to real images in different environments. The aim is to obtain at least one blob for each vehicle in the image. If a vehicle gives rise to several blobs, the latter are merged at the stage that combines optical flow with blobs since both present similar velocity vectors and are located in close proximity. Undesired blobs (for example, inside the car, in the sky, or on the sides of the road) do not present a problem as many of these are later removed for having no associated velocity vector.

5.1.1 Highway with two-way traffic

This sequence shows four vehicles traveling in the same direction as the car camera (our vehicle) and an oncoming truck. One of the vehicles (furthest to the right) travels in the same direction at a medium distance, and the rest are far away. Figure 13 shows the original image (a), the result after applying the smoothing filter (b), the edges once the contours have been closed (c), and finally, the blobs obtained after the search for connected components and the required filtering have been performed (d).

A single blob is obtained for the truck coming from the opposite direction, containing everything but the cabin. In the same lane, another blob is obtained that merges various vehicles and some of the trees in the area. Three blobs are obtained in our lane, one for the nearest vehicle, one for the intermediate one, and one that merges a truck and another vehicle that are close together. Another blob is also obtained on the road, which

merges part of the shoulder with a white line. There are also many blobs found inside the car and to the left of the mirror, but they are clearly invalid and must be removed.

5.1.2 Highway with heavy traffic in one direction

This sequence presents higher traffic density at different distances as well as diverse vegetation on the sides, and a bridge in the background, than the sequence described in Section 5.1.1. It is not an easy sequence to segment, although it also has the advantage that the vehicles closer to the camera have colors that strongly contrast with the background, making their contours easier to identify.

The segmentation result is shown in Figure 14, which shows that at least one blob has been obtained for each of the nearby vehicles, but in some cases, up to three blobs have been found. A blob has been obtained corresponding to a portion of the road's left shoulder, another for a house, and another for vegetation on the right side. As in the previous sequence, blobs have been obtained inside the vehicle and in the rearview mirror, which must be removed.

6 Combination of clusters and blobs

To obtain the final results, the partial results obtained from both the segmentation of the optical flow (clusters) and the image segmentation (blobs) need to be merged, assigning one, several or no blob to each cluster. The idea is to use the clusters and blobs computed in the previous steps to obtain sets of pixels with an associated velocity vector. Each set of pixels identifies an object with apparent movement. Each blob determines the shape, position, and size of the object, and the cluster represents its dynamic

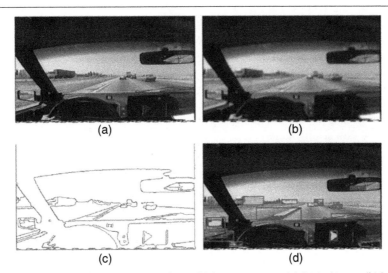

(a) (b)

(c) (d)

Figure 13 Simple example of an image (static) segmentation from a highway sequence. (a) Original image. **(b)** Smoothed image. **(c)** Contours closed. **(d)** Blobs.

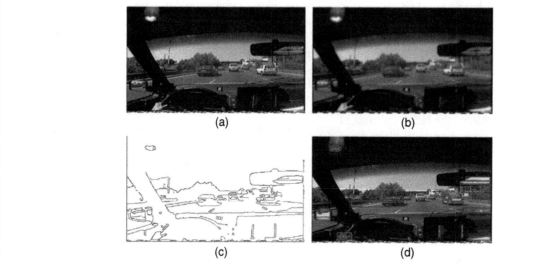

Figure 14 Complex example of an image (static) segmentation from a highway sequence. (a) Original image. **(b)** Smoothed image. **(c)** Contours closed. **(d)** Blobs.

properties, i.e., the velocity vector. However, the association between clusters and blobs is not trivial, since a single object can consist several blobs and/or several clusters.

The strategy used to calculate the optical flow clusters of an image is based on obtaining the smallest possible number of clusters, and if possible, only for moving objects, without considering their shape or size, because the optical flow does not preserve these properties. However, the strategy for the computation of blobs is completely different; the idea in this case is to obtain potential blobs in the image, in such a way that each group of pixels with relatively homogeneous values should result in a blob. The resulting large number of blobs does not pose a problem since any blobs clearly separated from any cluster are subsequently discarded as image background. As clusters necessarily need to be close to an object, any cluster without at least one associated blob is interpreted as erroneous and discarded. Therefore, according to the strategy used for the computation of blobs and clusters, clusters lead the combined process, as more importance and reliability is assigned to them than to blobs. As the search is oriented to finding objects in motion and this information is provided by the optical flow, the focus is on the clusters as they are generated by the optical flow segmentation.

For the final results, the shape, position, and size of the objects are derived from the blobs and only the velocity vector from the clusters. Cluster positions are discarded because the pixels inside uniform objects do not generate optical flow at all. Only their edges cause optical flow; therefore, object shapes are not preserved. A cluster can be associated to more than one blob and is associated mainly by the size of their intersection area or by their proximity. For reasons of efficiency, the intersection area is not computed by using the actual pixels of the blob and

the cluster, but by an estimate based on the minimum rectangle containing both.

The algorithm works through the full blob list, one at a time, trying to associate the best possible cluster to each blob, and if no suitable cluster is found, the blob is discarded. Next, all the blobs associated with the same cluster are grouped together in a single blob, recomputing its mass center where the cluster velocity vector will be placed. Finally, clusters with no associated blob are discarded, too. To select the most appropriate cluster to be associated with a blob, the following cases must be considered:

1. The blob intersects with exactly one cluster: if the rectangle overlying blob B intersects with the rectangle of a single cluster C, the blob is associated to this cluster, as shown in Figure 15, where I is the intersection rectangle. The result, shown in Figure 15, has the shape of the blob and the velocity

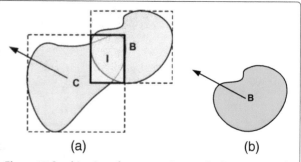

Figure 15 Combination of segmentation results: intersection of a unique blob with one cluster. (a) Intersection of blob and cluster. **(b)** Result.

vector of the cluster starting from the geometric center of the blob.

2. The blob intersects with several clusters: if the rectangle overlying blob B intersects with more than one cluster, as shown in Figure 16 in which blob B intersects with clusters C_1 and C_2, then the blob is associated to the cluster with the largest intersection area. In the example shown in Figure 16, area I_1 is greater than I_2; therefore, blob B is associated to cluster C_1.

3. The blob does not intersect with any cluster: when the rectangle covering blob B does not intersect with any cluster, the nearest cluster is considered. If the distance between the blob and cluster does not exceed a certain threshold, blob B is associated to this cluster; otherwise, the blob is discarded and not associated to any cluster. The example in Figure 17 shows blob B not intersecting with any cluster, but being close to clusters C_1 and C_2, so the distances to both clusters d_1 and d_2 are calculated. As the minimum distance is d_2 and does not exceed the maximum threshold, the blob is associated to cluster C_2, as shown in Figure 17.

This algorithm associates one or more blobs to each cluster, because the usual case is a moving vehicle generating a single cluster but with many blobs, due to the diversity of its component parts (wheels, windows, body, etc.). All of the parts generate a similar optical flow but different blobs. This algorithm is very efficient as the computation of a rectangle intersection is almost trivial, the result either being void or another rectangle.

6.1 Results of associating clusters and blobs
Figure 18 is an example of the association of clusters and blobs. This figure shows five vehicles traveling in the same direction as the vehicle carrying the camera, but driving at a slower speed. One of them is quite close, and the four others quite far from the camera. Figure 18a shows the blobs found, one obtained for the closest car, and only

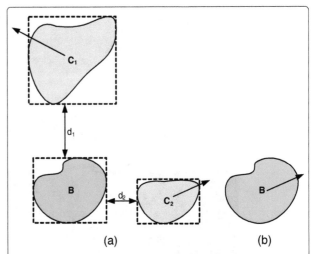

Figure 17 Combination of image and optical flow segmentation results if there is no blob-cluster intersection. **(a)** Intersection of blob and cluster. **(b)** Result.

three more for the four remote vehicles, because they are quite close together. Two blobs are also found in the central reservation. Figure 18b shows the clusters: one near the first car and two more related to the remote vehicles. Furthermore, a cluster is also found in the middle of the road. After associating (Figure 18c), it can be seen that all the blobs related to the distant vehicles have been grouped and associated to a single cluster, the one closest, while discarding the other cluster in spite of its proximity. Another successful association was obtained for the close car, and finally, the blobs and cluster related to the road were removed as there is no association between them due to their relative distances.

Figure 19 shows a more complex example. In addition to the vehicles present on the road, there is vegetation on the sides and a bridge in the background. There is a truck driving very close to the vehicle with the camera in the same direction, but at a slower speed, and two vehicles in the background with a relative speed close to zero. In the opposite direction, some small approaching vehicles can be observed, with similar textures as the background objects: central reservation, vegetation, or bridge.

The results after image segmentation, shown in Figure 19a, consist of seven blobs related to the truck due to its large size and the diversity of its component parts. There is also another blob for the bridge, one more for a truck close to one side of the bridge piers, and finally, one more for the central reservation.

Regarding the results of the optical flow segmentation, shown in Figure 19b, eleven clusters have been found. There are four clusters related to the truck: one for the pier on the right of the bridge, one for the car traveling in the same direction, two for the pier on the left of the bridge

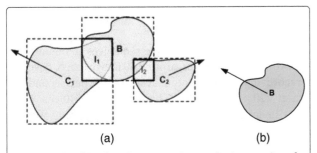

Figure 16 Combination of segmentation results: intersection of a unique blob with more than one cluster. **(a)** Intersection of blob and cluster. **(b)** Result.

Figure 18 Simple example of blob-cluster associations. **(a)** Blobs. **(b)** Clusters. **(c)** Association results.

(mixed with one of the trucks circulating in the opposite direction), two for a tree on the left, and finally, a cluster due to noise next to the windshield of the camera vehicle.

The association of clusters and blobs, Figure 19c, shows the truck perfectly identified by two objects, obtained by grouping several blobs together. Also, the distant bridge is identified but with a small velocity vector due to its distance. Regarding the opposite lanes, one object has been located near the left pier of the bridge, but it is mixed with an object from the truck due to their similar distance and texture. Finally, one blob in the central reservation has been associated with a cluster generated by a vehicle traveling in the opposite direction, leading to a false result. This is mainly due to the absence of blobs for these vehicles as they have a very small size and are very similar to the background texture.

7   Results

This section looks at the segmentation of multiple image sequences, in which all process steps are considered: image segmentation, blob computation, optical flow computation followed by segmentation, cluster recognition, and finally, cluster-blob association. The process followed is described below:

1. Starting from the original image, the segmentation process described in Section 5 is applied, obtaining a list of blobs in an XML file.
2. Optical flow is generated for the image sequence using the Lucas-Kanade algorithm.
3. Optical flow segmentation is applied to obtain a list of clusters in an XML file.
4. Blobs and clusters created in the previous steps are associated.

The only input data is the image sequences to be analyzed. Several test sequences, around 50 images each, have been recorded with a 25 interleaved frames per second camera at 720×576 pixels. Therefore, every 40 ms, a complete image frame is generated, after combining two image fields provided by the interleaved camera at 20-ms intervals. The main problem of using an interleaving camera derives from the delay in capturing both image fields, 20 ms, causing a mismatch in the final image. For example, a car traveling at 90 km/h (25 m/s) will advance

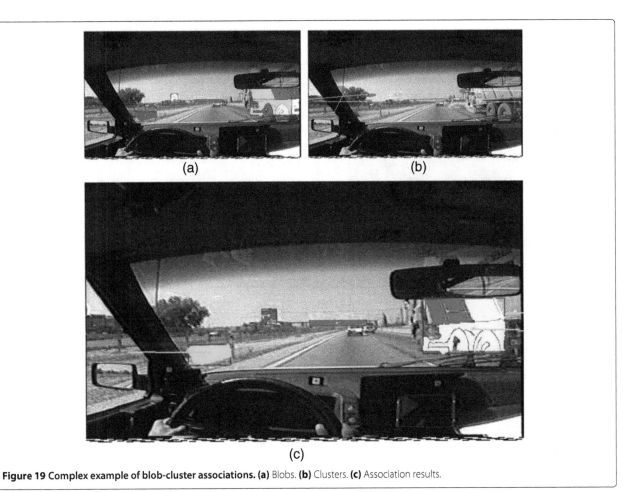

Figure 19 Complex example of blob-cluster associations. **(a)** Blobs. **(b)** Clusters. **(c)** Association results.

50 cm in 20 ms. One solution to fix this problem is to use only the even or the odd image fields and to ignore the other half of the original image, or to use a more expensive full-frame camera. The results in this section analyze both 720×576 interleaved and 720×288 non-interleaved images.

The camera is placed inside the experiment vehicle, and the images acquired include the road but also part of the experimental vehicle such as the dashboard, steering wheel, and roof areas. To simplify the localization process, the search will only consider the area of the image showing the road.

7.1 Two-way road

This sequence shows a two-way road with heavy traffic including different sized vehicles, speeds, and distances from the vehicle camera. In the image shown in Figure 20a, a group of distant vehicles and a truck traveling in the opposite direction can be seen. The result of the image segmentation and blob searching algorithm is shown in Figure 20b.

Vehicles traveling in the same direction as the camera are grouped in two blobs, one which comprises a single

vehicle and another grouping of two vehicles. The truck moving in the opposite direction is converted into one blob, but including some parts of the horizon because of its similar color. In this case, two more blobs appear, but they are considered noise: the first one is close to the truck, and the other represents the right road shoulder.

In the optical flow segmentation shown in Figure 21, several clusters are obtained for the vehicles traveling in the same direction as the camera and for the oncoming truck. Other clusters such as those near the edge of the windshield as well as the one corresponding to the central reservation are considered as noise.

The association of the partial results obtained in the previous steps shown in Figure 22 removes all noise clusters and blobs. The objects are correctly identified for vehicles traveling in the same direction as the experimental vehicle. However, some are grouped, because they are far away and the images acquired do not allow distinguishing them clearly. Furthermore, an object is obtained for the oncoming truck with an additional blob due to noise because both objects are very close. Finally, the results are considered satisfactory, because every moving vehicle is

(a)

(b)

Figure 20 Example of image segmentation results from a two-way road sequence. (a) Original image. **(b)** Blobs found.

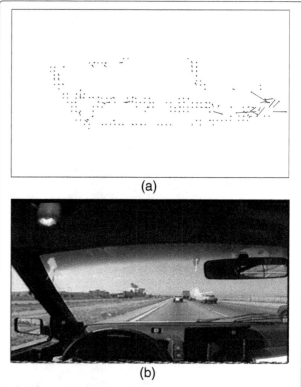

(a)

(b)

Figure 21 Optical flow segmentation results for the frame shown in Figure 20. (a) Optical flow. **(b)** Clusters.

identified and the noise objects obtained in intermediate steps are removed.

7.2 One-way highway

This example shows a one-way highway image in which the vehicle with the camera is traveling faster than the other vehicles. As shown in Figure 23a, there is a car close to the right of the experimental vehicle preceded by a small van, and there is another vehicle in front of the experimental car driving on the same lane. All three vehicles are approaching the experimental vehicle due to their lower speeds. An added difficulty compared to the previous example is that the road sides are lined by a wall on the right and a kind of overhanging roof on the left.

In the image segmentation result shown in Figure 23b, several blobs are obtained for the car on the right side, because of its large size. This effect does not cause a problem, because a subsequent step will group all of the blobs belonging to the same object and associate them to a cluster. The other vehicles are correctly located: a blob has been assigned for each one. Finally, some other blobs appear on the roof structure and around the road lines.

Figure 24b shows the optical flow segmentation in which the right-hand car is identified by two clusters, because of its large size and the multiple parts composing it. Two distant vehicles are detected with a cluster

assigned to each one. Finally, several clusters are obtained for the roof on the left side of the road, and even though they do not represent actual movement, they do show apparent motion, their detection thus being correct.

Figure 25 shows the final result after associating the clusters and blobs obtained in the previous steps. Two objects have been obtained for the car close on the right by grouping a large number of blobs into two clusters. Several blobs and clusters have been grouped for two distant vehicles and for the roof structure on the left. In the latter case, the roof appears to be moving with respect to the

Figure 22 Final result for the combination of segmentation results applied to the image shown in Figure 20.

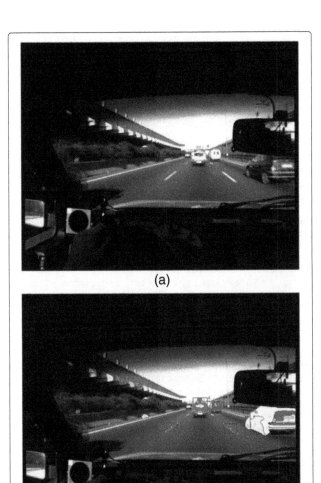

(a)

(b)

Figure 23 Image segmentation result for a one-way highway example. **(a)** Original image. **(b)** Blobs found in the previous image.

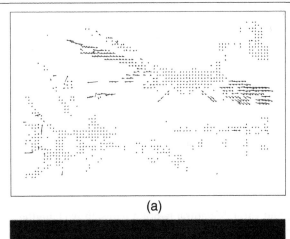

(a)

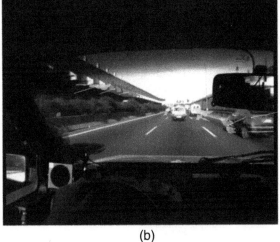

(b)

Figure 24 Optical flow segmentation for the one-way highway example of Figure 23. **(a)** Optical flow. **(b)** Clusters.

camera, resulting in several blobs being associated to their corresponding clusters.

The results are satisfactory in spite of the great complexity of the scene, because all vehicles except one have been located. The exception is related to the small vehicle on the left which is far from the experimental car and is almost hidden by the background.

8 Conclusion

This paper has addressed the search and detection of moving objects in an image sequence using a moving camera. Starting from the optical flow and image segmentation processes, the objects in the scene and their motion (both direction and magnitude) are obtained.

To obtain an estimate of the apparent movement, the optical flow of each image in the sequence is calculated. This optical flow is then segmented, and similar vectors

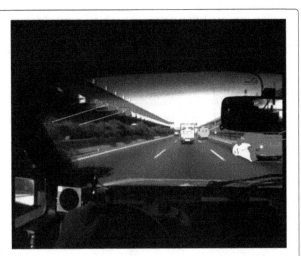

Figure 25 Final cluster and blob association for the one-way highway example of Figure 23.

are grouped since they are expected to belong to the same object. In a third step, the segmentation of images is addressed to distinguish the objects present in the scene. Finally, the results of the two kinds of segmentation are grouped to associate each object to its apparent motion.

The method described has been applied to detect moving objects as perceived by a driver which could interfere with the driver's behavior, either by causing a distraction or by posing real dangers that require immediate attention. The input data consists of video sequences recorded by a camera mounted on a conventional vehicle driving on public roads, implying several challenges when calculating the optical flow: moving camera (all objects appear to move) and variable natural lighting (constantly changing shadows and reflections).

The results show that most of the relevant objects from the scene are properly detected and associated to their corresponding movement, while unrelated objects are only grouped when they are quite far and very difficult to distinguish, even to the human eye.

Endnote

[a] The speedup is defined as the sequential execution time divided by the parallel execution time to know how much a parallel algorithm is faster than a corresponding sequential algorithm.

Competing interests

The authors declare that they have no competing interests.

References

1. A Garcia-Dopico, JL Pedraza, M Nieto, A Pérez, S Rodríguez, J Navas, Parallelization of the optical flow computation in sequences from moving cameras. EURASIP J. Image Video Process. **2014**, 18 (2014)
2. J Barron, D Fleet, SS Beauchemin, Performance of optical flow techniques. Int. J. Comput. Vis. **12**(1), 43–47 (1994)
3. T Brox, A Bruhn, N Papenberg, J Weickert, ed. by T Pajdla, J Matas, High accuracy optical flow estimation based on a theory for warping, in *Lecture Notes in Computer Science (LNCS): European Conference on Computer Vision (ECCV)*, vol. 3024 (Springer Berlin, 2004), pp. 25–36
4. SN Tamgade, VR Bora, Motion vector estimation of video image by pyramidal implementation of Lucas-Kanade optical flow. Paper presented at the 2nd international conference on emerging trends in engineering and technology (ICETET), Nagpur, 16–18 Dec 2009, pp. 914–917
5. K Pauwels, MM Van Hulle, Optic flow from unstable sequences through local velocity constancy maximization. Image Vis. Comput. **27**(5), 579–587 (2009)
6. A Doshi, AG Bors, Smoothing of optical flow using robustified diffusion kernels. Image Vis. Comput. **28**(12), 1575–1589 (2010)
7. A Bruhn, J Weickert, C Schnörr, Lucas/Kanade meets Horn/Schunck: combining local and global optic flow methods. Int. J. Comput. Vis. **61**(3), 211–231 (2005)
8. M Drulea, IR Peter, S Nedevschi, Optical flow a combined local-global approach using L1 norm. Paper presented at the 2010 IEEE 6th international conference on intelligent computer communication and processing, Cluj-Napoca, 26–28 Aug 2010, pp. 217–222
9. T Brox, J Malik, Large displacement optical flow: descriptor matching in variational motion estimation. IEEE Trans. Pattern Anal. Mach. Intell. **33**(3), 500–513 (2011)
10. JS Zelek, Towards Bayesian real-time optical flow. Image Vis. Comput. **22**(12), 1051–1069 (2004)
11. S Tan, J Dale, A Anderson, A Johnston, Inverse perspective mapping and optic flow: a calibration method and a quantitative analysis. Image Vis. Comput. **24**(2), 153–165 (2006)
12. H Liu, TH Hong, M Herman, R Chellappa, ed. by B Buxton, R Cipolla, Accuracy vs. efficiency trade-offs in optical flow algorithms, in *LNCS: 4th European Conference on Computer Vision*, vol. 1065 (Springer Berlin, 1996), pp. 271–286
13. B Buxton, B Stephenson, H Buxton, Parallel computations of optic flow in early image processing. IEEE Proc. F: Commun. Radar Signal Process. **131**(6), 593–602 (1984)
14. K Sakurai, S Kyo, S Okazaki, Overtaking vehicle detection method and its implementation using IMAPCAR highly parallel image processor. IEICE Trans. **91-D**(7), 1899–1905 (2008)
15. H Bulthoff, J Little, T Poggio, A parallel algorithm for real-time computation of optical flow. Nature. **337**(6207), 549–553 (1989)
16. A Del Bimbo, P Nesi, Optical flow estimation on Connection-Machine 2. Paper presented at the computer architectures for machine perception, New Orleans, 15–17 Dec 1993, pp. 267–274
17. H Wang, J Brady, I Page, A fast algorithm for computing optic flow and its implementation on a transputer array. Paper presented at the British machine vision conference (BMVC90), Oxford, 24–27 Sept 1990, pp. 175–180
18. C Colombo, A Del Bimbo, S Santini, A multilayer massively parallel architecture for optical flow computation. Paper presented at the 11th IAPR international conference on pattern recognition, 1992. Vol. IV. Conference D: architectures for vision and pattern recognition, The Hague, 30 Aug–3 Sept 1992, pp. 209–213
19. MG Milanova, AC Campilho, MV Correia, Cellular neural networks for motion estimation. Paper presented at the 15th international conference on pattern recognition (ICPR'00), Barcelona, 3–7 Sept 2000, pp. 819–822
20. J Sosa, J Boluda, F Pardo, R Gómez-Fabela, Change-driven data flow image processing architecture for optical flow computation. J. Real-Time Image Process. **2**(4), 259–270 (2007)
21. J Díaz, E Ros, R Agís, JL Bernier, Superpipelined high-performance optical-flow computation architecture. Comput. Vis. Image Underst. **112**(3), 262–273 (2008)
22. N Devi, V Nagarajan, FPGA based high performance optical flow computation using parallel architecture. Int. J. Soft. Comput. Eng. **2**(1), 433–437 (2012)
23. Y Mizukami, K Tadamura, Optical flow computation on compute unified device architecture. Paper presented at the the 14th international conference image analysis and processing (ICIAP), Modena, 10–14 Sept 2007, pp. 179–184
24. M Gong, Real-time joint disparity and disparity flow estimation on programmable graphics hardware. Comput. Vis. Image Underst. **113**(1), 90–100 (2009)
25. MV Correia, AC Campilho, ed. by AC Campilho, MS Kamel, A pipelined real-time optical flow algorithm, in *LNCS: Image Analysis and Recognition*, vol. 3212 (Springer Berlin, 2004), pp. 372–380
26. J Chase, B Nelson, J Bodily, Z Wei, DJ Lee, Real-time optical flow calculations on FPGA and GPU architectures: a comparison study. Paper presented at the 16th international symposium on field programmable custom computing machines, Palo Alto, 14–15 April 2008, pp. 173–182
27. K Pauwels, M Tomasi, JD Alonso, E Ros, NM Van-Hulle, A Comparison of FPGA and GPU for real-time phase-based optical flow, stereo, and local image features. IEEE Trans. Comput. **61**(7), 999–1012 (2012)
28. B Lucas, T Kanade, An iterative image registration technique with an application to stereo vision. Paper presented at 7th international joint conference on artificial intelligence (IJCAI), Vancouver, 24–28 Aug 1981, pp. 674–679
29. B Lucas, Generalized image matching by method of differences. PhD Thesis, Department of Computer Science, Carnegie-Mellon University, 1984
30. Top 500 Supercomputer Sites (2014). http://www.top500.org. Accessed 25 April 2014
31. M Fleury, AF Clark, AC Downton, Evaluating optical-flow algorithms on a parallel machine. Image Vis. Comput. **19**(3), 131–143 (2001)
32. A García Dopico, M Correia, J Santos, L Nunes, ed. by M Bubak, G van Albada, P Sloot, and J Dongarra, Distributed computation of optical flow,

in *LNCS: Computational Science*, vol. 3037 (Springer Berlin, 2004), pp. 380–387

33. T Kohlberger, C Schnorr, A Bruhn, J Weickert, Domain decomposition for variational optical-flow computation. IEEE Trans. Image Process. **14**(8), 1125–1137 (2005)

34. EM Kalmoun, H Köstler, U Rüde, 3D optical flow computation using a parallel variational multigrid scheme with application to cardiac C-arm CT motion. Image Vis. Comput. **25**(9), 1482–1494 (2007)

35. A Pérez, MI García, M Nieto, JL Pedraza, S Rodríguez, J Zamorano, Argos: an advanced in-vehicle data recorder on a massively sensorized vehicle for car driver behavior experimentation. IEEE Trans. Intell. Transport. Syst. **11**(2), 463–473 (2010)

36. G Adiv, Determining three-dimensional motion and structure from optical flow generated by several moving objects. IEEE Trans. Pattern Anal. Mach. Intell. **7**(4), 384–401 (1985)

37. W Thompson, T Pong, Determining moving objects. Int. J. Comput. Vis. **4**(1), 39–57 (1990)

38. JG Choia, SD Kim. Multi-stage segmentation of optical flow field. Signal Process. **54**(2), 109–118 (1996)

39. D Chung, WJ MacLean, S Dickinson, Integrating region and boundary information for spatially coherent object tracking. Image Vis. Comput. **24**(7), 680–692 (2006)

40. J Klappstein, T Vaudrey, C Rabe, A Wedel, R Klette, ed. by T Wada, F Huang, and S Lin, Moving object segmentation using optical flow and depth information, in *LNCS: Advances in image and Video Technology*, vol. 5414 (Springer Berlin, 2009), pp. 611–623

41. K Pauwels, N Krüger, F Wörgötter, NM Van-Hulle. J. Vis. **10**(10), 18 (2010)

42. H Samija, I Markovic, I Petrovic, Optical flow field segmentation in an omnidirectional camera image based on known camera motion. Paper presented at the 34th international convention MIPRO, Opatija, 23–27 May 2011, pp. 805–809

43. R Namdev, A Kundu, K Krishna, C Jawahar, Motion segmentation of multiple objects from a freely moving monocular camera. Paper presented at the IEEE international conference on robotics and automation (ICRA), Saint Paul, MN, USA, 14–18 May 2012, pp. 4092–4099

44. M Correia, A Campilho, J Santos, L Nunes, Optical flow techniques applied to the calibration of visual perception experiments. Paper presented at the 13th international conference on pattern recognition (ICPR), Vienna, 25–29 Aug 1996, pp. 498–502

45. M Correia, A Campilho, Implementation of a real-time optical flow algorithm on a pipeline processor. Paper presented at the international conference of computer based experiments, learning and teaching, Szklarska Poreba. 28 Sept–1 Oct 1999

46. B Fornberg, Generation of finite difference formulas on arbitrarily spaced grids. Math. Comput. **51**, 699–706 (1988)

47. E Simoncelli, E Adelson, D Heeger, Probability distributions of optical flow. Paper presented at the IEEE conference on computer vision and pattern recognition, Maui, 3–6 June 1991, pp. 310–315

48. J Canny, A computational approach to edge detection. IEEE Trans. Pattern Anal. Mach. Intell. **8**(6), 679–698 (1986)

49. R Deriche, J Cocquerez, G Almouzny, An efficient method to build early image description. Paper presented at the 9th international conference on pattern recognition, Rome, 14–17 Nov 1988, pp. 588–590

11

Subjective assessment of HDTV with superresolution function

Seiichi Gohshi[1*], Takayuki Hiroi[1] and Isao Echizen[2]

Abstract

Superresolution (SR) is a means of image enhancement, and some recent high-definition television (HDTV) sets and digital cameras are equipped with it. However, the resolution of such HDTV sets has not been tested as to whether it is actually better than that of HDTV sets without the function, in part because the resolution difference between HDTV sets is not always clearly visible. This paper proposes a subjective assessment for this purpose. The method is a combination of Scheffe's paired comparison and part of BT.500. Using this method, we performed a subjective assessment on an HDTV set with the SR function and other sets. The assessment data was statistically analyzed, and the results prove that the HDTV set with the SR function was not superior in resolution to the others.

Keywords: Superresolution; Superresolution image reconstruction; HDTV

1 Introduction

Digital high-definition television (HDTV) broadcasting has started in many countries, and large LCD TV sets have become common. The image quality of these systems is much higher than those of analogue systems such as NTSC and PAL. LCD manufacturers are selling various HDTV systems, and their catalogues are filled with sales points, such as superresolution (SR) [1-3], 240-Hz frame rates [4], etc.

There is a variety of SR technologies [5-9], and they obviously improve the resolution of still images [9-12]. However, SR technologies are complex, and it is not easy to develop a real-time SR function for HDTV. All of the SR proposals in the literature only include computer simulations and either do not work in real time or work only for a limited range of video sequence types [5-10,12-14]. However, we need to discuss real-time SR technology since it is now being used in commercial TV sets [1-3]. Note as well that there is another resolution enhancement method called enhancer or unsharp mask that does not actually improve the resolution but instead enhances edges. Unlike a SR function, it is very easy to make real-time enhancer hardware for HDTV [15,16].

All HDTV sets in use today receive broadcasting bit streams, such as MPEG-2 or MPEG-4, and decode them. After decoding, the sets have different functions to produce better image quality for LCDs. The functions, such as enhancers and noise reducers and so on, vary depending on the manufacturer and set in question. It is impossible to access the video signal inside an HDTV set and show it on another display. If we want to compare individual HDTV sets, we have to compare them with only their displays and with their functions. Although consumers want to buy HDTV sets with better image quality, the methods including the paired comparisons that have been reported in the literature are not useful to compare more than two displays at the same time. For this comparison, HDTV sets should be assessed with all of their functions and on their own displays.

Most HDTV sets are equipped with some kind of image enhancement or image-improving technology. In fact, manufacturers do not always state that their sets are equipped with enhancement technologies. Recently, HDTV sets with SR have become available. According to the information provided by the manufacturers, the SR function is different from that of conventional enhancers. However, the SR function developed for HDTV has not been assessed yet. If HDTV sets with SR cannot actually create frequency elements higher than those of the conventional enhancers, it is questionable whether HDTV

*Correspondence: gohshi@cc.kogakuin.ac.jp
[1] Kogakuin University, 1-24-2 Nishi-Shinjuku, Shinjuku-ku, Tokyo 163-8677, Japan
Full list of author information is available at the end of the article

sets with SR show better resolution than the conventional HDTV sets without SR.

In this paper, therefore, HDTV sets with enhancement technologies other than SR will be categorized as sets without SR, and those whose manufacturers say are equipped with SR functions will be categorized as sets with SR. This distinction mirrors the situation when shoppers go to an electronics store to buy an HDTV and find that it is not easy to tell the differences in resolution between HDTV sets with and without SR functions. They may end up relying on the claims of the manufacturers or question whether sets equipped with SR have better resolutions than sets without it.

The goal of our study is to see whether SR functions actually improve the resolution of HDTV sets [17,18]. Although there are several types of SR, so far, superresolution image reconstruction (SRR) is the only SR technology that has been embodied in a real-time system [1-3,19]. As mentioned above, the details about SR on most HDTV sets are not released by their manufacturers, so there is no proof that sets are actually equipped with an actual SR function or not. SR is an established research field. However, if the SR functions of HDTVs are not based on researchers' understanding, they may cause confusion not only among researches but also among consumers. We can theoretically analyze the resolution of the video if the HDTV set can be made to output video signals before and after the SR signal process. However, the SR processed image is only sent to the LCD, and there is no method to take the unprocessed image from the set. The only practical way to analyze the capability of SRR on HDTV sets is subjective assessment. There are many subjective assessment methods for evaluating image quality, and they give various results. There is no 'standard' method, but psychology and psychophysics provide plenty of methods to carry out this evaluation.

Subjective assessments are the alternative way to clarify the capabilities of HDTVs equipped with SR. These methods measure the reactions of volunteers who view television systems and are used to judge the performances of the systems. Although there are a couple of subjective assessment candidates [20-22], they are not appropriate for the purpose. All of them are designed to assess the image quality with a single display. P.910 is mainly designed for videophone systems, and P.912 is for surveillance systems because content for them are very limited. Videophone sequences mainly show a couple of people, and surveillance sequences tend to show people in corridors or vehicles on streets. Broadcasting has much more varied content, including news, dramas, and sports whose images do not usually resemble the above.

One of the most common and useful subjective assessments is BT.500 [20]. However, BT.500 has been standardized to evaluate the relationship between the video stream bitrate and subjective image quality, and also only one display can be used during the entire assessment test.

We have to use a number of HDTV sets showing the same bit streams to compare individual HDTV sets. The same bit stream was sent to the non-SR and SRR TV sets in order to compare their image qualities, but there is no standard for this sort of evaluation.

To be able to make a comparison, we decided that a couple of capabilities of BT.500 must be combined with other measuring factors.

We thought that a paired comparison would be useful. The notion of a paired comparison is exploited whenever we go to a store and do comparison shopping of similar items. Shoppers would likely want to compare the image qualities of two (or more) TV sets if all other features such as price, reliability, etc. are equivalent. The paired comparison does have an issue in that a lot of time would be consumed if we wanted to compare numerous HDTV sets. The number of TV manufacturers with established brands, however, is limited, and here, we only compare one HDTV set with an SRR function with four other HDTV sets. However, despite their potential utility and despite that paired comparison methods have been used to make video quality assessments, the ones described in the literature use only one display to make comparisons of individual signal processing methods or make changes to parameters. Such paired comparisons have not been used to compare different displays [23-25].

This paper is organized as follows: Section 2 discusses the eligibility of the observers in the assessment and the length of the test video in reference to BT.500. Section 3 explains the subjective assessment. Section 4 describes the statistical analysis of the subjective assessment, and Section 5 is the conclusion.

2 Observers and length of test sequence

BT.500 was used when digital video coding technology was first implemented in broadcasting, and it was an important standard at the time digital broadcasting was just starting. Our study followed the guidelines laid out in BT.500 as to how we selected the observers and how we determined the length of the test video sequences. BT.500 specifies that the observers must be non-video experts who do not work in the video industry and the number of observers should be more than 15. It specifies that the number of sequences should be at least four. BT.500 is still widely used to assess the video image quality, and this means that non-specialist observers can recognize differences in quality. Many analysts and critics of HDTV image quality can easily recognize differences in image quality, but non-video experts can do so as well. BT.500 calls for the length of each video sequence for the assessment to be from 10 to 15 s long. The ITE/ARIB Hi-Vision Test Sequences (ITE sequences) were made for HDTV assessments, and the period of each sequence is 15 s [26,27]. Although these sequences have been used for subjectively assessing HDTV video coding technologies, they are in YUV422 format. We have to process the sequences with the same MPEG-2 video encoder as broadcasting companies use, including the horizontal resolution conversion.

The sequences for the assessment should be selected from terrestrial broadcasting content because of the issues discussed above. However, it is not easy to find appropriate sequences in actual broadcasting content. The appropriate sequences must have very high frequency elements that are details in images that have no panning. Since panning causes motion blur in the whole image on the display, there are no high-frequency elements in the image at all. Blurry video sequences are thus of no use to assessments seeking to determine how high the resolution of an image is on a display. In accordance with the above considerations, we recorded various pieces of terrestrial HDTV broadcasting content onto a Blu-ray Disc (BD) player (capable of showing 1,920 × 1,080i/59.94-Hz HDTV video) and conducted many subjective assessments on them in order to select the appropriate sequences. Five sequences, each lasting from 10 to 15 s, were selected. The sequences are described in Section 3.2.

3 Subjective assessment
3.1 Scheffe's paired comparison
Before describing the assessment procedure, we should note that the 'pre-assessments' conducted beforehand proved that the results of paired comparisons were reproducible. We selected Scheffe's paired comparison, which is a round-robin comparison. The video signal paths are shown in Figure 1; a pair of HDTV sets are used in one

assessment. The same HDTV video bit stream was used to make non-SR and SRR processed video sequences. Figure 2 shows an example of comparing an HDTV with an SRR function and one without SR. All signal paths are 1,920 × 1,080/59.94 Hz.

Commercial HDTV sets have several display modes, and the names of these modes vary from one manufacturer to another. Most commercial HDTV sets have a dynamic mode, cinema mode, and standard mode. The dynamic mode is used in stores, and it gives an excessive enhancement. The cinema mode is used for showing Blu-ray and DVD movies. The standard mode is for home use, and we chose this mode since it is recommended by HDTV manufacturers for viewing over long periods and reducing energy consumption. The standard mode includes all parameters such as contrast, sharpness, color mode, and those recommended by the manufacturer. Most consumers likely do not have sufficient knowledge to control the many parameters of recent HDTV sets. Hence, they tend to use HDTV sets only in the recommended standard mode. In each assessment, observers assess a pair of HDTV sets at a time (this is the basic rule of Scheffe's paired comparison, that is, they do not compare the image quality of all five TV sets at once). Synchronized HDTV video is sent to both sets.

The observers we recruited for the experiment were allowed to move freely and check the image quality since it gave them more chances to check for very small resolution differences between sets. People would make such checks when they go to a shop to buy a HDTV set. Moreover, while they are in the shop, they would freely move around the sets and compare their image quality characteristics, including the resolutions. If they cannot find any difference in resolution regardless of how close they get to the screen, they would not need to worry about which set had the SR functions. For this reason, we asked the observers to move freely and look for differences in resolution. Scheffe's paired comparison is used for many purposes and has been used for the image quality assessment for HDTV sets [18,28].

HDTV sets are usually set in living rooms. Thus, normal lighting conditions for a living room were used. The same video sequence was repeated until the observer made the decision between the two sets. Five TV sets were selected for the experiment (the selection included the HDTV with SRR). A round-robin paired comparison was conducted since Scheffe's paired comparison was used. That is, one sequence was assessed five times by each observer, using the pair of HDTV A and HDTV B, the pair of HDTV B and HDTV C, and the pair of HDTV C and HDTV A, etc. Each observer was shown two HDTV sets and asked to choose the one with the higher resolution. Odd grades, such as three or five grades, are commonly used when a paired comparison is conducted. Observers scored +2

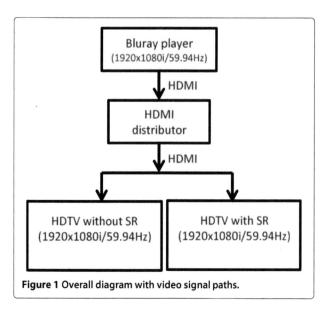

Figure 1 Overall diagram with video signal paths.

Figure 2 Subjective assessment.

for excellent, +1 for good resolution, 0 for fair, −1 for poor, and −2 for bad resolution in each assessment. There was no time limitation on an assessment. Observers could assess the TV sets as long as they wanted in order to make their decision. Each of the observers assessed the image quality on their own without anyone else in the test room. Figure 3 shows a photo of the experiment. As the photo shows the conditions were similar to when someone goes to a shop to buy a TV. In each test sequence, the observer made 20 assessments since there were five TV set round robins per sequence. Since there were five test sequences, the total number of assessments that one observer had to make was 100.

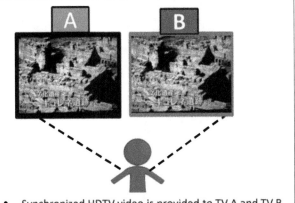

- Synchronized HDTV video is provided to TV A and TV B
- Observers can move freely to assess resolution

Figure 3 Paired HDTV assessment.

3.2 Test sequences

Still images such as test patterns and high-resolution photos are usually used to assess the resolution of displays. However, the SRR function on an HDTV set is supposed to work on digital broadcasting content, not on still photos. Since SRR cannot improve resolution with a single image such as a test pattern, we have to use video sequences taken with a HDTV video camera. As described in Section 2, the lengths were from 10 to 15 s. The test video sequences were selected from terrestrial HDTV digital broadcasting content in Japan. Content was recorded on a BD at HDTV resolution, and the repeat function of the BD player was used to show the sequences to the observers during the assessment. A limited amount of recorded broadcasting content was deemed appropriate for this assessment since most of it did not show any differences in the pre-assessment involving several observers. BT.500 recommends using at least four video sequences. Five sequences were selected. The test video sequences are shown in Figures 4, 5, 6, 7 and 8. The circles in each figure are high-resolution areas that were the objectives of the assessments.

Before starting the assessment, we prepared a couple of test video sequences to help non-video specialists understand what was meant by high-resolution HDTV video sequences. This training procedure is described in BT.500, and the recruited observers indicated that they understood the instructions after going through the training procedure. Dummy video sequences were shown to observers to stabilize their opinion, as specified in BT.500. Especially high resolution areas in the video sequences

Figure 4 Sequence 1 (news).

Figure 5 Sequence 2 (skyscraper).

Figure 6 Sequence 3 (river).

Figure 7 Sequence 4 (grass).

were pointed out by the indicators who conducted the assessments with the observers. We did not use the assessment results of the training video sequences. After the training, the observers were asked to concentrate on watching the texture in the circled areas and decide which HDTV set had the higher resolution. In tests such as these, it is generally difficult for non-experts to detect differences in resolution in the whole image. Thus, after the training, we asked the observers to concentrate on watching the texture in the circles and decide which HDTV set had the higher resolution. Furthermore, the observers were also asked to evaluate only the resolution and ignore other things. Sequences 1 (Figure 4) to 5 (Figure 8) were selected for the actual test. All of the circled areas have high-frequency elements and details.

4 Statistical analysis

Twenty-five observers participated in the assessment. All of them were university students ranging in age from 20 to 23 years old (average, 21). Prior to each test, a training session was held to introduce them to the test methodology of using broadcasting content that had high-resolution areas. The stimuli numbered five since five HDTV sets were used.

The outline of the analysis process of Scheffe's comparison test is as follows: A round-robin is performed on the five samples by comparing a pair of samples each time. The cross table for the whole results is made, and an analysis of variance is conducted. F_0 is calculated. We go forward to the yardstick analysis only when a significant difference is detected in the analysis of variance and F_0. The results for sequence 1 (news) are shown in Table 1. n means the number of stimuli (five HDTV sets), and N means the number of observers (25). The results in the deviations column and the biased deviations column were calculated in order to analyze the assessments [28,29]. F at a 1% provability, $F_{1\%}$, values were derived from F table using the degrees of freedom of the residual (369) and

Figure 8 Sequence 5 (night scenery).

Table 1 Analysis of variance

Factors		Deviation	Degrees of freedom		Biased deviation	F_0	$F_{1\%}$
Stimuli	S_α	687.672	$(n-1)$	4	171.918	75.84872[a]	3.398
Stimuli × observers	$S_{\alpha(k)}$	85.028	$(n-1)(N-1)$	96	0.885708	0.3907668[a]	1.568
Combination	S_β	38.428	$(n-1)(n-2)/2$	6	6.404667	2.8256828	2.287
Residual	S_ϵ	836.372	$n^2N - n^2/2 - 2nN$	369	2.2666	-	-
Overall result	S_τ	965		500	-	-	-

[a]Significant difference in the stimuli × observers row (1%).

those of the second parameter (4, 96, and 6). F_0 values are obtained with the biased deviation values. The biased deviation of the stimuli value (171.918) was divided by the biased deviation of the residual value (2.2666). Thus, the F_0 value of the stimuli was 75.84872. The F_0 value of the stimuli × observers row was calculated in a similar fashion. The biased deviation of the stimuli × observers row (0.3907668) was divided by the biased deviation of the residual value (2.2666). The F_0 value of the stimuli × observers was 0.3907668. If F_0 is bigger than $F_{1\%}$, there is a significant difference, and indeed, the table shows that the F_0 values of the stimuli are bigger than those of F. There is a significant difference in the stimuli × observers row (1%), which is indicated with 'a' in the F_0 column.

The yardstick method can only be used on significant differences in the analysis of variance [28,29]. Although the details of the analysis cannot be discussed in full due to space limitations, it is a typical combination of Scheffe's paired comparisons and a yardstick analysis of the results of the Scheffe's paired comparisons.

The α values for HDTV sets ($\alpha_{\text{HDTV A}}$, $\alpha_{\text{HDTV B}}$, $\alpha_{\text{HDTV C}}$, $\alpha_{\text{HDTV D}}$, and $\alpha_{\text{HDTV E}}$) were determined from the degrees of freedom and Figure 9. Figure 9 is called the cross table, and it is used in Scheffe's paired comparison. There are two degrees of freedom: the number of observers (25) and the number of HDTV sets (5). $\alpha_{\text{HDTV A}}$ is the value in Figure 9, i.e., the row ($X_{.j.} - X_{i..}$) and the column (HDTV A) divided by $2nN$, i.e., the stimuli values (HDTV sets: $n = 5$, observers: $N = 25$). ($X_{.j.} - X_{i..}$, HDTV A)(-252) are divided by $2nN$ as follows [28,29]:

$$\alpha_{\text{HDTV A}} = -252/(2 \times 25 \times 5) = -1.008 \qquad (1)$$

$\alpha_{\text{HDTV B}}$, $\alpha_{\text{HDTV C}}$, $\alpha_{\text{HDTV D}}$, and $\alpha_{\text{HDTV E}}$ are calculated in a similar way.

$$\alpha_{\text{HDTV B}} = -0.148, \quad \alpha_{\text{HDTV C}} = 0.6, \quad \alpha_{\text{HDTV D}} = 1.052,$$
$$\alpha_{\text{HDTV E}} = -0.496.$$

$$(2)$$

In Scheffe's paired comparison, all HDTVs become the reference. For example, HDTV A starts out as the reference, and HDTV B, C, D, and E are evaluated against it. Then, HDTV B becomes the reference, and all other HDTVs are evaluated against it. Although the evaluation of HDTV B is +2 with reference HDTV A, the evaluation might not be -2 but be -1 when HDTV A is assessed against the reference HDTV B. The reverse assessment is not always symmetrical.

The order of resolution is HDTV D, HDTV C, HDTV B, HDTV E, and HDTV A. HDTV A is equipped with SRR. According to the subjective assessments, the resolution of HDTV A is the lowest.

zw	HDTV A	HDTV B	HDTV C	HDTV D	HDTV E	$X_{i..}$
HDTV A	zw	27	41	41	12	121
HDTV B	-35	zw	30	34	-3	26
HDTV C	-41	-11	zw	23	-34	-63
HDTV D	-38	-34	-22	zw	-35	-129
HDTV E	-17	7	38	36	zw	64
$X_{.j.}$	-131	-11	87	134	-60	$X_{...}$
$X_{.j.} - X_{i..}$	-252	-37	150	263	-124	0

Figure 9 Cross table.

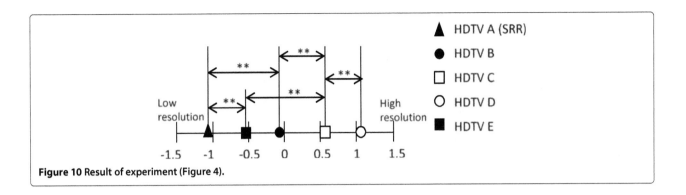

Figure 10 Result of experiment (Figure 4).

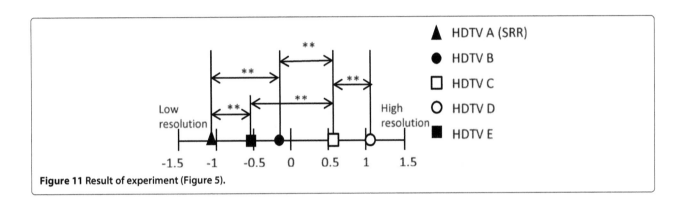

Figure 11 Result of experiment (Figure 5).

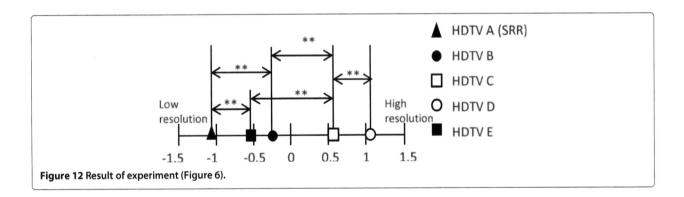

Figure 12 Result of experiment (Figure 6).

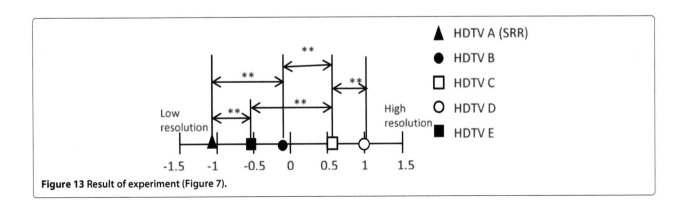

Figure 13 Result of experiment (Figure 7).

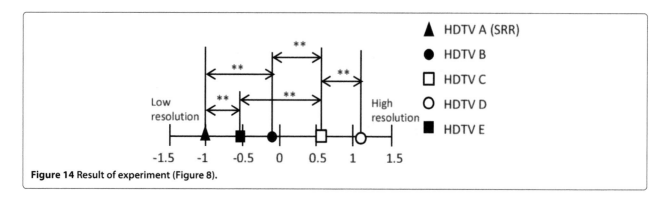

Figure 14 Result of experiment (Figure 8).

An analysis was conducted to see if the order had statistically significant differences. A Y value for 1% was used, and it can be derived using Equation 3:

$$Y_\alpha = q\sqrt{\frac{V_\epsilon}{2nN}}. \tag{3}$$

Different tables give the provability at 1% of the $F_{1\%}$ distribution [29]; thus, $Y_{\alpha 0.01} = 0.44847$.

The yardstick values are shown in Figure 10. The differences in the yardstick values in relation to $Y_{\alpha 0.01}$ are as follows. The difference between the lowest resolution HDTV A and the second lowest HDTV E is calculated as follows:

$$\alpha_{\text{HDTV E}} - \alpha_{\text{HDTV A}} = 0.512 \tag{4}$$

Here,

$$\alpha_{\text{HDTV E}} - \alpha_{\text{HDTV A}} > Y_{\alpha 0.01}. \tag{5}$$

The percentage 1% in Equation 5 means a false provability of 1%, and the result is 99% true. The resolution of HDTV set A with SRR is thus inferior to that of HDTV set E, the second lowest resolution at a provability of 99%.

$$\alpha_{\text{HDTV B}} - \alpha_{\text{HDTV A}} = 0.86, \quad \alpha_{\text{HDTV C}} - \alpha_{\text{HDTV B}} = 0.748,$$
$$\alpha_{\text{HDTV D}} - \alpha_{\text{HDTV C}} = 0.452. \tag{6}$$

All of these values are greater than $Y_{\alpha 0.01} = 0.44847$. There are statistical differences and their false provability of 1%. These relations are marked with double asterisk in Figure 10. Thus, the HDTV set with SRR was actually poorer in resolution than the other HDTV sets. Figures 11, 12, 13 and 14 show the assessment results of Figures 5, 6, 7 and 8. All of them have the similar tendencies. Our assessments have proven that the resolution of the HDTV set with SRR is the lowest of the manufacturers' HDTV sets tested.

5 Conclusions

Our subjective assessment of HDTV with an SRR function used Scheffe's paired comparison, observers who

were not video experts, as called for by BT.500, and content chosen from terrestrial digital HDTV broadcasting. The assessment results were statistically analyzed (analysis of variance). A yardstick method was conducted on the points of significant difference. It was statistically proven that the SRR function on the HDTV set did not improve the resolution.

The resolution of the HDTV set with SRR was found to be the lowest of the HDTV sets tested. This result accords with most observers' opinions just after the assessment test. The assessment method described here can be used for other items such as frame rate conversion from 60 to 240 Hz and noise reduction on digital HDTV sets. It is necessary to conduct further validation of this method with various content and TV sets.

Competing interests
The authors declare that they have no competing interests.

Author details
[1] Kogakuin University, 1-24-2 Nishi-Shinjuku, Shinjuku-ku, Tokyo 163-8677, Japan. [2] National Institute of Informatics, The Graduate University for Advanced Studies (SOKENDAI), 2-1-2, Hitotsubashi, Chiyoda-ku, Tokyo 101-8430, Japan.

References
1. S Tokumitsu, From REGZA to Cell REGZA. http://www.chinacom.tw/ngn2009/pdf/Toshiba_Presentation_Web_REVISED.pdf. Accessed 12 Feb 2014
2. N Matsumoto, T Ida, Reconstruction-based super-resolution using self-congruency around image edges. J. IEICE. **J93-D**(2), 118–126 (2010). (in Japanese)
3. Toshiba. http://www.toshiba.co.jp/regza/detail/superresolution/resolution.html (in Japanese). Accessed 12 Feb 2014
4. Sony. https://www.sony.jp/bravia/technology/mf/ (in Japanese). Accessed 12 Feb 2014
5. S Farsiu, D Robinson, M Elad, P Milanfar, Fast and robust multi-frame super-resolution. IEEE Trans. Image Process. **13**(10), 1327–1344 (2004)
6. S Panda, RS Prasad, G Jena, POCS based super-resolution image reconstruction using an adaptive regularization parameter. IJCSI Int. J. Comput. Sci. Issues. **8**(5), 1694–0814 (2011)
7. SC Park, MK Park, MG Kang, Super-resolution image reconstruction: a technical overview. IEEE Signal Process. Mag. **20**, 21–36 (2003)
8. AWM Eekeren, K Schutte, LJ Vliet, Multiframe super-resolution reconstruction of small moving objects. IEEE Trans. Image Process. **19**(11), 2901–2912 (2010)
9. A Katsaggelos, R Molina, J Mateos, *Synthesis Lectures on, Images, Video and Multimedia Processing*. (Morgan & Claypool Publishers, San Rafael, 2007)

10. D Glasner, S Bagon, M Irani, Super-resolution from a single image. 2009 IEEE 12th International Conference on Computer Vision, Kyoto, October 2009, pp. 349–356

11. V Bannore, Iterative-Interpolation Super-Resolution Image Reconstruction, Studies in Computational Intelligence, vol. 195, chapter 5 (Springer Milton, Keynes, 2010), pp. 77–103

12. S Chaudhuri, J Manjunath, *Motion-Free Super-Resolution*. (Springer, New York, 2005), pp. 202–214

13. S Baker, T Kanade, Limitation on super-resolution and how to break them. PAMI. **24**(9), 1167–1183 (2002)

14. O Shahar, A Faktor, M Irani, Space-time super-resolution from a single video, in *CVPR '11 Proceedings of the 2011 IEEE Conference on, Computer Vision and Pattern Recognition* (IEEE Piscataway, 2011), pp. 3353–3360

15. WF Schreiber, Wirephoto quality improvement by unsharp masking. J. Pattern Recognit. **2**, 111–121 (1970)

16. J-S Lee, Digital image enhancement and noise filtering by use of local statistics, in *IEEE Transactions on Pattern Analysis and Machine Intelligence, PAMI-2* (IEEE Piscataway, 1980), pp. 165–168

17. S Gohshi, Limitation of super resolution image reconstruction for video, in *Fifth International Conference on Computational Intelligence, Communication Systems and Networks* (IEEE Madrid, 5–7 June 2013), pp. 217–221

18. S Gohshi, I Echizen, Subjective assessment for HDTV with super-resolution function, in *Seventh International Workshop on Video Processing and Quality Metrics for Consumer Electronics - VPQM2013 2013* (Scottsdale, 30 January–1 February 2013), pp. 32-36

19. N Matsumoto, T Ida, A study on one frame reconstruction-based super-resolution using image segmentation. IEICE Technical Report (2008). (in Japanese)

20. http://www.itu.int/rec/R-REC-BT.500/en. Accessed 12 Feb 2014

21. http://www.itu.int/rec/T-REC-P.910/en. Accessed 12 Feb 2014

22. http://www.itu.int/rec/T-REC-P.912-200808-I

23. J-S Lee, FD Simone, T Ebrahimi, Subjective quality evaluation via paired comparison: application to scalable video coding. Multimedia IEEE Trans. **13**(5), 882–893 (2011)

24. DA Silverstein, JE Farrell, Quantifying perceptual image quality. Proc. IS&T Image Process. Image, Qual., Image Capture, Syst. Conf. **1**, 242246 (1998)

25. J Li, M Barkowsky, PL Callet, Subjective assessment methodology for preference of experience in 3DTV, in *Proceedings of the 11th IEEE IVMSP Workshop: 3D Image/Video Technologies and Applications,* Seoul (IEEE Piscataway, 2013)

26. http://www.ite.or.jp/en/. Accessed 12 Feb 2014

27. http://www.nes.or.jp/gaiyo/pdf/ite_hyoujundouga_sample.pdf. Accessed 12 Feb 2014

28. H Scheffe, An analysis of variance for paired comparisons. J. Am. Stat. Assoc. **47**(259), 381–400 (1952)

29. T Fukuda, R Fukuda, *Ergonomics Handbook*. (Scientist Press Co. Ltd, Tokyo, 2009). (in Japanese)

12

Two-way partitioning of a recursive Gaussian filter in CUDA

Chang Won Lee, Jaepil Ko and Tae-Young Choe[*]

Abstract

Recursive Gaussian filters are more efficient than basic Gaussian filters when its filter window size is large. Since the computation of a point should start after the computation of its neighborhood points, recursive Gaussian filters are line oriented. Thus, the degree of parallelism is restricted by the length of the data image. In order to increase the parallelism of recursive Gaussian filters, we propose a two-way partitioned recursive Gaussian filter. The proposed filter partitions a line into two lines and a point, which is used for Gaussian blur effect across the two lines. This partition increases the parallelism because the filter is applied to the two blocks in parallel. Experimental results show that the process time of the proposed filter is half compared to the time of an one-way parallel recursive Gaussian filter while the peak signal-to-noise ratio is maintained within an acceptable rate of 26 to 33 dB.

Introduction

A Gaussian blur filter, or Gaussian filter, is one of the fundamental and widely used image processing techniques. A typical use of the filter is denoising. It is also used as a preprocessing step for down/up sampling, edge detection [1,2], or scale space representation [3]. Contrast enhancement techniques such as Retinex [4-6] or unsharp filters [7] are the other uses for Gaussian blur where it approximates the illumination component of an image at a large scale.

According to the definition of Gaussian filter, filtered value of a pixel in a two-dimensional image is computed using nearby pixel values. The range of the pixels to be used is determined by filter window size $N \times N$. It is known that the filtered value of a pixel can be computed by pixels in a horizontal line and a vertical line that pass through the pixel. Let us call the Gaussian filter that computes filtered value of a pixel using the crossing two lines as *finite impulse response* (FIR) filter. FIR filter has $4N \times width \times height$ computation steps if the size of given image is width × height.

Although FIR filter implements Gaussian blur filter in the exact discrete way, the processing time of the filter depends on the filter window size $N \times N$. Recursive Gaussian filters that implement Gaussian filter are

developed in order to eliminate effect of the filter window size. A recursive Gaussian filter computes filtered value of a pixel using differential values of its neighborhood pixels [8]. Since the differential values of neighborhood pixels contain all approximated data within the range of the filter window size, the filter window size is not involved in the number of computation steps. Computation step of a recursive Gaussian filter proposed by van Vliet et al. is about $32 \times width \times height$. Thus, recursive Gaussian filters is faster than the FIR filter if a filter window size is greater than 8. Unfortunately, recursive Gaussian filters make dependence between pixels and restrict the degree of parallelism. Pixel $p[i][j]$ must wait until the filtered value of pixel $p[i-1][j]$ is computed in the row-oriented step.

As graphic processing unit (GPU) cores can be used for general purpose computation, many image processing algorithms have been implemented in general purpose GPU (GPGPU). NVIDIA supports Compute Unified Device Architecture (CUDA) as a GPGPU architecture and a development environment. Since recursive Gaussian filters make dependencies between pixels, it is conventional to allocate a line into a thread in a core processes. On the other side, the bitmap Gaussian filter can allocate 1 pixel per 1 thread, which fully utilizes available cores. Thus, recursive Gaussian filters shows better performance in the restricted area where the number of cores is small and the filter window size is large.

---

*Correspondence: choety@kumoh.ac.kr
Department of Computer Engineering, Kumoh National Institute of Technology, Gumi, Gyeongbuk 730-701, Korea

We propose a refined recursive Gaussian filter for GPGPU that partitions working domain into two ways. The proposed filter combines a recursive Gaussian filter and FIR filter in order to minimize error rate that occurs by splitting the working domain. The remainder of this paper is structured as follows: 'Problem environment and related work' section explains the problem environment and reviews related work. 'Proposed filter' section gives details of the proposed refined recursive Gaussian filter. 'Experimental results' section gives the experimental results of the proposed filter. Finally, 'Conclusions' section concludes with future works.

Problem environment and related work

Recursive Gaussian filter

Gaussian blur uses the Gaussian distribution function. Equation 1 shows a Gaussian distribution function for a two-dimensional space represented as two-dimensional array in$[x, y]$ [9]:

$$g(x, y) = \frac{1}{\sqrt{2\pi}\sigma} e^{-\frac{d^2}{2\sigma^2}}, \tag{1}$$

where $d = \sqrt{(x - x_c)^2 + (y - y_c)^2}$ is the distance of the neighborhood pixel in$[x, y]$ from the center pixel in$[x_c, y_c]$, and σ denotes the Gaussian half-width [10]. Since discrete two-dimensional space like image is filtered, integer value N is used instead of real value σ. For the simplicity, N is set to $2 \times \sigma$, and filter window size $N \times N$ is used. Since a basic Gaussian blur (FIR) filter is a type of a separable filter [11], the filter computes the filtered pixel out$[x, y]$, the discrete convolution of pixel in$[x, y]$ with the sampled Gaussian, as follows:

$$w[x, y] = \sum_{k=x-N/2}^{x+N/2} \text{in}[k - x, y] g(k, y),$$

$$\text{out}[x, y] = \sum_{l=y-N/2}^{y+N/2} w[x, l - y] g(x, l), \tag{2}$$

where out[ ] is computed after the two-dimensional array w[ ] is computed. Thus, the time complexity of the basic Gaussian filter for 1 pixel depends on the filter window size and is about $2N + 1$ additions and $2N + 2$ multiplications.

Such computational complexity can be reduced to a constant if a recursive Gaussian filter is used [8,12]. Young and van Vliet proposed a recursive Gaussian filter, which we call it YVRG filter, using an approximation by the Fourier transform [8]. A recursive Gaussian filtering process requires two *steps* where each step is composed of two *passes* as follows:

1. Row-oriented step

   (a) Forward pass generates w[ ] using in[ ]
   (b) Backward pass generates out[ ] using w[ ]

2. Column-oriented step

   (c) Downward pass generates w[ ] using out[ ]
   (d) Upward pass generates in[ ] using w[ ]

where the two-dimensional array in[ ] stores the input image, and another two-dimensional array out[ ] stores the intermediate image after the row-oriented step finishes. A one-dimensional array w[ ] temporarily stores the intermediate data during each pass of the lines. After the filtering finishes, array in[ ] is overwritten by the filtered image. These steps are shown in Figure 1. Since the column-oriented step is the same as the row-oriented step except for its direction, only the row-oriented step will be discussed in the paper as shown in Figure 2. During a forward pass, input pixels are processed in the forward direction and the intermediate pixels are stored in a temporary array named w[ ]. During a backward pass, the pixels in w[ ] are processed in the backward direction. The resulting pixels are stored in data array out[ ] and used as input data in the column-oriented step.

Let us show the detailed step of YVRG filter. The resulting pixel out$[x, y]$ is computed from the following two recursive passes:

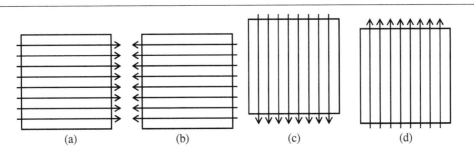

Figure 1 Passes of recursive Gaussian filter. Sequence of a recursive Gaussian filter: **(a)** row-oriented step forward pass, **(b)** row-oriented step backward pass, **(c)** column-oriented step forward pass, and **(d)** column-oriented step backward pass.

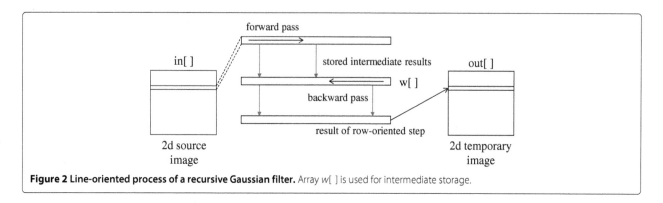

Figure 2 Line-oriented process of a recursive Gaussian filter. Array w[ ] is used for intermediate storage.

Forward pass:

$$w[x,y] = B \cdot \text{in}[x,y] + (b_1 \cdot w[x-1,y] + b_2 \cdot w[x-2,y] + b_3 \cdot w[x-3,y]) / b_0, \tag{3}$$

Backward pass:

$$\text{out}[x,y] = B \cdot w[x,y] + (b_1 \cdot \text{out}[x+1,y] + b_2 \cdot \text{out}[x+2,y] + b_3 \cdot \text{out}[x+3,y]) / b_0. \tag{4}$$

The precalculated constants are

$$b_0 = 1.57825 + 2.44413q + 1.4281q^2 + 0.422205q^3$$
$$b_1 = 2.44413q + 2.85619q^2 + 1.26661q^3$$
$$b_2 = -(1.4281q^2 + 1.26661q^3)$$
$$b_3 = 0.422205q^3$$
$$B = 1 - ((b_1 + b_2 + b_3)/b_0)$$
$$q = \begin{cases} 0.11477050185203552246093750 & \text{if } N < 0.5 \\ 3.97156 - 4.14554\sqrt{1 - 0.26891N} & \text{if } 0.5 \le N < 2.5 \\ 0.98711N - 0.96330 & \text{otherwise.} \end{cases}$$

Since filter window size N is used to calculate constant q only, it does not affect the time complexity of the YVRG filter. Equations 3 and 4 show that pixels in a line are bound by precedence relations. The resulting value of pixel $\text{out}[x,y]$ needs the value of $\text{out}[x+1,y]$ and the intermediate pixel value $w[x,y]$ needs the value of $w[x-1,y]$. Thus all pixel values in a line are restricted by a linear precedence order.

While the recursive process needs three previous neighborhood pixels for each pixel according to Equations 3 and 4, there are no sufficient neighborhood pixels near the image boundaries for the process. For example, pixels $w[-1,y]$, $w[-2,y]$, and $w[-3,y]$ required by pixel $w[0,y]$ are not available in the image. Thus, boundary pixels are duplicated as shown in Figure 3. In the case of a row-oriented step, $\text{in}[x,0]$ is copied to $w[x,-3]$ through $w[x,-1]$ and these are used to calculate $w[x,0]$ through $w[x,2]$.

A forward pass uses five multiplications and three additions per pixel as same as the backward pass does. In order to compute the filtered value of a pixel, four passes are required. Thus 20 multiplications and 12 additions are required per pixel. A recursive Gaussian filter of any filter window size has a similar time complexity as a basic Gaussian filter with filter window size seven.

Unfortunately, the precedence relation of YVRG filter causes a disadvantage if the filter is applied to a small-sized image on massive parallel computers. For example, the YVRG filter uses a maximum of 512 processors in parallel in order to process a 512×512 image because the pixels in a line are bound by precedence relations. Most high-end NVIDIA graphic processors have more than 1,000 cores [13], of which about half are idle during the filtering process. This means that the YVRG filter cannot fully utilize graphic processors if the number of cores exceeds the image length. Although the basic Gaussian filter can fully utilize graphic processors, it requires a

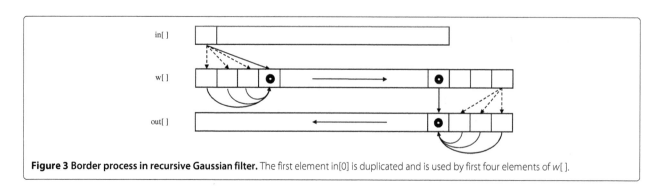

Figure 3 Border process in recursive Gaussian filter. The first element in[0] is duplicated and is used by first four elements of w[ ].

massive computation time when the filter window size is large. In order to solve such a dilemma, we refine the YVRG filter in order to increase the degree of parallelism by partitioning each line into three parts: two sub-lines and a point. The three parts execute in parallel in order to theoretically reduce process time by half and double the graphic processor's utilization.

System environments

Let us consider the hardware systems on which recursive Gaussian filters run. Currently, many types of parallel computers are available. At the standalone computer level, openCL based on multiple cores [14] and CUDA using NVIDIA graphic processors [15] are popular. At the networked computing system level, cluster computing, grid computing, and cloud computing systems are available [16]. Since image processing shares a heavy amount of data between nearby pixels, little communication overhead is required. Thus, standalone computer systems with multiple processing cores are preferable to network computing systems.

CUDA is a parallel computing platform. It requires GPUs produced by NVIDIA. CUDA is provided with libraries and a compiler called 'nvcc.' CUDA allows a programmer to make a general-purpose function called a kernel and run it in a core, a processing unit of an NVIDIA graphic card. The kernel function is mapped to a process unit called a thread that runs in a core. A block is composed of multiple threads and is mapped to a streaming multiprocessor (SM) that is composed of multiple CUDA cores. Since the number of cores in an SM is static, there should be a sufficient number of threads in a block to maximize GPU utilization.

In a traditional parallel computer, an optimal static mapping of threads into processors is possible. However, it is not a good idea to allocate a specific number of threads to an SM, since the CUDA cores' configuration in SM is different for each GPU model. CUDA provides an automatic scheduler for allocating threads to cores. Thus, a programmer only needs to allocate enough threads in a block in order to maximize the utilization of CUDA cores in SMs. The programmer also needs to take care of making enough number of blocks in order to keep SMs work as much as possible. After all, defining domain range per thread and the amount of threads per block determines the utilization of a CUDA GPU.

There are four levels of memory in CUDA: constant memory, local memory, shared memory, and global memory. Since the size and access times of memory levels are different, careful variable allocation is required.

Related work

If FIR filter is used in parallel computing systems, an input image can be partitioned into any types, for example, line-oriented, column-oriented, checkerboard-oriented partition [11,17], or bitwise allocation [2,18], because there is no precedence dependency between pixels. Although the FIR filter is highly suitable for parallelism, it requires large process time for big filter window because its processing step is linear to the filter window size. Ryu and Nishimura tried to reduce process time of FIR filter using a look-up table and integer-only operations [19]. Although the process time of the filter is reduced, the time complexity is still linear to the filter window size.

Recursive Gaussian filters exploit differences of previous nearby pixels in order to eliminate effect of filter window size from process time. Two representative recursive Gaussian filters are proposed by Deriche [20] and YVRG filter proposed by van Vliet et al. [12]. Since the filter window size is used not as an iteration number but as a parameter for calculating coefficients in the recursive computation, the filters have steady process time even if the filter window size becomes large. Process steps of the two recursive Gaussian filters are almost the same, except that Deriche's filter works better if the filter window size is less that 64 and YVRG filter works better otherwise [10].

However, the YVRG filter binds all pixels into a line because of the precedence dependencies of adjacent pixels. For example, $w[x, y]$ should be computed after $w[x - 1, y]$ in a forward pass of a row-oriented step, and $out[x, y]$ should be computed after $out[x + 1, y]$ in a backward pass.

Because of these dependencies, the parallel version of recursive Gaussian filters should partition an image into lines such that each processor computes a output line from an input line using an intermediate buffer $w[\ ]$, as shown in Figure 2. The degree of parallelism of the YVRG filter is $min(v, h)$ where the image size is $v \times h$. If the number of available processors exceeds the degree of parallelism, the remainder of the processors become idle. For example, an NVIDIA graphic processor GTX780 has 2304 CUDA cores. Assume that a filter program processes a 512×512 image. While 512 CUDA cores are working, the other 1792 CUDA cores stay idle, leading to a 22.2% processor utilization.

A parallel version of a recursive Gaussian filter (one-way recursive Gaussian filter) is already included in the CUDA Toolkit. The version is a parallelized implementation of the YVRG algorithm proposed by Young and van Vliet [8]. This implementation partitions an image into lines and allocates each line to a thread. Thus, its parallelism is restricted by the height or width of the input image. Other papers have partitioned image domains in a similar manner while implementing similar algorithms [17,21,22].

Gaussian KD-Trees algorithm was proposed for accelerating a broad class of nonlinear filters like bilateral filters

[23]. It adapts three schemes to achieve less computation. One is ignoring interactions further than three standard deviations apart. Another is taking important sampling in which values are averaged with other values that are considered nearby. The other is computing the filter at a lower resolution and then interpolating the result. This method is superior to the previous grid approach [24] in terms of memory size and processing time aspects. However, it has a tree building overload and it is also difficult to implement tree traversal due to its extremely irregular algorithm that results in debilitating the advantage of GPU implementation.

Podlozhnyuk proposed an efficient parallel image convolution method that uses shared memory in CUDA [11]. Since values in the boundary pixels of a block should be exchanged between neighborhood blocks, a careful communication schedule is required. The paper proposes a schedule that enables data loading and filtering process concurrently. Although the method works well on FIR filter, it does not show the same performance if recursive Gaussian filters are used. Recursive Gaussian filters prefer temporary memory access. Thus, local memory is more efficient than shared memory in the case of recursive filters.

Proposed filter

Two-way partitioning

In order to increase the parallelism of a recursive Gaussian filter, we propose a two-way recursive Gaussian filter. The filter partitions an image in line-based orientation and partitions each line into three blocks again. The first and third blocks use the recursive Gaussian filter, while the second block uses a general Gaussian filter. One major problem is that all pixels in a line are related by a precedence dependency, as shown in Equations 3

and 4. However, we note two facts that circumvent the dependencies in a line:

- When out$[x, y]$ is computed in backward pass, out$[x + 1, y]$ through out$[x + 3, y]$ are required. Pixels out$[x + 1, y]$ through out$[x + 3, y]$ are the results of a row-oriented step. If the pixels have already been computed using the basic Gaussian filter, out$[x, y]$ has no precedence dependency on out$[x + k, y]$ where $k > 3$.
- There is no priority between forward and backward passes. Thus, any pass can start in any order.

These facts motivate us to partition a line into the following three parts:

- B_l: the left half of the line from index 0 to width$/2-1$, where *width* is the number of horizontal pixels in the picture.
- P_c: the pixel located at width$/2$.
- B_r: the right half of the line from index width$/2 + 1$ to width-1.

The proposed filter uses two passes for each step. In the first pass, the filter in block B_l works similarly to a one-way recursive Gaussian filter. It starts from the leftmost pixel in$[0, y]$ and generates intermediate data $w[\ ]$ until it arrives at index width$/2 - 1$, as shown in Figure 4. The filter for pixel P_c computes the horizontal value of the basic Gaussian filter $w[$width$/2, y]$ for pixel in$[$width$/2, y]$ with its filter window size. Thus, the time complexity of P_c is depend on the filter window size. The filter in block B_r works similarly to the filter in block B_l but in the reverse direction. It starts from the rightmost pixel in$[$width $- 1, y]$ and generates

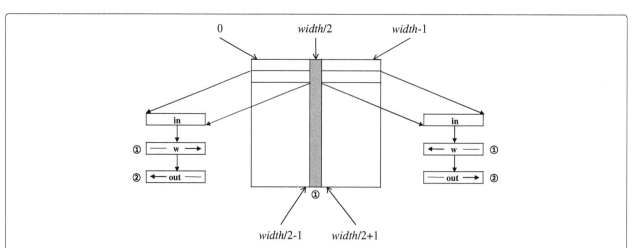

Figure 4 Partition to three blocks. Each line is divided into three blocks B_l (index range 0 ~ width$/2 - 1$), P_c (index width$/2$), and B_r (index range width$/2 + 1$ ~ width $- 1$).

intermediate data $w[\ ]$ until index width/2 + 1. In other words, the filter in block B_r starts from a backward pass.

Since forward and backward passes are used to reflect the left-side and right-side neighborhood pixels, respectively, the execution order of the forward and backward passes does not affect the filtering results. After finishing the first pass, that is, computation of $w[]$, each block starts a reverse directed pass. It is important to notice the filtering boundary pixels. Boundary pixels like $w[0,y]$, $w[1,y]$, and $w[2,y]$ need values $w[-3,y]$, $w[-2,y]$, and $w[-1,y]$. Since these values are not available, $w[0,y]$ is used instead. When the direction of computation is changed, pixel out[width/2 − 1, y] needs value out[width/2, y], out[width/2 + 1, y], and out[width/2 + 2, y]. Although these indexes have been computed in B_r, they are not the same values as in Equation 4 because those values are generated by the second pass while the values in B_r are generated by the first pass.

In order to solve this mismatch, pixel P_c, computed by the basic Gaussian filter, is used as a buffer zone. The computed value of pixel P_c, that is, out[width/2, y], is used instead of the three values out[width/2, y], out[width/2 + 1, y], and out[width/2 + 2, y] as shown in Figure 5. This is the reason for computing P_c concurrently with the other two blocks. In addition, block B_r uses pixel P_c in the same manner but in the inverse order. Figure 6 shows the parallelism of the proposed filter. Three processors can execute in parallel in the first pass and two processors can execute in parallel in the second pass.

Algorithm 1 shows the detailed process of row-oriented step of the proposed two-way filter. Three threads are assigned to each row calculated in line 1. Thus a block takes charge of adjacent lines in an image. For example, if four lines are allocated to each block (blockDim.x = 4), the third block filters line 12 ∼ 15. The three threads are identified by pre-assigned value *threadIdx.y*. If a thread has index (blockIdx.x = 2, threadIdx.x = 2, threadIdx.y = 1), the thread tasks charge of central pixel P_c of line 10. Neighborhood values for boundary pixels are initialized at line 3, 9, 14, and 21. Intermediate array $w[row]$ [] is divided to two sub arrays w_l and w_r in order to prevent race condition in $w[row]$ [width/2 − 2] ∼ $w[row]$ [width/2 + 2],

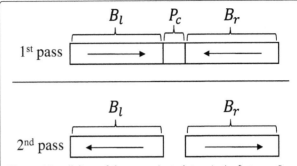

Figure 6 Parallelism of the row-oriented step. In the first pass, B_l, P_c, and B_r are computed in parallel. In the second pass, inverse directions of blocks B_l and B_r are computed in parallel.

which are overlapped and are accessed concurrently by two threads.

The time complexity of the proposed filter is determined by two factors: line width and filter window size. Assuming that there are enough processors, three processors are allocated to each line. If l = max(width, height), then $3l$ processors are required in order to maximize the performance. A processor for block B_l or B_r computes half of the $l/2$ pixels in a pass. Since each pixel requires eight multiplications and four additions, $6l$ operations are required for each pixel. The center pixel P_c requires $3N$ operations, where $N \times N$ is the filter window size. Thus, max($6l, 3N$)+$6l$ operations are required per step and max($12l, 6N$)+$12l$ steps are required during the proposed filter. In short, the process time of the filter is halved or speedup is doubled compared to those of a one-way recursive Gaussian filter if the number of cores is equal to or greater than $3l$.

Double speedup with the cost of triple cores is not highly efficient. The proposed two-way recursive Gaussian filter is useful if lots of small-sized images compared to the number of cores should be processed in sequence. An typical example is the application that filters multiple different windows of an image in order to find the best parameters.

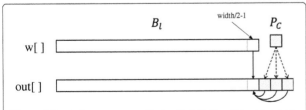

Figure 5 Start of reverse pass. Pixel out[width/2 − 1] is computed using pixel w[width/2 − 1], out[width/2], out[width/2 + 1], and out[width/2 + 2] which are copied from P_c.

Table 1 Experimental environment

	Description
CPU	Intel core i5 750 (2.67 GHz)
GPU	Geforce GTX 670 (GK104)
	Compute capability, 3.0
	Number of CUDA cores 1,344
	Graphic clock, 915 MHz
	Processor clock, 980 MHz
Compiler	Visual Studio 2010
Library	CUDA 5.0
Image	512 × 512 bitmap

Compile and execution environment.

Algorithm 1: TWO-WAY RECURSIVE GAUSSIAN FILTER, row-oriented step

---

Input: An 2-d image array in[ ][ ] with $height \times width$, filter window size N

Output: An filtered 2-d image array out[ ][ ] with the same size of in[ ][ ]

1 $row \leftarrow blockDim.x * blockIdx.x + threadIdx.x$

2 **if** $threadIdx.y = 0$ **then**   /* left side block B_l */

3 $\quad$ $w_l[row][2], w_l[row][1], w_l[row][0] \leftarrow in[row][0]$

4 $\quad$ **for** $i \leftarrow 3$ **to** $width/2 - 1$ **do**

5 $\quad\quad$ $w_l[row][i] \leftarrow B * in[row][i] + (b_1 * w_l[row][i-1] + b_2 * w_l[row][i-2] + b_3 * w_l[row][i-3])/b_0$

6 **else if** $threadIdx.y = 1$ **then**   /* center pixel P_c */

7 $\quad$ $w_l[row][width/2], w_r[row][width/2] \leftarrow bitwiseRowGaussianFilter(in, row, width/2, N)$

8 **else**   /* right side block B_r */

9 $\quad$ $w_r[row][width], w_r[row][width+1], w_r[row][width+2] \leftarrow in[row][width-1]$

10 $\quad$ **for** $i \leftarrow width - 1$ **downto** $width/2 + 1$ **do**

11 $\quad\quad$ $w_r[row][i] \leftarrow B * in[row][i] + (b_1 * w_r[row][i+1] + b_2 * w_r[row][i+2] + b_3 * w_r[row][i+3])/b_0$

12 synchronize threads

13 **if** $threadIdx.y = 0$ **then**   /* left side block B_l */

14 $\quad$ $w_l[row][width/2+1], w_l[row][width/2+2] \leftarrow w_l[row][width/2]$

15 $\quad$ **for** $i \leftarrow width/2 - 1$ **downto** 0 **do**

16 $\quad\quad$ $w2_l[row][i] \leftarrow B * w_l[row][i] + (b_1 * w_l[row][i+1] + b_2 * w_l[row][i+2] + b_3 * w_l[row][i+3])/b_0$

17 $\quad\quad$ $out[row][i] = w2_l$

18 **else if** $threadIdx.y = 1$ **then**   /* center pixel P_c */

19 $\quad$ do nothing

20 **else**   /* right side block B_r */

21 $\quad$ $w_r[row][width/2-1], w_r[row][width/2-2] \leftarrow w_r[row][width/2]$

22 $\quad$ **for** $i \leftarrow width/2 + 1$ **to** $width - 1$ **do**

23 $\quad\quad$ $w2_r[row][i] \leftarrow B * w_r[row][i] + (b_1 * w_r[row][i-1] + b_2 * w_r[row][i-2] + b_3 * w_r[row][i-3])/b_0$

Experimental results

The proposed two-way recursive Gaussian filter was implemented in the C programming language using the CUDA library. The experimental environment is shown in Table 1. The experiment used the image commonly known as Lena, shown in Figure 7. For comparison, a parallel version of the one-way recursive Gaussian filter proposed by Young and van Vliet was also implemented.

Gaussian filters usually have been used to de-noise in differential operations for image processing or to achieve image blurring effects. For the differential operations, the typical filter window size is 3×3. To obtain a proper blurring effect, we should carefully determine the filter window size according to image sizes. One of the thumb rules suggests 1%~5% of the image size for the Gaussian half-width σ and two times of σ for the filter window size [25]. If we take 3% of σ for a 512×512 resolution image, the filter window size becomes about 30. Bilateral filters require 10% of σ, then the mask size becomes 102 for the same image resolution. The larger image size requires much larger mask size. In this paper, we take 3×3 and 30×30 mask size for Lena image.

Two filter window sizes, 3 and 30, were used, as shown in Figure 8. Filter window size 3 is the minimum size for

Figure 7 Data image. 512×512-sized image.

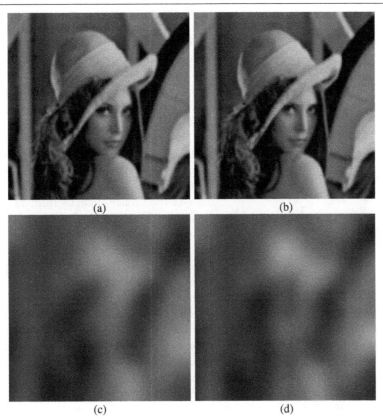

Figure 8 Filtered images. Comparison of the recursive Gaussian filter and proposed two-way recursive Gaussian filter: **(a)** the recursive Gaussian filter with filter window size 3, **(b)** the proposed two-way recursive Gaussian filter with filter window size 3, **(c)** the recursive Gaussian filter with filter window size 30, and **(d)** the proposed two-way recursive Gaussian filter with filter window size 30.

Gaussian filter because only adjacent pixels are used for filtering. Hale proposed 64 as a boundary filter window size for choosing among different two recursive Gaussian functions: smaller window size for Deriche's algorithm [20] and bigger window size for van Vliet et al.'s YVRG algorithm [12]. Since the proposed algorithm is based on van Vliet et al.'s algorithm, filter window size 30 is chosen as a medium stable value. The original image was changed to gray scale in order to analyze the results quantitatively.

Validity of the proposed filter

The peak signal-to-noise ratio (PSNR) was used for quantitative analysis. PSNR is computed as follows:

$$\text{MSE} = \frac{1}{mn} \sum_{i=0}^{m-1} \sum_{j=0}^{n-1} \left[I(i,j) - K(i,j) \right]^2$$

$$\text{PSNR} = 10 \log_{10} \frac{\text{MAX}_I^2}{\text{MSE}}, \qquad (5)$$

where MSE is the mean squared error, m is the width of the images, n is the height of the images, I and J are the two compared images, and MAX_I is the maximum value of a pixel in image I. Since the images are converted to gray

scale for the comparison, MAX_I is 255. The smaller the difference between the two images is, the smaller the MSE is. Thus, a large PSNR indicates that the two images are similar. Table 2 shows the PSNR values between a one-way recursive, two-way recursive, and basic Gaussian filter. For image comparison, a tolerable PSNR range is between 30 and 50 dB. It is known that two images are not easy to distinguish with the naked eye if the PSNR is 30 dB or more. Although the PSNR between the results of one-way and two-way recursive Gaussian filters is smaller than 30 dB when the filter window size is 3, the one-way recursive Gaussian filter has a worse PSNR value when it is compared to the basic Gaussian filter. The table shows that the result of a two-way recursive Gaussian filter is closer to that of the basic Gaussian filter. Thus, the proposed two-way recursive Gaussian filter is usable in the general case.

Performance comparison

Measure using cudaEventRecord()

Since the parallel CUDA code runs in a GPU, general clock measure functions like `gettimeofday()` or `clock()` cannot measure its process time correctly.

Table 2 PSNR comparison

Image size	Filter window size	One-way vs. two-way	FIR vs. one-way	FIR vs. two-way
SD	3	29.4	26.2	29.7
	30	31.1	32.8	31.4
	90	29.5	33.4	29.4
HD	3	33.0	30.9	33.6
	30	30.6	39.7	30.8
	90	24.7	33.0	26.3
Full HD	3	30.5	26.6	29.2
	30	32.9	36.7	33.2
	90	30.1	34.8	31.4

PSNR between three images: non-recursive Gaussian filter (the basic Gaussian filter), one-way recursive Gaussian filter, and proposed two-way recursive Gaussian filter. Unit of the PSNR value is dB (decibel).

CUDA provides the cudaEvent family of functions in order to measure process time in a GPU.

Before the process times are measured, the allocation of threads to blocks should be considered in order to maximize parallelism. A *thread* is a logical process unit in CUDA. The *kernel code* is a description of a thread and a *block* is a set of threads. The maximum number of threads in a block is 1,024, in the case of the GeForce GTX 670 GPU. However, this does not mean that all 1,024 threads run concurrently in a block. Although a SM is mapped to a block in CUDA and each SM contains 32 processing cores [26], this does not mean that 32 threads in a block will maximize the parallelism. Because of this uncertainty, we decided to allocate various numbers of threads to blocks to find an allocation that minimizes the process time. Figure 9 shows the process times of different numbers of allocated threads. The x-axis indicates the number of allocated lines per block, and the y-axis indicates the process time in the GPU kernel. One-way recursive Gaussian filter

allocates one thread per line, and the proposed two-way recursive Gaussian filter allocates three threads per line. The one-way recursive Gaussian filter has the minimum process time when the number of threads per block is 8 as shown in Figure 9a. Filter window size $N \times N$ does not affect the process time in the recursive Gaussian filters, as we expected. Thus, filter window size 30×30 is used for the following experiments.

The proposed two-way recursive Gaussian filter has the minimum process time when the number of threads per block is 16 as shown in Figure 9b. In Figure 9a, the process times increase as the lines per block exceed 8. Figure 9b shows the similar anomaly from 32 lines per block. The main reason of the larger process time in the case of the smaller number of lines per block is that the number of threads is not sufficient to fully utilize cores allocated to each block. As the number of lines per block increases, utilization of cores in each block increases, but the number of blocks decreases. If the number of blocks is not sufficient, blocks are not scheduled evenly. If 32 lines of an image with 512 lines are allocated to each block, 16 blocks should be allocated 7 SMs of NVIDIA GPX670 graphic card. Then a SM runs 2 or 3 blocks, which makes imbalance between SMs.

From the two process times, the speedup of the proposed two-way filter over the one-way filter is shown in Figure 10a, where the speedup value is double if the number of threads per block is greater than or equal to 16. Also, the figure shows that overheads invoked by sequential global memory access and FIR filter computation in the center point P_c do not affect performance of the two-way filter.

Measure using Nsight

Nsight is a development tool provided by NVIDIA and it tells occupancy of parallel applications in GPU [27]. Thus, Nsight can be used to investigate GPU utilization.

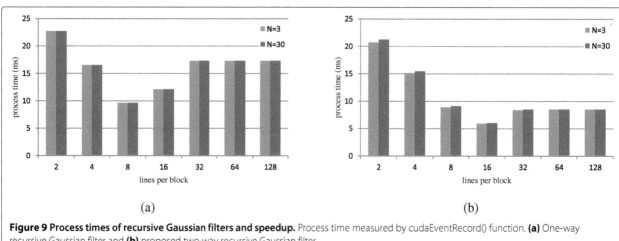

Figure 9 Process times of recursive Gaussian filters and speedup. Process time measured by cudaEventRecord() function. **(a)** One-way recursive Gaussian filter and **(b)** proposed two-way recursive Gaussian filter.

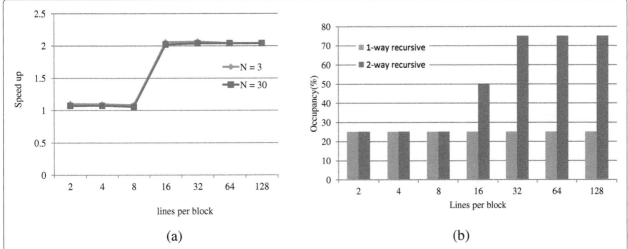

Figure 10 Speed up and occupancy comparison of recursive Gaussian filters. (a) Speed up of the proposed two-way recursive Gaussian filter against one-way recursive Gaussian filter. **(b)** Occupancies of recursive Gaussian filters.

Occupancy is the percentage of active warps against the maximum active warps, where a warp means a group of 32 threads. The amount of active warps is decided by the number of allocated threads per block, amount of available registers, and amount of shared memory. Allocating more threads to block increases occupancy.

Figure 10b shows an occupancy comparison between one-way recursive Gaussian filter and two-way recursive Gaussian filter. Since the total number of threads is fixed to data image width or height, that is, 512 in the case of Lena image, many CUDA cores are idle and it makes the CUDA occupancy at the low value. On the other side, two-way recursive Gaussian filter increases its occupancy as the number of lines per block increases over 16 as shown in Figure 10b.

Improvement using local memory
Figure 9 shows that performances of recursive Gaussian filters degrade as the number of lines per block exceeds 16. The imbalanced block allocation to SMs and sequential global memory access are assumed to be the main reasons of the degradation. Since the balanced allocation policy changes by different graphic card models, finding efficient memory access is focused in order to improve the proposed filter. CUDA provides following four-level hierarchical memory model: constant memory, per-thread local memory, per-block shared memory, and global memory [28]. Constant memory is used to store constant values. Thus, constants in Equations 3 and 4 are stored in constant memory. Image data is stored in the global memory in order to be accessed by all threads. During a forward pass, each pixel in array in[ ] is read once or twice according to filter window size. Thus it is not highly required to copy it in shared or local memory. Since array $w[\ ]$ is generated and frequently accessed by each thread, it is

good target for locating in local memory. Pixel P_c is read six times by adjacent two threads. Since P_c is stored in cache of the thread after being read, its memory location does not highly affect the performance of the filtering. As the result, major variables are located in each memory as follows:

- Constant memory: constants for Equations 3 and 4
- Per-thread local memory: $w[\ ]$, temporary memory for thread
- Global memory: in[ ], out[ ] (including P_c)

Figure 11 shows the improved process time by moving temporary array $w[\ ]$ from global memory to local memory. Note that the process time do not increase

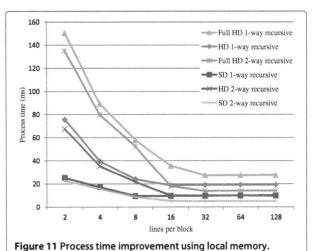

Figure 11 Process time improvement using local memory. Improved process time by allocating intermediate array variable $w[\ ]$ to local memory. Filter window size is set to 30 × 30. SD sized image is 512 × 512 Lena.bmp file, HD sized image is 1280 × 720 Mountain.bmp file, and Full HD sized image is 1920 × 1080 Lake.bmp file.

although the number of lines per block increases, which is a different tendency compared to the case of global memory access shown in Figure 9. The imbalanced block allocation to SMs still exists even in the case of the local memory access. However, local memory can be accessed in parallel by each thread while global memory should be accessed sequentially by blocks. As the result, the effect of imbalance allocation is assumed to be reduced by the local memory access. In order to prove the assumption, process time in each thread is analyzed as shown in Table 3. A process time is mainly composed of data request time on memory, execution time of instructions, and synchronization time. If the data request time is subtracted from the process time, remaining execution and synchronization times become similar for both memory access cases.

Figure 11 includes process time of HD and full HD-sized images. One-way recursive Gaussian filter is also improved by local memory access. Process times are stabilized after 32 lines per block. Two-way recursive Gaussian filter has 1.96, 1.90, and 1.98 speedup compared to one-way recursive Gaussian filter in the case of SD, HD, and full HD images, respectively. The figure shows the proposed two-way recursive Gaussian filter generates steady speedup and performance against bigger images.

Figure 12 shows performance comparison between a CPU-based implementation and the GPU-based implementation. GPU-based implementation configures the number of lines per block as 32. Multi-threaded two-way recursive Gaussian filter is implemented on a PC with Intel Quad Core i5-750 Processor 2.67 GHz. Although the CPU-based implementation has better performance on SD-sized image, the situation is reversed when HD and full HD-sized image is used.

Conclusions

In this paper, we have noticed that line-oriented recursive Gaussian filter can be partitioned more and proposed a two-way recursive filter that increases CUDA GPGPU utilization. The proposed filter divides each line into two sub-lines and a central point. The central point is used to

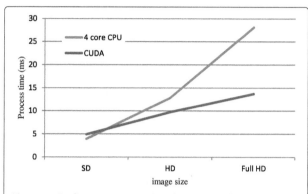

Figure 12 Performance comparison between 4 core CPU and 1344 core GPU. The proposed two-way recursive Gaussian filter is executed. Intel i5 with four cores uses four threads that fully utilize the multi-core CPU. CUDA configures 64 lines per block.

compensate mismatches occurred by dividing a line into two parts. PSNR shows that the quality of the filter locates between non-recursive Gaussian filter and the one-way line-oriented recursive Gaussian filter. The process time of the proposed filter is reduced to half by setting the number of lines per block to the same or greater than 16.

The research can be expanded by considering following various concerns. Starting from the proposed two-way recursive Gaussian filter, a line can be partitioned to three or more blocks, where quality and speedup are major concerns. Another consideration is the central points. The central points or boundary points between blocks in the partitioned line can be designed differently. The central points are required as boundary points in each block. If recursive equations are designed carefully, it could be possible to partition a line without any central point or boundary point.

Competing interests
The authors declare that they have no competing interests.

Authors' contributions
The work presented here was carried out in collaborated process of all authors. JPK and TYC defined the research theme. CWL and TYC designed methods, algorithm, and implementation, and carried out the laboratory experiments. CWL, JPK, and TYC analyzed the data, interpreted the results, and wrote the paper. All authors have contributed to inspection and approved the manuscript.

Table 3 Kernel process time components

Lines per block	Process time (ms)		Data request percentage		Execution and sync (ms)	
	Local	Global	Local	Global	Local	Global
4	15.2	15.1	1.2%	12.3%	15.0	13.5
8	8.4	8.9	2.9%	25.2%	8.2	6.8
16	5.1	5.9	6.1%	41.9%	4.8	3.5
32	4.9	8.4	10.2%	48.9%	4.4	4.3
64	5.1	8.5	10.2%	48.9%	4.4	4.3

Extraction of execution times and synchronization time among entire processing time in the case of two-way recursive Gaussian filter: 'Data request' means the percentage of memory access time among the entire filtering process. 'Execution and Sync' means the processing time where memory access time is subtracted.

References
1. J Canny, A computational approach to edge detection. IEEE Trans. Pattern Anal. Mach. Intell. **8**(6), 679–698 (1986)
2. Y Luo, R Duraiswami, Canny edge detection on NVIDIA CUDA, in *IEEE Computer Society Conference on Computer Vision and Pattern Recognition Workshops, 2008. CVPRW'08* (IEEE Anchorage, AK, USA, 2008), pp. 1–8
3. DG Lowe, Distinctive image features from scale-invariant keypoints. Int. J. Comput. Vis. **60**(2), 91–110 (2004)
4. EH Land, The Retinex theory of color vision. Sci Am. **237**(6), 108–128 (1977)
5. DJ Jobson, Z Rahman, GA Woodell, Properties and performance of a center/surround retinex. IEEE Trans. Image Process. **6**(3), 451–462 (1997)

6. DJ Jobson, Z-U Rahman, GA Woodell, A multi-scale retinex for bridging the gap between colour images and the human observation of scenes. IEEE Trans. Image Process. **6**(7), 965–976 (1997)

7. R Haralick, L Shapiro, *Computer and Robot Vision*. (Addison-Wesley, Boston, USA, 1992)

8. IT Young, LJ van Vliet, Recursive implementation of the Gaussian filter. Signal Process. **44**, 139–151 (1995)

9. LG Shapiro, GC Stockman, Image smoothing, in *Computer Vision* (Prentice Hall Upper Saddle River, NJ, USA, 2001), p. 137

10. D Hale, Recursive gaussian filters. CWP-546 (2006). http://www.cwp. mines.edu/Meetings/Project06/cwp546.pdf

11. V Podlozhnyuk, Image convolution with CUDA. NVIDIA Corporation White Paper, June. **2097**(3) (2007). https://cluster.earlham.edu/trac/bccd-ng/export/2037/branches/cuda/trees/software/bccd/software/cuda-0.2. 1221/sdk/projects/convolutionSeparable/doc/convolutionSeparable.pdf

12. LJV Vliet, IT Young, PW Verbeek, Recursive Gaussian derivative filters, in *Proceedings of the Fourteenth International Conference on Pattern Recognition, 1998*, vol. 1 (IEEE Brisbane, Queensland, Australia, 1998), pp. 509–514

13. NVIDIA Corporation, White Paper NVIDIA GeForce GTX 680 (2012). http:// www.geforce.com/Active/en_US/en_US/pdf/GeForce-GTX-680-Whitepaper-FINAL.pdf

14. P Jaaskelainen, CS de La Lama, P Huerta, JH Takala, OpenCL-based design methodology for application-specific processors, in *2010 International Conference on Embedded Computer Systems* (IEEE Samos, Greek, 2010), pp. 223–230s

15. CUDA Parallel computing platform. http://www.nvidia.com/object/ cuda_home_new.html, Jan. 2014

16. I Foster, Y Zhao, I Raicu, S Lu, Cloud computing and grid computing 360-degree compared, in *Grid Computing Environments Workshop, 2008. GCE'08* (IEEE, 2008), pp. 1–10

17. Y Su, Z Xu, X Jiang, GPGPU-based Gaussian filtering for surface metrological data processing, in *IV* (IEEE Computer Society, 2008), pp. 94–99. http://dx.doi.org/10.1109/IV.2008.14

18. A Trabelsi, Y Savaria, A 2D Gaussian smoothing kernel mapped to heterogeneous platforms, in *2013 IEEE 11th International New Circuits and Systems Conference (NEWCAS)* (IEEE Paris, France, 2013), pp. 1–4

19. J Ryu, TH Nishimura, Fast image blurring using Lookup Table for real time feature extraction, in *IEEE International Symposium on Industrial Electronics, 2009. ISIE 2009* (IEEE Seoul, Korea, 2009), pp. 1864–1869

20. R Deriche, Recursively implementating the Gaussian and its derivatives (1993). http://hal.archives-ouvertes.fr/docs/00/07/47/78/PDF/RR-1893. pdf

21. Y Ma, K Xie, M Peng, A parallel Gaussian filtering algorithm based on color difference, in *IPTC* (IEEE, 2011), pp. 51–54. http://ieeexplore.ieee.org/xpl/ mostRecentIssue.jsp?punumber=6099690

22. D Nehab, A Maximo, RS Lima, H Hoppe, GPU-efficient recursive filtering and summed-area tables. ACM Trans. Graph. **30**(6), 176:1–176:11 (2011)

23. A Adams, N Gelfand, J Dolson, MsLevoy, Gaussian KD-trees for fast high-dimensional filtering, in *ACM Transactions on Graphics (TOG), Volume 28* (ACM, 2009), p. 21

24. S Paris, F Durand, A fast approximation of the bilateral filter using a signal processing approach, in *Computer Vision–ECCV 2006* (Springer Graz, Austria, 2006), pp. 568–580

25. SK Park, BS Kim, EY Chung, KH Lee, A new illumination estimation method based on local gradient for retinex, in *IEEE International Symposium on Industrial Electronics, 2009. ISIE 2009* (IEEE Seoul, Korea, 2009), pp. 569–574

26. J Luitjens, S Rennich, CUDA warps and occupancy. GPU Computing Webinar (2011). http://on-demand.gputechconf.com/gtc-express/2011/ presentations/cuda_webinars_WarpsAndOccupancy.pdf

27. NVIDIA Nsight Visual Studio Edition. https://developer.nvidia.com/nvidia-nsight-visual-studio-edition June 2014

28. NVIDIA, Programming model, in *CUDA C Programming Guide, Design Guide* (NVIDIA, 2013), pp. 12–13. http://docs.nvidia.com/cuda/cuda-c-programming-guide/index.html#axzz34o3nNnUF June 2014

13

Low-complexity background subtraction based on spatial similarity

Sangwook Lee and Chulhee Lee[*]

Abstract

Robust detection of moving objects from video sequences is an important task in machine vision systems and applications. To detect moving objects, accurate background subtraction is essential. In real environments, due to complex and various background types, background subtraction is a challenging task. In this paper, we propose a pixel-based background subtraction method based on spatial similarity. The main difficulties of background subtraction include various background changes, shadows, and objects similar in color to background areas. In order to address these problems, we first computed the spatial similarity using the structural similarity method (SSIM). Spatial similarity is an effective way of eliminating shadows and detecting objects similar to the background areas. With spatial similarity, we roughly eliminated most background pixels such as shadows and moving background areas, while preserving objects that are similar to the background regions. Finally, the remaining pixels were classified as background pixels and foreground pixels using density estimation. Previous methods based on density estimation required high computational complexity. However, by selecting the minimum number of features and deleting most background pixels, we were able to significantly reduce the level of computational complexity. We compared our method with some existing background modeling methods. The experimental results show that the proposed method produced more accurate and stable results.

Keywords: Background subtraction; Background modeling; Structural similarity; Kernel density estimation

Introduction

As security monitoring emerges as an important issue, there has been an increasing demand for intelligent surveillance systems. Key operations in intelligent surveillance include object tracking, abnormal behavior detection, and behavior understanding. Accurate background subtraction plays an important role. The goal of background subtraction is to eliminate background components and detect meaningful moving objects. In real environments, due to various and complex background types such as moving escalators, waving tree branches, water fountains, and flickering monitors, background subtraction is a difficult task. Researchers have overcome these problems by using background modeling. Simple background models assume static background images. Background components can generally be eliminated by computing the difference between an input image and the background image that was modeled using average, low-pass filtering, and median filtering [1-4]. For instance, in [1], the median background image was used to subtract the background components.

Since temporal median filtering is time-consuming, a fast algorithm utilizing the characteristics of adjacent frames was proposed [2]. Cheng et al. applied a recursive mean procedure to compute background images [3]. In [4], low-pass filtering was utilized to estimate a static background image. However, these approaches cannot handle dynamic backgrounds and are sensitive to threshold values.

In order to handle various background types, statistical approaches were introduced. Among these approaches, Gaussian modeling methods have been widely used. Initially, uni-modal distribution was used to model pixel values [5]. In [6], a background subtraction method using the HSV color space was presented based on single Gaussian modeling. A fast and stable linear discriminant approach based on uni-modal distribution and Markov random field was proposed [7]. Rambabu and Woo proposed a background subtraction method which is robust against noisy and changing illumination based on single Gaussian modeling [8]. Although these models have low complexity levels and produce satisfactory performances in controlled backgrounds, it is difficult to use them for dynamic scenes. The Gaussian mixture model (GMM) is usually used to

* Correspondence: chulhee@yonsei.ac.kr
Yonsei University, 134 Sinchon-dong, Seodaemun-gu, Seoul 120-749, Korea

model various background types. Stuffer and Grimson used the GMM for background subtraction in [9], and it is still a popular method for background subtraction [10-20]. A spatio-temporal GMM (STGMM) was proposed to handle complex background [10]. Using a GMM, a statistical framework was investigated to localize a foreground object [11] and a dynamic background was modeled for highly dynamic conditions such as active cameras and high motion activities in background regions [12]. Also, the subtraction of two Gaussian kernels (difference of Gaussians) was used to eliminate background regions in embedded platforms [13]. A general framework of regularized online classification EM for GMM was proposed [14]. Wang et al. proposed an adaptive local-patch GMM to detect moving objects in dynamic background regions [15]. In [16], a new update algorithm was proposed for learning adaptive mixture models, and Bin et al. proposed a self-adaptive moving object detection algorithm. The method improved the original GMM in order to adapt to sudden or gradual illumination changes [17]. In [18], in order to improve GMM performance, a new rate control method based on high-level feedback was developed. An improved adaptive-K GMM method was presented for updating background regions [19], and GMM was used for modeling background regions in a Bayer-pattern domain [20]. A disadvantage of these multimodal Gaussian modeling methods is that they require pre-defined parameters such as the number of the Gaussian distributions and the standard deviations of those distributions. Also, dynamic backgrounds cannot be accurately modeled by a few Gaussian distributions. In order to overcome parameter background modeling methods, nonparametric background modeling techniques have been developed for estimating background probabilities. Nonparametric background modeling methods have been used to estimate background distribution based on pixel values observed in the past. In [21], the Gaussian kernel was used for pixel-based background modeling. This nonparametric method is usually used to handle multiple modes of dynamic backgrounds without pre-defined parameters. However, these nonparametric methods use kernel density estimation (KDE), which requires heavy computational complexity and a large amount of memory. Various efforts have been made to address these problems. Using Parzen density estimation and foreground object detection, a fast estimation method was presented [22] and an automatic background modeling based on multivariate non-parametric KDE was proposed [23]. In [24], a non-parametric method was proposed for foreground and background modeling, which did not require any initialization. Han et al. proposed an efficient algorithm for recursive density approximation based on density mode propagation [25]. Also, depth information, on-line auto-regressive modeling, and Gaussian family distribution were used to eliminate

background regions [26-28]. In [29], new object segmentation was proposed based on a recursive KDE. It used the mean-shift method to approximate the local maximum value of the density function. The background was modeled using real-time KDE based on online histogram learning [30].

Also, alternative approaches were proposed based on neural network techniques or the support vector machine (SVM) method [31-35]. A method was proposed based on self-organization through artificial neural networks [31]. Furthermore, a self-organization method was combined with fuzzy approach to update background [32]. In [33-35], an automatic algorithm was proposed to perform background modeling using SVM.

To develop a robust model with low complexity, we used a pixel-based background subtraction method based on spatial similarity computed using the structural similarity method (SSIM) [36]. Using spatial similarity, we measured the pixel similarity and eliminated background pixels. The remaining pixels were classified as either background or foreground pixels using KDE. Since we eliminated most background pixels and used only two features for KDE, the complexity of the proposed method was significantly reduced. The proposed method was evaluated using two datasets (Wallflower's and Li's datasets) and showed favorable performance over some existing methods.

The overall algorithm for efficient background subtraction
Preparation
The structure similarity for eliminating background components

To eliminate background components while preserving potential foreground components, we first computed the spatial similarity using the SSIM method that was developed for image quality assessment [36]. The SSIM was computed as follows:

$$\text{Luminance}: l(x, y) = \frac{2\mu_x\mu_y + C_1}{\mu_x^2 + \mu_y^2 + C_1}$$

$$\text{Contrast}: c(x, y) = \frac{2\sigma_x\sigma_y + C_2}{\sigma_x^2 + \sigma_y^2 + C_2}$$

$$\text{Structure}: s(x, y) = \frac{\sigma_{xy} + C_3}{\sigma_x\sigma_y + C_3} \quad (1)$$

$$\text{SSIM}(x, y) = [l(x,y)]^\alpha [c(x,y)]^\beta [s(x,y)]^\gamma$$
$$= \frac{\left(2\mu_x\mu_y + C_1\right)\left(2\sigma_{xy} + C_2\right)}{\left(\mu_x^2 + \mu_y^2 + C_1\right)\left(\sigma_x^2 + \sigma_y^2 + C_2\right)}$$

where α, β, and γ are parameters which determine the relative importance of $l(x, y)$, $c(x, y)$, and $s(x, y)$ and we set α, β, and γ to 1. μ_x and μ_y are the local means, σ_x and σ_y are the local standard deviations, σ_{xy} is the local covariance coefficient between regions x and y, and we set C_3 to $C_2/2$ and C_1 and C_2 are constants that were set to 6.5025 and 58.5225 as proposed in [36]. In Equation 1, l, c, and s represent the luminance, contrast, and structure of two images. In this paper, we computed the SSIM for local regions (e.g., a 3×3 block) to eliminate background components. Figure 1a and b show the input and reference background images, respectively. Figure 1c and g show the intensity and hue difference images between Figure 1a and b, respectively. The SSIM difference image between Figure 1a and b is shown in Figure 1k. Thresholding (if a pixel value of the difference image was larger than the given threshold value, the pixel was eliminated) was applied to the difference images with various threshold values (low, medium, large), and the resulting images are shown in Figure 1d,e,f,h,i,j,l,m,n. For the intensity component (Figure 1c,d,e,f), the differences between the shadow regions and the corresponding background regions were high. The thresholding operation still left shadows when using a low threshold value (e.g., 80). When we used a larger threshold value (e.g., 120) to eliminate the shadows, potential foreground objects were also eliminated (Figure 1f).

For the hue component (Figure 1g,h,i,j), shadows were not retained, but many of the background regions contained high difference values. To eliminate these background regions, we tried using a larger threshold value (e.g., 120). However, the top portion of the person with the blue jacket and the red portion of the person on the right were also eliminated. Furthermore, the small object in the lower-left corner was almost deleted when the intensity component or the hue component was used. However, the method based on the SSIM correctly retained the object (Figure 1k,l,m,n). In the SSIM, global intensity and contrast changes were not determined as forms of distortion [36]. Therefore, the proposed method proved to be robust against shadows with lower intensity values while retaining internal structures. Furthermore, since the proposed method used the variances and covariance of two local regions, it could detect objects with similar colors. In

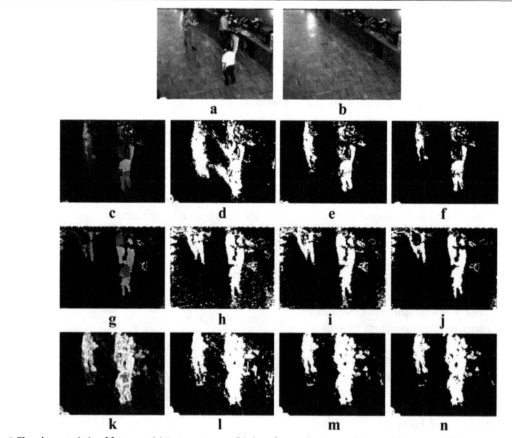

Figure 1 The characteristic of features. (a) An input image, **(b)** the reference background image, **(c)** intensity difference image between **(a)** and **(b)**, **(d)** thresholding of **(c)** with a low value (80), **(e)** thresholding of **(c)** with a middle value (100), **(f)** thresholding of **(c)** with a large value (120), **(g)** hue difference image between **(a)** and **(b)**, **(h)** thresholding of **(g)** with a low value (80), **(i)** thresholding of **(g)** with a middle value (100), **(j)** thresholding of **(g)** with a large value (120), **(k)** SSIM difference image between **(a)** and **(b)**, **(l)** thresholding of **(k)** with a low value (0.4), **(m)** thresholding of **(k)** with a middle value (0.5), and **(n)** thresholding of **(k)** with a large value (0.6).

Figure 2a, a person's head color was similar to the background regions. The proposed method showed improved performance compared to the other method [31] (http://www.na.icar.cnr.it/~maddalena.l/MODLab/SoftwareSOBS.html). Similarly, in Figure 2b, the woman's jacket color was similar to the background regions. The proposed method correctly classified the woman as a foreground object while the other method missed the jacket.

To apply the SSIM to local regions, we used a sliding window approach. For each pixel, we computed the SSIM of a 3×3 window centered at the pixel. Let $\mathbf{A}(i,j) = \lfloor A^R(i,j), A^G(i,j), A^B(i,j) \rfloor$ be a pixel in the RGB color space. Then, the similarity image (SI) between intensity images $A^I(i,j)$ and $B^I(i,j)$ was calculated as follows:

$$SI_{A^I,B^I}(i,j) = SSIM\left(A^I(i,j), B^I(i,j)\right) \qquad (2)$$

where

$$A^I(i,j) = \frac{1}{3}\left(A^R(i,j) + A^G(i,j) + A^B(i,j)\right), \mu_{A^I(i,j)}$$
$$= \frac{1}{9}\left(\sum_{v=-1}^{1}\sum_{u=-1}^{1} A^I(i+u,j+v)\right) \qquad (3)$$

$$\sigma^2_{A^I(i,j)} = \frac{1}{9}\left(\sum_{v=-1}^{1}\sum_{u=-1}^{1}\left(A^I(i+u,j+v)^2 - \mu_{A^I(i,j)}\right)\right),$$

$$\sigma_{A^I(i,j)B^I(i,j)} = \frac{1}{9}\left(\sum_{v=-1}^{1}\sum_{u=-1}^{1}\left(A^I(i+u,j+v) - \mu_{A^I(i,j)}\right)\right.$$
$$\left. \times \left(B^I(i+u,j+v) - \mu_{B^I(i,j)}\right)\right)$$

$A^I(i,j)$ represents an intensity value, $\mu_{A^I(i,j)}$ and $\mu_{B^I(i,j)}$ are intensity means, $\sigma_{A^I(i,j)}$ and $\sigma_{B^I(i,j)}$ are intensity standard deviations, and $\sigma_{A^I B^I(i,j)}$ is the intensity covariance. $SI_{A^I,B^I}(i,j)$ is close to 1 when two window regions were similar. C_1 and C_1 were set to 6.5025 and 58.5225, respectively [36]. By assuming that one image was a reference background image, we obtained a binary background image (BBI) by applying a thresholding operation:

$$BBI_{A^I,B^I}(i,j) = \begin{cases} 0(\text{background}) & \text{if } \left(SI_{A^I,B^I}(i,j) > T_1\right) \\ 1(\text{foreground candidate}) & \text{otherwise} \end{cases}$$
$$(4)$$

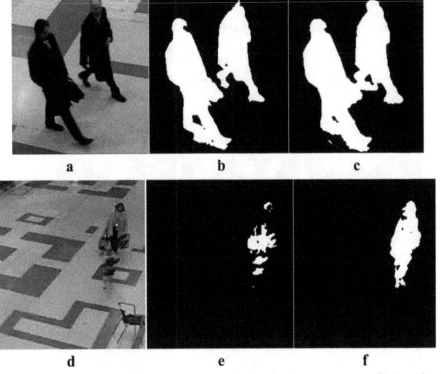

Figure 2 The effect for detecting the objects which are similar with backgrounds. (a) An input image 1, **(b)** the results of other method [31], **(c)** the results of the proposed method, **(d)** an input image 2, **(e)** the results of other method [31], and **(f)** the results of the proposed method.

T_1 is a threshold value which was empirically determined and set to 0.55. Figure 3 shows the effect of the threshold value. When we used a small value for T_1, most pixels were classified as background regions (Figure 3c). When we used a large value for T_1, most pixels were classified as foreground regions (Figure 3o). Based on this observation, we set T_1 to 0.55, though any value between 0.1 and 0.9 provided good performance.

Since we calculated the means and the variances, the computational complexity was low. However, some background pixels were still retained. In order to eliminate the background pixels, we used nonparametric kernel density estimation.

Determining foreground and background areas using KDE

Generally, KDE can model multi-modal probability distributions without requiring any prior information. It is effective for modeling the arbitrary densities of real environments. KDE was applied to each pixel of the training images. In other words, we extracted training samples at each pixel location of the training images. Let $s_1, s_2, ..., s_N$ be training samples and we used the Gaussian kernel function. Then, the probability of x_t was calculated as follows [21]:

$$p(x_t) = \frac{1}{N} \sum_{i=1}^{N} \frac{1}{\sqrt{2\pi}\sigma} e^{-\frac{1}{2\sigma}(s_i - x_t)^2} \tag{5}$$

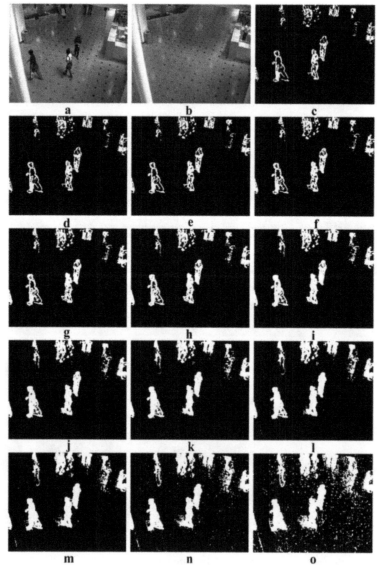

Figure 3 The effect of threshold T_1. (a) An input image, (b) the reference background image, (c) $T_1 = 0.1$, (d) $T_1 = 0.2$, (e) $T_1 = 0.3$, (f) $T_1 = 0.35$, (g) $T_1 = 0.4$, (h) $T_1 = 0.45$, (i) $T_1 = 0.50$, (j) $T_1 = 0.55$, (k) $T_1 = 0.60$, (l) $T_1 = 0.65$, (m) $T_1 = 0.70$, (n) $T_1 = 0.80$, and (o) $T_1 = 0.90$.

where σ represents the kernel function bandwidth and N is the number of training samples. A pixel was classified as a background pixel if the estimated probability was larger than the given threshold. It was observed that a large value of N produced more robust results. Consequently, a typical KDE method requires a large number of operations. On the other hand, we first eliminated most background pixels using the spatial similarity (SS) method and used only two features (one of the RGB components and one of the normalized RGB components). Also, we used a small number of samples (one hundred samples). Therefore, we were able to significantly reduce the computational complexity of the KDE without sacrificing performance. Figure 4 shows an example of the proposed method. We eliminated most background pixels using the SS method (Figure 4c). However, some background pixels were still retained and we eliminated these pixels using KDE. In this case, the candidate pixels made up 5% to 6% of the entire image. The processing time was also reduced accordingly.

Based on this observation, we propose a computationally efficient background subtraction method by eliminating background regions using spatial similarity in the spatial domain and the KDE method in the temporal domain. By combining spatial and temporal features, the proposed method produced better performance than the conventional KDE method. Figure 5 shows the comparison results. These sequences contain dynamic background regions. Tree branches were swaying and the curtain was moving in the wind. In dynamic background regions, it is difficult to accurately model the background in the conventional KDE method. Therefore, many background components are often classified as foreground components. However, since most of the background components in the proposed method were eliminated with spatial similarity, most of the background components misclassified as foreground components were correctly classified as background components.

The proposed method
Determine the background type
The reference background image (RBI) was computed as the average of the training intensity images:

$$\text{RBI}^I(i,j) = \frac{1}{N}\sum_{t=0}^{N-1} A_t^I(i,j) \tag{6}$$

where $A_t^I(i,j)$ represents a pixel of the t-th intensity image of a video sequence and N is the number of training images, which was set to 100. In other words, the first 100 images of a given video sequence generally were used as training images. We also computed the averages of the RGB channels of the training images:

$$\text{RBI}^\Omega(i,j) = \frac{1}{N}\sum_{t=0}^{N-1} A_t^\Omega(i,j) \text{ where } \Omega \in \{R, G, B\} \tag{7}$$

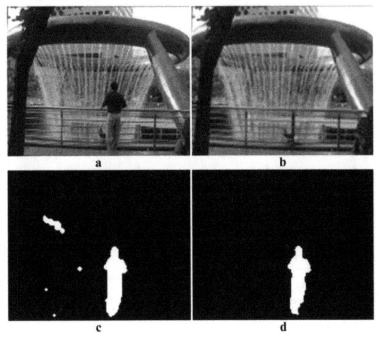

Figure 4 An example of the proposed method. (a) An input image, (b) the reference background image, (c) the similarity image, and (d) the final result.

Figure 5 The results of the proposed method and the single KDE method. First column: input image; second column: results of single KDE method; and third column: the proposed method.

Then, a similarity image between the reference background and training intensity images was computed using Equation 2 and the reference binary background image (RBBI) was computed:

For each pixel (i,j)

$$r(i,j) = \frac{1}{N}\sum_{t=0}^{N-1} \text{SI}_{\text{RBI}^I, A_t^I}(i,j)$$

$$\text{RBBI}(i,j) = \begin{cases} 0 \quad \text{(static background)} & \text{if } (r(i,j) > 0.8) \\ 1 \quad \text{(moving background)} & \text{otherwise} \end{cases}$$

$$(8)$$

The RBBI successfully detected moving background components such as moving escalators, waving tree branches, and water fountains.

Determine the foreground candidate pixels

When a new image was entered, a BBI was computed between the RBI and the input intensity image using Equations 3 to 4. If $\text{BBI}(i, j) = 1$, the pixel could have been either a foreground pixel or a moving background pixel. If $\text{RBBI}(i, j) = 1$ (moving background), we computed the difference between the intensity input image and the RBI^I. If the difference between the input

intensity image and the RBI^I was small, the pixel could have been a background pixel. Also, the pixel was classified as a foreground candidate when the difference was larger than the given threshold, and the pixel was classified as a foreground candidate if $\text{BBI}(i, j) = 1$ and $\text{RBBI}(i, j) = 0$. The following procedure was used to classify a pixel:

For each pixel (i, j)

$\quad$ If $\left(\text{BBI}_{\text{RBI}^I, I_k^I}(i,j) = 1\right)$, then

$\quad\quad$ If $(\text{RBBI}(i,j) = 1)$, then

$$\text{FCI}_k(i,j) = \begin{cases} if \left(\left|\text{RBI}^I(i,j) - I_k^I(i,j)\right| > T_2\right) \\ 1 \quad \text{(foreground candidate)} \\ \text{otherwise} \\ 0 \quad \text{(background)} \end{cases}$$

$\quad$ Otherwise
$$\text{FCI}_k(i,j) = 1 \quad \text{(foreground candidate)}$$

$$(9)$$

where $\text{FCI}_k(i, j)$ represents a candidate image, $I_k^I(i,j)$ represents the k-th input intensity image (see Equation 3), and T_2 was empirically set to 30. If T_2 was too large, most pixels were classified as background pixels. In other words, many foreground pixels were misclassified as background pixels when T_2 was too large. Figure 6 shows the results for various values of T_2. Figure 6a,b shows an input image and the BBI. Figure 6c,d,e,f shows the FCI for various values of T_2. Most foreground pixels were eliminated when T_2 was set to 80 (Figure 6f), while most moving background pixels were retained when T_2 was set to 10 (Figure 6c). In order to choose an optimal threshold value, we tested the proposed method with various values of T_2 using some video sequences with dynamic background regions and chose the threshold value ($T_2 = 30$). At this point, most background regions were removed.

Subtract the background pixels using KDE

We classified only the foreground candidate pixels (i.e., $FCI_k(i, j) = 1$) using KDE. Since there were high correlations among the R, G, and B components, and using all three channels produced only slight improvements, we used only the color with the largest difference. To improve performance, we also used one of the normalized RGB components that were robust against illumination changes and that represented the chrominance information well. We selected one of the RGB component channels as follows:

$$
\begin{aligned}
&\text{For each pixel } (i,j) \text{ of the } k\text{-th frame} \\
&\quad \text{If } (FCI_k(i,j) = 1) \\
&\quad\quad d_{max} = \max(\text{Diff}_R, \text{Diff}_G, \text{Diff}_B)
\end{aligned}
\tag{10}
$$

where

$$
\begin{aligned}
\text{Diff}_R &= \left| \text{RBI}^R(i,j) - I_k^R(i,j) \right| \\
\text{Diff}_G &= \left| \text{RBI}^G(i,j) - I_k^G(i,j) \right| \\
\text{Diff}_B &= \left| \text{RBI}^B(i,j) - I_k^B(i,j) \right|
\end{aligned}
$$

where d_{max} represents the maximum difference. Let Ω_{max} be the channel with the maximum difference.

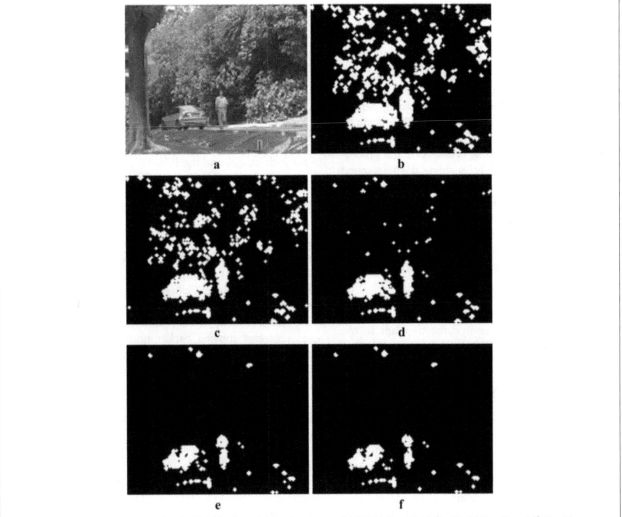

Figure 6 The results with various threshold (T_2) values. (a) An input image, **(b)** BBI, **(c)** $T_2 = 10$, **(d)** $T_2 = 30$, **(e)** $T_2 = 60$, and **(f)** $T_2 = 80$.

A foreground candidate pixel was classified as a background pixel when the estimated probability density function of the pixel value was larger than the given threshold as follows:

$$\text{if } \frac{1}{N}\sum_{m=0}^{N-1}\frac{1}{\sqrt{2\pi\sigma}}e^{-\frac{1}{2\sigma}\left(I_k^{\Omega_{max}}(i,j)-A_m^{\Omega_{max}}(i,j)\right)^2} > T_3,$$

    decide the pixel as background
  otherwise,
    decide the pixel as foreground

$$(11)$$

where σ represents the kernel width. Since the probability density function of the background pixel was unknown, we assumed that the probability densities for all intensity values were identical. Therefore, we set T_3 to 1/256. We used the standard deviation of the training images as the kernel width. This procedure was repeated using the normalized RGB color components, which were computed as follows:

$$I_{normalized}^{\Omega}(i,j) = \frac{255 \cdot I^{\Omega}(i,j)}{I^R(i,j) + I^G(i,j) + I^B(i,j)} \quad \text{with } \Omega \in \{R, G, B\}$$

$$(12)$$

where $I(i, j)$ represents the input image. If either the estimated probability density function of the pixel using the original RGB channels or the estimated probability density function of the pixel value of the normalized RGB channels was classified as a foreground component, the pixel was determined to be a foreground component. After this procedure, there were several small holes inside the foreground regions and some noise elements in the background regions. Most pixel-based methods suffer from this kind of problem. In order to address this, we applied a morphological operation to remove the small holes and noise elements. In particular, we used erosion followed by dilation and then a region filling technique was applied to the results [37].

Updating

After the decision procedure, the RBI and the pixels of the training images had to be updated to adapt to the changing background areas. We used a simple IIR filter to update the RBI as follows [38]:

  If pixel(i,j) is classified as background,
    $\text{RBI}^{\Omega}(i,j) = (1-\alpha)\text{RBI}^{\Omega}(i,j) + \alpha I_k^{\Omega}(i,j)$
    where $\Omega \in \{R, G, B\}$

$$(13)$$

where α represents the learning rate and was set to 0.01. The training images were updated by replacing the oldest pixel with the new background pixel. There is a trade-off in the choice of α. If a value for α was large, the RBI quickly reflected background changes. Figures 7

and 8 show the RBI changes for various learning rate values. As can be seen in Figure 7, the RBI was affected by shadows when we used a large value for α. Figure 7a, b shows the 372nd input and the initial RBI images. Figure 7c shows the RBI image when α was 0.6. Because of a large value for α, the RBI was quickly affected by the shadows. If we used a small value for α, the RBI did not quickly reflect background changes.

In some test sequences, the background gradually became brighter over a period (Figure 8). The RBI did not reflect this gradual background change with a small value of α (Figure 8c). Thus, we set $\alpha = 0.01$, and the learning rate was able to handle background changes adequately (Figure 8d).

If sudden background changes occurred, the results may have been erroneous. In order to handle such sudden background changes, we calculated the image intensity difference between the input image and the RBI and determined that sudden background changes occurred if the difference was larger than the given threshold:

$$\text{if } \left(\frac{1}{N_x \cdot N_y}\sum_{i=0,j=0}^{i=N_x-1,j=N_y-1}\left|I_k^I(i,j)-\text{RBI}^I(i,j)\right| > 30\right),$$

    a sudden background change occurs
    at the k-th sequence.

$$(14)$$

When a sudden background change was detected at the k-th image, we calculated the image differences between the previous 100 images (from the $(k$-99$)$-th image to the k-th image) and the RBI. We selected the previous images that had larger frame differences than the threshold. The selected images were temporarily used as the training images. If the number of selected images was smaller than 15, all the pixels of the k-th image were classified as background components. However, the RBI was not updated when sudden changes were detected.

Figure 9 shows an example of the proposed background subtraction procedure. Figure 9a is an input image, and Figure 9b shows the reference background image. Figure 9c is the reference binary background image where the white areas represent moving backgrounds (the waving trees). Figure 9d shows the binary background image between Figure 9a and b. Figure 9e shows the foreground candidate image. Figure 9f shows the result obtained using the original RGB components, and Figure 9g shows the final result using the normalized RGB components and the morphological operation.

Experimental results

Experiments were performed using two datasets (Li's dataset and the Wallflower's dataset). Li's dataset contained several dynamic background video sequences (water surface (WS), campus (CAM), fountain (FT), and meeting

Figure 7 The RBI images at different values of the learning rate 1. (a) Initial RBI', **(b)** 372th input image, **(c)** RBI' with the $\alpha = 0.6$, **(d)** RBI' with the $\alpha = 0.3$, **(e)** RBI' with the $\alpha = 0.05$, and **(f)** RBI' with the $\alpha = 0.01$.

room (MR)) and static background video sequences (shopping center (SC), subway station (SS), airport (AP), lobby (LB), bootstrap (B)). The Wallflower's dataset contained various background types (bootstrap (B), camouflage (C), foreground aperture (FA), light switch (LS), moved object (MO), time of day (TD), and waving tree (WT)).

First, we measured the processing time of the proposed method. The proposed method took about 0.015 s per 10,000 pixels, while the processing time of a conventional method [38] was about 1.475 s per 10,000 pixels (using a 2.8-GHz Pentium IV with 1 GB of RAM) when the number of sample images was 100. For instance, the proposed method processed 66.7 frames of video per second when working with 160×128 video sequences. The complexity of KDE is $O_{\text{KDE}}(MN)$ evaluations (the kernel function, multiplications and additions), assuming N image pixels and M sample points (N pixels per image and M training images). In the proposed method, we applied 'spatial similarity' to eliminate potential background pixels using a window processing operation (size of window = w). The computational complexity for calculating spatial similarity is $O_{\text{similarity}}(w^2 N)$ operations (multiplications and additions). Then, the remaining pixels (the number of remaining pixels: $K = \tau N$) are further processed using KDE ($O_{\text{KDE}}(KM)$). Therefore, the computational complexity of the proposed method is calculated as follows:

$$\begin{aligned} \text{Number of operation} &= O_{\text{similarity}}(w^2 N) + O_{\text{KDE}}(KM) \\ &= O_{\text{similarity}}(w^2 N) + O_{\text{KDE}}(\tau NM) \end{aligned}$$

(15)

In the proposed method, the window size is 3 ($w = 3$), and the average remaining pixels were about 5% ~ 6% of the entire image pixels ($\tau \cong 0.05$). In other words, the KDE operation was reduced by approximately 95%. Although we needed to compute additional spatial similarity, it had a minor effect on the overall complexity. With 100 training images, the computational complexity for KDE and

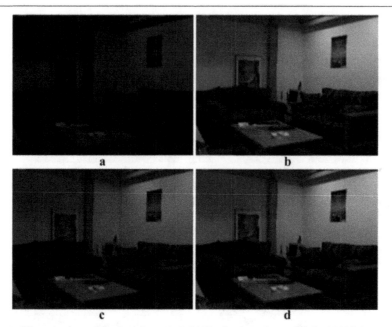

Figure 8 The RBI images at different values of the learning rate 2. (a) The first input image, **(b)** the 1,386th input image, **(c)** the 1,386th RBI^I with the $a = 0.001$, and **(d)** the 1,386th RBI^I with the $a = 0.01$.

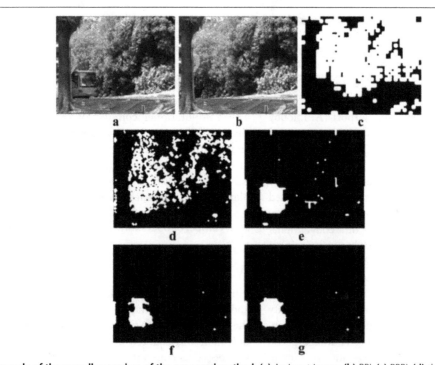

Figure 9 An example of the overall procedure of the proposed method. (a) An input image, **(b)** RBI, **(c)** RBBI, **(d)** the BBI between **(a)** and **(b)**, **(e)** the foreground candidate image, **(f)** the result obtained using the original RGB components, and **(g)** the final result.

the proposed method was $O(100\,N)$ and $O((9 + 0.05 \times 100)$ $N) = O(14\,N)$, respectively. In this case, the complexity of the proposed method was about 14% of KDE.

Next, the proposed method was compared with some existing algorithms [31,38-40]. The Jaccard similarity was used as a performance measure [41]:

$$JS = \frac{TP}{TP + FP + FN} \qquad (16)$$

where TP represents the number of true positive pixels, FP represents the number of false positive pixels, and FN represents the number of false negative pixels. Generally, a higher Jaccard similarity index indicates better performance.

Results using Li's dataset

Table 1 shows a performance comparison with Li's dataset based on Jaccard similarity.

Figure 10 shows the background subtraction results of the proposed method and Li's method using Li's dataset. The first column shows a test image, the second column shows the ground truth data of the test image, the third column shows the results of Li's method, and the fourth column shows the results of the proposed method. Using spatial similarity, the proposed method was robust against shadows. Noticeable improvements were observed in the SC, LB, B, and AP sequences which contained significant shadows. For these sequences, the proposed method showed about $8.4\% \sim 14.9\%$, $7.8\% \sim 20.6\%$, and $2.91\% \sim 12.7\%$ improvement compared to SOBS, Li's method, and Park's method, respectively, in terms of the Jaccard similarity. Since the proposed method used covariance, the variances of two local regions, and the normalized RGB color components, it was able to detect some objects that were similar to the background intensity. Therefore, in the WS and the FT sequences that contained objects whose intensity values were similar to the background regions, the

proposed method showed improved performance compared to the other methods. For instance, a main difficulty of the WS sequence was detecting a person's leg when the intensity value of the leg was similar to the background intensity value. The other methods missed parts of the leg while the proposed method accurately detected the leg. For this WS sequence, the proposed method showed about 10.4%, 7.8%, and 2.91% improvements compared to SOBS, Li's method, and Park's method. A main difficulty of the FT sequence was that a person's pants color was similar to the background region when the person stood against the fountain. For the FT sequence, the Jaccard similarity of the proposed method was 0.820, and the proposed method showed about 16.5%, 14.6%, and 10.3% improvements compared to SOBS, Li's method, and Park's method, respectively. However, some sequences (e.g., CAM, SS, and MR) contained complex dynamic background sequences. For instance, in the CAM sequence, the background included tree branches that were constantly swayed by a strong wind. The SS sequence contained moving escalators and the MR sequence contained moving curtains). In these kinds of dynamic background sequences, Park's method (in CAM, SS, and MR) and Li's method (in MR) performed slightly better than the proposed method.

Results using Wallflower's dataset

Table 2 shows a performance comparison with Wallflower's dataset based on FP + FN. Figure 11 shows the results of the proposed method and Wallflower method using the Wallflower's dataset. The first column shows a test image, the second column shows the ground truth data of the test image, the third column shows the results of Wallflower method, and the fourth column shows the results of the proposed method. The proposed method showed noticeable improvements for the C and B sequences. In the B sequence, the proposed method successfully detected objects that were similar to the background areas. On the other hand, since some moving trees of the WT sequence were classified as foreground components, the proposed method was not as good as Park's method. The LS sequence contained a sudden background change and the proposed method showed better performance. In the MO sequence, the proposed method classified the relocated objects (the chair and the phone) as foreground components. To handle this kind of problem, higher level processing such as that used in the Wallflower method might be required. The proposed method missed an object whose color was similar to that of the background area in the TD sequence.

The effects of thresholds

Next, we investigated the effects of thresholds (T_1 and T_2 in Equations 8 to 9). Figure 12 shows the Jaccard similarity of the proposed method as the T_1 and T_2 values increased with Li's dataset and wallflower's dataset. In order to

Table 1 Performance comparison with Jaccard similarity (Li's dataset)

Jaccard similarity	Proposed method	SOBS [31]	Li [39]	Park [38]
WS	0.929	0.825	0.851	0.8999
FT	0.820	0.655	0.674	0.7917
SC	0.752	0.668	0.645	0.6485
CAM	0.791	0.696	0.683	0.7935
LB	0.798	0.649	0.706	0.6706
SS	0.645	0.577	0.534	0.6826
B	0.723	0.602	0.564	0.6483
AP	0.714	0.594	0.508	0.6774
MR	0.852	0.817	0.911	0.8994
Average	0.780	0.676	0.675	0.746

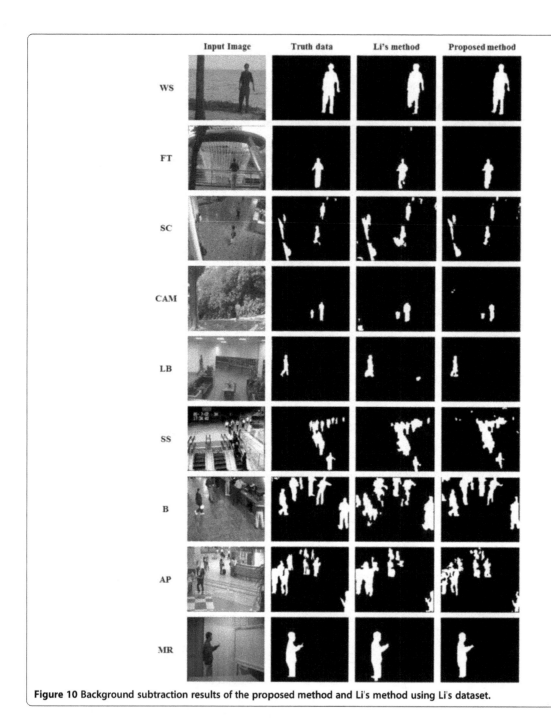

Figure 10 Background subtraction results of the proposed method and Li's method using Li's dataset.

analyze the effect of T_1, we computed the false positive ratio (FPR) and false negative ratio (FNR) metrics as follows:

$$
\begin{aligned}
\text{FPR} &= \frac{\text{FP}}{\text{TP} + \text{FP} + \text{FN}} \\
\text{FNR} &= \frac{\text{FN}}{\text{TP} + \text{FP} + \text{FN}}
\end{aligned}
\tag{17}
$$

When we used a large value for T_1, most foreground pixels were correctly classified as foreground pixels. However, many background pixels also were classified as foreground pixels. Therefore, FPR increased and FNR decreased. When we used a small value for T_1, most background pixels were classified as background pixels. However, many foreground pixels were classified as background pixels. Therefore, FPR decreased and FNR increased when we used a small value for T_1. Figure 13 shows the Jaccard similarity, and the FPR and FNR metrics with various values for T_1 (T_2 was fixed and set at 30).

We selected the optimal value for T_1 and T_2. When we set T_1 and T_2 to 0.55 and 30 respectively, the foreground candidate pixels were about 5% of the entire

Table 2 Performance comparison with the number of false positive and false negative pixels (Wallflower's dataset)

FP + FN	Proposed method	Wallflower [40]	Park [38]
C	325	2,395	1,492
WT	487	2,876	249
LS	1,140	1,322	2,260
MO	1,263	0	1,423
TD	685	986	306
FA	2,105	969	2,743
B	883	2,390	1,643
Sum	6,888	11,478	10,116

number of pixels, and the Jaccard similarity of the proposed method was about 0.78 with Li's dataset and the FP and FN numbers were about 6,888 with Wallflower's dataset. Experiments with various values of T_1 and T_2 show that the proposed method produced stable performance when the value of T_1 was from 0.5 to 0.65 and the value of T_2 was from 25 to 35.

Conclusions

In this paper, we proposed a background subtraction method that utilized structural similarity, which was robust against various background areas. The proposed method also significantly reduced the level of computational complexity since most pixels were eliminated using the similarity image. We tested the proposed method with two datasets and then compared the proposed method with some existing methods. The experimental results demonstrated that the proposed method

Figure 11 Background subtraction results of the proposed method and the Wallflower method using the Wallflower's dataset.

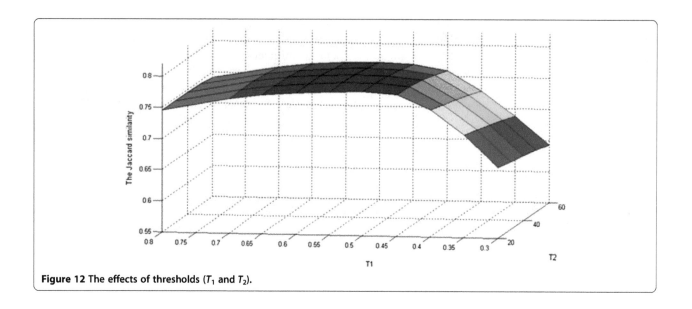

Figure 12 The effects of thresholds (T_1 and T_2).

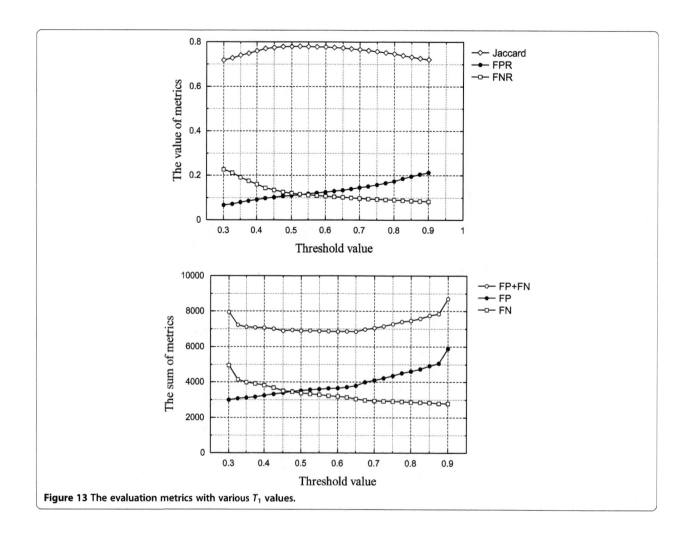

Figure 13 The evaluation metrics with various T_1 values.

was effective for various background scenes and compared favorably with some existing algorithms.

Competing interests
The authors declare that they have no competing interests.

Authors' information
Sangwook Lee received the BS and MS degrees in electrical and electronic engineering from Yonsei University, Seoul, Repiblic of Korea in 2004 and 2006, respectively. He is currently working toward the PhD degree from Yonsei University and a senior engineer at Samsung Electronics Co. Ltd., Republic of Korea. His research interests include machine vision, image/signal processing, and video quality measurement.

Chulhee Lee received the BS and MS degrees in electronic engineering from Seoul National University in 1984 and 1986, respectively, and a PhD degree in electrical engineering from Purdue University, West Lafayette, Indiana, in 1992. In 1996, he joined the faculty of the Department of Electrical and Computer Engineering, Yonsei University, Seoul, Republic of Korea. His research interests include image/signal processing, pattern cognition, and neural networks.

Acknowledgements
This work was supported by grant no. R01-2006-000-11223-0 from the Basic Research Program of the Korea Science & Engineering Foundation.

References
1. NJB McFarlane, CP Schofield, Segmentation and tracking of piglets in images. Mach. Vision App. **8**(1), 187–193 (1995)
2. MH Hung, CH Hsieh, Speed up temporal median filter for background subtraction, in *Proceedings of the PCSPA, vol. 1* (Harbin, 2004), pp. 297–300
3. F Cheng, S Huang, S Ruan, Advanced motion detection for intelligent video surveillance systems, in *Proceedings of the ACM SAC, vol. 1* (984, Sierra, 2010), pp. 983–984
4. S Cohen, Background estimation as a labeling problem, in *Proceedings of ICCV, vol. 2* (Beijing, 2005), pp. 1034–1041
5. C Wren, A Azarbayejani, T Darrell, A Pentland, Pfinder: Real-time tracking of the human body. IEEE Trans. Pattern Anal. Mach. **19**(7), 780–785 (1997)
6. M Zhao, J Bu, C Chen, Robust background subtraction in HSV color space, in *Proceedings of SPIE MSAV, vol. 1* (Boston, 2002), pp. 325–332
7. X Pan, Y Wu, GSM-MRF based classification approach for real-time moving object detection. J. Zhejiang Univ. Sci. A **9**(2), 250–255 (2008)
8. C Rambabu, W Woo, Robust and accurate segmentation of moving objects in real-time video, in *Proceedings of International Symposium on Ubiquitous VR, vol. 191* (Yanji City, 2006), pp. 65–69
9. C Stauffer, E Grimson, Adaptive background mixture models for real-time tracking, in *Proceedings of IEEE Conf. Computer Vision Patt. Recog, vol. 2* (Fort Collins, 1999), pp. 246–252
10. W Zhang, X Fang, X Yang, Q Wu, Spatiotemporal Gaussian mixture model to detect moving objects in dynamic scenes. J. Electron. Imaging **16**(2), 023013-1–023013-6 (2007)
11. T Su, J Hu, Background removal in vision servo system using Gaussian mixture model framework, in *Proceedings of ICNSC, vol. 1* (Singapore, 2004), pp. 70–75
12. A Doulamis, Dynamic background modeling for a safe road design, in *Proceedings of PETRA, vol. 1* (Samos, 2010), pp. 1–9
13. MH Khan, I Kypraios, U Khan, A robust background subtraction algorithm for motion based video scene segmentation in embedded platforms, in *Proceedings of FIT, vol. 1* (Abbottabad, 2009), pp. 1–8
14. H Wang, P Miller, Regularized online mixture of Gaussians for background with shadow removal, in *Proceedings of AVSS, vol. 1* (Klagenfurt, 2011), pp. 249–254
15. SC Wang, TF Su, SH Lai, Detection of moving objects from dynamic background with shadow remova, in *Proceedings of ICASSP, vol. 1* (Prague, 2011), p. 925
16. L Zhao, X He, daptive Gaussian mixture learning for moving object detection, in *Proceedings of IC-BNMT, vol. 1* (Beijing, 2010), pp. 1176–1180
17. Z Bin, Y Liu, Robust moving object detection and shadow removing based on improved Gaussian model and gradient information, in *Proceedings of ICMT2010, vol. 1* (Ningbo, 2010), pp. 1–5
18. HH Lim, JH Chuang, TL Liu, Regularized background adaptation: a novel learning rate control scheme for Gaussian mixture modeling. IEEE Trans. Image Process. **20**(3), 822–836 (2011)
19. H Zhou, X Zhang, Y Gao, P Yu, Video background subtraction using improved adaptive-K Gaussian mixture model, in *Proceedings of ICACTE, vol. 5* (Chengdu, 2010), pp. 363–366
20. J Suhr, H Jung, G Li, J Kim, Mixture of Gaussians-based background subtraction for Bayer-pattern image sequences. IEEE Trans. Circuits Syst. Video Technol. **21**(3), 365–370 (2011)
21. A Elgammal, D Harwood, L Davis, Non-parametric model for background subtraction, in *Proceedings of ECCV, vol. 1* (Dublin, 2000), pp. 751–767
22. T Tanaka, A Shimada, D Arita, R Taniguchi, A fast algorithm for adaptive background model construction using Parzen density estimation, in *Proceedings of IEEE Conf. AVSS, vol. 1* (London, 2007), pp. 528–553
23. A Tavakkoli, M Nicolescu, G Bebis, Automatic robust background modeling using multivariate non-parametric kernel density estimation for visual surveillance, in *Proceedings of the International Symposium of Advances in Visual Computing LNCS, vol. 1* (Nevada, 2005), pp. 363–370
24. N Martel-Brisson, A Zaccarin, Unsupervised approach for building non-parametric background and foreground models of scenes with significant fore-ground activity, in *Proceedings of VNBA, vol. 1* (Vancouver, 2008), pp. 93–100
25. B Han, DCY Zhu, L Davis, Sequential kernel density approximation through mode propagation: applications to background modeling, in *Proceedings of ACCV, vol. 1* (Jeju, 2004), pp. 1–6
26. G Gordon, T Darrell, M Harville, J Woodfill, Background estimation and removal based on range and color, in *Proceedings of CVPR, vol. 1* (Fort Collins, 1999), pp. 2459–2464
27. A Monnet, A Mittal, N Paragios, V Ramesh, Background modeling and subtraction of dynamic scenes, in *Proceedings of ICCV, vol. 2* (Beijing, 2003), pp. 1–8
28. H Kim, R Sakamoto, I Kitahara, T Toriyama, K Kogure, Robust foreground extraction technique using Gaussian family model and multiple thresholds, in *Proceedings of ACCV, vol. 1* (Tokyo, 2007), pp. 758–768
29. Q Zhu, G Liu, Z Wang, H Chen, Y Xie, A novel video object segmentation based on recursive kernel density estimation, in *Proceedings of ICINFA, vol. 1* (Shenzhen, 2011), pp. 843–846
30. A Kolawole, A Tavakkoli, Robust foreground detection in videos using adaptive color histogram thresholding and shadow removal, in *Proceedings of ISVC, vol. 2* (Las Vegas, 2011), pp. 496–505
31. L Maddalena, A Petrosino, A self-organizing approach to background subtraction for visual surveillance applications. IEEE Trans. Image Process. **13**(4), 1168–1177 (2008)
32. L Maddalena, A Petrosino, Self organizing and fuzzy modelling for parked vehicles detection, in *Proceeding of ACVIS, vol. 1* (Bordeaux, 2009), pp. 422–433
33. H Lin, T Liu, J Chuang, A probabilistic SVM approach for background scene initialization, in *Proceedings of ICIP, vol. 3* (Rochester, 2002), pp. 893–896
34. L Cheng, M Gong, D Schuurmans, T Caelli, Real-time discriminative background subtraction. IEEE Trans. Image Process. **20**(5), 1401–1414 (2011)
35. I Junejo, A Bhutta, H Foroosh, Dynamic scene modeling for object detection using single-class SVM, in *Proceeding of International Conference on Image Processing, vol. 1* (Hong Kong, 2010), pp. 1541–1544
36. Z Wang, AC Bovik, HR Sheikh, EP Simoncelli, Image quality assessment: from error visibility to structural similarity. IEEE Trans. Image Process. **13**(4), 1–14 (2004)
37. R Gonzalez, R Woods, *Digital Image Processing*, 2nd edn. (Prentice Hall, Englewood Cliffs, 2002)
38. JG Park, C Lee, Bayesian rule-based complex background modeling and foreground detection. Opt. Eng. **49**(2), 027006-1–027006-11 (2010)
39. L Li, W Huang, IYH Gu, Q Tian, Statistical modeling of complex backgrounds for foreground object detection. IEEE Trans. Image Process. **13**(1), 1459–1472 (2004)
40. K Toyama, L Krumm, B Brumitt, B Meyers, Wallflower: principles and practice of background maintenance, in *Proceedings of IEEE ICCV, vol. 1* (Kerkyra, 1999), pp. 255–261
41. P Jaccard, The distribution of flora in the alpine zone. New Phytol. **11**(2), 37–50 (1912)

14

Thermal spatio-temporal data for stress recognition

Nandita Sharma[1][*], Abhinav Dhall[1], Tom Gedeon[1] and Roland Goecke[1,2]

Abstract

Stress is a serious concern facing our world today, motivating the development of a better objective understanding through the use of non-intrusive means for stress recognition by reducing restrictions to natural human behavior. As an initial step in computer vision-based stress detection, this paper proposes a temporal thermal spectrum (TS) and visible spectrum (VS) video database *ANUStressDB* - a major contribution to stress research. The database contains videos of 35 subjects watching *stressed* and *not-stressed* film clips validated by the subjects. We present the experiment and the process conducted to acquire videos of subjects' faces while they watched the films for the ANUStressDB. Further, a baseline model based on computing local binary patterns on three orthogonal planes (LBP-TOP) descriptor on VS and TS videos for stress detection is presented. A LBP-TOP-inspired descriptor was used to capture dynamic thermal patterns in histograms (HDTP) which exploited spatio-temporal characteristics in TS videos. Support vector machines were used for our stress detection model. A genetic algorithm was used to select salient facial block divisions for stress classification and to determine whether certain regions of the face of subjects showed better stress patterns. Results showed that a fusion of facial patterns from VS and TS videos produced statistically significantly better stress recognition rates than patterns from VS or TS videos used in isolation. Moreover, the genetic algorithm selection method led to statistically significantly better stress detection rates than classifiers that used all the facial block divisions. In addition, the best stress recognition rate was obtained from HDTP features fused with LBP-TOP features for TS and VS videos using a hybrid of a genetic algorithm and a support vector machine stress detection model. The model produced an accuracy of 86%.

Keywords: Stress classification; Temporal stress; Thermal imaging; Support vector machines; Genetic algorithms; Watching films

1 Introduction

Stress is a part of everyday life, and it has been widely accepted that stress, which leads to less favorable states (such as anxiety, fear, or anger), is a growing concern to a person's health and well-being, functioning, social interaction, and financial aspects. The term *stress* was coined by Hans Selye, which he defined as 'the non-specific response of the body to any demand for change' [1]. Stress is a natural alarm, resistance, and exhaustion system [2] for the body to prepare for a fight or flight response to either defend or make the body adjust to threats and changes. The body shows stress through symptoms such as frustration, anger, agitation, preoccupation, fear, anxiety, and tenseness

[3]. When chronic and left untreated, stress can lead to incurable illnesses (e.g., cardiovascular diseases [4], diabetes [5], and cancer [6]), relationship deterioration [7,8], and high economic costs, especially in developed countries [9,10]. It is important to recognize stress early to diminish the risks. Stress research is beneficial to our society with a range of benefits, motivating interest and posing technical challenges in computer science in general and affective computing in particular.

Various computational techniques have been used to objectively recognize stress using models based on techniques such as Bayesian networks [11], decision trees [12], support vector machines [13], and artificial neural networks [14]. These techniques have used a range of physiological (e.g., heart activity [15,16], brain activity [17,18], galvanic skin response [19], and skin temperature [12,20]) and physical (e.g., eye gaze [11], facial information [21]) measures

* Correspondence: nandita.sharma@anu.edu.au
[1]Information and Human Centred Computing Research Group, Research School of Computer Science, Australian National University, Canberra, ACT 0200, Australia
Full list of author information is available at the end of the article

for stress as inputs. Physiological signal acquisition requires sensors to be in contact with a person, and this can be obtrusive [3]. In addition, the physiological sensors are usually required to be placed on specific locations of the body, and sensor calibration time is usually required as well, e.g., approximately 5 min is needed for the isotonic gel to settle before galvanic skin response readings can be taken satisfactorily using the BIOPAC System [22]. The trend in this area of research is leading towards obtaining symptom of stress measures through less or non-intrusive methods. This paper proposes a stress recognition method using facial imaging and does not require body contact with sensors unlike the usual physiological sensors.

A relatively new area of research is recognition of stress using facial data in the thermal (TS) and visible (VS) spectrums. Blood flow through superficial blood vessels, which are situated under the skin and above the bone and muscle layer of the human body, allows TS images to be captured. It has been reported in the literature that stress can be successfully detected from thermal imaging [23] due to changes in skin temperature under stress. In addition, facial expressions have been analyzed [24] and classified [25-27] using TS imaging. Commonly, VS imaging has been used for modeling facial expressions, and associated robust facial recognition techniques have been developed [28-30]. However, from our understanding, the literature has not developed computational models for stress recognition using both TS and VS imaging together as yet. This paper addresses the gap and presents a robust method to use information from temporal and texture characteristics of facial regions for stress recognition.

Automatic facial expression analysis is a long researched problem. Techniques have been developed for analyzing the temporal dynamics of facial muscle movements. A detailed survey of facial expression recognition methods can be found in [31]. Further, vision-based facial dynamics have been used for affective computing tasks such as pain monitoring [32] and depression analysis [30]. This motivated us to explore vision-based stress analysis where inspiration can be taken from the vast field of facial expression analysis. Descriptors such as the local binary pattern (LBP) have been developed for texture analysis and have been successfully applied to facial expression analysis [25,33,34], depression analysis [30], and face recognition [35]. A particular LBP extension for analysis of temporal data - local binary patterns on three orthogonal planes (LBP-TOP) - has gained attention and is suitable for the work in this study. LBP-TOP provides features that incorporate appearance and motion, and is robust to illumination variations and image transformations [25]. This paper presents an application of LBP-TOP to TS and VS videos.

Various facial dynamics databases have been proposed in the literature. For facial expression analysis, one of the most popular databases is the Cohn-Kanade + [32], which contains facial action coding system (FACS) and generic expression labels. Subjects were asked to pose and display various expressions. There are other databases in the literature which are spontaneous or close to spontaneous, such as RU-FACS [36], Belfast [37], VAM [38], and AFEW [39]. However, these are limited to emotion-related labels which do not serve the problem in the paper, i.e., stress classification. Lucey et al. [32] proposed the UNBC McMasters database comprising video clips where patients were asked to move the arm up and their reaction was recorded. For creating ANUStressDB, subjects were shown stressful and non-stressful video clips. This database is similar to that in [32].

There are various forms of *stressors*, i.e., demands or stimuli that cause stress [23,40-42] validated by self-reports (e.g., self-assessment [43,44]) and observer reports (e.g., human behavior coder [42]). Some examples of stressors are playing video (action) games [45,46], solving difficult mathematical/logical problems [47], and listening to energetic music [45]. Among these stressors are films, which were used to stimulate stress in this work. In this work, we develop a *computed stress measure* [3] using facial imaging in VS and TS. Our work analyzes dynamic facial expressions that are as natural as possible elicited by a typical stressful, tense, or fearful environment from film clips. Unlike the previous work in the literature that uses posed facial expressions for classification [48], the work presented in this paper provides an investigation of spontaneous facial expressions as responses or reactions to environments portrayed by the films.

This paper describes a method for collecting and computationally analyzing data for stress recognition from TS and VS videos. A stress database (ANUStressDB) of videos of faces is presented. An experiment was conducted to collect the data where experiment participants watched stressful and non-stressful film clips. ANUStressDB contains videos of 35 subjects watching film clips that created stressed and not-stressed environments validated by the person. Facial expressions in the videos were stimulated by the film clips. Spatio-temporal features were extracted from the TS and VS videos, and these features were provided as inputs to a support vector machine (SVM) classifier to recognize stress patterns. A hybrid of a genetic algorithm (GA) and SVM was used to select salient divisions of facial block regions and determine whether using the block regions improved the stress recognition rate. The paper compares the quality of the stress classifications produced from using LBP-TOP and HDTP (our thermal spatio-temporal descriptor) features from TS and VS data with and without using facial block selection.

The organization of the paper is as follows: Section 2 presents the experiment for TS, VS, and self-reported data collection. Section 3 describes the facial imaging processing steps for the TS and VS data. The new thermal spatio-temporal descriptor, HDTP, is proposed in Section 4. Stress classification models are described in Section 5. Section 6 presents the results, an analysis of the results, and suggestions for future work.

2 Data collection from the film experiment

After receiving approval from the Australian National University Human Research Ethics Committee, an experiment was conducted to collect TS and VS videos of faces of individuals while they watched films. Thirty-five graduate students consisting of 22 males and 13 females between the ages of 23 and 39 years old volunteered to be experiment participants. Each participant had to understand the experiment requirements from written experiment instructions with the guidance of an experiment instructor before they filled in the consent form. The participant was provided information about the experiment and its purpose from a script to ensure that there was consistency in the experiment information provided across all participants. After providing consent, the participant was seated in front of a LCD display (placed between two speakers). The distance between the screen and subject was in the range between 70 and 90 cm. The instructor started the films, which triggered a blank screen with a countdown of the numbers 3, 2, and 1 transitioning in and out slowly with one before the other. The reason for the countdown display and the blank screen was for participants to move away from their thoughts at the time and get ready to pay attention to the films that were about to start. This approach was like that used in experiments for similar work in [49]. Subsequent to the countdown display, a blank screen was shown for 15 s, which was followed by a sequence of film clips with 5-s blank screens in between. After watching the films, the participant was asked to do a survey, which related to the films they watched and provided validation for the film labels. The experiment took approximately 45 min for each participant. An outline of the process of the experiment for an experiment participant is shown in Figure 1.

Participants watched two types of films either labeled as *stressed* or *not-stressed*. Stressed films had stressful content (e.g., suspense with jumpy music), whereas not-stressed films created illusions of meditative environments (e.g., swans and ducks paddling in a lake) and had content that was not stressful or at least was relatively less stressful compared with films labeled as stressed. There were six film clips for each type of film. The survey done by experiment participants validated the film labels. The survey asked participants to rate the films they watched in terms of levels of stress portrayed by the film and the degree of tension and relaxation they felt. Participants found the films that were labeled *stressed* as stressful and films labeled *not-stressed* as not stressful with a statistical significance of $p < 0.001$ according to the Wilcoxon test.

While the participants watched the film clips, TS and VS videos of their faces were recorded. A schematic diagram of the experiment setup is shown in Figure 2. TS videos were captured using a FLIR infrared camera (model number SC620, FLIR Systems, Inc. Notting Hill, Australia), and VS videos were recorded using a Microsoft webcam (Microsoft Corporation, Redmond, WA, USA). Both the videos were recorded with a sampling rate of 30 Hz, and the frame width and height were 640 and 480 pixels, respectively. Each participant had a TS and VS video for each film they watched. As a consequence, a participant had 12 video clips made up of six stressed videos and six not-stressed videos. We name the database that has the collected labeled video data and its protocols as the *ANU Stress database* (*ANUStressDB*).

Note the usage of the terms *film* and *video* in this paper. We use the term *film* to refer to a video portraying entertaining content, colloquially called a 'film' or 'movie', which a participant watched during the experiment. We use the term *video* to refer to a visual recording of a participant's face and its movement during the time period while they watched a film. Thus in this paper, a film is something which is watched, while a video is something recorded about the watcher.

3 Face pre-processing pipeline

Facial regions in VS videos were detected using the Viola-Jones face detector. However, facial regions could not be recognized satisfactorily using the Viola-Jones algorithm in thermal spectrum (TS) videos, so a face detection method based on eye coordinates [50,51] and a template matching algorithm was used. A template of a facial region was developed from the first frame of a

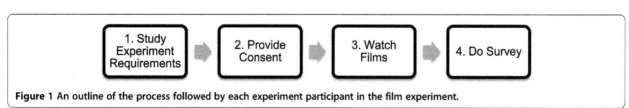

Figure 1 An outline of the process followed by each experiment participant in the film experiment.

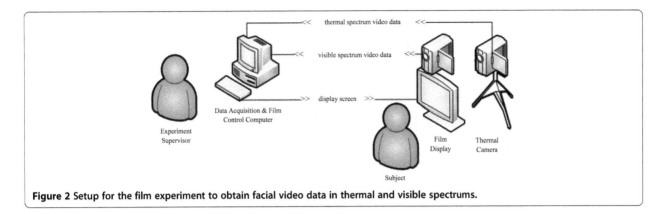

Figure 2 Setup for the film experiment to obtain facial video data in thermal and visible spectrums.

TS video. The facial region was extracted using the Pretty Helpful Development Functions toolbox for Face Recognition [50-52], which calculated the intraocular displacement to detect a facial region in an image. This facial region formed a template for facial regions in each video frame of the TS videos, which were extracted using MATLAB's Template Matcher system [53]. The Template Matcher was set to search the minimum difference pixel by pixel to find the area of the frame that best matched the template. Examples of facial regions that were detected in the VS and TS videos for a participant are presented in Figure 3.

Facial regions were extracted from each frame of a VS video and its corresponding TS video. Grouped and arranged in order of time of appearance in a video, the facial regions formed *volumes* of the facial region frames. Examples of facial blocks in TS and VS are shown in Figure 4.

4 Spatio-temporal features

There are claims in the literature that features from segmented image blocks of a facial image region can provide more information than features directly extracted from an image of a full facial region in VS [25]. Examples of full facial regions are shown in Figure 4, and blocks of a full facial region are presented in Figure 5. To illustrate the claim, features from each of the blocks used in conjunction with features from the other blocks in Figure 5 (i) can offer more information than features obtained from Figure 4a (i). The claim aligns with the results from classifying stress based on facial thermal characteristics [23]. As a consequence, the facial regions in this work were segmented into a grid of 3 × 3 blocks for each video segment, or facial volume, forming 3 × 3 blocks. A *block* has X, Y, and T components where X, Y, and T represent the width, height, and time components of an image sequence, respectively. Each block represented a division of a full facial block region or facial volume. LBP-TOP features were calculated for each block.

LBP-TOP is the temporal variant of local binary patterns (LBP). In LBP-TOP, LBP is applied to three planes - XY, XT,

and YT - to describe the appearance of an image, horizontal motion, and vertical motion, respectively. For a center pixel O_p of an orthogonal plane O and its neighboring pixels N_i, a decimal value is assigned to it:

$$d = \sum_{O}^{XY,XT,YT} \sum_{p} \sum_{i=1}^{k} 2^{i-1} I\left(O_p, N_i\right) \qquad (1)$$

According to a study that investigated facial expression recognition using LBP-TOP features, VS and near-infrared images produced similar facial expression recognition

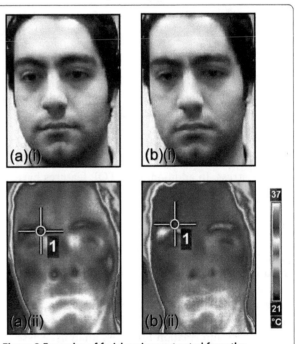

Figure 3 Examples of facial regions extracted from the ANUStressDB database. The facial regions are of an experiment participant watching the different types of film clips. **(a)** The participant was watching a not-stressed film clip. **(b)** The participant was watching a stressed film clip. **(i)** A frame in the visual spectrum. **(ii)** The corresponding frame in the thermal spectrum. The crosshairs in the thermal frame were added by the recording software and represents the camera auto-focus.

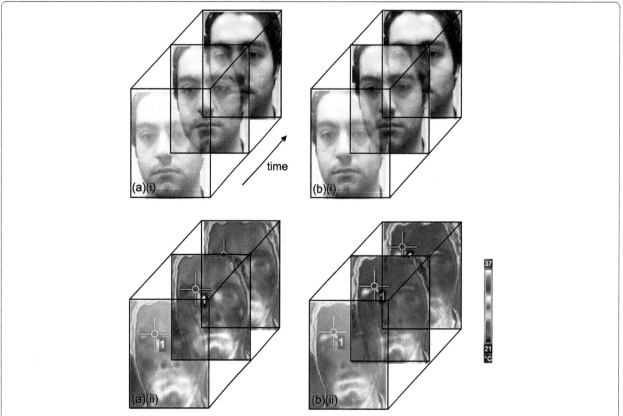

Figure 4 Examples of facial volumes extracted from the ANUStressDB database. The facial volumes are of an experiment participant watching the different types of film clips. **(a)** The participant was watching a not-stressed film clip. **(b)** The participant was watching a stressed film clip. (i) A facial volume in the visual spectrum. (ii) The corresponding facial volume in the thermal spectrum.

rates, provided that VS images had strong illumination [33]. Due to the fact that TS videos are defined by colors and different color variations, LBP-TOP features may not be able to fully exploit thermal information provided in TS videos and in particular capture thermal patterns for stress. In addition, LBP-TOP features have been mainly extracted from image sequences of people told to show some facial expression, which is not like the image sequences obtained from our film experiment. In our film experiment, participants watched films and involuntary facial expressions were captured. The recordings may have more subtle facial expressions of the kind of facial expressions analyzed in the literature using LBP-TOP. With the subtleness in facial movement, it is possible that LBP-TOP may not be able to offer as much information for stress analysis. These points motivate the development of a new set of features that exploits thermal patterns in TS videos for stress recognition. We propose a new type of feature for TS videos that captures dynamic thermal patterns in histograms (HDTP). This feature makes use of thermal data in each frame of a TS video of a face over the course of the video.

4.1 Histogram of dynamic thermal patterns

HDTP captures normalized dynamic thermal patterns, which enables individual-independent stress analysis. Some people may be more tolerant to some stressors than others [54,55]. This could mean that some people may show higher degree responses to stress than others. Additionally in general, the baseline for human response can vary from person to person. To consider these characteristics in features used for individual-independent stress analysis, ways have been developed to normalize data for each participant for their type of data [42]. HDTP is defined in terms of a participant's overall thermal state to minimize individual bias in stress analysis.

A HDTP feature is calculated for each facial block region. Firstly, a statistic (consider the standard deviation) is calculated for each facial region frame for a participant for a particular block (e.g., facial block region situated at the top right corner of the facial region in the XY plane) for all the videos. The statistic values from all these frames are partitioned to define empty *bins*. A bin has a continuous value range with a location defined from the statistic values. The bins are used to partition statistic values for each facial block region where the value for

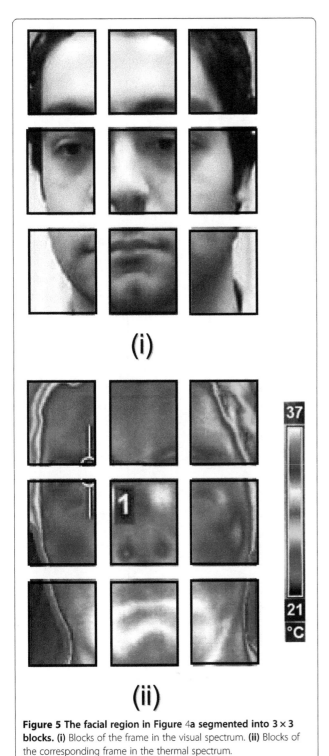

(i)

(ii)

37

1

21

°C

Figure 5 The facial region in Figure 4a segmented into 3 × 3 blocks. (i) Blocks of the frame in the visual spectrum. **(ii)** Blocks of the corresponding frame in the thermal spectrum.

in thermal videos for a participant who has a set of facial videos is provided in Figure 6.

As an illustration, consider that the statistic used is the standard deviation and the facial block region for which we want to develop a histogram is situated at the top right corner of the facial region in the XY plane (FBR$_1$) for video V_1 when a participant P_i was watching film F_1. In order to create a histogram, the bin locations and sizes need to be calculated. To do this, the standard deviation needs to be calculated for all frames in FBR$_1$ in all videos ($V_{1\text{-}12}$) for P_i. This will give standard deviation values from which the global minimum and maximum can be obtained and used to calculate the bin location and sizes. Then, the histogram for FBR$_1$, for V_1, and for P_i is calculated by filling the bins with the standard deviation values for each frame in FBR$_1$. This method then provides normalized features that also take into account the image and motion, and can be used as inputs to a classifier.

5 Stress classification system using a hybrid of a support vector machine and a genetic algorithm

SVMs have been widely used in the literature to model classification problems including facial expression recognition [27,33,34]. Provided a set of training samples, a SVM transforms the data samples using a nonlinear mapping to a higher dimension with the aim to determine a *hyperplane* that partitions data by class or labels. A hyperplane is chosen based on *support vectors*, which are training data samples that define maximum *margins* from the support vectors to the hyperplane to form the best decision boundary.

It has been reported in the literature that thermal patterns for certain regions of a face provide more information for stress than other regions [23]. The performance of the stress classifier can degrade if irrelevant features are provided as inputs. As a consequence and due to its benefits noted in literature, the classification system was extended to include a feature selection component, which used a GA to select facial block regions appropriate for the stress classification. GAs are inspired by biological evolution and the concept of survival of the fittest. A GA is a global search technique and has been shown to be useful for optimization problems and problems concerning optimal feature selection for classification [56].

The GA evolves a population of candidate solutions, represented by *chromosomes*, using *crossover*, *mutation*, and *selection* operations in search for a better quality population based on some fitness measure. Crossover and mutation operations are applied to chromosomes to achieve diversity in the population and reduce the risk of the search being stuck with a local optimal population. After each generation during the search, the GA selects chromosomes, probabilistically mostly made up of better quality chromosomes, for

each bin is the frequency of statistic values in the block that falls within the bounds of the bin range. Consequently, a histogram for each block can be formed from the frequencies. An algorithm presenting the approach for developing histograms of dynamic thermal patterns

Algorithm: HDTP. Find histograms that capture normalized dynamic thermal patterns in thermal videos for a participant

Inputs:

* p, a participant video data set that represents a set of all videos watched by the participant

* F, a function that calculates a statistic for a two dimensional matrix

Output:

* H, a set of histograms for p based on values obtained by F

Method:

for each video v(p)

    for each block location loc(p)

        for each facial block region b(v,loc)

            for each frame f(b)

            $s_{vbf} \leftarrow F(f(b))$

            end for

        end for

    end for

end for

for each block location loc(p)

    for each facial block region b(loc)

    bin_width(b) $\leftarrow$ calculate_bin_width(b)

    bin_locs(b) $\leftarrow$ calculate_bin_locations(bin_width(b))

    end for

end for

for each video v(p)

    for each block location loc(p)

        for each facial block region b(v,loc)

        h $\leftarrow$ partition_data(b, bin_locs(b))

        end for

    end for

end for

Figure 6 The HDTP algorithm captures dynamic thermal patterns in histograms from thermal image sequences.

the population in the next generation to direct the search to more favorable chromosomes.

Given a population of subsets of facial block regions with corresponding features, a GA was defined to evolve sets of blocks by applying crossover and mutation operations, and selecting block sets during each iteration of the search to determine sets of blocks that produce better quality SVM classifications. Each block set was represented by a binary fixed-length chromosome where an index or locus symbolized a facial block region; its value or allele depicted whether or not the block was used in the classification and the length of the chromosome matched the number of blocks for a video. The search space had 3×3 blocks (as shown in Figure 5) with

an addition of blocks that overlapped each other by 50%. The architecture for the GA-SVM classification system is shown in Figure 7. The characteristics of the GA implemented for facial block region selection is provided in Table 1.

In summary, various stress classification systems using a SVM were developed which differed in terms of the following input characteristics:

* $VS_{LBP-TOP}$: LBP-TOP features for VS videos
* $TS_{LBP-TOP}$: LBP-TOP features for TS videos
* TS_{HDTP}: HDTP features (as described in Section 4.1) for TS videos
* $VS_{LBP-TOP} + TS_{LBP-TOP}$: $VS_{LBP-TOP}$ and $TS_{LBP-TOP}$

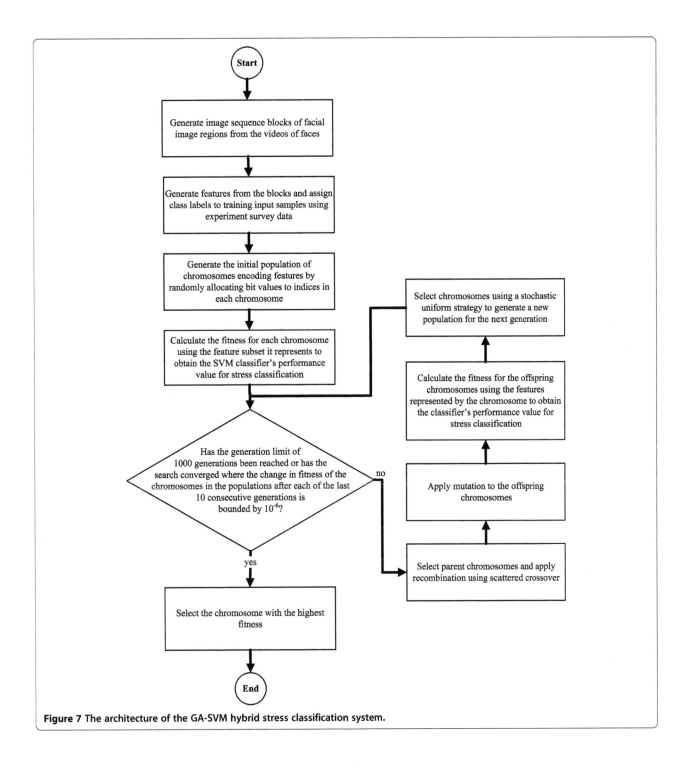

Figure 7 The architecture of the GA-SVM hybrid stress classification system.

- $VS_{LBP-TOP} + TS_{HDTP}$: $VS_{LBP-TOP}$ and TS_{HDTP}
- $TS_{LBP-TOP} + TS_{HDTP}$: $TS_{LBP-TOP}$ and TS_{HDTP}
- $VS_{LBP-TOP} + TS_{LBP-TOP} + TS_{HDTP}$

These inputs were also provided as inputs to the GA-SVM classification systems to determine whether the system produced better stress recognition rates.

6 Results and discussion

Each of the different features is derived from VS and TS facial videos using LBP-TOP and HDTP facial descriptors on standardized data and provided as inputs to a SVM for stress classification. Facial videos of participants watching stressed films were assigned to the stressed class, and videos associated with not-stressed films were assigned to the

Table 1 GA implementation settings for facial block region selection

GA parameter	Value/setting
Population size	100
Number of generations	2,000
Crossover rate	0.8
Mutation rate	0.01
Crossover type	Scattered crossover
Mutation type	Uniform mutation
Selection type	Stochastic uniform selection

not-stressed class. Furthermore, their corresponding features were assigned to corresponding classes. Recognition rates and F-scores for the classifications were obtained using 10-fold cross-validation for each type of input. The results are shown in Figure 8.

Results show that when HDTP features for TS videos (TS_{HDTP}) were provided as input to the SVM classifier, there were improvements in the stress recognition measures. The best recognition measures for the SVM were obtained when $VS_{LBP-TOP} + TS_{HDTP}$ was provided as input. It produced a recognition rate that was at least 0.10 greater than the recognition rate for inputs without TS_{HDTP} where the range for recognition rates was 0.13. This provides evidence that TS_{HDTP} had a significant contribution towards the better classification performance and suggests that TS_{HDTP} captured more patterns associated with stress than $VS_{LBP-TOP}$ and $TS_{LBP-TOP}$.

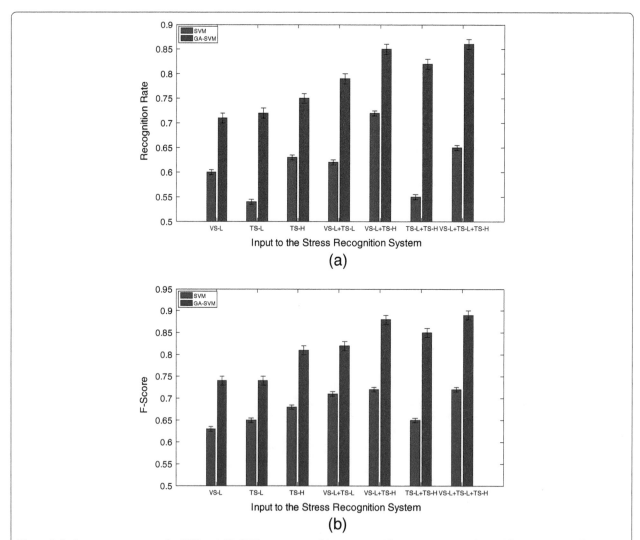

Figure 8 Performance measures for SVM and GA-SVM stress recognition systems. The measures were obtained for various input features based on 10-fold cross-validation. The labels on the horizontal axes are shortened to improve readability. L and H stand for LBP-TOP and HDTP, respectively. **(a)** Recognition rate measure for the stress recognition systems. **(b)** F-score measure for the stress recognition systems.

The performance for the classification was the lowest when $TS_{LBP-TOP}$ was provided as input.

The features were also provided as inputs to a GA which selected facial block regions with a goal to disregard irrelevant facial block regions for stress recognition and to improve the SVM-based recognition measures. Performances of the classifications using 10-fold cross-validation on the different inputs are provided in Figure 8. For all types of inputs, GA-SVM produced significantly better stress recognition measures. According to the Wilcoxon non-parametric statistical test, the statistical significance was $p < 0.01$. Similar to the trend observed for stress recognition measures produced by the SVM, TS_{HDTP} also contributed to the improved results in GA-SVM. The best recognition measures were obtained when $VS_{LBP-TOP} + TS_{LBP-TOP} + TS_{HDTP}$ was provided as input to the GA-SVM classifier. The performance of the classifier was highly similar when it received $VS_{LBP-TOP} + TS_{HDTP}$ as inputs with a difference of 0.01 in the recognition rate. Results show that when a combination of at least two of $VS_{LBP-TOP}$, $TS_{LBP-TOP}$, and TS_{HDTP} was provided as input, then it performed better than when only one of $VS_{LBP-TOP}$, $TS_{LBP-TOP}$, or TS_{HDTP} was used.

Further, stress recognition systems provided with TS_{HDTP} as input produced significantly better stress recognition measures than inputs with TS_{HDTP} replaced by $TS_{LBP-TOP}$ ($p < 0.01$). This suggests that stress patterns were better captured by TS_{HDTP} features than $TS_{LBP-TOP}$ features.

In addition, blocks selected by the GA in the GA-SVM classifier for the different inputs were recorded. When $VS_{LBP-TOP}$ was given as inputs to a GA, the blocks that produced better recognition results were the blocks that corresponded to the cheeks and mouth regions on the XY plane. For $VS_{LBP-TOP}$, fewer blocks were selected and they were situated around the nose. On the other hand for TS_{HDTP}, more blocks were used in the classification - nose, mouth, and cheek regions and regions on the forehead were selected by the GA. Future work could extend the investigation by more complex block definitions to find and use more precise regions showing symptoms of stress for classification.

Future work could also investigate other block selection methods different from the GA used in this work. The GA search took approximately 5 min to reach convergence, but it could take longer if the chromosome is extended to encode more general information for a block, e.g., coordinate values and the size for the block. The literature has claimed that a GA usually takes longer execution times than other types of feature selection techniques, such as correlation analysis [57]. Therefore in future, other block selection methods could be investigated that do not require execution times as long as a GA and still produce stress recognition measures comparable to the GA hybrid.

7 Conclusions

The ANU Stress database (ANUStressDB) was presented which has videos of faces in temporal thermal (TS) and visible (VS) spectrums for stress recognition. A computational classification model of stress using spatial and temporal characteristics of facial regions in the ANUStressDB was successfully developed. In the process, a new method for capturing patterns in thermal videos was defined - HDTP. The approach was defined so that it reduced individual bias in the computational models and enhanced participant-independent recognition of symptoms of stress. For computing the baseline for stress classification, a SVM was used. Facial block regions selected informed by a genetic algorithm improved the rates of the classifications regardless of the type of video - videos in TS or VS. The best recognition rates, however, were obtained when features from TS and VS videos were provided as inputs to the GA-SVM classifier. In addition, stress recognition rates were significantly better for classifiers provided with HDTP features instead of LBP-TOP features for TS. Future work could extend the investigation by developing features for facial block regions to capture more complex patterns and examining different forms of facial block regions for stress recognition.

Competing interests
The authors declare that they have no competing interests.

Author details
[1]Information and Human Centred Computing Research Group, Research School of Computer Science, Australian National University, Canberra, ACT 0200, Australia. [2]Vision & Sensing Group, Information Sciences & Engineering, University of Canberra, Bruce ACT 2601, Australia.

References

1. H Selye, The stress syndrome. Am. J. Nurs. **65**, 97–99 (1965)
2. L Hoffman-Goetz, BK Pedersen, Exercise and the immune system: a model of the stress response? Immunol. Today **15**, 382–387 (1994)
3. N Sharma, T Gedeon, Objective measures, sensors and computational techniques for stress recognition and classification: a survey. Comput. Methods Prog. Biomed. **108**, 1287–1301 (2012)
4. GE Miller, S Cohen, AK Ritchey, Chronic psychological stress and the regulation of pro-inflammatory cytokines: a glucocorticoid-resistance model. Health Psychology Hillsdale **21**, 531–541 (2002)
5. RS Surwit, MS Schneider, MN Feinglos, Stress and diabetes mellitus. Diabetes Care **15**, 1413–1422 (1992)
6. L Vitetta, B Anton, F Cortizo, A Sali, Mind body medicine: stress and its impact on overall health and longevity. Ann. N. Y. Acad. Sci. **1057**, 492–505 (2005)
7. JA Seltzer, D Kalmuss, Socialization and stress explanations for spouse abuse. Social Forces **67**, 473–491 (1988)
8. PR Johnson, J Indvik, Stress and violence in the workplace. Employee Counsell. Today **8**, 19–24 (1996)
9. The American Institute of Stress. (05/08/10), America's no. 1 health problem - why is there more stress today? http://www.stress.org/. Accessed 5 August 2010
10. Lifeline Australia, Stress costs taxpayer $300K every day, 2009. http://www.lifeline.org.au Accessed 10 August 2010
11. W Liao, W Zhang, Z Zhu, Q Ji, A real-time human stress monitoring system using dynamic Bayesian network, in *Computer Vision and Pattern Recognition - Workshops, CVPR Workshops*. San Diego, CA, USA, 25 June 2005.

12. J Zhai, A Barreto, Stress recognition using non-invasive technology, in *Proceedings of the 19th International Florida Artificial Intelligence Research Society Conference FLAIRS*. Melbourne Beach, Florida, 2006, pp. 395–400

13. J Wang, M Korczykowski, H Rao, Y Fan, J Pluta, RC Gur, BS McEwen, JA Detre, Gender difference in neural response to psychological stress. Soc. Cogn. Affect. Neurosci. **2**, 227 (2007)

14. N Sharma, T Gedeon, in *Stress Classification for Gender Bias in Reading - Neural Information Processing vol. 7064*, ed. by B-L Lu, L Zhang, J Kwok (Springer, Berlin, 2011), pp. 348–355

15. T Ushiyama, K Mizushige, H Wakabayashi, T Nakatsu, K Ishimura, Y Tsuboi, H Maeta, Y Suzuki, Analysis of heart rate variability as an index of noncardiac surgical stress. Heart Vessel. **23**, 53–59 (2008)

16. H Seong, J Lee, T Shin, W Kim, Y Yoon, The analysis of mental stress using time-frequency distribution of heart rate variability signal, in *Annual International Conference of Engineering in Medicine and Biology Society, 2004*. San Francisco, CA, USA, 1–4 September 2004, vol 1, pp. 283–285

17. DA Morilak, G Barrera, DJ Echevarria, AS Garcia, A Hernandez, S Ma, CO Petre, Role of brain norepinephrine in the behavioral response to stress. Prog. Neuro-Psychopharmacol. Biol. Psychiatry **29**, 1214–1224 (2005)

18. M Haak, S Bos, S Panic, LJM Rothkrantz, Detecting stress using eye blinks and brain activity from EEG signals, in *Proceeding of the 1st Driver Car Interaction and Interface (DCII 2008)*. Chez Technical University, Prague, 2008.

19. Y Shi, N Ruiz, R Taib, E Choi, F Chen, Galvanic skin response (GSR) as an index of cognitive load, in *CHI '07 extended abstracts on Human factors in computing systems*. San Jose, CA, USA, 2007, 28 April - 3 May 2007, pp. 2651–2656

20. S Reisman, Measurement of physiological stress, in *Bioengineering Conference*. 1997, 4–6 April 1997, pp. 21–23

21. DF Dinges, RL Rider, J Dorrian, EL McGlinchey, NL Rogers, Z Cizman, SK Goldenstein, C Vogler, S Venkataraman, DN Metaxas, Optical computer recognition of facial expressions associated with stress induced by performance demands. Aviat. Space Environ. Med. **76**, B172–B182 (2005)

22. BIOPAC Systems Inc, BIOPAC Systems, 2012. http://www.biopac.com/. Accessed 10 February 2011

23. P Yuen, K Hong, T Chen, A Tsitiridis, F Kam, J Jackman, D James, M Richardson, L Williams, W. Oxford, Emotional & physical stress detection and classification using thermal imaging technique, in *3rd International Conference on Crime Detection and Prevention (ICDP 2009)*. London, 2009, 3 December 2009, pp. 1–6

24. S Jarlier, D Grandjean, S Delplanque, K N'Diaye, I Cayeux, MI Velazco, D Sander, P Vuilleumier, KR Scherer, Thermal analysis of facial muscles contractions. IEEE Trans. Affect. Comput. **2**, 2–9 (2011)

25. G Zhao, M Pietikainen, Dynamic texture recognition using local binary patterns with an application to facial expressions. IEEE Trans. Pattern Anal. Mach. Intell. **29**, 915–928 (2007)

26. B Hernández, G Olague, R Hammoud, L Trujillo, E Romero, Visual learning of texture descriptors for facial expression recognition in thermal imagery. Comput. Vis. Image Underst. **106**, 258–269 (2007)

27. L Trujillo, G Olague, R Hammoud, B Hernandez, Automatic feature localization in thermal images for facial expression recognition, in *IEEE Computer Society Conference on Computer Vision and Pattern Recognition - Workshops, 2005. CVPR Workshops*. San Diego, CA, USA, 2005, 20, 21 and 25 June 2005, p. 14

28. PK Manglik, U Misra, HB Maringanti, Facial expression recognition, in *IEEE International Conference on Systems, Man and Cybernetics*. 2004, The Hague, Netherlands, 10–13 October 2004, pp. 2220–2224

29. N Neggaz, M Besnassi, A Benyettou, Application of improved AAM and probabilistic neural network to facial expression recognition. J. Appl. Sci. **10**, 1572–1579 (2010)

30. G Sandbach, S Zafeiriou, M Pantic, D Rueckert, Recognition of 3D facial expression dynamics. Image Vis. Comput. **30**, 762–773 (2012)

31. Z Zeng, M Pantic, GI Roisman, TS Huang, A survey of affect recognition methods: audio, visual, and spontaneous expressions. IEEE Trans. Pattern Anal. Mach. Intell. **31**, 39–58 (2009)

32. P Lucey, JF Cohn, KM Prkachin, PE Solomon, I Matthews, Painful data: The UNBC-McMaster shoulder pain expression archive database, in *IEEE International Conference on Automatic Face & Gesture Recognition and Workshops (FG 2011)*. 2011, Santa Barbara, CA, USA, 21–25 March 2011, pp. 57–64

33. M Taini, G Zhao, SZ Li, M Pietikainen, Facial expression recognition from near-infrared video sequences, in *19th International Conference on Pattern Recognition (ICPR)*. 2008, Tampa, Florida, USA, 8–11 December 2008, pp. 1–4

34. P Michel, RE Kaliouby, Real time facial expression recognition in video using support vector machines, in *the Proceedings of the 5th International Conference on Multimodal Interfaces, 2003*. Vancouver, British Columbia, Canada, 5–7 November 2003

35. T Ahonen, A Hadid, M Pietikainen, Face description with local binary patterns: application to face recognition. IEEE Trans. Pattern Anal. Mach. Intell. **28**, 2037–2041 (2006)

36. MS Bartlett, GC Littlewort, MG Frank, C Lainscsek, IR Fasel, JR Movellan, Automatic recognition of facial actions in spontaneous expressions. J. Multimed. **1**, 22–35 (2006)

37. E Douglas-Cowie, R Cowie, M Schröder, A new emotion database: considerations, sources and scope, in *ISCA Tutorial and Research Workshop (ITRW) on Speech and Emotion*, 2000, pp. 39–44

38. M Grimm, K Kroschel, S Narayanan, The Vera am Mittag German audio-visual emotional speech database, in *IEEE International Conference on Multimedia and Expo*. Hannover, Germany, 23–26 June 2008, 2008, pp. 865–868

39. A Dhall, R Goecke, S Lucey, T Gedeon, A semi-automatic method for collecting richly labelled large facial expression databases from movies. IEEE Multimedia **19**, 34–41 (2012)

40. J Zhai, A Barreto, Stress detection in computer users based on digital signal processing of noninvasive physiological variables, in *Proceedings of the 28th IEEE EMBS Annual International Conference*. 2006, New York City, NY, USA, 30 August - 3 September 2006, pp. 1355–1358

41. N Hjortskov, D Rissén, A Blangsted, N Fallentin, U Lundberg, K Søgaard, The effect of mental stress on heart rate variability and blood pressure during computer work. Eur. J. Appl. Physiol. **92**, 84–89 (2004)

42. JA Healey, RW Picard, Detecting stress during real-world driving tasks using physiological sensors. IEEE Trans. Intell. Transport. Syst. **6**, 156–166 (2005)

43. A Niculescu, Y Cao, A Nijholt, Manipulating stress and cognitive load in conversational interactions with a multimodal system for crisis management support, in *Development of Multimodal Interfaces: Active Listening and Synchrony* (Springer, Dublin Ireland, 2010), pp. 134–147

44. LM Vizer, L Zhou, A Sears, Automated stress detection using keystroke and linguistic features: an exploratory study. Int. J. Hum. Comput. Stud. **67**, 870–886 (2009)

45. T Lin, L John, Quantifying mental relaxation with EEG for use in computer games, in *International Conference on Internet Computing, 2006*. Las Vegas, NV, USA, 26–29 June 2006, pp. 409–415

46. T Lin, M Omata, W Hu, A Imamiya, Do physiological data relate to traditional usability indexes? in *Proceedings of the 17th Australia Conference on Computer-Human Interaction: Citizens Online: Considerations for Today and the Future* (Narrabundah, Australia, 2005), pp. 1–10

47. WR Lovallo, *Stress & Health: Biological and Psychological Interactions* (Sage Publications, Inc., California, 2005)

48. P Lucey, JF Cohn, T Kanade, J Saragih, Z Ambadar, I Matthews, The extended Cohn-Kanade dataset (CK+): a complete dataset for action unit and emotion-specified expression, in *IEEE Computer Society Conference on Computer Vision and Pattern Recognition Workshops (CVPRW)* (San Francisco, CA, USA, 2010), pp. 94–101

49. JJ Gross, RW Levenson, Emotion elicitation using films. Cognit. Emot. **9**, 87–108 (1995)

50. V Struc, N Pavesic, The complete Gabor-Fisher classifier for robust face recognition. EURASIP Advances in Signal Processing **2010**, 26 (2010)

51. V Struc, N Pavesic, Gabor-based kernel partial-least-squares discrimination features for face recognition. Informatica (Vilnius) **20**, 115–138 (2009)

52. V Struc, *The PhD Toolbox: Pretty Helpful Development Functions for Face Recognition*, 2012. http://luks.fe.uni-lj.si/sl/osebje/vitomir/face_tools/PhDface/. Accessed 12 September 2012

53. Mathworks, Vision TemplateMatcher System Object R2012a. (2012). http://www.mathworks.com.au/help/vision/ref/vision.templatematcherclass.html. Accessed 12 September 2012

54. APA, *American Psychological Association, Stress in America* (APA, Washington, DC, 2012)

55. CJ Holahan, RH Moos, Life stressors, resistance factors, and improved psychological functioning: an extension of the stress resistance paradigm. J. Pers. Soc. Psychol. **58**, 909 (1990)

56. H Frohlich, O Chapelle, B Scholkopf, Feature selection for support vector machines by means of genetic algorithm, in *15th IEEE International Conference on Tools with Artificial Intelligence*. Sacramento, California, USA, 3–5 November 2003, 2003, pp. 142–148

57. L Yu, H Liu, Feature selection for high-dimensional data: a fast correlation-based filter solution, in *12th International Conference on Machine Learning*. Los Angeles, CA, 23–24 June 2003, 2003, pp. 856–863

15

Saliency detection in complex scenes

Linfeng Xu*, Liaoyuan Zeng, Huiping Duan and Nii Longdon Sowah

Abstract

Detecting multiple salient objects in complex scenes is a challenging task. In this paper, we present a novel method to detect salient objects in images. The proposed method is based on the general 'center-surround' visual attention mechanism and the spatial frequency response of the human visual system (HVS). The saliency computation is performed in a statistical way. This method is modeled following three biologically inspired principles and compute saliency by two 'scatter matrices' which are used to measure the variability within and between two classes, i.e., the center and surrounding regions, respectively. In order to detect multiple salient objects of different sizes in a scene, the saliency of a pixel is estimated via its saliency support region which is defined as the most salient region centered at the pixel. Compliance with human perceptual characteristics enables the proposed method to detect salient objects in complex scenes and predict human fixations. Experimental results on three eye tracking datasets verify the effectiveness of the method and show that the proposed method outperforms the state-of-the-art methods on the visual saliency detection task.

Keywords: Visual attention; Saliency model; Complex scene; Human fixation prediction

1 Introduction

Visual saliency is a state or quality which makes an item, e.g., an object or a person, prominent from its surroundings. Humans, as well as most primates, have a marvelous ability to interpret complex scenes and pay their attention to the salient objects or regions in the visual environment in real time. Two approaches for the deployment of algorithm based on visual attention have been proposed: the bottom-up and the top-down [1].

For many researches in physiology [2], neuropsychology [3], cognitive science [4], and computer vision [1], it is essential to study the mechanisms of human attention. The understanding of visual attention is helpful for object-of-attention image segmentation [5,6], adaptive coding [7], image registration [8], video analysis [9], and perceptual image/video representation [10]. Most models of attention are bottom-up and biologically inspired. Typically, these models posit that saliency is the impetus for selective vision. Saliency detection can be performed based on center-surround contrast [1], information theory [11,12], graph model [13], common similarity [14-16], or learning methods [17,18].

*Correspondence: lfxu@uestc.edu.cn
School of Electronic Engineering, University of Electronic Science and Technology of China, Xiyuan Avenue 2006, West Hi-Tech Zone, Chengdu, Sichuan 611731, China

The bottom-up saliency detection methods can be broadly classified into local and global schemes. The local contrast-based methods measure the visual rarity with respect to the local neighborhoods using multi-scale image features [1,19,20]. The saliency maps generated by such methods usually highlight the object boundary. Furthermore, without knowing the scale of the salient object, the local methods may not detect the salient object accurately. On the contrary, the global contrast-based methods measure the saliency of a pixel by integrating its contrast to all pixels in the image [12,21,22]. Generally, the global methods can generate saliency maps with full resolution and evenly highlighted salient regions. These methods can achieve good accuracy of saliency detection in a scene which consists of a single salient object and a simple background. However, it is hard to detect salient objects from complex scenes due to the global consideration. As shown in Figure 1, the pen container is the most salient according to the fixation density map from the MIT-1003 dataset [23], which shows the region attracting the attention of most subjects. The saliency map in Figure 1c highlights the object boundary, which is obtained from the local method [1]. The global method [22] cannot detect the container because the color of the container is similar to that of the wall and its contrast to all the pixels of the image is low, as shown in Figure 1d.

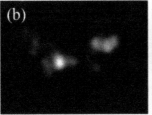

Figure 1 Saliency detection in a complex scene. (a) Original image. **(b)** Human fixation density map. **(c)** Saliency map of the local method [1]. **(d)** Saliency map of the global method [22].

In this paper, we focus on a bottom-up model of saliency detection, which is widely believed to be closely connected to the ubiquity of attention mechanisms in the early stages of biological vision [24]. In neuroscience, numerous studies show that the neuronal response is elevated by the stimulus within the classical receptive field (the center), while stimuli presented in the annular window surrounding the receptive field (the surround) inhibit the response [25]. According to the 'center-surround' mechanisms and the spatial frequency response of the human visual system (HVS) [26], we propose a saliency model based on the following principles of human visual attention:

1. Appearance distinctness between an object and its surroundings. It is generally considered that the response of neurons comes from the contrast of the center region and the surrounding regions [27]. For a pixel p which is inside an object, the pixel is salient if the object is distinct from its surroundings.
2. Unevenness of appearance within an object while appearance similarity within its surrounding region. For a pixel p inside a region (the center), the pixel is salient if the variability of the region is not too low since some intermediate spatial frequency stimuli may evoke a peak response [26]. Meanwhile, the stimuli from the surrounding region should be as weak as possible because the surround is antagonistic to the center and a stronger response will be evoked without the surrounding stimuli [25]. So, the surrounding region should have low variability.
3. Large object size. According to the neuropsychological experiments, attentive response increases when the stimulus size is large and the object is attended [28]. If multiple objects have the same distinctness with respect to their surroundings, humans may pay attention to the larger object first.

These principles reflect the common human characteristics about saliency perception. For example, according to the visual experiments, the spatial frequency response of the HVS, which is similar to the response of a band-pass filter, has a peak response at about 2 to 5 cycles per degree (cpd) and falls off at about 30 cpd [26]. As shown in Figure 2a, a cluttered image is hard to attract people's attention. Principle 2 demands HVS to be sensitive to stimuli from the center and not at the surroundings in order to create stronger center-surround contrast and make the object attentive. In the experiments, we find that each of the principles contributes to the performance of the saliency detector.

Extending our previous work [29], we propose a novel method to measure visual saliency based on biologically plausible saliency mechanisms with a reasonable mathematical formulation. We define the saliency of an image region in a statistical way by means of the scatter matrix. For a pixel in an image, the center region and the surrounding region are defined as the regions centered at the pixel. For a center and a surrounding region, the saliency value is determined by two scatter matrices of the visual features. The first is the 'within-classes scatter matrix' S_W which expresses the similarity between the features of the center region and the surrounding region. The second is the 'between-classes scatter matrix' S_B which describes how the feature statistics in the center region diverge from those in the surrounding region. For a pixel, there exist many concentric regions with different radii, which have different prominence with respect to their surroundings. In order to detect the most salient objects in the scenes, the saliency support region of a pixel is explored, which is the most salient center region among all the concentric center regions. In order to make the large object more salient, the saliency value is weighted using the radius of the saliency support region.

The proposed method has two advantages. First, it is based on the computational architecture of human visual attention. The mechanism of the method is consistent with human perceptual characteristics. So, the method has a good performance for human fixation prediction. Secondly, the proposed method searches the potential saliency support regions to measure the saliency of multiple objects at different scales. This mechanism enables the method to explore various salient objects adaptively. It is effective for saliency detection in complex scenes.

Figure 2 Two types of images. (a) A cluttered image. **(b)** A concise image. The two people in image **(b)** attract our attention.

The proposed method is evaluated on three eye tracking datasets which comprise natural images in different scenes and the corresponding human fixation data. Compared to 12 state-of-the-art methods and the human fixation data, the experimental results show that our method outperforms all other methods in terms of receiver operator characteristic (ROC) area metrics for the human fixation prediction task.

This paper is organized as follows: The related work is in Section 2. Section 3 describes the proposed method for saliency detection. The experimental results are provided in Section 4 to verify the effectiveness of the method. Finally, the conclusion is drawn in Section 5.

2   Related work

In the past few decades, a lot of bottom-up saliency-driven methods have been proposed in cognitive fields, which can be broadly classified as biologically inspired, purely computational, or an integration of the two [21].

Many attention models are based on the biologically inspired architecture proposed by Koch and Ullman [30], which is motivated from Treisman and Gelade's feature integration theory (FIT) [31]. This structure explains the human visual search strategies, i.e., the visual input is firstly divided into several feature types (e.g., intensity, color, or orientation) which are explored concurrently, and then the conspicuities of the features are combined into a saliency or master map which is a scalar, two-dimensional map providing higher intensities for the most prominent areas.

According to this biologically plausible architecture, a popular bottom-up attention model is proposed by Itti et al. [1]. In Itti's model, three multi-resolution extracted local feature contrasts, i.e., luminance, chrominance, and orientation, are mixed to produce a saliency map. Walther and Koch [19] extended Itti's model to infer proto-object regions from individual contrast maps at different spatial scales. These models obtained good results in applications from computer vision to robotics [19,32].

In the last decade, many purely computational methods came up to model saliency with less biological motivation. Ma and Zhang [33] proposed a fuzzy growing method to extract salient objects based on local contrast analysis. Achanta et al. [21] estimated the center-surround contrast by using a frequency-tuned technology. In order to solve the object scale problem, Achanta et al. extended their work by using a symmetric-surround method to vary the bandwidth of the center-surround filtering near image borders [34]. Hu et al. [35] presented a composite saliency indicator and a dynamic weighting strategy to estimate saliency. Hou and Zhang [36] extracted the saliency map from the spectral residual of the log-spectrum of an image. According to the global rarity principle of saliency, Zhai and Shah [37] and Cheng et al. [22] used the histogram-based method to detect the global contrast of a pixel or region. By filtering color values and position values, Perazzi et al. [38] computed the uniqueness and distribution to detect salient regions. Recently, based on a graph-based manifold ranking method, Yang et al. [39] detected saliency of the image elements by ranking the similarity to background and foreground queries. Li et al. [40] performed saliency detection by integrating the dense and sparse reconstruction errors of image regions. These state-of-the-art methods can extract salient regions effectively.

Some of the other methods model saliency based on both of the biological and computational models. Harel et al. [13] used Itti's model to create feature maps, which are integrated into activation maps by using a graph-based approach. Finally, saliency maps are generated by a Markovian algorithm. Bruce and Tsotsos [11] represented the probability distribution of local image patches by using the independent component analysis (ICA). They computed the self-information of image regions to implement a neurally plausible circuit that closely corresponds to visual saliency. Wang et al. [41] use the learned sparse codes to extract some sub-band feature maps which are represented by a random walk-based graph model to simulate the information transmission among the neurons.

Besides Bruce's work, some other saliency detectors also established models based on information theory. Itti and Baldi [42] presented a Bayesian definition of surprise to describe saliency. Gao and Vasconcelos [43] proposed a discriminant saliency detection model by maximizing the mutual information of the center and surrounding regions in an image. Klein and Frintrop [44] used the integral histograms to estimate the distributions of the center and surrounding region and expressed the saliency by the Kullback-Leibler divergence (KLD) of these distributions.

Statistical theory has also gotten into the field of saliency detection. Zhang et al. [45] computed saliency based on the self-information of local image features using natural image statistics. Also using natural image statistics, Vigo et al. [46] detected salient edge based on ICA.

We implement the computation of saliency based on the statistics of local image regions. Our work is most closely related to the within-classes scatter matrix and between-classes scatter matrix in Fisher's linear discriminant analysis (LDA) which is commonly used for dimensionality reduction before later classification [47]. We use these two scatter matrices to measure the variability within/between the center and surrounding regions which are defined in Section 3.1. Furthermore, we compute the visual saliency based on principles 1 and 2.

Some methods detect saliency at a single spatial scale [33,35], while others combine feature maps at multiple scales to the final saliency map [1,19,20]. Without knowing the scale of the object, these methods may not detect the most salient object accurately. The proposed method finds the saliency support region for a local area and computes the saliency of this region with respect to its surroundings to detect multiple salient objects adaptively.

3 Proposed method

In this section, we propose a computational method for saliency detection in images, which is performed in the CIELAB color space. We first define the center region and surrounding region that are used for the center-surround contrast computation. Secondly, a central stimuli sensitivity-based model is proposed to compute the saliency of the center region. Then, the saliency support region of a given pixel is searched to mimic the maximum response of the receptive field in the neurophysiological experiment. Finally, we introduce the visual saliency map generation.

3.1 Center region and surrounding region

The saliency computation of the method is based on the selection of two regions, i.e., the center region and surrounding region. According to the center-surround mechanism, the saliency of a pixel is determined by the contrast between the center object (which the pixel belongs to) and the surrounding region. Without *a priori* information of the center object, we assume that it is approximately within a circular region centered at the pixel, which is referred to as the center region. In this paper, the surrounding region of the center region is defined as the concentric annular region outside the center region, which has the maximal radius toward the nearest image border. For a pixel in the image, there are many center regions. As shown in Figure 3, three center regions for the center pixel of the circles are shown, which are the regions within the blue, purple, or red circles. The corresponding surrounding regions are the annular regions between these circles and the outmost yellow circle.

3.2 Central stimuli sensitivity-based saliency model

According to principles 1 and 2, the appearance distinctness between the object and its surrounding and the appearance similarity of each of them are key for visual saliency detection. In order to make an object prominent, the stimuli from the center region should make the HVS sensitive while the stimuli from the surrounding region should not. Following the band-pass characteristic of the spatial frequency response of the HVS [26], we measure the sensitivity in a statistics-theoretic way.

Inspired by the scatter matrices used in Fisher-LDA [47], we use the within-classes scatter matrix to measure the similarity of the center region, R_c, and the surrounding region, R_s, which is defined as

$$S_{\mathrm{W}} = \sum_{n \in \{1,2\}} \sum_{p \in R^n} \left(x_p - \mu_n \right) \left(x_p - \mu_n \right)^T \tag{1}$$

where R^1 denotes the region R_c, R^2 denotes the region R_s, x_p is the feature vector of pixel p (the vector contains the intensity and color features in the experiments), and μ_n is the mean feature vector of the region R^n. The matrix of each region is normalized by the number of the pixels in the region. The eigenvalues of the scatter matrix are related to the spatial frequency of the region. If a region is flat, the pixels in the region concentrate on their mean. In other words, the pixels in the region are not scattered. For two flat regions, the eigenvalues of S_{W} are small. According to principle 2, we define the sum of the eigenvalues of S_{W} to be inversely proportional to the saliency value in the method. However, a flat center region with low frequency may get a large saliency value, which violates principle 2. In order to measure the sensitivity to the center stimuli, which has a peak response at an intermediate frequency [26], we modify (1) by weighting the matrix of R_c, which can be represented as

$$S_{\mathrm{W}} = \omega_c \sum_{p \in R^1} \left(x_p - \mu_1 \right) \left(x_p - \mu_1 \right)^T + \sum_{p \in R^2} \left(x_p - \mu_2 \right) \left(x_p - \mu_2 \right)^T \tag{2}$$

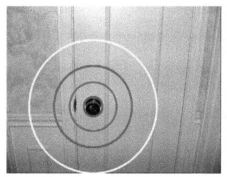

Figure 3 Examples of center regions and surrounding region. Three center regions for the pixel in the circle center are shown, which are the regions within the blue, purple, or red circles. The corresponding surrounding regions are the annular regions between these circles and the outmost yellow circle.

where ω_c is a empirically set parameter to control the contribution of the similarity of R_c to the computed saliency value. By setting ω_c to 1, a flat center region may produce a large saliency value. If ω_c is decreased, an uneven center region with a higher spatial frequency may generate a large saliency value. We will demonstrate in Section 4.5 that the weight ω_c plays a significant role in the saliency computing.

To measure the difference of R_c and R_s, the between-classes scatter matrix is used, which is defined as

$$S_{\mathrm{B}} = \sum_{n \in \{1,2\}} (\mu_n - \mu)(\mu_n - \mu)^T \qquad (3)$$

where μ is the overall mean feature vector of the pixels in $R_c \bigcup R_s$. For two regions which are distinct from each other, the eigenvalues of S_{B} are large.

The saliency of a particular center region depends on the traces of S_{W} and S_{B}, i.e., the sums of eigenvalues of the two scatter matrices, which is computed by

$$\mathrm{Sal}\,(R_c) = \frac{\mathrm{trace}\,(S_{\mathrm{B}})}{\mathrm{trace}\,(S_{\mathrm{W}})}. \qquad (4)$$

A center region which is distinct from its flat surrounding region has a high saliency value.

3.3   Saliency support region

As shown in Figure 3, many center regions exist for a pixel. Some of them are salient, such as the region within the blue circle, while some others are not, such as the regions within the red and purple circles. As mentioned in Section 2, some of the previous work preset multiple spatial scales or use a single scale to detect saliency, which may fail to find the salient object.

According to the spatial summation curves in the neurophysiological experiments, when the visual stimuli cover the area of receptive field center, the neural responses reach the peak [48]. We believe that for a salient object, there exists a support to form the saliency quality, which

generates a peak response in the neuron. We attempt to find the support region which generates the most intensive saliency with respect to its surrounding region, referred to as the saliency support region.

We define the saliency support region of a pixel as the center region which has the largest saliency value using (4). The saliency support region, SSR, can be formulated as

$$\mathrm{SSR} = \arg \max_{R_c \in \mathbb{A}} \mathrm{Sal}\,(R_c) \qquad (5)$$

where $\mathbb{A}$ is the set of all the possible center regions of a pixel. As shown in Figure 4, the saliency support region of the pixel in the middle of the flower is the region within the red circle, which consists of the stamens and has the largest saliency value with respect to its surrounding region of flower petals and green leaves. Other center regions are less salient than the saliency support region. We use the saliency value of the saliency support region to represent the saliency of the center pixel of the SSR. The exploration of the saliency support region intends to measure the maximal saliency of pixels and find salient objects with different sizes. For a pixel, there are many possible center regions that need to be compared. In order to reduce computational expense, we reduce the candidate center regions by sampling their radii at a fixed interval in the implementation, i.e., only the regions with the sampled radii are compared.

3.4   Visual saliency map

In the saliency map of the proposed method, the value of a pixel is determined by the saliency value of its saliency support region. According to the principle 3, large objects may attract more human attention than small details. For example, the large desk lamp in Figure 5 is more attentive than the small lights. In terms of saliency support region, if the most salient region is large, it may attract more attention. In the method, the saliency value is weighted

Figure 4 An example of the saliency support region. The region within the red circle is the saliency support region of the pixel in the middle of flower stamen, which has the largest saliency value with respect to its surrounding region of flower petals and green leaves.

by the radius of the saliency support region, which can be represented as

$$\mathrm{Sal}(p) = \mathrm{Sal}(\mathrm{SSR}) \cdot r(\mathrm{SSR}) \qquad (6)$$

where p is the center pixel of the saliency support region (SSR), and $r(\mathrm{SSR})$ denotes the radius of SSR.

Instead of measuring the saliency values of all the pixels, we sample the pixels at an interval (e.g., 10 pixels) for computation reduction. The lattice of the sampled pixels is interpolated bilinearly and Gaussian filtered with $\sigma = 25$

to generate the final saliency map of the image, as shown in Figure 6.

4 Experiments

In this section, we apply the proposed method on three public eye tracking datasets (two color image datasets and one gray image dataset) to evaluate the performance of human fixation prediction. These datasets comprise natural images, containing different objects and scenes, and the corresponding human fixations. The proposed

Figure 5 An example of large object size for saliency detection. The large desk lamp may attract more attention than the small lamps.

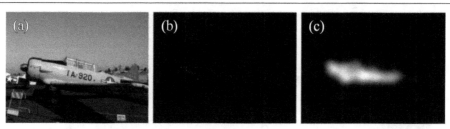

Figure 6 An example of the saliency map. (a) Original image. **(b)** Lattice of the sampled pixels. **(c)** Saliency map generated by interpolation and filtering.

method is compared with the state-of-the-art bottom-up methods based on a well-known validation approach. The qualitative and quantitative assessments of detection results are reported.

4.1 Parameter setting

There is a parameter in the proposed method: the weight ω_c of the within-classes scatter matrix of the center region in (2). We set the weight $\omega_c = 0.1$ because it can obtain large areas under the ROC curves in the experiments on the three datasets. The relationship between the parameter and the performance of the method is discussed in Section 4.5.

4.2 Experiments on BRUCE color image dataset

In the first experiment, we perform saliency computations on the popular color image dataset introduced by Bruce and Tsotsos [11], which consists of 120 images in indoor and outdoor scenes, such as human objects, furniture, phones, fruits, cars, buildings, streets, etc. All the image sizes are 681×511 pixels. In the dataset, 20 subjects' fixations are recorded for each image. To compare the saliency maps with the human fixations objectively, we use the popular validation approach as in [11]. The area under the ROC curve is used to quantitatively evaluate the performance of visual saliency detection.

We compare the proposed method with 12 state-of-the-art bottom-up saliency detection methods, i.e., Itti's model (IT) [1], attention information maximization (AIM) [11], spectral residual (SR) [36], graph-based visual saliency (GB) [13], site entropy rate (SER) [41], context aware (CA) [49], salient region detection (AC) [20], maximum symmetric surround (MSS) [34], region-based contrast (RC) [22], saliency filters (SF) [38], graph-based manifold ranking (MR) [39], and dense and sparse reconstruction (DSR) [40] which are listed in Table 1. These methods involve a variety of saliency models, such as biologically motivated (e.g., IT), computational (e.g., AC and MSS), frequency-based (e.g., SR), mixed (e.g., AIM and GB), local contrast (e.g., IT and AC), global contrast (e.g., RC), and state-of-the-art (e.g., SF, MR, and DSR) models. Some of the methods are used to predict human

fixations, such as AIM, GB, and SER, and some others show excellent performance in the salient region/object extraction task, such as RC, SF, MR, and DSR. For all these methods, we use the source codes or executable codes by the authors. The proposed method is implemented in Matlab.

Figure 7 qualitatively shows the comparison results of saliency maps for some test images of the BRUCE dataset. The original images are shown in Figure 7a, while the maps obtained from the state-of-the-art methods are given in Figure 7b,c,d,e,f,g,h,i,j,k,l,m, respectively. The results of the proposed method are shown in Figure 7n. The fixation density maps are shown in the final column, which are generated from the sum of 2D Gaussians corresponding to each fixation point of all the subjects [11]. It can be seen that most of the methods can detect the single salient object in a simple scene, such as the second row. However, it is challenging for the images which

Table 1 The state-of-the-art methods

Algorithm name	Reference	Implementation code
Itti's model (IT)	Itti [1]	Matlab code by Harel [13]
Attention information max. (AIM)	Bruce [11]	Matlab code by author
Spectral residual (SR)	Hou [36]	Matlab code by author
Graph-based visual saliency (GB)	Harel [13]	Matlab code by author
Site entropy rate (SER)	Wang [41]	Executable code by author
Context aware (CA)	Goferman [49]	Matlab code by author
Salient region detection (AC)	Achanta [20]	Executable code by author
Maximum symmetric surround (MSS)	Achanta [34]	Executable code by author
Region-based contrast (RC)	Cheng [22]	Executable code by author
Saliency filters (SF)	Perazzi [38]	C code by author
Graph-based manifold ranking (MR)	Yang [39]	Matlab code by author
Dense and sparse reconstruction (DSR)	Li [40]	Matlab code by author

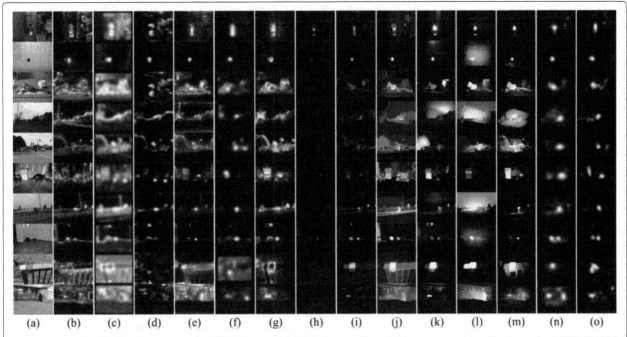

(a)　(b)　(c)　(d)　(e)　(f)　(g)　(h)　(i)　(j)　(k)　(l)　(m)　(n)　(o)

Figure 7 Examples of saliency maps over the BRUCE dataset. (a) Original images. **(b to n)** Saliency maps achieved by the methods IT [1], AIM [11], SR [36], GB [13], SER [41], CA [49], AC [20], MSS [34], RC [22], SF [38], MR [39], DSR [40], and the proposed method. **(o)** Human fixation density maps.

consist of multiple objects or complex scenes. The comparison results show that our maps which are based on the biological perception mechanisms are more consistent with the human fixation density maps. For example, in the third image, the scene is a bit complex. There are some objects, e.g., the tomatoes, cup, and knife, on a motley table mat. The two tomatoes have the stronger local contrast than the other objects. As a result, it is shown from the fixation density map that the tomatoes attract the attention of most of the subjects. However, most of the methods fail to do well. In the methods IT, AIM, SR, GB, and CA, saliency detection is performed by searching the high-frequency regions. So, the boundaries of the objects are detected as the most salient. In some methods, such as SER, MSS, and SF, the pixels in the cup, knife, or table mat are very salient due to the global consideration. The proposed method searches the saliency support region to explore the most salient region. So, the tomatoes are assigned the highest saliency value and recognized as the most salient region. Meanwhile, if multiple salient objects have the comparable local contrast, our method also can detect these objects. For example, for the eighth image, the two salient objects are detected by the proposed method.

In order to evaluate the quality of the proposed method, we perform a quantitative comparison by computing the salient degree between the extracted saliency map and the human fixations. The popular validation approach, the ROC area [11], is used to evaluate the performance of visual saliency detection. The results of ROC areas of

the compared methods on this dataset are shown in the second column of Table 2. Among the existing methods, the very recent method MR has the best fixation prediction performance on this dataset, whose ROC area is 0.7378. It shows that MR does well not only in the salient region detection task but also in this fixation prediction evaluation. However, it can be seen that the ROC

Table 2 The ROC areas on three eye tracking datasets

Method	BRUCE dataset	MIT-1003 dataset	DOVES dataset
IT [1]	0.5709	0.6835	0.5548
AIM [11]	0.6275	0.7662	0.6201
SR [36]	0.5315	0.6977	0.5429
GB [13]	0.5237	0.6857	0.5061
SER [41]	0.6632	0.7835	0.6716
CA [49]	0.6307	0.7585	0.6271
AC [20]	0.5520	0.6251	0.5312
MSS [34]	0.6107	0.6774	0.5530
RC [22]	0.6461	0.7568	0.6176
SF [38]	0.6601	0.7019	0.6492
MR [39]	0.7378	0.7766	0.7375
DSR [40]	0.7144	0.7908	0.7021
PM[a]	*0.7626*	*0.8027*	*0.7503*

[a]The proposed method. The numbers in italics show the best method which achieves the maximal ROC area on each dataset.

area of the proposed method is about 0.025 (3.4%) higher than MR. It demonstrates that the proposed method outperforms the 12 state-of-the-art methods on predicting human fixations on this eye tracking dataset.

The results listed in Table 2 are different from some of the reported results [11,13,41]. In the existing comparison methods, the fixation mask is obtained by setting a quantization threshold, i.e., the threshold classifies the locations in a fixation density map into fixations and non-fixations. So, different quantization thresholds lead to different results. To perform a fair comparison, we use the fixation points provided by the dataset as the ground truth for all the compared methods, i.e., only the points are fixations and the rest are non-fixations. The ROC areas of the compared methods are generated using the Matlab code provided by Harel et al. [13].

4.3   Experiments on MIT-1003 color image dataset

We perform saliency computations on another color image dataset introduced by Judd et al. [23]. The MIT-1003 dataset contains 1,003 natural images of varying dimensions (the maximal dimension of the width and height is 1,024 pixels), along with human fixation data from 15 subjects. The images in this dataset contain different scenes and objects, as well as many semantic objects, such as faces, people, body parts, and text, which are not modeled by bottom-up saliency [23].

We compare the proposed method with the same 12 methods listed in Table 1 on this dataset. Comparison results of saliency maps for some of the test images are shown in Figure 8. The original images are shown in Figure 8a, while the results from the state-of-the-art methods are given in Figure 8b,c,d,e,f,g,h,i,j,k,l,m, respectively. The results of the proposed method are shown in Figure 8n, and the fixation density maps provided in the dataset are given in Figure 8o. For the fifth and seventh images that contain complex background, the global contrast-based methods, e.g., RC and SF, are apt to highlight the noise regions, e.g., shadows, and overlook the key regions. Some local contrast-based methods, such as IT, AIM, SR, GB, and CA, detect the boundary of objects as the most salient like their performance on the BRUCE dataset. Although some methods preset multiple scales, such as IT and AC, they cannot effectively detect salient objects in the complex scenes. Method SER performs better than other existing methods. However, for the images with multiple objects, such as the sixth and seventh images, SER only detects one object. By following the biological perception mechanisms and exploring the saliency support region, the proposed method can achieve good performance to predict most of the fixations in the images that contain complex scenes and semantic objects. For example, in the fifth image, the proposed method detects the face of the

girl as the most salient, which is consistent with most of the subjects. However, most of the other methods fail to find the face of the girl and detect the boundaries of different objects. Another example is the sixth and seventh images, in which the proposed method detects two salient people due to the saliency support region exploration.

The results of ROC areas of the compared methods on this dataset are shown in the third column of Table 2. Among the existing methods, the very recent method DSR shows the best performance on this dataset. The proposed method achieves a slightly higher ROC area than DSR and also outperforms the state-of-the-art methods on this human fixation dataset. We notice that the improvement of our method on this dataset is not as overt as on the BRUCE dataset. The main reason is that the MIT-1003 dataset contains many semantic objects which put forward challenges to the bottom-up models. The detected results by our method are based on the bottom-up contrast, which may diverge from the fixations of the subjects. Using some high-level features may improve the results.

4.4   Experiments on DOVES gray image dataset

In the third experiment, we test the proposed method on a gray image dataset, DOVES, which is introduced by van der Linde et al. [50]. The DOVES dataset contains 101 natural images and the eye tracking data from 29 subjects. All the image sizes are $1,024 \times 768$ pixels. Because the first fixations of each eye movement trace of the subjects are forced at the center of the image [50], these fixations are removed in the experiments.

We also compare the proposed method with the 12 methods listed in Table 1 on the DOVES dataset. However, some of the methods are not compatible with gray images. For the methods AIM, CA, AC, and MSS, we use the RGB images whose three components are generated by duplicating the intensity of the gray images. Comparison results of saliency maps for some test images from this gray image dataset are shown in Figure 9. The original images are shown in Figure 9a, while the maps from the 12 previous methods are shown in Figure 9b,c,d,e,f,g,h,i,j,k,l,m, respectively. The results of the proposed method are given in Figure 9n and the human fixation density maps are shown in the final column. It can be seen that the cue of colors is key for most of the existing methods. For these gray images, most of the methods detect the bright sky or dark shadows as the salient regions, and method MR generally detects the image center as the salient region. However, the proposed method is less sensitive to the lack of colors, which mainly depends on the local statistical property of the image. The saliency maps generated by the proposed method are consistent with

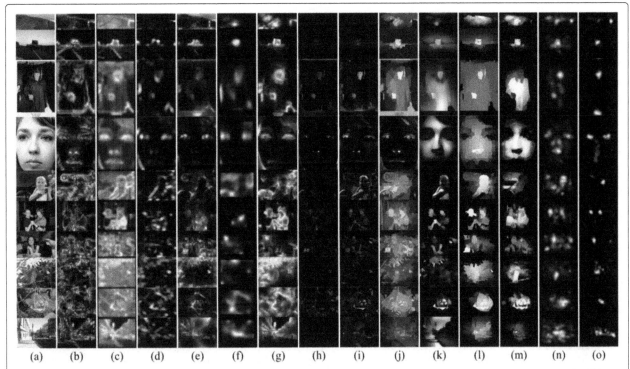

Figure 8 Examples of saliency maps over the MIT-1003 dataset. (a) Original images. **(b to n)** Saliency maps achieved by the methods IT [1], AIM [11], SR [36], GB [13], SER [41], CA [49], AC [20], MSS [34], RC [22], SF [38], MR [39], DSR [40], and the proposed method. **(o)** Human fixation density maps.

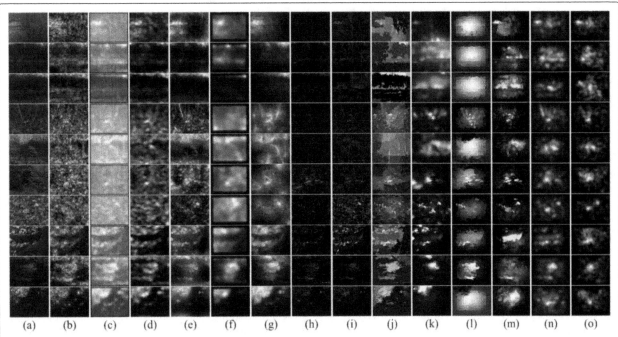

Figure 9 Examples of saliency maps over the DOVES dataset. (a) Original images. **(b to n)** Saliency maps achieved by the methods IT [1], AIM [11], SR [36], GB [13], SER [41], CA [49], AC [20], MSS [34], RC [22], SF [38], MR [39], DSR [40], and the proposed method. **(o)** Human fixation density maps.

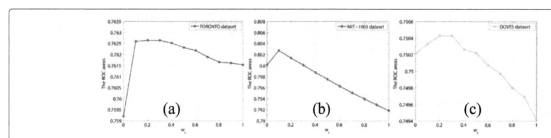

Figure 10 The relationship between the ROC area and the weight ω_c. Results on **(a)** the BRUCE dataset, **(b)** the MIT-1003 dataset, and **(c)** the DOVES dataset.

human fixations well. It shows that the proposed method has a good ability to predict fixations even for gray images.

The results of ROC area of all the compared methods on the DOVES dataset are presented in the fourth column of Table 2. Method MR shows the highest ROC area (0.7375) on this dataset compared to the previous methods. The main reason is that most of the subjects tend to focus their fixations on the image center if there are no very prominent regions. Compared with MR, the proposed method achieves about 2% improvement of ROC area. It shows that the proposed method outperforms the state-of-the-art methods on fixation prediction for gray images.

4.5 Discussion
In our model, the parameter ω_c is designed to determine the region of which frequency will be assigned a high saliency value. If ω_c is set to 1 and 0, the regions with very low and high frequency will be assigned high saliency values, respectively. According to the HVS principles, the very low and high frequency regions may weaken the response of the HVS. So, an inappropriate value of ω_c will lead to the wrong detection, i.e., the ROC area may be small.

Figure 10 shows the relationship between the ROC area and the weight ω_c in (2) on the three datasets. Generally, when the weight ω_c is bigger than 0.3, the ROC area decreases as the weight increases. That is to say, the salient objects are not necessarily flat according to the evaluation based on the human fixation data. On the contrary, if no constraints are imposed on the similarity of the center region, i.e., $\omega_c = 0$, the ROC area drops, especially on the BRUCE dataset, the ROC area in Figure 10a is the lowest when $\omega_c = 0$. That is to say, if the center region is rather cluttered, it may not attract human attention. This result is consistent with the spatial frequency response of the HVS [26]. The curves in Figure 10 are similar to the mirror of the spatial frequency response curve, which show that the response reaches a maximum when the spatial frequency

gets an intermediate frequency, ω_c is between 0.1 and 0.3, while it falls off rapidly at higher frequency, namely $\omega_c = 0$. The response decreases slowly as the frequency decreases to DC, i.e., $\omega_c = 1$, from the intermediate frequency. It is worth noting that our model is biologically plausible. It is difficult to denote the spatial frequency by specific values of ω_c.

The performance improvement of the proposed method in the fixation prediction experiments verifies the effectiveness of the scatter matrix-based saliency computation and the saliency support region exploration. However, since we use the pixel-wise processing manner and the SSR is searched for every processed pixel, the method is computationally expensive. We therefore adopt the sub-sampling method to reduce the cost. The average running time on the BRUCE dataset to generate the saliency map is 60.63 s when measured on an Intel 3.20-GHz CPU with 3-GB RAM in Matlab implementation. In the future, we will study the superpixel-based processing to make the algorithm more efficient.

5 Conclusions
In this paper, we propose a novel method to compute visual saliency in a statistical way. According to three principles of human visual attention, we use the within-classes scatter matrix and the between-classes scatter matrix to measure the similarity and distinctness within and between the center region and the surrounding region, respectively. Furthermore, the saliency of the center region is computed by the two scatter matrices. In order to detect the salient objects with different sizes, the saliency support region is explored and the saliency value of the center pixel of the region is obtained. To make the large object more salient, the saliency value is weighted by the radius of the saliency support region. Experimental results are obtained by applying the proposed method to three eye tracking datasets. The results show that the proposed method outperforms the state-of-the-art methods on saliency detection in complex scenes and human fixation prediction.

Competing interests
The authors declare that they have no competing interests.

Acknowledgements
This work was partially supported by NSFC (No. 61201274), National High Technology Research and Development Program of China (863 Program, No. 2012AA011503), and Fundamental Research Funds for the Central Universities (No. ZYGX2012J025).

References

1. L Itti, C Koch, E Niebur, A model of saliency-based visual attention for rapid scene analysis. IEEE Trans. Pattern Anal. Mach. Intell. **20**(11), 1254–1259 (1998)
2. S Kastner, LG Ungerleider, Mechanisms of visual attention in the human cortex. Ann. Rev. Neurosci. **23**, 315–341 (2000)
3. HE Egeth, S Yantis, Visual attention: control, representation, and time course. Ann. Rev. Psychol. **48**, 269–297 (1997)
4. R Desimone, J Duncan, Neural mechanisms of selective visual attention. Ann. Rev. Neurosci. **18**, 193–222 (1995)
5. H Li, KN Ngan, Saliency model based face segmentation in head-and-shoulder video sequences. J. Vis. Commun. Image Represen. **19**(5), 320–333 (2008)
6. H Li, KN Ngan, Learning to extract focused objects from low DOF images. IEEE Trans. Circuits Syst. Video Technol. **21**(11), 1571–1580 (2011)
7. KC Liu, Prediction error preprocessing for perceptual image compression. EURASIP J. Image Video Process. **2012**, 3 (2012)
8. D Mahapatra, Y Sun, Rigid registration of renal perfusion images using a neurobiology-based visual saliency model. EURASIP J. Image Video Process. **2010**, 195640 (2010)
9. J You, G Liu, A novel attention model and its application in video analysis. Appl. Math. Comput. **185**(2), 963–975 (2007)
10. M Mancas, B Gosselin, B Macq, Perceptual image representation. EURASIP J. Image Video Process. **2007**, 098181 (2007)
11. N Bruce, JK Tsotsos, Saliency based on information maximization. Adv. Neural Inform. Process. Syst. **18**, 155–162 (2006)
12. W Luo, H Li, G Liu, KN Ngan, Global salient information maximization for saliency detection. Signal Process.: Image Commun. **27**(3), 238–248 (2012)
13. J Harel, C Koch, P Perona, Graph-based visual saliency. Adv. Neural Inform. Process. Syst. **19**, 545–552 (2006)
14. H Li, KN Ngan, A co-saliency model of image pairs. IEEE Trans. Image Process. **20**(12), 3365–3375 (2011)
15. F Meng, H Li, G Liu, KN Ngan, Object co-segmentation based on shortest path algorithm and saliency model. IEEE Trans. Multimedia **14**(5), 1429–1441 (2012)
16. H Li, F Meng, KN Ngan, Co-salient object detection from multiple images. IEEE Trans. Multimedia **15**(8), 1896–1909 (2013)
17. T Liu, J Sun, NN Zheng, X Tang, HY Shum, Learning to detect a salient object, in *Proceedings of IEEE Conference on Computer Vision and Pattern Recognition (CVPR)* (Minneapolis, 18–23 June 2007), pp. 1–8
18. J Li, Y Tian, T Huang, W Gao, Multi-task rank learning for visual saliency estimation. IEEE Trans. Circuits Syst. Video Technol. **21**(5), 623–636 (2011)
19. D Walther, C Koch, Modeling attention to salient proto-objects. Neural Netw. **19**(9), 1395–1407 (2006)
20. R Achanta, F Estrada, P Wils, S Süsstrunk, Salient region detection and segmentation, in *Proceedings of International Conference on Computer Vision Systems (ICVS)*, vol. 5008 (Santorini, 12–15 May 2008), pp. 66–75
21. R Achanta, S Hemami, F Estrada, S Süsstrunk, Frequency-tuned salient region detection, in *Proceedings of IEEE Conference on Computer Vision and Pattern Recognition (CVPR)* (Miami, 20–25 June 2009), pp. 1597–1604
22. MM Cheng, GX Zhang, NJ Mitra, X Huang, SM Hu, Global contrast based salient region detection, in *Proceedings of IEEE Conference on Computer Vision and Pattern Recognition (CVPR)* (Colorado Springs, 20–25 June 2011), pp. 409–416
23. T Judd, K Ehinger, F Durand, A Torralba, Learning to predict where humans look, in *Proceedings of IEEE International Conference on Computer Vision (ICCV)* (Kyoto, 27 Sept–4 Oct 2009), pp. 2106–2113
24. D Gao, N Vasconcelos, Decision-theoretic saliency: computational principles, biological plausibility, and implications for neurophysiology and psychophysics. Neural Comput. **21**, 239–271 (2009)
25. KA Sundberg, JF Mitchell, JH Reynolds, Spatial attention modulates center-surround interactions in macaque visual area V4. Neuron **61**(6), 952–963 (2009)
26. DH Kelly, Motion and vision.I. Stabilized images of stationary gratings. J. Opt. Soc. Am. **69**, 1266–1274 (1979)
27. JR Cavanaugh, W Bair, JA Movshon, Nature and interaction of signals from the receptive field center and surround in macaque V1 neurons. J. Neurophysiol. **88**(5), 2530–2546 (2002)
28. K Herrmann, L Montaser-Kouhsari, M Carrasco, DJ Heeger, When size matters: attention affects performance by contrast or response gain. Nat. Neurosci. **13**(12), 1554–1559 (2010)
29. L Xu, H Li, L Zeng, Z Wang, G Liu, Saliency detection using a central stimuli sensitivity based model, in *Proceedings of IEEE International Symposium on Circuits and Systems (ISCAS)* (Beijing, 19–23 May 2013), pp. 945–949
30. C Koch, S Ullman, Shifts in selective visual attention: towards the underlying neural circuitry. Hum. Neurobiol. **4**, 219–227 (1985)
31. AM Treisman, G Gelade, A feature-integration theory of attention. Cogn. Psychol. **12**, 97–136 (1980)
32. S Frintrop, E Rome, HI Christensen, Computational visual attention systems and their cognitive foundation: a survey. ACM Trans. Appl. Percept. **7**, 6:1–6:39 (2010)
33. YF Ma, HJ Zhang, Contrast-based image attention analysis by using fuzzy growing, in *Proceedings of ACM International Conference of Multimedia* (Berkeley, 2–8 Nov 2003), pp. 374–381
34. R Achanta, S Süsstrunk, Saliency detection using maximum symmetric surround, in *Proceedings of IEEE International Conference on Image Processing (ICIP)* (Hong Kong, 26–29 Sept 2010), pp. 2653–2656
35. Y Hu, X Xie, W Ma, L Chia, D Rajan, Salient region detection using weighted feature maps based on the human visual attention model, in *Proceedings of Fifth Pacific Rim Conference on Multimedia* (Tokyo, 30 Nov–3 Dec 2004), pp. 993–1000
36. X Hou, L Zhang, Saliency detection: a spectral residual approach, in *Proceedings of IEEE Conference on Computer Vision and Pattern Recognition (CVPR)* (Minneapolis, 18–23 June 2007), pp. 1–8
37. Y Zhai, M Shah, Visual attention detection in video sequences using spatiotemporal cues, in *Proceedings of ACM International Conference of Multimedia* (Santa Barbara, 23–27 Oct 2006), pp. 815–824
38. F Perazzi, P Krähenbühl, Y Pritch, A Hornung, Saliency filters: contrast based filtering for salient region detection, in *Proceedings of IEEE Conference on Computer Vision and Pattern Recognition (CVPR)* (Providence, 16–21 June 2012), pp. 733–740
39. C Yang, L Zhang, H Lu, X Ruan, MH Yang, Saliency detection via graph-based manifold ranking, in *Proceedings of IEEE Conference on Computer Vision and Pattern Recognition (CVPR)* (Portland, 23–28 June 2013), pp. 3166–3173
40. X Li, H Lu, L Zhang, X Ruan, MH Yang, Saliency detection via dense and sparse reconstruction, in *Proceedings of IEEE International Conference on Computer Vision (ICCV)* (Sydney, 1–8 Dec 2013), pp. 2976–2983
41. W Wang, Y Wang, Q Huang, W Gao, Measuring visual saliency by site entropy rate, in *Proceedings of IEEE Conference on Computer Vision and Pattern Recognition (CVPR)* (San Francisco, 13–18 June 2010), pp. 2368–2375
42. L Itti, P Baldi, Bayesian surprise attracts human attention. Adv. Neural Inform. Process. Syst. **19**, 547–554 (2006)
43. D Gao, N Vasconcelos, Bottom-up saliency is a discriminant process, in *Proceedings of IEEE International Conference on Computer Vision (ICCV)* (Rio de Janeiro, 14–20 Oct 2007), pp. 1–6
44. DA Klein, S Frintrop, Center-surround divergence of feature statistics for salient object detection, in *Proceedings of IEEE International Conference on Computer Vision (ICCV)* (Barcelona, 6–13 Nov 2011), pp. 2214–2219
45. L Zhang, MH Tong, TK Marks, H Shan, GW Cottrell, SUN: a Bayesian framework for saliency using natural statistics. J. Vis. **8**(7), 1–20 (2008)
46. DR Vigo, J van de Weijer, T Gevers, Color edge saliency boosting using natural image statistics, in *Proceedings of IS&T's fifth European Conference on Colour in Graphics, Imaging, and Vision (CGIV)* (Joensuu, 14–17 June 2010), pp. 228–234

47. PN Belhumeur, JP Hespanha, DJ Kriegman, Eigenfaces Vs.Fisherfaces: recognition using class specific linear projection. IEEE Trans. Pattern Anal. Mach. Intell. **19**(7), 711–720 (1997)

48. MP Sceniak, DL Ringach, MJ Hawken, R Shapley, Contrast's effect on spatial summation by macaque V1 neurons. Nat. Neurosci. **2**(8), 733–739 (1999)

49. S Goferman, L Zelnik-Manor, A Talm, Context-aware saliency detection, in *Proceedings of IEEE Conference on Computer Vision and Pattern Recognition (CVPR)* (San Francisco, 13–18 June 2010), pp. 2376–2383

50. I van der Linde, U Rajashekar, AC Bovik, LK Cormack, DOVES: a database of visual eye movements. Spat. Vis. **22**(2), 161–177 (2009)

16

On required accuracy of mixed noise parameter estimation for image enhancement via denoising

Victoriya V Abramova[1], Sergey K Abramov[1], Vladimir V Lukin[1*], Karen O Egiazarian[2] and Jaakko T Astola[2]

Abstract

Characteristics of noise (type, statistics, spatial correlation) are nowadays exploited in many image denoising and enhancement methods. However, these characteristics are often unknown, and they have to be extracted from an image at hand. There are many powerful and accurate blind methods for noise variance estimation for the cases of additive and multiplicative noise models. However, more complicated noise models containing a mixture of signal-independent (SI) and signal-dependent (SD) components are often more adequate in practice. Parameters of both components have to be automatically estimated to be used in image enhancement. This paper addresses a question of required accuracy of such estimation. Analysis is carried out for color images processed by a filter based on discrete cosine transform. The influence of errors in mixed noise parameters estimation is studied in terms of filtering efficiency. This efficiency is characterized by the conventional criterion peak signal-to-noise ratio (PSNR) and two visual quality metrics, PSNR human visual system masking (PSNR-HVS-M) and multi-scale structural similarity (MSSIM). If a reduction of filtering efficiency exceeds 0.5 dB (in terms of PSNR and PSNR-HVS-M) or 0.005 (in terms of MSSIM), mixed noise parameters estimation is assumed to be unacceptable. As the result, it is shown that SI and SD noise parameters have to be estimated with a relative error not exceeding 20%…30%.

Keywords: Mixed noise; Blind variance estimation; Filtering efficiency; Visual quality

1. Introduction

Imaging systems (sensors) are widely used in various applications such as remote sensing, non-destructive control, medical diagnostics, photography, etc. [1]. Some acquired images need a special pre-processing (e.g., denoising, deblurring, edge detection, compression [2-4], etc.) for further exploitation (e.g., object recognition, visual inspection, diagnostics, etc.). In order to enhance an image using, e.g., modern image denoising methods based on wavelets [5-7] or discrete cosine transform (DCT) [8,9] transforms, one has to know a noise type and its basic characteristics such as probability density function (PDF), variance, or two-dimensional (2D) spatial correlation function (if the observed noise is not independent and identically distributed (i.i.d.)). Proper thresholds in edge detection and image segmentation depend on noise statistics as well [1,10]. In lossy image compression, a

quantization step has to be adaptively adjusted depending on noise variance [11].

A practical problem is that *a priori* information on noise type and basic characteristics is not always available. Although there are such applications as synthetic aperture radar (SAR) imaging with known number of looks and image forming mode for which speckle characteristics can be accurately predicted [10], it appears a more practical situation when noise characteristics are fully or partly unknown (unavailable). For example, for color images acquired by digital cameras, noise properties are determined by camera settings, illumination conditions, and other factors [9,11-13]. Similarly, noise characteristics might be considerably different in sub-band images of multi- and hyperspectral remote sensing data acquired from airborne and space-borne platforms [14-16].

Then, a task of blind estimation of noise characteristics for each particular image subject to further processing, in particular, denoising [9,11,12] becomes of prime importance. General requirements to the methods intended for

* Correspondence: lukin@ai.kharkov.com
[1]National Aerospace University, Kharkov 61070, Ukraine
Full list of author information is available at the end of the article

blind (automatic) estimation of additive and multiplicative noise variance can be found in [8,17]. Clearly, it is desirable to provide almost unbiased estimates with estimation variance as small as possible. It is also needed to ensure applicability of a method to images of different content (including highly textural ones) and different noise levels (intensities) including non-intensive noise. A blind estimation method is practical if it is fast enough.

Moreover, for the methods of pure additive or multiplicative noise variance estimation, it has been established that the estimation relative error in practice should not be larger than ±20% [8,18]. If an obtained variance estimate is outside this limit, under- or oversmoothing takes place in image denoising based on blind estimation result.

With a new generation of sensors, signal-dependent noise models have become more popular since they describe noise statistics better [8,9,11-13,15,16,19,20]. There is an essential interest in design and testing the methods for blind estimation of mixed noise parameters [9,12,15,16,21,22]. However, to our best knowledge, it has not been studied yet how accurate have to be these estimates. It is worth mentioning that dependence of noise variance on signal (local mean in images) can be set parametrically, i.e., by some polynomial [9,12,15,22]. To avoid difficulties of polynomial order choice, we consider below a simplest case of mixed noise where SD and SI components are characterized by one parameter each. This model is typical in raw data in digital photos [9,11], sub-band images of hyperspectral remote sensing data [15,16] and radar images formed by multi-look SARs and side-look aperture radars [21,22].

Being applied at the first stage of image processing chain [8,9,11,12], blind estimation of noise parameters provides data for next stages. Therefore, accuracy of blind estimation has to be analyzed in the combination with efficiency of further image processing. Since image filtering is one of the most common operations (stages) of image processing chain, we have decided to carry out our analysis just from the viewpoint of filtering efficiency. We consider estimation accuracy acceptable if estimation errors that always happen in practice do not produce essential reduction of image denoising efficiency. In the next sections of the paper, we give quantitative definition of what is essential. We characterize image filtering efficiency not only by the conventional criteria, such as peak signal-to-noise ratio (PSNR) (or mean square error (MSE)), but also using metrics that describe image visual quality [23]. This is important since for many considered applications, visual quality of filtered images has a great importance (e.g., digital photography, medical imaging). The main goal of this paper is to give practical recommendations (requirements) on accuracy of mixed noise parameters estimation to ensure efficient image filtering.

2. Noise models and estimated parameters

In general, noise is considered signal-dependent if its statistical characteristics (variance, PDF) depend upon information signal (image). A typical example of signal-dependent noise is Poisson noise for which variance is equal to the true value of image pixel $\sigma_{sd}^2 = I^{tr}$ and noise PDF changes. It is close to Gaussian for large true values but considerably differs from Gaussian if I^{tr} is small (less than 12). Other examples of signal-dependent noise are film-grain noise and speckle [24,25]. For all these cases, a dependence of signal-dependent noise variance on true value $\sigma_{sd}^2 = f(I^{tr})$ is monotonically increasing (although other character of this dependence is, in general, possible).

The aforementioned examples relate to the cases when there is a single source of noise. However, noise can originate from several different sources, for example, image pixel generation (photon counting, coherent processing of registered signals) and circuitry (thermal) noise [19]. Then, one deals with a mixed noise, such as mixed additive and impulse noise [26,27] where impulse noise usually originates from coding/decoding errors at image transmission via communication channels. However, here, we address another type of mixed noise that has SI and SD components. A prominent example is noise in modern imaging sensors namely dark noise, thermal noise, and photon-counting noise [19].

Here, we assume that noise sources are independent, and consider two typical models of the mixed noise consisting of two components, SI and SD. For the first model, noise variance depends on image true value as

$$\sigma_{sd}^2 = \sigma_{si}^2 + kI^{tr}, \tag{1}$$

where σ_{si}^2 is variance of SI noise, e.g., of dark current noise and k is a proportionality factor for SD component [9,15]. The model is valid for raw images acquired by digital cameras and sub-band images formed by hyperspectral sensors.

For the second model, typical for radar images [28], one has

$$\sigma_{sd}^2 = \sigma_{si}^2 + k(I^{tr})^2. \tag{2}$$

In both cases, we have dependencies that are fully described by two parameters, σ_{si}^2 and k, that have to be estimated in a blind manner and used in filtering (we assume that we know *a priori* which model, (1) or (2), fits the data). Moreover, in both cases, it is possible to find such I_t^{tr} that for $I^{tr} > I_t^{tr}$ the SD component is dominant and vice versa. It is also possible to determine which component is dominant for an entire considered test image. For this purpose, one has to calculate

$$\text{MSE}_{\text{inp}} = \sigma_{\text{si}}^2 + k \sum_{i=1}^{I_{IM}} \sum_{j=1}^{J_{IM}} I_{ij}^{tr} / (I_{IM} J_{IM}) \qquad (3)$$

for the model (1) and

$$\text{MSE}_{\text{inp}} = \sigma_{\text{si}}^2 + k \sum_{i=1}^{I_{IM}} \sum_{j=1}^{J_{IM}} \left(I_{ij}^{tr} \right)^2 / (I_{IM} J_{IM}) \qquad (4)$$

for the model (2), where I_{IM}, J_{IM} define image size. If MSE_{inp} is twice larger than σ_{si}^2, the impact of SD noise can be considered prevailing (the SD noise is considered dominant) and vice versa. Note that MSE_{inp} can be also treated as equivalent variance of the noise in original images.

Such preliminary analysis can be useful since both situations can be met in practice. For example, SI noise is usually assumed to be dominant for sub-band images formed by old generation sensors, e.g., AVIRIS [14,15] while SI is prevailing for new generation sensors [15,16]. Thus, it is desirable to study both situations in our further analysis.

It is also supposed that noise is spatially uncorrelated. Although this is often not true in practice, this assumption simplifies our analysis. In the future, we plan to carry out similar analysis for spatially correlated noise as well.

3. Denoising method and quantitative criteria

There is a great number of denoising methods, especially for processing color images (note that just color image case for which enhancement is of great value will be analyzed below) [27,29,30]. However, here, we are not interested in image denoising methods that do not exploit information on noise type and statistics in their operation. Instead, we have to focus on filtering methods able to adapt to quite complex types of signal-dependent noise [8,9,31] described by the models (1) and (2).

Then, there are two possible approaches. The first one is to apply a variance-stabilizing transformation [32,33] that converts an image corrupted by a given type of signal-dependent noise to an image corrupted by an additive noise and then to apply a filter designed to suppress an additive noise. For the model (1), this can be done by, e.g., generalized Anscombe transformation [33].

The second possibility is to apply denoising methods that can be adapted to signal-dependent nature of the noise. Since the DCT-based filtering allows to do this easily [34,35], we concentrate below on this method of denoising. The DCT-based filtering [34,35] is carried out in blocks of a limited support, usually 8 × 8 pixels. This feature of the DCT-based filtering allows easy adaptation to non-stationary (signal-dependent) properties of the noise. Direct DCT is performed in each block. Then, a

thresholding of DCT coefficients (hard, soft, or combined [36]) is performed for all coefficients except DC. Here, we focus on hard thresholding since it is simple and the most efficient in terms of provided output PSNR [36].

For signal-dependent noise, absolute values of DCT coefficients in an 8 × 8 block, $D(n, m, q, s)$, have to be compared with a threshold $T(n,m) = \beta \sqrt{f(\bar{I}_{nm})}$, where indices n,m define a block upper left corner, $q = 0,..,7$, $s = 0,...,7$ are indices of DCT coefficients in 8 × 8 blocks, $\bar{I}_{nm}$ is nm-th block local mean, and β is a constant. Hard thresholding operation is resulting in assigning to zero those coefficients ($D(n, m, q, s)$, $q = 0,...,7$, $s = 0,...,7$ (except DC component with $q = 0$ and $s = 0$) which absolute value is below the threshold: $|D(n, m, q, s)| < T(n, m)$, and keeping all others unchanged (for each possible position of a block). After this, an inverse DCT is applied to the thresholded DCT coefficients in each block. Here, we consider the DCT-based filtering with full overlapping (shifting by one position to the next window), thus, multiple denoised (filtered) values are obtained for each image pixel (except those ones placed at the image corners). These multiple denoised values of the same pixel coming from different windows are averaged. This procedure is similar to a translation invariant wavelet shrinkage, where instead of block DCTs, wavelet transform of an image and all possible shifted version of it are performed. This allows to improve a denoising performance and to diminish blocking artifacts with respect to the case of filtering performed in non-overlapping blocks. Note also, that in the case of fully overlapping blocks, DCT-based filtering efficiency is close to that of the state-of-the-art filters [23] such as, e.g., BM3D [37]. This is one more reason why the DCT-based filtering was selected in our analysis.

Usually, the value of β recommended in hard thresholding is 2.6 [36] although one can find slightly different recommendations [38] which we will discuss later.

Then, for the spatially uncorrelated signal-dependent noise models (1) and (2), one gets

$$T(n, m) = 2.6 \sqrt{\sigma_{si}^2 + k \bar{I}_{nm}} \qquad (5)$$

and

$$T(n, m) = 2.6 \sqrt{\sigma_{si}^2 + k \bar{I}_{nm}^2}, \qquad (6)$$

respectively. In practice, if σ_{si}^2 and k are estimated, the obtained estimates of these parameters are to be used in (5) and (6).

A traditional approach to filter efficiency characterization and comparison to other filters is to calculate and analyze output MSE or PSNR. In this paper, we mainly consider R component of RGB color image.

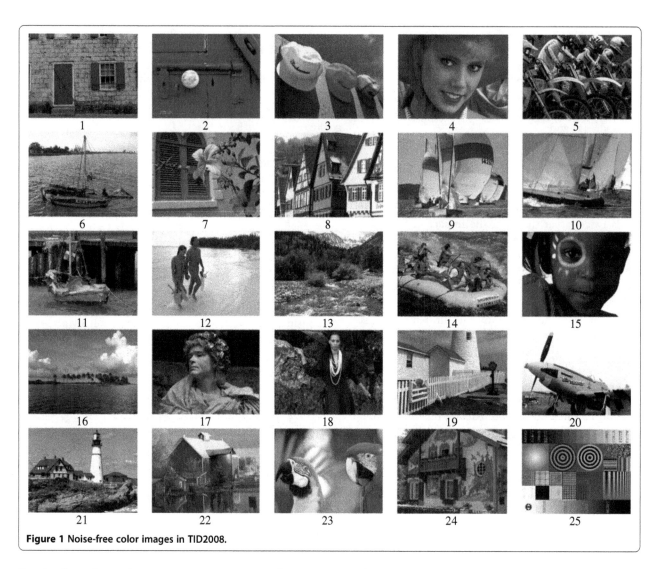

Figure 1 Noise-free color images in TID2008.

Results for other color components are in good agreement with those for the R component denoising (this will be shown by particular examples).

Since we deal with color images (and their components) that are usually intended for visual inspection, visual quality of processed images is of a value. Thus, alongside with the conventional output PSNR (PSNR $= 10 \log_{10}(255^2/MSE_{out})$ where MSE_{out} denotes MSE after denoising), it is worth using visual quality metrics.

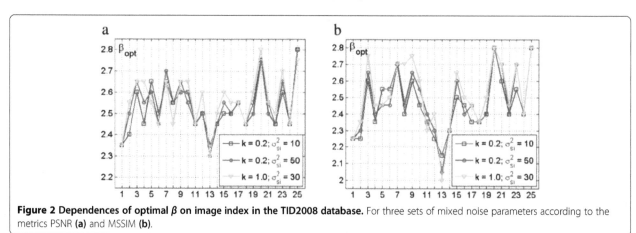

Figure 2 Dependences of optimal β on image index in the TID2008 database. For three sets of mixed noise parameters according to the metrics PSNR **(a)** and MSSIM **(b)**.

In our analysis, we have used two quality metrics inspired by human visual system (HVS). A first one is the recently proposed metric PSNR human visual system masking (PSNR-HVS-M) [39] (available at [40] and defined as PSNR-HVS-M = $10 \log_{10}(255^2/\text{MSE}_{\text{out}}^{\text{HVS}})$, where $\text{MSE}_{\text{out}}^{\text{HVS}}$ is a specific MSE determined in DCT domain that takes into account such peculiarities of human vision system as different sensitivity to distortions in different spatial frequencies and masking effects). This metric is among the best in characterizing visual quality of images corrupted by a noise as well as images with distortions due to filtering and compression [41]. PSNR-HVS-M is intended to assess visual quality of both grayscale and color images. Similarly to the conventional PSNR, the metric PSNR-HVS-M is expressed in decibels and larger values correspond to better visual quality. If PSNR-HVS-M exceeds 40 dB, distortions can be hardly noticed [42].

Another widely used HVS metric is multi-scale structural similarity (MSSIM) [43]. It takes into account human's ability to adapt to a structural similarity at different scales and HVS sensitivity to distortions of luminance and contrast. The metric values vary from 0 (extremely bad quality) to 1 (perfect or ideal quality). As it is seen, this metric has another range of variation where the value 0.99 corresponds to practical invisibility of distortions if they are spread over entire image [42]. While PSNR-HVS-M exploits discrete cosine transform in blocks for its calculation, MSSIM is based on wavelets. Thus, we can expect that if analysis of both metrics leads to drawing similar conclusions, then these conclusions will be well grounded.

Note that performance analysis of filtering efficiency is usually carried out under an assumption that noise characteristics are known in advance (or accurately pre-estimated) and filter parameters are set according to certain recommendations [6,9,31]. Recall that, in our case, the thresholds for blocks are set to

$$T(n, m) = \beta \sqrt{\hat{\sigma}_{si}^2 + \hat{k} \bar{I}_{nm}} \quad \text{or} \quad T(n, m) = \beta \sqrt{\hat{\sigma}_{si}^2 + \hat{k} \bar{I}_{nm}^2}$$

depending on the considered model where $\hat{\sigma}_{si}^2$ and $\hat{k}$ are model parameter estimates obtained by some technique. Thus, all three parameters, β, $\hat{\sigma}_{si}^2$ and $\hat{k}$, can influence filter performance. Besides, image properties have also an impact on efficiency of filtering.

Assume that statistical characteristics of the noise are not known in advance. Properties of image signal component (for example, its spatial spectrum in DCT or

PSNR = 30.99; PSNR-HVS-M = 35.42;
MSSIM = 0.931

PSNR = 30.53; PSNR-HVS-M = 34.93;
MSSIM = 0.927

Figure 3 The fragment of noise-free test image #13 and filtered results for accurate and erroneous estimates. The fragment of noise-free test image #13 **(a)**, its noisy ($k = 0.2$; $\sigma_{si}^2 = 50$) **(b)** version for red component and filtered results for accurate estimates ($\delta_V = 0$; $\delta_k = 0$) **(c)** and for erroneous estimates ($\delta_V = 0.4$; $\delta_k = 0.3$) **(d)** of the noise parameters.

wavelet domain) are also unknown since an observed image is noisy. Thus, to partly simplify the situation, we have, at least, to set the parameter β fixed. Let us demonstrate that setting β equal to 2.6 is a good choice for the considered hard threshold DCT filter with full overlapping of blocks.

To demonstrate this, we have considered several sets (combinations) of the parameters σ_{si}^2 and k for the model (1) to simulate the cases of dominant additive noise and dominant signal-dependent noise with different intensities. Besides, we have carried out tests for 25 color images from the database TID2008 [41]. It contains noise-free images where there are 24 images of natural scenes (Kodak images) and one (the 25th) is artificially created (see Figure 1). This allows simulating noisy images with pre-determined statistical characteristics of the mixed noise described by the considered models (1) and (2) easily.

The optimal values of β that provide minimal output MSE (maximal output PSNR) for the red component are presented for three sets of the parameters σ_{si}^2 and k for the model (1) in Figure 2a (the corresponding dependences for other color components are very similar).

The model parameters are set so that either additive noise is prevailing ($k = 0.2$; $\sigma_{si}^2 = 50$), or signal-dependent noise is dominant ($k = 1$; $\sigma_{si}^2 = 30$), or impact of both noise components is comparable ($k = 0.2$, $\sigma_{si}^2 = 10$).

The observed tendencies are the following. First, the average value of β is really about 2.6 for all three sets of the noise parameters. Second, there are complex structure images (e.g., the test images #1 and #13) for which optimal β are slightly smaller than 2.6. There are also simple structure images (#3, 7, 20, 23, 25) for which the optimal β can be slightly larger than 2.6, especially if noise is quite intensive (e.g., $k = 1$ and $\sigma_{si}^2 = 30$).

Dependences for the metric MSSIM (Figure 2b) are very similar. The only difference is that optimal values of β are by about 3% smaller than for the corresponding cases in Figure 2a. This tendency has been earlier observed in [38]. It can be explained by the fact that by setting a slightly smaller β one provides better edge/detail/texture preservation while noise suppression in homogeneous image regions becomes worse. This is just the case when a filtered image is perceived as having better visual quality. Dependences of optimal β for another HVS metric, PSNR-HVS-M (not presented in the paper),

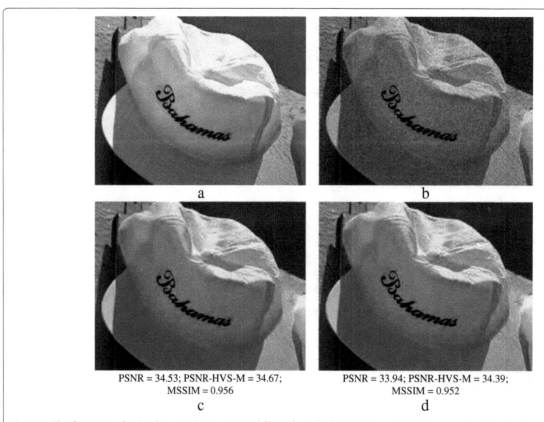

a	b
PSNR = 34.53; PSNR-HVS-M = 34.67; MSSIM = 0.956 c	PSNR = 33.94; PSNR-HVS-M = 34.39; MSSIM = 0.952 d

Figure 4 The fragment of noise-free test image #03 and filtered results for accurate and erroneous estimates. The fragment of noise-free test image #03 **(a)**, its noisy ($k = 1.0$; $\sigma_{si}^2 = 30$) **(b)** version for red component and filtered results for accurate estimates ($\delta_V = 0$; $\delta_k = 0$) **(c)** and for erroneous estimates ($\delta_V = -0.5$; $\delta_k = -0.2$) **(d)** of the noise parameters.

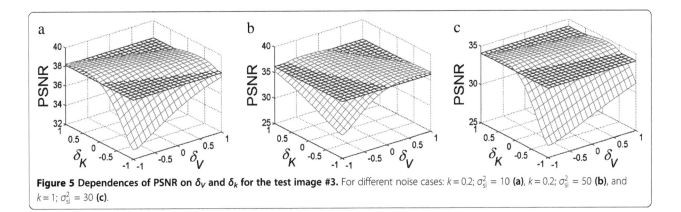

Figure 5 Dependences of PSNR on δ_V and δ_k for the test image #3. For different noise cases: $k = 0.2$; $\sigma_{si}^2 = 10$ **(a)**, $k = 0.2$; $\sigma_{si}^2 = 50$ **(b)**, and $k = 1$; $\sigma_{si}^2 = 30$ **(c)**.

are similar to those ones for PSNR. The difference is again in smaller optimal β similarly to MSSIM.

For more detailed analysis, we have further concentrated on two color images from the database TID2008 [41], namely the test image #3 (one of the simplest) and the test image #13 (the most complex one) (see Figure 1) since, according to our previous experience [17,18], just these marginal cases determine basic requirements. The test image #25 has not been chosen since it is artificial and we are more interested in enhancing natural scene images. The test image #20 has not been used for the analysis since clipping (overexposure) effects occur for it in bright upper region that corresponds to sky.

Our idea is that a joint analysis of filtering efficiency for these two images carried out for different noise parameters' sets can produce initial insight on basic requirements to an accuracy of blind estimation of noise parameters σ_{si}^2 and k. We assume that these requirements will be correct for the majority of real-life images. At the end of the paper, we will check validity of these requirements for two extreme cases and for entire database of images corrupted by mixed noise with different sets of parameters.

Thus, we assume that the DCT-based filter parameter β is set to be equal to 2.6 but the estimates of σ_{si}^2 and k obtained by some technique and then used in filtering can be erroneous. To characterize these estimates, let us use the parameters

$$\delta_V = \left(\hat{\sigma}_{si}^2 - \sigma_{si}^2\right)/\sigma_{si}^2 \quad \text{and} \quad \delta_k = \left(\hat{k} - k\right)/k, \qquad (7)$$

where $\hat{\sigma}_{si}^2$ and k are estimates of σ_{si}^2 and k, respectively. Then, $\delta_V = 0$ and $\delta_k = 0$ correspond to true values of σ_{si}^2 and k; $\delta_V = -1$ relates to the case when the additive noise component is absent. Similarly, $\delta_k = -1$ corresponds to assumption that the signal-dependent noise component is absent and the present noise is pure additive. The case $\delta_V = -1$ and $\delta_k = -1$ relates to the case of no filtering applied, i.e., to a noisy image.

In our experiments, we have analyzed δ_V and δ_k ranging from -1 to $+1$ (from -100% to $+100\%$), that is for $\delta_V = 1$ and/or $\delta_k = 1$, it is assumed that the estimates of $\hat{\sigma}_{si}^2$ and $\hat{k}$ are twice (by 100%) larger than the true values of these parameters. According to our experience [22], practical estimates are rarely outside these limits.

An important question is what is considerable (essential) impact of errors in parameter estimation on filtering efficiency? Our proposition is to consider that impact is essential if PSNR or PSNR-HVS-M reduction is more than 0.5 dB compared to PSNR or PSNR-HVS-M observed for $\delta_V = 0$ and $\delta_k = 0$, i.e., for perfect (recommended) settings. The value 0.5 dB is selected since such a difference in output PSNR or PSNR-HVS-M is noticeable if filtered images are visually inspected together (compared). This statement follows from our experience in creation and exploitation of the database TID2008 [41] (e.g., the difference equal to 3 dB for a given filtered image is easily recognized by any observer). To partly prove this, Figure 3 presents a fragment of the noise-free color image #13 (Figure 3a), its noisy version for the red components (model (1), $\sigma_{si}^2 = 50$ and $k = 0.2$, Figure 3b), the filtered image fragment under assumption that one has accurate estimates of the noise parameters ($\delta_V = 0$ and $\delta_k = 0$, Figure 3c) and the same fragment in the case of erroneous estimates ($\delta_V = 0.4$ and $\delta_k = 0.3$, i.e., noise parameters are both overestimated, Figure 3d). For the latter two images, the values of all three metrics are presented. Reduction of PSNR and PSNR-HVS-M for the image in Figure 3d compared to the image in Figure 3c is about 0.5 dB. Due to

Table 1 Simulation data for the test image #3, noise model (1), PSNR metric

k	σ_{si}^2	MSE_{inp}	PSNR ($\delta_V =$ -1, $\delta_k = -1$)	PSNR ($\delta_V =$ -0, $\delta_k = -0$)	max_{PSNR}	δ_{Vmax}	δ_{kmax}
0.2	10	32.66	32.99	38.64	38.65	0.3	−0.1
0.2	50	72.62	29.52	36.58	36.62	0.4	−0.7
1.0	30	144.01	26.55	34.52	34.57	1	−0.2

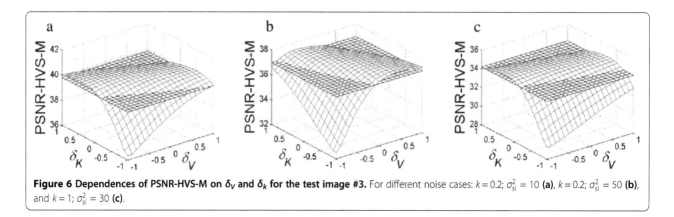

Figure 6 Dependences of PSNR-HVS-M on δ_V and δ_k for the test image #3. For different noise cases: $k = 0.2$; $\sigma_{si}^2 = 10$ **(a)**, $k = 0.2$; $\sigma_{si}^2 = 50$ **(b)**, and $k = 1$; $\sigma_{si}^2 = 30$ **(c)**.

overestimation of both parameters of the mixed noise, oversmoothing is observed. It mainly appears itself in smearing low contrast texture (bushes) in the central part of the picture in Figure 3d. The reduction of the metric MSSIM is observed as well. For the case considered in Figure 3, reduction is equal to 0.004.

Besides, Figure 4 represents images for another case. The simple structure image #3 (its noise-free color version is presented in Figure 4a) is corrupted by rather intensive signal-dependent noise with $\sigma_{si}^2 = 30$ and $k = 1.0$ (Figure 4b, red component). Noise is well visible, especially in image homogeneous regions. Figure 4c presents the denoised image under assumption that mixed noise parameters are estimated absolutely accurately. Meanwhile, Figure 4d represents the output image obtained in the case of underestimation of mixed noise parameters. As it is seen, underestimation leads to residual noise that appears itself clearly in image homogeneous regions. Again, reduction of PSNR and PSNR-HVS-M is close to 0.5 dB while decrease of MSSIM is close to 0.005.

Thus, both underestimation and overestimation of the mixed noise parameters are undesirable. Underestimation is crucial for simple structure images and overestimation is undesired for complex structure images.

We have checked other test images and other noise parameter sets. Analysis carried out for all images in TID2008 has shown that reduction of PSNR and PSNR-HVS-M by about 0.5 dB approximately corresponds to MSSIM reduction by 0.005. Note that all three dependences are nonlinear and there is no strict relationship between them. The only observation is that if PSNR-HVS-M decreases, MSSIM usually diminishes as well and vice versa.

Thus, our approach to analysis consists in the following. The first task is to determine 2D areas of δ_V and δ_k where reduction is smaller than 0.5 dB according to the metrics PSNR and PSNR-HVS-M or smaller than 0.005 according to MSSIM for each considered image and each set of mixed noise parameters. It is assumed that if the mixed noise parameters' estimates are within these areas, the estimation errors do not essentially influence the filtering accuracy.

Note that in addition to three aforementioned sets of mixed noise parameters for the model (1), we consider below one set (combination) of σ_{si}^2 and k for the model (2) to simulate the real-life situation for which the multiplicative noise is dominant. Then, at the second stage, the obtained areas have to be aggregated by AND rule to provide final requirements to estimation accuracy under assumption that neither noise statistics nor image properties are available in advance.

4. Analysis of results

The obtained dependences of output PSNR on δ_V and δ_k are presented as 2D surfaces (see Figure 5) of red color. Black color horizontal surface corresponds to the levels PSNR($\delta_V = 0$, $\delta_k = 0$) – 0.5, dB and PSNR-HVS-M($\delta_V = 0$, $\delta_k = 0$) – 0.5, dB, respectively. Thus, it is easy to see for which area of δ_V and δ_k filtering efficiency is acceptable for each particular case (red color surface is over black one).

Three combinations of k and σ_{si}^2 are considered, namely, $k = 0.2$, $\sigma_{si}^2 = 10$; $k = 0.2$, $\sigma_{si}^2 = 50$; and $k = 1$, $\sigma_{si}^2 = 30$. For each combination, Table 1 presents the following data: MSE_{inp} to discriminate the cases of dominant signal-dependent or signal-independent noise; PSNR ($\delta_V = -1$, $\delta_k = -1$), i.e., for original noisy image; PSNR ($\delta_V = 0$, $\delta_k = 0$), i.e., for the image filtered with the recommended parameter under condition of absolutely accurate estimation of σ_{si}^2 and k; max $_{PSNR}$, i.e., maximal attained value and the values δ_{Vmax}, δ_{kmax} for which max$_{PSNR}$ has been provided.

Table 2 Simulation data for the test image #3, noise model (1), PSNR-HVS-M metric

k	σ_{si}^2	MSE_{inp}	PSNR-HVS-M ($\delta_V = -1$, $\delta_k = -1$)	PSNR-HVS-M ($\delta_V = -0$, $\delta_k = -0$)	max$_{PSNR-}$ HVS-M	$\delta_{Vmaxvis}$	$\delta_{kmaxvis}$
0.2	10	32.66	36.32	40.29	40.30	0.2	−0.1
0.2	50	72.62	32.45	37.45	37.47	0.2	−0.5
1.0	30	144.01	29.22	34.67	34.68	0.7	−0.2

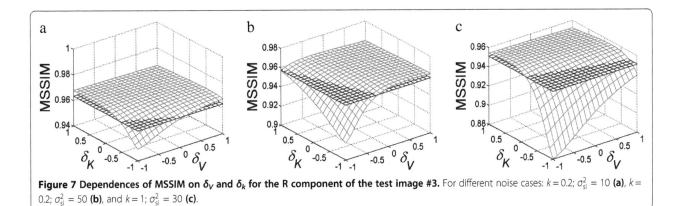

Figure 7 Dependences of MSSIM on δ_V and δ_k for the R component of the test image #3. For different noise cases: $k = 0.2$; $\sigma_{si}^2 = 10$ **(a)**, $k = 0.2$; $\sigma_{si}^2 = 50$ **(b)**, and $k = 1$; $\sigma_{si}^2 = 30$ **(c)**.

As it is seen, for two cases ($k = 0.2$, $\sigma_{si}^2 = 10$ and $k = 1$, $\sigma_{si}^2 = 30$), the SD noise component is dominant ($MSE_{inp} > 2$ σ_{si}^2). For the case $k = 0.2$, $\sigma_{si}^2 = 50$, the SI noise component is dominant. The first observation is that if noise is more intensive (compare the case $k = 1$, $\sigma_{si}^2 = 30$ to the case $k = 0.2$, $\sigma_{si}^2 = 10$), the DCT-based filtering is more efficient (PSNR($\delta_V = 0$, $\delta_k = 0$) differs more from the corresponding PSNR($\delta_V = -1$, $\delta_k = -1$)). In particular, PSNR ($\delta_V = 0$, $\delta_k = 0$) is larger by about 8 dB than PSNR ($\delta_V = -1$, $\delta_k = -1$) for the case $k = 1$, $\sigma_{si}^2 = 30$.

If the SD noise component is dominant (see the plots in Figure 5a, c), it does not matter too much how accurate the estimates $\hat{\sigma}_{si}^2$ are. It is considerably more important how accurate is the estimate of the SD noise parameter k. If $\hat{\sigma}_{si}^2$ is quite accurate (let us say, $|\delta_V| \leq 0.5$), then $|\delta_k|$ should be smaller than about 0.4. Thus, if the SD noise component is dominant, then the requirement to accuracy of k is stricter than the requirement to accuracy of $\hat{\sigma}_{si}^2$. This appears itself in the fact that a red surface 'strip' that is 'over' the corresponding threshold (black color surface) is oriented more parallel to the axis δ_V.

Another situation is observed if SI noise component is dominant (see the plot in Figure 5b). Then accuracy of estimating the parameter k is less important, but the requirement to estimation of σ_{si}^2 is stricter. In fact, for the considered case, it is desirable to provide $|\delta_V|$ less than 0.3...0.4. The red surface 'strip' is oriented more parallel to the axis δ_k. Thus, initial conclusion is quite trivial - it is necessary to more accurately estimate the parameter for the noise component which is dominant.

If one parameter is overestimated, then it is desirable to have another parameter underestimated ($\hat{k} < k$) to provide rather efficient filtering (see the values δ_{Vmax} and δ_{kmax} in Table 1). It is better, if $\hat{\sigma}_{si}^2 > \sigma_{si}^2, \delta_V > 0$. The worst case is if both parameters, σ_{si}^2 and k, are underestimated. Then, undersmoothing is observed (look at data for $\delta_V \rightarrow -1$, $\delta_k \rightarrow -1$) and filtering efficiency is far from optimal (attainable). One more interesting observation that follows from analysis of data in Table 1 is that max_{PSNR} is only slightly (by 0.01...0.05 dB) larger than PSNR($\delta_V = 0$, $\delta_k = 0$). This shows that the practical recommendation (5) works well enough.

Consider now the dependences for the metric PSNR-HVS-M presented in Figure 6. The corresponding data are collected in Table 2. For each combination, Table 2 presents the values of PSNR-HVS-M($\delta_V = -1$, $\delta_k = -1$)for original noisy images; PSNR-HVS-M($\delta_V = 0$, $\delta_k = 0$), i.e., for the images filtered with the recommended parameter under condition of absolutely accurate estimation of σ_{si}^2 and k; $max_{PSNR-HVS-M}$, i.e., maximal reachable value and the values $\delta_{Vmaxvis}$, $\delta_{kmaxvis}$ for which $max_{PSNR-HVS-M}$ has been attained.

From the very beginning, let us stress that the values PSNR-HVS-M($\delta_V = -1$, $\delta_k = -1$) are larger than the corresponding PSNR($\delta_V = -1$, $\delta_k = -1$). This is due to the masking effects [39]. As it is according to the metric PSNR, PSNR-HVS-M increases for the recommended setting of the DCT filter parameter β (compare PSNR-HVS-M ($\delta_V = 0$, $\delta_k = 0$) to PSNR-HVS-M($\delta_V = -1$, $\delta_k = -1$)). Visual quality improvement due to filtering is essential - from

Table 3 Simulation data for the test image #13, noise model (1), PSNR metric

k	σ_{si}^2	MSE_{inp}	PSNR ($\delta_V = -1, \delta_k = -1$)	PSNR ($\delta_V = -0, \delta_k = -0$)	max_{PSNR}	δ_{Vmax}	δ_{kmax}
0.2	10	32.0	33.08	33.91	33.96	−0.6	0
0.2	50	71.93	29.56	30.99	31.09	−0.3	0
1.0	30	140.24	26.66	28.64	28.77	−0.6	−0.1

Table 4 Simulation data for the test image #13, noise model (1), PSNR-HVS-M metric

k	σ_{si}^2	MSE_{inp}	PSNR-HVS-M ($\delta_V = -1, \delta_k = -1$)	PSNR-HVS-M ($\delta_V = -0, \delta_k = -0$)	$max_{PSNR-HVS-M}$	$\delta_{Vmaxvis}$	$\delta_{kmaxvis}$
0.2	10	32.0	40.08	40.36	40.45	−0.1	−0.4
0.2	50	71.93	34.90	35.42	35.56	−0.4	0
1.0	30	140.24	31.30	32.01	32.24	−0.7	−0.2

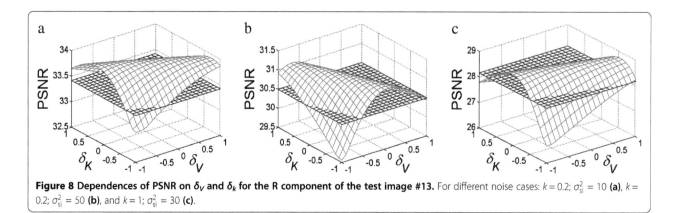

Figure 8 Dependences of PSNR on δ_V and δ_k for the R component of the test image #13. For different noise cases: $k = 0.2$; $\sigma_{si}^2 = 10$ **(a)**, $k = 0.2$; $\sigma_{si}^2 = 50$ **(b)**, and $k = 1$; $\sigma_{si}^2 = 30$ **(c)**.

about 4 dB for non-intensive noise ($k = 0.2$; $\sigma_{si}^2 = 10$), it reaches 5.5 dB for the case $k = 1$, $\sigma_{si}^2 = 30$. Note that PSNR-HVS-M($\delta_V = 0$, $\delta_k = 0$) for $k = 0.2$; $\sigma_{si}^2 = 10$ exceeds 40 dB, i.e., residual distortions in the filtered image are almost invisible [35].

The observed values $\max_{\text{PSNR–HVS-M}}$ practically do not differ from the corresponding PSNR-HVS-M($\delta_V = 0$, $\delta_k = 0$). Interestingly, all $\delta_{V\text{maxvis}}$ are larger than 0 while all $\delta_{k\text{maxvis}}$ are smaller than 0. This means that it is less risky to overestimate SI noise variance and underestimate the parameter k than to fall into other possible situations. Meanwhile, all $\delta_{V\text{maxvis}}$ (Table 2) are smaller than the corresponding $\delta_{V\text{max}}$ (see Table 1). This shows that for providing higher visual quality, it is undesirable to have considerable overestimation of mixed noise parameters. In some sense, it is equivalent to the recommendation to have β slightly smaller than 2.6 in threshold setting (5) to guarantee good visual quality of filtered image [38].

Figure 7 shows dependences of the metric MSSIM on δ_V and δ_k for the test image #3. The conclusions that can be drawn from their analysis are similar to those presented above. Overestimation of mixed noise parameters is less risky than underestimation. It is more important to correctly estimate the parameter of mixed noise

that corresponds to the dominant component of the noise.

Consider now the results for the test image #13 (Figures 1 or 3a). Again, we present data only for R component processed but the dependences for other color components are very similar. The dependences obtained for PSNR and PSNR-HVS-M are represented in Figures 8 and 9, respectively. Particular data are collected in Tables 3 and 4. Note that the cases $k = 0.2$, $\sigma_{si}^2 = 10$ and $k = 1$; $\sigma_{si}^2 = 30$, as earlier, correspond to the dominant SD noise component while the SI noise component is prevailing if $k = 0.2$; $\sigma_{si}^2 = 50$.

At the first glance, the dependences in Figures 8 and 9 are quite similar to the corresponding dependences in Figures 5 and 6. However, there are several distinctive differences. One of them is that filtering of the test image #13 is considerably less efficient than of the test image #3. Only for the most intensive noise ($k = 1$; $\sigma_{si}^2 = 30$), the difference between PSNR($\delta_V = 0$, $\delta_k = 0$) and PSNR for the original image (PSNR($\delta_V = -1$, $\delta_k = -1$)) reaches 2 dB. This difference is only 0.83 dB for the case $k = 0.2$; $\sigma_{si}^2 = 10$. The value $\max_{\text{PSNR}}$ is 0.05...0.13 dB larger than the corresponding PSNR($\delta_V = 0$, $\delta_k = 0$), and this takes place if $\delta_{V\text{max}} < 0$, i.e., if SI noise variance is underestimated and the parameter k is estimated properly (without error).

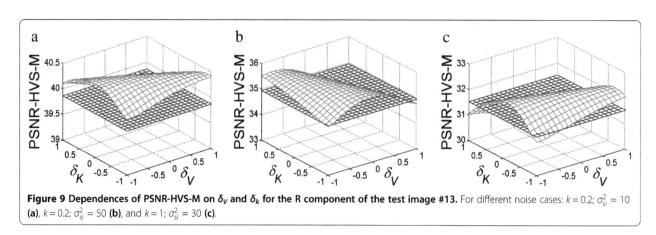

Figure 9 Dependences of PSNR-HVS-M on δ_V and δ_k for the R component of the test image #13. For different noise cases: $k = 0.2$; $\sigma_{si}^2 = 10$ **(a)**, $k = 0.2$; $\sigma_{si}^2 = 50$ **(b)**, and $k = 1$; $\sigma_{si}^2 = 30$ **(c)**.

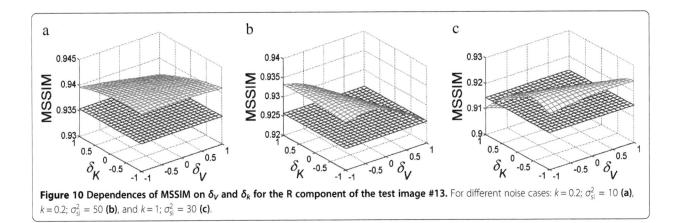

Figure 10 Dependences of MSSIM on δ_V and δ_k for the R component of the test image #13. For different noise cases: $k = 0.2$; $\sigma_{si}^2 = 10$ **(a)**, $k = 0.2$; $\sigma_{si}^2 = 50$ **(b)**, and $k = 1$; $\sigma_{si}^2 = 30$ **(c)**.

Overestimation of both parameters is severely undesirable since this leads to reduction of filtering efficiency and image oversmoothing (analyze data for $\delta_V \to 1$, $\delta_k \to 1$ where the dependences PSNR(δ_V, δ_k) rapidly decrease if δ_V and δ_k increase).

Analysis of plots in Figure 9 and data in Table 4 leads to the same conclusions. Note that in the case $k = 0.2$; $\sigma_{si}^2 = 10$, PSNR-HVS-M increase due to filtering is only 0.28 dB, i.e., it is practically invisible. Only for $k = 1$;

$\sigma_{si}^2 = 30$ the value PSNR-HVS-M($\delta_V = 0$, $\delta_k = 0$) is by 0.71 dB larger than for the original image, i.e., there is a small noticeable improvement of visual quality. This means that if filtering is applied to improve visual quality of highly textural images based on mixed noise parameters estimated in a blind manner, then these estimates should not be essentially larger than true values of these parameters (i.e., in fact, it is desirable to have $\delta_V \leq 0$, $\delta_k \leq 0$).

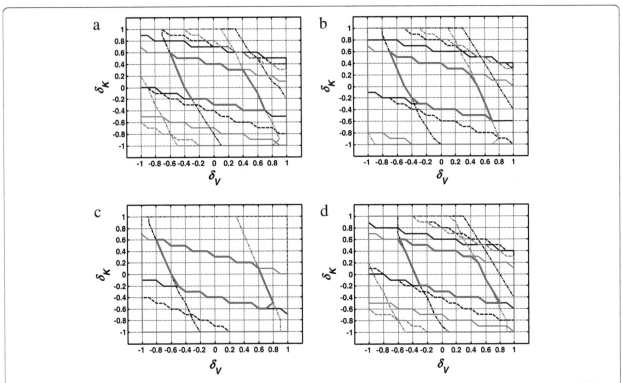

Figure 11 Areas of acceptable δ_V and δ_k for different noise cases with marked boundaries for appropriate estimation accuracy. (a) For PSNR; **(b)** for PSNR-HVS-M and **(c)** for MSSIM metrics for red color component and **(d)** for PSNR for green color component. Notations used: black color for image #3, red color for image #13, solid line for the case $k = 1$; $\sigma_{si}^2 = 30$; dashed line for the case $k = 0.2$; $\sigma_{si}^2 = 10$; dashed-dotted line for the case $k = 0.2$; $\sigma_{si}^2 = 50$.

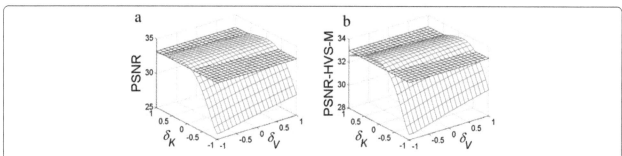

Figure 12 Dependences of PSNR (a) and PSNR-HVS-M (b) on δ_V and δ_k for the test image #3. With noise simulated according model (2) for $k = 0.01$ and $\sigma_{si}^2 = 20$.

Figure 10 presents the obtained results for the metric MSSIM. Their analysis also shows that overestimation of mixed noise parameters is severely undesirable for this (highly textural) test image. Parameter that relates to a dominant component of the mixed noise has to be estimated more accurately.

Let us now aggregate the obtained results for three noise parameter combinations and two test images of sufficiently different complexity. For this purpose, we have marked the 'allowed' 2D areas of mixed noise parameter estimates to be acceptable (see Figure 11 and description of notations used) and determined a joint acceptable area (where all areas overlap). This area is indicated by solid (blue) line and is located in the central part (horizontal axis corresponds to δ_V and vertical to δ_k). Although all particular areas are of rather large size, their intersection is, certainly, smaller. However, it is still quite large. In the worst case, $|\delta_k| = 0.2$ and $|\delta_V| = 0.3$ (see Figure 11a). The conclusions that can be drawn from analysis of the area according to the metric PSNR-HVS-M (Figure 11b) are practically the same. The intersection area obtained for the metric MSSIM (Figure 11c) almost coincides with that for the metric PSNR.

To show that the results obtained for other color components are similar to the results obtained for the red component, Figure 11d presents intersection areas for the green component according to the metric PSNR. Comparison of the obtained acceptable areas to the corresponding areas presented in Figure 11a shows that there is no essential difference.

Let us consider now the data for the model (2). Only one case has been simulated: $k = 0.01$, $\sigma_{si}^2 = 20$. The dependences of PSNR and PSNR-HVSM on δ_V and δ_k for the R component of the test image #3 are presented in Figure 12. The data are collected in Tables 5 and 6.

As it is seen, the multiplicative noise is dominant. Because of this, the parameter k has to be estimated with higher accuracy than the parameter σ_{si}^2. PSNR and PSNR-HVS-M improvement due to filtering is quite large, about 8 dB for PSNR and about 5 dB for PSNR-

HVS-M. Similarly, Figure 13 presents dependences of PSNR and PSNR-HVS-M on δ_V and δ_k for the R component of the test image #13.

The data are given in Tables 5 and 6, respectively. In this case, PSNR and PSNR-HVS-M improvement for accurately estimated k and σ_{si}^2 (see data for $\delta_V = 0$, $\delta_k = 0$) is considerably smaller than for the test image #3. The requirement to accuracy of the parameter k estimation is stricter than to estimation accuracy of the parameter σ_{si}^2 although the estimation errors with $|\delta_k| \leq 0.2$ are still acceptable. Overestimation of the parameter k is especially undesirable.

A shortcoming of the analysis carried out above is that only two test images (although with essentially different properties) and only four (totally) sets of mixed noise parameters (although quite different) have been considered. Thus, let us also study two extreme cases. According to the previous analysis, the strictest restrictions are observed for the following cases: (a) a complex structure image corrupted by non-intensive noise with obvious dominance of one component, for example, additive; (b) a simple structure image corrupted by intensive noise with one prevailing component, for example, signal dependent of the model (2).

For the case a, we have used the test image #1 from the database TID2008 (Figure 1). The model (1) noise has been simulated with $k = 0.01$ and $\sigma_{si}^2 = 25$. These settings relate to, e.g., the practical case of noisy (junk) component images acquired by old generation hyperspectral sensors [8]. For the case b, the test image #23 from TID2008 (Figure 1) that is one of the simplest

Table 5 Simulation data for the test image #3 and 13, noise model (2), PSNR metric

Image no.	k	σ_{si}^2	MSE_{inp}	PSNR ($\delta_V = -1$, $\delta_k = -1$)	PSNR ($\delta_V = -0$, $\delta_k = -0$)	max_{PSNR}	δ_{Vmax}	δ_{kmax}
3	0.01	20	171.67	25.78	33.66	33.70	0.6	0
13	0.01	20	168.90	25.85	28.02	28.10	−0.6	−0.1

Table 6 Simulation data for the test image #3 and 13, noise model (2), PSNR-HVS-M metric

Image No	k	σ^2_{si}	MSE_{inp}	PSNR-HVS-M ($\delta_V = -1$, $\delta_k = -1$)	PSNR-HVS-M ($\delta_V = -0$, $\delta_k = -0$)	$max_{PSNR-HVS-M}$	$\delta_{Vmaxvis}$	$\delta_{kmaxvis}$
3	0.01	20	171.67	28.46	33.48	33.49	0.6	−0.1
13	0.01	20	168.90	30.32	31.24	31.39	−0.8	−0.2

has been exploited. The model (2) noise has been generated with $k = 0.1$ and $\sigma^2_{si} = 10$. Such noise can be observed in images formed by multi-look synthetic aperture radars.

The obtained dependences of PSNR, PSNR-HVS-M, and MSSIM on δ_V and δ_k for the case a are presented in Figure 14. Obviously, σ^2_{si} has to be estimated with high accuracy and its overestimation is strongly undesirable. Quality improvement due to filtering is small even for the best settings.

The dependences for the case b are shown in Figure 15. It is seen that the parameter k has to be estimated correctly. Its underestimation can lead to considerable undersmoothing and is undesirable. In both extreme cases, it is still enough to estimate the dominant noise parameter with relative error not exceeding 0.2.

Finally, we have obtained intersection areas for two metrics (PSNR and PSNR-HVS-M) for all images (three components for each image) and all considered sets of signal-dependent noise models. These areas are shown in Figure 16. The first observation is that these acceptable areas are only slightly smaller than those ones presented earlier in Figure 11. Conclusions that follow from the analysis of these areas are the following. First, absolute values of both errors δ_V and δ_k should not, in general, be larger than 0.2. Second, as exceptional situation, it is possible that absolute values of one of these errors can be slightly larger than 0.2 (but in this case, another error should have the opposite sign). This property appears itself in non-circular (quasi-elliptical) shape of acceptable areas). Third, the acceptable area for the metric PSNR-HVS-M is slightly shifted with respect

to the acceptable area for the metric PSNR toward smaller values of both errors. In fact, this means that overestimation of mixed noise parameters is more risky for providing high visual quality of filtered images compared to the case of conventional analysis of denoising efficiency in terms of output MSE or PSNR.

Clearly, the way we followed in our analysis is not the only one possible. It is also possible to study tolerance of filtering techniques to ambiguity or inaccuracy of available *a priori* information in other ways. One of them can be based on simulating some estimates of noise parameters and using them instead of true values in denoising with statistical assessment of filtering efficiency. Following this way, we have assumed unbiased estimation of both parameters for the noise model (1) and estimates modeled as $\hat{k} = k + \Delta k$, $\hat{\sigma}^2_{si} = \hat{\sigma}^2_{si} + \Delta \hat{\sigma}^2_{si}$, where Δk and $\Delta \hat{\sigma}^2_{si}$ are mutually independent zero mean random variables supposed to be Gaussian with standard deviations δ_k and δ_v, respectively. Then, varying δ_k, δ_v, it is possible to simulate erroneous estimation for a set of realizations, to determine what are filtering criteria values (PSNR, PSNR-HVS-M, MSSIM) for each realization and to statistically process them with obtaining mean and standard deviation for each considered metric as well as confidence intervals.

Note that erroneous estimation of noise parameters leads to degradation of all metrics (reduction of their mean values compared to the corresponding optimal ones). Because of this, we have determined confidence interval width as $MCW = |MO - MM| + 3MS$, where MO determines optimal value of a visual quality metric for errorless noise parameters estimates; MM is mean

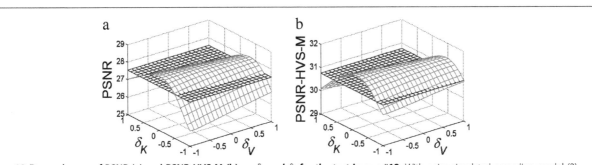

Figure 13 Dependences of PSNR (a) and PSNR-HVS-M (b) on δ_V and δ_k for the test image #13. With noise simulated according model (2) for $k = 0.01$ and $\sigma^2_{si} = 20$.

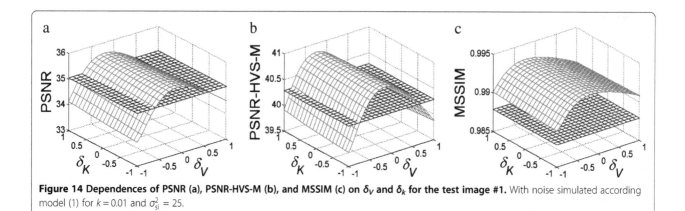

Figure 14 Dependences of PSNR (a), PSNR-HVS-M (b), and MSSIM (c) on δ_V and δ_k for the test image #1. With noise simulated according model (1) for $k = 0.01$ and $\sigma_{si}^2 = 25$.

value of a visual quality metric; MS is standard deviation of a visual quality metric.

Simulation results for the test images #3 and #13 for two sets of parameters for model (1) are presented in Table 7. Recall that we need MCW less than 0.5 dB for the metrics PSNR and PSNR-HVS-M and less than 0.005 for the metric MSSIM. Conditions for which these requirements are satisfied depend upon a test image and noise parameters. The larger values of δ_k, δ_v result in larger degradations of all metrics. However, the aforementioned requirements are usually satisfied if both δ_k, δ_v are smaller than 0.15. If these standard deviations are both equal to 0.25, requirements can be not satisfied. Thus, we come approximately to the same conclusions as in our previous analysis.

5. Conclusions and future work

The question of influence of mixed noise parameters estimation accuracy on filtering efficiency in image enhancement applications is studied. It is demonstrated that the parameter that corresponds to a dominant noise type has to be estimated with a higher accuracy. This accuracy is characterized by a relative error that should be less than 20% for the dominant noise type and less than 30% for another type of noise. Then, decrease of filtering

efficiency characterized by PSNR or PSNR-HVS-M drop compared to the optimum does not exceed 0.5 dB (MSSIM drop does not exceed 0.005), and thus, it is practically not noticeable (crucial). Note that these requirements practically coincide with requirements to accuracy of pure additive or pure multiplicative noise variance estimation [17] - an estimate has to differ from a true value by less than 20%. It is also important to stress that even the most advanced modern methods of blind estimation of mixed noise parameters do not always provide the required accuracy of parameters' estimation [44].

It is also shown that for highly textural images it is better to have underestimation of the mixed noise parameters than overestimation. Unfortunately, it happens in practice that mixed noise parameters are usually overestimated for complex structure images [22]. This motivates a design of more accurate methods for blind estimation including analysis of dependences between the estimates of components of the mixed noise.

Besides, in the future, we plan to concentrate on considering spatially correlated noise which is rather typical in practice. Other filters based on using estimated parameters of mixed noise can be studied as well since restrictions for them can differ from restrictions obtained for the DCT-based denoising.

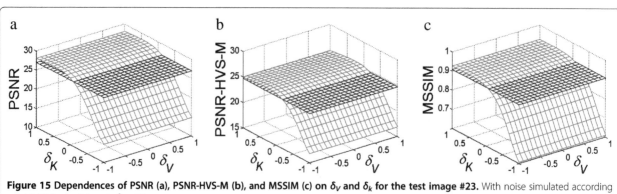

Figure 15 Dependences of PSNR (a), PSNR-HVS-M (b), and MSSIM (c) on δ_V and δ_k for the test image #23. With noise simulated according model (2) for $k = 0.1$ and $\sigma_{si}^2 = 10$.

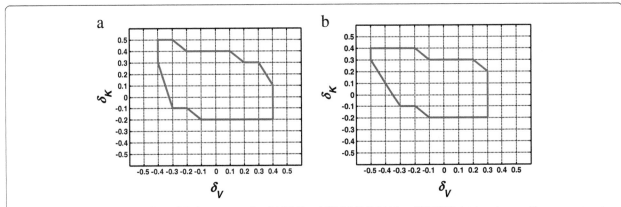

Figure 16 Areas of acceptable δ_V and δ_k for two metrics. (a) PSNR and **(b)** PSNR-HVS-M for all TID2008 database images (three components for each image) and all considered sets of signal-dependent noise models.

Table 7 Simulation data for the test image #3 and 13, noise model (1), all considered metrics

δ_k, δ_v	PSNR				PSNR-HVS-M				MSSIM			
	MO	MM	MS	MCW	MO	MM	MS	MCW	MO	MM	MS	MCW
Image 03												
Case $k = 0.2$; $\sigma_{si}^2 = 50$												
0.05	36.58	36.57	0.013	0.046	37.40	37.40	0.006	0.017	0.9841	0.9841	0.0001	0.0002
0.10		36.55	0.045	0.160		37.38	0.030	0.103		0.9840	0.0002	0.0007
0.15		36.52	0.103	0.364		37.37	0.059	0.207		0.9839	0.0005	0.0016
0.20		36.49	0.158	0.557		37.34	0.091	0.328		0.9838	0.0007	0.0025
0.25		36.41	0.244	0.900		37.29	0.142	0.534		0.9834	0.0011	0.0041
Case $k = 1.0$; $\sigma_{si}^2 = 30$												
0.05	34.53	34.52	0.020	0.065	34.67	34.67	0.004	0.018	0.9756	0.9764	0.0002	0.0005
0.10		34.51	0.051	0.173		34.66	0.026	0.095		0.9764	0.0004	0.0012
0.15		34.44	0.132	0.480		34.63	0.071	0.260		0.9760	0.0009	0.0031
0.20		34.37	0.336	1.162		34.58	0.189	0.662		0.9756	0.0023	0.0077
0.25		34.35	0.347	1.218		34.56	0.198	0.710		0.9755	0.0023	0.0079
Image 13												
Case $k = 0.2$; $\sigma_{si}^2 = 50$												
0.05	31.00	31.00	0.034	0.102	35.42	35.42	0.046	0.138	0.9828	0.9828	0.0003	0.0008
0.10		30.98	0.066	0.215		35.40	0.087	0.277		0.9827	0.0005	0.0016
0.15		30.96	0.100	0.343		35.37	0.126	0.426		0.9825	0.0008	0.0025
0.20		30.97	0.151	0.479		35.40	0.194	0.598		0.9827	0.0012	0.0036
0.25		30.93	0.164	0.555		35.36	0.217	0.709		0.9825	0.0013	0.0043
Case $k = 1.0$; $\sigma_{si}^2 = 30$												
0.05	28.64	28.64	0.041	0.127	32.01	32.01	0.054	0.164	0.9713	0.9713	0.0005	0.0017
0.10		28.64	0.080	0.246		32.01	0.101	0.308		0.9712	0.0010	0.0031
0.15		28.61	0.109	0.356		31.98	0.137	0.443		0.9710	0.0014	0.0045
0.20		28.62	0.143	0.450		32.00	0.185	0.563		0.9713	0.0019	0.0059
0.25		28.55	0.241	0.810		31.93	0.299	0.975		0.9706	0.0031	0.0098

Competing interests

The authors declare that they have no competing interests.

Author details

[1]National Aerospace University, Kharkov 61070, Ukraine. [2]Tampere University of Technology, Tampere FI-33101, Finland.

References

1. WK Pratt, *Digital Image Processing*, 4th edn. (Wiley-Interscience, New York, 2007). p. 807
2. M Elad, Sparse and Redundant Representations, in *From Theory to Applications in Signal and Image Processing*, ed. by M Elad. vol. 20 (Springer Science, Business Media, LLC, Philadelphia, PA, 2010), p. 376
3. OK Al-Shaykh, RM Mersereau, Lossy compression of noisy images. IEEE Trans. on Image Process. 7(12), 1641–1652 (1998). doi:10.1109/83.730376
4. A Bovik, *Handbook on Image and Video Processing* (Waltham, MA, Academic Press, 2000), p. 1384
5. DL Donoho, De-noising by soft thresholding. IEEE Trans. on Information Theory IT-41(3), 613–627 (1995)
6. S Mallat, *A Wavelet Tour of Signal Processing* (Academic, San Diego, CA, 1998), p. 620
7. L Sendur, IW Selesnick, Bivariate shrinkage with local variance estimation. IEEE Sig. Process. Letters 9(12), 438–441 (2002)
8. V Lukin, S Abramov, N Ponomarenko, M Uss, M Zriakhov, B Vozel, K Chehdi, J Astola, Methods and automatic procedures for processing images based on blind evaluation of noise type and characteristics. SPIE J. Adv. Remote Sens (2011). doi: 10.1117/1.3539768
9. A Foi, *Pointwise Shape-Adaptive DCT Image Filtering and Signal-Dependent Noise Estimation, Thesis for the degree of Doctor of Technology* (Tampere University of Technology, Tampere, 2007)
10. C Oliver, S Quegan, *Understanding Synthetic Aperture Radar Images* (Raleigh, NC, SciTech Publishing, 2004), p. 479
11. N Ponomarenko, V Lukin, K Egiazarian, L Lepisto, Color image lossy compression based on blind evaluation and prediction of noise characteristics, in *Proceedings of the SPIE 7870 of Image Processing: Algorithms and Systems VII* (San Francisco, 23 Jan 2011)
12. C Liu, R Szeliski, SB Kang, CL Zitnick, WT Freeman, Automatic estimation and removal of noise from a single image. IEEE Trans. Pattern Anal. Mach. Intell. 30(2), 299–314 (2008)
13. SH Lim, Characterization of Noise in Digital Photographs for Image Processing, in *Proceedings of the SPIE 6069 of Digital Photography II* (San Jose, 15 Jan 2006)
14. PJ Curran, JL Dungan, Estimation of signal-to-noise: a new procedure applied to AVIRIS data. IEEE Trans. Geosci. Remote Sens. 27, 620–628 (1989)
15. M Uss, B Vozel, V Lukin, K Chehdi, Local signal-dependent noise variance estimation from hyperspectral textural images. IEEE J. Select. Topics Signal Process 5, 469–486 (2011)
16. B Aiazzi, L Alparone, A Barducci, S Baronti, P Marcoinni, I Pippi, M Selva, Noise modelling and estimation of hyperspectral data from airborne imaging spectrometers. Ann. Geophys. 49, 19 (2006)
17. B Vozel, S Abramov, K Chehdi, V Lukin, N Ponomarenko, M Uss, J Astola, Multivariate Image Processing, in *Blind Methods for Noise Evaluation in Multi-Component Images*, ed. by C Collet, J Chanussot, K Chehdi (Toulouse, Wiley&Iste, 2010), pp. 263–302
18. S Abramov, V Lukin, N Ponomarenko, K Egiazarian, O Pogrebnyak, Influence of multiplicative noise variance evaluation accuracy on MM-band SLAR image filtering efficiency, in *Proceedings of the MSMW 2004*. vol 1, (Kharkov, 21–26 Jun 2004), pp. 250–252
19. JP Kerekes, JE Baum, Hyperspectral imaging system modeling. Lincoln Laboratory J. 14(1), 117–130 (2003)
20. A Barducci, D Guzzi, P Marcoionni, I Pippi, CHRIS-Proba performance evaluation: signal-to-noise ratio, instrument efficiency and data quality from acquisitions over San Rossore (Italy) test site, in *Proceedings of the 3rd ESA CHRIS/Proba Workshop*, 21–23 Mar 2005
21. S Abramov, V Zabrodina, V Lukin, B Vozel, K Chehdi, J Astola, Improved method for blind estimation of the variance of mixed noise using weighted LMS line fitting algorithm, in *Proceedings of the ISCAS* (Paris, 30 May–2 Jun 2010), pp. 2642–2645
22. S Abramov, V Zabrodina, V Lukin, B Vozel, K Chehdi, J Astola, Methods for Blind Estimation of the Variance of Mixed Noise and Their Performance Analysis, in *Numerical Analysis – Theory and Applications*, ed. by J Awrejcewicz (Richardson, TX, InTech, 2011), pp. 49–70. doi: 10.5772/1829
23. D Fevralev, V Lukin, N Ponomarenko, S Abramov, K Egiazarian, J Astola, Efficiency analysis of color image filtering. EURASIP J. Adv. Signal Process. 2011, 41 (2011). doi:10.1186/1687-6180-2011-41
24. R Oktem, K Egiazarian, Transform domain algorithm for reducing the effect of film-grain noise in image compression. Electronic Letters 35(21), 1830–1831 (1999)
25. G Ramponi, R D'Alvise, Automatic Estimation of the Noise Variance in SAR Images for Use in Speckle Filtering, in *Proceedings of the IEEE-EURASIP Workshop on Non-linear Signal and Image Processing* (Antalya, 20–23 Jun 1999), pp. 835–838
26. J Astola, P Kuosmanen, *Fundamentals of nonlinear digital filtering* (CRC Press LLC, Boca Raton, 1997). 276
27. VI Ponomaryov, Real time 2D-3D filtering using order statistics based algorithms. J. of Real-Time Image Process. 1, 173–194 (2007)
28. V Lukin, N Ponomarenko, S Abramov, B Vozel, K Chehdi, Improved noise parameter estimation and filtering of MM-band SLAR images, in *Proceedings of the MSMW 2007*. vol 1, (Kharkov, 25–30 Jun 2007), pp. 439–441
29. KN Plataniotis, AN Venetsanopoulos, *Color Image Processing and Applications* (Springer, New York, 2000). 355
30. J Astola, P Haavisto, Y Neuvo, Vector median filter. Proc. IEEE 4, 678–689 (1990)
31. R Touzi, A review of speckle filtering in the context of estimation theory. IEEE Trans. on Geosci. and Remote Sens. 40(11), 2392–2404 (2002)
32. A Foi, Clipped noisy images: heteroskedastic modeling and practical denoising. Signal Process. 89(12), 2609–2629 (2009)
33. F Murtagh, JL Starck, A Bijaoui, Image restoration with noise suppression using a multiresolution support. Astron. Astrophys. Suppl. Ser. 112, 179–189 (1995)
34. V Lukin, N Ponomarenko, S Abramov, B Vozel, K Chehdi, J Astola, Filtering of radar images based on blind evaluation of noise characteristics, in *Proceedings of the Image and Signal Processing for Remote Sensing XIV*. vol 7109 (Cardiff, 15–18 Sep 2008)
35. R Oktem, K Egiazarian, VV Lukin, NN Ponomarenko, OV Tsymbal, Locally adaptive DCT filtering for signal-dependent noise removal. EURASIP J. Adv. Signal Process (2007). doi:10.1155/2007/42472
36. D Fevralev, S Krivenko, V Lukin, A Zelensky, K Egiazarian, Speeding-up DCT based Filtering of Images, in *CD ROM Proceedings of the Modern Problems of Radioengineering, Telecommunications and Computer Science (TCSET)* (Lviv-Slavsko, 23–27 Feb 2010)
37. K Dabov, A Foi, V Katkovnik, K Egiazarian, Image denoising by sparse 3-D transform-domain collaborative filtering. IEEE Trans. Image Process. 16(8), 2080–2095 (2007)
38. V Lukin, N Ponomarenko, K Egiazarian, HVS-Metric-Based Performance Analysis Of Image Denoising Algorithms, in *Proceedings of the EUVIP* (Paris, 4–6 Jul 2011)
39. N Ponomarenko, F Silvestri, K Egiazarian, M Carli, J Astola, V Lukin, On between-coefficient contrast masking of DCT basis functions, in *CD-ROM Proceedings of the VPQM* (Scottsdale, 25–26 Jan 2007)
40. N Ponomarenko, *PSNR-HVS-M download page*, 2009. http://www.ponomarenko.info/psnrhvsm.htm. Accessed 28 Mar 2013
41. N Ponomarenko, V Lukin, A Zelensky, K Egiazarian, M Carli, F Battisti, TID2008 - a database for evaluation of full-reference visual quality assessment metrics. Advances of Modern Radioelectronics 10, 30–45 (2009)
42. V Lukin, M Zriakhov, S Krivenko, N Ponomarenko, Z Miao, Lossy compression of images without visible distortions and its applications, in *Proceedings of the ICSP 2010* (Beijing, 24–28 Oct 2010), pp. 694–697
43. Z Wang, EP Simoncelli, AC Bovik, Multi-scale Structural Similarity for Visual Quality Assessment, in *Proceedings of the 37th IEEE Asilomar Conference on Signals, Systems and Computers*. vol 2 (Monterey, 9–12 Nov 2003), pp. 1398–1402
44. ML Uss, B Vozel, V Lukin, K Chehdi, Image Informative Maps for Component-wise Estimating Parameters of Signal-Dependent Noise. J. Electron. Imag 22(1) (2013). doi:10.1117/1.JEI.22.1.013019

17

Soft computing-based colour quantisation

Gerald Schaefer

Abstract

Soft computing techniques have shown much potential in a variety of computer vision and image analysis tasks. In this paper, an overview of recent soft computing approaches to the colour quantisation problem is presented. Colour quantisation is a common image processing technique to reduce the number of distinct colours in an image. Those selected colours form a colour palette, while the resulting image quality is directly determined by the choice of colours in the palette. The use of generic optimisation techniques such as simulated annealing and soft computing-based clustering algorithms founded on fuzzy and rough set ideas to formulate colour quantisation algorithms is discussed. These methods are capable of deriving good colour palettes and are shown to outperform standard colour quantisation techniques in terms of image quality. Furthermore, a hybrid colour quantisation algorithm which combines a generic optimisation approach with a common clustering algorithm is shown to lead to improved image quality. Finally, it is demonstrated how optimisation-based colour quantisation can be employed in conjunction with a more appropriate measure for image quality.

Keywords: Colour quantisation; Colour palette; Soft computing; Clustering; Optimisation; Image quality

1 Introduction

Colour quantisation is a common image processing technique that allows the representation of true colour images using only a small number of colours. True colour images typically use 24 bits per pixel resulting overall in 2^{24}, i.e. more than 16 million, different colours. Colour quantisation uses a colour palette that contains only a small number of distinct colours (usually between 8 and 256), and pixel data are then stored as indices to this palette. Since each pixel in the image now takes on one of the colours of the palette, the choice of the colours that make up the palette is of crucial importance for the quality of the quantised image.

A common way of expressing this quality is to calculate the difference between the original (unquantised) image O and its colour-quantised counterpart Q for which the mean-squared error (MSE) is the most widely used measure:

$$\text{MSE}(O, Q) = \frac{1}{3nm} \sum_{i=1}^{n} \sum_{j=1}^{m} ((R_O(i,j) - R_Q(i,j))^2$$
$$+ (G_O(i,j) - G_Q(i,j))^2 + (B_O(i,j) - B_Q(i,j))^2), \quad (1)$$

where $R(i,j)$, $G(i,j)$, and $B(i,j)$ are the red, green, and blue pixel values at location (i,j), and n and m are the dimensions of images.

However, the selection of the optimal colour palette is known to be an NP-complete problem [1]. In the image processing literature, many different algorithms have been introduced that aim to find a palette that allows for good image quality of the quantised image. A relatively simple approach is the popularity algorithm [2], which - typically following a uniform quantisation to 5 bits per channel - selects the N colours that are represented most often to form the colour palette. In median cut quantisation [2], an iterative procedure repeatedly splits (by a plane through the median point) colour cells into sub-cells. In octree quantisation [3], the colour space is represented as an octree where sub-branches are successively merged to form the palette, while Neuquant [4] employs a one-dimensional self-organising Kohonen neural network to generate the colour map.

In this paper, we present several soft computing approaches to colour quantisation. In particular, in Section 2.1, we show how general purpose optimisation algorithms such as simulated annealing can be used to derive a good colour palette. Colour quantisation can also be regarded as a clustering problem. Consequently, in Section 2.2, several soft computing-based clustering algorithms, namely fuzzy based clustering, rough set

Correspondence: gerald.schaefer@ieee.org
Department of Computer Science, Loughborough University, Loughborough, UK

based clustering and a combined fuzzy-rough clustering approach, and their application to the colour quantisation problem, are discussed. In Section 2.3, we present experimental results that confirm that these soft computing-based methods do indeed make effective approaches for colour quantisation, outperforming several standard algorithms. A hybrid optimisation scheme for colour quantisation is described in Section 2.4 and shown to lead to improved performance. In Section 2.5, we show that by adapting the objective function, optimisation-based colour quantisation can be formulated, employing a more appropriate image quality metric. Finally, Section 3 concludes the paper.

2 Review

2.1 Soft computing-based optimisation for colour quantisation

The main advantage of black-box optimisation algorithms is that they do not require any domain-specific knowledge yet are able to provide a near-optimal solution. This makes them suitable for a variety of problems, and in the following, we show how they can be employed to lead to an effective colour quantisation algorithm.

While there are many different optimisation algorithms (e.g. in [5], genetic algorithms were used for colour quantisation, while in [6], particle swarm optimisation [7] was utilised), the approach in [8] employs a modification of the well-known simulated annealing algorithm. Simulated annealing (SA) was first introduced as a general optimisation method by Kirkpatrick et al. [9], and it simulates the annealing of metal, in which the metal is heated up to a temperature near its melting point and then slowly cooled down. This allows the particles to move towards a minimum energy state, with a more uniform crystalline structure. The process therefore permits some control over the microstructure.

Simulated annealing is a variation of the hill-climbing algorithm. Both start from a randomly selected point within the search space of all possible solutions. Each point in search space has a measurable error value, E, associated with it, which indicates the quality of the solution. From the current point in search space, new trial solutions are selected for testing from the neighborhood of the current solution. This is usually done by moving a small step in a random direction. Typically, small and equally distributed random numbers from the interval $[-s_{max}, s_{max}]$ are added to each component of the current solution vector, where s_{max} is called the maximum step width and is chosen from the interval between 0 and the upper limit of the search space dimension.

If the decrease in error values, denoted as ΔE, is negative (i.e. the error of a trial solution is below that of the current one), then the trial solution is accepted as the current solution. However unlike hill-climbing, SA does not automatically reject a new candidate solution if ΔE is positive. Instead, it becomes the current solution with probability $p(T)$ which is usually determined using

$$p(T) = e^{-\Delta E/T}, \tag{2}$$

where T is referred to as 'temperature', an abstract control parameter for the cooling schedule. For a given temperature and positive values of ΔE, the probability function shown in Equation 2 has a defined upper limit of 1 and tends towards 0 for large positive values of ΔE.

The algorithm starts with a high temperature, i.e. with a high transition probability. The temperature is then reduced towards 0, usually in steps, according to a cooling schedule such as

$$T_{n+1} = \alpha T_n, \tag{3}$$

where T_n is the temperature at step n and α is a cooling coefficient (usually between 0.8 and 0.99).

During each step, the temperature must be held constant for an appropriate number of iterations in order to allow the algorithm to settle into a 'thermal equilibrium', i.e. a balanced state. If the number of iterations is too small, the algorithm is likely to converge to a local minimum.

For both continuous parameter optimisation and discrete parameters with large search ranges, it is practically impossible to choose direct neighbours of the current solution as new candidate solutions due to the vast number of points in the search space. Therefore, it is necessary to choose new candidates at some distance in a random direction of the current solution in order to navigate through the search space in an acceptable time. This distance could either be a fixed step width s or it could have an upper limit, s_{max}. The maximum step width s_{max} is crucial to the success of SA. If s_{max} is too small and the start point for a search run is too far away from the global optimum, the algorithm might not be able to get near that optimum. If, on the other hand, the step width is too large and the peak of the optimum very narrow, the algorithm might never reach the top because most of the steps are too large.

Step width adapting simulated annealing (SWASA) [10] overcomes the problems associated with constant values for s_{max} using a scaling function to adapt the maximum step width to the current iteration by

$$s_{max}(n) = \frac{2s_0}{1 + e^{\beta n/n_{max}}}, \tag{4}$$

where $s_{max}(n)$ is the maximum step width at iteration n, s_0 is the initial maximum step width, n_{max} the maximum number of iterations, and β is an adaptation constant.

For colour quantisation, the objective is, as mentioned, to minimise the total error introduced through the application of a colour palette. The colour palette C for an image I, a codebook of k colour vectors, should then be chosen so as to minimise the error function

$$E(C,I) = \frac{1}{\sum_{j=1}^{k} l_j} \sum_{i=1}^{k} \sum_{j=1}^{l_i} ||C_i - I_j|| + p(C,I), \qquad (5)$$

with

$$p(C,I) = \sum_{i=1}^{k} \delta a_i, \quad a_i = \begin{cases} 1 & \text{if } l_i = 0 \\ 0 & \text{otherwise} \end{cases}, \qquad (6)$$

where l_i is the number of pixels I_j represented by colour C_i of the palette, $||.||$ is the Euclidean distance in RGB (red-green-blue) space, and δ is a constant (set to $\delta = 10$ in [8]). The objective function $E(C,I)$ used is hence a combination of the mean Euclidean distance, i.e. the error measure of Equation 1, and a penalty function. The purpose of the penalty function $p(C,I)$ is to avoid unused palette colours by adding a constant penalty value to the error for each entry in the codebook that is not used in the resulting picture.

2.2 Soft computing-based clustering for colour quantisation

Colour quantisation can also be seen as a clustering problem where the task is to identify those clusters that best represent the colours in an image. Consequently, soft computing-based clustering algorithms can be readily adapted to derive a good colour palette. In the following, we discuss how fuzzy c-means, rough c-means, and a combined fuzzy-rough clustering algorithm can be employed for colour quantisation.

2.2.1 Fuzzy c-means

Fuzzy c-means (FCM) is based on the idea of finding cluster centres by iteratively adjusting their positions and evaluation of an objective function as in (hard) c-means, yet allows more flexibility by introducing the possibility of partial memberships to clusters. The general FCM algorithm is illustrated in Figure 1.

For colour quantisation, the error function follows the form

$$E = \sum_{j=1}^{C} \sum_{i=1}^{N} \mu_{ij}^{k} ||x_i - c_j||^2, \qquad (7)$$

where μ_{ij}^{k} is the fuzzy membership of pixel x_i and the colour cluster identified by its centre c_j, and k is a constant that defines the fuzziness of the resulting partitions.

E can reach the global minimum when pixels nearby the centroid of corresponding clusters are assigned higher membership values, while lower membership values are assigned to pixels far from the centroid [11]. Here, the membership is proportional to the probability that a pixel belongs to a specific cluster where the probability is only dependent on the distance between the image pixel and each independent cluster centre. The membership functions and the cluster centres are updated by

$$\mu_{ij} = \frac{1}{\sum_{m=1}^{C} \left(\frac{||x_j - c_i||}{||x_j - c_m||^{2/(k-1)}} \right)}, \qquad (8)$$

and

$$c_i = \frac{\sum_{j=1}^{N} \mu_{ij}^{k} x_j}{\sum_{j=1}^{N} \mu_{ij}^{k}}. \qquad (9)$$

Fuzzy c-means operates iteratively though the following steps [12]:

Step 1. Initialise the cluster centres c_i and let $t = 0$.
Step 2. Initialise the fuzzy partition memberships functions μ_{ij} according to Equation 8.
Step 3. Let $t = t + 1$ and compute new cluster centres c_i using Equation 9.
Step 4. Repeat steps 2 to 3 until convergence.

An initial setting for each cluster centre is required, and FCM is guaranteed to converge to a local minimisation solution. The efficiency of FCM has been comprehensively investigated in [13]. To address the inefficiency of the original FCM algorithm, several variants of the fuzzy c-means algorithm have been introduced which are discussed in the following.

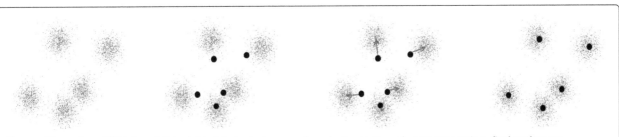

Figure 1 Illustration of FCM, from left to right: data to clusters - random cluster centres - clusters converging - final settlement.

2.2.2 Fuzzy c-means variants

While FCM often provides good clustering results, it also suffers from a relatively high computational complexity, especially when there are many samples as is the case for colour quantisation. However, a number of faster FCM variants have been developed and have also been shown to work well for colour quantisation [14].

To combat the computational complexity of FCM, Cheng et al. [15] proposed a multistage random sampling strategy. This method has a lower number of feature vectors and also needs fewer iterations to converge. The basic idea is to randomly sample and obtain a small subset of the dataset in order to approximate the cluster centres of the full dataset. This approximation is then used to reduce the number of iterations. Random sampling FCM (RSFCM) consists of two phases. First, a multistage iterative process of a modified FCM is performed. In the second phase, standard FCM is performed with the cluster centres approximated by the final cluster centres from the first phase. It has been shown that RSFCM is able to reduce the computational complexity compared to the classical FCM method.

Ahmed et al. [16] introduced an alternative to classical FCM by adding a term that enables the labelling of a pixel to be associated with its neighbourhood. As a regulator, the neighbourhood term can change the solution towards piecewise homogeneous labelling. As a further extension, in [17], the enhanced FCM (EnFCM) algorithm was presented. In order to reduce the computational complexity, a linearity-weighted sum image is formed from the original image, and a modified objective function is employed. EnFCM considers a number of pixels with similar colours as a weight. Thus, this approach can accelerate the convergence of searching for global similarity.

Anisotropic mean shift-based FCM (AMSFCM) is an efficient approach to fuzzy c-means clustering which utilises an anisotropic mean shift algorithm coupled with fuzzy clustering [14]. Mean shift-based techniques have been shown to be capable of estimating the local density gradients of similar pixels. These gradient estimates are iteratively performed so that all pixels can find similar pixels in the same image [18]. AMSFCM combines fuzzy c-means and anisotropic mean shift, a mean shift variant that does not suffer of shortcomings due to radially symmetric kernels [19]. Importantly, the AMSFCM algorithm continuously inherits and updates the states, based on the mutual correction of FCM and mean shift.

2.2.3 Rough c-means

Lingras and West [20] introduced a rough set-inspired clustering algorithm based on the well-known c-means algorithm. In this rough c-means (RCM) approach, each cluster c_k is described not only by its centre m_k, but also contains additional information, in particular its lower

approximation $\underline{c_k}$, its upper approximation $\overline{c_k}$, and its boundary area $c_k^b = \overline{c_k} - \underline{c_k}$. The clustering algorithm proceeds in the following steps:

Step 1. Each data sample is randomly assigned to one lower approximation. Since the lower approximation of a cluster is a subset of its upper approximation, this also automatically assigns the sample to the upper approximation of the same cluster.

Step 2. The cluster centres are updated as

$$
m_k = \begin{cases} \omega_l \sum_{x_i \in \underline{c_k}} \dfrac{x_i}{|\underline{c_k}|} + \omega_b \sum_{x_i \in c_k^b} \dfrac{x_i}{|c_k^b|} & \text{if } c_k^b \neq \{\} \\ \omega_l \sum_{x_i \in \underline{c_k}} \dfrac{x_i}{|\underline{c_k}|} & \text{otherwise} \end{cases}.
$$

(10)

The cluster centres are hence determined as a weighted average of the samples belonging to the lower approximation and the boundary area, where the weights ω_l and ω_b define the relative importance of the two sets.

Step 3. For each data sample, the closest cluster centre is determined and the sample is assigned to its upper approximation. Then, all clusters that are at most ϵ further away than the closest cluster are determined. If such clusters exist, the sample will also be assigned to their upper approximations. If no such cluster exists, the sample is assigned also to the lower approximation of the closest cluster.

Step 4. If the algorithm has converged (i.e. if the cluster centres do not change any more, or after a pre-set number of iterations), terminate; otherwise, go to step 2.

Strictly speaking, this algorithm does not implement all properties set out for rough sets [21] and hence belongs to the reduced interpretation of rough sets as lower and upper approximations of data [22].

Peters [23] pointed out some potential pitfalls of the algorithm in terms of objective function and numerical stability and suggested some improvements to overcome these. Equation 10 is revised to

$$
m_k = \omega_l \sum_{x_i \in \underline{c_k}} \frac{x_i}{|\underline{c_k}|} + \omega_u \sum_{x_i \in \overline{c_k}} \frac{x_i}{|\overline{c_k}|},
$$

(11)

with $\omega_l + \omega_u = 1$, i.e. as a convex combination of lower and upper approximation means. In order to overcome the possibility of situations with empty lower approximations, the calculation of cluster centres can be modified so that for empty lower approximations, the cluster centre is calculated as the average of samples in the upper approximation or by ensuring that each lower approximation has at least one member.

In [24], an RCM-based colour quantisation is introduced which follows the clustering approach from [20] and [23], assigning the data sample closest to the cluster centre to its lower approximation, though with a different initialisation approach where rather than randomly assigning samples to clusters, random cluster centres are generated first and then the algorithm proceeds with steps 3, 2, and 4 (i.e., steps 2 and 3 reversed) in order to derive a colour palette.

2.2.4 Fuzzy-rough c-means

Fuzzy-rough c-means (FRCM) clustering [25] utilises, in addition to the fuzziness of fuzzy c-means, concepts of rough set theory to provide an effective clustering algorithm that can also be adapted for colour quantisation [26]. In particular, as in rough c-means, each cluster is represented by a lower and an upper approximation. However, while the lower approximation is defined as crisp, the boundary area is fuzzy. While the aim is to minimise the same error function E as in Equation 7, memberships are defined as

$$\mu_{ij} = \begin{cases} 1 & \forall x_i \in \underline{c_j} \\ \dfrac{1}{\sum_{l=1}^{C} \left(\dfrac{||x_i - m_j||}{||x_i - m_l||} \right)^{2/(\alpha-1)}} & \forall x_i \in c_j^b \end{cases} \tag{12}$$

Calculation of cluster centres m_j remains as given in Equation 9, while lower and upper approximations are defined as detailed in Section 2.2.3 for rough c-means. The difference between fuzzy c-means and fuzzy-rough c-means is hence that the membership values in the lower approximation are 1 (i.e. crisp), while those in the boundary region are fuzzy memberships. In other words, fuzzy-rough c-means first partitions the data into two classes: lower approximation and boundary area, and only those points in the boundary region are fuzzified. This in turn leads to faster convergence when compared to FCM [25]. In contrast to rough c-means, samples in the boundary region are not all treated equally but are rather assigned membership values depending on their distance to the cluster centroids. In addition, there is no need to specify weights for the calculation for cluster centroids.

2.3 Colour quantisation performance

In order to evaluate the various colour quantisation algorithms, we performed a set of experiments on a set of six test images. These images, Lenna, Peppers, Mandrill, Sailboat, Airplane, and Pool, are commonly used in the colour quantisation literature and hence present a good test bed for evaluation purposes. We applied all seven discussed algorithms, that is SWASA, FCM, RSFCM, EnFCM, AMSFCM, RCM, and FRCM, to all images to generate quantised images with a palette of 16 colours.

For the simulated annealing algorithm, a population-based version of the SWASA algorithm with a population size of 10 was employed. The start temperature T_0 was chosen to be 20, and the cooling coefficient α was set to 0.9. The parameters s_0 and β were set to 100 and 5.3, respectively. The temperature was kept constant for over 20 iterations, and the maximum number of iterations was set to 10,000. For the rough c-means approach, we adopted the parameters $\omega_l = 0.7$, $\omega_u = 0.3$, and $\tau = 0.001$ (image pixel values are normalised to $[0; 3]^3$). For the fuzzy c-means and fuzzy rough c-means algorithms, the fuzziness exponent α was set to 1.2.

To put the results we obtained into context, we also implemented four popular colour quantisation algorithms (which are often integrated in typical image processing software) to generate corresponding quantised images with palette size 16. The algorithms we tested were as follows:

- *Popularity algorithm* [2]: Following a uniform quantisation to 5 bits per channel, the N colours that are represented most often form the colour palette.
- *Median cut quantisation* [2]: An iterative algorithm that repeatedly splits (by a plane through the median point) colour cells into sub-cells.
- *Octree quantisation* [3]: The colour space is represented as an octree where sub-branches are successively merged to form the palette.
- *Neuquant* [4]: A one-dimensional self-organising Kohonen neural network is applied to generate the colour map.

For all algorithms, pixels in the quantised images were assigned to their nearest neighbours in the colour palette to provide the best possible image quality.

The obtained results are listed in Table 1, expressed in terms of average (over 10 runs of the algorithms) peak-signal-to-noise ratio (PSNR) defined as

$$PSNR(O, Q) = 10 \log_{10} \frac{255^2}{MSE(O, Q)}, \tag{13}$$

with $MSE(O, Q)$ calculated as in Equation 1. A higher PSNR hence indicates better image quality.

As can be seen from Table 1, all the soft computing algorithms provide very good results and clearly outperform standard colour quantisation algorithms. The results

Table 1 Quantisation results, given in terms of PSNR (dB) with the best result for each image in boldface

	Lenna	Peppers	Mandrill	Sailboat	Pool	Airplane	average
Popularity algorithm [2]	22.24	18.56	18.00	8.73	19.87	15.91	17.22
Median cut [2]	23.79	24.10	21.52	22.01	24.57	24.32	23.39
Octree [3]	27.45	25.80	24.21	26.04	29.39	28.77	26.94
Neuquant [4]	27.82	26.04	24.59	26.81	27.08	28.24	26.73
SWASA [8]	27.79	26.16	24.46	26.69	29.84	29.43	27.40
FCM [14]	**28.81**	26.77	**25.03**	27.25	31.03	30.23	28.17
RSFCM [14]	28.70	26.70	24.98	27.32	30.81	30.73	28.20
EnFCM [14]	28.61	26.74	24.87	27.22	31.11	29.92	28.08
AMSFCM [14]	28.63	26.71	24.66	27.24	30.87	29.96	28.01
RCM [24]	28.63	26.67	25.02	**27.62**	29.40	30.50	27.98
FRCM [26]	28.44	**26.80**	**25.03**	27.47	**31.20**	**31.24**	**28.73**

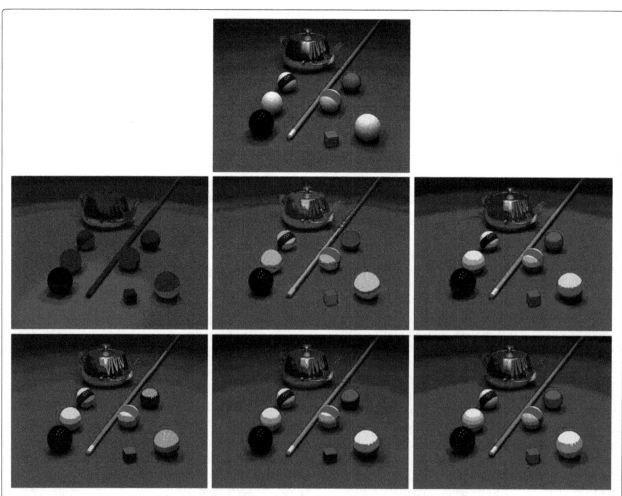

Figure 2 Results of colour quantisation algorithms applied to the Pool image (top row). Shown are the quantised images after applying (from left to right, top to bottom) popularity, median cut, octree, Neuquant, rough c-means, and fuzzy-rough c-means algorithms.

of the different fuzzy clustering approaches are fairly similar which suggests that the computationally more efficient versions (RSFCM, EnFCM, AMSFCM) can be employed without sacrificing image quality. Also, the rough set approach gives similar performance and the presented rough colour quantisation approach hence adds to the applications of rough sets in the field of imaging and vision. The best performance is achieved by the combined fuzzy-rough c-means approach, which gives the best image quality for four of the six images and overall provides a PSNR improvement of more than 0.5 compared to the next ranked algorithm.

Figure 2 shows the Pool image together with the images colour quantised by the popularity, median cut, octree, and Neuquant algorithms as well as two of the soft-computing based techniques, namely the rough c-means and fuzzy-rough c-means approaches. It is clear that the popularity algorithm performs poorly on this image and assigns virtually all of the colours in the palette to green and achromatic colours. Median cut is better but still provides a fairly poor colour reproduction; most of the colours in the quantised image are fairly different from the original. The same holds true for the images produced by Neuquant. Here, the most obvious artefact is the absence of an appropriate red colour in the colour palette. A far better result is achieved by the octree algorithm, although here also, the red is not very accurate and the colour of the cue is greenish instead of brown. Clearly better image quality is maintained by applying the rough c-means algorithm. Although the colour palette has only 16 entries, all colours of the original image are accurately presented including the red ball and the colour of the billiard cue. A further improvement is achieved by the fuzzy-rough c-means colour quantisation technique which achieves even better colour reproduction, e.g. in the reflections on the black ball.

2.4 Hybrid optimisation-based colour quantisation

Figure 3 shows a typical run of the simulated annealing optimisation method applied to colour quantisation as explained in Section 2.1. The solid line represents the average quantisation error over time (iterations) while the dashed line represents the best solution of each iteration.

As can be seen in Figure 3, there is always a variation in error values within the population which indicates that although simulated annealing is able to find good solutions (as was confirmed in Section 2.3), i.e. solutions from within the region around the global optimum, it rarely exploits that region completely. Therefore, in [27], SWASA was combined with a standard c-means clustering algorithm [28] to provide a stacked hybrid optimisation method. C-means clustering is guaranteed to converge towards the local clustering minimum by iteratively carrying out the following two steps:

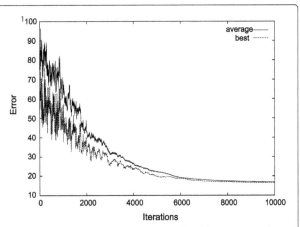

Figure 3 Typical run of SA optimisation for colour quantisation [27].

- Each input vector is mapped to its closest codeword by a nearest neighbour search.
- The input vectors assigned in each class (i.e. for each codeword) are represented by the centroid of the vectors in that class.

In this hybridised algorithm, the SA component is hence responsible for identifying the region in the search space that will contain the global optimum while the c-means component will then descend into the minimum present in that region.

To show the effect of this hybridisation, we ran the combined algorithm on the same image dataset that was used in Section 2.3, and show the results, again in terms of PSNR, in Table 2. As can be seen from there, the further adjustment through application of a subsequent clustering step does indeed improve image quality significantly, resulting in a colour quantisation algorithm that also outperforms all algorithms from Table 1.

2.5 Image quality metric-based colour quantisation

Although many colour quantisation algorithms have been proposed, virtually all of them define the goal of quantisation as that of finding a palette that minimises the MSE, given in Equation 1, of the resulting image. It is however well known that metrics such as MSE and PSNR do not correspond very well to how the human visual system operates and how humans judge differences between images. An image with a higher MSE does not necessarily have perceptually lower image quality; similarly, two images that are perceived with equal quality are likely to have different values in terms of MSE or PSNR.

Furthermore, RGB, the device space, is poorly related to the human visual system. Colour differences calculated as Euclidean distances between RGB co-ordinates do not

Table 2 Quantisation results, given in terms of PSNR (dB), of the hybrid SA algorithm

	Lenna	Peppers	Mandrill	Sailboat	Pool	Airplane	average
SWASA [8]	27.79	26.16	24.46	26.69	29.84	29.43	27.40
Hybrid SWASA [27]	29.70	27.17	25.37	27.95	31.57	32.94	28.97

correspond well to how humans perceive colour differences. Much research has been done on deriving colour spaces such as CIELAB and CIELUV that are designed to be perceptually uniform, i.e. where Euclidean distances correspond to perceived distances in all regions of the colour space [29]. Uniform colour spaces have been used in colour quantisation algorithms and have been shown to perform better compared to algorithms based on the RGB space [30].

However, the application of a perceptual uniform colour space alone does not guarantee improved image quality. Uniform colour spaces were developed for and hence only accurately model the colour differences between large patches of uniformly coloured samples. Real images on the other hand seldomly comprise such large areas. Therefore, it is crucial to also take into account the spatial characteristics of images when developing an appropriate image quality metric [31].

S-CIELAB (for spatial CIELAB [32]) first converts the RGB image into an opponent colour space. The individual channels are then convolved with a kernel whose shape is estimated from the visual spatial sensitivity to that channel. This convolution simulates the blurring that occurs in the human visual system. Both the opponent colour space and the convolution kernels were derived following a series of experiments on the pattern-colour separability of the visual system [33]. After the filtering, the image is converted to XYZ and then to CIELAB to provide spatial CIELAB co-ordinates. The difference between two images can then be expressed as the average colour difference, expressed in terms of ΔE units, between the two S-CIELAB representation, where the colour difference is usually calculated as the Euclidean distance between two colours.

In contrast to colour spaces such as CIELAB, for which colour quantisation can be easily adapted [30] by converting the RGB image to the new colour space and then applying the quantisation algorithm, this is not possible for S-CIELAB. The reason is that S-CIELAB does not simply provide a new colour space but takes into account the spatial interaction between neighbouring pixels. It is therefore image dependent, and identical S-CIELAB co-ordinates in two different images can originate from fairly different original RGB values. In the context of colour quantisation, this means that converting an image to S-CIELAB and performing the quantisation there will not lead to an optimal palette. Rather, the palette has to be found in the palette search space, and then the image quality is calculated based on the quantised image. This is possible using optimisation techniques such as the SWASA algorithm explained in Section 2.1 to develop an image metric-based colour quantisation algorithm [34]. The objective function to be minimised here is defined as the average ΔE between the original image O and the image quantised using the colour palette.

That this leads indeed to improved performance is again evaluated on the same image dataset as in Section 2.3. The results are given in Table 3. From there, it is evident that optimisation-based colour quantisation based on minimising MSE clearly outperforms conventional algorithms also when expressed in terms of S-CIELAB image quality. However, directly optimising with respect to this image metric leads to a significant further improvement, reducing the average ΔE from 6.65 to 4.37.

3 Conclusions

In this paper, we have given an overview of recent soft computing-based colour quantisation approaches and have shown that this family of algorithms work very well, resulting in quantised images with high image quality. In particular, we have discussed the use of optimisation algorithms such as simulated annealing and of soft computing-based clustering algorithms including fuzzy c-means, rough c-means, and combined fuzzy-rough

Table 3 Quantisation results, given in terms of $\Delta E_{S-CIELAB}$

	Lenna	Peppers	Mandrill	Sailboat	Pool	Airplane	average
Popularity algorithm [2]	11.92	21.81	20.54	41.03	9.31	15.59	20.03
Median cut [2]	10.34	8.89	10.66	10.10	7.73	7.05	9.13
Octree [3]	7.20	7.92	9.36	6.66	4.85	3.57	6.59
Neuquant [4]	7.13	7.84	9.79	5.50	5.65	4.21	6.68
SWASA/MSE [8]	6.78	7.77	9.28	6.48	5.69	3.87	6.65
SWASA/S-CIELAB [34]	4.57	6.33	6.27	3.50	3.06	2.47	4.37

c-means approaches in this context. All techniques were compared against standard colour quantisation methods and were shown to clearly outperform them. A hybrid colour quantisation algorithm, combining simulated annealing with a c-means clustering algorithm, was shown to lead to improved performance, while by modifying the objective function, optimisation-based colour quantisation algorithms can be tuned with respect to a particular image quality metric. Although the compiled results convincingly demonstrate that soft computing-based methods are well suited for the colour quantisation problem, it should also be noted that they typically have higher demands in terms of computational complexity and might hence be suitable only for situations where the quantisation stage is not time critical.

Competing interests
The author declares that he has no competing interests.

References

1. X Wu, Color quantization by dynamic programming and principal analysis. ACM Trans. Graph. **11**(4), 348–372 (1992)
2. P. S Heckbert, Color image quantization for frame buffer display. ACM Comput. Graph. (ACM SIGGRAPH '82 Proc.) **16**(3), 297–307 (1982)
3. M Gervautz, W Purgathofer, A simple method for color quantization: octree quantization, in *Graphics Gems*, ed. by A. S. Glassner (ACM, San Diego, 1990), pp. 287–293
4. A. H Dekker, Kohonen neural networks for optimal colour quantization. Network: Comput. Neural Syst. **5**, 351–367 (1994)
5. P Scheunders, A genetic c-means clustering algorithm applied to color image quantization. Pattern Recognit. **30**(6), 859–866 (1997)
6. M Omran, A Engelbrecht, A Salman, A color image quantization algorithm based on particle swarm optimization. Informatica. **29**, 263–271 (2005)
7. J Kennedy, R Eberhart, Particle swarm optimization. IEEE Int. Conference on Neural Networks. **4**, 1942–1948 (1995)
8. G Schaefer, L Nolle, An optimisation approach to colour palette generation. Int. J. Pattern Recognit. Mach. Intell. **1**(1), 40–46 (2006)
9. S Kirkpatrick, CD Gelatt, MP Vecchi, Optimization by simulated annealing. Science. **220**(4598), 671–680 (1983)
10. L Nolle, On the effect of step width selection schemes on the performance of stochastic local search strategies, in *18th European Simulation Multi-Conference, ESM 2004*, Magdeburg (Gruner, Druck, Erlangen, 2004), pp. 149–153
11. K Chuang, S Tzeng, H Chen, J Wu, T Chen, Fuzzy c-means clustering with spatial information for image segmentation. Comput. Med. Imaging Graph. **30**, 9–15 (2006)
12. J Bezdek, A convergence theorem for the fuzzy isodata clustering algorithms. IEEE Trans. Pattern Anal. Mach. Intell. **2**, 1–8 (1980)
13. R Hu, L Hathaway, On efficiency of optimization in fuzzy c-means. Neural, Parallel Sci. Comput. **10**, 141–156 (2002)
14. G Schaefer, H Zhou, Fuzzy clustering for colour reduction in images. Telecommun. Syst. **40**(1–2), 17–25 (2009). doi:10.1007/s11235-008-9143-8
15. T Cheng, D Goldof, L Hall, Fast fuzzy clustering. Fuzzy Sets Syst. **93**, 49–56 (1998)
16. M Ahmed, S Yamany, Mohamed N, A Farag, T Moriaty, A modified fuzzy c-means algorithm for bias field estimation and segmentation of MRI data. IEEE Trans. Med. Imaging. **21**, 193–199 (2002)
17. L Szilagyi, Z Benyo, SM Szilagyii, HS Adam, MR brain image segmentation using an enhanced fuzzy c-means algorithm, in *25th IEEE International Conference on Engineering in Medicine and Biology*, vol. 1 (IEEE, Piscataway, 2003), pp. 724–726
18. D Comaniciu, P Meer, Mean shift: a robust approach toward feature space analysis. IEEE Trans. Pattern Anal. Mach. Intell. **24**, 603–619 (2002)
19. J Wang, B Thiesson, Y Xu, M Cohen, Image and video segmentation by anisotropic kernel mean shift, in *8th European Conference on Computer Vision* (Springer, Berlin, 2004), pp. 238–2492
20. P Lingras, C West, Interval set clustering of web users with rough k-means. J. Intell. Inform. Syst. **23**, 5–16 (2004)
21. Z Pawlak, Rough sets. Int. J. Inform. Comput. Sci. **11**, 145–172 (1982)
22. YY Yao, X Li, TY Lin, Q Liu, Representation and classification of rough set models, in *Soft Computing: Third International Workshop on Rough Sets and Soft Computing : (RSSC94)*, ed. by TY Lin, A Martin Wildberger (Society for Computer Simulation International, San Diego, 1994), pp. 630–637
23. G Peters, Some refinements of rough k-means clustering. Pattern Recognit. **39**, 1481–1491 (2006)
24. G Schaefer, H Zhou, M Celebi, A Hassanien, Rough colour quantisation. Int. J. Hybrid Inform. Syst. **8**(1), 25–30 (2011). doi10.3233/HIS-2011-0128
25. Q Hu, D Yu, An improved clustering algorithm for information granulation, in *Fuzzy Systems and Knowledge Discovery*, ed. by L Wang, Y Jin (Springer, Heidelberg, 2005), pp. 494–504
26. G Schaefer, G Hu, H Zhou, J Peters, A Hassanien, Rough c-means and fuzzy rough c-means for colour quantisation. Fundam. Inform. **119**(1), 113–120 (2012). doi10.3233/FI-2012-729
27. L Nolle, G Schaefer, Color map design through optimization. Eng. Optimization. **39**(3), 327–343 (2007)
28. Y Linde, A Buzo, RM Gray, An algorithm for vector quantizer design. IEEE Trans. Commun. **28**, 84–95 (1980)
29. B Hill, T Roger, FW Vorhagen, Comparative-analysis of the quantization of color spaces on the basis of the CIELAB color-difference formula. ACM Trans. Graph. **16**(2), 109–154 (1997)
30. RS Gentile, JP Allebach, E Walowit, Quantization of color images based on uniform color spaces. J. Imaging Technol. **16**, 11–21 (1990)
31. MP Eckert, AP Bradley, Perceptual quality metrics applied to still image compression. Signal Process. **70**, 177–200 (1998)
32. X Zhang, BA Wandell, A spatial extension of CIELAB for digital color image reproduction. Journal of the Society for Information Display. **5**(1), 61–63 (1997)
33. AB Poirson, BA Wandell, Pattern-colour separable pathways predict sensitivity to simple coloured patterns. Vis. Res. **36**(4), 515–526 (1996)
34. G Schaefer, L Nolle, Quality metric based colour palette optimisation, in *2006 IEEE International Conference on Image Processing* (IEEE, Piscataway, 2006), pp. 1793–1796

18

Automatic prediction of age, gender, and nationality in offline handwriting

Somaya Al Maadeed* and Abdelaali Hassaine

Abstract

The classification of handwriting into different categories, such as age, gender, and nationality, has several applications. In forensics, handwriting classification helps investigators focus on a certain category of writers. However, only a few studies have been carried out in this field. Classification of handwriting into a demographic category is generally performed in two steps: feature extraction and classification. The performance of a system depends mainly on the feature extraction step because characterizing features makes it possible to distinguish between writers. In this study, we propose several geometric features to characterize handwritings and use these features to perform the classification of handwritings with regards to age, gender, and nationality. Features are combined using random forests and kernel discriminant analysis. Classification rates are reported on the QUWI dataset, reaching 74.05% for gender prediction, 55.76% for age range prediction, and 53.66% for nationality prediction when all writers produce the same handwritten text and 73.59% for gender prediction, 60.62% for age range prediction, and 47.98% for nationality prediction when each writer produces different handwritten text.

Keywords: Writer demographic category classification; Handwriting analysis; Chain code; Edge-based directional features; Writer identification

1 Introduction

Handwritings can be classified into many categories including gender, age, handedness, and nationality. This type of classification has several applications. For example, in the forensic domain, handwriting classification can help the investigators to focus on a certain category of suspects. Additionally, processing each category separately leads to improved results in writer identification and verification applications.

There are only a few studies in the literature that investigate the automatic detection of gender, age, and handedness from handwritings. Bandi et al. [1] proposed a system that classifies the handwritings into demographic categories using the 'macro-features' introduced in [2]. These features focus on measures such as pen pressure, writing movement, stroke formation, and word proportion. The authors reported classification accuracies of 77.5%, 86.6%, and 74.4% for gender, age, and handedness classification, respectively. However, in this study, all the writers had to produce the same letter.

Unfortunately, this is not always the case in real forensic caseworks. Moreover, the dataset used in this study is not publicly available.

Liwicki et al. [3] also performed the classification of gender and handedness in the online mode (which means that the temporal information about the handwriting is available). The authors used a set of 29 features extracted from the online information and its offline representation and applied support vector machines and Gaussian mixture models to perform the classification. The authors reported a performance of 67.06% for gender classification and 84.66% for handedness classification. In a recent study [4], the authors reported separately the performance of the offline mode, the online mode and their combination. The performance reported for the offline mode was 55.39%, which is slightly better than chance.

In this paper, we propose a new method for the detection of the age range, gender, and nationality of the writer of a handwritten document. A set of novel features are proposed and described, including directions, curvatures, tortuosities, chain codes, and edge-based directional features. These features are combined using several classifiers, including random forests and kernel discriminant

---

* Correspondence: s_alali@qu.edu.qa
Computer Science and Engineering Department, College of Engineering, Qatar University, Doha, Qatar

analysis. This method is evaluated using the QUWI database, which is the only available public dataset containing annotations regarding gender, age range, and nationality.

The remainder of this paper is organized as follows: Sections 2 and 3 give a detailed description of our feature extraction and classification methods. Section 4 presents the dataset used in this study and the detailed results. Section 5 concludes this work and draws some perspectives. Our method consists of two main steps: feature extraction and classification. These two steps are illustrated in Figure 1.

2 Feature extraction

In this step, the characterizing features are extracted from the handwriting. To make the system pen independent, images are first binarized using the Otsu thresholding algorithm [5]. The following subsections describe the features considered in this study. These features do not correspond to a single value, but are defined by a probability distribution function (PDF) extracted from the handwriting images to characterize the writer's individuality [6,7]. The PDF describes the relative likelihood for a certain feature to take on a given value.

Note that all these developed features or their equivalents are used by forensic document examiners as well as graphologists in order to distinguish between different categories of writers [8].

1.1 Direction feature (f1)

This method has been used in writer identification [7,9], and its implementation closely resembles the one proposed by Matas et al. [10]. First, we compute the Zhang skeleton of the binarized image. This skeleton is well known for not producing parasitic branches unlike most skeletonization algorithms [11]. The skeleton is then segmented at its junction pixels. Then, we traverse the pixels of the obtained segments of the skeleton using the predefined order favoring the four-connectivity neighbors as shown in Figure 2a. A result of such an ordering is shown in Figure 2b. For each pixel p, we consider the $2 \cdot N + 1$ neighboring pixels centered at position

p. A linear regression of these pixels gives a good estimation of the tangent at the pixel p (Figure 2c). The value of N has empirically been set to 5 pixels throughout this paper.

The PDF of the resulting directions is computed as a vector of probabilities for which the size has been empirically set to 10. It is worth noting that this is the first time that such a method of computing directions has been proposed for categorization applications.

2.2 Curvature feature (f2)

In forensic document examination, curvature is commonly accepted as a characterizing feature [7,8]. We have adapted this method to handwriting as follows: for each pixel p belonging to the contour, we consider a neighboring window of size t. Inside this window, we compute the number of pixels n_1 and the number of pixels n_2 that belong to the background and foreground, respectively (see Figure 3a). The difference $n_1 - n_2$ is positive at the points on which the contour is convex and negative at the points on which the contour is concave and is therefore a good indicator of the local curvature of the contour. Therefore, we estimate the curvature as being: $C = \frac{n_1 - n_2}{n_1 + n_2}$. The value C is illustrated in Figure 3b on a binary shape for which t has been empirically set to 5. The PDF of curvatures is computed in a vector with a size empirically set to 100. This way of computing curvatures is also novel in the field of offline writer identification and categorization, and to the extent of our knowledge, it has never been used before.

2.3 Tortuosity feature (f3)

This feature makes it possible to distinguish between fast writers who produce smooth handwriting and slow writers who produce 'tortuous'/twisted handwriting. To estimate tortuosity, for each pixel p of the text, we determine the longest line segment that traverses p and is completely included inside the foreground (Figure 4a). An example of estimated tortuosities is shown in Figure 4b.

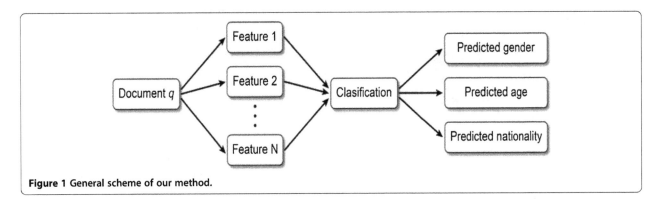

Figure 1 General scheme of our method.

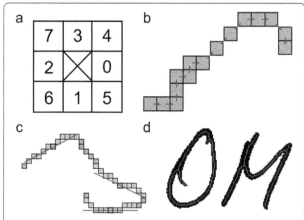

Figure 2 Computing local directions. The predefined order for traversing shapes **(a)**. Example of an ordered shape **(b)**. Estimating directions by computing linear regression of neighbors of the three pixels in bold **(c)**. Binary image and its corresponding Zhang skeleton **(d)**; the red color corresponds to a $\pi/2$ tangent, and the blue color corresponds to a zero tangent.

The PDF of the angles of the longest traversing segments is produced in a vector with the size set to 10, as mentioned previously.

2.4 Chain code features (f4 to f7)

Chain codes are generated by scanning the contour of the text and assigning a number to each pixel according to its location with respect to the previous pixel. Figure 5 shows a contour and its corresponding chain code.

Chain codes have been applied to writer identification in [12]. These features make it possible to characterize a detailed distribution of curvatures in the handwriting. Chain codes might be applied at different orders:

f4: The PDF of i patterns in the chain code list such that $i \in 0,1,...,7$. This PDF has a size of 8.

f5: The PDF of (i, j) patterns in the chain code list such that $i,j \in 0,1,...,7$. This PDF has a size of 64.

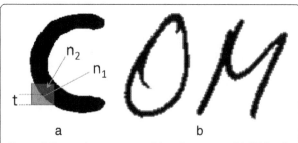

Figure 3 Computing curvatures (a) and curvatures highlighted on binary image (b). Red corresponds to the maximum curvature and blue corresponds to the minimum one.

Figure 4 Computing tortuosity. Longest traversing segment for four different pixels **(a)**. Length of maximum traversing segment: red corresponds to the maximum length, blue to the minimum one **(b)**.

Similarly, f6 and f7 correspond to the PDF of (i, j, k) and (i, j, k, l) in the chain code list with sizes of 512 and 4,096, respectively. Not all successions of chain code patterns can be obtained. For example, the chain code pattern $(1, 5)$ is not a possible succession, and therefore its corresponding distribution in the PDF will always be nil.

2.5 Edge-based directional features (f8 to f26)

Initially introduced in [9], these features provide a detailed distribution of directions and can also be applied at several sizes by positioning a window centered at each contour pixel and counting the occurrences of each direction, as shown in Figure 6a. These features have been computed from size 1 (f8, which has a PDF size of 4) to size 10 (f17, which has a PDF size of 40). We have also extended these features to include not only the contour of the moving window but also the whole window (Figure 6b) [7]. This feature has been computed from size 2 (f18, which has a PDF size of 12) to size 10 (f26, which has a PDF size of 220).

3 Classification

In this step, the features previously presented are used to decide which category each handwriting belongs to. When performing the classification, each element of the feature vectors will be used as a separate input for the classifier. (For example, f1 will be an input vector of 10 elements for the classifier.)

We have combined these features using a Random Forest classifier [13] with kernel discriminant analysis using spectral regression (SR-KDA). Descriptions of the random forests classifier and the SR-KDA [14] are given below.

The use of these two classifiers is justified by their ability to train on large datasets for features and achieving high classification rates [15].

3.1 Random forest classifier

Random forests is an ensemble learning method for classification that operates by constructing a multitude of decision trees at training time and outputting the class that is

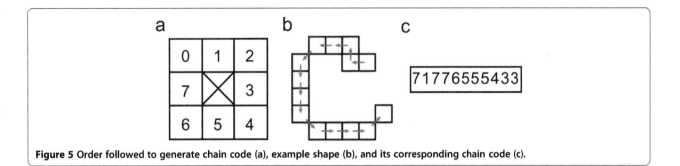

Figure 5 Order followed to generate chain code (a), example shape (b), and its corresponding chain code (c).

the mode of the classes output by individual trees. Each decision tree is constructed as follows:

1. If the number of cases in the training set is N, sample n cases such as $n < N$ at random but with replacement from the original data. This sample will be the training set for growing the tree.
2. If there are M input variables, a number $m < < M$ is specified such that at each node, m variables are selected at random from M and the best split on these m is used to split the node. The value of m is held constant during the forest growing.
3. Each tree is grown to the largest extent possible. There is no pruning.

In our case, we built the random forest classifiers for the cases of age, gender, and nationality using the R random forest library [16].

3.2 Kernel discriminant analysis using spectral regression

Let $x_i \in R^d$, $i = 1,..., m$ be training vectors represented as an $m \times m$ kernel matrix K such that $K(x_i, x_j) = \langle \Phi(x_i), \Phi(x_j) \rangle$, where $\Phi(x_i)$ and $\Phi(x_j)$ are the embeddings of data items x_i and x_j. If v denotes a projective function into the kernel feature space, then the objective function for KDA is [17]:

$$\max_v D(v) = \frac{v^T C_b v}{v^T C_t v}, \tag{1}$$

where C_b and C_t denote the between-class and total scatter matrices in the feature space, respectively. Equation 1 can be solved by the eigen-problem $C_b = \lambda C_t$. It is proved in [18] that Equation 1 is equivalent to:

$$\max_\alpha D(\alpha) = \frac{\alpha^T KWK_\alpha}{\alpha^T KK_\alpha}, \tag{2}$$

where $\alpha = [\alpha_1, \alpha_2,..., \alpha_m]^T$ is the eigenvector satisfying $KWK\alpha = \lambda KK\alpha$.

$W = (W_l)_{l = 1,...,n}$ is an $(m \times m)$ block diagonal matrix of labels arranged such that the upper block corresponds to positive examples and the lower one corresponds to negative examples of the class. Each eigenvector α yields a projection function v in the feature space.

It is also shown in [4] that instead of solving the eigen-problem in KDA, the KDA projections can be obtained by the following two linear equations:

$$W\phi = \lambda\phi \quad (K + \delta I)\alpha = \phi \tag{3}$$

where ϕ is an eigenvector of W, I is the identity matrix, and $\delta > 0$ is a regularization parameter. $W = (W_l)_{l = 1,...,n}$ is an $(m \times m)$ block diagonal matrix of labels arranged such that the upper block corresponds to positive examples and the lower one corresponds to negative examples of the class. Eigenvectors ϕ are obtained directly from the Gram-Schmidt method. Because $(K + \delta I)$ is positive definite, a Cholesky decomposition is used to solve the

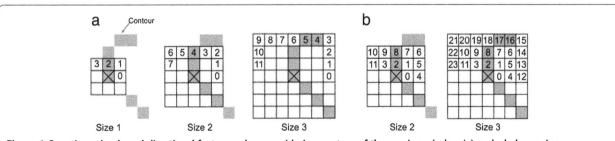

Figure 6 Counting edge-based directional features when considering contour of the moving window (a) and whole moving window (b).

linear equations in (3). Thus, for the resolution of the linear system of Equation 3, the system becomes:

$$(K + \delta I)\alpha = \phi \Leftrightarrow \begin{cases} R^T \theta = \phi \\ R\alpha = \theta \end{cases} \tag{4}$$

i.e., solve the system to first find vector θ and then find vector α. In summary, SR-KDA only needs to solve a set of regularized regression problems, and there is no eigenvector computation involved. This results in a significant improvement of computational complexity and

allows large kernel matrices to be handled. After obtaining α, the decision function for the new data item is calculated from:

$$f(x) = \sum_{i=1}^{n} \alpha_i K(x, x_i). \tag{5}$$

The classification results of those classifiers for all the presented features on the QUWI dataset will be shown in the next Section.

Table 1 Correct classification rates for gender detection using random forests (RF) and kernel discriminant analysis (KDA)

	Arabic				English				Both			
	Same text (%)		Different text (%)		Same text (%)		Different text (%)		Same text (%)		Different text (%)	
Feature	RF	KDA	RF	KDA	RF	KDA	RF	KDA	RF	KDA	RF	KDA
f1	59.4	65.5	62.1	62.9	62.0	64.1	63.3	62.9	63.3	64.7	63.0	59.2
f2	68.3	63.9	66.9	63.1	63.4	62.8	69.2	62.2	64.9	68.5	67.5	60.6
f3	58.1	59.9	62.1	60.6	62.7	58.3	63.0	54.3	61.3	60.2	61.1	59.9
f4	53.0	60.6	54.8	57.1	64.1	53.5	59.2	53.3	57.8	61.6	56.1	62.7
f5	68.9	64.8	65.2	65.3	65.5	62.4	66.8	65.7	66.6	69.2	67.0	64.4
f6	67.0	68.6	68.6	66.1	67.3	69.3	71.6	70.2	66.9	68.2	70.3	68.0
f7	65.7	70.0	68.3	71.8	68.7	69.3	69.9	73.7	66.3	74.1	69.3	73.6
f8	57.1	58.9	54.8	59.1	52.8	57.2	58.5	54.9	54.6	58.5	56.3	60.2
f9	55.2	58.2	56.6	57.4	59.9	57.2	60.6	54.9	57.8	57.8	57.5	59.9
f10	55.9	58.7	56.6	61.9	57.8	57.2	55.7	60.0	56.3	58.8	54.4	59.5
f11	58.4	61.5	59.7	58.1	59.9	61.7	56.8	60.6	57.8	61.6	58.7	56.0
f12	63.8	61.5	62.8	62.4	64.1	58.6	59.5	62.9	62.6	63.0	60.8	59.5
f13	64.4	62.0	64.5	62.8	63.7	63.5	63.0	60.3	63.9	62.3	63.0	60.9
f14	63.8	63.6	65.2	60.8	64.4	60.0	62.3	61.3	63.3	63.3	64.9	62.0
f15	64.4	63.6	66.9	62.9	65.1	66.2	61.6	62.5	65.3	59.2	66.2	67.3
f16	65.1	63.0	69.3	63.8	62.7	63.8	64.7	61.3	63.6	60.6	67.7	62.3
f17	66.7	61.8	68.6	59.4	61.6	66.2	64.4	61.3	62.6	57.8	67.4	60.2
f18	56.5	59.1	58.6	59.6	61.3	58.3	60.9	56.8	58.1	59.2	63.2	62.7
f19	56.5	61.8	58.3	62.3	60.6	55.5	59.5	61.9	57.9	65.1	60.3	61.6
f20	60.3	64.1	60.3	63.8	58.8	59.7	60.9	64.8	60.1	67.5	60.3	60.6
f21	62.5	64.8	62.4	64.1	62.7	62.4	61.6	63.2	61.3	67.5	63.0	62.3
f22	65.7	65.3	63.5	63.6	62.7	61.7	61.9	63.2	64.4	65.4	63.6	64.1
f23	67.9	63.7	63.5	66.1	67.6	62.1	63.0	65.4	66.4	63.3	64.1	64.1
f24	67.9	64.4	66.2	65.9	70.8	63.1	64.4	64.1	68.8	63.7	65.5	65.9
f25	68.3	66.5	65.2	66.8	69.7	64.8	64.7	65.4	68.3	66.1	66.3	65.1
f26	68.3	66.8	67.6	66.4	69.7	66.9	65.7	68.6	69.3	64.7	66.7	64.1
f1 + f2 + f3	65.4	68.6	66.6	69.5	64.8	66.6	74.7	68.3	62.8	72.0	69.1	64.1
f4 +,…, + f7	67.3	68.9	68.6	70.1	69.0	69.0	70.2	70.8	64.8	70.2	69.8	69.0
f8 +,…, + f17	67.6	65.8	67.6	63.6	66.2	64.5	63.7	63.8	66.9	63.7	67.7	66.9
f18 +,…, + f26	67.3	67.2	64.8	66.8	71.1	64.5	64.0	66.4	68.8	66.8	66.1	65.1
f1 +,…, + f26	71.1	68.4	69.0	71.6	69.7	68.6	68.2	66.4	69.8	72.3	68.7	70.8

4 Evaluation

In this section, we describe the QUWI handwriting database on which the experiments have been conducted. We also present the results obtained for each individual feature as well as their combination using random forests and kernel discriminant analysis. The results are then analyzed and discussed.

4.1 Dataset

To the best of our knowledge, the only publicly available handwriting dataset annotated with respect to age, gender, and nationality is the QUWI dataset [19]. This dataset contains handwritings of 1,017 writers in both English and Arabic. In each language, writers produced one text that is the same for all the writers and another text that is different for every writer. Moreover, writers in this dataset have different genders, age ranges, and nationalities. Because very few writers are left-handed (around fifty writers), this dataset can only be useful for handedness detection.

To perform the classification, 70% of this dataset has been used for training and 30% for testing as is often the case in data mining [18]. We have computed the presented

Table 2 Correct classification rates for age range detection using random forests (Rf) and kernel discriminant analysis (Kda)

	Arabic				English				Both			
	Same text (%)		Different text (%)		Same text (%)		Different text (%)		Same text (%)		Different text (%)	
Feature	RF	KDA	RF	KDA	RF	KDA	RF	KDA	RF	KDA	RF	KDA
f1	53.7	56.5	56.9	52.1	47.2	58.3	53.6	49.2	50.4	52.9	53.2	47.2
f2	56.2	52.0	59.3	53.6	51.1	51.4	57.4	53.0	55.4	49.8	58.7	50.4
f3	55.9	54.9	56.2	49.9	49.7	52.1	53.3	51.1	52.4	54.0	53.5	45.4
f4	56.5	54.4	50.7	51.9	49.3	53.1	50.9	51.1	51.9	50.5	52.5	46.8
f5	55.9	48.9	56.6	48.9	50.4	43.8	54.0	48.9	54.1	43.6	55.8	47.2
f6	58.7	48.2	60.7	48.6	50.4	49.3	55.4	50.5	55.1	45.7	58.4	46.1
f7	59.1	53.9	61.4	55.3	50.7	53.1	56.8	54.6	54.6	51.6	58.7	48.9
f8	49.8	57.2	51.7	52.6	48.2	55.9	50.5	56.5	49.6	55.4	52.0	49.7
f9	56.2	53.9	55.5	53.4	49.7	56.9	54.7	56.2	54.8	48.8	54.6	47.2
f10	57.1	56.0	55.5	52.9	48.2	53.8	52.6	54.0	54.4	55.7	54.8	48.6
f11	55.6	53.4	55.2	54.8	47.9	47.2	52.9	56.5	53.4	54.3	53.2	49.3
f12	54.0	53.5	53.1	53.3	50.4	49.7	56.4	53.7	52.8	52.9	54.9	52.5
f13	55.2	53.5	55.5	52.6	50.4	47.9	55.7	53.0	52.6	54.0	56.1	47.9
f14	56.2	53.7	54.1	52.4	53.2	51.0	54.7	55.9	54.1	51.2	56.5	47.9
f15	56.2	50.8	56.2	52.3	52.8	48.6	54.7	50.5	54.4	51.9	57.2	51.1
f16	55.9	49.6	57.2	52.8	50.4	48.3	57.8	48.6	53.9	50.9	56.3	51.4
f17	55.2	51.0	58.3	52.8	48.9	49.0	55.4	50.2	53.4	50.9	54.9	50.4
f18	55.6	54.1	58.6	52.8	49.3	55.2	55.1	56.2	53.1	49.8	55.1	49.3
f19	57.1	54.9	56.6	53.8	50.4	53.8	55.4	56.2	54.4	51.9	55.3	48.6
f20	58.1	53.0	55.2	52.9	50.7	51.0	54.2	54.9	54.4	52.6	54.6	49.7
f21	57.5	51.3	54.1	53.4	49.7	48.3	54.6	56.8	54.3	51.6	54.2	50.0
f22	57.1	50.3	55.9	53.8	50.7	47.2	53.7	54.3	54.3	50.9	54.1	50.4
f23	55.2	49.9	58.3	53.3	49.7	47.6	54.9	53.3	53.1	51.9	54.8	47.5
f24	54.9	50.3	58.3	52.4	50.7	48.3	56.5	53.0	53.8	51.9	56.3	49.7
f25	56.2	50.4	60.0	54.4	51.8	49.3	58.0	53.3	54.1	53.6	58.6	51.1
f26	56.8	51.8	58.6	54.8	51.8	49.3	58.7	51.4	54.9	53.6	57.7	51.4
f1 + f2 + f3	58.7	53.9	62.4	50.4	52.8	54.1	59.9	49.5	55.8	54.0	60.6	46.8
f4 +,..., + f7	58.4	50.8	60.7	52.3	50.0	48.6	56.4	53.0	54.4	47.1	58.5	48.6
f8 +,..., + f17	57.1	49.1	58.3	54.1	48.9	50.7	54.7	51.4	54.1	49.5	56.7	53.2
f18 +,..., + f26	55.9	50.1	57.2	53.9	50.7	49.7	56.4	55.9	53.1	53.3	56.8	49.3
f1 +,..., + f26	58.1	53.0	59.3	55.8	51.4	53.5	57.4	53.3	55.1	49.8	59.4	53.9

features on this dataset. As mentioned previously, each feature corresponds to a PDF of several values with each of them used as a separate predictor. These predictors were combined using a random forest classifier, which is well suited for this category of features [13], as well as the kernel discriminant analysis using spectral regression.

Three classification tasks were defined for this dataset:

- Gender classification. Note that a random classification would predict approximately 50%, as this is a two-class classification.

- Age range classification. To avoid classes with very small patterns, seven age ranges were defined: (1950 to 1965), (1966 to 1975), (1976 to 1985), (1986 to 1990), (1991 to 1995), (1996 to 2000), and (2001 to 2012). A random classification would therefore predict approximately 14%.

- Nationality prediction. To avoid small classes, only writers of eight different nationalities were considered. Each of these classes has more than 30 writers. A random classification would only predict approximately 12%.

Table 3 Correct classification rates for nationality detection using random forests (Rf) and kernel discriminant analysis (Kda)

| | Arabic | | | | English | | | | Both | | | |
| | Same text (%) | | Different text (%) | | Same text (%) | | Different text (%) | | Same text (%) | | Different text (%) | |
Feature	RF	KDA	RF	KDA	RF	KDA	RF	KDA	RF	KDA	RF	KDA
f1	42.1	39.6	37.5	42.4	35.8	36.4	37.2	39.2	39.4	43.5	38.7	40.3
f2	37.8	38.0	38.2	43.4	36.2	36.4	38.9	41.0	42.6	41.1	40.	37.5
f3	44.0	38.0	39.8	42.8	33.7	36.4	35.2	39.9	38.6	38.6	39.6	37.5
f4	37.1	39.6	37.5	47.7	36.2	34.6	34.7	37.4	37.8	41.1	38.3	44.4
f5	42.1	39.6	39.8	36.3	42.4	37.1	41.8	39.6	43.8	38.2	43.0	41.5
f6	42.5	44.2	42.1	39.7	42.0	44.1	43.9	41.0	45.5	47.2	44.8	43.2
f7	43.2	47.3	42.1	38.6	41.6	45.2	44.8	49.6	44.0	53.7	42.4	48.0
f8	29.3	35.1	28.6	42.8	28.0	33.1	30.1	37.4	30.1	39.0	32.7	35.5
f9	38.2	37.3	33.6	42.2	35.8	33.5	36.4	39.2	34.9	38.6	35.5	37.5
f10	39.4	40.9	38.2	42.2	32.1	36.0	36.4	40.7	36.6	41.1	40.4	36.3
f11	42.1	41.5	41.7	43.4	34.2	40.8	36.0	40.7	38.8	37.8	41.4	39.1
f12	44.8	42.3	44.0	43.4	35.8	41.9	37.2	43.2	40.8	38.6	42.6	37.9
f13	45.6	40.9	44.4	40.9	36.2	45.2	34.3	41.7	42.6	35.4	42.0	38.7
f14	44.4	40.5	43.6	41.4	37.5	40.8	36.4	41.7	40.4	32.1	42.2	39.9
f15	42.1	40.0	42.9	41.1	38.3	42.7	38.5	42.8	43.2	32.5	42.4	40.7
f16	40.2	39.6	43.2	42.2	38.7	40.4	37.2	42.8	42.0	32.9	42.2	38.7
f17	39.4	39.2	43.6	44.5	35.4	40.4	37.7	39.2	42.4	39.4	43.0	39.9
f18	41.3	40.9	36.3	43.7	37.0	34.6	38.1	42.1	39.0	41.1	41.8	38.7
f19	41.3	43.2	36.3	44.1	37.0	35.7	38.1	40.7	39.0	41.9	41.8	37.5
f20	43.2	42.1	37.8	44.7	35.4	40.4	39.8	43.2	42.4	42.3	43.8	40.3
f21	46.0	42.9	38.6	46.4	36.2	40.4	38.9	42.8	42.4	41.5	43.6	38.7
f22	47.1	42.7	40.2	44.3	37.0	40.1	40.2	43.5	43.4	41.5	44.6	39.1
f23	46.3	43.1	44.0	43.7	38.3	43.0	38.5	44.6	44.0	40.7	44.4	39.5
f24	46.0	43.6	44.8	42.4	38.3	44.5	38.9	45.7	44.2	39.0	44.6	37.1
f25	45.6	43.6	45.6	44.9	39.5	44.9	40.2	44.6	44.6	39.8	44.6	37.1
f26	45.2	41.9	43.6	44.3	39.5	43.0	40.6	45.7	44.6	39.8	45.0	37.9
f1 + f2 + f3	41.7	41.3	40.4	45.1	42.3	39.3	45.1	44.2	42.6	43.9	44.0	40.3
f4 +,…, + f7	43.5	47.7	40.8	46.2	47.2	44.5	44.7	45.7	44.5	51.6	41.3	46.0
f8 +,…, + f17	45.7	41.3	46.0	44.3	42.3	44.5	40.7	46.4	44.7	38.2	42.9	41.5
f18 +,…, + f26	46.8	44.4	47.1	45.1	44.0	43.8	39.0	45.3	44.3	41.9	43.1	37.1
f1 +,…, + f26	48.9	47.7	47.4	46.2	44.4	48.9	44.3	47.1	**46.4**	44.3	**46.7**	44.8

4.2 Results

Tables 1, 2, and 3 depicts the correct classification rates for each category of features using a random forest of 5,000 random trees and kernel discriminant analysis for every gender, age range, and nationality classification. The classification is performed for the Arabic and English languages separately in the first step and jointly in the second step. The results are reported for the case of similar texts written by all the writers and different texts for each writer. Figure 7 summarizes the best results for gender, age range, and nationality using two classification methods.

4.3 Discussion and analysis

To test which feature combination is optimal for each classification problem, we plotted the average performance (for similar and different texts using random forest

and KDA) for the proposed geometric features (f1 to f3), chain code features (f4 to f7), edge-based directional features (f8 to 17), and filled edge-based directional features (f18 to f26). The results are shown in Figure 8. It is important to note that the performances are seemingly very high for nationality, low for age range and even lower for nationality detection. This is due to the fact that nationality prediction is a binary classification problem in which even a random prediction would score 50%, whereas age range and nationality detection are respectively seven- and eight-class classification problems in which a random classifier would only score 14% and 12%, respectively.

The results show that chain code-based features generally outperform using other features for predicting the gender and the nationality which suggests that the detailed distribution of curvatures in the handwriting is of a high importance in characterizing the gender and nationality. Note as well that the proposed geometric features outperforms other features for predicting the age range which suggests that all of the directions, curvatures, and tortuosity are essential for determining the age through handwriting.

We also plotted the average performance of random forests and KDA classifiers when combining all the features (f1 to f26). The results are shown in Figure 9. Random forests are generally preferred for the prediction of age range and nationality, whereas KDA is preferred for the prediction of gender. This clearly suggests that random forests are to be preferred when predicting patterns with many classes whereas KDA are to be preferred for binary classification problems.

The average performance when combining all the features (f1 to f26) on the same and different texts is shown in Figure 10. Notice that handwritings produced by the same writer yield slightly better results for the prediction of gender but not for the prediction of age range or nationality. This suggests that working on the same texts or different texts do not have any benefits in improving the classification results.

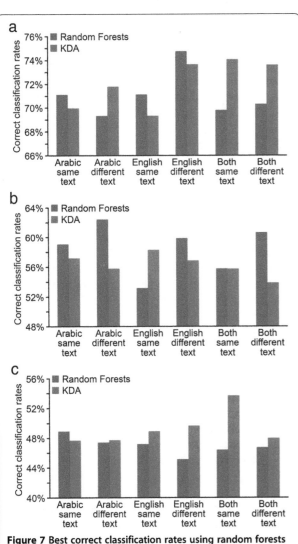

Figure 7 Best correct classification rates using random forests and kernel discriminant analysis. (a) Gender, **(b)** age range, and **(c)** nationality.

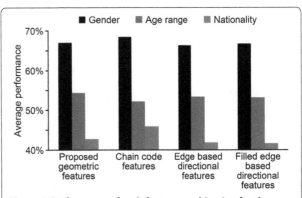

Figure 8 Performance of each feature combination for the detection of gender, age range, and nationality.

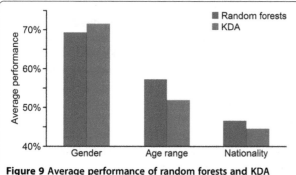

Figure 9 Average performance of random forests and KDA classifiers for the prediction of gender, age range, and nationality.

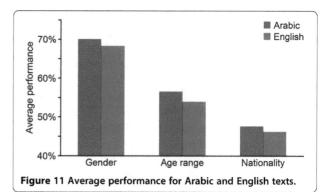

Figure 11 Average performance for Arabic and English texts.

The average performance when combining all the features (f1 to f26) on Arabic and English texts is shown in Figure 11. Generally, Arabic handwritings yield better prediction results. This is explained by the complexity of the Arabic script which tends to help better categorize writers.

Additionally, the combination of several features does not always yield better results. There are many cases in which one feature alone outperforms a combination of several features. Indeed, some features might be redundant or irrelevant and contain no useful information in which case they need to be removed for obtaining better performance.

The classification systems described here are promising; however, there remains a lot of room for improvement in terms of using new features and classification methods. Comparison of results, obtained in this research, with other researchers is difficult because of differences in experimental details, the actual handwriting used, the method of data collection, and dealing with cursive off-line handwritten text. If this work is compared to writer demographic identification research [1,4], it is the first one that implemented on offline cursive Arabic and English writers. This also means that it uses different sets of features and classification techniques. Unfortunately, both datasets used in [1,4] are not publically available. The dataset used in this research is available for research purposes.

Finally, for the comparison purposes, the average correct gender classification results are over 73%, which exceeds the results reported in [4] for offline gender identification (55.39%) on a different dataset consisting of 200 writers. The results also compare well with the 77.5% reported in [1] on a smaller dataset (800 individuals wrote the same letter). The authors of [1] also report an age range classification accuracy of 86.6%, which seemingly outperforms our 55%. However, the authors only included two age range categories (below 24 and above 45) and included only 650 individuals.

5 Conclusion

We have presented a method that uses several geometric features for the classification of age range, gender, and nationality of handwritings, which is applicable for both Arabic and English documents. This study is the first that reported classification results for those subcategories on the QUWI dataset [19]. The results are reported for both text-dependent and text-independent category classification.

Experiments show that using chain code-based features generally outperforms using other features for predicting the gender and the nationality, and the proposed geometric features outperforms other features for predicting the age range. The results suggest that random forests are generally preferred for the prediction of age range and nationality, whereas KDA is preferred for the prediction of gender. We have also noticed that handwritings produced by the same writer yield slightly better results for the prediction of gender but not for the prediction of age range or nationality. It has also shown that experiments on Arabic handwritings attained generally better prediction results. Future work includes exploring ways of combining the proposed features and using other classifiers. The use of the proposed features for predicting the handedness of writers is also planned.

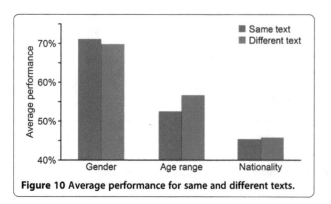

Figure 10 Average performance for same and different texts.

Competing interests
The authors declare that they have no competing interests.

Acknowledgements
This work is supported by the Qatar National Research Fund through National Priority Research Program (NPRP) No. 09 – 864 – 1 – 128. The contents of this publication are solely the responsibility of the authors and do not necessarily represent the official views of the Qatar National Research Fund or Qatar University.

References
1. K Bandi, SN Srihari, Writer demographic identification using bagging and boosting, in *Proceedings of the International Graphonomics Society Conference (IGS)* (Salerno, Italy, 2005), pp. 133–137. 26–29 June
2. S Srihari, SH Cha, H Arora, S Lee, Individuality of handwriting: a validation study, in *2001 Proceedings of the Sixth International Conference on Document Analysis and Recognition* (Seattle, 2001), pp. 106–109. 10–13 September
3. M Liwicki, A Schlapbach, P Loretan, H Bunke, Automatic detection of gender and handedness from on-line handwriting, in *Proceedings of the 13th Conference of the International Graphonomics Society* (Melbourne, 2007), pp. 179–183. 11–14 Novembers
4. M Liwicki, A Schlapbach, H Bunke, Automatic gender detection using on-line and off-line information. Pattern. Anal. Appl. **14**, 87–92 (2011)
5. N Otsu, A threshold selection method from gray-level histograms. IEEE Trans. Syst. Man Cybern. **9**(1), 62–66 (1979)
6. A Hassaine, S Al-Maadeed, J Alja'am, A Jaoua, A Bouridane, The ICDAR2011 Arabic Writer Identification Contest, in *Proceedings of the Eleventh International Conference on Document Analysis and Recognition* (Beijing, China, 2011). 18–21 September
7. A Hassaïne, S Al-Maadeed, A Bouridane, A set of geometrical features for writer identification, in *The 19th International Conference of Neural Information Processing Doha, Qatar* (Springer, Berlin Heidelberg, 2012), pp. 584–591. 12–15 November
8. K Koppenhaver, *Forensic Document Examination: principles and practice* (Humana Press, New York, 2007)
9. M Bulacu, L Schomaker, Text-independent writer identification and verification using textural and allographic features. IEEE Trans. Pattern Anal. Mach. Intell. **29**(4), 701–717 (2007)
10. J Matas, Z Shao, J Kittler, Estimation of curvature and tangent direction by median filtered differencing, in *The 8th International Conference on Image Analysis and Processing*. Lecture notes in computer science. vol 974 (Springer-Verlag, Berlin, 1995), pp. 83–88. 13–15 September
11. TY Zhang, A fast parallel algorithm for thinning digital patterns. Commun. ACM **27**(3), 236–239 (1984)
12. I Siddiqi, N Vincent, Text independent writer recognition using redundant writing patterns with contour-based orientation and curvature features. Pattern Recogn. **43**(11), 3853–3865 (2010)
13. L Breiman, Random forests. Mach. Learn. **45**, 5–32 (2001)
14. D Cai, X He, J Han, *Proceedings of the ICDM* (Omaha, Nebraska, 2007). 28–31 October
15. HH Bock, E Diday, *Analysis of Symbolic Data: Exploratory Methods for Extracting Statistical Information from Complex Data* (Springer, Heidelberg, 2000)
16. A Liaw, M Wiener, Classification and regression by randomforest. NANR News **2**(3), 18–22 (2002). http://CRAN.R-project.org/doc/Rnews
17. S Mika, G Ratsch, J Weston, B Scholkopf, KR Mullers, Fisher discriminant analysis with kernels, in *Neural Networks for Signal Processing IX, 1999*. Proceedings of the 1999 IEEE Signal Processing Society Workshop, Madison (IEEE, Piscataway, 1999), pp. 41–48. 23–25 August
18. TY Lin, Y Xie, A Wasilewska, CJ Liau, *Data Mining: Foundations and Practice, vol. 118* (Springer, Heidelberg, 2008)
19. S Al-Ma'adeed, W Ayouby, A Hassaine, J Aljaam, QUWI: an Arabic and English handwriting dataset for offline writer identification, in *International Conference on Frontiers in Handwriting Recognition* (Bari, Italy, 2012). 18–20 September

19

A context-adaptive SPN predictor for trustworthy source camera identification

Xiangui Kang[*], Jiansheng Chen, Kerui Lin and Peng Anjie

Abstract

Sensor pattern noise (SPN) has been recognized as a reliable device fingerprint for camera source identification (CSI) and image origin verification. However, the SPN extracted from a single image can be contaminated largely by image content details from scene because, for example, an image edge can be much stronger than SPN and hard to be separated. So, the identification performance is heavily dependent upon the purity of the estimated SPN. In this paper, we propose an effective SPN predictor based on eight-neighbor context-adaptive interpolation algorithm to suppress the effect of image scene and propose a source camera identification method with it to enhance the receiver operating characteristic (ROC) performance of CSI. Experimental results on different image databases and on different sizes of images show that our proposed method has the best ROC performance among all of the existing CSI schemes, as well as the best performance in resisting mild JPEG compression, especially when the false-positive rate is held low. Because trustworthy CSI must often be performed at low false-positive rates, these results demonstrate that our proposed technique is better suited for use in real-world scenarios than existing techniques. However, our proposed method needs many such as not less than 100 original images to create camera fingerprint; the advantage of the proposed method decreases when the camera fingerprint is created with less original images.

Keywords: Context-adaptive interpolation; Edge-adaptive predictor; Sensor pattern noise; Camera source identification

1. Introduction

Digital images are easy to modify and edit via image-editing software. Image content becomes unbelievable. Using this kind of forged image should be avoided as evidence in a court of law, as news, as part of a medical record, or as financial documents. There are some works focused on image component forensics in recent years [1-3]. The work in [3] first proposed using the imaging sensor pattern noise (SPN) to trace back the imaging device and solve the camera source identification (CSI) problem. They extracted SPN from wavelet high-frequency coefficients using the wavelet-based denoising filter [4]. A camera reference SPN is built by averaging residual noise from multiple images taken by the same camera. In [5], an innovative and recently introduced denoising filter, namely, a sparse 3D transform-domain collaborative filtering (BM3D) [6], is used to extract the SPN. This filter is based on an enhanced sparse representation in a transform domain. A maximum likelihood method is proposed in [7] to estimate the camera reference SPN. It will be named the MLE CSI method for short in this paper. Later, [8] proposed a more stable detection statistic, the peak-to-correlation energy measure (PCE), to suppress periodic noise contamination and enhance CSI performance. The authors of [9] proposed a forgery-detection method using SPN to determine if an image is tampered. Li [10] demonstrated that the SPN extracted from a single image can be contaminated by image scene details and proposed some models to attenuate the strong signal component of noise residue. However, attenuating strong components from scene details may also attenuate the useful SPN components [11]. Kang et al. [11] proposed a detection statistic correlation over circular correlation norm (CCN) to lower the false-positive rate and a white-camera reference SPN to enhance the ROC performance [12]. The noise residues extracted from the original images are whitened first and then averaged to generate the white-camera phase reference SPN. We call it the phase CSI method for short in the rest of this paper.

Although there have been some prior studies dedicated to improving the performance of CSI based on SPN in

---

[*] Correspondence: isskxg@mail.sysu.edu.cn
School of Information Science and Technology, Sun Yat-sen University, Guangzhou 510006, People's Republic of China

recent years, an effective method to eliminate the contamination of the image scene details is still lacking. In order to reduce the impact of scene details while preserving SPN at the same time, an edge-adaptive SPN predictor based on a four-neighbor context-adaptive interpolation (PCAI4) [13] was proposed and has been proved to have improvement on CSI performance via extensive experiments. This paper is an extension work of our conference paper [13]. Because the method PCAI4 only predicts the center pixel from its four-neighboring pixels, in this paper, we will extend this method by making use of all the eight-neighboring pixels and propose an edge-adaptive SPN predictor based on eight-neighbor context-adaptive interpolating prediction, as well as a CSI method with this advanced predictor. We have also conducted extensive experiments on different image datasets and reported new results in this paper. Thanks to its adaptability to image edge and context, the predicted SPN is much purer and performs better for CSI. The experimental results on different image databases show that our proposed method can achieve the best ROC performance among all of the existing CSI schemes on different sizes of images and has the best performance in resisting mild JPEG compression.

The rest of this paper is organized as follows. In Section II, we will first introduce our context-adaptive interpolating prediction algorithm. Then, an eight-neighbor SPN predictor is proposed to improve the CSI performance. In Section III, we evaluate the performance of our proposed algorithm and compare its performance with state-of-the-art CSI methods on different image databases. The conclusion of this paper is made in Section IV.

2. Advance SPN predictor based on adaptive interpolation

2.1 Context-adaptive interpolator

The context-adaptive interpolation (CAI) method predicts a center pixel from its four-neighbor pixels. We will call it the 'CAI4' in this paper. The SPN predictor using CAI4 [13] is based on the CAI [14] interpolation algorithm which is adapted from the gradient-adaptive predictor (GAP) [15]. In the CAI4 method, the local regions are classified into four types: smooth, horizontally edged, vertically edged, and other. A mean filter is used to estimate the center-pixel value in smooth region; in edged regions, the center pixel is predicted along the edge. In other regions, a median filter is applied. Taking p to be a center-pixel value to be predicted, and $\mathbf{t} = [n, s, e, w]^T$ to be a vector of its four-neighboring pixels as in Figure 1, the predicted pixel value $\hat{p}$ using CAI4 method can be formulated as

$$\hat{p} = \begin{cases} \text{mean}(\mathbf{t}) & (\max(\mathbf{t}) - \min(\mathbf{t}) \le 20) \\ (n+s)/2 & (|e-w| - |n-s| > 20) \\ (e+w)/2 & (|n-s| - |e-w| > 20) \\ \text{median}(\mathbf{t}) & (\text{otherwise}). \end{cases} \quad (1)$$

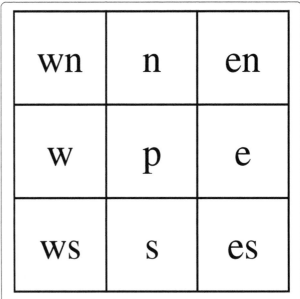

Figure 1 Neighborhood of the center pixel to be predicted.

In (1), a smooth region will never be estimated as the edged region, and the interpolation prediction in the edged regions are adapted from the GAP [15]. The center pixel is predicted according to different types of edge regions, which is classified by the four-neighboring pixel values with an empirical threshold. The threshold has little impact on the experimental results and set to be 20 according to the former work [15].

2.2 Extending CAI4 to CAI8

The CAI4 method only predicts the center pixel from its four-neighbor pixels because it is proposed as an adaptive interpolation algorithm and is not aware of the other four diagonal pixels. As we are using it to predict SPN knowing all the neighbor pixels in Figure 1, we can extend and enhance the CAI4 method by making use of all the eight-neighboring pixels. We call this method 'CAI8' in short form.

In CAI8 method, the local regions are classified into six types: smooth, horizontally edged, vertically edged, left-diagonal edge, right-diagonal edge, and others. In the smooth region, a mean filter is used to estimate the center pixel from the eight-neighboring pixels; in the horizontal and vertical edge regions, the center-pixel value is predicted along the edge as the same as CAI4. In the diagonal-edge region, the center-pixel value is also estimated along the corresponding edge; in other regions, a median filter is applied. Taking p' to be the center-pixel value to be predicted by CAI8, $\mathbf{t}' = [n, s, e, w, en, es, wn, ws]^T$ to be a vector of its eight-neighboring pixels as shown in Figure 1, then the predicted pixel value $\hat{p}'$ using the CAI8 method can be formulated as follows:

$$\hat{p}' = \begin{cases} \text{mean}(\mathbf{t}') & (\max(\mathbf{t}')-\min(\mathbf{t}') \leq 20) \\ (n+s)/2 & (|e{-}w|{-}|n{-}s| > 20) \\ (e+w)/2 & (|n{-}s|{-}|e{-}w| > 20) \\ (es+wn)/2 & (|en{-}ws|{-}|es{-}wn| > 20) \\ (en+ws)/2 & (|es{-}wn|{-}|en{-}ws| > 20) \\ \text{median}(\mathbf{t}') & (\text{otherwise}). \end{cases} \quad (2)$$

In (2), the center-pixel value is predicted along different directions of the edge, including in the diagonally edged region which is ignored by CAI4. So, the predicted result can suppress the interference of image edge better and has less prediction error.

2.3 Source camera identification with SPN predictor based on CAI8

SPN can be contaminated largely by the image scene, especially in the texture regions. Method CAI8 can predict a center-pixel value accurately in allusion to different local regions because it is adaptive to image edge and local context. So, the difference between the predicted value and actual value can suppress the impact of image edge better while preserving the SPN components at the same time.

Let $\mathbf{y} = \{y_i \mid i = 0, 1, ..., N{-}1\}$ be the camera reference SPN, and $\mathbf{x} = \{x_i\}$ be the noise residue extracted from a test image. For the null hypothesis, $\mathbf{y}$ is not the correct camera reference SPN of the noise residue $\mathbf{x}$ extracted from a test image, i. e., the test image is not taken by the reference camera. In other words, $\mathbf{x}$ is a negative sample for $\mathbf{y}$. For the affirmative hypothesis, $\mathbf{y}$ is the correct camera reference SPN of the noise residue $\mathbf{x}$ extracted from a test image, i.e., the test image is taken by the reference camera. In other words, $\mathbf{x}$ is a positive sample for $\mathbf{y}$.

In the following, we will propose a context-adaptive SPN predictor based on CAI8, which is called PCAI8 in short form, and a source camera identification method with PCAI8.

(1) Firstly, we take the difference D of the predicted value and actual value,

$$\mathbf{D} = \mathbf{I}{-}\text{CAI}(\mathbf{I}), \quad (3)$$

where CAI($\cdot$) means the pixel-wise CAI8 prediction as shown in Equation 2.

(2) In order to further eliminate the impact of the image scene and extract a more accurate camera reference SPN, we then perform a pixel-wise adaptive Wiener filter based on the statistics estimated from the neighborhood of each pixel, assuming that the SPN is a white Gaussian signal corrupted by image content. For each pixel (i, j), the optimal predictor for the estimated SPN is

$$\mathbf{W}(i,j) = \mathbf{D}(i,j)\frac{\sigma_0^2}{\hat{\sigma}^2(i,j) + \sigma_0^2}, \quad (4)$$

where $\hat{\sigma}2$ represents the estimated local variance for the original noise-free image, and σ_0^2 represents the overall variance of the additive white Gaussian noise (AWGN) signal, i.e., the SPN here. To a large extent, the performance of the predictor depends on the accuracy of the estimated local variance. We use the maximum *a posteriori* probability (MAP) estimation to estimate the local variance as following:

$$\hat{\sigma}^2(i,j) = \max\left(0, \frac{1}{m^2}\sum_{(p,q)\in N_m} \mathbf{D}^2(p,q){-}\sigma_0^2\right), \quad (5)$$

where m is the size of a neighborhood N_m for each pixel. Here, we take $m = 3$. The overall variance of the SPN σ_0^2 is also unknown. The detailed discussion of the choice of the parameter σ_0^2 can be found in [3]; the authors of [3] found that the choice of the parameter σ_0^2 has little impact on the experimental results, and our experiments also verified this point. We follow the work in [3] and use $\sigma_0^2 = 9$ in all experiments to make sure that the predictor extracts a relatively consistent level of the SPN.

Our proposed SPN predictor PCAI8 is adaptive to different image edge regions according to all eight-neighbor pixels, and the PCAI8 method is more accurate than PCAI4 in classifying edge's area, so it is expected that the predicted SPN has less scene noise from the original image than PCAI4 and other denoising filters.

(3) The estimated camera reference SPN y' is obtained by averaging all the residual noise W_k $\{W_k(i, j)\}$ (the estimated SPN from each image) extracted from the same camera as follows:

$$\mathbf{y}' = \frac{\sum_{k=0}^{L-1} \mathbf{W}_k}{L}, \quad (6)$$

where L denotes the total number of images used for the extraction of camera reference SPN. The residual noise $\mathbf{W}_k(i, j)$ is extracted pixel-wise according to Equation 4.

(4) In order to further suppress the unwanted artifacts caused by camera processing operations such as color interpolation and JPEG compression blocking artifacts, we adopt two pre-processing operations proposed in [7] to enhance the estimated SPN before it is used for identification. So, the final estimated camera reference SPN y can be expressed as

$$\mathbf{y} = WF(ZM(y')), \quad (7)$$

Table 1 Cameras used in the experiments

Camera brand[a]	Sensor	Resolution	Format
Canon PS A3000 IS	1/2.3" CCD	3,648 × 2,736	JPEG
Canon PS A610	1/1.8" CCD	2,592 × 1,944	JPEG
Canon PS A620	1/1.8" CCD	3,072 × 2,304	JPEG
Panasonic lumix DMC-FZ30	1/1.8" CCD	3,264 × 2,448	JPEG
Nikon D300	23.6 × 15.8 mm CMOS	4,288 × 2,848	JPEG
Nikon D40	23.7 × 15.6 mm CCD	3,040 × 2,012	NEF
Minolta A2	2/3" CCD	3,272 × 2,454	MRW

[a]Canon Inc., Tokyo, Japan; Panasonic Corp., Kadoma, Japan.

where the $ZM(\cdot)$ operation makes $\mathbf{y}'$ to have zero mean in every row and column, and the $WF(\cdot)$ operation makes $ZM(\mathbf{y}')$ to have a flat frequency spectrum using the Wiener filter in Fourier domain.

(5) Finally, calculate the detection statistic $c(\mathbf{x}, \mathbf{y})$ between the camera reference SPN y and the noise residue x extracted from a test image with Equation 4. We use the detection statistic CCN to measure the similarity between the image noise residue x and a camera's reference SPN y. We use CCN instead of PCE [8] because it can lower the false-positive rate at the same true-positive rate (please refer to [11] for details). The CCN value $c(\mathbf{x}, \mathbf{y})$ is defined as:

$$c(\mathbf{x}, \mathbf{y}) = \frac{\mathbf{xy}/N}{\sqrt{\frac{1}{N-|\mathbf{A}|}\sum_{m\notin\mathbf{A}} r_{\mathbf{xy}}^2(m)}} = \frac{r_{\mathbf{xy}}(0)}{\sqrt{\frac{1}{N-|\mathbf{A}|}\sum_{m\notin\mathbf{A}} r_{\mathbf{xy}}^2(m)}} \quad (8)$$

where $\mathbf{A}$ is a small neighbor area around zero where $r_{\mathbf{xy}}(0) = \frac{1}{N}\mathbf{xy} = \frac{1}{N}\sum_{i=0}^{N-1} x_i y_i$, and $|\mathbf{A}|$ is the size of $\mathbf{A}$. The size of $\mathbf{A}$ is chosen to be a block of 11×11 pixels. The circular shift vector $\mathbf{y}_m = \{y_{i\oplus m}\}$, where the operation $\oplus$ is modulo N addition in $\mathbb{Z}_N$. The circular cross-correlation $r_{\mathbf{xy}}(m)$ is defined as

$$r_{\mathbf{xy}}(m) = \frac{1}{N}\mathbf{xy}_m = \frac{1}{N}\sum_{i=0}^{N-1} x_i y_{i\oplus m}. \quad (9)$$

In the next section, we will evaluate the CSI performance of our proposed method.

3. Experimental results

In this section, we will compare the CSI performance of the proposed PCAI8 method with the existing state-of-the-art methods on two different image databases. In 'Part A' section, an image database built by ourselves is used. In this database, blue sky images can be used to extract more

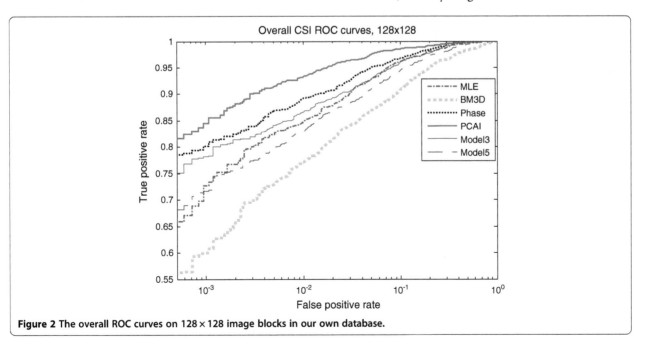

Figure 2 The overall ROC curves on 128 × 128 image blocks in our own database.

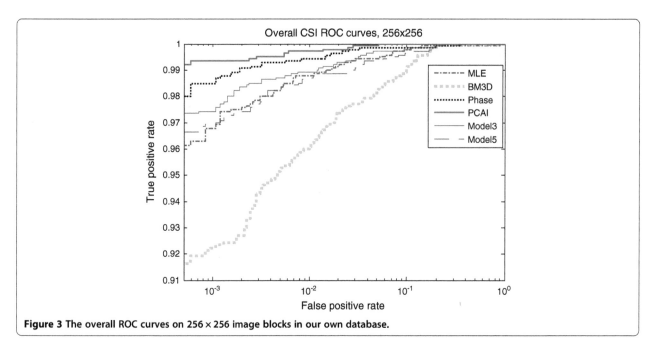

Figure 3 The overall ROC curves on 256 × 256 image blocks in our own database.

accurate reference patterns. In 'Part B' section, we use a public image database, the 'Dresden Image Database' (DID) [16], which can be downloaded from the internet [17]. Cameras in this image database cover different camera brands or models and different devices of the same camera model. We choose two of Li's models, 'model 3' and 'model 5', in our experimental comparison because they show better results according to Li's work [10]. Furthermore, all model parameters are chosen the same as those in Li's work, and we use model 3 or model 5 to denote the image noise residue attenuated by model

3 or model 5 in our results. As a result, we compare our PCAI8 method with the MLE method from [7], BM3D method [5], PCAI4 method [13], phase method [11], and Li's method [10] (i.e., model 3 and model 5).

The CSI experiments are performed on the image block with different sizes cropped from the center of the full-size images. Our experiments are performed in the luminance channel of all images because the luminance channel contains information of all the three RGB channels. In fact, experiments in the other channel are also performed and have similar results.

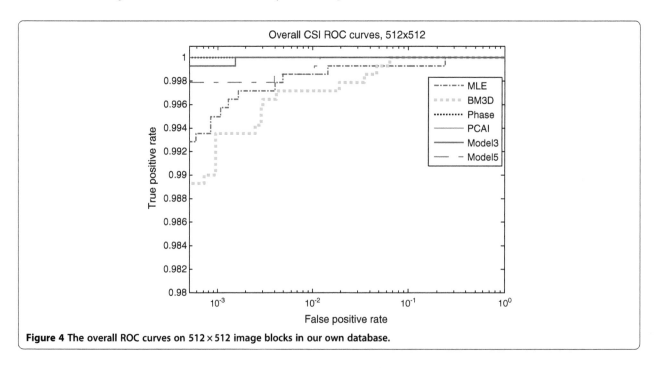

Figure 4 The overall ROC curves on 512 × 512 image blocks in our own database.

Table 2 The TPR of the different methods at a low FPR of 10^{-3}

Method	Image size (pixels)		
	128 × 128	256 × 256	512 × 512
PCAI4	0.838	0.986	1.000
PCAI8	0.848	0.993	1.000
Phase	0.803	0.980	1.000
MLE	0.727	0.968	0.995
BM3D	0.601	0.922	0.993
Model 3	0.781	0.974	0.999
Model 5	0.716	0.969	0.998

The detection statistic CCN is used to measure the similarity between the image noise residue **x** and a camera's reference SPN **y** for all methods. In order to make a fair comparison, before the calculation of detection statistic, for all four methods, we performed the same pre-processing operations as shown in (7) on the estimated reference PRNU/SPN **y** before the calculation of detection statistic. The experiments on different image databases demonstrate that our method always has the best performance among all existing methods regardless of using CCN, PCE, or correlation as a detection statistic. So, we report the experimental results with detection statistic CCN to measure the similarity between the image noise residue **x** and a camera's reference SPN **y** for all methods.

3.1 Part A

On the first image database, we use seven different cameras in our experiments. Table 1 shows the image format, native

resolution, and imaging sensor property of the cameras (PS means PowerShot). All images are in JPEG format with the highest JPEG quality factor provided by the cameras, except in raw data format for the Nikon D40 (Shanghai, China) and Minolta A2 (Konica, Tokyo, Japan). For each camera, we have two sub-image datasets which are the test image dataset and original image dataset, respectively. The original image dataset is used for camera reference SPN extraction. It has been proved that a more accurate camera reference SPN can be extracted by using blue sky images [7]. So, the original images are taken on a sunny day of the blue sky whose content is flat or near flat. The test images are taken under a variety of environments, from indoor furniture to outdoor sight. The images in the test image dataset are used as test samples for CSI. The CSI experiment is performed on the image block with different sizes from 128 × 128 to 512 × 512. The image block is cropped from the center of a full-size photo.

For each chosen camera, we extract the camera reference SPN using $L = 100$ images from the original image dataset, 200 test images of this camera are selected as the positive samples, and 1,200 test images of the other six cameras (each camera is responsible for 200) are selected as the negative samples. All the test images are chosen randomly from the test image dataset. Totally, we get 200 positive and 1,200 negative samples of CCN values for each chosen camera.

To obtain the *overall ROC curve*, for a given detection threshold, we count the number of true-positive decisions and the number of false-positive decisions for each camera and then sum them up to obtain the total number of true-positive decisions and false-positive decisions. Then, the

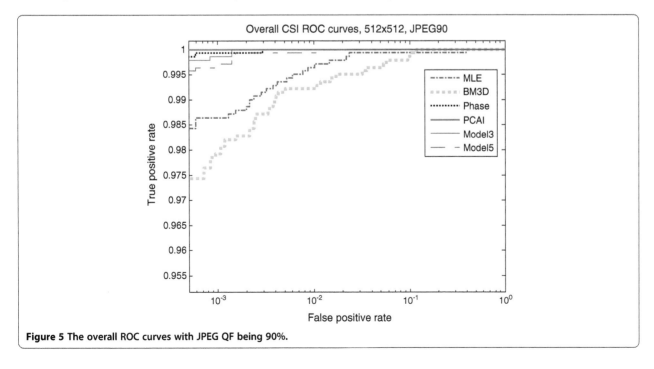

Figure 5 The overall ROC curves with JPEG QF being 90%.

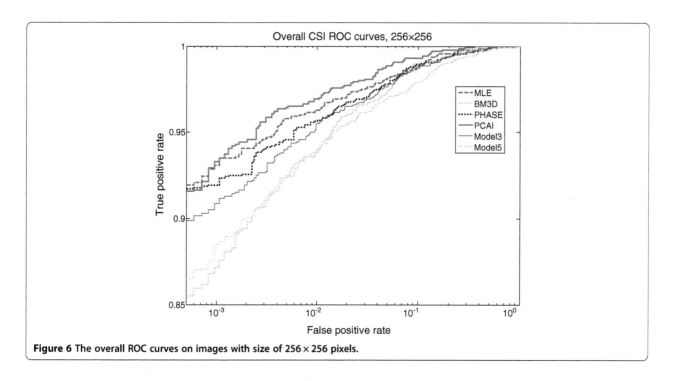

Figure 6 The overall ROC curves on images with size of 256 × 256 pixels.

total true-positive rate (TPR) and total false-positive rate (FPR) are calculated to draw the overall ROC curve.

The overall ROC curve performances of our proposed PCAI method compared with other SPN CSI methods are shown in Figures 2, 3 and 4. In practical applications, it is often necessary to ensure a sufficiently low FPR;

Table 3 Cameras in the Dresden Image Database

Camera brand[a]	Device ID	Image no.	Resolution
Casio_EX-Z150	C0	181	3,264 × 2,448
	C1	189	
	C2	187	
	C3	187	
	C4	181	
FujiFilm_FinePixJ50	C5	210	3,264 × 2,448
	C6	205	
	C7	215	
Olympus_mju_1050SW	C8	204	3,648 × 2,736
	C9	209	
	C10	218	
	C11	207	
	C12	202	
Sony_DSC-T77	C13	181	3,648 × 2,736
	C14	171	
	C15	189	
	C16	184	

[a]Casio Electronics Co., Tokyo, Japan; Fujifilm Holdings Corp., Tokyo, Japan; Olympus Corp., Tokyo, Japan; Sony Corp., Tokyo, Japan.

therefore, the ROC performance in low FPR case is more critical. So, the horizontal axis of all the ROC curves in this paper is in logarithmic scale, in order to show the detail of the ROC curves with a low FPR.

The experimental results show that the proposed PCAI8 method outperforms the others and enhances the ROC performance of CSI for images of different sizes. The proposed PCAI8 method, the PCAI4 method, and the phase SPN method can achieve a 100% TPR at a low FPR on an image block of 512 × 512 pixels in our experimental environment. From Figures 2, 3 and 4, we also notice that both PCAI methods, including PCAI4 and PCAI8, achieve better ROC performance than other methods because of the SPN predictor PCAI has less scene noise residue. Compared to PCAI4, PCAI8 always achieves better performance than PCAI4, which means that the PCAI8method can suppress the scene noise better than PCAI4.

Table 2 shows the TPR of the different methods at a low FPR of 10^{-3}. From the table data, we find that the TPR of the proposed method is always the largest regardless of the image size. The experimental results indicate that the proposed method raises the TPR prominently in the case of trustworthy identification which is with a low FPR. For example, on small image block size of 256 × 256, the TPR of our proposed PCAI8 method is 99.3%, the TPR of the MLE, phase, PCAI4, BM3D, model 3, and model 5 methods is 96.8%, 98%, 98.6%, 92.2%, 97.4%, and 96.9%, respectively. The improvement is 2.5%, 1.3%, 0.7%, 7.1%, 1.9%, and 2.5%, respectively.

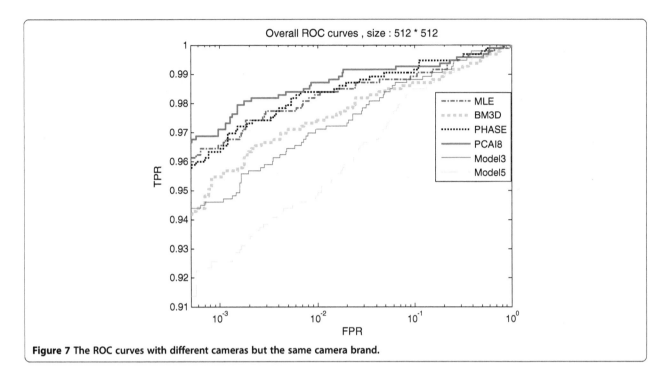

Figure 7 The ROC curves with different cameras but the same camera brand.

When an image is JPEG-compressed, the SPN is impaired at the same time, so it becomes more difficult to use SPN for CSI. Figure 5 shows the overall ROC curves performance on JPEG-compressed images of 512×512 pixels, with a quality factor (QF) of 90%. The number of test images is the same as that mentioned above. The results with the other sizes are not shown here because they are also similar. The experimental results show that the proposed PCAI8 method also has the best performance in resisting mild JPEG compression and achieves perfect detection.

Although camera fingerprint can be created with as much as possible original images, sometime we cannot have as much as 100 original images for camera finger-

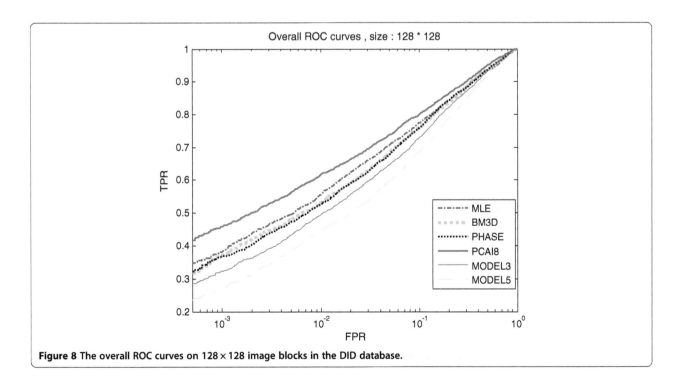

Figure 8 The overall ROC curves on 128×128 image blocks in the DID database.

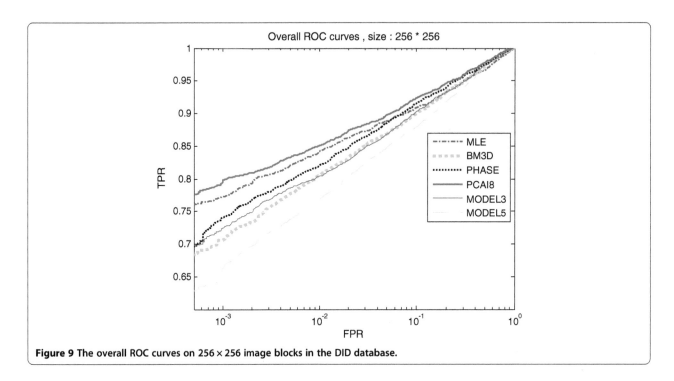

Figure 9 The overall ROC curves on 256 × 256 image blocks in the DID database.

print creation. So, we also investigate the performance when camera fingerprint is extracted using less than 100, e.g., 30, original images from the original image dataset; the other setup is the same as Figure 3. It is observed from Figure 6 that the advantage of the proposed PCAI decreases when the camera fingerprint is extracted using only 30 original images, but it still achieves similar performance as the state-of-the-art MLE method.

3.2 Part B

In this part, we report the experimental results on 3,320 images of 17 cameras from the Dresden Image Database. This image database contains some images with some special shooting environment and setting, such as a high ISO value which results in high shooting noises. It makes the CSI challenging on this image database. The 17 camera devices belong to four camera brands or

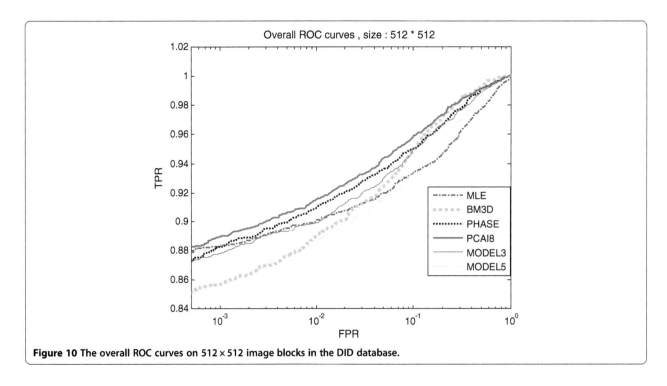

Figure 10 The overall ROC curves on 512 × 512 image blocks in the DID database.

models. Each camera model has 3 to 5 different camera devices. The different camera devices with the same camera model have the same in-camera processing, such as JPEG compress and color filter array (CFA) interpolation. Table 3 shows the information of each device. Device ID is the unique identification for each camera device. Image no. denotes the number of images in the camera devices, and the resolution is the native resolution of the camera devices.

Most settings of the experiments in this part are similar with the ones in 'Part A' section. We use the luminance channel of all the images to extract sensor pattern noises of test images and reference SPN of each camera device. All the image blocks are of three sizes (i.e., 128×128, 256×256, and 512×512 pixels) and are all cropped from the center of full-size images. In this image database, exactly blue sky images are not available. All the images are ordinary scene pictures in daily life. There are about 200 images of each camera device (Table 3).

In our experiments, we use the *five-fold cross-validation* method. Assume that one database contains $N \times K$ images taken by N cameras; each camera is responsible for K images. Firstly, we divide the images of each camera device into five groups averagely. In each fold, we randomly choose one group as the test image dataset (about $K/5$ images for each camera), and the other four groups as original images dataset (about $K \times 4/5$ images for each camera). The original image dataset is used for extracting the camera reference SPN, and images from the test image dataset may be used as positive test samples or negative test samples. For each chosen camera, we extract the camera reference SPN using its original image dataset; the test images (about $K/5$ images) of this camera are selected as the positive samples, and the test images of the other $N-1$ cameras (each camera is responsible for $K/5$ images) are selected as the negative samples. So, we get $K/5$ CCN values of positive samples and $K/5 \times (N-1)$ CCN values of negative samples for each chosen camera. After five folds, totally, we get K CCN values of positive samples and $K \times (N-1)$ CCN values of negative samples for each camera. At last, the overall ROC curve is obtained in a similar way as mentioned in 'Part A' section.

An obvious characteristic of this database is that some camera devices belong to the same brand. Most of the previous works, including the experiments in 'Part A' section, only considered different camera brands. It might lead to a problem that we cannot make a clear division of camera source identification and camera model identification because the extracted SPN might contain part of camera model noises, which could be regarded as fingerprints of a special camera model. These noises play different roles in experiments dependent on the models of tested cameras. So, if all the tested cameras come from different camera brands, the SPN with more

Table 4 The TPR of the four methods at a low FPR of 10^{-3}

Method	Image size (pixels)		
	128×128	256×256	512×512
PCAI4	0.423	0.784	0.887
PCAI8	0.462	0.794	0.890
MLE	0.391	0.772	0.881
Phase	0.377	0.741	0.881
BM3D	0.377	0.713	0.859
Model 3	0.322	0.724	0.878
Model 5	0.268	0.661	0.858

camera model noises might give a better performance than the more accurate one which is with less camera model noises in it. And, the results of such experiments are not very reliable when different camera devices of the same camera model are considered.

In order to make the experiments more convincing, we first compare the performance between our method and other methods in the same camera brand. Figure 7 shows the overall ROC curve performance on images of five camera devices (device ID: C0 to C4) in Casio_EX-Z150. We use the five-fold cross validation method in this experiment. Only the results on 512×512 sizes are showed since the results in other sizes are similar.

The experimental results show that our proposed method has the best performance in identifying the source of images taken by the same camera brand and model. The proposed method can achieve a high TPR of 97% at a low FPR of 10^{-3} for images with size of 512×512, which means that only few images are misjudged.

In the following, we report the CSI experimental results on the whole DID database. In plotting the overall ROC curves on all the images in the DID database, we totally get 3,320 CCN values of positive samples and 53,120 CCN values of negative samples. The results with three different image sizes are shown in Figures 8, 9 and 10.

The experimental results also show that both PCAI8 and PCAI4 have better performance than the other methods in identifying images of different source camera models regardless of different image sizes. Table 4 shows the TPR

Table 5 Computational time of the different methods

Methods	Time (s)
PCAI4	0.14
PCAI8	0.22
BM3D	0.34
Phase	1.73
MLE	1.73
Model 3	1.78
Model 5	1.75

of the different methods at a low FPR of 10^{-3}. It shows that the TPR of the proposed PCAI8 method is always the largest at a low FPR. For example, on small image block of size 128×128, the TPR of the PCAI8 method is 46.2%, the TPR of the MLE, phase, PCAI4, BM3D, model 3, and model 5 methods is 39.1%, 37.7%, 42.3%, 37.7%, 32.2%, and 26.8%, respectively. The improvement is 7.1%, 9.5%, 3.9%, 9.5%, 14.0%, and 19.4%, respectively. The performance of PCIA8 achieves little better than that of PCAI4.

The experimental results in both 'Part A' and 'Part B' sections show that the propose method achieves better performance for CSI whether the influence of camera model is considered or not. In 'Part A' section, we compare all methods on seven cameras with different camera models in our image database. In 'Part B' section, we test all methods on five camera devices with the same model and also test all methods on 17 camera devices with the same model or different models. All the experiments on images with different sizes show that our proposed method has the best ROC performance among all of the existing CSI schemes.

The computation time to get the noise residue **x** from a test image of each method with Intel® (Santa Clara, CA, USA) Xeon®CPU E5-2603 1.80 GHz and Matlab (MathWorks, Bangalore, India) is shown in Table 5. It is observed that both PCAI4 and PCAI8 methods have the best efficiency.

4 Conclusion

In this paper, we propose a source camera identification scheme based on an eight-neighbor context-adaptive SPN predictor to enhance the ROC performance of CSI. The SPN predictor can suppress the effect of image content better and lead to a more accurate SPN estimation because of its adaptability of different image edge regions. Extensive experiment results on different image databases and on different sizes of images show that our proposed PCAI method achieves the best ROC performance among all of the state-of-the-art CSI schemes and also has the best performance in resisting mild JPEG compression (e.g., with a quality factor of 90%) simultaneously, especially when the false-positive rate is held low (e.g., $P_{fp} = 10^{-3}$). Because trustworthy CSI must often be performed at low false-positive rates, these results demonstrate that our proposed technique is better suited for use in real-world scenarios than existing techniques. However, our proposed method needs many such as not less than 100 original images to create a camera fingerprint; the advantage of the proposed method decreases when the camera fingerprint is created with less original images.

Competing interests
The authors declare that we have no competing interests.

Acknowledgements
This work was supported by NSFC (grant nos. 61379155 and U1135001), 973 Program (grant no. 2011CB302204), the Research Fund for the Doctoral Program of Higher Education of China (grant no. 20110171110042), NSF of Guangdong Province (grant no.s2013020012788), and the National Science & Technology Pillar Program (grant no. 2012BAK16B06).

References
1. A Swaminathan, M Wu, KJR Liu, Nonintrusive component forensics of visual sensors using output images. IEEE. T. Inf. Foren. Sec. **2**(1), 91–106 (2007)
2. A Swaminathan, M Wu, KJR Liu, Digital image forensics via intrinsic fingerprints. IEEE. T. Inf. Foren. Sec. **3**(1), 101–117 (2008)
3. J Lukáš, J Fridrich, M Goljan, Digital camera identification from sensor pattern noise. IEEE. T. Inf. Foren. Sec. **1**(2), 205–214 (2006)
4. MK Mihcak, I Kozintsev, K Ramchandran, *Spatially adaptive statistical modeling of wavelet image coefficients and its application to denoising. Paper presented at the IEEE international conference on acoustics, speech, and signal processing*, vol. 6 (Phoenix, AR, USA, May1999), pp. 3253–3256
5. A Cortiana, V Conotter, G Boato, FGB de Natale, *Performance comparison of denoising filters for source camera identification. Paper presented at the SPIE conference on media watermarking, security, and forensics III*, vol. 7880 (San Jose, CA, USA, Jan. 2011), p. 778007
6. K Dabov, A Foi, V Katkovnik, K Egiazarian, Image denoising by sparse 3D transform-domain collaborative filtering. IEEE Trans. Image Process **16**(8), 2080–2095 (2007)
7. M Chen, J Fridrich, M Goljan, J Lukáš, Determining image origin and integrity using sensor noise. IEEE. T. Inf. Foren. Sec. **3**(1), 74–90 (2008)
8. M Goljan, *Digital camera identification from images - estimating false acceptance probability. Paper presented at the international workshop on digital-forensics and watermarking* (LNCS 5450, Busan, Korea, Dec. 2008), pp. 454–468
9. J Fridrich, M Chen, M Goljan, *Imaging sensor noise as digital X-ray for revealing forgeries. Paper presented at the 9th international workshop on information hiding* (Saint Malo, France, July 2007), pp. 342–358
10. C-T Li, Source camera identification using enhanced sensor pattern noise. IEEE. T. Inf. Foren. Sec. **5**(2), 280–287 (2010)
11. X Kang, Y Li, Z Qu, J Huang, Enhancing source camera identification performance with a camera reference phase sensor pattern noise. IEEE. T. Inf. Foren. Sec. **7**(2), 393–402 (2012)
12. X Kang, Y Li, Z Qu, J Huang, *Enhancing ROC performance of trustworthy camera source identification. Paper presented at the SPIE conference on electronic imaging-media watermarking, security, forensics XIII*, vol. 7880 (San Francisco, CA, USA, Jan. 2011), pp. 788001–78800109
13. G Wu, X Kang, KJR Liu, *A context adaptive predictor of sensor pattern noise for camera source identification. Paper presented at the 19th international conference on image processing* (Orlando, FL, USA, 15–20 Sept. 2012), pp. 237–240
14. W Liu, W Zeng, L Dong, Q Yao, Efficient compression of encrypted grayscale images. IEEE Trans. Image Process **19**(4), 1097–1102 (2010)
15. X Wu, N Memon, Context-based adaptive lossless image coding. IEEE. T. Commun **45**(4), 437–444 (1997)
16. T Gloe, R Böhme, *Proceedings of the 25th Symposium on Applied Computing*, vol.2 (Springer, New York, 2010), pp. 1585–1591
17. Dresden Image Database, (Technische Universitaet Dresden, Dresden, 2009–2014). http://forensics.inf.tu-dresden.de/ddimgdb. Accessed 3 May 2013

Permissions

The contributors of this book come from diverse backgrounds, making this book a truly international effort. This book will bring forth new frontiers with its revolutionizing research information and detailed analysis of the nascent developments around the world.

We would like to thank all the contributing authors for lending their expertise to make the book truly unique. They have played a crucial role in the development of this book. Without their invaluable contributions this book wouldn't have been possible. They have made vital efforts to compile up to date information on the varied aspects of this subject to make this book a valuable addition to the collection of many professionals and students.

This book was conceptualized with the vision of imparting up-to-date information and advanced data in this field. To ensure the same, a matchless editorial board was set up. Every individual on the board went through rigorous rounds of assessment to prove their worth. After which they invested a large part of their time researching and compiling the most relevant data for our readers.

The editorial board has been involved in producing this book since its inception. They have spent rigorous hours researching and exploring the diverse topics which have resulted in the successful publishing of this book. They have passed on their knowledge of decades through this book. To expedite this challenging task, the publisher supported the team at every step. A small team of assistant editors was also appointed to further simplify the editing procedure and attain best results for the readers.

Apart from the editorial board, the designing team has also invested a significant amount of their time in understanding the subject and creating the most relevant covers. They scrutinized every image to scout for the most suitable representation of the subject and create an appropriate cover for the book.

The publishing team has been an ardent support to the editorial, designing and production team. Their endless efforts to recruit the best for this project, has resulted in the accomplishment of this book. They are a veteran in the field of academics and their pool of knowledge is as vast as their experience in printing. Their expertise and guidance has proved useful at every step. Their uncompromising quality standards have made this book an exceptional effort. Their encouragement from time to time has been an inspiration for everyone.

The publisher and the editorial board hope that this book will prove to be a valuable piece of knowledge for researchers, students, practitioners and scholars across the globe.

List of Contributors

Tiago de Freitas Pereira
CPqD Telecom & IT Solutions, School of Electrical and Computer Engineering, University of Campinas (UNICAMP), Campinas, São Paulo 13083-970, Brazil

Jukka Komulainen
Center for Machine Vision Research, Department of Computer Science and Engineering, University of Oulu, Oulu FI-90014, Finland

André Anjos
IDIAP Research Institute, Martigny CH-1920, Switzerland

José Mario De Martino
School of Electrical and Computer Engineering, University of Campinas (UNICAMP), Campinas, São Paulo 13083-970, Brazil

Abdenour Hadid
Center for Machine Vision Research, Department of Computer Science and Engineering, University of Oulu, Oulu FI-90014, Finland

Matti Pietikäinen
Center for Machine Vision Research, Department of Computer Science and Engineering, University of Oulu, Oulu FI-90014, Finland

Sébastien Marcel
IDIAP Research Institute, Martigny CH-1920, Switzerland

Jinming Duan
College of Information Engineering, Qingdao University, Qingdao 266071, China

Zhenkuan Pan
College of Information Engineering, Qingdao University, Qingdao 266071, China

Xiangfeng Yin
College of Information Engineering, Qingdao University, Qingdao 266071, China

Weibo Wei
College of Information Engineering, Qingdao University, Qingdao 266071, China

Guodong Wang
College of Information Engineering, Qingdao University, Qingdao 266071, China

Junqiu Wang
Aviation Industry Cooperation China, Beijing, China

Yasushi Yagi
The Institute of Scientific and Industrial Research, Osaka University, 8-1 Mihogaoka, Ibaraki, Osaka 567-0047, Japan

Tong Zhu
School of Electrical, Computer & Energy Engineering, Arizona State University, Tempe, AZ 85287, USA

Lina Karam
School of Electrical, Computer & Energy Engineering, Arizona State University, Tempe, AZ 85287, USA

Mingjing Zhang
School of Computing Science, Simon Fraser University, Vancouver, British Columbia V5A 1S6, Canada

Mark S Drew
School of Computing Science, Simon Fraser University, Vancouver, British Columbia V5A 1S6, Canada

Bulent Cavusoglu
Electrical-Electronics Engineering Department, Ataturk University, Erzurum 25240, Turkey

Antonio Garcia-Dopico
DATSI, Facultad de Informática, Universidad Politécnica de Madrid Boadilla del Monte, Madrid 28660, Spain José Luis Pedraza

Manuel Nieto
DATSI, Facultad de Informática, Universidad Politécnica de Madrid Boadilla del Monte, Madrid 28660, Spain José Luis Pedraza

Antonio Pérez
DATSI, Facultad de Informática, Universidad Politécnica de Madrid Boadilla del Monte, Madrid 28660, Spain José Luis Pedraza

Santiago Rodríguez
DATSI, Facultad de Informática, Universidad Politécnica de Madrid Boadilla del Monte, Madrid 28660, Spain José Luis Pedraza

Juan Navas
DATSI, Facultad de Informática, Universidad Politécnica de Madrid Boadilla del Monte, Madrid 28660, Spain José Luis Pedraza

Rocio A Lizarraga-Morales
Universidad de Guanajuato DICIS, Salamanca, Guanajuato 36885, Mexico

Yimo Guo
Center for Machine Vision Research, Department of Computer Science and Engineering, University of Oulu, P.O. Box 4500, ulu FI-90014, Finland

Guoying Zhao
Center for Machine Vision Research, Department of Computer Science and Engineering, University of Oulu, P.O. Box 4500, ulu FI-90014, Finland

Matti Pietikäinen
Center for Machine Vision Research, Department of Computer Science and Engineering, University of Oulu, P.O. Box 4500, ulu FI-90014, Finland

Raul E Sanchez-Yanez
Universidad de Guanajuato DICIS, Salamanca, Guanajuato 36885, Mexico

Zhenhua Chai
National Laboratory of Pattern Recognition, Institute of Automation, Chinese Academy of Science, P.O. Box 2728, Beijing 100190, People's Republic of China

Heydi Mendez-Vazquez
Advanced Technologies Application Center, 7th Avenue #21812 b/ 218 and 222, Havana, Cuba

Ran He
National Laboratory of Pattern Recognition, Institute of Automation, Chinese Academy of Science, P.O. Box 2728, Beijing 100190, People's Republic of China

Zhenan Sun
National Laboratory of Pattern Recognition, Institute of Automation, Chinese Academy of Science, P.O. Box 2728, Beijing 100190, People's Republic of China

Tieniu Tan
National Laboratory of Pattern Recognition, Institute of Automation, Chinese Academy of Science, P.O. Box 2728, Beijing 100190, People's Republic of China

Antonio Garcia-Dopico
DATSI, Facultad de Informática, Universidad Politécnica de Madrid, Boadilla del Monte 28660, Spain José Luis Pedraza Manuel Nieto

Antonio Pérez
DATSI, Facultad de Informática, Universidad Politécnica de Madrid, Boadilla del Monte 28660, Spain José Luis Pedraza Manuel Nieto

Santiago Rodríguez
DATSI, Facultad de Informática, Universidad Politécnica de Madrid, Boadilla del Monte 28660, Spain José Luis Pedraza Manuel Nieto

Luis Osendi
DATSI, Facultad de Informática, Universidad Politécnica de Madrid, Boadilla del Monte 28660, Spain José Luis Pedraza Manuel Nieto

Seiichi Gohshi
Kogakuin University, 1-24-2 Nishi-Shinjuku, Shinjuku-ku, Tokyo 163-8677, Japan

Takayuki Hiroi
Kogakuin University, 1-24-2 Nishi-Shinjuku, Shinjuku-ku, Tokyo 163-8677, Japan

Isao Echizen
National Institute of Informatics, The Graduate University for Advanced Studies (SOKENDAI), 2-1-2, Hitotsubashi, Chiyoda-ku, Tokyo 101-8430, Japan

Chang Won Lee
Department of Computer Engineering, Kumoh National Institute of Technology, Gumi, Gyeongbuk 730-701, Korea

Jaepil Ko
Department of Computer Engineering, Kumoh National Institute of Technology, Gumi, Gyeongbuk 730-701, Korea

Tae-Young Choe
Department of Computer Engineering, Kumoh National Institute of Technology, Gumi, Gyeongbuk 730-701, Korea

Sangwook Lee
Yonsei University, 134 Sinchon-dong, Seodaemun-gu, Seoul 120-749, Korea

Chulhee Lee
Yonsei University, 134 Sinchon-dong, Seodaemun-gu, Seoul 120-749, Korea

Nandita Sharma
Information and Human Centred Computing Research Group, Research School of Computer Science, Australian National University, Canberra, ACT 0200, Australia

Abhinav Dhall
Information and Human Centred Computing Research Group, Research School of Computer Science, Australian National University, Canberra, ACT 0200, Australia

Tom Gedeon
Information and Human Centred Computing Research Group, Research School of Computer Science, Australian National University, Canberra, ACT 0200, Australia

Roland Goecke
Information and Human Centred Computing Research Group, Research School of Computer Science, Australian National University, Canberra, ACT 0200, Australia

Vision & Sensing Group, Information Sciences & Engineering, University of Canberra, Bruce ACT 2601, Australia

Linfeng Xu
School of Electronic Engineering, University of Electronic Science and Technology of China, Xiyuan Avenue 2006, West Hi-Tech Zone, Chengdu, Sichuan 611731, China

Liaoyuan Zeng
School of Electronic Engineering, University of Electronic Science and Technology of China, Xiyuan Avenue 2006, West Hi-Tech Zone, Chengdu, Sichuan 611731, China

Huiping Duan
School of Electronic Engineering, University of Electronic Science and Technology of China, Xiyuan Avenue 2006, West Hi-Tech Zone, Chengdu, Sichuan 611731, China

Nii Longdon Sowah
School of Electronic Engineering, University of Electronic Science and Technology of China, Xiyuan Avenue 2006, West Hi-Tech Zone, Chengdu, Sichuan 611731, China

Victoriya V Abramova
National Aerospace University, Kharkov 61070, Ukraine

Sergey K Abramov
National Aerospace University, Kharkov 61070, Ukraine

Vladimir V Lukin
National Aerospace University, Kharkov 61070, Ukraine

Karen O Egiazarian
Tampere University of Technology, Tampere FI-33101, Finland

Jaakko T Astola
Tampere University of Technology, Tampere FI-33101, Finland

Gerald Schaefer
Department of Computer Science, Loughborough University, Loughborough, UK

Somaya Al Maadeed
Computer Science and Engineering Department, College of Engineering, Qatar University, Doha, Qatar

Abdelaali Hassaine
Computer Science and Engineering Department, College of Engineering, Qatar University, Doha, Qatar

Xiangui Kang
School of Information Science and Technology, Sun Yat-sen University, Guangzhou 510006, People's Republic of China

Jiansheng Chen
School of Information Science and Technology, Sun Yat-sen University, Guangzhou 510006, People's Republic of China

Kerui Lin
School of Information Science and Technology, Sun Yat-sen University, Guangzhou 510006, People's Republic of China

Peng Anjie
School of Information Science and Technology, Sun Yat-sen University, Guangzhou 510006, People's Republic of China

Printed in the USA
CPSIA information can be obtained
at www.ICGtesting.com
JSHW051428221024
72173JS00006B/1409